The Hebraic Tongue Restored

The Hebraic Tongue Restored

And the True Meaning of the Hebrew Words Re-established and Proved by their Radical Analysis

By

Fabre d'Olivet

Done into English by
Nayán Louise Redfield

יהוה

"He who can rightly pronounce it, causeth heaven and earth to tremble, for it is the
NAME
which rusheth through the universe."

Samuel Weiser, Inc.
New York

First Published in this Edition 1921

Reprinted 1976

Second Impression 1978

International Standard Book Number

0 87728 332 X

Library of Congress Catalogue Card Number

76 15542

Samuel Weiser, Inc.
740 Broadway
New York, N.Y. 10003

Printed in the U.S.A. by
Noble Offset Printers, Inc., New York, N.Y. 10003

To the Torch-bearers of the Seven-Tongued-Flame
who have ever been the Path-Finders and
Lights on the Way-of-Knowing
and Being, I offer at the
Dawn-of-the-New-Day
this volume

TO THE READER

I would direct attention to the English word-for-word translation given in the Literal Version of the Cosmogony of Moses. This translation is *d'Olivet's,* and in the footnotes which accompany it I have retained his selection of words some of which are now obsolete. In the "Correct Translation" at the close of the volume I have, however, set aside some of the quaint words making choice of more modern ones.

N. L. R.

TRANSLATOR'S FOREWORD.

THE HEBRAIC TONGUE RESTORED is a strong appeal to those who, realizing that the time of philosophy is past and the time of religion at hand, are seeking for those higher truths the spreading knowledge of which has already altered the complexion of the world and signalled the approaching end of materialism.

In this prodigious work of Fabre d'Olivet, which first appeared in 1815, he goes back to the origin of speech and rebuilds upon a basis of truly colossal learning the edifice of primitive and hieroglyphic Hebrew, bringing back the Hebraic tongue to its constitutive principles by deriving it wholly from the *Sign,* which he considers the symbolic and living image of the generative ideas of language. He gives a neoteric translation of the first ten chapters of the SEPHER OF MOSES (*Genesis*) in which he supports each with a scientific, historic and grammatical commentary to bring out the three meanings: literal, figurative and hieroglyphic, corresponding to the natural, psychic and divine worlds. He asserts plainly and fearlessly that the Genesis of Moses was symbolically expressed and ought not to be taken in a purely literal sense. Saint Augustine recognized this, and Origen avers that "if one takes the history of the creation in the literal sense, it is absurd and contradictory."

Fabre d'Olivet claims that the Hebrew contained in Genesis is the *pure idiom of the ancient Egyptians,* and considering that nearly six centuries before Jesus Christ, the Hebrews having become Jews no longer spoke nor understood their original tongue, he denies the value of the Hebrew as it is understood today, and has undertaken to restore this tongue lost for twenty-five centuries. The truth of this opinion does not appear doubtful, since the Hebrews according to *Genesis* itself remained some four hundred years in Egypt. This idiom, therefore, having become separated from a tongue which had attained its highest perfection and was composed entirely of universal, intellectual, abstract expressions, would naturally fall from degeneracy to degeneracy, from restriction to restriction, to its most material elements; all that was spirit would become substance; all that was intellectual would become sentient; all that was universal, particular.

According to the Essenian tradition, every word in this *Sepher of Moses* contains three meanings—the positive or simple, the comparative or figurative, the superlative or hieratic. When one has penetrated to this last meaning, all things are disclosed through a radiant illumination and the soul of that one attains to heights which those bound to the narrow limits of the positive meaning and satisfied with the letter which killeth, never know.

The learned Maimonides says "Employ you reason, and you will be able to discern what is said allegorically, figuratively and hyperbolically, and what is meant literally."

NAYÁN LOUISE REDFIELD

HARTFORD, CONN.,
October, 1918.

NOTE.

It may be noted by the careful student that the Syriac characters in this volume are in some instances not exactly correct. Unfortunately, the impossibility of securing better types necessitated the use of these unsatisfactory forms. For this the author and the publishers ask the indulgence of the reader.

THE HEBRAIC TONGUE RESTORED
AND THE TRUE MEANING OF THE HEBREW WORDS RE-ESTABLISHED AND PROVED BY THEIR RADICAL ANALYSIS.

In this work is found:

1st.—INTRODUCTORY DISSERTATION upon the Origin of Speech, the study of the tongues which can lead to this origin and the purpose that the Author has in view;

2nd.—HEBRAIC GRAMMAR founded upon new principles, and made useful for the study of tongues in general;

3rd.—SERIES OF HEBRAIC ROOTS considered under new relations, and destined to facilitate the understanding of language, and that of etymological science;

4th.—PRELIMINARY DISCOURSE;

5th.—Translation into English of the first ten chapters of the Sepher, containing the COSMOGONY OF MOSES

This translation, destined to serve as proof of the principles laid down in the Grammar and in the Dictionary, is preceded by a LITERAL VERSION, in French and in English, made upon the Hebrew Text presented in the original with a transcription in modern characters and accompanied by critical and grammatical notes, wherein the interpretation given to each word is proved by its radical analysis and its comparison with the analogous word in Samaritan, Chaldaic, Syriac, Arabic or Greek.

CONTENTS

OF PART FIRST

INTRODUCTORY DISSERTATION.

		PAGE
§I.	Upon the Origin of Speech and upon the Study of the Tongues which can lead to it	3
§II.	Hebraic Tongue: Authenticity of the Sepher of Moses; Vicissitudes experienced by this book..	21
§III.	Continuation of the Revolutions of the Sepher. Origin of the Principal Versions which have been made	37

HEBRAIC GRAMMAR.

Chapter I. General Principles.

§I.	The Real Purpose of this Grammar............	55
§II.	Etymology and Definition...................	60
§III.	Division of Grammar: Parts of Speech..........	65
§IV.	Hebraic Alphabet: Comparative Alphabet	70-71

Chapter II. Signs Considered as Characters.

| §I. | Hebraic Alphabet: its vowels: its origin........ | 73 |

CONTENTS

		PAGE
§II.	Origin of the Vowel Points.................	77
§III.	Effects of the Vowel Points. Samaritan Text....	84

Chapter III. Characters Considered as Signs.

§I.	Traced Characters, one of the elements of Language: Hieroglyphic Principle of their Primitive Form	89
§II.	Origin of Signs and Their Development: Those of the Hebraic Tongue....................	93
§III.	Use of the Signs: Example drawn from the French	99

Chapter IV. The Sign Producing the Root.

§I.	Digression on the Principle and the Constitutive Elements of the Sign...................	103
§II.	Formation of the Root and of the Relation......	107
§III.	Preposition and Interjection..................	114

Chapter V. The Noun.

§I	The Noun Considered under seven relations: Etymology	119
§II.	Quality	124
§III.	Gender	132
§IV.	Number	135
§V.	Movement	139
§VI.	Construct State	147
§VII.	Signification	150

Chapter VI. Nominal Relations.

§I.	Absolute Pronouns..........................	151
§II.	Affixes	155
§III.	Use of the Affixes...........................	161

Chapter VII. The Verb.

§I.	Absolute Verb and Particular Verbs............	167

CONTENTS

		PAGE
§II.	Three Kinds of Particular Verbs	172
§III.	Analysis of Nominal Verbs: Verbal Inflection	177

Chapter VIII. Modifications of the Verb.

§I.	Form and Movement	183
§II.	Tense	187
§III.	Formation of Verbal Tenses by Means of Pronominal Persons	192

Chapter IX. Conjugations.

§I.	Radical Conjugation	197
	Remarks upon the Radical Conjugation	207
§II.	Derivative Conjugation	212
	Remarks upon the Derivative Conjugation	220
§III.	Compound Radical Conjugation with the Initial Adjunction י	225
	Remarks on the Compound Radical Conjugation. Initial Adjunction י	230
§IV.	Compound Radical Conjugation with the Initial Adjunction נ	233
	Remarks on the Compound Radical Conjugation	238
§V.	Compound Radical Conjugation with the Terminative Adjunction	241
	Remarks on the Compound Radical Conjugation	246
§VI.	Irregular Conjugations	250

Chapter X. Construction of Verbs: Adverbial Relations: Paragogic Characters: Conclusion.

§I.	Union of Verbs with Verbal Affixes	255
§II.	Adverbial Relations	262
§III.	Paragogic Characters	271
§IV.	Conclusion	275

CONTENTS

Radical Vocabulary : Prefatory Note.............. 279

HEBRAIC ROOTS.

		PAGE
א	A.	287
ב	B.	300
ג	G.	310
ד	D.	318
ה	H. E.	326
ו	O. OU. W.	334
ז	Z.	339
ח	E. H. CH.	345
ט	T.	356
י	I.	361
כ	CH. KH.	368
ל	L.	377
מ	M.	385
נ	N.	394
ס	S.	405
ע	U. H. WH.	413
פ	PH.	422
צ	TZ.	430
ק	KQ.	438
ר	R.	446
ש	SH.	455
ת	TH.	465

The Hebraic Tongue Restored

PART FIRST

I

INTRODUCTORY DISSERTATION

INTRODUCTORY DISSERTATION.

§ I.

UPON THE ORIGIN OF SPEECH AND UPON THE STUDY OF THE TONGUES WHICH CAN LEAD TO IT.

The origin of speech is generally unknown. It is in vain that savants of the centuries past have endeavoured to go back to the hidden principles of this glorious phenomenon which distinguishes man from all the beings by which he is surrounded, reflects his thought, arms him with the torch of genius and develops his moral faculties; all that they have been able to do, after long labours, has been to establish a series of conjectures more or less ingenious, more or less probable, founded in general, upon the physical nature of man which they judged invariable, and which they took as basis for their experiments. I do not speak here of the scholastic theologians who in order to extricate themselves from perplexity upon this difficult point, taught that man had been created possessor of a tongue wholly formed; nor of Bishop Walton who, having embraced this convenient opinion, gave as proof, the conversation of God Himself with the first man, and the discourses of Eve with the serpent;[1] not reflecting that this so-called serpent which conversed with Eve, and to which God also spoke, might, therefore, have drawn from the same source of speech and participated in the tongue of the Divinity. I refer to those savants who, far from the dust and clamours of the school, sought in good faith the truth that the school no longer possessed. Moreover, the theologians themselves had been abandoned long since by their disciples. Richard Simon, the priest,[2] from

[1] Walton, *Prolegom* I.
[2] Rich. Sim. *Histoire crit.* L. I, ch. 14 et 15.

whom we have an excellent critical history of the Old Testament, did not fear, relying upon the authority of Saint Gregory of Nyssa, to reject theological opinion in this respect, and to adopt that of Diodorus Siculus and even that of Lucretius, who attribute the formation of language to the nature of man and to the instigation of his needs.[3]

It is not because I here oppose the opinion of Diodorus Siculus or Lucretius to that of the theologians, that one should infer that I consider it the best. All the eloquence of J. J. Rousseau could not make me approve of it. It is one extreme striking another extreme, and by this very thing departing from the just mean where truth abides. Rousseau in his nervous, passionate style, pictures the formation of society rather than that of language: he embellishes his fictions with most vivid colours, and he himself, drawn on by his imagination, believes real what is only fantastic.[4] One sees plainly in his writing a possible beginning of civilization but no probable origin of speech. It is to no purpose that he has said that the meridional tongues are the daughters of pleasure and those of the North, of necessity: one still asks, how pleasure or necessity can bring forth simultaneously, words which an entire tribe agrees in understanding and above all agrees in adopting. Is it not he who has said, with cold, severe reason, that language could be instituted only by an agreement and that this agreement could not be conceived without language? This vicious circle in which a modern theosophist confines it, can it be eluded? "Those who devote themselves to the pretension of forming our tongues and all the science of our understanding, by the expedients of natural circumstances alone, and by our human means alone," says this theosophist,[5] "expose

---

[3] Diod-Sic. L. II. "At varios linguæ sonitus natura subegit
    Mittere, et utilitas expressit nomina rerum."
    —LUCRET.

[4] *Essai sur l'origine des Langues.*

[5] St.-Martin *Esprit des choses*, T. II p. 127.

themselves voluntarily to this terrible objection that they themselves have raised; for he who only denies, does not destroy, and he does not refute an argument because he disapproves of it: if the language of man is an agreement, how is this agreement established without language?"

Read carefully both Locke and his most painstaking disciple Condillac;[6] you will, if you desire, have assisted at the decomposition of an ingenious contrivance; you will have admired, perhaps, the dexterity of the decomposer; but you will remain as ignorant as you were before, both concerning the origin of this contrivance, the aim proposed by its author, its inner nature and the principle which moves its machinations. Whether you reflect according to your own opinion, or whether long study has taught you think according to others, you will soon perceive in the adroit analyst only a ridiculous operator who, flattering himself that he is explaining to you how and why such an actor dances in the theatre, seizes a scalpel and dissects the legs of a cadaver. Your memory recalls Socrates and Plato. You hear them again rebuking harshly the physicists and the metaphysicians of their time;[7] you compare their irresistible arguments with the vain jactancy of these empirical writers, and you feel clearly that merely taking a watch to pieces does not suffice to give reason for its movement.

But if the opinion of the theologians upon the origin of speech offends reason, if that of the historians and the philosophers cannot hold out against a severe examination, it is therefore not given to man to know it. Man, who according to the meaning of the inscription of the temple of Delphi,* can know nothing only so far as he

[6] Locke. *Essay concern. Human Understand.* B. III; Condillac *Logique.*

[7] Plat. *dial Theaet. Phaedon. Crat.*

* This famous inscription, *Know thyself* was, according to Pliny, a saying of the sage Chilo, a celebrated Greek philosopher who lived about 560 B. C. He was from Lacedæmon and died of joy, it was said, embracing his son, victor in the Olympic games.

knows himself, is therefore condemned to be ignorant of what places him in the highest rank among sentient beings, of what gives him the sceptre of the earth, of what constitutes him veritably man,—namely Speech! no! that cannot be, because Providence is just. Quite a considerable number of the sages among all nations have penetrated this mystery, and if, notwithstanding their efforts, these privileged men have been unable to communicate their learning and make it universal, it is because the means, the disciples or the favourable conditions for this, have failed them.

For the knowledge of speech, that of the elements and the origin of language, are not attainments that can be transmitted readily to others, or that can be taken to pieces after the manner of the geometricians. To whatever extent one may possess them, whatever profound roots they may have thrown into the mind, whatever numerous fruits they may have developed there, only the principle can ever be communicated. Thus, nothing in elementary nature is propagated at the same time: the most vigorous tree, the most perfect animal do not produce simultaneously their likeness. They yield, according to their specie, a germ at first very different from them, which remains barren if nothing from without coöperates for its development.

The archæological sciences, that is to say, all those which go back to the principles of things, are in the same category. Vainly the sages who possess them are exhausted by generous efforts to propagate them. The most fertile germs that they scatter, received by minds uncultivated or badly prepared, undergo the fate of seeds, which falling upon stony ground or among thorns, sterile or choked die there. Our savants have not lacked aid; it is the aptitude for receiving it that has been lacking. The greater part of them who ventured to write upon tongues, did not even know what a tongue was; for it is not enough merely to have compiled grammars, or to have toiled laboriously to find the difference between a supine and a gerund; it is necessary to have explored many idioms, to have compared them assiduously and without prejudices; in order to penetrate, through the points of contact of their particular genius, to the universal genius which presides over their formation, and which tends to make only one sole and same tongue.

Among the ancient idioms of Asia, are *three* that it is absolutely imperative to understand if one would proceed with assurance in the field of etymology and rise by degrees to the source of language. These idioms, that I can justly name tongues, in the restricted meaning which one has given to this word, are Chinese, Sanskrit and Hebrew. Those of my readers who are familiar with the works of the savants of Calcutta and particularly those of Sir William Jones, may perhaps be astonished that I name Hebrew in place of the Arabic from which this estimable writer derives the Hebraic idiom, and which he cites as one of the mother-tongues of Asia. I shall explain my thought in this respect, and at the same time state why I do not name either Persian, or Uigurian Tataric, which one might think I had forgotten.

When Sir William Jones, glancing with observant eye over the vast continent of Asia and over its numerous dependent isles, placed therein the five ruling nations, among which he divided the heritage, he created a geographical tableau of happy conception and great interest that the historian ought not to overlook.[8] But in establishing this division his consideration was rather of the power and extent of the peoples that he named, than of their true claims to anteriority; since he did not hesitate to say that the Persians, whom he ranked among the five ruling nations, draw their origin from the Hindus and Arabs,[9] and that the Chinese are only an Indian colony;[10]

[8] *Asiat. Research.* T. I.
[9] *Ibid.* T. II. p. 51.
[10] *Asiat. Research.* T. II. p. 368, 379.

therefore, recognizing only three primordial sources, viz., that of the Tatars, that of the Hindus and that of the Arabs.

Although I may not agree wholly with him in this conclusion, I infer nevertheless, as I have already said, that this writer, in naming the five principal nations of Asia, considered their power more than their true rights to anteriority. It is evident, to say the least, that if he had not been obliged to yield to the *éclat* with which the Arabic name is surrounded in these modern times, due to the appearance of Mohammed, to the propagation of the cult, and of the Islamic empire, Sir William Jones would not have chosen the Arabic people instead of the Hebrew people, thus making the former one of the primordial sources of Asia.

This writer had made too careful a study of the Asiatic tongues not to have known that the names which we give to the Hebrews and to the Arabs, however much dissimilar they may appear, owing to our manner of writing them, are in substance only the same epithet modified by two different dialects. All the world knows that both these peoples attribute their origin to the patriach Heber :* now, the name of this so-called patriarch, signifies nothing less than that which is placed *behind* or *beyond*, that which is *distant, hidden, deceptive, deprived of light;* that which *passes*, that which *terminates*, that which is *occidental*, etc. The Hebrews, whose dialect is evidently anterior to that of the Arabs, have derived from it *hebri* and the Arabs *harbi*, by a transposition of letters which is a characteristic of their language. But whether it be pronounced *hebri*, or *harbi*, one or the other word expresses always that the people who bear it are found placed either beyond, or at the extremity, at the confines, or at the occidental borders of a country. From

* Following the Hebraic orthography עבר *habar*, following the Arabic عبر *habar*. The Hebraic derivative is עברי *habri*, a Hebrew: the Arabic derivative is عربي *harbi*, an Arab.

the most ancient times, this was the situation of the Hebrews or the Arabs, relative to Asia, whose name in its primitive root signifies the unique continent, the land, in other words, the Land of God.

If, far from all systematic prejudice, one considers attentively the Arabic idiom, he discovers there the certain marks of a dialect which, in surviving all the dialects emanated from the same branch, has become successively enriched from their *débris,* has undergone the vicissitudes of time, and carried afar by a conquering people, has appropriated a great number of words foreign to its primitive roots; a dialect which has been polished and fashioned upon the idioms of the vanquished people, and little by little shown itself very different from what it was in its origin; whereas the Hebraic idiom on the contrary (and I mean by this idiom that of Moses), long since extinct in its own country and lost for the people who spoke it, was concentrated in one unique book, where hardly any of the vicissitudes which had altered the Arabic had been able to assail it; this is what distinguishes it above all and what has made it my choice.

This consideration has not escaped Sir William Jones. He has clearly seen that the Arabic idiom, toward which he felt a strong inclination, had never produced any work worthy of fixing the attention of men prior to the Koran,[11] which is, besides, only a development of the Sepher of Moses; whereas this Sepher, sacred refuge of the Hebrew tongue, seemed to him to contain, independent of a divine inspiration,[12] more true sublimity, exquisite beauties, pure morals, essential history and traits of poetry and eloquence, than all the assembled books written in any tongue and in any age of the world.

However much may be said and however much one may, without doing the least harm to the Sepher, compare and even prefer certain works equally famous among

[11] *Asiat. Research.* T. II. p. 13.
[12] *Ibid.* T. II. p, 15.

the nations, I affirm that it contains for those who can read it, things of lofty conception and of deep wisdom; but it is assuredly not in the state in which it is shown to the vulgar readers, that it merits such praise. Sir William Jones undoubtedly understood it in its purity and this is what I like to believe.

Besides, it is always by works of this nature that a tongue acquires its right to veneration. The books of universal principles, called *King,* by the Chinese, those of divine knowledge, called *Veda* or *Beda,* by the Hindus, the Sepher of Moses, these are what make illustrious the Chinese, the Sanskrit and the Hebrew. Although Uigurian Tataric may be one of the primitive tongues of Asia, I have not included it as one that should be studied by the student who desires to go back to the principle of speech; because nothing could be brought back to this principle in an idiom which has not a sacred literature. Now, how could the Tatars have had a sacred or profane literature, they who knew not even the characters of writing? The celebrated Genghis Khan, whose empire embraced an immense extent, did not find, according to the best writers, a single man among his Mongols capable of writing his dispatches.[13] Tamerlane, ruler in his turn of a part of Asia, knew neither how to read nor write. This lack of character and of literature, leaving the Tataric idioms in a continual fluctuation somewhat similar to that which the rude dialects of the savage peoples of America experienced, makes their study useless to etymology and can only throw uncertain and nearly always false lights in the mind.

One must seek the origin of speech only from authentic monuments, whereon speech itself has left its ineffaceable imprint. If time and the scythe of revolutions had respected more the books of Zoroaster, I doubtless might have compared with the Hebrew, the ancient tongue of the Parsees, called *Zend,* in which are written the fragments

[13] *Traduct. franc. des Recher. Asiat.* T. II. P. 49. *Notes.*

ORIGIN OF SPEECH

which have come down to us; but after a long and impartial examination, I cannot refrain from believing, notwithstanding all the recognition that I feel for the extraordinary labours of Anquetil-Duperron who has procured them for us, that the book called today, the *Zend-Avesta*, by the Parsees, is only a sort of breviary, a compilation of prayers and litanies wherein are mingled here and there certain fragments from the sacred books of Zeradosht, the ancient Zoroaster, translated in the living tongue; for this is precisely what the word *Zend* signifies—living tongue. The primitive Avesta was divided into twenty-one parts, called *Nosk*, and entered into all the details of nature,[14] as do the Vedas and Pouranas of the Hindus, with which it had perhaps more affinity than one imagines. The Boun-Dehesh, which Anquetil-Duperron has translated from the *Pehlevi*, a sort of dialect more modern still than the *Zend*, appears to be only an abridgment of that part of the Avesta which treated particularly of the origin of Beings and the birth of the Universe.

Sir William Jones, who believes as I do that the original books of Zoroaster were lost, thinks that the Zend, in which are written the fragments that we possess, is a dialect of Sanskrit, in which Pehlevi, derived from the Chaldaic and from the Cimmerian Tatars, has mingled many of its expressions.[15] This opinion, quite comformable with that of the learned d'Herbelot who carries the Zend and Pehlevi back to Nabatæan Chaldaic,[16] that is, to the most ancient tongue of Assyria, is therefore most probable since the characters of Pehlevi and Zend are obviously of Chaldaic origin.

I do not doubt that the famous inscriptions which are found in the ruins of ancient Isthakr,[17] named Persepolis by the Greeks, and of which no savant, up to this time,

[14] *Zend-Avesta*, T. I. *part* II. p. 46.
[15] *Asiat. Research*, T. II. p. 52 *et suiv.*
[16] *Bibl. ori.* p. 514.
[17] Millin: *Monumens inédits*.

has been able to decipher the characters, belong to the tongue in which the sacred books of the Parsees were originally written before they had been abridged and translated in Pehlevi and Zend. This tongue, whose very name has disappeared, was perhaps spoken at the court of those monarchs of Iran, whom Mohsenal-Fany mentions in a very curious book entitled *Dabistan*,* and whom he assures had preceded the dynasty of the Pishdadians, which is ordinarily regarded as the earliest.

But without continuing further upon this digression, I believe I have made it sufficiently understood that the study of Zend cannot be of the same interest, nor produce the same results as that of Chinese, Sanskrit or Hebrew, since it is only a dialect of Sanskrit and can only offer sundry fragments of the sacred literature translated from an unknown tongue more ancient than itself. It is enough to make it enter as a sort of supplement in the research of the origin of speech, considering it as a link which binds Sanskrit to Hebrew.

It is the same with the Scandinavian idiom, and the Runic poetry preserved in the Edda.[18] These venerable relics of the sacred literature of the Celts, our ancestors, ought to be regarded as a medium between the tongues of ancient Asia and that of modern Europe. They are not to be disdained as an auxiliary study, the more so since they are all that remains to us really authentic pertaining to the cult of the ancient Druids, and as the other Celtic dialects, such as Basque, Armoric Breton, Welsh Breton or *Cymraeg*, possessing no writings, can merit no sort of confidence in the important subject with which we are engaged.

But let us return to the three tongues whose study I recommend: Chinese, Sanskrit and Hebrew; let us

* This work which treats of the manners and customs of Persia, is not known except for a single extract inserted in the *New Asiatic Miscellany*, published by Gladwin, at Calcutta, 1789.

[18] *Edda Islandorum* Haoniæ, 1665, in-4.°

ORIGIN OF SPEECH

glance at them without concerning ourselves for the present, with their grammatical forms; let us fathom their genius and see in what manner they principally differ.

The Chinese tongue is, of all the living tongues today, the most ancient; the one whose elements are the simplest and the most homogeneous. Born in the midst of certain rude men, separated from other men by the result of a physical catastrophe which had happened to the globe, it was at first confined to the narrowest limits, yielding only scarce and material roots and not rising above the simplest perceptions of the senses. Wholly physical in its origin, it recalled to the memory only physical objects: about two hundred words composed its entire lexicon, and these words reduced again to the most restricted signification were all attached to local and particular ideas. Nature, in thus isolating it from all tongues, defended it for a long time from mixture, and when the men who spoke it, multiplied, spread abroad and commingled with other men, art came to its aid and covered it with an impenetrable defense. By this defense, I mean the symbolic characters whose origin a sacred tradition attributes to Fo-Hi. This holy man, says the tradition, having examined the heavens and the earth, and pondered much upon the nature of intermediate things, traced the eight *Koua*, the various combinations of which sufficed to express all the ideas then developed in the intelligence of the people. By means of this invention, the use of knots in cords, which had been the custom up to that time, ceased.*

Nevertheless, in proportion as the Chinese people extended, in proportion as their intelligence made progress and became enriched with new ideas, their tongue followed these different developments. The number of its words fixed by the symbolic *Koua*, being unable to be augmented, was modified by the accent. From being par-

* This tradition is drawn from the great history *Tsee-tchi-Kien-Kang-Mou*, which the Emperor *Kang-hi* ordered translated into Tataric and embellished with a preface.

ticular they became generic; from the rank of nouns they were raised to that of verbs; the substance was distinguished from the spirit. At that time was felt the necessity for inventing new symbolic characters, which, uniting easily, the one with the other, could follow the flight of thought and lend themselves to all the movements of the imagination.[19] This step taken, nothing further arrested the course of this indigenous idiom, which, without ever varying its elements, without admitting anything foreign in its form, has sufficed during an incalculable succession of ages for the needs of an immense nation; which has given it sacred books that no revolution has been able to destroy, and has been enriched with all the profoundness, brilliancy and purity that moral and metaphysical genius can produce.

Such is this tongue, which, defended by its symbolic forms, inaccessible to all neighbouring idioms, has seen them expiring around it, in the same manner that a vigorous tree sees a host of frail plants, which its shade deprives of the generating heat of day, wither at its feet.

Sanskrit did not have its origin in India. If it is allowable for me to express my thought without promising to prove it, since this would be neither the time nor the place; I believe that a people much older than the Hindus, inhabiting another region of the earth, came in very remote times to be established in *Bharat-Wersh*, today Hindustan, and brought there a celebrated idiom called *Bali* or *Pali,* many indications of which are found in *Singhala,* of the island of Ceylon, in the kingdoms of Siam, of Pegu, and in all that part which is called the empire of the Burmans. Everywhere was this tongue considered sacred.[20] Sir William Jones, whose opinion is the same as mine relative to the exotic origin of Sanskrit, without however giving the Pali tongue as its primitive source,

---

[19] *Mém. concer. les Chinois.* T. I. p. 273 *et suiv. Ibid.* T. VIII. p 133 *et suiv. Mém. de l'Acad. des Inscrip.* T. XXXIV. in-4. p. 25.
[20] *Descript. de Siam.* T. I. p. 25. *Asiat. Resear.* T. VI. p. 307.

ORIGIN OF SPEECH

shows that the pure Hindi, originating in Tatary, rude jargon of the epoch of that colonization, has received from some sort of foreign tongue its grammatical forms, and finding itself in a convenient position to be, as it were, grafted by it, has developed a force of expression, harmonious and copious, of which all the Europeans who have been able to understand it speak with admiration.[21]

In truth, what other tongue ever possessed a sacred literature more widespread? How many years shall yet pass ere Europeans, developed from their false notions, will have exhausted the prolific mine which it offers!

Sanskrit, in the opinion of all the English writers who have studied it, is the most perfect tongue that men have ever spoken.[22] It surpasses Greek and Latin in regularity as in richness, and Persian and Arabic in poetic conceptions. With our European tongues it preserves a striking analogy that holds chiefly to the form of its characters, which being traced from left to right have served, according to Sir William Jones, as type or prototype of all those which have been and which still are in use in Africa and in Europe.

Let us now pass on to the Hebraic tongue. So many abstract fancies have been uttered concerning this tongue, and the systematic or religious prejudice which has guided the pen of its historians, has so obscured its origin, that I scarcely dare to say what it is, so simple is what I have to say. This simplicity will, nevertheless, have its merit; for if I do not exalt it to the point of saying with the rabbis of the synagogue or the doctors of the Church, that it has presided at the birth of the world, that angels and men have learned it from the mouth of God Himself, and that this celestial tongue returning to its source, will become that which will be spoken by the blessed in heaven; neither shall I say with the modern philosophists, that

[21] *Ibid.* T. I. p. 307.
[22] Wilkin's *Notes on the Hitopadesa.* p. 294. Halhed, *dans la préface de la Gramm. du Bengale, et dans le Code des lois des Gentoux.*

it is a wretched jargon of a horde of malicious, opinionated, suspicious, avaricious and turbulent men; I shall say without any partiality, that the Hebrew contained in the Sepher, is the pure idiom of the ancient Egyptians.

This truth will not please those prejudiced *pro* or *con*, I am certain of this; but it is no fault of mine if the truth so rarely flatters their passions.

No, the Hebraic tongue is neither the first nor the last of the tongues; it is not the only one of the mother-tongues, as a modern theosophist, whom I esteem greatly otherwise, has inopportunely believed, because it is not the only one that has sprung from the divine wonders;[23] it is the tongue of a powerful, wise and religious people; of a thoughtful people, profoundly learned in moral sciences and friend of the mysteries; of a people whose wisdom and laws have been justly admired. This tongue separated from its original stem, estranged from its cradle by the effect of a providential emigration, an account of which is needless at the moment, became the particular idiom of the Hebrew people; and like a productive branch, which a skillful agriculturist has transplanted in ground prepared for this purpose, so that it will bear fruit long after the worn out trunk whence it comes has disappeared, so has this idiom preserved and brought down to us the precious storehouse of Egyptian learning.

But this storehouse has not been trusted to the caprice of hazard. Providence, who willed its preservation, has known well how to shelter it from storms. The book which contains it, covered with a triple veil, has crossed the torrent of ages respected by its possessors, braving the attention of the profane, and never being understood except by those who would not divulge its mysteries.

With this statement let us retrace our steps. I have said that the Chinese, isolated from their birth, having departed from the simplest perceptions of the senses, had reached by development the loftiest conceptions of intel-

[23] St-Martin: *Esprit des choses*, T. II. p. 213.

ligence; it was quite the contrary with the Hebrew: this distinct idiom, entirely formed from a most highly perfected tongue, composed wholly of expressions universal, intelligible and abstract, delivered in this state to a sturdy but ignorant people, had, in its hands fallen from degeneracy to degeneracy, and from restriction to restriction, to its most material elements; all that was intelligible had become sentient; all that was universal had become particular.

Sanskrit, holding a sort of mean between the two, since it was the result of a formed tongue, grafted upon an unformed idiom, unfolded itself at first with admirable promptness: but after having, like the Chinese and the Hebrew, given its divine fruits, it has been unable to repress the luxury of its productions: its astonishing flexibility has become the source of an excess which necessarily has brought about its downfall. The Hindu writers, abusing the facility which they had of composing words, have made them of an excessive length, not only of ten, fifteen and twenty syllables, but they have pushed the extravagance to the point of containing in simple inscriptions, terms which extend to one hundred and even one hundred and fifty. [24] Their vagabond imagination has followed the intemperance of their elocution; an impenetrable obscurity has spread itself over their writings; their tongue has disappeared.

But this tongue displays in the *Vedas* an economical richness. It is there that one can examine its native flexibility and compare it with the rigidity of the Hebrew, which beyond the amalgamation of root and sign, does not admit of any composition: or, compare it with the facility with which the Chinese allows its words, all monosyllables, to be joined without ever being confused. The principal beauties of this last idiom consist in its characters, the symbolic combination of which offers a tableau more or less perfect, according to the talent of the writer. It

---

[24] *Asiat. Research.* T. I. p. 279, 357, 366, etc.

can be said without metaphor, that they paint pictures in their discourse.[25] The written tongue differs essentially from the spoken tongue.[26] The effect of the latter is very mediocre, and as it were, of no importance; whereas, the former, carries the reader along presenting him with a series of sublime pictures. Sanskrit characters say nothing to the imagination, the eye can run through them without giving the least attention; it is to the happy composition of its words, to their harmony, to the choice and to the blending of ideas that this idiom owes its eloquence. The greatest effect of Chinese is for the eyes; that of Sanskrit, for the ears. The Hebrew unites the two advantages but in a less proportion. Sprung from Egypt where both hieroglyphic and literal characters were used at the same time,[27] it offers a symbolic image in each of its words, although its sentence conserves in its *ensemble* all the eloquence of the spoken tongue. This is the double faculty which has procured for it so much eulogy on the part of those who felt it and so much sarcasm on the part of those who have not.

Chinese characters are written from top to bottom, one under the other, ranging the columns from right to left; those of Sanskrit, following the direction of a horizontal line, going from left to right; Hebraic characters, on the contrary, proceed from right to left. It appears that in the arrangement of the symbolic characters, the genius of the Chinese tongue recalls their origin, and makes them still descend from heaven as, it was said, their first inventor had done. Sanskrit and Hebrew, in tracing their lines in an opposite way, also make allusion to the manner in which their literal characters were invented; for, as Leibnitz very well asserted, everything has its sufficient reason; but as this usage pertains especially to the history of peoples, this is not the place to enter in-

[25] *Mém. concern. les Chinois.* T. I.
[26] *Ibid.* T. VIII. p. 133 à 185.
[27] Clem. Alex. *Strom.* L. V. Herodot. L. II. 36.

to the discussion that its examination would involve. I shall only observe that the method which the Hebrew follows was that of the ancient Egyptians, as related by Herodotus.[28] The Greeks, who received their letters from the Phœnicians, wrote also for some time from right to left; their origin, wholly different, made them soon modify this course. At first they traced their lines in forms of furrows, going from right to left and returning alternately from left to right;[29] afterward, they fixed upon the sole method that we have to-day, which is that of Sanskrit, with which the European tongues have, as I have already said, much analogy. These three styles of writing merit careful consideration, as much in the three typical tongues as in the derivative tongues which are directly or indirectly attached to them. I conclude here this parallelism: to push it further would be useless, so much the more as, not being able to lay before the reader at once the grammatical forms of Chinese, Sanskrit and Hebrew, I should run the risk of not being understood.

If I had felt sure of having the time and the assistance necessary, I should not have hesitated to take first the Chinese, for basis of my work, waiting until later to pass on from Sanskrit to Hebrew, upholding my method by an original translation of the King, the Veda and the Sepher; but being almost certain of the contrary, I have decided to begin with the Hebrew because it offers an interest more direct, more general, more within the grasp of my readers and promises besides, results of an early usefulness. I trust that if the circumstances do not permit me to realize my idea in regard to Sanskrit and Chin-

[28] Herodot. *Ibid.*
[29] *Mém. de l'Acad. des Inscript.* T. XXXIX. in-12 p. 129. Court-de-Gébelin, *Orig. du Lang.* p. 471.

ese, that there will be found men sufficiently courageous, sufficiently obedient to the impulse which Providence gives toward the perfecting of the sciences and the welfare of humanity, to undertake this laborious work and terminate what I have commenced.

§ II.

HEBRAIC TONGUE: AUTHENTICITY OF THE SEPHER OF MOSES; VICISSITUDES EXPERIENCED BY THIS BOOK.

In choosing the Hebraic tongue, I have not been ignorant of any of the difficulties, nor any of the dangers awaiting me. Some knowledge of speech, and of tongues in general, and the unusual course that I had given to my studies, had convinced me long since that the Hebraic tongue was lost, and that the Bible which we possess was far from being the exact translation of the Sepher of Moses. Having attained this original Sepher by other paths than that of the Greeks and Latins, and carried along from the Orient to the Occident of Asia by an impulse contrary to the one ordinarily followed in the exploration of tongues, I saw plainly that the greater part of the vulgar interpretations were false, and that, in order to restore the tongue of Moses in its primitive grammar, it would be necessary to clash violently with the scientific or religious prejudices that custom, pride, interest, the rust of ages and the respect which it attached to ancient errors, concurred in consecrating, strengthening and preserving.

But if one had to listen always to these pusillanimous considerations, what things would ever be perfected? Has man in his adolescence the same needs that he has in his infancy? Does he not change his apparel as well as his nourishment? Are not the lessons of manhood different from those of youth? Do not the savage nations advance toward civilization and those which are civilized toward the acquisition of sciences? Does not one see the cave of the troglodyte make way for the lodge of the hunter, the tent of the herdsman, the hut of the agriculturist, and this cabin transformed successively, thanks to the progressive development of commerce and the arts, into a commodious house, castle, magnificent palace or sumptuous temple? This superb city that we inhabit and this Louvre which spreads before our eyes such rich architecture, do not these all repose upon the same soil where a few miserable hovels of fishermen stood not long ago?

Be not deceived: there are moments indicated by Providence, when the impulse that it gives toward new ideas, undermining precedents useful in their beginning but now superfluous, forces them to yield, even as a skillful architect clears away the rough framework which has supported the arches of his edifice. It would be just as foolish or culpable to attack these precedents or to disturb this framework, when they still support either the social edifice or the particular one, and proceeding, under pretext of their rusticity, their ungracefulness, their necessary obstruction, to overthrow them as out of place; as it would be ridiculous or timid to leave them all there by reason of a foolish or superannuated respect, or a superstitious and condemnatory weakness, since they are of no further use, since they encumber, since they are an obstruction, since they detract from the wisest institutions or the noblest and loftiest structures. Undoubtedly, in the first instance, and following my comparison, either the prince or the architect should stop the audacious ignoramus and prevent him from being buried beneath the inevitable ruins: but in the second instance, they should, on the contrary, welcome the intrepid man who, presenting himself with either torch or lever in hand, offers them, notwithstanding certain perils, a service always difficult.

Had I lived a century or two earlier, even if fortunate circumstances assisted by steadfast labour had placed the same truths within my grasp, I would have kept silent about them, as many savants of all nations have been obliged to do; but the times are changed. I see in looking about me that Providence is opening the portals of a New Day. On all sides, institutions are putting themselves in harmony with the enlightenment of the century. I have not hesitated. Whatever may be the success of my efforts, their aim has been the welfare of humanity and this inner consciousness is sufficient for me.

I am about therefore, to restore the Hebraic tongue in its original principles and show the rectitude and force of these principles, giving by their means a new translation of that part of the Sepher which contains the Cosmogony of Moses. I feel myself bound to fulfill this double task by the very choice that I have made, the motives of which it is useless to explain further. But it is well, perhaps, before entering into the details of the Grammar, and of the numerous notes preceding my translation which prepare and sustain it, that I reveal here the true conditions of things, so as to fortify upright minds against the wrong direction that might be given them, showing the exact point of the question to exploring minds, and make it clearly understood to those whose interests or prejudices, of whatever sort, might lead them astray, that I shall set at naught all criticism which may come from the limits of science, whether supported by delusory opinions or authorities, and that I shall recognize only the worthy champion who shall present himself upon the field of truth, armed with *truth*.

It is well known that the Fathers of the Church have believed, until Saint Jerome, that the Hellenistic version called the *Septuagint*, was a divine work written by prophets rather than by simple translators, often even unaware, from what Saint Augustine says, that another original existed;[30] but it is also known that Saint Jerome, judging this version corrupt in innumerable passages, and by no means exact,[31] substituted a Latin version for it

[30] Walton. *Proleg.* IX. Rich. Simon, *Hist. crit.* L. II. ch. 2. August. L. III. c. 25.

[31] Hieron. *in quæst. hebr.* Rich. Simon. *Ibid.* L. II. ch. 3.

that was considered the only authentic one by the Council of Trent, and in defense of which the Inquisition has not feared to kindle the flames of the stake.[32] Thus the Fathers have contradicted beforehand the decision of the Council, and the decision of the Council has, in its turn, condemned the opinion of the Fathers; so that one could not find Luther entirely wrong, when he said that the Hellenistic interpreters had not an exact knowledge of Hebrew, and that their version was as void of meaning as of harmony,[33] since he followed the sentiment of Saint Jerome, sanctioned in some degree by the Council; nor even blame Calvin and the other wise reformers for having doubted the authenticity of the Vulgate, notwithstanding the infallible decision of the Council,[34] since Saint Augustine had indeed condemned this work according to the idea that every Church had formed in his time.

It is therefore, neither the authority of the Fathers, nor that of the Councils that can be used against me; for the one destroying the other, they remain ineffectual. It will be necessary to demonstrate by a complete and perfect knowledge of Hebrew, and not by Greek and Latin citations to which I take exception, but by interpretations founded upon better principles than mine, to prove to me that I have misunderstood this tongue, and that the bases upon which I place my grammatical edifice are false. One clearly realizes, at this time in which we are living, that it is only with such arguments one can expect to convince me.*

[32] Mariana: *pr. Edit. vulg.* c. I.
[33] Luther *sympos. Cap. de Linguis.*
[34] Fuller, *in miscell.* Causabon. *adv. Baron.*

* The Fathers of the Church can unquestionably be quoted like other writers, but it is upon things *de facto*, and in accordance with the rules of criticism. When it is a question of saying that they have believed that the translation of the Septuagint was a work inspired of God, to quote them in such case is unobjectionable; but if one pretends thus to prove it, the quotation is ridiculous. It is necessary, before engaging in a critical discussion, to study the excellent rules

AUTHENTICITY OF THE SEPHER 25

But if honest minds are astonished that after more than twenty centuries, I alone have been able to penetrate the genius of the tongue of Moses, and understand the writings of this extraordinary man, I shall reply frankly that I do not believe that it is so; I think, on the contrary, that many men have, at different times and among different peoples, possessed the understanding of the Sepher in the way that I possess it; but some have prudently concealed this knowledge whose divulgence would have been dangerous at that time, while others have enveloped it with veils so thick as to be attacked with difficulty. But if this explanation will not be accepted, I would invoke the testimony of a wise and painstaking man, who, being called upon to reply to a similar objection explained thus his thought: "It is very possible that a man, secluded in the confines of the Occident and living in the nineteenth century after Christ, understands better the books of Moses, those of Orpheus, and the fragments which remain to us of the Etruscans, than did the Egyptian, Greek and Roman interpreters of the age of Pericles and Augustus. The degree of intelligence required to understand the ancient tongues is independent of the mechanism and the material of those tongues. It is not only a question of grasping the meaning of the words, it is also necessary to enter into the spirit of the ideas. Often words offer in their vulgar relation a meaning wholly opposed to the spirit that has presided at their *rapprochement....*" [35]

I have said that I consider the Hebraic idiom contained in the Sepher, as a transplanted branch of the Egyptian tongue. This is an assertion the historic proof of which I cannot give at this moment, because it would draw me into details too foreign to my subject; but it seems to me that plain, common sense should be enough

---

laid down by Fréret the most judicious critic that France has possessed. Voyez *Acad. de Belles-Let.* T. VI. *Mémoir.* p. 146. T. IV. p. 411. T. XVIII. p. 49. T. XXI. *Hist.* p. 7.

[35] Court-de Gébelin: *Mond. primit.* T. I, p. 88.

here: for, in whatever manner the Hebrews may have escaped, one cannot deny that they made a long sojourn in Egypt. Even though this sojourn were of only four or five centuries duration as everyone is led to believe;* I ask in all good faith, whether a rude tribe deprived of all literature, without civil or religious institutions that might hold it together, could not assume the tongue of the country in which it lived; a tribe which, transported to Babylon for only seventy years, and while it formed a corps of the nation, ruled by its particular law, submissive to an exclusive cult, was unable to preserve its maternal tongue and bartered it for the Syriac-Aramæan, a sort of Chaldaic dialect;[36] for it is well known that Hebrew, lost from this epoch, ceased to be the vulgar tongue of the Jews.

Therefore, I believe that one cannot, without voluntarily ignoring the evidence, reject so natural an assertion and refuse to admit that the Hebrews coming out from Egypt after a sojourn of more than four hundred years, brought the tongue with them. I do not mean by this to destroy what Bochart, Grotius, Huet, Leclerc,[37] and other erudite moderns have advanced concerning the radical identity which they have rightly admitted between Hebrew and Phœnician; for I know that this last dialect brought into Egypt by the Shepherd kings became identified with the ancient Egyptian long before the arrival of the Hebrews at the banks of the Nile.

Thus the Hebraic idiom ought therefore to have very close relations with the Phœnician, Chaldaic, Arabic and all those sprung from the same source; but for a long time cultivated in Egypt, it had acquired intellectual developments which, prior to the degeneracy of which I have spoken, made it a moral tongue wholly different

---

* In the Second Book of the Sepher, entitled ואלה שמות *W'âleh-Shemoth* ch. 12 v. 40, one reads that this sojourn was 430 years.

[36] Walton *Proleg.* III. Rich. Simon: *Hist. crit. L.* II. ch. 17.

[37] Bochart, *Chanaan* L. II. ch. I. Grotius: *Comm. in Genes.* c. II. Huet: *Démonst. Evan. prop.* IV. c. 3. Leclerc: *Diss. de Ling. hebr.*

AUTHENTICITY OF THE SEPHER

from the vulgar Canaanitish tongue. Is it needful to say to what degree of perfection Egypt had attained? Who of my readers does not know the stately eulogies given it by Bossuet, when, laying aside for a moment his theological partiality, he said, that the noblest works and the most beautiful art of this country consisted in moulding men;[38] that Greece was so convinced of this that her greatest men, Homer, Pythagoras, Plato, even Lycurgus and Solon, those two great legislators, and others whom it is unnecessary to name, went there to acquire wisdom.

Now, had not Moses been instructed in all the sciences of the Egyptians? Had he not, as the historian of the Acts of the Apostles insinuated,[39] begun there to be "mighty in words and deeds?" Think you that the difference would be very great, if the sacred books of the Egyptians, having survived the *débris* of their empire, allowed you to make comparison with those of Moses? Simplicius who, up to a certain point had been able to make this comparison, found so much that was conformable,[40] that he concluded that the prophet of the Hebrews had walked in the footsteps of the ancient *Thoth*.

Certain modern savants after having examined the Sepher in incorrect translations, or in a text which they were incapable of understanding, struck with certain repetitions, and believing they detected in the numbers taken literally, palpable anachronisms, have imagined, now, that Moses had never existed, and then, that he had worked upon scattered memoirs, whose fragments he himself or his secretaries had clumsily patched together.[41] It has also been said that Homer was an imaginary being; as if the existence of the Iliad and the Odyssey, these master-pieces of poetry, did not attest the existence of

[38] Bossuet: *Hist. Univers.* III. part. § 3.
[39] Act. VII. v. 22.
[40] Simplic. *Comm. phys. arist.* L. VIII p. 268.
[41] Spinosa: *tract. theol.* c. 9. Hobbes: *Leviath. Part.* III, c. 33. Isaac de la Peyrère: *Syst. theol. Part.* I. L. IV. c. I. Leclerc, Bolinbroke, Voltaire, Boulanger, Fréret, etc.

their author! He must have little poetic instinct and poor understanding of the arrangement and plan of an epic work, who could conceive such a false idea of man and his conceptions, and be persuaded that a book like the Sepher, the King or the Veda could be put forward as genuine, be raised by fraud to the rank of divine Writings, and be compiled with the same heedlessness that certain authors display in their crude libels.

Undoubtedly certain notes, certain commentaries, certain reflections written at first marginally, have slipped into the text of the Sepher; Esdras has restored badly some of the mutilated passages; but the statue of the Pythian Apollo on account of a few slight breaks, remains none the less standing as the master-piece of an unrivalled sculptor whose unknown name is a matter of less consequence. Not recognizing in the Sepher the stamp of a grand man shows lack of knowledge; not wishing that this grand man be called Moses shows lack of criticism.

It is certain that Moses made use of more ancient books and perhaps of sacerdotal memoirs, as has been suspected by Leclerc, Richard Simon and the author of Conjectures upon Genesis.[42] But Moses does not hide it; he cites in two or three passages of the Sepher the title of the works which are before his eyes: the book of the *Generations of Adam;*[43] the book of the *Wars of the Lord;*[44] the book of the *Sayings of the Seers.*[45] The book of *Jasher* is mentioned in Joshua.[46] The compiling of old memoirs the causing of them to be compiled by scribes as these writers have advanced, or indeed the abridging them as Origen supposed, is very far from that.[47] Moses created in copying: this is what a real genius does. Can one im-

[42] Leclerc, *in Diss.* III. *de script. Pentateuch.* Richard Simon: *Hist. crit.* L. I. c. 7.
[43] *Gen.* c. 5. v. 1.
[44] *Num.* c. 21. v. 14.
[45] *Chron.* II. c. 33, v. 19.
[46] *Jos.* c. 10. v. 13.
[47] *Epist. ad Affric.*

agine that the sculptor of the Pythian Apollo had no models? Can one imagine, by chance, that Homer imitated nothing? The opening lines of the Iliad were copied from the *Demetréide* of Orpheus. The history of Helen and the war of Troy were preserved in the sacerdotal archives of Tyre whence this poet took it. It is asserted that he changed it to such an extent, that, of the simulacrum of the Moon he made a woman, and of the Eons, or celestial Spirits who contended for its possession, the men whom he called Greeks and Trojans. [48]

Moses had delved deeply into the sanctuaries of Egypt, and he had been initiated into the mysteries; it is easily discovered in examining the form of his Cosmogony. He undoubtedly possessed a great number of hieroglyphics which he explained in his writings, as asserted by Philo;[49] his genius and particular inspiration produced the rest. He made use of the Egyptian tongue in all its purity.* This tongue had at this time attained its highest degree of perfection. It was not long becoming deteriorated in the hands of a rude tribe left to their own fate in the deserts of Idumea. It was a giant that found itself suddenly among a troop of pygmies. The extraordinary movement which this tongue had stamped upon its nation could not last, but in order that the plans of Providence should be fulfilled it was sufficient that the sacred storehouse in the Sepher should be guarded carefully.

It appears, in the opinion of the most famous rabbis,[50] that Moses himself, foreseeing the fate to which his

[48] Beausobre, *Hist. du Manich.* T. II. p. 328.
[49] *De vitâ Mos.*

* I shall not stop to contend with the opinion of those who seem to believe that the Coptic differs not in the least from the ancient Egyptian; for can one imagine such an opinion as serious? One might as well say that the tongue of Boccaccio and Dante is the same as that of Cicero and Vergil. One can display his wit in upholding such a paradox; but he could prove it neither by criticism nor even by common sense.

[50] Moyse de Cotsi: *Pref. au grand Livre des Command. de la Loi.* Aben-Esra, *Jesud Mora,* etc.

book must be submitted and the false interpretations that must be given it in the course of time, had recourse to an oral law which he gave by word of mouth to reliable men whose fidelity he had tested, and whom he charged to transmit it in the secret of the sanctuary to other men who, transmitting it in their turn from age to age might insure its thus reaching the remotest posterity.[51] This oral law that the modern Jews are confident they still possess, is named Kabbala,* from a Hebrew word which signifies, that which *is received*, that which *comes from elsewhere*, that which *is passed from hand to hand*, etc. The most famous books that they possess, such as those of the *Zohar,* the *Bahir,* the *Medrashim,* the two *Gemaras,* which compose the *Talmud,* are almost entirely kabbalistic.

It would be very difficult to say today whether Moses has really left this oral law, or whether, having left it, it has not become altered, as the learned Maimonides seems to insinuate when he writes that his nation has lost the knowledge of innumerable things, without which it is almost impossible to understand the Law.[52] Be that as it may, it is quite possible that a like institution might have been in the mind of the Egyptians whose inclination for the mysteries is quite well known.

Besides, chronology, cultivated but little before the conquest of Chosroes, that famous Persian monarch whom we call Cyrus, hardly permits fixing the epoch of the appearance of Moses. It is only by approximation that one can place, about fifteen centuries before the Christian era, the issue of the Sepher. After the death of this theocratic lawgiver, the people to whom he had confided this sacred storehouse, remained still in the desert for some time and were established only after many struggles. Their wandering life influenced their lang-

---

[51] Boulanger: *Antiq. dev.* L. I. c. 22.

* קבל.

[52] Rambam. *More. Nebuch.* Part. I. c. 21.

uage which degenerated rapidly. Their character became harsh; their spirit was roused. They turned hands against each other. One of the twelve tribes, that of Benjamin, was almost wholly destroyed. Nevertheless, the mission that this people had to fulfill and which had necessitated their exclusive laws, alarmed the neighbouring peoples; their customs, their extraordinary institutions, their pride irritated them; they became the object of their attacks. In less than four centuries they were subjected six times to slavery, and six times they were delivered by the hand of Providence who willed their preservation. In the midst of these terrible catastrophes, the Sepher was respected: covered with a providential obscurity it followed the vanquished, escaped the victors, and for a long time remained unknown to its possessors themselves. Too much publicity would have brought about its loss. Whether it is true that Moses had left oral instructions for evading the corruption of the text, it is not to be doubted that he did not take all possible precaution to guard its preservation. It can therefore be regarded as a very probable thing that those who handed down in silence and in the most inviolable secrecy, the thoughts of the prophet, confided his book to each other in the same manner, and in the midst of troubles preserved it from destruction.

But at last after four centuries of disasters, a more peaceful day seemed to shine upon Israel. The theocratic sceptre was divided; the Hebrews gave themselves a king, and their empire although restricted by neighbouring powers did not remain without some glory. Here a new danger appeared. Prosperity came to do what the most frightful reverses had been unable to achieve. Indolence seated upon the throne crept into the lowest ranks of the people. Certain indifferent chronicles, certain misunderstood allegories, chants of vengeance and of pride, songs of voluptuousness, bearing the names of Joshua, Ruth, Samuel, David and Solomon, usurped the place of the

Sepher. Moses was neglected; his laws were unheeded. The guardians of his secrets, invested with luxury, a prey to all the temptations of avarice gradually forgot their oaths. The arm of Providence raised against this intractable people, struck them at the moment least suspected. They were stirred by intestine struggles, they turned against each other. Ten tribes separated themselves and kept the name of Israel. The other two tribes took the name of Judah. An irreconcilable hatred spread between these two rival peoples; they erected altar against altar, throne against throne; Samaria and Jerusalem had each its sanctuary. The safety of the Sepher was the outcome of this division.

Amid the controversies born of this schism each people recalled its origin, invoked its unheeded laws, cited the forgotten Sepher. Everything proves that neither one nor the other possessed this book any longer and that it was only by favour of heaven that it was found long afterward,[53] at the bottom of an old coffer covered with dust, but happily preserved beneath a heap of pieces of money, which avarice had in all probability accumulated secretly and hidden from all eyes. This event decided the fate of Jerusalem. Samaria deprived of her palladium, having been struck a century before by the power of the Assyrians, had fallen, and her ten tribes, captive, dispersed among the nations of Asia, having no religious bond, or to speak more clearly, entering no more in the conservative plans of Providence, were dissolved there; whereas Jerusalem, having recovered her sacred code in the moment of her greatest peril, attached herself to it with a strength that nothing could break. In vain were the peoples of Judah led away into bondage; in vain was their royal city destroyed as Samaria had been, the Sepher which followed them to Babylon was their safe-guard. They could indeed lose, during the seventy years of their captivity, even their mother tongue, but they could not

---

[53] Voyez *Chroniq.* II. c. 34. v. 14. *et suiv.;* et conférez *Rois* II. ch. 12.

be detached from the love of their laws. It was only needful that a man of genius should deliver these laws to them. This man was found; for genius never fails to come forth when summoned by Providence.

Esdras was the name of this man. His soul was strong and his constancy unflinching. He saw that the time was favourable, that the downfall of the Assyrian empire, overthrown by the hands of Cyrus, gave him the means for reëstablishing the Kingdom of Judah. He skillfully profited by this. From the Persian monarch he obtained the liberty of the Jews and led them to the ruins of Jerusalem. But previous even to their captivity, the politics of the Assyrian kings had reanimated the Samaritan schism. Certain tribes, Cuthæans or Scythians, brought into Samaria, had intermarried with certain surviving members of Israel and even with certain remnants of the Jews who had taken refuge there. At Babylon the plan had been conceived of opposing them to the Jews, whose religious obstinacy was disturbing.[54] A copy of the Hebraic Sepher had been sent to them with a priest devoted to the interests of the court. Accordingly when Esdras appeared, these new Samaritans opposed its establishment with all their strength.[55] They accused him before the great king, of fortifying a city and of making a citadel rather than a temple. It was even said that not content with calumniating him they advanced to fight.

But Esdras was hard to intimidate. Not only did he repulse these adversaries and thwart their intrigues, but anathematizing them, raised up between them and the Jews an insurmountable barrier. He did more: being unable to take away from them the Hebraic Sepher, a copy of which they had received from Babylon, he conceived the idea of giving another form to his and resolved upon the change of its characters.

This was comparatively easy, since the Jews, having

[54] *Kings* II ch. 17. v. 27.
[55] Joseph: *Hist. Jud.* L. XI. c. 4.

at that time not only become denaturalized, but having lost completely the idiom of their forefathers, read the ancient characters with difficulty, accustomed as they were to the Assyrian dialect and to the modern characters of which the Chaldeans had been the inventors. This innovation that politics alone seemed to order, and which without doubt was done from the loftiest motives, had most fortunate results for the preservation of the text of Moses, as I shall relate in my Grammar. It called forth between the two peoples an emulation which has contributed not inconsiderably to bring down to us a book to which the highest interests must ever be attached.

Furthermore, Esdas did not act alone in this matter. The anathema which he had hurled against the Samaritans having been approved by the doctors of Babylon, he convoked them and held with them that great synagogue, so famous in the books of the rabbis.[56] It was there that the changing of the characters was arrested; that the vowel points were admitted in the writing for the use of the vulgar, and the ancient Masorah began, which one should guard against confusing with the modern Masorah, a work of the rabbis of Tiberias, the origin of which does not go back beyond the fifth century of the Christian era.*

[56] R. Eleasar.

* The first *Mashorah*, whose name indicates Assyrian origin as I shall show in my Grammar, regulates the manner in which one should write the Sepher, as much for usage in the temple as for its particular use; the characters that should be employed, the different divisions in books, chapters and verses that should be admitted in the works of Moses; the second *Masorah*, that I write with a different orthography in order to distinguish it from the first, aside from the characters, vowel points, books, chapters and verses with which it is likewise occupied, enters into the most minute details pertaining to the number of words and letters which compose each of these divisions in parti cular, and of the work in general; it notes those of the verses where some letter is lacking, is superfluous, or else has been changed for another; it designates by the word *Kere* and *Ketib*, the diverse renditions that should be substituted in the reading of each; it marks the

Esdras did still more. As much to estrange the Samaritans as to humour the Jews, whom long custom and their sojourn at Babylon had attached to certain writings more modern than those of Moses and much less authentic, he made a choice from them, retouched those which appeared to him defective or altered, and made up a collection which he joined to the Sepher. The assembly over which he presided approved of this labour that the Samaritans deemed impious; for it is well to know that the Samaritans received absolutely only the Sepher of Moses,[57] and rejected all the other writings as apocryphal. The Jews themselves have not today the same veneration for all the books which constitute what we call the Bible. They preserved the writings of Moses with a much more scrupulous attention, learned them by heart and recited them much oftener than the others. The savants, who have been in a position to examine their various manuscripts, state that the part consecrated to the books of the Law is always much more exact and better treated than the rest.[58]

number of times that the same word is found at the beginning, the middle or the end of a verse; it indicates what letters should be pronounced, understood, inverted, suspended, etc., etc. It is because they have not studied to distinguish these two institutions from each other, that the savants of the past centuries have laid themselves open to such lively discussions: some, like Buxtorf who saw only the first *Mashorah* of Esdras, would not grant that it had anything of the modern, which was ridiculous when one considers the minutiæ of which I have just spoken: others, like Cappell, Morin, Walton and even Richard Simon who saw only the *Masorah* of the rabbis of Tiberias, denied that it had anything of the ancient, which was still more ridiculous, when one considers the choice of characters, vowel points, and the primitive divisions of the Sepher. Among the rabbis, all those who have any name, have upheld the antiquity of the *Mashorah;* there has been only Elijah Levita who has attributed it to more modern times. But perhaps he heard only the *Masorah* of Tiberias mentioned. Rarely do the rabbis say all that they think.

[57] Walton. *Proleg.* XI. Richard Simon. *Hist. crit.* L. I. ch. 10.

[58] Rich. Simon: *Hist. Crit.* L. I. ch. 8.

This revision and these additions have given occasion in later times for thinking that Esdras had been the author of all the writings of the Bible. Not only have the modern philosophists embraced this opinion,[59] which favoured their skepticism, but many Fathers of the Church, and many thinkers have ardently sustained it, believing it more consistent with their hatred of the Jews:[60] they rely chiefly upon a passage attributed to Esdras himself.[61] I think I have sufficiently proved by reasoning, that the Sepher of Moses could be neither a supposition nor a compilation of detached fragments: for one never takes for granted nor compiles works of this nature, and as to its integrity in the time of Esdras, there exists a proof *de facto* that cannot be challenged: this is the Samaritan text. It is well known, however little one may reflect, that considering the condition of things, the Samaritans, mortal enemies of the Jews, anathematized by Esdras, would never have received a book of which Esdras had been the author. They were careful enough not to receive the other writings, and it is also this which can make their authenticity doubted.[62] But it is not my plan here to enter into a discussion in regard to this. It is only with the writings of Moses that I am occupied; I have designated them expressly by the name Sepher, in order to distinguish them from the Bible in general, the Greek name of which, recalls the translation of the Septuagint and comprises all the additions of Esdras and even some more modern ones.

[59] Bolingbroke, Voltaire, Fréret, Boulanger, etc.

[60] St. Basil. *Epist. ad Chil.* St. Clém. Alex. *Strom.* I. Tertull. *de habit. mulier.* c. 35. St. Iren. L. XXXIII. c. 25. Isidor. *Etymol.* L. VI c. 1. Leclerc. *Sentim. de quelq. théolog.* etc.

[61] Esdras ch. IV. v. 14. This book is regarded as apocryphal.

[62] Rich. Simon. *Hist. crit.* L. I. ch. 10.

§ III.

CONTINUATION OF THE REVOLUTIONS OF THE SEPHER. ORIGIN OF THE PRINCIPAL VERSIONS WHICH HAVE BEEN MADE.

Let us rely firmly upon this important truth: the Hebraic tongue already corrupted by a gross people, and intellectual as it was in its origin, brought down to its most material elements, was entirely lost after the captivity of Babylon. This is an historic fact impossible to be doubted, whatever skepticism we may profess. The Bible shows it;[63] the Talmud affirms it;[64] it is the sentiment of the most famous rabbis;[65] Walton cannot deny it;[66] the best critic who has written upon this matter, Richard Simon, never wearies of repeating it.[67] Thus therefore, nearly six centuries before Jesus Christ, the Hebrews, having become Jews, no longer either spoke or understood their original tongue. They used a Syriac dialect called Aramaic, formed of the union of several idioms of Assyria and Phœnicia, and quite different from the Nabathæan which according to d'Herbelot was pure Chaldaic.[68]

On and after this epoch, the Sepher of Moses was always paraphrased in the synagogues. It is known that after the reading of each verse, an interpreter was charged with explaining it to the people, in the vulgar tongue. From this came the name of *Targum*.* It is somewhat

[63] *Nehem.* ch. 8.
[64] Thalm. *devot.* ch. 4.
[65] Elias, Kimchi, Ephode, etc.
[66] *Proleg.* III et XII.
[67] *Hist. crit.* L. I. ch. 8, 16, 17, etc.
[68] *Biblioth. ori.* p. 514.

* From the Chaldaic word, תַּרְגּוּם, *version, translation*: R. Jacob: *in compend. thalm.*

difficult to say today, whether these versions were at first written by the doctors or entrusted to the sagacity of the interpreters. However that may be, it appears certain that the meaning of the Hebraic words, becoming more and more uncertain, violent discussions arose concerning the diverse interpretations which were given to the Sepher. Some, claiming to possess the oral law secretly given by Moses, wished to introduce it for everyone in these explanations; others, denied the existence of this law, rejected all kinds of traditions and required that they hold to the most literal and the most material explanations. Two rival sects were born of these disputes. The first, that of the Pharisees was the most numerous and the most esteemed: it admitted the spiritual meaning of the Sepher, treated as allegories what appeared to be obscure, believed in divine Providence and in the immortality of the soul.[69] The second, that of the Sadducees, treated as fables all the traditions of the Pharisees, scorned their allegories, and as it found nothing in the material meaning of the Sepher which might prove or even express the immortality of the soul, denied it; seeing nothing in what their antagonists called soul, only a consequence of the organization of the body, a transient faculty which must become extinguished with it.[70] In the midst of these two contending sects, a third was formed, less numerous than the other two, but infinitely more learned: it was that of the Essenes. These held a median position between the Pharisees, who made every thing give way to the allegorical, and the Sadducees who, by the dryness of their interpretations perverted the dogmas of Moses. They preserved the letter and the material meaning outwardly, but guarded the tradition and the oral law for the secret of the sanctuary. The Essenes, living far from cities, formed particular societies, and in no wise

[69] Joseph. *Antiq.* L. XII. 22. XVII. 3.

[70] Joseph. *Ibid.* L. XIII. 9. Budd. *Introd. ad phil. hebr.* Basnage: *Hist. des Juifs.* T. I.

ORIGIN OF PRINCIPAL VERSIONS 39

jealous of the sacerdotal charges filled by the Pharisees, or of the civil honours intrigued for by the Sadducees, they applied themselves much to ethics and the study of nature. All that has been written upon the mode of life and intelligence of this sect has redounded greatly to its credit. [71] Wherever there were Jews, there were Essenes; but it was in Egypt that they were mostly found. Their principal retreat was in the environs of Alexandria, toward the lake, and Mount Moriah.

I beg the reader seriously interested in ancient secrets to give attention to this name;* for if it is true, as everyone attests, that Moses has left an oral law, it is among the Essenes that it has been preserved. The Pharisees who boasted so haughtily that they possessed it, had only its semblances, for which Jesus constantly reproaches them. It is from these Pharisees that the modern Jews descend, with the exception of certain true savants through whom the secret tradition goes back to that of the Essenes. The Sadducees have brought forth the present Karaites, otherwise called *Scripturalists*.

But even before the Jews possessed their Chaldaic targums, the Samaritans had a version of the Sepher made in the vulgar tongue; for they were even less able than the Jews to understand the original text. This version which we possess entire, being the first of all those which had been made, merits consequently more confidence than the targums, which succeeding and destroying one another do not appear of great antiquity: besides, the dialect in which the Samaritan version is written has more affinity with the Hebrew than with the Aramaic or the Chaldaic of the targums. To a rabbi, named Onkelos, has ordinarily been attributed the targum of the Sepher,

[71] Joseph: *de bello Jud.* L. II. c. 12. Phil. *de vitâ contempl.* Budd: *Introd. ad phil. hebr.* etc.

* It is unnecessary, I think, for me to say that Mount Moriah has become one of the symbols of Adonhiramite masonry. This word signifies *the reflected light, the splendour.*

properly so-called, and to another rabbi named Jonathan, that of the other books of the Bible; but the epoch of their composition has not been fixed. It can only be inferred that they are more ancient than the Talmud, because the dialect is more correct and less disfigured. The Talmud of Jerusalem particularly, is in a barbarous style, mixed with a quantity of words borrowed from neighbouring tongues and chiefly from Greek, Latin and Persian.[72] This was the vulgar idiom of the Jews in the time of Jesus Christ.

Nevertheless, the Jews, protected by the Persian monarchs, had enjoyed some moments of tranquillity; they had rebuilt their temples; they had raised again the walls of their city. Suddenly the face of things was changed: the empire of Cyrus crumbled; Babylon fell into the power of the Greeks; all bent beneath the laws of Alexander. But this torrent which burst forth in a moment, both upon Africa and upon Asia, soon divided its waves and turned them in different channels. Alexander died and his captains parcelled out his heritage. The Jews fell into the power of the Seleucidæ. The Greek tongue carried everywhere by the conquerors, modified the new idiom of Jerusalem and drew it further away from the Hebrew. The Sepher of Moses already disfigured by the Chaldaic paraphrases disappeared gradually in the Greek version.

Thanks to the discussions raised by the savants of the last centuries upon the famous version of the Hellenist Jews, vulgarly called the Septuagint version, nothing had become more obscure than its origin.[73] They questioned among themselves, at what epoch, and how, and why it had been done;[74] whether it was the first of all, and whether there did not exist an earlier version in Greek,

---

[72] *Hist. crit.* L. II. ch. 18.

[73] *Hist. crit.* L. II. c. 2.

[74] Despierres: *Auctor, script. tract.* II. Walton. *Proleg.* IX.

ORIGIN OF PRINCIPAL VERSIONS 41

from which Pythagoras, Plato and Aristotle had drawn their knowledge;[75] who the seventy interpreters were and whether they were or were not, in separate cells while labouring at this work;[76] whether these interpreters were, in short, prophets rather than simple translators.[77]

After having examined quite at length the divergent opinions which have been put forth on this subject, these are what I have judged the most probable. Anyone can, if he is so inclined, do this difficult labour over again, which after all will produce only the same results, if he is careful to exercise the same impartiality that I have shown.

It cannot be doubted that Ptolemy, son of Lagus, notwithstanding some acts of violence which marked the beginning of his reign and into which he was forced by the conspiracy of his brothers, was a very great prince. Egypt has not had a more brilliant epoch. There, flourished at the same time, peace, commerce, the arts, and the cultivation of the sciences, without which there is no true grandeur in an empire. It was through the efforts of Ptolemy that the splendid library in Alexandria was established, which Demetrius of Phalereus, to whom he had confided its keeping, enriched with all the most precious literature of that time. The Jews had long since been settled in Egypt.[78] I cannot conceive by what spirit of contradiction the modern thinkers insist that, in the course of circumstances such as I have just presented, Ptolemy did not have the thought that has been attributed to him of making a translation of the Sepher in order to place it in his library.[79] Nothing seems to me so simple. The

---

[75] Cyril. Alex. L. I. Euseb. *præp. evan.* c. 3. Ambros. *Epist.* 6. Joseph *Contr. Api.* L. I. Bellarmin. *de verbo Dei.* L. II. c. 5.

[76] St. Justin, *orat. par. ad gent.* Epiph. *Lib. de mens. et ponder.* Clem. Alex. *Strom.* L. I. Hieron. *Præf. in Pentat.* J. Morin. *Exercit.* IV.

[77] St. Thomas: *quæst.* II. art. 3. St. August. *de Civit. dei.* L. XVIII. c. 43. Iren. *adv. hæres.* c. 25, etc.

[78] Joseph. *Antiq.* L. XII. c. 3.

[79] *Horæ Biblicæ*: § 2.

historian Josephus is assuredly believable on this point as well as the author of the letter of Aristeas, [80] notwithstanding certain embellishments with which he loads this historic fact.

But the execution of this plan might offer difficulties; for it is known that the Jews communicated with reticence their books, and that they guarded their mysteries with an inviolable secrecy. [81] It was even a customary opinion among them, that God would punish severely those who dared to make translations in the vulgar tongue. The Talmud relates that Jonathan, after the appearance of his Chaidaic paraphrase, was sharply reprimanded by a voice from heaven for having dared to reveal to men the secrets of God. Ptolemy, therefore, was obliged to have recourse to the intercession of the sovereign pontiff Eleazar, showing his piety by freeing certain Jewish slaves. This sovereign pontiff whether touched by the bounty of the king, or whether not daring to resist his will, sent him an exemplar of the Sepher of Moses, permitting him to make a translation of it in the Greek tongue. It was only a question of choosing the translators. As the Essenes of Mount Moriah enjoyed a merited reputation for learning and sanctity, everything leads me to believe that Demetrius of Phalereus turned his attention upon them and transmitted to them the orders of the king. These sectarians lived as anchorites, secluded in separate cells, being occupied, as I have already said, with the study of nature. The Sepher was, according to them, composed of spirit and substance: by the substance they understood the material meaning of the Hebraic tongue; by the spirit, the spiritual meaning lost to the vulgar.[82] Pressed between the religious law which forbade the communication of the divine mysteries and the authority of the prince who ordered them to translate

[80] Joseph. *Ibid. præf.* et L. XII. c. 2.
[81] *Hist. crit.* L. II. ch. 2.
[82] Joseph. *de Bello Jud.* L. II. ch. 12. Phil. *de vitâ contempl.* Budd. *introd. ad phil. hebr.*

ORIGIN OF PRINCIPAL VERSIONS 43

the Sepher, they were astute enough to extricate themselves from such a hazardous step: for, in giving the substance of the book, they obeyed the civil authority, and in retaining the spirit, obeyed their conscience. They made a verbal version as exact as they could in the restricted and material expression, and in order to protect themselves still further from the reproaches of profanation, they made use of the text of the Samaritan version whenever the Hebraic text did not offer sufficient obscurity.

It is very doubtful whether there were seventy in number who performed this task. The name of the *Septuagint Version* comes from another circumstance that I am about to relate.

The Talmud states that at first there were only five interpreters, which is quite probable; for it is known that Ptolemy caused only the five books of Moses to be translated, those contained in the Sepher, without being concerned with the additions of Esdras.[83] Bossuet agrees with this in saying that the rest of the books were, in the course of time, put into Greek for the use of the Jews who were spread throughout Egypt and Greece, where they had not only forgotten their ancient tongue, the Hebrew, but even the Chaldaic which they had learned during captivity.[84] This writer adds, and I beg the reader to note this, that these Jews made a Greek mixture of Hebraisms which is called the Hellenistic tongue, and that the *Septuagint* and all the New Testament are written in this language.

It is certain that the Jews, dispersed throughout Egypt and Greece, having entirely forgotten the Aramaic dialect in which their Targums were written, and finding themselves in need of a paraphrase in the vulgar tongue, would naturally take the version of the Sepher which already existed in the royal library at Alexandria: this is

[83] Joseph. *Antiq.* L. XII. ch. 2.
[84] *Disc. sur l'Hist. univ.* I. part. 8.

what they did. They joined to it a translation of the additions of Esdras and sent the whole to Jerusalem to be approved as a paraphrase. The sanhedrin granted their demand, and as this tribunal happened to be of seventy judges in conformity with the law,[85] this version received the name of *Septuagint version,* that is to say, approved by the seventy.[86]

Such is the origin of the Bible. It is a copy in the Greek tongue of the Hebraic writings wherein the material forms of the Sepher of Moses are well enough preserved, so that those who see nothing beyond the material forms may not suspect the spiritual. In the state of ignorance in which the Jews were at that time, this book thus disguised suited them. It suited them to such an extent, that in many of the Greek synagogues, it was read not only as paraphrase, but in place of and in preference to the original text.[87] Of what use was the reading of the Hebrew text? The Jewish people had long since ceased to understand it even in its most restricted acceptance,* and among the rabbis, if one excepts certain

[85] Sepher. L. IV. c. 11. Elias Levita: *in Thisbi.*
[86] *Hist. crit.* L. II. c. 2.
[87] Walton: *Proleg.* IX. *Horæ biblicæ.* §. 2. *Hist. Crit.* L. I. c. 17.

* Philo, the most learned of the Jews of his time, did not know a word of Hebrew although he wrote a history of Moses. He praises much the Greek version of the Hellenists, which he was incapable of comparing with the original. Josephus himself, who has written a history of his nation and who should have made a special study of the Sepher, proves at every step that he did not understand the Hebrew text and that he often made use of the Greek. He laboured hard in the beginning of his work to understand why Moses, wishing to express the first day of creation, used the word *one* and not the word *first,* without making the very simple reflection that the word אחד in Hebrew, signifies both. It is obvious that he pays less attention to the manner in which the proper names were written, than to that in which they were pronounced in his time, and that he read them not by the Hebraic letter, but by the Greek letter. This historian who promises to translate and to render the meaning of Moses, without adding or diminishing anything, is however far from accomplishing this purpose. In the very first chapter of his book, he says that God

ORIGIN OF PRINCIPAL VERSIONS 45

Essenes initiated in the secrets of the oral law, the most learned scarcely pretended to go back of the Greek, the Latin, or the barbarous jargon of Jerusalem, to the Chaldaic Targums which had become for them almost as difficult as the text.*

It was during this state of ignorance and when the Greek Bible usurped everywhere the place of the Hebraic Sepher, that Providence wishing to change the face of the world and operating one of those necessary movements whose profound reason I believe it useless to reveal, raised up Jesus. A new cult was born. Christianity, at first obscure, considered as a Jewish sect, increased, was spread abroad and covered Asia, Africa and Europe. The Roman empire was enveloped by it. Jesus and his disciples had always quoted the Greek Bible, the Fathers of the Church attaching themselves to this book with a religious respect, believing it inspired, written by the prophets, scorned the Hebraic text, and as Saint Augustine clearly says, [88] were even ignorant of its existence. Nevertheless the Jews, alarmed at this movement which was beyond their comprehension, cursed the book which caused it. The rabbis, either by politics or because the oral law became known, openly scoffed it as an illusory version, decried it as a false work, and caused it to be considered by the Jews as more calamitous for Israel than the golden calf. They publicly stated that the earth had been enveloped in darkness during three days on account of this profanation of the holy Book, and as one

took away speech from the serpent, that he made its tongue venomous, that he condemned it henceforth to have feet no more; that he commanded Adam to tread upon the head of this serpent, etc. Now, if Philo and Josephus showed themselves so ignorant in the understanding of the sacred text, what must have been the other Jews? I make exception always of the Essenes.

* It is related in St. Luke that Jesus Christ read to the people a passage from Isaiah paraphrased in Chaldaic and that he explained it (ch. 4. v. 17). It is Walton who has made this observation in his Prolegomena. *Dissert.* XII.

[88] "Ut an alia esset ignorarent." August. L. III. c. 25.

can see in the Talmud, ordained an annual fast of three days in memory of this event.

These precautions came too late; the storehouse badly guarded had changed hands. Israel, resembling a crude coffer closed with a triple lock but worn out by time, afforded no longer a sufficiently sure shelter. A terrible revolution drew nigh: Jerusalm fell, and the Roman empire, a political moribund body, was destined to the vultures of the North. Already the clouds of ignorance were darkening the horizon; already the cries of the barbarians were heard in the distance. It was necessary to oppose these formidable enemies with an insurmountable obstacle. That obstacle was this same Book which was to subdue them and which they were not to understand.

Neither the Jews nor the Christians were able to enter into the profoundness of these plans. They accused each other of ignorance and of bad faith. The Jews, possessors of an original text which they could no longer comprehend, anathematized a version which rendered only the gross and exterior forms. The Christians, content with these forms which at least they grasped, went no further and treated with contempt all the rest. It is true that from time to time there appeared among them men who, profiting by a last gleam of light in those dark days, dared to fix the basis of their belief, and judging the version in its spirit to be identical with its forms, detached themselves abruptly and disdainfully from it. Such were Valentine, Basil, Marcion, Apelles, Bardesane, and Manes, the most terrible of the adversaries that the Bible has encountered. All treated as impious the author of a book wherein the Being, preëminently good, is represented as the author of evil; wherein this Being creates without plan, prefers arbitrarily, repents, is angered, punishes an innocent posterity with the crime of one whose downfall he has prepared.[89] Manes, judging Moses by the book that the Christians declared to be from him,

[89] Beausobre: *Hist. du Manich.* Passim. Epiphan, *hœres*, passim.

ORIGIN OF PRINCIPAL VERSIONS

regarded this prophet as having been inspired by the Genius of evil.[90] Marcion, somewhat less severe saw in him only the instrument of the Creator of the elementary world, very different from the Supreme Being.[91] All of them caused storms, more or less violent; according to the force of their genius. They did not succeed, because their attack was imprudent, unseasonable, and because without knowing it they brought their light to bear inopportunely upon a rough structure prepared for sustaining a most true and imposing edifice.

Those Fathers of the Church whose eyes were not wholly bli ded, sought for expedients to evade the greatest difficulties. Some accused the Jews of having foisted upon the books of Moses things false and injurious to the Divinity;[92] others had recourse to allegories.[93] Saint Augustine acknowledged that there was no way of conserving the literal meaning of the first three chapters of Genesis, without attributing to God things unworthy of him.[94] Origen declared that if the history of the creation was taken in the literal sense it was absurd and contradictory.[95] He complained of the ignorant ones who, led astray by the letter of the Bible, attributed to God sentiments and actions that one would not wish to attribute to the most unjust, the most barbarous of men.[96] The wise Beausobre in his *Histoire du Manichéisme,* and Pétau in his *Dogmes théologiques,* cite numerous similar examples.

The last of the Fathers who saw the terrible mistake of the version of the Hellenists and who wished to remedy it, was Saint Jerome. I give full justice to his inten-

[90] *Act. disput. Archel.* § 7.
[91] Tertull. *Contr. Marci.*
[92] *Recognit.* L. II. p. 52. *Clément. Homel.* III. p. 642-645.
[93] Pétau: *Dogm. théol. de opif.* L. II. 7.
[94] August. *Contr. Faust.* L. XXXII. 10. *De Genes. Contr. Manich.* L. II. 2.
[95] Origen. *philocal.* p. 12.
[96] Origen. *Ibid.* p. 6 et 7.

tions. This Father, of an ardent character and searching mind, might have remedied the evil, if the evil had been of a nature to yield to his efforts. Too prudent to cause a scandal like that of Marcion or of Manes; too judicious to restrict himself to vain subtleties as did Origen or Saint Augustine, he felt deeply that the only way of arriving at the truth was to resort to the original text. This text was entirely unknown. The Greek was everything. It was from the Greek, strange and extraordinary fact, that had been made, according as was needed, not only the Latin version, but the Coptic, Ethiopic, Arabic, and even the Syriac, Persian and others.

But in order to resort to the original text it would be necessary to understand the Hebrew. And how was it possible to understand a tongue lost for more than a thousand years? The Jews, with the exception of a very small number of sages from whom the most horrible torments were unable to drag it, understood it hardly better than Saint Jerome. Nevertheless, the only way that remained for this Father was to turn to the Jews. He took a teacher from among the rabbis of the school of Tiberias. At this news, all the Christain church cried out in indignation. Saint Augustine boldly censured Saint Jerome. Rufinus attacked him unsparingly. Saint Jerome, exposed to this storm, repented having said that the version of the Septuagint was wrong; he used subterfuges; sometimes, to flatter the vulgar, he said that the Hebraic text was corrupt; sometimes, he extolled this text concerning which, he declared that the Jews had not been able to corrupt a single line. When reproached with these contradictions, he replied that they were ignorant of the laws of dialectics, that they did not understand that in disputes one spoke sometimes in one manner and sometimes in another, and that one did the opposite of what one said.[97] He relied upon the example of Saint Paul; he quoted Origen. Rufinus charged him with

[97] P. Morin. *Exercit. Bibl.* Rich. Simon. *Hist. crit.*

ORIGIN OF PRINCIPAL VERSIONS 49

impiety, and replied to him that Origen had never forgotten himself to the point of translating the Hebrew, and that only Jews or apostates could undertake it.[98] Saint Augustine, somewhat more moderate, did not accuse the Jews of having corrupted the sacred text; he did not treat Saint Jerome as impious and as apostate; he even agreed that the version of the Septuagint is often incomprehensible; but he had recourse to the providence of God,[99] which had permitted that these interpreters should translate the Scripture in the way that was judged to be the most fitting for the nations who would embrace the Christian religion.

In the midst of these numberless contradictions, Saint Jerome had the courage to pursue his plan; but other contradictions and other obstacles more alarming awaited him. He saw that the Hebrew which he was so desirous of grasping escaped from him at each step; that the Jews whom he consulted wavered in the greatest uncertainty; that they did not agree upon the meaning of the words, that they had no fixed principle, no grammar; that, in fact, the only lexicon of which he was able to make use was that very Hellenistic version which he aspired to correct.[100] What was the result of his labour? A new translation of the Greek Bible in Latin, a little less barbarous than the preceding translations and compared with the Hebraic text as to the literal forms. Saint Jerome could do nothing further. Had he penetrated the inner principles of the Hebrew; had the genius of that tongue been unveiled to his eyes, he would have been constrained by the force of things, either to keep silence or to restrict it within the version of the Hellenists. This version, judged the fruit of a divine inspiration, dominated the minds in such a manner, that one was obliged to lose one's way like Marcion, or follow it into its necessary

[98] Ruffin. *Invect.* Liv. II. Richard Simon. *Ibid.* L. II. chap. 2.
[99] August. *de doct. Christ.* Walton: *Proleg.* X.
[100] Rich. Simon. *Ibid.* L. II. ch. 12.

obscurity. This is the Latin translation called ordinarily, the Vulgate.

The Council of Trent has declared this translation authentic, without nevertheless, declaring it infallible; but [101] the Inquisition has sustained it with all the force of its arguments,[102] and the theologians with all the weight of their intolerance and their partiality.*

I shall not enter into the irksome detail of the numberless controversies which the version of the Hellenists and that of Saint Jerome have brought about in the more modern times. I shall pass over in silence the translations which have been made in all the tongues of Europe, whether before or after the Reformation of Luther, because they were all alike, only copies more or less removed from the Greek and Latin.

No matter how much Martin Luther and Augustine Eugubio say about the ignorance of the Hellenists, they still use their lexicon in copying Saint Jerome. Though Santes Pagnin or Arias Montanus endeavour to discredit the Vulgate; though Louis Cappell pass thirty-six years of his life pointing out the errors; though Doctor James or Father Henri de Bukentop, or Luc de Bruges, count minutely the mistakes of their work, brought according to some to two thousand, according to others, four thousand; though Cardinal Cajetan, or Cardinal Bellarmin perceive them or admit them; they do not advance one iota the

[101] *Hist. crit.* L. II. ch. 12.
[102] Palavic. *Hist.* M. VI. ch. 17. Mariana: *pro. Edit. vulg.* c. I.

* Cardinal Ximenes having caused to be printed in 1515, a polyglot composed of Hebrew, Greek and Latin, placed the Vulgate between the Hebraic text and the Septuagint version: comparing this Bible thus ranged in three columns, to Jesus Christ between the two robbers: the Hebrew text according to his sentiment, represented the wicked robber, the Hellenistic version the good robber and the Latin translation Jesus Christ! The editor of the Polyglot of Paris, declares in his preface that the Vulgate should be regarded as the original source wherein all the other versions and the text itself should agree. When one has such ideas, one offers little access for truth.

intelligence of the text. The declamations of Calvin, the labours of Olivetan, of Corneille, Bertram, Ostervald and a host of other thinkers do not produce a better effect. Of what importance the weighty commentaries of Calmet, the diffuse dissertations of Hottinger? What new lights does one see from the works of Bochard, Huet, Leclerc, Lelong and Michaelis? Is the Hebrew any better understood? This tongue, lost for twenty-five centuries, does it yield to the researches of Father Houbigant, or to the indefatigable Kennicott? Of what use is it to either or both, delving in the libraries of Europe, examining, compiling and comparing all the old manuscripts? Not any. Certain letters vary, certain vowel points change, but the same obscurity remains upon the meaning of the Sepher. In whatever tongue one turns it, it is always the same Hellenistic version that one translates, since it is the sole lexicon for all the translators of the Hebrew.

It is impossible ever to leave the vicious circle if one has not acquired a true and perfect knowledge of the Hebraic tongue. But how is one to acquire the knowledge? How? By reëstablishing this lost tongue in its original principles: by throwing off the Hellenistic yoke: by reconstructing its lexicon: by penetrating the sanctuaries of the Essenes: by mistrusting the exterior doctrine of the Jews: by opening at last that holy ark which for more than three thousand years, closed to the profane, has brought down to us, by a decree of Divine Providence, the treasures amassed by the wisdom of the Egyptians.

This is the object of a part of my labours. With the origin of speech as my goal, I have found in my path Chinese, Sanskrit and Hebrew. I have examined their rights. I have revealed them to my readers, and forced to make a choice between these three primordial idioms I have chosen the Hebrew. I have told how, being composed in its origin of intellectual, metaphorical and universal expressions, it had insensibly become wholly gross in its nature because restricted to material, literal and particular expressions. I have shown at what epoch and how it was entirely lost. I have followed the revolutions of the Sepher of Moses, the unique book which contains this tongue. I have developed the occasion and the manner in which the principal versions were made. I have reduced these versions to the number of four; as follows: the Chaldaic paraphrases or targums, the Samaritan version, that of the Hellenists, called the Septuagint version, and finally that of Saint Jerome, or the Vulgate. I have indicated sufficiently the idea that one ought to follow.

It is now for my Grammer to recall the forgotten principles of the Hebraic tongue, to establish them in a solid manner, and to connect them with the necessary results: it is for my translation of the Cosmogony of Moses and the notes which accompany it, to show the force and concordance of these results. I shall now give myself fearlessly to this difficult labour, as certain of its success as of its utility, if my readers vouchsafe to follow me with the attention and the confidence that is required.

Hebraic Grammar

HEBRAIC GRAMMAR

CHAPTER I.

GENERAL PRINCIPLES.

§ I.

THE REAL PURPOSE OF THIS GRAMMAR.

Long ago it was said, that grammar was the art of writing and of speaking a tongue correctly: but long ago it ought also to have been considered that this definition good for living tongues was of no value applied to dead ones.

In fact, what need is there of knowing how to speak and even write (if composing is what is meant by writing) Sanskrit, Zend, Hebrew and other tongues of this nature? Does one not feel that it is not a question of giving to modern thoughts an exterior which has not been made for them; but, on the contrary, of discovering under a worn-out exterior ancient thoughts worthy to be revived under more modern forms? Thoughts are for all time, all places and all men. It is not thus with the tongues which express them. These tongues are appropriate to the customs, laws, understanding and periods of the ages; they become modified in proportion as they advance in the centuries; they follow the course of the civilization of peoples. When one of these has ceased to be spoken it can only be understood through the writings which have survived. To continue to speak or even to write it when its genius is extinguished, is to wish to resuscitate a dead body; to affect the Roman toga, or to appear in the streets of Paris in the robe of an ancient Druid.

I must frankly say, despite certain scholastic precedents being offended by my avowal, that I cannot approve of those sorry compositions, whether in prose or in verse, where modern Europeans rack their brains to clothe the forms long since gone, with English, German or French thoughts. I do not doubt that this tendency everywhere in public instruction is singularly harmful to the advancement of studies, and that the constraint of modern ideas to adapt themselves to ancient forms is an attitude which checks what the ancient ideas might pass on in the modern forms. If Hesiod and Homer are not perfectly understood; if Plato himself offers obscurity, for what reason is this so? For no other reason save that instead of seeking to understand their tongue, one has foolishly attempted to speak or write it.

The grammar of the ancient tongues is not therefore, either the art of speaking or even of writing them, since the sound is extinct and since the signs have lost their relations with the ideas; but the grammar of these tongues is the art of understanding them, of penetrating the genius which has presided at their formation, of going back to their source, and by the aid of the ideas which they have preserved and the knowledge which they have procured, of enriching modern idioms and enlightening their progress.

So then, while proposing to give an Hebraic grammar, my object is assuredly not to teach anyone either to speak or to write this tongue; that preposterous care should be left to the rabbis of the synagogues. These rabbis, after tormenting themselves over the value of the accents and the vowel points, have been able to continue their cantillation of certain barbarous sounds; they have been indeed able to compose some crude books, as heterogeneous in substance as in form, but the fruit of so many pains has been to ignore utterly the signification of the sole Book which remained to them, and to make themselves more and more incapable of defending their law-

PURPOSE OF THIS GRAMMAR 57

maker, one of the noblest men that the earth has produced, from the increased attacks that have never ceased to be directed against him by those who knew him only through the thick clouds with which he had been enveloped by his translators.* For, as I have sufficiently intimated, the Book of Moses has never been accurately translated. The most ancient versions of the Sepher which we possess, such as those of the Samaritans, the Chaldaic Targums, the Greek version of the Septuagint and the Latin Vulgate, render only the grossest and most exterior forms without attaining to the spirit which animates them in the original. I might compare them appropriately with those disguises which were used in the ancient mysteries,[1] or even with those symbolic figures which were used by the initiates; the small figures of satyrs and of Sileni that were brought from Eleusis. There was nothing more absurd and grotesque than their outward appearance, upon opening them, however, by means of a secret spring, there were found all the divinities of Olympus. Plato speaks of this pleasing allegory in his dialogue of the Banquet and applies it to Socrates through the medium of Alcibiades.

It is because they saw only these exterior and material forms of the Sepher, and because they knew not how to make use of the secret which could disclose its spiritual and divine forms, that the Sadducees fell into materialism and denied the immortality of the soul.[2] It is well known how much Moses has been calumniated by modern philosophers upon the same subject.[3] Fréret has not failed to quote all those who, like him, have ranked him among the materialists.

* The most famous heresiarchs, Valentine, Marcion and Manes rejected scornfully the writings of Moses which they believed emanated from an evil principle.

1 Apul. I. XL.
2 Joseph. *Antiq.* I. XIII. g.
3 Fréret: *des Apol. de la Rel. chrét.* ch. II.

When I say that the rabbis of the synagogues have put themselves beyond the state of defending their lawgiver, I wish it to be understood that I speak only of those who, holding to the most meticulous observances of the *Masorah,* have never penetrated the secret of the sanctuary. Doubtless there are many to whom the genius of the Hebraic tongue is not foreign. But a sacred duty imposes upon them an inviolable silence.[4] It is said, that they hold the version of the Hellenists in abomination. They attribute to it all the evils which they have suffered. Alarmed at its use against them by the Christians in the early ages of the Church, their superiors forbade them thereafter to write the Sepher in other characters than the Hebraic, and doomed to execration those among them who should betray the mysteries and teach the Christians the principles of their tongue. One ought therefore to mistrust their exterior doctrine. Those of the rabbis who were initiated kept silence, as Moses, son of Maimon, called Maimonides, expressly said:[5] those who were not, had as little real knowledge of Hebrew, as the least learned of the Christians. They wavered in the same incertitude over the meaning of the words, and this incertitude was such that they were ignorant even of the name of some of the animals of which it was forbidden them, or commanded by the Law, to eat.[6] Richard Simon who has furnished me with this remark, never wearies of repeating how obscure is the Hebraic tongue:[7] he quotes Saint Jerome and Luther, who are agreed in saying, that the words of this tongue are equivocal to such an extent that it is often impossible to determine the meaning.[8] Origen, according to him, was persuaded of this truth; Calvin felt it and Cardinal Cajetan himself, was convinced.[9] It

[4] Richard Simon, *Hist. Crit.* L. I. ch. 17
[5] *Mor. Nebuc.* P. II. ch. 29.
[6] Bochart: *de Sacr. animal.*
[7] *Ibid.* I. III. ch. 2.
[8] Hieron. *Apelog. adv. Ruff.* I. 1. Luther, *Comment. Genes.*
[9] Cajetan, *Comment. in Psalm.*

was Father Morin who took advantage of this obscurity to consider the authors of the Septuagint version as so many prophets;[10] for, he said, God had no other means of fixing the signification of the Hebrew words.

This reason of Father Morin, somewhat far from being decisive, has not hindered the real thinkers, and Richard Simon particularly, from earnestly wishing that the Hebraic tongue lost for so long a time, might finally be reëstablished.[11] He did not conceal the immense difficulties that such an undertaking entailed. He saw clearly that it would be necessary to study this tongue in a manner very different from the one hitherto adopted, and far from making use of the grammars and dictionaries available, he regarded them, on the contrary, as the most dangerous obstacles; for, he says, these grammars and these dictionaries are worth nothing. All those who have had occasion to apply their rules and to make use of their interpretations have felt their insufficiency.[12] Forster who had seen the evil sought in vain the means to remedy it. He lacked the force for that: both time and men, as well as his own prejudices were too much opposed.*

I have said enough in my Dissertation concerning what had been the occasion and the object of my studies. When I conceived the plan with which I am now occupied, I knew neither Richard Simon nor Forster, nor any of the thinkers who, agreeing in regarding the Hebraic tongue as lost, had made endeavours for, or had hoped to succeed in its reëstablishment; but truth is absolute, and it is truth which has engaged me in a difficult undertaking; it is truth which will sustain me in it; I now pursue my course.

10 *Exercit. Bibl.* L. I. ex. VI. ch. 2.
11 *Hist. crit.* I. III. ch. 2.
12 *Hist. Crit.* I. III. ch. 3.

* The rabbis themselves have not been more fortunate, as one can see in the grammar of Abraham de Balmes and in several other works.

§ II.

ETYMOLOGY AND DEFINITION.

The word *grammar* has come down to us from the Greeks, through the Latins; but its origin goes back much further. Its real etymology is found in the root קר, כר, גר (*gre, cre, kre*), which in Hebrew, Arabic or Chaldaic, presents always the idea of engraving, of character or of writing, and which as verb is used to express, according to the circumstances, the action of engraving, of characterizing, of writing, of proclaiming, of reading, of declaiming, etc. The Greek word γραμματική signifies properly the science of characters, that is to say, of the characteristic signs by means of which man expresses his thought.

As has been very plainly seen by Court de Gébelin, he who, of all the archæologists has penetrated deepest into the genius of tongues, there exist two kinds of grammars: the one, universal, and the other, particular. The universal grammar reveals the spirit of man in general; the particular grammars develop the individual spirit of a people, indicate the state of its civilization, its knowledge and its prejudices. The first, is founded upon nature, and rests upon the basis of the universality of things; the others, are modified according to opinion, places and times. All the particular grammars have a common basis by which they resemble each other and which constitutes the universal grammar from which they emanate:[13] for, says this laborious writer, "these particular grammars, after having received the life of the universal grammar, react in their turn upon their

---

[13] *Mond. prim. Gramm. univ.* t. I, ch. 13, 14 et 15.

ETYMOLOGY AND DEFINITION

mother, to which they give new force to bring forth stronger and more fruitful off-shoots."

I quote here the opinion of this man whose grammatical knowledge cannot be contested, in order to make it understood, that wishing to initiate my readers into the inner genius of the Hebraic tongue, I must needs give to that tongue its own grammar; that is to say, its idiomatic and primitive grammar, which, holding to the universal grammar by the points most radical and nearest to its basis, will nevertheless, be very different from the particular grammars upon which it has been modelled up to this time.

This grammar will bear no resemblance to that of the Greeks or that of the Latins, because it is neither the idiom of Plato nor that of Titus Livius which I wish to teach, but that of Moses. I am convinced that the principal difficulties in studying Hebrew are due to the adoption of Latin forms, which have caused a simple and easy tongue to become a species of scholastic phantom whose difficulty is proverbial.

For, I must say with sincerity, that Hebrew is not such as it has ordinarily been represented. It is necessary to set aside the ridiculous prejudice that has been formed concerning it and be fully persuaded that the first difficulties of the characters being overcome, all that is necessary is six months closely sustained application.

I have said enough regarding the advantages of this study, so that I need not dwell further on this subject. I shall only repeat, that without the knowledge of this typical tongue, one of the fundamental parts of universal grammar will always be unknown, and it will be impossible to proceed with certainty in the vast and useful field of etymology.

As my intention is therefore to differ considerably from the method of the Hebraists I shall avoid entering into the detail of their works. Besides they are sufficiently well known. I shall limit myself here to indicate summarily, those of the rabbis whose ideas offer some analogy to mine.

The Hebraic tongue having become absolutely lost during the captivity of Babylon, all grammatical system was also lost. From that time nothing is found by which we can infer that the Jews possessed a grammar. At least, it is certain that the crude dialect which was current in Jerusalem at the time of Jesus Christ, and which is found employed in the Talmud of that city, reads more like a barbarous jargon than like an idiom subject to fixed rules. If anything leads me to believe that this degenerated tongue preserved a sort of grammatical system, before the captivity and while Hebrew was still the vulgar tongue, it is the fact that a great difference is found in the style of writing of certain writers. Jeremiah, for example, who was a man of the people, wrote evidently without any understanding of his tongue, not concerning himself either with gender, number or verbal tense; whilst Isaiah, on the contrary, whose instruction had been most complete, observes rigorously these modifications and prides himself on writing with as much elegance as purity.

But at last, as I have just said, all grammatical system was lost with the Hebraic tongue. The most learned Hebraists are agreed in saying, that although, from the times of the earliest Hellenist interpreters, it had been the custom to explain the Hebrew, there had been, however, no grammar reduced to an art.

The Jews, dispersed and persecuted after the ruin of Jerusalem, were buried in ignorance for a long time. The school of Tiberias, where Saint Jerome had gone, possessed no principle of grammar. The Arabs were the first to remedy this defect. Europe was at that time plunged in darkness. Arabia, placed between Asia and Africa, reanimated for a moment their ancient splendour.

The rabbis are all of this sentiment. They assert that those of their nation who began to turn their attention to grammar did so only in imitation of the Arabs. The first books which they wrote on grammar were in Arabic. After Saadia-Gaon, who appears to have laid the foundation, the most ancient is Juda-Hayyuj. The opinion of the latter is remarkable.[14] He is the first to speak, in his work, of the letters which are hidden and those which are added. The greatest secret of the Hebraic tongue consists, according to him, of knowing how to distinguish these sorts of letters, and to mark precisely those which are of the substance of the words, and those which are not. He states that the secret of these letters is known to but few persons, and in this he takes up again the ignorance of the rabbis of his time, who, lacking this understanding were unable to reduce the words to their true roots to discover their meaning.

The opinion of Juda-Hayyuj is confirmed by that of Jonah, one of the best grammarians the Jews have ever had. He declares at the beginning of his book, that the Hebraic tongue has been lost, and that it has been reëstablished as well as possible by means of the neighbouring idioms. He reprimands the rabbis sharply for putting among the number of radicals, many letters which are only accessories. He lays great stress upon the intrinsic value of each character, relates carefully their various peculiarities and shows their different relations with regard to the verb.

The works of Juda-Hayyuj and those of Jonah have never been printed, although they have been translated from the Arabic into rabbinical Hebrew. The learned Pocock who has read the books of Jonah in Arabic, under the name of Ebn-Jannehius, quotes them with praise. Aben Ezra has followed the method indicated by these two ancient grammarians in his two books entitled *Zahot* and *Moznayim*. David Kimchi diviates more. The Christian Hebraists have followed Kimchi more willingly than they have Aben Ezra, as much on account of the clear-

[14] Richard Simon, *Hist. Crit.* L. I. ch. 31.

ness of his style, as of his method which is easier. But in this they have committed a fault which they have aggravated further by adopting, without examining them, nearly all of the opinions of Elijah Levita, ambitious and systematic writer, and regarded as a deserter and apostate by his nation.

I dispense with mentioning other Jewish grammarians.* I have only entered into certain details with regard to Juda-Hayyuj, Jonah and Aben Ezra, because I have strong reasons for thinking, as will be shown in the development of the work, that they have penetrated to a certain point, the secret of the Essenian sanctuary, either by the sole force of their genius or by the effect of some oral communication.

* Although Maimonides is not, properly speaking, a grammarian, his way of looking at things coincides too well with my principles to pass over them entirely in silence. This judicious writer teaches that as the greater part of the words offer, in Hebrew, a generic, universal and almost always uncertain meaning, it is necessary to understand the sphere of activity which they embrace in their diverse acceptations, so as to apply that which agrees best with the matter of which he is treating. After having pointed out, that in this ancient idiom, very few words exist for an endless series of things, he recommends making a long study of it, and having the attention always fixed upon the particular subject to which the word is especially applied. He is indefatigable in recommending, as can be seen in the fifth chapter of his book, long meditation before restricting the meaning of a word, and above all, renunciation of all prejudices if one would avoid falling into error,

§ III.

DIVISION OF GRAMMAR:

PARTS OF SPEECH.

I have announced that I was about to reëstablish the Hebraic tongue in its own grammar. I claim a little attention, since the subject is new, and I am obliged to present certain ideas but little familiar, and also since it is possible that there might not be time for me to develop them to the necessary extent.

The modern grammarians have varied greatly concerning the number of what they call, parts of speech. Now, they understand by parts of speech, the classified materials of speech; for if the idea is one, they say, the expression is divisible, and from this divisibility arises necessarily in the signs, diverse modifications and words of many kinds.

These diverse modifications and these words of many kinds have, as I have said, tried the sagacity of the grammarian. Plato and his disciples only recognized two kinds, the noun and the verb;[15] neglecting in this, the more ancient opinion which, according to the testimony of Dionysius of Halicarnassus and Quintilian, admitted three, the noun, the verb and the conjunction.[16] Aristotle, more to draw away from the doctrine of Plato than to approach that of the ancients, counted four: the noun, the verb, the article and the conjunction.[17] The Stoics acknowledged five, distinguishing the noun as proper and appellative.[18] Soon the Greek grammarians, and after

---
[15] Plat. *in Sophist*. Prisc. L. II. Apollon. *Syn*.
[16] Denys Halyc, *de Struct. orat*. 2. Quint. *Inst*. L. I. ch. 4.
[17] Arist. *Poet*. ch. 20.
[18] Diog. Lært. L. VIII, §. 57.

them the Latins, separated the pronoun from the noun, the adverb from the verb, the preposition from the conjunction and the interjection from the article. Among the moderns, some have wished to distinguish the adjective from the noun; others, to join them; again, some have united the article with the adjective, and others, the pronoun with the noun. Nearly all have brought into their work the spirit of the system or prejudices of their school. Court de Gébelin [19] who should have preferred the simplicity of Plato to the profusion of the Latin grammatists, has had the weakness to follow the latter and even to surpass them, by counting ten parts of speech and giving the participle as one of them.

As for me, without further notice of these vain disputes, I shall recognize in the Hebraic tongue only three parts of speech produced by a fourth which they in their turn produce. These three parts are the Noun, the Verb, and the Relation : שם *shem*, פעל *phahal*, מלה *millah*. The fourth is the Sign, אות *aoth*.*

Before examining these three parts of speech, the denomination of which is quite well known let us see what

[19] *Gramm. univ.* L. II. ch. 2. 3 et 4.

* An English grammarian named Harris, better rhetorician than able dialectician, has perhaps believed himself nearer to Plato and Aristotle, by recognizing at first only two things in nature, the *substance* and the *attribute*, and by dividing the words into *principals* and *accessories*. According to him one should regard as principal words, the *substantive* and the *attributive*, in other words, the noun and the verb; as accessory words, the *definitive* and the *connective*, that is to say, the article and the conjunction. Thus this writer, worthy pupil of Locke, but far from being a disciple of Plato, regards the verb only as an attribute of the noun. "*To think*," he said, "is an attribute of man; *to be white*, is an attribute of the swan; *to fly*, an attribute of the eagle, etc." (*Hermes*, L. I. ch. 3.) It is difficult by making such grammars, to go far in the understanding of speech. To deny the absolute existence of the verb, or to make it an attribute of the substance, is to be very far from Plato, who comprises in it the very essence of language; but very near to Cabanis who makes the soul a faculty of the body.

is the fourth, which I have just mentioned for the first time.

By *Sign,* I understand all the exterior means of which man makes use to manifest his ideas. The elements of the sign are voice, gesture and traced characters: its materials, sound, movement and light. The universal grammar ought especially to be occupied with, and to understand its elements: it ought, according to Court de Gébelin, to distinguish the sounds of the voice, to regulate the gestures, and preside at the invention of the characters.[20] The more closely a particular grammar is related to the universal grammar, the more it has need to be concerned with the *sign*. This is why we shall give very considerable attention to this in regard to one of its elements,— the traced characters; for, as far as the voice and gesture are concerned, they have disappeared long ago and the traces they have left are too vague to be taken up by the Hebraic grammar, such as I have conceived it to be.

Every sign produced exteriorly is a noun; for otherwise it would be nothing. It is, therefore, the noun which is the basis of language; it is, therefore, the noun which furnishes the substance of the verb, that of the relation, and even that of the sign which has produced it. The noun is everything for exterior man, everything that he can understand by means of his senses. The verb is conceived only by the mind, and the relation is only an abstraction of thought.

There exists only one sole Verb, absolute, independent, creative and inconceivable for man himself whom it penetrates, and by whom it allows itself to be felt: it is the verb *to be-being,* expressed in Hebrew by the intellectual sign ו *o,* placed between a double root of life הוה, *hoeh.*

It is this verb, unique and universal, which, penetrating a mass of innumerable nouns that receive their

[20] *Gramm. univ.* L. I, ch. 8, et 9.

existence from the sign, forms particular verbs. It is the universal soul. The particular verbs are only animated nouns.

The relations are abstracted by thought from signs, nouns or verbs, and incline toward the sign as toward their common origin.

We shall examine in particular each of these four parts of speech in the following order: the *Sign,* the *Relation,* the *Noun* and the *Verb,* concerning which I have as yet given only general ideas. In terminating this chapter, the Hebrew alphabet, which it is indispensable to understand before going further, is now added. I have taken pains to accompany it with another comparative alphabet of Samaritan, Syriac, Arabic and Greek characters; so as to facilitate the reading of words in these tongues, which I shall be compelled to cite in somewhat large number, in my radical vocabulary and in my notes upon the Cosmogony of Moses.

It must be observed, as regards the comparative Alphabet, that it follows the order of the Hebraic characters. This order is the same for the Samaritan and Syriac; but as the Arabs and Greeks have greatly inverted this order, I have been obliged to change somewhat the idiomatic arrangement of their characters, to put them in relation to those of the Hebrews. When I have encountered in these last two tongues, characters which have no analogues in the first three, I have decided to place them immediately after those with which they offer the closest relations,

Hebraic Alphabet
and
Comparative Alphabet

HEBRAIC ALPHABET

א	A, a.	as mother-vowel, this is *a*: as consonant, it is a very soft aspiration.
ב	B, b, bh.	English *b*.
ג	G, g, gh.	English *g* before a, o, u.
ד	D, d, dh.	English *d*.
ה	H, hè, h.	as mother-vowel, this is *è*: as consonant, it is a simple aspiration: *h*.
ו ו ו	O, o, W or U, u, y.	as mother-vowel, this is *o, u, ou*: as consonant, it is *v, w* or *f*.
ז	Z, z.	English *z*.
ח	H, hê, h, ch.	as mother-vowel, this is *hê*: as consonant, it is a chest aspiration: *h*, or *ch*.
ט	T, t.	English *t*.
י	I, i, J, j.	as mother-vowel, this is *i* or *aï*: as consonant, it is a whispering aspiration: *j*.
כ ך	C, c, ch.	German *ch*, Spanish iota, Greek χ.
ל	L, l.	
מ ם	M, m.	same as English analogues.
נ ן	N, n.	
ס	S, s.	
ע	H, ho, gh, gho	as mother-vowel, it is the Arabic ع *ho*: as consonant, it is a guttural aspiration, the nasal *gh*, the Arabic غ.
פ	PH, ph.	Greek φ.
צ ץ	TZ, tz.	
ק	K, k, qu.	Same as English.
ר	R, r.	
ש	SH, sh.	French *ch* or English *sh*.
ת	TH, th.	English *th* or Greek θ.

Comparative Alphabet

Hebrew		Samaritan	Syriac	Arabic	Greek	French
א	aleph.	ᐱ	ܐ	ا	A α	A a.
ב	beth.	ᕳ	ܒ	ب	B β ϐ	B b.
ג	ghimel.	ᒣ	ܓ	ج	Γ γ Γ	G g gh.
ד	daleth.	ᑫ	ܕ	د	Δ δ	D d.
				ذ		DZ dz, d *weak*.
				ض		DH dh, d *strong*.
ה ה	hè.	ᘁ	ܗ	ه	E ε	E, Hè.
ו ו ו	wao.	ᔑ	ܘ	و	O o, Ω ω, Υ υ	O o, OU ou, U u.
ז	zaïn.	ᔓ	ܙ	ز	Z ζ	Z z.
ח	heth.	ᕼ	ܚ	ح	H η	H hè.
				خ	X χ	CH ch.
ט	teth.	ᐁ	ܛ	ت ث	T τ ?	T t.
				ط		TH th, t *strong*.
י	ïod.	ᛖ	ܝ	ي	I ι	I i.
כ ך	caph.	᙭	ܟ	ق ك		KH kh.
ל	lamed.	2	ܠ	ل	Λ λ	L l
ם מ	mëm.	ᓕ	ܡ	م	M μ	M. m.
נ ן	noun.	ᒐ	ܢ	ن	N ν	N n.
ס	samech.	ᗅ	ܣ	س	Σ ς σ ϲ	S s.
				ص		SS ss, s *strong*.
ע	haïn.	∇	ܥ	ع غ	OY υ	H ho, wh.
				غ		GH gh
פ ף	phè.	ᒷ	ܦ	ف	Φ φ	PH ph, F f.
					Π π ϖ	P p.
					Ψ ψ	PS ps.
צ ץ	tzad.	ᛗ	ܨ	ظ		TZ tz.
ק	coph.	ᑭ	ܩ	ق	K κ	C c, K k, Q q.
ר	resch.	ᕁ	ܪ	ر	Ρ ρ	R r.
ש	shin.	ᙍ	ܫ	ش		SH sh.
ת ת	thao.	ᐱ	ܬ	ت ث	Θ θ ϑ	TH th.

CHAPTER II.

SIGNS CONSIDERED AS CHARACTERS.

§ I.

HEBRAIC ALPHABET: ITS VOWELS: ITS ORIGIN.

Before examining what the signification of the characters which we have just laid down can be, it is well to see what is their relative value.

The first division which is established here is that which distinguishes them as vowels and as consonants. I would have much to do if I related in detail all that has been said, for and against the existence of the Hebraic vowels. These insipid questions might have been solved long ago, if those who had raised them had taken the trouble to examine seriously the object of their dispute. But that was the thing concerning which they thought the least. Some had only a scholastic erudition which took cognizance of the material of the tongue; others, who had a critical faculty and a philosophic mind were often ignorant even of the form of the Oriental characters.

I ask in all good faith, how the alphabet of the Hebrews could have lacked the proper characters to designate the vowels, since it is known that the Egyptians who were their masters in all the sciences, possessed these characters and made use of them, according to the report of Demetrius of Phalereus, to note their music and to solmizate it; since it is known, by the account of Horus-Apollonius, that there were seven of these characters;[1] since it is known that the Phœnicians, close neighbours of the Hebrews, used these vocal characters to designate the seven planets.[2] Porphyry testifies positively to this in his

[1] *Hyeroglyph.* L. II. 29.
[2] Cedren. p. 169.

Commentary upon the grammarian Dionysius Thrax,[3] which confirms unquestionably, the inscription found at Milet, and concerning which we possess a learned dissertation by Barthelemy.[4] This inscription includes invocations addressed to the seven planetary spirits. Each spirit is designated by a name composed of seven vowels and beginning with the vowel especially consecrated to the planet which it governs.

Let us hesitate no longer to say that the Hebrew alphabet has characters whose primitive purpose was to distinguish the vowels; these characters are seven in number.

א soft vowel, represented by *a*.
ה stronger vowel, represented by *e, h*.
ח very strong pectoral vowel, represented by *e, h, ch*.
ו indistinct, dark vowel, represented by *ou, u, y*.
ו brilliant vowel, represented by *o*.
י hard vowel, represented by *i*.
ע deep and guttural vowel, represented by *ho, who*.

Besides these vocal characters, it is further necessary to know that the Hebrew alphabet admits a vowel which I shall call consonantal or vague, because it is inherent in the consonant, goes with it, is not distinguishable, and attaches to it a sound always implied. This sound is indifferently *a, e, o,* for we ought not to believe that the vocal sound which accompanies the consonants has been as fixed in the ancient tongues of the Orient as it has become in the modern tongues of Europe. The word מלך, which signifies a *king*, is pronounced indifferently *malach, melech, moloch,* and even *milich;* with a faint sound of the voice. This indifference in the vocal sound would not have existed if a written vowel had been inserted between the consonants which compose it; then the sound would have become fixed and striking, but of

---

[3] *Mém. de Gotting.* T. I. p. 251. *sur l'ouvrage de Démétrius de Phal* Περὶ Ἑρμηνείας.

[4] *Mém. de l'Acad. des Belles-Lettres,* T. XLI. p. 514.

ten the sense would also have been changed. Thus, for example, the word מלך, receiving the mother vowel א, as in מלאך , signifies no longer simply *a king,* but a divine, eternal emanation; *an eon, an angel.*

When it was said that the Hebrew words were written without vowels, it was not understood, and Boulanger who has committed this mistake in his encyclopædic article, proves to me by this alone, that he was ignorant of the tongue of which he wrote.

All Hebrew words have vowels expressed or implied, that is to say, mother vowels or consonantal vowels. In the origin of this tongue, or rather in the origin of the Egyptian tongue from which it is derived, the sages who created the alphabet which it has inherited, attached a vocal sound to each consonant, a sound nearly always faint, without aspiration, and passing from the *æ* to the *œ,* or from the *a* to the *e,* without the least difficulty; they reserved the written characters for expressing the sounds more fixed, aspirate or striking. This literal alphabet, whose antiquity is unknown, has no doubt come down to us as far as its material characters are concerned; but as to its spirit, it has come down in sundry imitations that have been transmitted to us by the Samaritans, Chaldeans, Syrians and even the Arabs.

The Hebraic alphabet is that of the Chaldeans. The characters are remarkable for their elegance of form and their clearness. The Samaritan much more diffuse, much less easy to read, is obviously anterior and belongs to a more rude people. The savants who have doubted the anteriority of the Samaritan character had not examined it with sufficient attention. They have feared besides, that if once they granted the priority of the character, they would be forced to grant the priority of the text; but this is a foolish fear. The Samaritan text, although its alphabet may be anterior to the Chaldaic alphabet, is nevertheless only a simple copy of the Sepher of Moses, which the politics of the kings of Assyria caused to pass into Samaria, as I have already said in my Dissertation; if this copy differs it is because the priest who was charged with it, as one reads in the Book of Kings,[5] either conformed to the ideas of the Samaritans with whom he wished to keep up the schism, or he consulted manuscripts by no means accurate. It would be ridiculous to say with Leclerc,[6] that this priest was the author of the entire Sepher; but there is not the least absurdity in thinking that he was the author of the principal different readings which are encountered there; for the interest of the court of Assyria which sent him was, that he should estrange as much as possible the Samaritans and the Jews, and that he should stir up their mutual animosity by all manner of means.

It is therefore absolutely impossible to deny the Chaldean origin of the characters of which the Hebraic alphabet is composed today. The very name of this alphabet demonstrates it sufficiently. This name written thus כתיבה אשורית (*chathibah ashourith*) signifies, Assyrian writing: an epithet known to all the rabbis, and to which following the genius of the Hebraic tongue, nothing prevents adding the formative and local sign מ to obtain כתיבה מאשורית (*chathibah mashourith*), writing in the Assyrian style. This is the quite simple denomination of this alphabet; a denomination in which, through a very singular abuse of words, this same Elijah Levita, of whom I have had occasion to speak, insisted on seeing the Masorites of Tiberias; thus confusing beyond any criticism, the ancient Mashorah with the modern Masorah, and the origin of the vowel points with rules infinitely newer, that are followed in the synagogues relative to their employment.*

[5] *Kings* L. II. ch. 17. v. 27.

[6] Leclerc: *Sentimens de quelq. theol. de Hollande.* L. VI.

* No one is ignorant of the famous disputes which were raised among the savants of the last centuries concerning the origin of the vowel points. These points had always been considered as contem-

§ II.

ORIGIN OF THE VOWEL POINTS.

Thus therefore, the Hebraic alphabet, whatever might have been the form of its characters at the very remote epoch when Moses wrote his work, had seven written vowels: ע, י, ו, ו, ח, ה, א; besides a vague vowel attached to each consonant which I have called on account of this, consonantal vowel. But by a series of events which hold to principles too far from my subject to be explained here, the sound of the written vowels became altered, materialized, hardened as it were, and changed in such a way that the characters which expressed them were con-

poraries of the Hebraic characters and belonging to the same inventors; when suddenly, about the middle of the sixteenth century, Elijah Levita attacked their antiquity and attributed the invention to the rabbis of the school of Tiberias who flourished about the fifth century of our era. The entire synagogue rose in rebellion against him, and regarded him as a blasphemer. His system would have remained buried in obscurity, if Louis Cappell, pastor of the Protestant Church at Saumur, after having passed thirty-six years of his life noting down the different readings of the Hebraic text, disheartened at being unable to understand it, had not changed his idea concerning these same points which had caused him so much trouble and had not taken to heart the opinion of Elijah Levita.

Buxtorf, who had just made a grammar, opposed both Elijah Levita and Cappell, and started a war in which all the Hebrew scholars have taken part during the last two centuries, never asking themselves, in their disputes for or against the points, what was the real point of question. Now, this is the real point. Elijah Levita did not understand Hebrew, or if he did understand it, he was very glad to profit by an equivocal word of that tongue to start the war which drew attention to him.

The word אשורי (*ashouri*), signifies in Hebrew, as in Chaldaic, *Assyrian*, that which belongs to Assyria, its root שר or שור indicates all that which tends to rule, to be lifted up; all that which emanates from an original principle of force, of grandeur and of *éclat*. The

fused with the other consonants. The vowels א, ה and ח offered only an aspiration more or less strong, being deprived of all vocal sound; ו and ו became the consonants *v* and *w*; י was pronounced *ji*, and ע took a raucous and nasal accent.*

If, as has very well been said by the ancients, the vowels are the soul and the consonants the body of the words,[7] the Hebraic writing and all which, generally

alphabet of which Esdras made use in transcribing the Sepher, was called כתיבה אשורית *Assyrian writing*, or in a figurative sense, sovereign, primordial, original writing. The addition of the sign מ having reference to the intensive verbal form, only gives more force to the expression. כתיבה מאשורית, signifies therefore, *writing in the manner of the Assyrian*, or writing emanated from the sovereign radiant principle. This is the origin of the first *mashorah*, the real mashorah to which both the Hebraic characters and vowel points which accompany them must be related.

But the word אסור *assour*, signifies all that which is *bound*, *obliged* and *subject to rules*. אסירה *a college, a convention*, a thing which receives or which gives certain laws in certain circumstances. This is the origin of the second *Masorah*. This latter does not invent the vowel points; but it fixes the manner of using them; it treats of everything which pertains to the rules that regulate the orthography as well as the reading of the Sepher. These *Masorites* enter, as I have said, into the minutest details of the division of the chapters, and the number of verses, words and letters which compose them. They know, for example, that in the first book of the Sepher called *Berœshith*, the *Parshioth*, or great sections, are twelve in number; those named *Sedarim* or orders, forty-three in number; that there are in all one thousand five hundred and thirty-four verses, twenty thousand seven hundred and thirteen words, seventy-eight thousand, one hundred letters; and finally, that the middle of this book is at chapter 27, v. 40, at the centre of these words: וְעַל חַרְבְּךָ תִחְיֶה "And by thy sword (extermination) shalt thou live."

* I render it by *gh* or *wh*.

[7] Priscian L. I.

ORIGIN OF THE VOWEL POINTS

speaking, belonged to the same primitive stock, became by this slow revolution a kind of body, if not dead, at least in a state of lethargy wherein remained only a vague, transitory spirit giving forth only uncertain lights. At this time the meaning of the words tended to be materialized like the sound of the vowels and few of the readers were capable of grasping it. New ideas changed the meaning as new habits had changed the form.

Nevertheless, certain sages among the Assyrians, called Chaldeans, a lettered and savant caste which has been inappropriately confused with the corps of the nations;* certain Chaldean sages, I say, having perceived the successive change which had taken place in their tongue, and fearing justly that notwithstanding the oral tradition which they strove to transmit from one to the other, the meaning of the ancient books would become lost entirely, they sought a means to fix the value of the vocal characters, and particularly to give to the implied consonantal vowel, a determined sound which would prevent the word from fluctuating at hazard among several significations.

For it had come to pass that at the same time that the mother vowels, that is to say, those which were designated by the written characters, had become consonantal, the consonants, so to speak, had become vocalized by means of the vague vowel which united them. The

---

* The Chaldeans were not a corps of the nations, as has been ridiculously believed; but a corps of savants in a nation. Their principal academies were at Babylon, Borseppa, Sippara, Orchoe, etc. Chaldea was not, properly speaking, the name of a country, but an epithet given to the country where the Chaldeans flourished. These sages were divided into four classes, under the direction of a supreme chief. They bore, in general, the name of כשדאין, *Chashdaïn* or of כלדאין, *Chaldaïn*, according to the different dialects. Both of these names signified alike, *the venerables, the eminent ones, those who understand the nature of things*. They are formed of the assimilative article ל, and the words שדי or חלד which have reference to excellence, to eminence, to infinite time and to eternal nature.

many ideas which were successively attached to the same root, had brought about a concourse of vowels that it was no longer possible to blend as formerly with the spoken language, and as the written language afforded no assistance in this regard, the books became from day to day more difficult to understand.

I beg the readers but little familiar with the tongues of the Orient, to permit me to draw an example from the French. Let us suppose that we have in this tongue, a root composed of two consonants *bl*, to which we attach an idea of roundness. If we conceive trifling objects under this form, we say indifferently *bal, bel, bil, bol, bul boul;* but in proportion as we distinguish the individuals from the species in general, we would know that a *bale* is neither a *bille*, nor a *boule;* we would be careful not to confuse the *bol* of an apothecary, with the *bôl* which is used for liquors, nor the *bill* of the English parliament with a *bulle* of the pope; in short, we make a great difference between this last *bulle* and a *bulle* of soap and a *balle* of merchandize, etc.

Now it is in this manner that the Chaldeans thought to obviate the ever growing confusion which was born of the deviation of the mother vowels and of the fixation of the vague vowels. They invented a certain number of small accents, called today vowel points, by means of which they were able to give to the characters of the alphabet under which they placed them, the sound that these characters had in the spoken language. This invention, quite ingenious, had the double advantage of preserving the writing of the ancient books, without working any change in the arrangement of the literal characters, and of permitting the noting of its pronunciation such as usage had introduced.

Here is the form, value and name of these points, which I have placed under the consonant ב solely for the purpose of serving as example; for these points can be placed under all the literal characters, consonants as well as vowels.

Long Vowels	Short Vowels
בָּ bâ—*kametz*	בַּ ba—*patah*
בֵּ bê—*zere*	בֶּ be—*segol*
בִּ bî—*hirck*	בֻּ bu—*kibbuz*
בֹּ bô—*holem*	בָּ bo—*kamez-hatef*

The point named *shewa*, represented by two points placed perpendicularly under a character, in this manner בְּ, signifies that the character under which it is placed lacks the vowel, if it is a consonant, or remains mute if it is a vowel.

The consonant שׁ always bears a point, either at the right of the writer, שׁ, to express that it has a hissing sound as in *sh;* or at the left שׂ, to signify that it is only aspirate. This difference is of but little importance; but it is essential to remark that this point replaces on the character שׁ, the vowel point called *holem*, that is to say *o*. This vocal sound precedes the consonant שׁ when the anterior consonant lacks a vowel, as in מֹשֶׁה *moshe,* it follows it when this same consonant שׁ is initial, as in שָׁנָה *shone.*

Besides these points, whose purpose was to fix the sound of the vague vowels and to determine the vocal sound which remained inherent, or which was attached to the mother vowels either as they were by nature or as they became consonants, the Chaldeans invented still another kind of interior point, intended to give more force to the consonants or to the mother vowel, in the bosom of which it is inscribed. This point is called *dagesh*, when applied to consonants, and *mappik*, when applied to vowels. The interior point *dagesh*, is inscribed in all of the consonants except ר. It is soft in the following six, ת ,פ ,כ ,ד ,ג ,ב when they are initial or preceded by the mute point called *shewa;* it is hard in all the others and even in those alluded to, when they are preceded by any vowel whatever; its effect is to double their value. Certain Hebrew grammarians declare that this point, inscribed in the bosom of the consonant פ, pronounced ordinarily *ph,* gives it the force of the simple *p;* but here their opinion is sharply contested by others who assert that the Hebrews, as well as the Arabs, have never known the articulation of our *p*. But as my object is not to teach the pronunciation of Hebrew, I shall not enter into these disputes.

Indeed it is of no importance whatever in understanding the sole Hebrew book which remains to us, to know what was the articulation attached to such or such character by the orators of Jerusalem; but rather, what was the meaning that Moses, and the ancient writers who have imitated him, gave to these characters.

Let us return to the point *mappik*. This inner point is applied to three vowels י, ו, ה and gives them a new value. The vowel ה, is distinguished from the word, and takes an emphatic or relative meaning; the vowel ו ceases to be a consonant, and becomes the primitive vowel *ou*, and if the point is transposed above it, וֹ it takes the more audible sound of *o* or *u*. The vowel י, is distinguished from the word, even as the vowel ה, and takes an emphatic sound or becomes audible from the mute that it had been.

The diphthongs, however, are quite rare in Hebrew. Nevertheless, according to the Chaldaic pronunciation, when the pure vowels ו or י, are preceded by any vowel point, or joined together, they form real diphthongs as in the following words: עֲשָׂו *heshaou*, שָׁלֵו *shaleou*, פְּנַי *phanai* גוֹי *goi,* גלוי *galoui,* etc.

The reading of the Hebraic text which I give further on in the original, and its carefully made comparison with the transcription in modern characters, will instruct those who desire to familiarize themselves with the Hebrew characters, much more than all that I might be able to tell them now, and above all they will acquire these same characters with less *ennui*.

§ III.

EFFECTS OF THE VOWEL POINTS.

SAMARITAN TEXT.

Such was the means invented by the Chaldeans to note the pronunciation of the words without altering their characters. It is impossible, lacking monuments, to fix today even by approximation, the time of this invention; but one can without deviating from the truth, determine when it was adopted by the Hebrews. Everything leads to believe that this people, having had occasion during its long captivity in Babylon to become acquainted with the Assyrian characters and the Chaldaic punctuation, found in its midst men sufficiently enlightened to appreciate the advantage of each, and to sacrifice the pride and national prejudice which might hold them attached to their ancient characters.

To Esdras is due the principal honour; a man of great genius and uncommon constancy. It was he who, shortly after the return of the Jews to Jerusalem, revised the sacred Book of his nation, repaired the disorder brought upon it by the numerous revolutions and great calamities, and transcribed it completely in Assyrian characters. It is needless to repeat here the motives and occasion of the additions which he judged proper to make. I have spoken sufficiently of this in my Introductory Dissertation. If any fault was committed in the course of a work so considerable, the evil which resulted was slight; while the good of which it became the source was immense.

For if we possess the very work of Moses in its integrity, we owe it to the particular care of Esdras and to

SAMARITAN TEXT

his bold policy. The Samaritan priests who remained obstinately attached to the ancient character, finally corrupted the original text and this is how it was done.

Since they no longer pronounced the words in the same manner, they believed the changing of the orthography immaterial, and since they were deprived of means for determining the sound of the vague vowels which were fixed, they inserted mother vowels where there were none.* These vowels whose degeneration was rapid, became consonants; these consonants were charged with new vague vowels which changed the meaning of the words, besides taking from them what had been hieroglyphic, and finally the confusion became such that they were forced, in order to understand their Book, to have recourse to a translation in the language of the time. Then all was lost for them; for the translators, whatever scruples they might have brought to bear in their work, could translate only what they understood and as they understood.

What happened, however, to the rabbis of the Jewish synagogue? Thanks to the flexibility of the Chaldaic punctuation, they were able to follow the vicissitudes of

*Only a glance at the Samaritan text is sufficient to see that it abounds in the added mother vowels. Father Morin and Richard Simon have already remarked this: but neither has perceived how this text could in that way lose its authenticity. On the contrary, Morin pretended to draw from this abundance of mother vowels, a proof of the anteriority of the Samaritan text. He was ignorant of the fact that the greater part of the mother vowels which are lacking in the Hebraic words, are lacking designedly and that this want adds often an hieroglyphic meaning to the spoken meaning, according to the Egyptian usage. I know well that, particularly in the verbs, the copyists prior to Esdras, and perhaps Esdras himself, have neglected the mother vowels without other reason than that of following a defective pronunciation, or through indolence; but it was an inevitable misfortune. The Masorites of Tiberias may also have followed bad rules, in fixing definitely the number of these vowels. One ought in this case to supply them in reading, and an intelligent person will do so.

the pronunciation without changing anything in the substance, number or arrangement of the characters. Whereas the greater part yielding to the proneness of their gross ideas, lost as had the Samaritans, the real meaning of the sacred text; this text remained entirely concealed in its characters, the knowledge of which was preserved by an oral tradition. This tradition called Kabbala, was especially the portion of the Essenes who communicated it secretly to the initiates, neglecting the points or suppressing them wholly.

This has been the fate of the Sepher of Moses. This precious Book more and more disfigured from age to age, at first by the degeneration of the tongue, afterward by its total loss, given over to the carelessness of the ministers of the altars, to the ignorance of the people, to the inevitable digressions of the Chaldaic punctuation, was preserved by its characters which like so many of the hieroglyphics have carried the meaning to posterity. All of those whom the synagogue has considered as enlightened men, all of those whom the Christian church itself has regarded as true savants, the sages of all the centuries, have felt this truth.

Therefore, let us leave to the Hebraist grammarians the minute and ridiculous care of learning seriously and at length, the rules, wholly arbitrary, which follow the vowel points in their mutations. Let us receive these points in the Hebraic tongue, as we receive the vowels which enter in the composition of the words of other tongues without concerning ourselves as to their origin or their position. Let us not seek, as I have already said, to speak Hebrew, but to understand it. Whether such or such word is pronounced in such or such fashion in the synagogue, matters not to us. The essential thing is to know what it signifies. Let us also leave the musical notes which the rabbis call the accents, and without disturbing ourselves as to the tones in which the first chapters of the Sepher were cantillated at Jerusalem, let us consider what profound meaning was attached to it by Moses, and with that object let us seek to penetrate the inner genius of the Egyptian idiom which he has employed under its two relations, literal and hieroglyphic. We shall attain this easily by the exploration of the roots, few in number, which serve as the basis of this idiom and by an understanding of the characters, still fewer in number, which are as their elements.

For, even in the richest tongues, the roots are few in number. The Chinese tongue, one of the most varied in the whole earth, which counts eighty-four thousand characters, has scarcely more than two hundred or two hundred and thirty roots, which produce at the most, twelve or thirteen hundred simple words by variations of the accent.

CHAPTER III.

CHARACTERS CONSIDERED AS SIGNS.

§ I.

TRACED CHARACTERS, ONE OF THE ELEMENTS OF LANGUAGE:

HIEROGLYPHIC PRINCIPLE OF THEIR PRIMITIVE FORM.

We are about to examine the alphabetical form and value of the Hebrew characters; let us fix our attention now upon the meaning which is therein contained. This is a matter somewhat novel and I believe it has not been properly investigated.

According to Court de Gébelin, the origin of speech is divine. God alone can give to man the organs which are necessary for speaking; He alone can inspire in him the desire to profit by his organs; He alone can establish between speech and that multitude of marvelous objects which it must depict, that admirable *rapport* which animates speech, which makes it intelligible to all, which makes it a picture with an energy and truthfulness that cannot be mistaken. This estimable writer says, "How could one fail to recognize here the finger of the All Powerful? how could one imagine that words had no energy by themselves? that they had no value which was not conventional and which might not always be different; that the name of lamb might be that of wolf, and the name of vice that of virtue, etc." [1]

[1] *Monde primi. Orig. du lang.* p. 66.

Indeed a person must be the slave of system, and singularly ignorant of the first elements of language to assert with Hobbes and his followers, that there is nothing which may not be arbitrary in the institution of speech;[2] that "we cannot from experience conclude that anything is to be called just or unjust, true or false, or any proposition universal whatsoever, except it be from remembrance of the use of names imposed arbitrarily by men."[3]

Again if Hobbes, or those who have followed him, having delved deeply in the elements of speech, had demonstrated the nothingness or absolute indifference of it by a rational analysis of tongues or even simply by the analysis of the tongue that they spoke; but these men, compilers of certain Latin words, believed themselves so wise that the mere declaration of their paradox was its demonstration. They did not suspect that one could raise his grammatical thoughts above a supine or a gerund.

May I be pardoned for this digression which, distant as it appears from the Hebraic grammar, brings us, however, back to it; for it is in this grammar that we shall find the consoling proof, stated above by Gébelin and the response to the destructive paradoxes of Hobbes and all his acolytes. It is even one of the motives which has caused me to publish this grammar, and which, being connected with that of giving to my translation of the Cosmogony of Moses an incontrovertible basis, engages me in a work to which I had not at first destined myself.

I shall show that the words which compose the tongues in general, and those of the Hebraic tongue in particular, far from being thrown at hazard, and formed by the explosion of an arbitrary caprice, as has been asserted, are, on the contrary, produced by a profound reason. I shall prove that there is not a single one that may not, by means of a well made grammatical analysis,

[2] Hobb. *de la nat. hum.* ch. 4. 10.
[3] *Ibid:* ch. 5. § 10. **Leviath. ch. 4.**

CHARACTERS CONSIDERED AS SIGNS

be brought back to the fixed elements of a nature, immutable as to substance, although variable to infinity as to forms.

These elements, such as we are able to examine here, constitute that part of speech to which I have given the name of *sign*. They comprise, as I have said, the voice, the gesture, and the traced characters. It is to the traced characters that we shall apply ourselves; since the voice is extinct, and the gesture disappeared. They alone will furnish us a subject amply vast for reflections.

According to the able writer whom I have already quoted, their form is by no means arbitrary. Court de Gébelin proves by numerous examples that the first inventors of the literal alphabet, unique source of all the literal alphabets in actual use upon the earth, and whose characters were at first only sixteen in number, drew from nature itself the form of these characters, relative to the meaning which they wished to attach to them. Here are his ideas upon this subject, to which I shall bring only some slight changes and certain developments necessitated by the extent of the Hebraic alphabet and the comparison that I am obliged to make of several analogous letters; in order to reduce the number to the sixteen primordial characters, and make them harmonize with their hieroglyphic principle.

א   A.—Man himself as collective unity, principle: master and ruler of the earth.

ב פ   B. P. PH.—The mouth of man as organ of speech; his interior, his habitation, every central object.

ג כ   G. C. CH.—The throat: the hand of man half closed and in action of taking: every canal, every enclosure, every hollow object.

ד ת   D. DH. TH.—The breast: every abundant, nutritive object: all division, all reciprocity.

ה   H. EH. AH.—The breath: all that which animates: air, life, being.

ו O. U.—The eye: all that which is related to the light, to brilliancy, to limpidness, to water.

עוו OU. W. WH.—The ear: all that which is related to sound, to noise, to wind: void, nothingness.

זשׂסן Z. S. SH.—A staff, an arrow, a bow; the arms, the instruments of man: every object leading to an end.

ח H. HE. CH.—A field, image of natural existence: all that which requires work, labour, effort: all that which excites heat.

טצ T. TZ.—A roof: a place of surety, of refuge: a haven, a shelter; a term, an aim: an end.

י I.—The finger of man, his extended hand: all that which indicates the directing power and which serves to manifest it.

ל L.—The arm: everything which is extended, raised, displayed.

מ M.—The companion of man, woman: all that which is fruitful and creative.

נ N.—The production of woman: a child: any fruit whatsoever: every produced being.

ק Q. K.—A positive arm: all that which serves, defends, or makes an effort for man.

ר R.—The head of man: all that which possesses in itself, a proper and determining movement.

Now it must be observed that these characters received these symbolic figures from their first inventors only because they already contained the idea; that in passing to the state of signs, they present only abstractly to the thought the faculties of these same objects: but, as I have stated, they can fulfill the functions of the *signs*, only after having been veritable *nouns:* for every *sign* manifested exteriorly is at first a *noun*.

§ II.

ORIGIN OF SIGNS AND THEIR DEVELOPMENT:

THOSE OF THE HEBRAIC TONGUE.

Let us try to discover how the *sign*, being manifested exteriorly, produced a *noun*, and how the *noun*, characterized by a figured type produced a *sign*. Let us take for example, the sign מ M, which, expressing by means of its primordial elements, the sound and organs of the voice, becomes the syllable aM or Ma, and is applied to those faculties of woman which eminently distinguish her, that is to say, to those of mother. If certain minds attacked by skepticism ask me why I restrict the idea of mother in this syllable aM or Ma, and how I am sure that it is applied effectively there, I shall reply to them that the sole proof that I can give them, in the material sphere which envelops them is, that in all the tongues of the world from that of the Chinese to that of the Caribs, the syllable aM or Ma is attached to the idea of mother, and aB, Ba, or aP, Pa, to that of father. If they doubt my assertion let them prove that it is false; if they do not doubt it, let them tell me how it is that so many diverse peoples, thrown at such distances apart, unknown to each other, are agreed in the signification of this syllable, if this syllable is not the innate expression of the sign of maternity.

This is a grammatical truth that all the sophisms of Hobbes and his disciples knew not how to overthrow.

Let us settle upon this fundamental point and proceed. What are the relative or abstract ideas which are attached to, or which follow from, the primordial idea represented by the syllable aM or Ma? Is it not the idea of fecundity, of multiplicity, of abundance? Is it not the idea of fecundation, of multiplication, of formation? Does not one see from this source, every idea of excited and passive action, of exterior movement, of plastic force, of characteristic place, of home, of means, etc?

It is useless to pursue this examination: the mass of ideas contained in the primordial idea of mother, is either attached to the figured sign, to the typical character which represents it, or is derived from and follows it.

Each *sign* starts from the same principles and acquires the same development. Speech is like a sturdy tree which, shooting up from a single trunk begins with a few branches; but which soon extends itself, spreads, and becomes divided in an infinity of boughs whose interlaced twigs are blended and mingled together.

And do not wonder at this immense number of ideas following from so small a number of *signs*. It is by means of the eight keys called *Koua,* that the Chinese tongue, at first reduced to two hundred and forty primordial characters, is raised to eighty and even eighty-four thousand derivative characters, as I have already said.

Now the newer a tongue is and closer to nature, the more the *sign* preserves its force. This force dies out insensibly, in proportion as the derivative tongues are formed, blended, identified and mutually enriched with a mass of words which, belonging to several tribes at first isolated and afterward united, lose their synonymy and finally are coloured with all the nuances of the imagination, and adapt themselves to every delicacy of sentiment and expression. The force of the *sign* is the grammatical touchstone by means of which one can judge without error the antiquity of any tongue.

In our modern tongues, for example, the *sign*, because of the idiomatic changes brought about by time, is very difficult to recognize; it yields only to a persistent analysis. It is not thus in Hebrew. This tongue, like a vigorous shoot sprung from the dried trunk of the pri-

ORIGIN OF SIGNS OF HEBRAIC TONGUE

mitive tongue, has preserved on a small scale all the forms and all the action. The *signs* are nearly all evident, and many even are detached: when this is the case, I shall give them name of *relations* for I understand by *sign* only the constitutive character of a root, or the character which placed at the beginning or at the end of a word, modifies its expression without conserving any in itself.

I now pass, after these explanations, to what the Hebraic *signs* indicate, that is to say, to a new development of the literal characters of the Hebraic tongue considered under the relation of the primitive ideas which they express, and by which they are constituted representative *signs* of these same ideas.

א A.—This first character of the alphabet, in nearly all known idioms, is the sign of power and of stability. The ideas that it expresses are those of unity and of the principle by which it is determined.

ב B. P.—Virile and paternal sign: image of active and interior action.

ג G.—This character which offers the image of a canal, is the organic sign; that of the material covering and of all ideas originating from the corporeal organs or from their action.

ד D.—Sign of nature, divisible and divided: it expresses every idea proceeding from the abundance born of division.

ה H. He.—Life and every abstract idea of being.

ו OU. W.—This character offers the image of the most profound, the most inconceivable mystery, the image of the knot which unites, or the point which separates nothingness and being. It is the universal, convertible sign which makes a thing pass from one nature to another; communicating on the one side, with the sign of light and of spiritual sense ו, which is itself more elevated, and connecting on the other side, in its degeneration, with the sign of darkness and of material sense ע which is itself still more abased.

ז Z. C. S.—Demonstrative sign: abstract image of the link which unites things: symbol of luminous refraction.

ח H. HE. CH.—This character, intermediary between ה and כ, the former designating life, absolute existence; the latter, relative life, assimilated existence, —is the sign of elementary existence: it offers the image of a sort of equilibrium, and is attached to ideas of effort, of labour, and of normal and of legislative action.

ט T.—Sign of resistance and of protection. This character serves as link between ד and ת, which are both much more expressive.

I.—Image of potential manifestation: of spiritual duration, of eternity of time and of all ideas relating thereunto: remarkable character in its vocal nature, but which loses all of its faculties in passing to the state of consonant, wherein it depicts no more than a material duration, a sort of link as ז, or of movement as שׁ.

כ C. CH.—Assimilative sign: it is a reflective and transient life, a sort of mould which receives and makes all forms. It is derived from the character ח which proceeds itself from the sign of absolute life ה. Thus holding, on the one side, to elementary life, it joins to the signification of the character ח, that of the organic sign ג, of which it is, besides, only a kind of reinforcement.

ל L.—Sign of expansive movement: it is applied to all

ORIGIN OF SIGNS OF HEBRAIC TONGUE

ideas of extension, elevation, occupation, possession. As final sign, it is the image of power derived from elevation.

מ M.—Maternal and female sign: local and plastic sign: image of exterior and passive action. This character used at the end of words, becomes the collective sign ם. In this state, it develops the being in indefinite space, or it comprises, in the same respect, all beings of an identical nature.

נ N.—Image of produced or reflected being: sign of individual and of corporeal existence. As final character it is the augmentative sign ן, and gives to the word which receives it all the individual extension of which the expressed thing is susceptible.

ס S. X.—Image of all circumscription: sign of circular movement in that which has connection with its circumferential limit. It is the link ז reinforced and turned back upon itself.

ע H. WH.—Sign of material meaning. It is the sign ו considered in its purely physical relations. When the vocal sound ע, degenerates in its turn into consonant, it becomes the sign of all that which is bent, false, perverse and bad.

פ PH. F.—Sign of speech and of that which is related to it. This character serves as link between the characters ב and ו, B and V, when the latter has passed into state of consonant; it participates in all their significations, adding its own expression which is the emphasis.

צ TZ.—Final and terminative sign being related to all ideas of scission, of term, solution, goal. Placed at the beginning of words, it indicates the movement which carries toward the term of which it is the sign: placed at the end, it marks the same term where it has tended; then it receives this form ץ, It is derived from the character ס and from the character ז, and it marks equally scission for both.

ק   Q. K.—Sign eminently compressive, astringent and trenchant; image of the agglomerating or repressive form. It is the character כ wholly materialized and is applied to objects purely physical. For this is the progression of the signs: ה, universal life; ח, elementary existence, the effort of nature; כ, assimilated life holding the natural forms; ק material existence giving the means of forms.

ר   R.—Sign of all movement proper, good or bad: original and frequentative sign: image of the renewal of things as to their movement.

ש   SH.—Sign of relative duration and of movement therewith connected. This character is derived from the vocal sound י, passed into the state of consonant; it joins to its original expression the respective significations of the characters ז and ס.

ת   TH.—Sign of reciprocity: image of that which is mutual and reciprocal. Sign of signs. Joining to the abundance of the character ר, to the force of the resistance and protection of the character ט, the idea of perfection of which it is itself the symbol.

Twenty-two signs: such are the simple bases upon which reposes the Hebraic tongue, upon which are raised the primitive or derivative tongues which are attached to the same origin. From the perfect understanding of these bases, depends the understanding of their **genius**: their possession is a **key which unlocks the roots**.

§ III.

USE OF THE SIGNS: EXAMPLE DRAWN FROM

THE FRENCH.

I might expatiate at length upon the signification of each of these characters considered as *Signs*, especially if I had added to the general ideas that they express, some of the particular, relative or abstract ideas which are necessarily attached; but I have said enough for the attentive reader and he will find elsewhere in the course of this work quite a considerable number of examples and developments to assure his progress and level all doubts which he might have conceived.

As I have not yet spoken of the *noun*, fundamental part of speech, and as it would be difficult for those of my readers, who have of the Hebraic tongue only the knowledge that I am giving them, to understand me if I proceeded abruptly to the composition or the decomposition of the Hebraic words by means of the sign, I shall put off demonstrating the form and utility of this labour. In order, however, not to leave this chapter imperfect and to satisfy the curiosity as much as possible, without fatiguing too much the attention, I shall illustrate the power of the sign by a French word, taken at hazard, of a common acceptation and of obvious composition.

Let it be the word *emplacement*.* Only a very super-

* At the very moment of writing this, I was at the *Bureau des Opérations militaires du Ministère de la guerre*, where I was then employed. Just as I was seeking for the French word announced in the above paragraph, the chief of the division interrupted me, in order to give me some work to do relative to an *emplacement* of troops. My administrative labour terminated, I again took up my grammatical work, retaining the same word which had engaged my attention.

ficial knowledge of etymology is necessary to see that the simple word here is *place*. Our first task is to connect it with the tongue from which it is directly derived; by this means we shall obtain an etymology of the first degree, which will set to rights the changes which might be effected in the characters of which it is composed. Now, whether we go to the Latin tongue, or whether we go to the Teutonic tongue, we shall find in the one *platea*, and in the other *platz*. We shall stop there without seeking the etymology of the second degree, which would consist in interrogating the primitive Celt, common origin of the Latin and the Teutonic; because the two words that we have obtained suffice to enlighten us.

It is evident that the constitutive root of the French word *place*, is *aT* or *aTz*. Now, the sign in *at*, indicates to us an idea of resistance or of protection, and in *atz* an idea of term, of limit, of end. It is, therefore, a thing resisting and limited, or a thing protective and final. But what is the sign which governs this root and which makes it a noun, by proceeding from right to left following the Oriental manner? It is the sign L, that of all extension, of all possession. *Lat* is therefore, a thing extended as *læt,* or extended and possessed as *latitude*. This is unimpeachable.

Next, what is the second sign which stamps a new meaning on these words? It is the sign P, that of active and central action; inner and determinative character; which, from the word *læt,* an extended thing, makes a thing of a fixed and determined extent, a *plat,* or a *place* by changing the *t* into *c,* as the etymology of the first degree has proved to us the reality of this change.

Now that we understand clearly in the word *em-placement,* the simple word *place* of which it is composed, let us search for the elements of its composition. Let us examine first the termination *ment,* a kind of adverbial relation, which added to a noun, determines, in French, an action implied. The etymology of the first degree gives us *mens,* in Latin, and *mind* in Teutonic. These two words mutually explain each other, therefore it is unnecessary for us to turn to the second degree of etymology. Whether we take *mens* or *mind,* it remains for us to explore the root *eN* or *iN,* after dropping the initial character M, and the final S or D, that we shall take up further on. To the root *en,* expressing something even in the tongue of the Latins, we shall now direct our attention.

Here we see the sign of absolute life E, and that of reflective or produced existence N, joined together to designate every particular being. This is precisely what the Latin root EN, signfies, *lo, behold;* that is to say, *see; examine* this individual existence. It is the exact translation of the Hebrew הן *hen!* If you add to this root the luminous sign as in the Greek αἰών (*æon*), you will have the individual being nearest to the absolute being; if, on the contrary, you take away the sign of life and substitute that of duration as in the Latin *in,* you will have the most restricted, the most centralized, the most interior being.

But let the root EN be terminated by the conscriptive and circumferential sign S, and we shall obtain *ens,* corporeal mind, the intelligence peculiar to man. Then let us make this word rule by the exterior and plastic sign M, and we shall have the word *mens,* intelligence manifesting itself outwardly and producing. This is the origin of the termination sought for: it expresses the exterior form according to which every action is modified.

As to the initial syllable *em,* which is found at the head of the word *em-place-ment,* it represents the root EN, and has received the character M, only because of the consonant P, which never allows N in front of it, and this, as though the being generated could never be presented prior to the generating being. This syllable comes therefore from the same source, and whether it be derived from the corresponding Latin words *en* or *in,* it always characterizes restricted existence in a determined or inner point.

According to these ideas, if I had to explain the French word *em-place-ment*, I would say that it signifies the proper mode according to which a fixed and determined extent, as *place,* is conceived or is presented exteriorly.

Moreover, this use of the sign which I have just illustrated by a word of the French tongue, is much easier and more sure in the Hebrew, which, possessing in itself nearly all the constitutive elements, only obliges the etymologist on very rare occasions to leave his lexicon; whereas, one cannot analyze a French word without going back to Latin or Teutonic, from which it is derived, and without making frequent incursions into Celtic, its primitive source, and into Greek and Phœnician, from which it has received at different times a great number of expressions.

CHAPTER IV.

THE SIGN PRODUCING THE ROOT.

§ I.

DIGRESSION ON THE PRINCIPLE AND THE CONSTITUTIVE ELEMENTS OF THE SIGN.

I have endeavoured to show in the preceding chapter, the origin of the sign and its power: let us again stop a moment upon this important subject, and though I might be accused of lacking method, let us not fear to retrace our steps, the better to assure our progress.

I have designated as elements of speech, the voice, the gesture and the traced characters; as means, the sound, the movement and the light: but these elements and these means would exist in vain, if there were not at the same time a creative power, independent of them, which could take possession of them and put them into action. This power is the Will. I refrain from naming its principle; for besides being difficult to conceive, it would not be the place here to speak of it. But the existence of the will cannot be denied even by the most determined skeptic; since he would be unable to call it in question without willing it and consequently without giving it recognition.

Now the articulate voice and the affirmative or negative gesture are, and can only be, the expression of the will. It is the will which, taking possession of sound and movement, forces them to become its interpreters and to reflect exteriorly its interior affections.

Nevertheless, if the will is absolute, all its affections although diverse, must be identical; that is to say, be respectively the same for all individuals who experience them. Thus, a man willing and affirming his will by gesture or vocal inflection, experiences no other affection than any man who wills and affirms the same thing. The gesture and sound of the voice which accompany the affirmation are not those destined to depict negation, and there is not a single man on earth who can not be made to understand by the gesture or by the inflection of the voice, that he is loved or that he is hated; that he wishes or does not wish the thing presented. There would be nothing of agreement here. It is an identical power which is manifested spontaneously and which radiating from one volitive centre reflects itself upon the other.

I would it were as easy to demonstrate that it is equally without agreement and by the sole force of the will, that the gesture or vocal inflection assigned to affirmation or negation is transformed into different words, and how it happens, for example, that the words לא, *no*, and כה, *yes*, having the same sound and involving the same inflection and the same gesture, have not, however, the same meaning; but if that were so easy, how has the origin of speech remained till now unknown? How is it that so many savants armed with both synthesis and analysis, have not solved a question so important to man? There is nothing conventional in speech, and I hope to prove this to my readers; but I do not promise to prove to them, a truth of this nature in the manner of the geometricians; its possession is of too high an importance to be contained in an algebraic equation.

Let us return. Sound and movement placed at the disposition of the will is modified by it; that is to say, that by certain appropriate organs, sound is articulated and changed into voice; movement is determined and changed into gesture. But voice and gesture have only an instantaneous, fugitive duration. If it is of importance to the will of man, to make the memory of the affections that it manifests exteriorly survive the affections themselves (for this is nearly always of importance to him); then,

THE SIGN PRODUCING THE ROOT 105

finding no resource to fix or to depict the sound, it takes possession of movement and with the aid of the hand, its most expressive organ, finds after many efforts, the secret of drawing on the bark of trees or cutting on stone, the gesture upon which it has at first determined. This is the origin of traced characters which, as image of the gesture and symbol of the vocal inflection, become one of the most fruitful elements of language, which extend its empire rapidly and present to man an inexhaustible means of combination. There is nothing conventional in their principle; for *no* is always *no,* and *yes* always *yes:* a man is a man. But as their form depends much upon the designer who first tests the will by depicting his affections, enough of the arbitrary can be insinuated, and it can be varied enough so that there may be need of an agreement to assure their authenticity and authorize their usage. Also, it is always in the midst of a tribe advanced in civilization and subject to the laws of a regular government, that the use of some kind of writing is encountered. One can be sure that wherever traced characters are found, there also are found civilized forms. All men, however savage they may be, speak and impart to each other their ideas; but all do not write, because there is no need of agreement for the establishment of a language, whereas there is always need of one for writing.

Nevertheless, although traced characters infer an agreement, as I have already said, it must not be forgotten that they are the symbol of two things which are not inferred, the vocal inflection and the gesture. These are the result of the spontaneous outburst of the will. The others are the fruit of reflection. In tongues similar to Hebrew, where the vocal inflection and the gesture have long since disappeared, one must devote himself to the characters, as the sole element which remains of the language, and regard them as the complete language itself, not considering the agreement by which they have been established. This is what I have done, in constituting them representative signs of the fundamental ideas of the Hebraic tongue. I shall follow the same method showing successively how this small quantity of signs has sufficed for the formation of the roots of this tongue, and for the composition of all the words which have been derived therefrom. Let us examine first what I mean by a root.

§ II.

FORMATION OF THE ROOT AND OF THE RELATION.

A root is, and can never be anything but, monosyllabic: it results from the union of two signs at the least, and of three at the most. I say two signs at the least, for a single sign cannot constitute a root, because the fundamental idea that it contains, being, as it were, only in germ, awaits the influence of another sign in order to be developed. It is not that the sign before being constituted such, may not have represented a noun, but this noun becomes effaced, as I have said, to constitute the sign. When the sign is presented alone in speech, it becomes, in Hebrew, what I call an article; that is to say, a sort of relation whose expression entirely abstract, determines the diverse relations of nouns and verbs to each other.

The root cannot be composed of more than three signs, without being dissyllabic and consequently without ceasing to be of the number of primitive words. Every word composed of more than one syllable is necessarily a derivative. For, two roots are either united or contracted; or else one or several signs have been joined to the radical root for its modification.

Although the etymological root may be very well employed as noun, verb or relation, all that, however, does not matter, so long as one considers it as root; seeing that it offers in this respect no determined idea of object, action or abstraction. A noun designates openly a particular object of whatever nature it may be, a verb expresses some sort of action, a relation determines a *rapport:* the root presents always a meaning universal as noun, absolute as verb, and indeterminate as relation.

Thus the root אִי, formed of the signs of power and of manifestation, designates, in general, the centre toward which the will tends, the place where it is fixed, its sphere of activity. Employed as noun, it is a desire, a desired object: a place distinct and separate from another place; an isle, a country, a region, a home, a government: as verb, it is the action of desiring a thing eagerly, of tending toward a place, of delighting therein: as relation, it is the abstract connection of the place where one is, of the object to which one tends, of the sphere wherein one acts.

Thus the root אוֹ, which unites to the sign of power, the universal, convertible sign, image of the mysterious knot which brings nothingness to being, offers even a vaguer meaning than the root אִי, of which I have spoken, and of which it seems to be a modification. Nor is it yet a desire, even in general; it is, so to speak, the germ of a desire, a vague appetence, without aim and without object; a desirous uneasiness, an obtuse sense. Employed as noun, it designates the uncertainty of the will; if it is made a verb, it is the indeterminate action of willing; if it is used as relation, it is the abstract expression of the affinity that the uncertainty or indetermination of the will, establishes between one or the other object which attracts it. This root, considered rightly as primitive, produces a great number of derivative roots by becoming amalgamated with other primitive roots, or receiving them by the adjunction of the signs which modify it. One finds, for example, the following, which are worthy of closest attention.

אוֹב All desire acting inwardly and fructifying. It is, as noun, the matrix of the Universe, the vessel of Isis, the Orphic egg, the World, the Pythonic spirit; etc.

אוֹר Every desire acting outwardly and being propagated. As noun, it is that which binds cause to effect, the causality; any sort of emanation; as verb, it is the action of emanating, of passing from cause to effect; as relation, it is the abstract affinity according to which one conceives that a thing exists, or takes place *because* of another.

אוּל Every expansive desire being projected into space. As noun, it is an interval of time or place; a duration, a distance; as verb, it is the action of being extended, of filling, of invading time or space; that of waiting or lasting; as relation, it is the abstract affinity expressed by *perhaps*.

אוֹן Every desire spreading into infinity, losing itself in vacuity, vanishing: as noun, it is everything and nothing according to the manner in which one considers infinity.

אוֹף Every desire subjugating another and drawing it into its vortex: as noun, it is the sympathetic force, the passion; a final cause: as verb, it is the action of drawing into its will, of enveloping in its vortex: as relation, it is the abstract affinity expressed by *same, likewise*.

אוֹץ Every desire leading to a goal. As noun, it is the very limit of desire, the end to which it tends; as verb, it is the action of pushing, of hastening, of pressing toward the desired object: as relation, it is the abstract affinity expressed by *at*.

אוּר Every desire given over to its own impulse. As noun, it is ardour, fire, passion: as verb, it is that which embraces, burns, excites, literally as well as figuratively.

אוֹת All sympathizing desire; being in accord with another. As noun it is a symbol, a character, any object whatever: as verb, it is the action of sympathizing, of being in accord with, of agreeing, of being *en rapport*, in harmony; as relation it is the abstract affinity expressed by *together*.

I shall give no more examples on this subject since my plan is to give, in the course of this Grammar, a series of all the Hebraic roots. It is there that I invite the reader to study their form. I shall be careful to distinguish the primitive roots from the compound, intensive or onomatopoetic roots. Those of the latter kind are quite rare in

Hebrew. One finds them in much greater numbers in Arabic where many local circumstances have called them into existence. This concurrence of imitative sounds, very favourable to poetry and to all the arts of imitation, must have been greatly prejudicial to the development of universal ideas toward which the Egyptians directed their greatest efforts.

It is an unfortunate mistake to imagine that the examination of Hebraic roots is as difficult as it is in the modern idioms. In these idioms, raised, for the most part, upon the *débris* of many united idioms, the roots deeply buried beneath the primitive materials, can deceive the eye of the observer; but it cannot do thus in Hebrew. This tongue, thanks to the form of the Chaldaic characters which have changed scarcely anything but its punctuation, offers still to an observant reader who does not wish to concern himself with the vowel points, the terms used by Moses in their native integrity. If, notwithstanding the precautions of Esdras, there have crept in certain alterations in the mother vowels and even in the consonants, these alterations are slight and do not prevent the root, nearly level with the ground, if I may thus express it, from striking the eye of the etymologist.

Let us examine now what I mean by the relations.

The relations are, as I have said, extracted by thought from the signs, nouns or verbs. They express always a connection of the sign with the noun, of the noun with the noun, or of the noun with the verb. Thence, the simple and natural division which I establish, in three kinds, according to the part of speech with which they preserve the greatest analogy. I call designative relation or *article,* that which marks the connection of the sign with the noun: nominal relation or *pronoun,* that which indicates the connection of the noun with the noun, or of the noun with the verb; and finally adverbial relation or *adverb,* that which characterizes the connection of the verb with the verb, or of the verb with the noun. I use here these

FORMATION OF ROOT AND RELATION 111

denominations known as article, pronoun and adverb to avoid prolixity; but without admitting in Hebrew the distinctions or the definitions that grammarians have admitted in other tongues.

The relations, forming together a kind of grammatical bond which circulates among the principal parts of speech, must be considered separately, kind by kind, and according as they are connected with the sign, noun or verb. I am about to speak of the designative relation or article, since I have already made known the sign: but I shall put off speaking of the nominal relation, because I have already spoken of the noun, and shall deal later with the adverbial relation having already dealt with the verb.

The designative relation or article, is represented under three headings in the Hebraic tongue, namely: under that of the relation properly speaking, or *article,* of the prepositive relation, or *preposition,* and of the interjective relation, or *interjection.* The article differs principally from the sign, by what it preserves of its own peculiar force, and by what it communicates to the noun to which it is joined; a sort of movement which changes nothing of the primitive signification of this noun; nevertheless it is strictly united there and is composed of but one single character.

I enumerate six articles in Hebrew, without including the designative preposition את, of which I shall speak later. They have neither gender nor number. The following are the articles with the kind of movement that they express.

ה DETERMINATIVE ARTICLE.—It determines the noun; that is to say, that it draws the object which it designates from a mass of similiar objects and gives it a local existence. Derived from the sign ה, which contains the idea of universal life, it presents itself under several acceptations as article. By the first, it points out simply the noun that it modifies and is rendered by the corresponding articles *the; this, that, these, those:*

by the second, it expresses a relation of dependence or division, and is translated *of the; of this, of that, of these, of those:* by the third, it adds to the noun before which it is placed, only an emphatic meaning, a sort of exclamatory accent. In this last acceptation, it is placed indifferently at the beginning or at the end of words and is joined with the greater part of the other articles without being harmful to their movement. Therefore I call it *Emphatic article,* and when I translate it, which I rarely do lacking means, I render it by *o! oh! ah!* or simply by the exclamation point (!).

ל DIRECTIVE ARTICLE.—It expresses, with nouns or actions whose movement it modifies, a direct relation of union, of possession, or of coincidence. I translate it by *to, at, for, according to, toward,* etc.

מ EXTRACTIVE OR PARTITIVE ARTICLE.—The movement which this article expresses, with nouns or actions that it modifies, is that by which a noun or an action is taken for the means, for the instrument, by which they are divided in their essence, or drawn from the midst of several other nouns or similar actions. I render it ordinarily by *from, out of, by; with, by means of, among, between,* etc.

ב MEDIATIVE OR INTEGRAL ARTICLE.—This article characterizes with nouns or actions, almost the same movement as the extractive article מ, but with more force, and without any extraction or division of the parts. Its analogues are: *in, by, with, while,* etc.

כ ASSIMILATIVE ARTICLE.—The movement which it expresses, with nouns or actions is that of similitude, of analogy, and of concomitance. I render it by: *as, similar; such as, according to,* etc.

ו CONJUNCTIVE OR CONVERTIBLE ARTICLE.—This article, in uniting nouns, causes the movement of nothingness, of which the character ו becomes the sign, as we have seen: in making actions pass from one time to another.

it exercises upon them the convertible faculty of which this same character is the universal emblem. Its conjunctive movement can be rendered by: *and, also, thus, then, afterward, that,* etc. But its convertible movement is not expressible in our tongue and I do not know of any in which it can be expressed. In order to perceive it one must feel the Hebraic genius.

The chapters wherein I shall treat of the noun and the verb will contain the necessary examples to illustrate the use of these six articles whether relative to the noun or the verb.

§ III.

PREPOSITION AND INTERJECTION.

Articles, which we shall now examine, remain articles, properly speaking, only so far as they are composed of a single literal character and as they are joined intimately to the noun, the verb or the relation which they govern; when they are composed of several characters and when they act apart or are simply united to words by a hyphen, I call them prepositive articles or *prepositions*: they become *interjections* when, in this state of isolation, they offer no longer any relation with the noun or the verb, and express only a movement of the mind too intense to be otherwise characterized.

Prepositions, intended to serve as link between things, and to show their respective function, lose their meaning when once separated from the noun which they modify. Interjections, on the contrary, have only as much force as they have independence. Differing but little in sound, they differ infinitely in the expression, more or less accentuated, that they receive from the sentiment which produces them. They belong, as a learned man has said, "to all time, to all places, to all peoples": they form an universal language.[1]

I am about to give here, the prepositions and interjections which are the most important to understand, so as to fix the ideas of the reader upon the use of these kinds of relations. I am beginning with those prepositions which take the place of the articles already cited.

הֶ‎אָ: *determinative prep.* replaces the article ה.
עַל or אֶלֽי‎,אֶל *directive*   "   "   "   " ל.
מִמֶּֽנִי‎ or מָנִי‎,מִן *extractive*   "   "   "   " מ.

[1] Court de Geb: *Gramm. Univ.* p. 353.

PREPOSITION AND INTERJECTION

בְּ.	*mediative*	*prep.* replaces the article	בִּ׳, בְּדִי or בְּמוֹ:
כְּ.	*assimilative*	" " " "	כִּ׳, כֶּה or כְּמוֹ:

The **conjunctive and convertible article** וְ is **not replaceable**.

אֶת, אוֹת: *designative preposition:* has **no corresponding article**.

גַּם same, also, as ⎫
כִּי׃ that   ⎪
עִם with   ⎬ *conjunctive prepositions*   גַּם, גַּם כִּי׃ / כִּי׃ / עִם, עִמָּד׃
אַף likewise, even ⎭

אוֹ either, or   ⎫
בַּל׃ neither, nor   ⎬ *disjunctive prepositions*   בְּלִי, בִּלְתִּי, מִבְּלִי׃
without   ⎭

אַךְ but, except   ⎫
אוּלָם nevertheless ⎬ *restrictive prepositions*
רַק save, at least ⎭

אִם if, but if ⎫ *conditional prepositions*   אִם, כִּי אִם׃
אוּלַי perhaps ⎭

יוֹתֵר besides, moreover ⎬ *additive prepositions*
מְאֹד very, more   ⎭

אֵצֶל near, with   ⎬ *final prepositions*
עַד at, as far as   ⎭   עַד עֲדֵי׃

בְּעַד for   ⎫
כְּפִי, לְפִי׃ according to ⎪
כִּי׃ for, because   ⎪
חֵלֶף on account of   ⎬ *discursive prepositions*
יַעַן כִּי׃ since   ⎪
לָכֵן therefore   ⎪
עַל־כֵּן now then, so ⎪
לְמַעַן as   ⎭
etc., etc.,

INTERJECTIONS.

אָח, אוֹי, אוֹיחַ:	ah! woe! alas!
הָ, הָא:	oh! heavens!
חֶאָח:	now then! come **now**!
הָבָה:	take care! mind!
הוֹי:	indeed!
לוּ, אַחֲלִי:	would to God!
	etc., etc.,

I believe it quite useless to prolong this list and to dwell upon the particular signification of each of these relations; however, there is one of which I must speak, because its usage is very frequent in the tongue of Moses, and also because we shall see it soon figuring in the nominal inflection, and joining its movement to that of the articles. This is the designative preposition אֶת, which I have mentioned as having no corresponding article.

The movement which expresses this preposition with the nouns which it modifies, is that by which it puts them *en rapport* as governing or governed, as independent one of the other and participating in the same action. I name it *designative,* on account of the sign of signs, ת, from which it is derived. It characterizes sympathy and reciprocity when it is taken substantively. Joined to a noun by a hyphen אֶת־, it designates the substance proper and individual, the identity, the selfsameness, the seity, the *thou-ness,* if I may be permitted this word; that is to say, that which constitutes *thou,* that which implies something apart from *me,* a thing that is not *me;* in short, the presence of another substance. This important preposition, of which I cannot give the exact meaning, indicates the coincidence, the spontaneity of actions, the liaison, the *ensemble* and the dependence of things.

The designative relation that I am considering in connection with the article, preposition and interjection, will

PREPOSITION AND INTERJECTION

be easily distinguished from the nominal relation concerning which I shall speak later on; because this relation is not intended either to modify nouns or to set forth the confused and indeterminate movements of the mind; but serves as supplement to nouns, becomes their lieutenant, so to speak, and shows their mutual dependence. This same relation will not be, it is true, so easy to distinguish from the adverbial relation, and I admit that often one will meet with some that are, at the same time, prepositions and adverbs. But this very analogy will furnish the proof of what I have advanced, that the relation extracted by thought, from the sign, the noun and the verb, circulates among these three principal parts of speech and is modified to serve them as common bond.

One can observe, for example, that the designative relation tends to become adverbial and that it becomes thus whenever it is used in an absolute manner with the verb, or when the article is joined, making it a sort of adverbial substantive. Therefore one can judge that *upon, in, outside,* are designative relations, or prepositions when one says: *upon that; in the present; outside this point:* but one cannot mistake them for adverbials when one says: *I am above; I am within; I am without.* It is in this state that they are taken to be inflected with the article. *I see the above, the within, the without; I come from above, from within, from without; I go above, within, without;* etc. The Hebraic tongue, which has not these means of construction, makes use of the same words עַל, חוּץ בֵּית to express equally *upon, above, the upper part; in, the inside; out, beyond, the outside.* It is to these fine points that great attention must be given in translating Moses.

As to the vowel points which accompany the different relations of which I shall speak, they vary in such a way, that it would be vainly wasting precious time to consider them here; so much the more as these variations change nothing as to the meaning, which alone concerns me, and alters only the pronunciation, which does not concern me.

I am always surprised, in reading the majority of the Grammars written upon the Hebraic tongue, to see with what scruples, with what tedious care they treat a miserable *kamez,* or a still more miserable *kamez-hatif;* whereas they hardly deign to dwell upon the meaning of the most important words. Numberless pages are found jumbled with the uncouth names of *zere, segol, patah, holem,* and not one where the sign is mentioned, not one where it is even a question of this basis, at once so simple and so fecund, both of the Hebraic language and of all the languages of the world.

CHAPTER V.

THE NOUN.

THE NOUN CONSIDERED UNDER SEVEN RELATIONS.

§ I.

ETYMOLOGY

The noun, I repeat, is the basis of speech; for, although it may be the product of the sign, the sign without it would have no meaning, and if the sign had no meaning, there would exist neither relations nor verbs.

We shall consider the nouns of the Hebraic tongue, under seven relations, namely: under the first six, of Etymology, Quality, Gender, Number, Movement and Construction, and then, under the seventh relation of Signification, which includes them all.

The Hebraist grammarians, dazzled by the *éclat* of the verb and by the extensive use of the verbal faculties, have despoiled the noun of its etymological rank to give it to the verb, thus deriving from the verb not only the equi-literal substantives, that is to say, compounds of the same number of characters, but even those which offer less: claiming, for example, that גַל *a heap*, is formed from גָלַל *he heaps up;* that אָב *father,* is derived from אָבָה *he willed;* that אֵשׁ *the fire,* finds its origin in אָשֵׁשׁ *he was strong and robust,* etc.

It is needless for me to say into how many errors they have fallen by this false course, and how far distant they are from the real etymological goal. The lexicons also, of these Hebraists, all constructed after this method, are only crude vocabularies, where the simplest words, thrown more or less far from their root, according as the verb bids it, are presented almost never in their real place, or in the true light which would facilitate their comprehension.

I have spoken sufficiently of the sign and its value, of the root and its formation; I now intend to give certain simple rules to lead to the etymological understanding of the noun.

Often a *noun* properly speaking, is, in the tongue of the Hebrews, only its root used in a more restricted sense: as when uniting the idea of paternity and maternity upon a single subject, one pronounces אב, *father,* or אם *mother.* It is then a movement of the thought upon itself, which makes of a thing that it had conceived in general, a determined thing, by which it qualifies a particular subject. This movement is very common in the idiom of Moses, and it merits so much the more attention, because, not having observed it, the greater part of the translators have been mistaken in the meaning of the words and have ridiculously particularized what was universal. As when, for example, in עץ, a vegetable substance, a vegetation in general, they have seen *a wood,* or *a tree:* or in גן, an enclosure, a circumscription, a sphere, only a *garden*: or even in דם, the universal idea of an assimilation of homogeneous parts, they have seen only *blood;* etc.

When a noun is composed of three or more consonants, and when it is of more than one syllable, it is obviously a derivative. It is in the examination of its root that the art of the etymologist shines. He must master both the value of each sign and the position that it takes, whether at the beginning or the end of words, and the different modifications which it brings about; for, to understand the root clearly, it is necessary to know how to distinguish it from the sign, or from the article by which it is modified. If the etymologist would acquire a science which opens the door to the loftiest conceptions, he must be provided with the faculties and the necessary means. If long study of tongues in general, and the Hebraic tongue in particular, can lend a little confidence in my abilities, I beg the reader, interested in an art too little cultivated, to study carefully, both the series of Hebraic roots which I give him at the close of this Grammar and the numerous notes which accompany my translation of the Cosmogony of Moses.

The work of Court de Gébelin is a vast storehouse of words, which one ought to possess without being a slave to it. This painstaking man had intellect rather than etymological genius; he searched well; he classed well his materials; but he constructed badly. His merit, is having introduced the Primitive tongue; his fault, is having introduced it to his reader in a thousand scattered fragments. The genius will consist in reassembling these fragments to form a whole. I offer in this Grammar an instrument to attain this end. It is THE HEBRAIC TONGUE DERIVED WHOLLY FROM THE SIGN.

Here are the general principles which can be drawn from the work of Gébelin relative to etymological science. I add some developments that experience has suggested to me.

Particular tongues are only the dialects of an universal tongue founded upon nature, and of which a spark of the Divine word animates the elements. This tongue, that no people has ever possessed in its entirety, can be called *the Primitive tongue.* This tongue, from which all others spring as from an unique trunk, is composed only of monosyllabic roots, all adhering to a small number of signs. In proportion as the particular tongues become mingled with one another and separated from their primitive stock, the words become more and more altered: therefore it is essential to compare many languages in order to obtain the understanding of a single one.

It is necessary to know that all vowels tend to become consonants, and all consonants to become vowels;

to consider this movement; to follow it in its modifications; to distinguish carefully the mother vowel from the vague vowel and when one is assured that the vocal sound which enters into the composition of a word, descends from a vague vowel, give it no further attention. One will attain to this final understanding, by the study of the Hebraic tongue, where the difference which exists between these two sorts of vowels is decisive.

It is necessary to consider besides, that, in the generation of tongues, the consonants are substituted for one another, particularly those of the same organic sound. Therefore it is well to classify them by the sound and to know them under this new relation.

Labial sound: ב, פ, ו: B, P, PH, F, V. This sound, being the easiest, is the first of which children make use; it is generally that of gentleness and mildness considered as onomatopoetic.

Dental sound: ד, ט: D, T. It expresses, on the contrary, all that which touches, thunders, resounds, resists, protects.

Lingual sound: ל, ר: L, LL, LH, R, RH. It expresses a rapid movement, either rectilinear or circular, in whatever sense one imagines it, always considered as onomatopoetic.

Nasal sound: מ, נ: M, N, GN. It expresses all that which passes from without within, or which emerges from within without.

Guttural sound: ג, כ, ע, ק: GH, CH, WH, K, Q. It expresses deep, hollow objects, contained one within the other, or modelled by assimilation.

Hissing sound: ז, ס, צ: Z, S, X, TZ, DZ, PS. It is applied to all hissing objects, to all those which have relation with the air, or which cleave it in their course.

Sibilant sound: י, ש, ת: J, G, CH, SH, TH. It expresses light movements, soft and durable sounds; all pleasing objects.

The consonants thus distinguished by sound, become the general signs from which the onomatopoetic roots of which I have spoken, are formed, and are very easily put one in the place of the other. In the derivative tongues they even lend mutual aid in passing from one sound to another, and it is then that they render the etymology of the words more and more uncertain. The etymologist can only surmount the numerous obstacles in the modern idioms, by having stored in his mind a number of tongues whose radical words can assist him readily in going back to the idiomatic or primitive root of the word which he analyzes. Never can one hope by the aid of a single tongue, to form good etymology.

As to the mother vowels, א, ה, ח, ו, י, ', ע; A, E, Ê, OU, O, I, HO; they are substituted successively one for the other, from א to ע; they all incline to become consonants and to become extinct in the deep and guttural sound כ, which can be represented by the Greek χ or the German *c̀h*. I always mark this *c̀h* with an *accent grave* in order to distinguish it from the French *ch*, which is a hissing sound like the ש of the Hebrews, or the *sh* of the English.

After having set forth these etymological principles, I pass on to the next rules, relative to their employment; very nearly such as Court de Gébelin gives them.

One should not take for granted any alteration in a word that one may not be able to prove by usage or by analogy; nor confuse the radical characters of a word with the accessory characters, which are only added signs or articles. The words should be classified by families and none admitted unless it has been grammatically analyzed: primitives, should be distinguished from compounds and all forced etymology carefully avoided: and finally, an historical or moral proof should corroborate the etymology; for the sciences proceed with certain step only as they throw light upon each other.

§ II.

QUALITY

I call Quality, in the Hebraic nouns, the distinction which I establish among them and by means of which I divide them into four classes, namely: substantives, qualificatives, modificatives, and facultatives.

Substantives are applied to all that has physical or moral substance, the existence of which the thought of man admits either by evidence of the senses, or by that of the intellectual faculties. Substantives are proper or common: *proper* when they are applied to a single being, or to a single thing in particular, as מֹשֶׁה *Mosheh* (Moses), נֹחַ *Noah,* מִצְרַיִם *Mitzraim* (Egypt) etc.; *common,* when they are applied to all beings, or to all things of the same kind, as אִישׁ *man* (intelligent being); רֹאשׁ *head* (that which rules or enjoys by its own movement); מֶלֶךְ *king* (a temporal and local deputy); etc.

Qualificatives express the qualities of the substantives and offer them to the imagination under the form which characterizes them. The grammarians in naming them *adjectives,* have given them a denomination too vague to be preserved in a grammar of the nature of this one. This class of nouns expresses more than a simple adjunction; it expresses the very quality or the form of the substance, as in טוֹב *good,* גָּדוֹל *great,* צַדִּיק *just,* עִבְרִי *Hebrew;* etc.

The tongue of Moses is not rich in qualificatives, but it obviates this lack by the energy of its articles, by that of its verbal facultatives and by the various extensions which it gives to its substantives by joining them to certain initial or terminative characters. It has, for example, in the emphatic article ה, a means of intensity of which it

QUALITY

makes great use, either in placing it at the beginning or the end of words. Thus, of נַחַל *a torrent*, it makes נַחֲלָה *a very rapid torrent;* of קָפָד *disappearance, absence,* it makes קְפָדָה *an eternal absence, a total disappearance;* מוֹת *death,* it makes הַמוֹתָה *a violent, cruel, sudden death,* etc. Sometimes it adds to this article, the sign of reciprocity ת, to augment its force. Then one finds for עֵזֶר *a support, an aid,* עֶזְרָתָה *a firm support, an accomplished aid;* for אֵימָה *terror,* אֵימָתָה *extreme terror, frightful terror;* for יְשׁוּעָה *safety, refuge,* יְשׁוּעָתָה *an assured safety, an inaccessible refuge;* etc.

The assimilative article כ, forms a kind of qualificative of the noun which it governs. It is thus that one should understand כֵּאלֹהִים *like unto the Gods,* or *divine;* כְּכֹהֵן *like unto the priest,* or *sacerdotal;* כְּעָם *like unto the people,* or *vulgar;* כְּהַיּוֹם *like to-day,* or *modern;* etc.

On the other hand, the sign ת placed at the beginning of a word expresses reciprocity. אֲנִיָה signifies *pain,* תַּאֲנִיָה *mutual pain.*

The sign מ, when it is initial, is related to exterior action; when final, on the contrary, it becomes expansive and collective. אוֹל signifies *any force whatever,* מָאוֹל *a circumscribed and local force;* אוֹלָם *an exterior, invading force.*

The sign נ, is that of passive action when it is at the head of words; but at the end, it constitutes an augmentative syllable which extends its signification. אָפְדָה signifies *a veil,* אֹפֶדֶן *an immense veil, the enclosure of a tent;* גֵוָא characterizes *an extension,* and גְוָאן *an unlimited extension, inordinate;* הֵם expresses *a noise,* and הָמוֹן *a frightful noise, a terrible tumult, a revolt;* etc.

I pass over these details of which my footnotes on

the Cosmogony of Moses will afford sufficient examples. It will be enough for me here to indicate the grammatical forms.

The rabbis, in writing modern Hebrew, form the qualificatives by the addition of the character י to the masculine, and the syllable ית, to the feminine. They say, for example, אלהי *divine* (mas.) and אלהית *divine* (fem.). נפשי *spiritual* (mas.) and נפשית *spiritual* (fem.). Then they draw from these qualificatives a mass of substantive nouns, such as אלהות *the divinity;* אולות *fortitude;* נפשות *spirituality;* ידרות *tenderness;* etc. These forms do not belong to primitive Hebrew.

The comparative among qualificatives is not strictly characterized in the Hebraic tongue. When it is established, which is somewhat rare, it is by means of the extractive article מ, or by the preposition מן which corresponds.

The superlative is expressed in many ways. Sometimes one finds either the substantive or the qualificative doubled, in order to give the idea that one has of their force or their extent; sometimes they are followed by an absolute relative to designate that nothing is comparable to them. At other times the adverbial relation מְאֹד *very, very much, as much as possible,* indicates that one conceives them as having attained their measure in good or in evil, according to their nature. Finally one meets different periphrases and different formulas of which I herewith offer several examples.

QUALITY 127

נֹחַ אִישׁ צַדִּיק תָּמִים	Noah, intelligent being (man), just with integrity (as just as upright).
טוֹב שֵׁם מִשֶּׁמֶן טוֹב :	a good name, of good essence (a name of high repute is the best essence).
טוֹבִים הַשְּׁנַיִם מִן־הָאֶחָד .	good the two of a single one (two are better than one).
רַע רַע : מַטָּה מָטָּה :	bad, evil (wicked); down, down (beneath).
מִן־הָאָדֹם הָאָדֹם :	among the red, red (much redder).
קָטֹן בַּגּוֹיִם :	small among people (very small).
הָהָר הַטּוֹב הַזֶּה :	a mountain, the good, that one (the best of all).
טוֹב מְאֹד :	good exceedingly (as much as possible).
הַשָּׁמַיִם וּשְׁמֵי הַשָּׁמָיִם :	the heavens and the heaven of heavens.
אֱלֹהֵי אֱלֹהִים וַאֲדֹנֵי הָאֲדֹנִים :	God of Gods and Lord of Lords.
עֶבֶד עֲבָדִים :	servant of the servants.
חֹשֶׁךְ־אֲפֵלָה :	the obscurity of darkness.
שַׁלְהֶבֶתְיָה : מַאְפֵּלְיָה :	the flame of Jah! the darkness of Jah! (extremes).
אַרְזֵי־אֵל :	the cedars of God! (admirable, very beautiful).
עִיר גְּדוֹלָה לֵאלֹהִים ;	a great city! according to Him-the-Gods!
אַמִּץ לַאדֹנָי :	strong according to the Lord! (very strong).
בֹּעֲרָה : בִּמְאֹד מְאֹד :	a burning; with might of might.

Modificatives are the substantives or the qualificatives modified either by a simple abstraction of thought, or by the addition of an adverbial relation, so as to become the expression of an action understood. It is not unusual to find in Hebrew, nouns which can be taken, at the same time, as substantives, qualificatives or modificatives; all by a movement of abstraction, and this is easy when the idiom is not far removed from its source. Thus, for example טוֹב *good,* signifies equally *the good,* and the *good* manner in which a thing is done: רַע *evil,* signifies equally that which is *evil,* and the *evil* manner in which a thing is done. One perceives that the words *good* and *evil,* have exactly the same signification as the Hebraic words טוֹב and רַע, as substantives, and that they contain the same qualificative and modificative faculties. I have chosen them expressly so as to show how this abstraction of thought of which I have spoken, is accomplished.

Modificative nouns which are formed by the addition of a designative or adverbial relation as in French, *à-la-mode* (in the fashion), *à-outrance* (to the utmost), *forte-ment* (strongly), *douce-ment* (gently), are very rare in Hebrew. One finds, however, certain ones such as בְּרֵאשׁ־ית, *in the beginning, in-principle;* יְהוּד־ית, *in Jewish;* מֵאַשּׁוּר־ית *from the Assyrian;* etc. The nouns of number belong at the same time to substantives, qualificatives and modificatives. אֶחָד, *one,* can signify alike, *unity, unique* and *uniquely.*

Facultative nouns are the substantives, *verbalized,* as it were, and in which the absolute verb הוֹה, *to be-being,* begins to make its influence felt. The grammarians have called them up to this time *participles,* but I treat this weak denomination, as I have treated the one which they have given to qualificatives. I replace it by another which I believe more just.

Facultatives merit particular attention in all tongues, but especially in that of Moses, where they present more openly than in any other, the link which unites the substantive to the verb, and which, by an inexplicable power, makes of a substance inert and without action, an animated substance being carried suddenly toward a determined end. It is by means of the sign of light and of intellectual sense, וֹ, that this metamorphosis is accomplished. This is remarkable. If I take, for example, the substantive רָגַז, which expresses all physical movement all moral affection; if I introduce between the first and second character which compose it, the verbal sign וֹ, I obtain immediately the *continued* facultative, רוֹגֵז, *to be-moving, affecting, agitating.* If I modify this sign, that is to say, if I give it its convertible nature וֹ, and if I place it between the second and third character of the substantive in question, I obtain then the *finished* facultative רָגוֹז, *to be-moved, affected, agitated.* It is the same with מֶלֶךְ *a king,* whose continued and finished facultatives are מוֹלֵךְ *to be-ruling, governing;* מָלוּךְ *to be-ruled, governed,* and many others.

It can be observed that I name *continued facultative,* what the grammarians call *present participle,* and *finished* that which they call *past;* because in effect, the action expressed by these facultatives is not, properly speaking, present or past, but continued or finished in any time whatever. One says clearly *it was burning, it is burning, it will be burning; it was burned, it is burned, it will be burned.* Now who cannot see that the facultatives *burning* and *burned,* are by turns, both past, present and future? They both participate in these three tenses with the difference, that the first is always continued and the other always finished.

But let us return. It is from the finished facultative that the verb comes, as I shall demonstrate later on. This facultative, by means of which speech receives verbal life, is formed from the primitive root by the introduction of the sign וֹ between the two characters of which it is composed. Thus, for example:

The root שׁם contains every idea of elevation, erection, or monument, raised as indication of a place or thing:

thence: שָׁם or שׁוֹם to be erecting, stating, decreeing, designating:

שׁוֹם to be erected, stated, etc., whence the verb שׁוּם *to erect.*

The root כל contains every idea of consummation, of totalization, of agglomeration, of absorption:

thence: כָּל or כּוֹל to be consummating, totalizing, agglomerating:

כּוֹל to be consummated, agglomerated: whence the verb כּוּל, *to consummate.*

The root גל expresses every idea of heaping up, lifting up, of movement which carries upward from below:

thence: גָּל or גּוֹל to be heaping up, lifting up, pushing, leaping:

גּוֹל to be heaped up, lifted up; whence the verb גּוּל, *to heap up.*

As I shall be obliged to return to this formation of the facultatives, in the chapter in which I shall treat of the verb, it is needless for me to dwell further upon it now. I cannot, however, refrain from making the observation that since the institution of the Chaldaic punctuation, the points *kamez, holem,* and even *zere,* have often **replaced the verbal sign** וֹ in the continued facultative,

QUALITY 131

whether of compound or radical origin, and that one finds quite commonly רגן *to be moving;* מלך *to be ruling;* קם *to be establishing;* מת *to be dying;* etc. But two things prove that this is an abuse of punctuation. The first is, that when the continued facultative presents itself in an absolute manner, and when nothing can determine the meaning, then the sign reappears irresistibly; as in the following examples, קום *the action of establishing,* or *to be establishing:* מות *the action of dying,* or *to be dying.* The second thing which proves the abuse of which I am speaking, is that the rabbis who preserve to a certain point the oral tradition, never fail to make the mother vowel ו׳ appear in these same facultatives unless they deem it more suitable to substitute its analogues ׳ or א׳, writing קום, קים or קאים, *to be establishing, to establish, the action of establishing.*

I shall terminate this paragraph by saying that facultatives both continued and finished, are subject to the same inflections as the substantive and qualificative nouns, that is, of gender, number, movement and construction. The modificative noun does not have the inflections of the others because it contains an implied action, and since it has, as I shall demonstrate, the part of itself which emanates from the verb *to be,* wholly immutable and consequently inflexible.

§ III.

GENDER

Gender is distinguished at first by the sex, male or female, or by a sort of analogy, of similitude, which appears to exist among things, and the sex which is assigned to them by speech. The Hebraic tongue has two genders only, the masculine and the feminine; notwithstanding the efforts that the grammarians have made to discover in it a third and even a fourth which they have called common or epicene. These so-called genders are only the liberty allowed the speaker of giving to such or such substantive the masculine or feminine gender, indifferently, and according to the circumstance: if these genders merit any attention, it is when passing into the derivative tongues, and in taking a particular form there, that they have constituted the neuter gender which one encounters in many of them.

The feminine gender is derived from the masculine, and is formed by adding to the substantive, qualificative or facultative noun, the sign ה which is that of life. The modificative nouns have no gender, because they modify actions and not things, as do the other kinds of words.

I beg the reader who follows me with any degree of interest, to observe the force and constancy with which is demonstrated everywhere, the power that I have attributed to the *sign*, a power upon which I base the whole genius of the tongue of Moses.

I have said that the feminine gender is formed from the masculine by the addition of the sign of life ה׃ was it possible to imagine a sign of happier expression, to indicate the sex by which all beings appear to owe life, this blessing of the Divinity?

GENDER

Thus מֶלֶךְ *a king*, produces מַלְכָּה *a queen;* חָכָם *a wise man*, חֲכָמָה *a wise woman;* דָּג *a male fish*, דָּגָה *a female fish*.

Thus טוֹב *good* (mas.), becomes טוֹבָה *good* (fem.); גָּדוֹל *great* (mas.), גְּדוֹלָה *great* (fem.).

Thus מוֹלֵךְ *to be ruling* (mas.), becomes מוֹלְכָה *to be ruling* (fem.): שׂוֹם *or* שָׂם *to be raising* (mas.), שׂוֹמָה *to be raising* (fem.).

It must be observed, in respect to this formation, that when the qualificative masculine is terminated with the character ה, which is then only the emphatic sign, or by the character י, sign of manifestation, these two characters remain wholly simple, or are modified by the sign of reciprocity ת, in the following manner: יָפֶה *beautiful* (mas.), יָפָה or יָפַת (fem.); שֵׁנִי *second* (mas.), שְׁנִיָה or שֵׁנִית (fem.).

Besides, this sign ת, image of all that is mutual, replaces in almost every case the character ה, when it is a question of the feminine termination of qualificative or facultative nouns; it seems even, that the genius of the Hebraic tongue is particularly partial to it in the latter. One finds נוֹפֶלֶת, rather than נוֹפְלָה, *to be falling;* בּוֹרַחַת, rather than בּוֹרְחָה *to be fleeing;* etc.

It is useless, in a Grammar which treats principally of the genius of a tongue, to expatiate much upon the application of the genders; that is a matter which concerns the dictionary. Let it suffice to know, that, in general, the proper names of men, of occupations, of titles, peoples, rivers, mountains and months, are masculine; whereas the names of women, of countries, of cities, the members of the body, and all substantives terminating with the sign ה, are feminine.

As to the common gender, that is to say, that of the substantive nouns which take the masculine and feminine alike, it is impossible to apply any rule even approximately; it is by use alone that it can be shown. These are the substantives of the common gender which come to my mind at the moment: גַן *enclosure, organic sphere;* שֶׁמֶשׁ *sun;* אֶרֶץ *earth;* אוֹת *sign;* עֵת *time;* רוּחַ *spirit, expansive breath;* נֶפֶשׁ *soul;* אָרוֹן *chain of mountains;* חֲזִיר *pig;* אֲרִי *lion;* etc.

§ IV.

NUMBER

There exist only two characteristic numbers in Hebrew; these are *the singular* and *the plural;* the third number, called *dual,* is but a simple restriction of thought, a modification of the plural which tradition alone has been able to preserve by aid of the Chaldaic punctuation. This restricted number, passing into certain derivative tongues, has constituted in them a characteristic number, by means of the forms which it has assumed; but it is obvious that the Hebraic tongue, had it at first either alone, or else distinguished it from the plural only by a simple inflection of the voice, too little evident to be expressed by the sign; for it should be carefully observed that it is never the sign which expresses it, but the punctuation, at least in masculine nouns: as to feminine nouns, which, in the *dual* number, assume the same characters which indicate the masculine plural, one might, strictly speaking, consider them as belonging to common gender.

Masculine nouns, whether substantive, qualificative or facultative, form their plural by the addition of the syllable ם׳, which, uniting the signs of manifestation and of exterior generation. expresses infinite succession, the immensity of things.

Feminine nouns of the same classes form their plural by the addition of the syllable ת׳, which, uniting the signs of light and of reciprocity, expresses all that is mutual and similar, and develops the idea of the identity of things.

The two genders of the dual number are formed by the addition of the same syllable ם׳, designating the masculine plural, to which one adds, according to the Chaldaic punctuation, the vague vowel named *kamez* or *patah*, in this manner: יִם or יָם. One should realize now that this number is not really characteristic, as I have stated, since, if we remove the Chaldaic punctuation, and if we read the tongue of Moses without points, which should always be done in order to go back to hieroglyphic source, this number disappears entirely; the dual masculine being absorbed in the plural of the same gender, and the feminine being only an extension of the common number. The modern rabbis who have clearly seen this difficulty (considering the disadvantage of the Chaldaic punctuation, and furthermore, not wishing to loose this third number which presented certain beauties, and had been orally transmitted to them), have adopted the plan of expressing the inflection of the voice which constituted it in its origin, by doubling the sign of manifestation י, in this manner: רַגְלַיִם *the two feet* יָדַיִם *the two hands.* This number, furthermore, is usually applied to the things which nature has made double, or which the mind conceives as double, as the following examples will demonstrate.

Examples of the masculine plural.

צַדִיק *king,* מְלָכִים *kings;* סֵפֶר *book,* סְפָרִים *books;* מֶלֶךְ *just one,* צַדִיקִים *just ones;* נָקִי *innocent,* נְקִיִים *innocents;* פָּקוֹד *to be visiting, caring for,* פּוֹקְדִים *(plural);* פָּקוּד *to be visited, cared for,* פְּקוּדִים *(plural);* etc.

Examples of the feminine plural.

מַלְכָּה *queen,* מַלְכוֹת *queens;* אֵם *mother,* אִמּוֹת *mothers;* צַדִיקָה *just one,* צַדִיקוֹת *just ones;* פּוֹקְדָה or פּוֹקֶדֶת *to be visiting, caring for,* פּוֹקְדוֹת *(plural);* פְּקוּדָה *to be visited, cared for,* פְּקֻדוֹת *(plural);* etc.

Examples of the dual.

שַׁד *breast,* שָׁדַיִם *both breasts;* יָרֵךְ *thigh,* יְרֵכַיִם *both thighs;* שָׂפָה *lip,* שְׂפָתַיִם *both lips;* מֵי *water,* מַיִם *the waters;* שְׁמֵי *heaven (singular obsolete),* שָׁמַיִם *the heavens;* יָד *hand,* יָדַיִם *both hands;* etc.

NUMBER

It can be observed in these examples that the final character י is sometimes preserved in the plural as in נָקִי *innocent,* נְקִיִּים *innocents;* or in אֲרִי *lion,* אֲרָיִים *lions;* but it is, however, more customary for this final character י, to become lost or amalgamated with the plural, as in יְהוּדִי *a Jew,* יְהוּדִים *the Jews.*

It can also be observed that feminine nouns which terminate in ה in the singular, lose this character in taking the plural, and that those which take the dual number, change this same character to ת, as in שָׂפָה *lip,* שְׂפָתַיִם *both lips;* חוֹמָה *wall,* חֹמָתַיִם *both walls.*

Sometimes the plural number of the masculine in ים, is changed into ין, after the Chaldaic manner, and one finds quite frequently אַחֵר *other,* אַחֲרִין *others;* בֵּן *son,* בְּנִין *sons,* etc.

Sometimes also the feminine plural in וֹת, loses its essential character and preserves only the character ת, preceded thus by the vowel point *ḥolem* as in תּוֹלְדֹת *the symbol of generations* (genealogical tree) : צִדְקֹת *righteous acts,* etc. This is also an abuse born of the Chaldaic punctuation, and proves what I have said with regard to the facultatives. The rabbis are so averse to the suppression of this important sign וֹ in the feminine plural, that they frequently join to it the sign of manifestation י, to give it more force; writing אוֹת *sign, symbol, character,* and אוֹתִיּוֹת *signs, symbols,* etc.

One finds in Hebrew, as in other tongues, nouns which are always used in the singular and others which are always in the plural. Among the former one observes proper names, names of metals, of liquors, of virtues, of vices, etc. Among the latter, the names of ages, and of conditions relative to men.

One finds equally masculine or feminine nouns in the singular which take, in the plural, the feminine or masculine termination inconsistent with their gender; as אָב *father,* אָבוֹת *fathers;* עִיר *city,* עָרִים *cities;* etc. One also finds the gender called common or epicene, which takes indifferently the masculine or feminine plural, as I have already remarked; as הֵיכָל *palace,* הֵיכָלִים or הֵיכָלוֹת *palaces.* But these are anomalies which the grammar of an unspoken tongue can only indicate, leaving to the dictionary the care of noting them in detail.

§ V.

MOVEMENT

I call *Movement,* in the Hebraic nouns, that accidental modification which they undergo by the articles of which I have spoken in the second section of chapter IV.

In the tongues where this Movement takes place by means of the terminations of the nouns themselves, the grammarians have treated it under the denomination of *case;* a denomination applicable to those tongues, but which can only be applied to a tongue so rich in articles as the Hebrew, by an abuse of terms and in accordance with a scholastic routine wholly ridiculous.

I say that the denomination of *case* was applicable to those tongues, the nouns of which experience changes of termination to express their respective modifications; for, as Court de Gébelin has already remarked, these cases are only articles added to nouns, and which have finally amalgamated with them.[1] But the grammarians of the past centuries, always restricted to the Latin or Greek forms, saw only the material in those tongues, and never even suspected that there might have been something beyond. The time has come to seek for another principle in speech and to examine carefully its influence.

As I have dilated sufficiently upon the signification of each article in particular, as well as upon those of the corresponding prepositions, I now pass on without other preamble to the kind of modification which they bring in the nouns and which I call *Movement.*

Now, movement is inflicted in Hebraic nouns according to the number of the articles. We can, therefore, admit seven kinds of movements in the tongue of Moses, including the designative movement which is formed by

---

[1] Gramm. univers., p. 379.

means of the designative preposition אֶת and without including the enunciative which is expressed without an article.

I shall call this series of movements *Inflection,* and by this term I replace that of declension which should not be used here.

Example of nominal inflection.

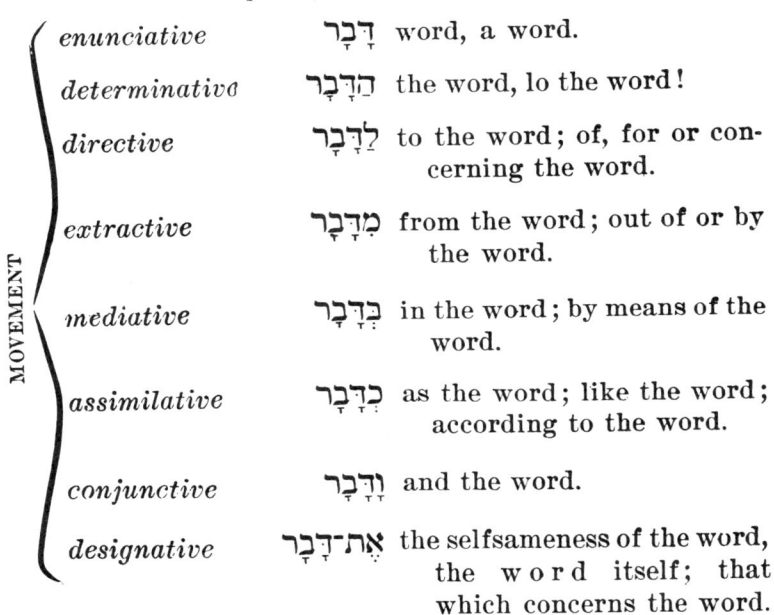

MOVEMENT
{
enunciative	דָּבָר	word, a word.
determinative	הַדָּבָר	the word, lo the word!
directive	לַדָּבָר	to the word; of, for or concerning the word.
extractive	מִדָּבָר	from the word; out of or by the word.
mediative	בְּדָבָר	in the word; by means of the word.
assimilative	כְּדָבָר	as the word; like the word; according to the word.
conjunctive	וְדָבָר	and the word.
designative	אֶת־דָּבָר	the selfsameness of the word, the w o r d itself; that which concerns the word.

The first remark to make with regard to this nominal inflection is, that the articles which constitute it, being of every gender and every number, are applied to the masculine as to the feminine, to the singular as to the plural or dual.

The second is, that they are often supplied by the corresponding prepositions of which I have spoken, and therefore, that the movement through them acquires greater force; for example, if it is a question of direct movement, the prepositions עַל־, אֱלִי־, אֶל־, which correspond with the article לֹ, have an energy, drawing nearer, imminent: it is the same with the prepositions מָמְנִי, מֶנִי, מִן, which correspond with the extractive article מ: with the prepositions בְּמוֹ, בְּדִי, בִּי, analogous to the mediative article בּ: the prepositions כְּמוֹ, כֹה, כִּי, which correspond with the assimilative article כּ: all of these augment in the same manner, the force of the movement to which they belong.

The third remark to make is, that the vague vowel which I have indicated by the Chaldaic punctuation, beneath each article, is the one which is found the most commonly used, but not the one which is always encountered. It must be remembered that as this punctuation is only a sort of vocal note applied to the vulgar pronunciation, nothing is more arbitrary than its course. All those Hebraists who are engrossed in the task of determining its variations by fixed rules, are lost in an inextricable labyrinth. I beg the reader who knows how much French or English deviates from the written language by the pronunciation, to consider what a formidable labour it would be, if it were necessary to mark with small accents the sound of each word, often so opposed to the orthography.

Without doubt there are occupations more useful, particularly for the extinct tongues.

The vague vowel, I cannot refrain from repeating, is of no consequence in any way to the meaning of the words of the Hebraic tongue, since one does not wish to speak this tongue. It is to the *sign* that one should give attention: it is its *signification* which must be presented. Considered here as article, it is invariable: it is always ה, ל, מ, ב, כ, or ו, which strikes the eye. What matters it to the ear, whether these characters are followed or not, by a *kamez*, a *patah* or a *zere*, that is to say, the indistinct vowels a, o, e? It is neither the *zere*, nor the *patah* nor the *kamez* which makes them what they are, but their nature as article. The vague vowel is there only for the compass of the voice. Upon seeing it written, it should be pronounced as it is pronounced in the modern tongues without giving it further attention, and if one insists on writing Hebrew from memory, which is, however, quite useless, one should learn to put it down as one learns the orthography, often very arbitrary, of French and English, by dint of copying the words in the manner in which they are written.

The meaning of the article in itself is already sufficiently difficult without still tormenting oneself as to how one shall place a fly speck.

Asiatic idioms in general, and Hebrew in particular, are far from affecting the stiffness of our European idioms. The nearer a word is to its root, the richer it is in pith, so to speak, and the more it can, without ceasing to be itself, develop various significations. The more distant it is, the less it becomes fitting to furnish new ramifications. Also one should guard against believing that an Hebraic word, whatever it may be, can be accurately grasped and rendered in all its acceptations by a modern word. This is not possible. All that can be done is to interpret the acceptation which it presents at the time when it is used. Here, for example, is the word דָּבָר, which I have used in the nominal inflection; I have rendered it by *word;* but in this circumstance where nothing has bound me as to the sense, I might have translated it quite as well by *discourse, precept, commandment, order, sermon, oration;* or by *thing, object, thought, meditation;* or by *term, elocution, expression;* or by the consecrated word *verb*, in Greek λόγος. All these significations and many others that I could add, feel the effects of the root דב, which, formed from the signs of natural abundance, and of active principle, develops the general idea of *effusion;* of the *course* given to anything whatsoever. This root being united by contraction with the root בר, all *creation* of being, offers in the compound דָּבָר, all the means of giving *course* to its ideas, of producing them, of distinguishing them, of creating them exteriorly, to make them known to others.

This diversity of acceptations which must be observed in the words of the Mosaic tongue, must also be observed in the different movements of the nominal inflection. These movements are not, in Hebrew, circumscribed in the limits that I have been obliged to give them. To make them felt in their full extent, it would be necessary to enter into irksome details. I shall give a few examples.

Let us remark first that the article ה, is placed, not only at the head of words as determinative, or at the end as emphatic, but that it becomes also redundant by resting at either place, whereas the other articles act. Thus, one finds הַשָּׁמַיִם, *the heavens,* שָׁמַיְמָה *heavens,* הַשָׁמַיְמָה *o heavens!* לְהַשָׁמַיִם *to the heavens, toward the heavens,* אֶת־הַשָׁמַיְמָה *the heavens themselves, that which constitutes the heavens.*

Such are the most common acceptations of this article: but the Hebraic genius by the extension which it gives them, finds the means of adding still a local, intensive, generative, vocative, interrogative and even relative force. Here are some examples.

Locative Force.

הָעִיר : הַפְּלִשְׁתִּים :   in the city; toward Palestine.
הָאֹהֱלָה שָׂרָה אִמּוֹ :   in the tent of Sarah his mother.
אַרְצָה : שָׁמַיְמָה :   on earth; in heaven.
צָפוֹנָה וָנֶגְבָּה וָקֵדְמָה וָיָמָּה :   toward the north and toward the south, and the east and the west.

Intensive Force.

נַחְלָה : עֲפָתָה :   a rapid torrent: a profound obscurity.

אִימָתָה : הַמּוֹתָה : an extreme terror; a violent death.

Generative Force.

אֶת־הָאָרֶץ : selfsameness of the earth: that which constitutes it.
הַמִּזְבַּח הַנְחֹשֶׁת : the altars of brass.
הַמַּמְלְכוֹת הָאָרֶץ : the kingdoms of the earth.
הַמִּסְגְּרוֹת הַגּוֹיִם : the abomination of the peoples.

Vocative Force.

הַיָּם הֶהָרִים : o waters! o mountains!
הַבַּת יְרוּשָׁלַיִם : o daughters of Jerusalem!
בֹּאִי הָרוּחַ : הַיֹּשְׁבִי : come, o spirit, o thou who dwellest!

Interrogative Force.

הַכְּתֹנֶת בִּנְךָ הוּא : is that the tunic of thy son?
הַיֵּיטַב : הַרְאִיתֶם : was it good? did you see?
הַאֱמֶת : הָעֵת : הָאָנֹכִי : is it the truth? is it the time? is it I?

Relative Force.

בֶּן־הַנֵּכָר הַנִּלְוָה : the son of the stranger who was come.
הַנּוֹלַד־לוֹ : he who was born to him.
הָרֹפֵא : הַגּוֹאֵל : he who is healing; he who is redeeming.

The other articles without having so extended a use, have nevertheless their various acceptations. I give here a few examples of each of the movements which they express.

MOVEMENT

Directive Movement.

מִזְמוֹר לְדָוִד׃	the canticle of David.
לְמֶלֶךְ׃ לְהָעָם׃ לְהַמִּזְבֵּחַ׃	for the king: for the people: for the altar.
לָנֶצַח׃ לְעַד׃ לְשֹׂבַע׃	forever: for eternity: to satiety.
אֶל־הַשָּׁמַיִם׃ עַל־הָאָרֶץ׃	toward the heavens: upon the earth.
לְמִינֵהוּ׃	according to his kind.

Extractive Movement.

מֵרֹב׃ מִכֹּהֵן׃	among the multitude: among the priesthood.
מֵיהוָֹה׃ מִלְאֹם׃	by Yahweh: by the nation.
מִגְּבוּרָתָם׃ מִלִּבּוֹ׃	by means of their power: from the depths of his heart.
מֵעָצְבֵּךְ וּמֵרָגְזֵךְ׃	with thy pain and thine emotion.
לְמִבָּרִאשׁוֹנָה׃	as it was from the beginning.
מִן־הָאָרֶץ׃	beyond the land.
מִימֵי רָע׃ מִקְצֵה הָאָרֶץ׃	from the days of evil: from the end of the earth.

Mediative Movement.

בְּשֵׁבֶט בַּרְזֶל׃	by means of a rod of iron.
בִּנְעָרֵינוּ וּבִזְקֵנֵנוּ.	with our young men and with our old men.
בֶּחֳדָשִׁים׃	in the festivals of the new moon.
בַּהַשָּׁמַיִם׃ בְּהַדֶּרֶךְ׃	to the heavens: on the way.

Assimilative Movement.

כְּעָם ׃ כַּכֹּהֵן ׃ כָּעֶבֶד ׃   like the p e o p l e : like the priest : like the servant.

כְּהֶחָכָם ׃ כְּהַיּוֹם ׃   like the wise man : the same as to-day.

כְּהַחַלֹּנוֹת ׃ כְּאַלְפַּיִם ׃   like the windows : about two thousand.

כַּגֵּר כָּאֶזְרָח ׃   stranger as well as native.

Conjunctive Movement.

חָכְמָה וְדַעַת ׃   wisdom and knowledge.

וְרֶכֶב וְסוּס ׃   the chariot and the horse.

עַם גָּדוֹל וְרַב וָרָם ׃   the great nation both numerous and powerful.

Designative Movement.

אֶת־הַשָּׁמַיִם וְאֶת־הָאָרֶץ ׃   the sameness of the heavens and the sameness of the earth.

אֶת־הַדָּבָר הַזֶּה ׃   the e s s e n c e of that same thing.

אֶת־נֹחַ ׃   with Noah.

אֶת־שֵׁם וְאֶת־חָם וְאֶת־יָפֶת ׃   Shem himself, and Ham himself, and Japheth himself.

These examples few in number, are sufficient to awaken the attention; but understanding can only be obtained **by study.**

§ VI.

CONSTRUCT STATE

Hebraic nouns, being classed in the **rhetorical sentence** according to the rank which they should occupy in developing the thought in its entirety, undergo quite commonly a slight alteration in the final character; now this is what I designate by the name of *construct state*.

In several of the derivative tongues, such as Greek and Latin, this accidental alteration is seen in the termination of the governed noun; it is quite the opposite in Hebrew. The governed noun remains nearly always unchanged, whereas the governing noun experiences quite commonly the terminative alteration of which we are speaking. I call the noun thus modified *construct,* because it determines the construction.

Here in a few words are the elements of this modification.

Masculine or feminine nouns in the singular, terminated by a character other than ה, undergo no other alteration in becoming constructs; when the Hebraic genius wishes, however, to make the construct state felt, it connects them with the noun which follows with a hyphen.

פֶּתַח־הָאֹהֶל׃ the door of the tent.

תָּם־לְבָבִי׃ the integrity of my heart.

This hyphen very frequently takes the place of the construct, even when the latter itself could be used.

סְאָה־סֹלֶת׃ a measure of meal.

עֲלֵה־זַיִת׃ a branch of the olive tree.

One recognizes, nevertheless, three masculine substantives which form their construct singular, by the addition of the character יִ: these are אָב *father,* אָח *brother,* and חָם *father-in-law;* one finds:

אֲבִי כְנָעַן: the father of Canaan.

אֲחִי יֶפֶת: חָמִיהָ: the brother of Japheth; father-in-law of her.

But these three substantives are rarely constructed in this manner except with proper nouns, or with the nominal relations called *affixes,* of which I shall speak in the chapter following.

Feminine nouns terminating in ה, and masculine nouns which have received this final character as emphatic article, change it generally into ת.

יְפַת מַרְאֶה: beautiful of form.

עֲשֶׂרֶת הַדְּבָרִים: the ten commandments.

עֲצַת גּוֹיִם: the counsel of the peoples.

Masculine nouns in the plural lose the final character ם, in becoming constructs; feminine nouns add to their plural the character י, and lose in the dual the character ם, as do the masculine. But feminine constructs in the plural are only used with *affixes.* Masculine constructs, in the plural and in the dual, like feminine constructs in the dual, are, on the contrary, constantly employed in the oratorical phrase, as can be judged by the following examples.

תּוֹרֵי זָהָב: the ornaments of gold.

מֵי הַמַּבּוּל: דְּגֵי הַיָּם: the waters of the deluge: the fish of the sea.

כְּלֵי בֵית־יְהוָֹה: the vessels of the house of Yahweh.

יְמֵי שְׁנֵי־חַיֵּי אַבְרָהָם: the days (or luminous periods) of the years (or temporal mutations) of the lives of Abraham.

It is easy to see in these examples that all the plurals terminating in םי, as שָׁנִים, יָמִים, כֵּלִים, דָגִים, מַיִם, תּוֹרִים, חַיִּים, have lost their final character in the construct state.

I refrain from enlarging my Grammar on this subject, for I shall have occasion to refer again to the construct state in speaking of the affixes which join themselves only to nominal and verbal constructs.

§ VII.

SIGNIFICATION

The Signification of nouns results wholly from the principles which I have laid down. If these principles have been developed with enough clarity and simplicity for an observant reader to grasp the *ensemble*, the signification of nouns should be no longer an inexplicable mystery whose origin he can, like Hobbes or his adherents, attribute only to chance. He must feel that this *signification*, so called from the primordial *signs* where it is in germ, begins to appear under a vague form and is developed under general ideas in the roots composed of these signs; that it is restrained or is fixed by aid of the secondary and successive signs which apply to these roots; finally, that it acquires its whole force by the transformation of these same roots into nouns, and by the kind of movement which the signs again impart to them, appearing for the third time under the denomination of articles.

CHAPTER VI.

NOMINAL RELATIONS.

§ I.

Absolute Pronouns.

I have designated the nominal relations under the name of *pronouns,* so as not to create needlessly new terms.

I divide the pronouns of the Hebraic tongue into two classes; each subdivided into two kinds. The first class is that of the *absolute pronouns,* or pronouns, properly so-called; the second is that of the *affixes,* which are derivatives, whose use I shall explain later.

The pronouns, properly so-called, are relative to persons or things; those relative to persons are called *personal;* those relative to things are named simply *relative.*

The affixes indicate the action of persons or things themselves upon things, and then I name them *nominal affixes;* or they can express the action of the verb upon persons or things and then I give them the name of *verbal affixes.* Below, is the list of the personal and relative pronouns.

Personal Pronouns.

	Singular		Plural	
1 {mas. / fem.}	אֲנִי or אָנֹכִי	I	1 {mas. / fem.}	נַחְנוּ or אֲנַחְנוּ we
2 {mas. / fem.}	אַתָּה / אַתְּ } thou		2 {mas. / fem.}	אַתֶּם / אַתֶּן } ye
3 {mas. / fem.}	הוּא he / הוּא or הִיא she		3 {mas. / fem.}	הֵם / הֵן } they

Relative Pronouns.

Of every Gender and of every Number.

אֵל or אֵלֶה this, that, these, those.

אֲשֶׁר who, which, whom, whose, that which; what.

דְּי, דָא or דַן this, that, these, those. (*Chaldaic.*)

זֶה, זוּ or זֹאת this, that, these, those.

הָא this, that, these, those; lo! behold!

הִנֵּה, הֵן lo! behold! is there?

הֲל is it ? (interrogation sign).

מִי who? מָה what?

פֶּה that thing there, that place there. (*Egyptian.*)

I have a few remarks to make concerning this class of pronouns. The first is, that I present the table according to the modern usage, which gives the first rank to the pronoun *I* or *me;* and that in this, I differ from the ideas of the rabbis, who, after a false etymology given to the verb, have judged that the rank belonged to the pronoun *he* or *him*. It is not that I am unaware of the mystical reasons which lead certain of them to think that the preëminence belongs to the pronoun of the third person הוּא, *he* or *him*, as forming the basis of the Sacred Name given to the Divinity. What I have said in my notes explaining the Hebraic names אֱלֹהִים and יְהֹוָה proves it adequately; but these reasons, very strong as they appear to them, have not determined me in the least to take away from the personal pronoun אֲנִי or אָנוֹכִי *I* or *me,* a rank which belongs to its nature. It is sufficient, in order to feel this rank, to put it into the mouth of the Divinity Itself, as Moses has frequently done : אָנוֹכִי יְהֹוָה אֱלֹהֶיךָ, *I am* YAHWEH (*the Being-Eternal*), ÆLOHIM (HE-*the-Gods*) *thine*. It is also sufficient to remember that one finds אֶהְוֶה written in the first person, and that therefore, this name has a greater force than YAHWEH.

ABSOLUTE PRONOUNS

The second remark that I have to make is, that all these pronouns, personal as well as relative when they are used in an absolute manner, always involve the idea of the verb *to be*, in its three tenses, following the meaning of the phrase, and without the need of expressing it, as in the greater part of the modern idioms. Thus אֲנִי, אַתָה, הוּא, etc., signifies literally: *I-being*, or *I am, I was, I shall be: thou-being, or thou art, thou wast, thou shalt be: he-being,* or *he is, he was, he shall be;* etc. It is the same with all the others indiscriminately.

The third remark finally, concerns the etymology of these pronouns; an etymology worthy of great attention, as it is derived from my principles and confirms them.

Let us content ourselves with examining the first three persons אֲנִי, אַתָה and הוּא, so as not to increase the examples too much, besides leaving something for the reader to do, who is eager to learn.

Now, what is the root of the first of these pronouns? It is אן, where the united signs of power and of produced being, indicate sufficiently a sphere of activity, an individual existence, acting from the centre to the circumference. This root, modified by the sign of potential manifestation י, which we shall presently see become the affix of possession, designates the *I*, active, manifested and possessed.

The root of the second pronoun אַתָה, is not less expressive. One sees here as in the first, the sign of power א, but which, united now to that of the reciprocity of things ת, characterizes a mutual power, a coexistent being. One associates with this idea, that of veneration, in joining to the root את, the emphatic and determinative article ה.

But neither the pronoun of the first person, nor that of the second, is equal in energy to that of the third הוּא particularly when it is used in an absolute manner: I must acknowledge it, notwithstanding what I have said concerning the grammatical rank that ought to be accorded the pronoun אֲנִי. This energy is such that uttered in an universal sense, it has become throughout the Orient, one of the sacred names of the Divinity. The Arabs and all the peoples who profess Islamism, pronounce it even in this day, with the greatest respect. One can still remember the righteous indignation of the Turkish ambassador, when this sacred name was profaned in our theatre in the farce of *le Bourgeois-Gentilhomme*, and travestied in the ridiculous syllable *hou! hou!*

Here is its composition. The sign of power א, which as we have seen, appears in the first two pronouns, אֲנִי and אַתָה, forms also the basis of this one. As long as this sign is governed only by the determinative article ה, it is limited to presenting the idea of a determined being, as is proved by the relative הא: even though the convertible sign ו, adds to it a verbal action, it is still only the pronoun of the third person; a person, considered as acting beyond us, without reciprocity, and that we designate by a root which depicts splendour and elevation, *he* or *him*: but when the character ה, instead of being taken as a simple article, is considered in its state of the sign of universal life, then this same pronoun הוא, leaving its determination, becomes the image of the All-Powerful: that which can be attributed only to GOD!

§ II.

Affixes.

Those of the affixes which I have called *nominal,* are joined without intermediary to the construct noun, to express dependence and possession in the three pronominal persons; for the Hebraic tongue knows not the use of the pronouns called by our grammarians, *possessive.*

Verbal affixes are those which are joined without intermediaries to verbs, whatever their modifications may be, and express the actual action either upon persons or upon things: for neither do the Hebrews know the pronouns that our grammarians call *conjunctive.*

Without further delay, I now give a list of the nominal and verbal affixes.

Nominal.

Singular

1 { m. / f. }   י or נִי   my, mine

2 { m. ךָ or כָה / f. ךְ or כִי }   thy, thine

3 { m. הוּ, וֹ, וּ his, his / f. הָ or נָה her, hers }

Plural

1 { m. / f. }   נוּ   our, ours

2 { m. כֶם / f. כֶן }   your, yours

3 { m. הֶם, ָם, or מוֹ / f. הֶן, ָן }   their, theirs

Verbal.

Singular

$\left\{\begin{array}{l}1\left\{\begin{array}{l}\text{m.}\\ \text{f.}\end{array}\right\} \text{ נִי or יִ of me}\\ 2\left\{\begin{array}{l}\text{m. } \text{כָה or } \text{ךָ}\\ \text{f. } \text{כִי or } \text{ךְ}\end{array}\right\} \text{ of thee}\\ 3\left\{\begin{array}{l}\text{m. } \text{הוּ, וּ, or וֹ of him}\\ \text{f. } \text{נָה or הָ of her}\end{array}\right.\end{array}\right.$

Plural

$\left\{\begin{array}{l}1\left\{\begin{array}{l}\text{m.}\\ \text{f.}\end{array}\right\} \text{ נוּ of us}\\ 2\left\{\begin{array}{l}\text{m. } \text{כֶם}\\ \text{f. } \text{כֶן}\end{array}\right\} \text{ of you}\\ 3\left\{\begin{array}{l}\text{m. } \text{כה, ם or מוֹ}\\ \text{f. } \text{הֶן or } \text{ן}\end{array}\right\} \text{ of them}\end{array}\right.$

It can be seen, in comparing these two lists, that the nominal and verbal affixes in the Hebraic tongue differ not in the least as to form, but only as to sense. However I must mention that one finds the simplest of these pronouns such as י, ה, ו, etc., used quite generally as nominal affixes, and the most composite such as הוּ, כָה, נִי, as verbal affixes, but it is not an invariable rule.

When the personal pronouns אֲנִי *I*, אַתָה *thou*, הוּא *he*, etc., are subject to the inflection of the articles, it is the nominal affixes which are used in determining the different movements as is shown in the following example:

AFFIXES

Example of the Pronominal Inflection.
Singular

MOVEMENT
- *Enunciative* — אֲנִי I
- *Determinative* — הָאנֹכִי it is **I**!
- *Directive* — לִי to me
- *Extractive* — מֶנִּי : מִמֶּנִּי from me
- *Mediative* — בִּי : כְּדִי in me, with **me**
- *Assimilative* — כִּי : כָּמוֹנִי as I
- *Conjunctive* — וְאֲנִי and I
- *Designative* — אוֹתִי : אוֹתָנִי myself, **me**

Plural

נַחְנוּ we

הָאֲנַחְנוּ us! it is **us**!

לָנוּ to us

מֶנּוּ : מִמֶּנּוּ from us

בָּנוּ in us, with **us**

כָּנוּ : כָּמוֹנוּ as we

וְנַחְנוּ and we

אוֹתָנוּ ourselves

I have chosen, in giving this example, the pronoun of the first person, which will suffice to give an idea of all the others. It will be noticed that I have added to the preposition את of the designative movement, the sign וֹ, because the Hebraic genius affects it in this case and in some others, as giving more importance to this movement.

The designative relations which I have made known under the name of prepositions, are joined to the nominal affixes in the same manner as the articles. Here are some examples of this liaison.

אֵלַי : אֵלֶיךָ : אֲלֵיהֶם :	unto me, unto thee, **unto them.**
אֶצְלוֹ : אִתּוֹ :	beside him; with him.
בַּעֲדוֹ : בַּעֲדֵיהֶם :	for him; for them.
עָלַי : תַּחְתַּי : עָדַי :	upon me; under me; as far as me.
עִמִּי : עִמְּךָ : עִמּוֹ :	with me; with thee; with him.

Relative pronouns are inflected with articles and with prepositions in the same manner as nouns. I shall not stop to give any particular examples of this inflection which has nothing very remarkable. I prefer to illustrate it by the following phrases:

אֵלֶּה תוֹלְדוֹת :	these are the symbols of the generations.
אֲשֶׁר עָשָׂה :	that which he had done.
אָנוֹכִי יְהוָה אֱלֹהֶיךָ אֲשֶׁר....	I am YAHWEH, HE-THE-GODS thine, who....
וְכָל אֲשֶׁר.....	and all that which...
מַה־זֹּאת עָשִׂיתָ :	why hast thou done that?
מִי־אָתְּ : מִי־אֵלֶּה :	who art thou? who are those?
מִי־שְׁמֶךָ : מֶה קוֹל :	what is thy name? what is this voice?
מֶה מִשְׁפַּט הָאִישׁ :	what is the fashion of this man?
מַה־טּוֹב וּמַה־נָּעִים :	how good it is! how pleasing!
מֶה־הָיָה לוֹ :	what has happened to him?
בַּת־מִי אַתְּ :	the daughter of whom art thou?

AFFIXES 159

לְמִי הַנַּעֲרָה הַזֹּאת: to whom belongs the young woman there?

לָמָה לִי: עַל־מֶה: why mine? upon what?

עַל־מֶה שָׁוְא: upon what futility?

הִנְנִי: הִנֶּנּוּ: כֻּלָּנוּ: כֻּלְּכֶם: here am I: behold us: both: them all.

כָּזֶה: כָּהֵנָה: like this one; like that one.

כָּזֶה וּכָזֶה: like this and like that.

בָּזֶה: כָּאֵלֶּה: in this one: in that one.

The relative אֲשֶׁר whose use I have just shown in several examples, has this peculiarity, that it furnishes a sort of pronominal article which is quite commonly employed.

This article, the only one of its kind, is reduced to the character שׁ, and comprises in this state all the properties of the sign which it represents. Placed at the head of nouns or verbs, it implies all the force of relative movement. Sometimes in uniting itself to the directive article לְ, it forms the pronominal preposition שֶׁל, which then participates in the two ideas of relation and direction contained in the two signs of which it is composed.

It is most important in studying Hebrew, to have the foregoing articles ever present in the mind, as well as those which I give below; for the Hebraists, unceasingly confusing them with the nouns that they inflect, have singularly corrupted the meaning of several passages. Here are a few examples which can facilitate understanding the prenominal articles in question.

עַד שֶׁקַּמְתִּי: as much as I was opposed, so much was I strengthened.

שֶׁהָיָה לָנוּ: שֶׁלִּי: who was for us? who, for me?

שֶׁאַתָּה: שֶׁהוּא: שֶׁיְהֹוָה: for whom thou: for whom he: for whom YAHWEH.

שֶׁכָּכָה ׃ בְּשֶׁגַּם ׃	whose fellow-creature? in what also?
שַׁלָּמָה ׃	what therefore? What is the why (the cause).
שֶׁאָהֲבָה ..... שֶׁיֵּרֵד	that which she loved... That which descends...
שעכרתי.....	that which I passed over...
כְּנַף־הַמְּעִיל־שֶׁל־שָׁאוּל ׃	the border of the tunic which was Saul's.
מִשֶּׁלָּנוּ ׃	of that which is ours.
בְּשֶׁלְּמִי הָרָעָה ׃	in that which is the why (the cause) of evil.

§ III.

Use of the Affixes.

Let us examine now, the use of nominal affixes with nouns: later on we shall examine that of verbal affixes with verbs. These affixes are placed, as I have already stated, without intermediary after the nouns, to express dependence or possession in the three pronominal persons. It is essential to recall here what I said in speaking of the construct state; for it is the affix which makes a construct of every noun.

Thus, among the masculine nouns which do not terminate with ה, three only take the character י, in the construct singular, that is: אבי *father*, אחי *brother*, and חמי *father-in-law*, the others remain inflexible.

Thus, among the masculine and feminine nouns, all those which terminate in ה, or which have received this character as an emphatic article, change this character in the singular, to ת.

Thus, all of the masculine nouns terminating in the plural with ים, lose the character ם in becoming constructs; it is the same with the dual for both genders.

Thus, generally, but in a manner less irresistible, the feminine whose plural is formed with ות, adds י to this final syllable in taking the nominal affix.

This understood, I pass now to the examples.

Mas. Sing.	{ enunciative construct }	דָּבָר	the **word**

SING. PERS.
- 1 { mas. / fem. } דְּבָרִי my word
- 2 { mas. דְּבָרְךָ / fem. דְּבָרֵךְ } thy word
- 3 { mas. דְּבָרוֹ his / fem. דְּבָרָהּ her } word

PLU. PERS.
- 1 { mas. / fem. } דְּבָרֵנוּ our word
- 2 { mas. דְּבַרְכֶם / fem. דְּבַרְכֶן } your word
- 3 { mas. דְּבָרָם / fem. דְּבָרָן } their word

Mas. Plu.	{ enunciative דְּבָרִים construct דִּבְרֵי }		the **words**

SING. PERS.
- 1 { mas. / fem. } דְּבָרַי my words
- 2 { mas. דְּבָרֶיךָ / fem. דְּבָרַיִךְ } thy words
- 3 { mas. דְּבָרָיו his / fem. דְּבָרֶיהָ her } words

USE OF AFFIXES

PLU. PERS.
- 1 { mas. / fem. } דְּבָרֵינוּ   our words
- 2 { mas. דְּבָרֵיכֶם / fem. דִּבְרֵיכֶן }   your words
- 3 { mas. דִּבְרֵיהֶם / fem. דִּבְרֵיהֶן }   their words

Fem. Sing. { enunciative צָרָה / construct צָרַת }   the distress

SING. PERS.
- 1 { mas. / fem. } צָרָתִי   my distress
- 2 { mas. צָרָתְךָ / fem. צָרָתֵךְ }   thy distress
- 3 { mas. צָרָתוֹ his / fem. צָרָתָהּ her } distress

PLU. PERS.
- 1 { mas. / fem. } צָרָתֵנוּ   our distress
- 2 { mas. צָרַתְכֶם / fem. צָרַתְכֶן }   your distress
- 3 { mas. צָרָתָם / fem. צָרָתָן }   their distress

Fem. Plu. { *enunciative* צָרוֹת } the distresses
{ *construct* צָרוֹתֵי }

SING. PERS.
1 { *mas.* / *fem.* } צָרוֹתַי my distresses
2 { *mas.* צָרוֹתֶיךָ / *fem.* צָרוֹתַיִךְ } thy distresses
3 { *mas.* צָרוֹתָיו his, / *fem.* צָרוֹתֶיהָ her } distresses

PLU. PERS.
1 { *mas.* / *fem.* } צָרוֹתֵינוּ our distresses
2 { *mas.* צָרוֹתֵיכֶם / *fem.* צָרוֹתֵיכֶן } your distresses
3 { *mas.* צָרוֹתֵיהֶם / *fem.* צָרוֹתֵיהֶן } their distresses

Mas. or fem. dual { *enunciative* עֵינַיִם } the eyes
{ *construct* עֵינֵי }

SING. PERS.
1 { *mas.* / *fem.* } עֵינַי my eyes
2 { *mas.* עֵינֶיךָ / *fem.* עֵינַיִךְ } thine eyes
3 { *mas.* עֵינָיו his / *fem.* עֵינֶיהָ her } eyes

USE OF AFFIXES

PLU. PERS.
1 mas./fem. עֵינֵינוּ our eyes
2 mas. עֵינֵיכֶם / fem. עֵינֵיכֶן your eyes
3 mas. עֵינֵיהֶם / fem. עֵינֵיהֶן their eyes

Nouns, whether masculine or feminine, which take the common or dual number, follow in the singular, one of the preceding examples according to their gender.

The anomalies relative to the vague vowel marked by the Chaldaic punctuation are still considerable: but they have no effect, and should not delay us. The only important remark to make is, that often the affix of the third person masculine of the singular, is found to be הוּ or מוֹ in place of וֹ and again in the plural מוֹ in place of ם, or of הם: so that one might find דְּבָרֵהוּ or דְּבָרְמוֹ *his word*, and דְּבָרִימוֹ *his words* or *their words;* or צָרָתֵהוּ or צָרָתֵמוֹ *his distress,* and צָרוֹתֵימוֹ *his distresses* or *their distresses.* Besides it seems that the affix הוּ, may be applied to the emphatic style, and the affix מוֹ, to poetry.

CHAPTER VII.

THE VERB

§ I.

Absolute Verb and Particular Verbs.

If in the course of this Grammar I have been compelled, in order to be understood, to speak often of the plural verbs, it must not be thought for this reason, that I have forgotten my fundamental principle, namely, that there exists but one sole Verb: a principle which I believe fixed. The plural verbs, of which I have spoken, should only be understood as nouns *verbalized* as it were, by the unique Verb הוה *to be-being,* in which it develops its influence with more or less force and intensity. Let us forget therefore, the false ideas which we have kept through habit, of a mass of verbs existing by themselves, and return to our principle.

There is but one Verb.

The words to which one has ordinarily given the name of verbs, are only substantives animated by this single verb, and determined toward the end peculiar to them: for now we can see that the verb, in communicating to nouns the verbal life which they possess, changes in no respect their inner nature, but only makes them living with the life whose principles they held concealed within themselves. Thus the flame, communicated to all combustible substance, burns not only as flame but as enflamed substance, good or evil, according to its intrinsic quality.

The unique Verb of which I speak is formed in Hebrew, in a manner meriting the attention of the reader. Its principle is light, represented by the intellectual sign ו; its substance is life universal and absolute, represented by the root הה. This root, as I have before stated, never leaves the noun: for when it is a question of designating life proper, or, to express it better, *existence,*—which men ought never to confuse with *life,* the Hebraic tongue employs the root חי, in which the character ח, carries the idea of some sort of effort causing equilibrium between two opposed powers. It is by means of intellectual light, characterized by the sign ו, that this unique Verb dispenses its verbal force to nouns, and transforms them into particular verbs.

The verb in itself is immutable. It knows neither number nor gender; it has no kind of inflection. It is foreign to forms, to movement and to time, as long as it does not leave its absolute essence and as long as the thought conceives it independent of all substance. הוה *to be-being,* belongs to the masculine as well as to the feminine, to the singular as to the plural, to active movement as to passive movement; it exercises the same influence upon the past as upon the future; it fulfills the present; it is the image of a duration without beginning and without end: הוה *to be-being* fulfills all, comprehends all, animates all.

But in this state of absolute immutability and of universality, it is incomprehensible for man. When it acts independently of substance man cannot grasp it. It is only because of the substance which it assumes, that it is sentient. In this new state it loses its immutability. The substance which it assumes transmits to it nearly all its forms; but these same forms that it influences, acquire particular modifications through which an experienced eye can still distinguish its inflexible unity.

These details may appear extraordinary to the grammarians but little accustomed to find these sorts of speculations in their works; but I have forewarned them that it is upon the Hebraic grammar that I am writing and not

ABSOLUTE VERB AND PARTICULAR VERBS

upon any from their domain. If they consider my method applicable, as I think it is, they may adopt it; if they do not, nothing hinders them from following their own routine.

Let us continue. As the verb הוה becomes manifest only because of the substance which it has assumed, it participates in its forms. Therefore, every time that it appears in speech, it is with the attributes of a particular verb, and subject to the same modifications. Now, these modifications in particular verbs, or rather in facultative nouns verbalized, are four in number, namely, Form, Movement, Time and Person.

I shall explain later what these modifications are and in what manner they act upon the verbs; it is essential to examine first of all, how these verbs issue from the primitive roots or derivative nouns, subject to the unique Verb which animates them.

If we consider the unique Verb הוה, *to be-being,* as a particular verb, we shall see clearly that what constitutes it as such, is the intellectual sign ו, in which the verbal *esprit* appears wholly to reside. The root הה, by itself, is only a vague exclamation, a sort of expiration, which, when it signifies something, as in the Chinese tongue, for example, is limited to depicting the breath, its exhalation, its warmth, and sometimes the life that this warmth infers; but then the vocal sound *o* is soon manifest, as can be seen in *ho, houo, hoe,* Chinese roots, which express all ideas of warmth, of fire, of life, of action and of being.

The sign ו, being constituted, according to the genius of the Hebraic tongue, symbol of the universal verb, it is evident that in transferring it into a root or into any compound whatsoever of this tongue, this root or this compound will partake instantly of the verbal nature: for this invariably happens.

We have seen in treating particularly of the sign, that the one in question is presented under two distinct modifications, first, as the universal convertible sign ו, and second, as the luminous sign וֹ: these two modifications are employed equally in the formation of verbs. I have already spoken of this in dealing with the facultatives in the Second section of the Fifth chapter. Here it is only a matter of verbs.

The facultative by which the Hebraic genius brings out the verbal action, is the finished facultative. It is in this manner.

This facultative is formed from roots by the insertion of the sign ו, between the two characters which compose it, as שׂוּם *to be placed*, גוּל *to be exhausted;* and from compound nouns by the insertion of this same sign between the last two characters of these nouns, as רגוּן *to be moved*, מָלוּךְ *to be ruled.*

Now if we take the finished facultative coming from the root, it will be sufficient, by a simple abstraction of thought, to make a verb of it, in that sort of original state which the grammarians call *infinitive,* though I cannot very well see why, and which I call, *nominal,* because it is governed by the articles and is subject to the nominal inflection. And as to the finished facultative coming from the compounds, we make a nominal verb of it by enlightening the sign ו that is to say, replacing it with the sign וֹ, as the following example illustrates:

root	קָם:	every idea of substance and of material establishment
finished facultative	קוּם:	to be established
nominal verb	קוֹם:	the action of establishing
compound	רֶגֶן:	physical or moral movement; an emotion
finished facultative	רגוּן:	to be moved
nominal verb	רגוֹן:	the action of moving

It is well to observe that sometimes ו is enlightened in order to form the verb from the root, as in מוט *to waver,* and in some others. As to the nominal verbs coming from compounds, the rule is without exception in this respect. If the Chaldaic punctuation replaces this sign by the points *holem* or *kamez* these points have then the same value and that suffices. This abuse due to the indolence of the copyists was inevitable.

§ II.

Three kinds of Particular Verbs.

There is no need I think of calling attention to the effect of the convertible sign, which, insinuating itself into the heart of the primitive roots, makes them pass from the state of noun to that of verb, and which being enlightened or extinguished by turn, and changing its position in the compound substantives, produces the sentiment of an action, continued or finished, and as it were, fixes the verbal life by the successive formation of the two facultatives and the nominal verb. I believe that there is none of my readers who, having reached this point of my Grammar, and being impressed by this admirable development does not disdainfully reject any system tending to make of speech a mechanical art or an arbitrary institution.

Indeed! if speech were a mechanical art or an arbitrary institution as has been advanced by Hobbes, and before him by Gorgias and the sophists of his school, could it, I ask, have these profound roots which, being derived from a small quantity of signs and being blended not only with the very elements of nature, but also producing those immense ramifications which, coloured with all the fires of genius, take possession of the domain of thought and seem to reach to the limits of infinity? Does one see anything similar in games of chance? Do human institutions, however perfect they may be, ever have this progressive course of aggrandizement and force? Where is the mechanical work from the hand of man, that can compare with this lofty tree whose trunk, now laden with branches, slept not long since buried in an imperceptible germ? Does not one perceive that this mighty tree, which at first, weak blade of grass, pierced with difficulty the ground which concealed its principles, can in nowise be considered as the production of a blind and capricious force, but on the contrary, as that of wisdom enlightened and steadfast in its designs? Now speech is like this majestic tree; it has its germ, it spreads its roots gradually in a fertile nature whose elements are unknown, it breaks its bonds and rises upward escaping from terrestrial darkness and bursts forth into new regions where, breathing a purer element, watered by a divine light, it spreads its branches and covers them with flowers and fruit.

But perhaps the objection will be made that this comparison which could not be questioned for Hebrew, whose successive developments I have amply demonstrated, is limited to this tongue, and that it would be in vain for me to attempt the same labour for another. I reply, that this objection, to have any force must be as affirmative as is my proof, instead of being negative; that is to say, that instead of saying to me that I have not done it, it is still to be done; he must demonstrate to me, for example, that French, Latin or Greek are so constituted that they can not be brought back to their principles, or what amounts to the same thing, to the primordial signs upon which the mass of words which compose them rest; a matter which I deny absolutely. The difficulty of the analysis of these idioms, I am convinced, is due to their complexity and remoteness from their origin; however, the analysis is by no means impossible. That of Hebrew, which now appears easy owing to the method I have followed, was none the less before this test, the stumbling-block of all etymologists. This tongue is very simple; its material offers advantageous results; but what would it be if the reasons which have led me to chose Hebrew had also inclined me toward Chinese! what a mine to exploit! what food for thought!

I return to the formation of the Hebraic verbs. I have shown in the preceding section that it was by the intermediary of the facultatives that the convertible sign וֹ raised the noun to the dignity of the verb. It is essential that we examine what the idiomatic genius adds to this creation.

This genius affects particularly the words composed of three consonant characters; that is to say, words which come from a primitive root governed by a sign, or from two roots contracted and forming two syllables. It is this which has caused the superficial etymologists and those who receive things without examination, to believe that the tongue of the Hebrews was essentially dissyllabic and that its roots could consist only of three characters. Ridiculous error, which veiling the origin of the words, and confounding the auxiliary sign and even the article, with the root itself, has finally corrupted the primitive meaning and brought forth in Hebrew, a sort of jargon, wholly different from the Hebrew itself.

Primitive roots are, in all known tongues, monosyllabic. I cannot repeat this truth too strongly. The idiomatic genius can indeed, as in Hebrew, add to this syllable, either to modify its meaning or to reinforce its expression; but it can never denature it. When by the aid of the convertible sign וֹ, the nominal verb is formed, as I have said, it is formed either of the root, as can be seen in שׂוּם *to constitute, to put up, to decree;* or of the compound substantive מָלוֹךְ *to rule*: but one feels the primitive root always, even in the nominal מָלוֹךְ, when he is intellectually capable of feeling it, or when he is not fettered by grammatical prejudices. If the reader is curious to know what this root is, I will tell him that it is אך, and that the expansive sign ל, governs jointly with that of exterior and local action, מ . Now לאך, develops all idea of legation, of function to which one is linked: of vicariate, of mission, etc., thus the word מֶלֶךְ *a king*, the origin of which is Ethiopic, signifies properly, a delegate, an envoy absolute; a minister charged with representing the divinity on earth. This word has had in

THREE KINDS OF PARTICULAR VERBS 175

its origin, the same meaning as מַלְאָךְ, of which we have adopted the Greek translation ἄγγελος, *an angel*. The primitive root αγ, which forms the basis of the Greek word ἄγγελος, is precisely the same as the Hebraic root אך, and like it develops ideas of attachment and of legation. This root belongs to the tongue of the Celts as well as to that of the Ethiopians and the Hebrews. It has become, through nasalization, our idiomatic root *ang*, from which the Latins and all modern peoples generally, have received derivatives.

Taking up again the thread of my ideas, which this etymological digression has for a moment suspended, I repeat, that the Hebraic genius which is singularly partial to words of two syllables, rarely allows the verb to be formed of the root without adding a character which modifies the meaning or reinforces the expression. Now it is in the following manner that the adjunction is made and the characters especially consecrated to this use.

This adjunction is initial or terminative; that is to say, that the character added is placed at the beginning or the end of the word. When the adjunction is initial, the character added at the head of the root is י or נ; when it is terminative it is simply the final character which is doubled.

Let us take for example the verb שׁוֹם that I have already cited. This verb will become, by means of the initial adjunction יְשׁוֹם, or נְשׁוֹם, and by means of the terminative adjunction, שׁוֹמֵם: but then, not only will the meaning vary considerably and receive acceptations very different from the primitive meaning, but the conjugation also will appear irregular, on account of the characters having been added after the formation of the verb, and the root will not always be in evidence. The result of this confusion of ideas is that the Hebraists, devoid of all etymological science, take roots sometimes for radical verbs, relative to the new meaning which they offer, and sometimes for irregular verbs, relative to the anomalies that they experience in their modifications.

But the truth is, that these verbs are neither radical verbs nor irregular verbs: these are verbs of a kind, distinct and peculiar to the Hebraic tongue; verbs of which it is necessary to understand the origin and development, so as to distinguish them in speech and assign them a rank in grammar. I shall name them *compound radical* verbs, as holding a mean between those which come directly from the root and those which are formed from the derivative substantives.

I classify verbs in three kinds, with regard to conjugation, namely: the radical, the derivative and the compound radical. By the first, I mean those which are derived from the root and which remain monosyllables, such as שׁוּם, בּוּל, גּוּל etc. By the second, those which are derived from a substantive already compound, and which are always dissyllables such as מָלוֹךְ, רָגוֹז, פָּקוֹד etc. By the third, those which are formed by the adjunction of an initial or terminative character to the root, and which appear in the course of the conjugation sometimes monosyllabic and sometime dissyllabic, such as יָשׂוּם, שׁוֹמֵם, נָשׂוֹם etc.

§ III.

Analysis of Nominal Verbs: Verbal Inflection.

The signification of radical verbs depends always upon the idea attached to their root. When the etymologist has this root firmly in his memory, it is hardly possible for him to err in the meaning of the verb which is developed. If he knows well, for example, that the root שׁם contains the general idea of a thing, upright, straight, remarkable; of a monument, a name, a sign, a place, a fixed and determined time; he will know well that the verb שׁום, which is formed from it, must express the action of instituting, enacting, noting, naming, designating, placing, putting up, etc. according to the meaning of the context.

The compound radical verbs offer, it is true, a few more difficulties, for it is necessary to join to the etymological understanding of the root, that of the initial or terminative adjunction; but this is not impossible. The first step, after finding the root, is to conceive clearly the sort of influence that this same root and the character which is joined to it, exercise upon each other; for their action in this respect is reciprocal: here lies the only difficulty. The signification of the joined characters is not in the least perplexing. One must know that the characters י and נ express, in their qualities as sign, the first, a potential manifestation, an intellectual duration, and the second, an existence, produced, dependent and passive. So that one can admit as a general underlying idea, that the adjunction י, will give to the verbal action, an exterior force, more energetic and more durable, a movement more apparent and more determined; whereas the adjunction נ, on the contrary, will render this same action more interior and more involved, by bringing it back to itself.

As to the terminative adjunction, since it depends upon the duplication of the final sign, it also draws all its expression from this same sign whose activity it doubles.

But let us take as an example of these three modifications, the root שׁם, which we already know as radical verb, and let us consider it as compound radical verb. In taking this verb שׁוּם, in the sense of *setting up*, which is its simplest acceptation, we shall find that the initial adjunction manifesting its action, gives it in שׁוֹם, the sense of *exposing,* of *placing in sight,* of *putting in a prominent place:* but if this verb is presented in a more figurative sense as that of *elevating,* we shall see that the initial adjunction נ, bringing back its action in itself, makes it signify, *to elevate the soul, to be inspired, to be animated; to assume,* as it were, *the spirit of the loftiest and most radiant parts of universal spirituality.* These are the two initial adjunctions.

The terminative adjunction being formed by the duplication of the final character, it is expedient to examine this character in the root שׁם. Now, this character, considered as the sign of exterior action, is used here in its quality of collective sign. But this sign which already tends very much to extension, and which develops the being in infinite space as much as its nature permits, can not be doubled without reaching that limit where extremes meet. Therefore, the extension, of which it is the image, is changed to a dislocation, a sort of annihilation of being, caused by the very excess of its expansive action. Also the radical verb שׁוּם, which is limited to signifying the occupation of a distinguished, eminent place, presents in the compound radical שׁמם, only the action of *extending* in the void, of *wandering* in space, of *depriving of stability* of *making deserted,* of *being delirious,* etc.

In this manner should the radical and the compound radical verbs be analyzed. As to the derivative verbs, their analysis is no more difficult; for, as they come for

VERBAL INFLECTION 179

the most part from a triliteral substantive, they receive from it verbal expression. I shall have many occasions for examining these sorts of verbs in the course of my notes upon the *Cosmogony of Moses*, so that I shall dispense with doing so here: nevertheless, in order to leave nothing to be desired, in this respect, for the reader who follows me closely, I shall give two examples.

Let us take two verbs of great importance. בָּרוֹא *to create* and אָמוֹר *to speak, to say, to declare.* The first thing to do is to bring them both back to the substantives from which they are derived: this is simply done, by taking away the sign וֹ, which verbalizes them. The former presents to me in ברא, the idea of an emanated production, since בר signifies *a son, an exterior fruit;* the latter, in אמר, *a declaration, a thing upon which light is thrown*, since מאר signifies a *luminous focus, a torch.* In the first, the character א is a sign of stability; in the second, it is only a transposition from the middle of the word to the beginning to give more energy. Let us take the first.

The word בר, considered as primitive root, signifies not only *a son*, but develops the general idea of every production emanated from a generative being. Its elements are worthy of the closest attention. It is on the other hand, the sign of movement proper ר, united to that of interior action ב. The first of these signs, when it is simply vocalized by the mother vowel א as in אר, is applied to the elementary principle, whatever it may be, and under whatever form it may be conceived; ethereal, igneous, aerial, aqueous or terrestrial principle. The second of these signs is preëminently the paternal symbol. Therefore the elementary principle, whatever it may be, moved by an interior, generative force, constitutes the root באר whence is formed the compound substantive בָּרָא and the verb that I am analyzing, ברוא : that is to say, *to draw from an unknown element; to make pass from the principle to the essence; to make same that which was other;*

to bring from the centre to the circumference; in short, *to create.*

Now let us see the word מֵאר. This word is supported likewise by the elementary root אר, but this root being enlightened by the intellectual sign וֹ, has become אוֹר *the light*. In this state it assumes, not the paternal sign ב, as in the word ברא, that I have just examined, but the maternal sign מ, image of exterior action, so as to constitute the substantive מאר or מאוֹר : also, it is no longer an interior and creative action, but an action exterior and propagating, a *reflection;* that is to say, a luminous focus, a torch diffusing light from which it has received the principle.

Such is the image of speech. Such at least is the etymology of the Hebraic verb אָמוֹר, which is to say, *to spread abroad its light; to declare its thought, its will; to speak,* etc.

I have now shown how verbs are formed and analyzed; let us see how they are inflected with the aid of the designative relations which I have called articles. This inflection will prove that these verbs are really nominal, partaking, on the one hand, of the name from which they are derived by their substance, and on the other, of the absolute verb from which they receive the verbal life.

	enunciative	מְלוֹךְ	the action of ruling
	determinative	הַמְלוֹךְ	of the action of ruling
MOVEMENNT.	*directive*	לַמְלוֹךְ	to the action of ruling
	extractive	מִמְלוֹךְ	from the action of ruling
	mediative	בִּמְלוֹךְ	in the action of ruling
	assimilative	כִּמְלוֹךְ	conformable to the action of ruling
	conjunctive	וּמְלוֹךְ	and the action of ruling
	designative	אֶת־מָלוֹךְ	that which constitutes the action of ruling

I have a very important observation to make concerning this verbal inflection. It is with regard to the conjunctive article ו. This article which, placed in front of the nominal verb, expresses only the conjunctive movement as in the above example, takes all the force of the convertible sign, before the future or past tense of this same verb, and changes their temporal modification in such a way that the future tense becomes past and the past tense takes all the character of the future. Thus for example the future יִהְיָה *it shall be,* changes abruptly the signification in receiving the conjunctive article ו, and becomes the past וַיְהִי *and it was:* thus the past הָיָה *it was,* loses too its original meaning in taking the same article ו, and becomes the future וְהָיָה *and it shall be.*

It is impossible to explain in a satisfactory manner this idiomatic Hebraism without admitting the intrinsic force of the universal, convertible sign ו and without acknowledging its influence in this case.

Besides, we have an adverbial relation in our own tongue, that exercises an action almost similar, upon a past tense, which it makes a future. I do not recall having seen this singular idiomatism pointed out by any grammarian. It is the adverbial relation *if.* I am giving this example to the reader that he may see in what manner a past can become a future, without the mind being disturbed by the boldness of the ellipsis and without it even striking the attention. *They were* is assuredly of the past; it becomes future in this phrase: if *they were* in ten years at the end of their labours they would be happy!

The nominal verb participating, as I have said, in two natures, adopts equally the nominal and verbal affixes. One finds מָלוֹכִי and מָלְכָנִי *the action of ruling, mine* (my rule) : מָלוֹכוֹ and מָלְכֵהוּ *the action of ruling, his* (his rule) : etc.

One perceives that it is only the sense of the sentence which can indicate whether the affix added here is nominal or verbal. It is an amphibology that Hebrew writers would have been able to evade easily, by distinguishing the nominal affixes from the verbal.

Here is an example of the verbal and nominal affixes united to the nominal verb. I have followed the Chaldaic punctuation, which, always submissive to the vulgar pronunciation, replaces the verbal sign ו, on this occasion, by the weak vowel point, named *shewa*.

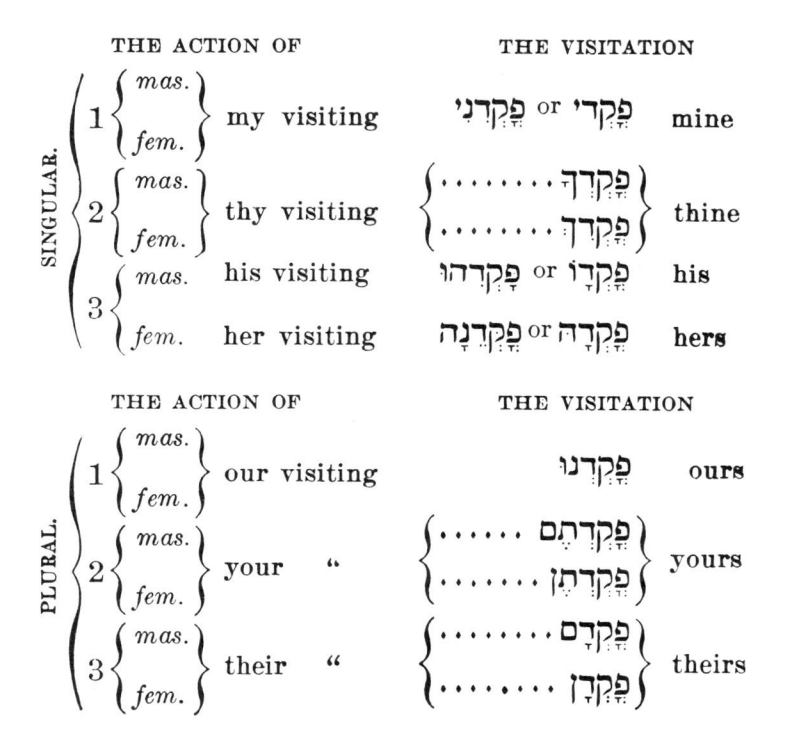

			THE ACTION OF		THE VISITATION	
SINGULAR.	1	mas. / fem.	my visiting	פָּקְדִי or פָּקְדֵנִי	mine
	2	mas. / fem.	thy visiting	פָּקְדְךָ / פָּקְדֵךְ	thine
	3	mas.	his visiting	פָּקְדוֹ or פָּקְדֵהוּ	his
		fem.	her visiting	פָּקְדָהּ or פָּקְדֶנָּה	hers

			THE ACTION OF		THE VISITATION	
PLURAL.	1	mas. / fem.	our visiting	פָּקְדֵנוּ	ours
	2	mas. / fem.	your "	פָּקְדְתֶם / פָּקְדְתֶן	yours
	3	mas. / fem.	their "	פָּקְדָם / פָּקְדָן	theirs

CHAPTER VIII.

MODIFICATIONS OF THE VERB.

§ I.

Form and Movement.

In the preceding chapter I have spoken of the absolute verb, of the particular verbs which emanate from it, and of the various kinds of these verbs. I have stated that these verbs were subject to four modifications: form, movement, time and person. I am about to make known the nature˙ of these modifications; afterward, I shall give models of the conjugations for all the kinds of verbs of the Hebraic tongue: for I conceive as many conjugations as I have kinds of verbs, namely: radical, derivative and compound radical conjugations. I do not know why the Hebraists have treated as irregular, the first and third of these conjugations, when it is obvious that one of them, the radical, is the type of all the others and particularly of the derivative, which they have chosen for their model in consequence of an absurd error which placed the triliteral verb in the first etymological rank.

I am beginning with an explanation of what ought to be understood by the *form* of the verb, and its *movement* which is here inseparable.

I call verbal form, that sort of modification by means of which the Hebraic verbs display an expression more or less forceful, more or less direct, more or less simple or compound. I recognize four verbal forms: positive, intensive, excitative and reflexive or reciprocal form.

The movement is active or passive. It is inherent in the form; for under whatever modification the verb may appear, it is indispensable that it present an active or passive action; that is to say, an action which exercises itself from within outwardly by an agent upon an object, or an action which exercises itself from without inwardly, by an object upon an agent. *One loves* or *one is loved; one sees* or *one is seen*, etc.

The verbs to which modern grammarians have given the somewhat vague name of *neuter verbs* and which appear indeed to be neither active nor passive, such as *to sleep, to walk, to fall, etc.*, are verbs, not which unite the two movements, as Harris[1] believed because this definition agrees only with the reflexive form; but verbs wherein the verbal action itself seizes the agent and suspends it between the two movements, making it object without taking from it any of its faculty of agent. Thus, when I say: *I sleep, I walk, I fall;* it is as if one said: *I devote myself to the action of sleeping, of walking, of falling, which now exercises itself upon me.* Far from having called these verbs *neuter*, that is to say, foreign to active and passive movement, the grammarians should have named them *superactives;* for they dominate the active movement, even as one has proof in considering that there is not a single active verb which, by an abstraction of thought, being taken in a general sense independent of any object, cannot take the character of the verbs in question. When one says, for example, *man loves, hates, wills, thinks*, etc., the verbs *to love, to hate, to will, to think* are in reality *superactives;* that is to say, that the verbal action which they express, dominates the agent and suspends in it the active movement, without in any manner rendering it passive.

But let us leave modern grammar which is not my domain and enter that of the Hebrews, to which I would confine myself. It is useless to speak of the superactive movement, which all verbs can take, which all can leave and which besides, differs in nothing from the active movement in its characteristic course. Let us limit ourselves to the two movements of which I have first spoken

[1] *Hermes*, L. I. c. 9.

and see how they are characterized according to their inherent form.

I call *positive,* the first of the four forms of Hebraic verbs. In this form the verbal action, active or passive, is announced simply and in accordance with its original nature. The passive movement is distinguished from the active by means of the two characters ‏נ‎ and ‏ה‎ ; the first, which is the sign of produced being, governs the continued facultative; the second, which is that of life, governs the nominal verb. Therefore one finds for the active movement, ‏קוֹם‎ or ‏קָם‎, *to be establishing,* ‏קוֹם‎, *the action of establishing;* and for the passive movement ‏נָקוֹם‎, *being established,* ‏הקוֹם‎, *the action of being established.*

The second form is what I name *intensive,* on account of the intensity which it adds to the verbal action. Our modern tongues which are deprived of this form, supply the deficiency by the aid of modificatives. This form, which a speaker can use with great force, since the accent of the voice is able to give energetic expression, is very difficult to distinguish today in writing, particularly, since the Chaldaic punctuation has substituted for the mother vowel ‏'‎, placed after the first character of the verb, the imperceptible point called *hirek.* The only means which remains to recognize this form, is the redoubling of the second verbal character, which being marked unfortunately again by the insertion of the interior point, is hardly more striking than the point *hirek.* The rabbis having recognized this difficulty have assumed the very wise part of giving to the mother vowel ‏'‎, the place which has been taken from it by this last mentioned point. It would perhaps be prudent to imitate them, for this form which is of the highest importance in the books of Moses, has scarcely ever been perceived by his translators. The active and passive facultative is governed by the character ‏מ‎, sign of exterior action, and the second character is likewise doubled in both movements; but in the active movement, the nominal verb adopts the mother vowel י, or the point *hirek* after the first character; in the passive movement it takes the mother vowel וּ, or the point *kibbuz*. For the active movement, one finds מְפַקֵּד, *to be visiting, inspecting with diligence:* פִּיקֵד or פַּקֵּד *the action of visiting*, etc.; for the passive movement מְפֻקָּד, *being visited, inspected with diligence*: פּוּקוֹד or פֻּקוֹד, *the action of being visited,* etc.

I qualify the third form by the name of *excitative*, in order to make understood as much as possible, by one single word, the kind of excitation that it causes in the verbal action, transporting this action beyond the subject which acts, upon another which it is a question of making act. This form is of great effect in the tongue of Moses. Happily it has a character that the Chaldaic point has never been able to supply and which makes it easily recognized: it is the sign of life ה, which governs the nominal verb in the two movements. For the active movement מֵקִים *to be establishing;* הֵקֵם or הָקִים *the action of establishing*: and for passive movement מוּקָם *being established;* הוּקַם *the action of being established.*

The fourth form is that which I name *reciprocal* or *reflexive,* because it makes the verbal action reciprocal or because it reflects it upon the very subject which is acting. It is easily recognized by means of the characteristic syllable הת composed of the united signs of life and of reciprocity. The second character of the verb, is doubled in this form as in the intensive, thus conserving all the energy of the latter. The two movements are also here united in a single one, to indicate that the agent which makes the action, becomes the object of its own action. One finds for the continued facultative מִתְפַּקֵּד *visiting each other;* הִתְפַּקֵּד *the action of visiting each other.*

I shall now enter into some new details regarding these four forms in giving models of the conjugations.

§ II.

Tense.

Thus Hebraic verbs are modified with respect to form and movement. I hope that the attentive reader has not failed to observe with what prolific richness the principles, which I have declared to be those of the tongue of Moses in particular, and those of all tongues in general, are developed, and I hope it will not be seen without some interest, that the sign, after having furnished the material of the noun, becomes the very substance of the verb and influences its modifications. For, let him examine carefully what is about to be explained—two movements being united to four forms. One of these movements is passive, and from its origin, is distinguished from the active, by the sign of produced being. The form, if intensive, is the sign of the duration and the manifestation which constitutes it: if it is excitative, it is the same sign united to that of life: if it is reflexive, it is the sign of that which is reciprocal and mutual, which is presented. There is such a continuous chain of regularity that I cannot believe it is the result of chance.

Now, let us pass on to the different modifications of Hebraic verbs under the relation of Tense. If, before seeing what these modifications are, I should wish to examine, as Harris[1] and some other grammarians, the nature of this incomprehensible being which causes them,—Time, what trouble would I not experience in order to develop unknown ideas; ideas that I would be unable to sustain with anything sentient! for how can Time affect our material organs since *the past* is no more; since *the future* is not; since *the present* is contained in an indivisible in-

[1] *Hermes,* L. I. ch. 7.

stant? Time is an indecipherable enigma for whatever is contained within the circle of the sensations, and nevertheless the sensations alone give it a relative existence. If they did not exist, what would it be?

It is measure of life. Change life and you will change Time. Give another movement to matter and you will have another space. Space and Time are analogous things. There, it is matter which is changed; here, it is life. Man, intelligent and sentient being, understands matter through his corporeal organs, but not through those of his intelligence; he has the intellectual sentiment of life, but he grasps it not. This is why Space and Time which appear so near, remain unknown to him. In order to understand them, man must needs awaken a third faculty within him, which being supported at the same time both by sensations and by sentiment, and enlightening at the same time the physical and mental qualities, unites in them the separated faculties. Then a new universe would be unveiled before his eyes; then he would fathom the depths of space, he would grasp the fugitive essence of Time; it would be known in its double nature.

Still if one asks me if this third faculty exists, or even if it can exist, I shall state that it is what Socrates called *divine inspiration* and to which he attributed the power of virtue.

But whatever Time may be, I have not dwelt a moment upon its nature, I have only tried to make its profound obscurity felt, in order that it be understood, that all peoples, not having considered it in the same manner, could not have experienced the same effects. Also it is very necessary in all idioms, that verbs conform to the tenses, and especially that the idiomatic genius should assign them the same limits.

The modern tongues of Europe are very rich in this respect, but they owe this richness, first, to the great number of idioms whose *débris* they have collected and of which they were insensibly composed; afterward, with the progress of the mind of man whose ideas, accumulating with the centuries, are refined and polished more and more, and are developed into a state of perfection. It is a matter worthy of notice, and which holds very closely to the history of mankind, that the tongues of the North of Europe, those whence are derived the idioms so rich today in temporal modifications, had in their origin only two simple tenses, the *present* and the *past*: they lacked the future; whereas the tongues of Occidental Asia, which appear of African origin, lacked the present, having likewise only two simple tenses, the *past* and the *future*.

Modern grammarians who have broached the delicate question of the number of tenses possessed by the French tongue, one of the most varied of Europe, and of the world in this regard, have been very far from being in accord. Some have wished to recognize only five, counting as real tenses, only the simplest ones, such as *I love, I loved, I was loving, I shall love, I should love;* considering the others as but temporal gradations. Abbé Girard has enumerated eight; Harris, twelve; Beauzée, twenty. These writers instead of throwing light upon this matter have obscured it more and more. They are like painters who, with a palette charged with colours, instead of instructing themselves or instructing others concerning their usage and the best manner of mixing them, amuse themselves disputing over their number and their rank.

There are three principal colours in light, as there are three principal tenses in the verb. The art of painting consists in knowing how to distinguish these principal colours, *blue, red* and *yellow;* the median colours *violet, orange* and *green;* and those median colours of infinite shades which can arise from their blending. Speech is a means of painting thought. The tenses of the verb are the coloured lights of the picture. The more the palette is rich in shades, the more a people gives flight to its imagination. Each writer makes use of this palette according to his genius. It is in the delicate manner of composing the shades and of mixing them, that painters and writers are alike distinguished.

It is well known that ancient painters were ignorant of the shades and half-tones. They used the primary colours without mixing them. A picture composed of four colours was regarded as a miracle of art. The colours of speech were not more varied. These shades of verbal light which we call compound tenses were unknown. The Hebrews were not poorer in this respect, than the Ethiopians and the Egyptians, renowned for their wisdom; the Assyrians, famous for their power; the Phœnicians, recognized for their vast discoveries and their colonies; the Arabs finally, whose high antiquity can not be contested: all of these had, properly speaking, only two verbal tenses: the *future* and the *past*.

But one must not think that in these ancient tongues, and particularly in the Hebrew, these two tenses were so determined, so decisive, as they have since become in our modern idioms, or that they signified precisely that which was, or that which must be, as we understand by *it has been, it shall be;* the temporal modifications הָיָה, and יְהִיֶ, express in Hebrew, not a rupture, a break in temporal continuity, but a continued duration, uniting, without the slightest interruption, the most extreme point of the past to the indivisible instant of the present, and this indivisible instant to the most extreme point of the future. So that it was sufficient by a single restriction of thought, by a simple inflection of the voice, to fix upon this temporal line, any point whatever from the past to the present, or from the present to the future, and to obtain thus by the aid of the two words הָיָה and יְהִיֶ, the same differences which modern tongues acquire with difficulty, through the following combinations: *I was, I have been, I had been, I shall be, I should be, I may have been, I might have been, I ought to be, I would be, I have to be, I had to be, I am about to be, I was about to be.*

I have purposely omitted from this list of tenses the indivisible instant *I am,* which makes the fourteenth, because this instant is never expressed in Hebrew except by the pronoun alone, or by the continued facultative, as in אָנֹכִי יְהוָֹה, *I am* YAHWEH: הִנְנִי מֵבִיא *behold me leading;* etc.

It is on this account that one should be careful in a correct translation, not always to express the Hebraic past or future, which are vague tenses, by the definite tenses. One must first examine the intention of the writer, and the respective condition of things. Thus, to give an example, although, in the French and English *word-for-word* translation, conforming to custom, I have rendered the verb בָּרָא, of the first verse of the Cosmogony of Moses, by *he created,* I have clearly felt that this verb signified there, *he had created;* as I have expressed it in the correct translation; for this antecedent nuance is irresistibly determined by the verb הָיְתָה, *it existed,* in speaking of the earth an evident object of an anterior creation.

Besides the two tenses of which I have just spoken, there exists still a third tense in Hebrew, which I call *transitive,* because it serves to transport the action of the past to the future, and because it thus participates in both tenses by serving them as common bond. Modern grammarians have improperly named it *imperative.* This name would be suitable if used only to express commands; but as one employs it as often in examining, desiring, demanding and even entreating, I do not see why one should refuse it a name which would be applicable to all these ideas and which would show its transitive action.

§ III.

Formation of Verbal Tenses by Means of Pronominal Persons.

After having thus made clear the modification of Hebraic verbs relative to tense, there remains only for me to say how they are formed. But before everything else it is essential to remember what should be understood by the three Pronominal Persons.

When I treated of nominal relations, known under the denomination of Personal and Relative pronouns, I did not stop to explain what should be understood by the three Pronominal Persons, deeming that it was in speaking of the verb that these details would be more suitably placed, so much the more as my plan was to consider *person*, as one of the four modifications of the verb.

Person and tense are as inseparable as form and movement; never can the one appear without the other; for it is no more possible to conceive person without tense, than verbal form without active or passive movement.

At the time when I conceived the bold plan of bringing back the Hebraic tongue to its constitutive principles by deriving it wholly from the *sign,* I saw that the sign had three natural elements: *voice, gesture* and *traced characters.* Now by adhering to the traced characters to develop the power of the sign, I think I have made it clearly understood, that I consider them not as any figures whatever, denuded of life and purely material, but as symbolic and living images of the generative ideas of language, expressed at first by the sundry inflections which the voice received from the organs of man. Therefore these characters have always represented to me, the voice, by means of the verbal inflections whose symbols they are; they have also represented to me, the gesture with which each inflection is necessarily accompanied, and when the sign has developed the three parts of speech, the noun, the relation and the verb, although there may not be a single one of these parts where the three elements of speech do not act together, I have been able to distinguish, nevertheless, that part where each of them acts more particularly. The voice, for example, appears to me to be the dominant factor in the verb; the vocal accent or the character in the noun, and the gesture finally in the relation. So that if man making use of speech follows the sentiment of nature he must raise the voice in the verb, accentuate more the noun and place the gesture upon the relation. It seems even as though experience confirms this grammatical remark especially in what concerns the gesture. The article and the prepositions which are designative relations, the pronouns of any kind which are nominal relations, the adverbs which are adverbial relations, always involve a gesture expressed or understood. Harris had already observed this coincidence of the gesture and had not hesitated to place in it the source of all pronouns, following in this the doctrine of the ancients, related by Apollonius and Priscian.[1]

Harris was right in this. It is the gesture which, always accompanying the nominal relations, has given birth to the distinction of the three persons, showing itself by turn identical, mutual, other or relative. The identical gesture produces the first person *I*, or *me*, אֲנִי: this is a being which manifests itself; the mutual gesture produces the second person, *thou* or *thee* אַתָּה: this is a mutual being; the other, or relative gesture, produces the third per-

[1] *Hermes.* Liv. I. Chap. 5 Apoll. de *Synt.*, Liv. II, Chap 5. Prisc. Liv. XII.

son, *he* or *him*, הוּא: this is another being, sometimes relative, as in the English pronoun, sometimes absolute, as in the Hebraic pronoun.

These personal pronouns whose origin I here explain, are like the substantive nouns which they replace in speech, subject to gender, number and inflection of the articles. I have explained them under these different relations and now we can see how in Hebrew, they determine the tense of the verbs. It is a matter worthy of attention and it has not escaped the sagacity of Court de Gébelin.[2] After being contracted in such a manner as not to be confused with the verbal affixes, the personal pronouns are placed before the nominal verb, when it is a question of forming the future, and to form the past, they are placed after the verb so as to express by this, that the action is already done.

By this simple yet energetic manner of showing verbal tenses, the Hebraic genius adds another which is none the less forceful and which proceeds from the power of the sign. It allows the luminous sign וֹ, which constitutes the nominal verb, to stand in the future; and not content with making it appear וֹ, in the finished facultative, makes it disappear wholly in the past; so that the third person of this tense, which is found without the masculine pronoun, is exactly the same as the root, or the compound whence the verb is derived. This apparent simplicity is the reason why the Hebraists have taken generally the third person of the past, for the root of the Hebraic verb and why they have given it this rank in all the dictionaries. Their error is having confounded the moment when it finishes, with that in which it begins, and not having had enough discernment to see that if the nominal verb

---

[2] *Grammaire Univ.* page 245. Court de Gébelin has put some obscurity into his explanation; but although he may be mistaken in respect to the tenses, it is plainly seen that what he said is exactly what I say.

FORMATION OF VERBAL TENSES

did not claim priority over all the tenses, this priority would belong to the transitive as the most simple of all.

Here is the new character which the personal pronouns take in order to form verbal tenses.

The affixes of the future placed before the verb, with the terminations which follow them.

SINGULAR.
- 1 { mas. / fem. } .... א   I
- 2 { mas. .... ת / fem. ....ת' } thou
- 3 { mas. ....י   he / fem. ....ת   she }

PLURAL.
- 1 { mas. / fem. } .....נ   we
- 2 { mas. ת..ו. / fem. ת..נה } ye
- 3 { mas. י..ו. / fem. ת..נה } they

Affixes of the past placed after the verb.

SINGULAR.
- 1 { mas. / fem. } ...תי   I
- 2 { mas. ....תָ / fem. ....תְ } thou
- 3 { mas. ......   he / fem. ....תָ   she }

PLURAL.
- 1 { mas. / fem. } ....נו   we
- 2 { mas. ...תֶם / fem. ....תֶן } ye
- 3 { mas. / fem. } .....ו   they

I do not speak of the affixes of the transitive, because this tense, which holds a sort of mean between the future and the past, has no affixes properly speaking, but has terminations which it borrows from both tenses.

Hebraic words moreover, do not recognize what we call verbal moods, by means of which we represent in our modern idioms, the state of the will relative to the verbal action, whether that will is influential or resolute, as in *I am doing, I have done, I shall do;* whether it is dubitative or irresolute, as in *I might have done, I should have done, I would do;* or whether it is influenced or constrained, as in *I must do, that I may do; I was obliged to do, that I might have done; I shall be obliged to do; I should be obliged to do;* the modern tongue is of an inexhaustible richness in this respect. It colours with the most delicate shades all the volitive and temporal modifications of verbs. The nominal verb and also the transitive show this fine shading of the meaning. *To do,* for example, is an indefinite nominal, but *I have just done, I am doing, I am going to do,* show the same nominal expression of the past, the present and the future. The transitive *do,* conveys visibly the action from one tense to the other, but if I say *may have done, may have to do,* this change marks first a past in a future, and afterward a future in a future.

After this data I now pass on to the models of the three verbal conjugations, according to their forms and their movements, supporting them with certain remarks concerning the most striking anomalies which can be found.

CHAPTER IX.

CONJUGATIONS.

§ I.

Radical Conjugation.

POSITIVE FORM.

ACTIVE MOVEMENT.
CONTINUED FACULTATIVE

mas. קָם or קוֹם } to be
fem. קוֹמָה } establishing

PASSIVE MOVEMENT.
CONTINUED FACULTATIVE

mas. נָקוֹם } being
fem. נְקוֹמָה } established

FINISHED.
mas. קוֹם }
fem. קוֹמָה } to be established

NOMINAL VERB.
absol. קוֹם } to establish : action
constr. קוֹם } of establishing

absol. }
constr. } הקוֹם } action of being established

TEMPORAL VERB. FUTURE.

SINGULAR	1	m. / f.	אָקוּם	I shall or will establish
	2	m.	תָּקוּם	thou shalt establish
		f.	תָּקוּמִי	
	3	m.	יָקוּם	he shall establish
		f.	תָּקוּם	she " "
PLURAL	1	m. / f.	נָקוּם	we shall or will establish
	2	m.	תָּקוּמוּ	you shall establish
		f.	תְּקוּמֶנָה	
	3	m.	יָקוּמוּ	they shall establish
		f.	תְּקוּמֶנָה	
SINGULAR	1	m. / f.	אֶקּוֹם	I shall or will be established
	2	m.	תִּקּוֹם	thou shalt be established
		f.	תִּקּוֹמִי	
	3	m.	יִקּוֹם	he shall be established
		f.	תִּקּוֹם	she " " "
PLURAL	1	m. / f.	נִקּוֹם	we shall or will be established
	2	m.	תִּקּוֹמוּ	you shall be established
		f.	תִּקּוֹמֶנָה	
	3	m.	יִקּוֹמוּ	they shall be established
		f.	תִּקּוֹמֶנָה	

CONJUGATIONS 199

TRANSITIVE.

SING.	2	m. f.	קוּם קוּמִי	} establish
PLU.	2	m. f.	קוּמוּ קוּמְנָה	} establish
SING.	2	m. f.	הִקוֹם הִקוֹמִי	} be established
PLU.	2	m. f.	הִקוֹמוּ הִקוֹמְנָה	} be established

PAST.

SINGULAR.	1	m. f.	קַמְתִּי	I established
	2	m. f.	קַמְתָּ קַמְתְּ	} thou established
	3	m. f.	קָם קָמָה	he established she "
PLURAL.	1	m. f.	קַמְנוּ	we established
	2	m. f.	קַמְתֶּם קַמְתֶּן	} you established
	3	m. f.	קָמוּ	they established

SINGULAR	1 m./f.	נְקוּמוֹתִי	I was established
	2 m.	נְקוּמוֹתָ	thou wast established
	2 f.	נְקוּמוֹת	
	3 m.	נָקוֹם	he was established
	3 f.	נָקוֹמָה	she " "
PLURAL	1 m./f.	נְקוּמוֹנוּ	we were established
	2 m.	נְקוּמוֹתֶם	you were established
	2 f.	נְקוּמוֹתֶן	
	3 m./f.	נָקוֹמוּ	they were established

INTENSIVE FORM.

ACTIVE MOVEMENT.   **PASSIVE MOVEMENT.**

FACULTATIVE.

CONTINUED.   CONTINUED.

mas. מְקוֹמֵם   *mas.* מְקוֹמָם

fem. מְקוֹמְמָה   *fem.* מְקוֹמְמָה

FINISHED.

mas. ....
fem. .... } like the passive

NOMINAL VERB.

absol. } קוֹמֵם   *absol.* } קוֹמָם
constr.   *constr.*

CONJUGATIONS

TEMPORAL VERB. FUTURE.

SINGULAR.	1 {m./f.}	אָקוֹמֵם		SINGULAR.	1 {m./f.}	אָקוֹמַם
	2 {m.}	תְּקוֹמֵם			2 {m.}	תְּקוֹמַם
	2 {f.}	תְּקוֹמְמִי			2 {f.}	תְּקוֹמְמִי
	3 {m.}	יְקוֹמֵם			3 {m.}	יְקוֹמַם
	3 {f.}	תְּקוֹמֵם			3 {f.}	תְּקוֹמַם
PLURAL.	1 {m./f.}	נְקוֹמֵם		PLURAL.	1 {m./f.}	נְקוֹמַם
	2 {m.}	תְּקוֹמְמוּ			2 {m.}	תְּקוֹמָמוּ
	2 {f.}	תְּקוֹמֵמְנָה			2 {f.}	תְּקוֹמַמְנָה
	3 {m.}	יְקוֹמְמוּ			3 {m.}	יְקוֹמָמוּ
	3 {f.}	תְּקוֹמֵמְנָה			3 {f.}	תְּקוֹמַמְנָה

TRANSITIVE.

SING.	2 {m.}	קוֹמֵם		SING.	2 {m. ......}	
	2 {f.}	קוֹמְמִי			2 {f. ......}	
PLU.	2 {m.}	קוֹמְמוּ		PLU.	2 {m. ......}	wanting
	2 {f.}	קוֹמֵמְנָה			2 {f. ......}	

PAST.

SINGULAR.	1 {m./f.}	קוֹמַמְתִּי		SINGULAR.	1 {m./f.}	קוֹמַמְתִּי
	2 {m.}	קוֹמַמְתָּ			2 {m.}	קוֹמַמְתָּ
	2 {f.}	קוֹמַמְתְּ			2 {f.}	קוֹמַמְתְּ
	3 {m.}	קוֹמֵם			3 {m.}	קוֹמֵם
	3 {f.}	קוֹמֵמָה			3 {f.}	קוֹמֵמָה

PLURAL. 1 {m. f.}	קוֹמַמְנוּ	PLURAL. 1 {m. f.}	קוֹמַמְנוּ
2 {m.	קוֹמַמְתֶּם	2 {m.	קוֹמַמְתֶּם
{f.	קוֹמַמְתֶּן	{f.	קוֹמַמְתֶּן
3 {m. f.}	קוֹמְמוּ	3 {m. f.}	קוֹמְמוּ

Excitative Form.

ACTIVE MOVEMENT.   PASSIVE MOVEMENT.

FACULTATIVE.

CONTINUED.   CONTINUED.

mas. מֵקִים   *mas.* מוּקָם

fem. מְקִימָה   *fem.* מוּקָמָה

FINISHED.

mas. .... ⎫
fem. .... ⎬ like the passive
              ⎭

NOMINAL VERB.

absol. הָקֵם   *absol.* ⎫
constr. הָקִים   *constr.* ⎬ הוּקַם

CONJUGATIONS 203

TEMPORAL VERB.

FUTURE.

SINGULAR.	1 {m. / f.}	אָקִים		SINGULAR.	1 {m. / f.}	אוּקַם
	2 {m.	תָּקִים			2 {m.	תוּקַם
	f.}	תָּקִימִי			f.}	תוּקְמִי
	3 {m.	יָקִים			3 {m.	יוּקַם
	f.}	תָּקִים			f.}	תוּקַם
PLURAL.	1 {m. / f.}	נָקִים		PLURAL.	1 {m. / f.}	נוּקַם
	2 {m.	תָּקִימִי			2 {m.	תוּקְמוּ
	f.}	תָּקִימֶינָה			f.}	תוּקַמְנָה
	3 {m.	יָקִימוּ			3 {m.	יוּקְמוּ
	f.}	תָּקִימְנָה			f.}	תוּקַמְנָה

TRANSITIVE.

SING.	2 {m.	הָקֵם	SING.	2 {m. . . . . . / f. . . . . . .}	
	f.}	הָקִימִי			} wanting
PLU.	2 {m.	הָקִימוּ	PLU.	2 {m. . . . . . / f. . . . . . .}	
	f.}	הָקֵמְנָה			

PAST.

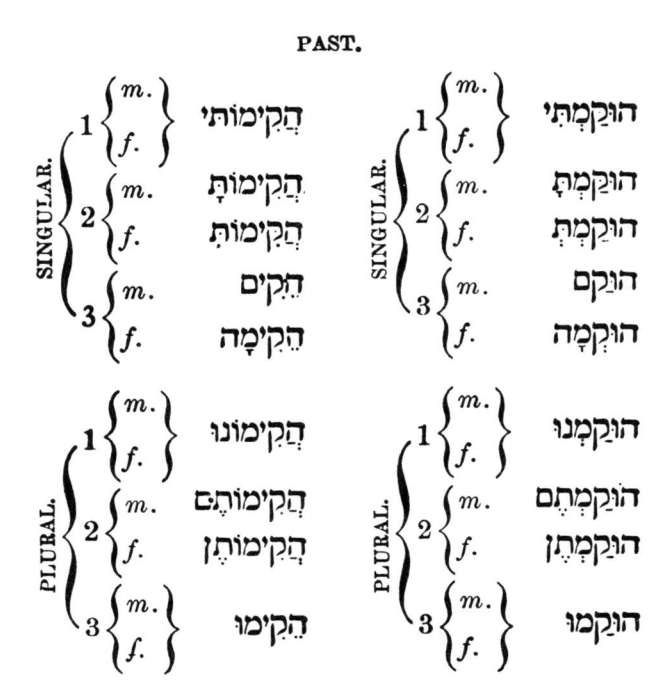

<table>
<tr><td rowspan="6">SINGULAR.</td><td rowspan="2">1</td><td>m.</td><td>הֲקִימוֹתִי</td><td rowspan="6">SINGULAR.</td><td rowspan="2">1</td><td>m.</td><td>הוּקַמְתִּי</td></tr>
<tr><td>f.</td><td></td><td>f.</td></tr>
<tr><td rowspan="2">2</td><td>m.</td><td>הֲקִימוֹתָ</td><td rowspan="2">2</td><td>m.</td><td>הוּקַמְתָּ</td></tr>
<tr><td>f.</td><td>הֲקִימוֹתְ</td><td>f.</td><td>הוּקַמְתְּ</td></tr>
<tr><td rowspan="2">3</td><td>m.</td><td>הֵקִים</td><td rowspan="2">3</td><td>m.</td><td>הוּקַם</td></tr>
<tr><td>f.</td><td>הֵקִימָה</td><td>f.</td><td>הוּקְמָה</td></tr>
</table>

<table>
<tr><td rowspan="6">PLURAL.</td><td rowspan="2">1</td><td>m.</td><td>הֲקִימוֹנוּ</td><td rowspan="6">PLURAL.</td><td rowspan="2">1</td><td>m.</td><td>הוּקַמְנוּ</td></tr>
<tr><td>f.</td><td></td><td>f.</td></tr>
<tr><td rowspan="2">2</td><td>m.</td><td>הֲקִימוֹתֶם</td><td rowspan="2">2</td><td>m.</td><td>הוּקַמְתֶּם</td></tr>
<tr><td>f.</td><td>הֲקִימוֹתֶן</td><td>f.</td><td>הוּקַמְתֶּן</td></tr>
<tr><td rowspan="2">3</td><td>m.</td><td>הֵקִימוּ</td><td rowspan="2">3</td><td>m.</td><td>הוּקְמוּ</td></tr>
<tr><td>f.</td><td></td><td>f.</td></tr>
</table>

REFLEXIVE FORM.

ACTIVE AND PASSIVE MOVEMENT UNITED.

FACULTATIVE.

CONTIN.
   mas.   מִתְקוֹמֵם
   fem.   מִתְקוֹמְמָה

FINISH.
   mas. .... } wanting
   fem. ....

CONJUGATIONS

NOMINAL VERB.

FUTURE.

absol. ⎫
constr. ⎭   הִתְקוֹמֵם

TEMPORAL VERB.

FUTURE.

SINGULAR.
- 1 *mas.* / *fem.* — אֶתְקוֹמֵם
- 2 *mas.* — תִּתְקוֹמֵם
- 2 *fem.* — תִּתְקוֹמְמִי
- 3 *mas.* — יִתְקוֹמֵם
- 3 *fem.* — תִּתְקוֹמֵם

PLURAL.
- 1 *mas.* / *fem.* — נִתְקוֹמֵם
- 2 *mas.* — תִּתְקוֹמְמוּ
- 2 *fem.* — תִּתְקוֹמֵמְנָה
- 3 *mas.* — יִתְקוֹמְמוּ
- 3 *fem.* — תִּתְקוֹמֵמְנָה

TRANSITIVE

SING.	2	*mas.*	הִתְקוֹמֵם
		fem.	הִתְקוֹמִי
PLU.	2	*mas.*	הִתְקוֹמְמוּ
		fem.	הִתְקוֹמֵמְנָה

PAST.

SINGULAR	1	*mas.* / *fem.*	הִתְקוֹמַמְתִּי
	2	*mas.*	הִתְקוֹמַמְתָּ
		fem.	הִתְקוֹמַמְתְּ
	3	*mas.*	הִתְקוֹמֵם
		fem.	הִתְקוֹמֵמָה
PLURAL	1	*mas.* / *fem.*	הִתְקוֹמַמְנוּ
	2	*mas.*	הִתְקוֹמַמְתֶּם
		fem.	הִתְקוֹמַמְתֶּן
	3	*mas.* / *fem.*	הִתְקוֹמְמוּ

CONJUGATIONS 207

Remarks upon the Radical Conjugation.

    I have already clearly shown why the conjugation which the Hebraists treat as irregular, should be considered as the first of all. The verbs which depend upon it are those which are formed directly from the root. The one that I have chosen as type is the same as that which the Hebraists have ordinarily chosen. As to the meaning, it is one of the most difficult of all the Hebraic tongue. The Latin *surgere* expresses only the least of its acceptations. As I shall often have occasion to speak of it in my notes, I am limiting myself to one simple analysis.

    The sign ק is, as we know, the sign of agglomerative or repressive force, the image of material existence, the means of the forms. Now this sign offers a different expression according as it begins or terminates the root. If it terminates it as in חק, for example, it characterizes that which is finished, definite, bound, arrested, cut, shaped upon a model, designed: if it begins it, as in קה, וק or קי, it designates that which is indefinite, vague, indeterminate, unformed. In the first case it is matter put in action; in the second, it is matter appropriate to be put in action. This last root, bearing in the word קום or קים, the collective sign, represents *substance* in general; employed as verb it expresses all the ideas which spring from substance and from its modifications: such as, *to substantialize, to spread out, to rise into space; to exist in substance, to subsist, to consist, to resist; to clothe in form and in substance, to establish, to constitute, to strengthen, to make firm,* etc. One must feel after this example, how difficult and dangerous it is to confine the Hebraic verbs to a fixed and determined expression; for this expression results always from the meaning of the phrase and the intention of the writer.

    As to the four forms to which I here submit the verb קום, I must explicitly state, not only as regards this conjugation but also for those which follow, that all verbs do not receive them indifferently; that some affect one form more than another, and finally, that there are some which one never finds under the positive form. But once again, what matter these variations? It is not a question of writing but of understanding Hebrew.

Positive Form.

Active movement. Although the modern Hebraists, with an unprecedented whimsicality, have taken the third person of the past for the theme of all verbs, they are forced to agree that in this conjugation, this third person is not in the least thematic: one also finds in dictionaries, the nominal קוּם presented as theme: and this ought to be, not only for all radical verbs such as this one, but for all kinds of verbs.

The continued facultative is often marked by the luminous, sign וֹ, as can be seen in אוֹר *to be shining.* The Chaldaic punctuation is not consistent in the manner of replacing this sign. Instead of the point *kamez* which is found here in קָם, one meets the *zere*, in עֵר *to be watching, vigilant,* and in some others. I state here once more, that the feminine facultative, in the continued active and passive, as well as in the finished, changes the character הָ into ת, and that one finds equally קוֹמָה or קוֹמֶת; נְקוֹמָה or נְקוֹמֶת; קוּמָה or קוּמֶת. I have already mentioned this variation in chapter V. § 3, in treating of gender. I do not mention the plural of the facultatives, since its formation offers no difficulties.

The future has sometimes the emphatic article הּ, as well as the transitive. One finds אָקוּמָה, *I shall establish, I shall raise up.* שׁוּבָה, *come! arise! return to thy first state,* etc.

The past, which, by its nature, ought to lose the luminous sign, conserves it, however, in certain verbs where it is identical; such as אוֹר, *it shone;* בּוֹשׁ, *it reddened,* etc. One also finds the *zere* substituted by the *kamez* in מָת *he died.* I observe at this point, that all verbs in general which terminate with ת, do not double this character, either in the first or second person of the past, but receive the interior point only as duplicative accent. One finds therefore מַתִּי *I was dying,* מַתָּ *thou wast dying,* מַתֶּם *you were dying,* etc.

Passive movement. The inadequate denomination which the Hebraists had given to the facultatives in considering them as *present* or *past* participles, had always prevented them from distinguishing the continued facultative of the passive movement, from the finished facultative belonging to the two movements. It was impossible in fact, after their explanations to perceive the delicate difference which exists in Hebrew between נָקוֹם *that which became, becomes* or *will become established,* and קוּם, *that which was, is* or *will be established.* When, for example, it was a matter of explaining how the verb הָיָה or הֱיוֹת *the action of being, of living,* could have a passive facultative, they are lost in ridiculous interpretations. They perceived not that the difference of these three facultatives הוֹיָה, נְהִיָה and הָיוֹה was in the continued or finished movement: as we would say *a being being, living; a thing being effected; a being realized, a thing effected.*

It is easy to see, moreover, in the inspection of the passive movement alone, that the Chaldaic punctuation has altered it much less than the other. The verbal sign is almost invariably found in its original strength.

Intensive Form.

Radical verbs take this form by redoubling the final character; so that its signification depends always upon the signification of this character as sign. In the case in question, the final character being considered as collective sign, its redoubling expresses a sudden and general usurpation. Thus the verb קֹמֵם, can be translated, according to the circumstance, by the action of *extending indefinitely, of existing in substance in an universal manner; of establishing, of establishing strongly, with energy; of resisting, of opposing vigorously,* etc.

In this state this verb is easily confused with a derivative verb, if the verbal sign, instead of being placed after the first character, as it is, was placed after the second, as is seen in פָּקוֹד *to visit*: notwithstanding this difference, the rabbis, not finding this form sufficiently characterized, have substituted for it the hyphen of the Chaldaic, some examples of which, one finds moreover, in the Sepher of the Hebrews. This form consists in substituting the sign of manifestation and duration, for that of light, and in saying, without doubling the final character, קִים instead of קוֹמֵם; חִית instead of חוֹבֵב, etc.

Sometimes too, not content with doubling the last character of the root as in קֹמֵם, the entire root is doubled, as in כִּלְכֵּל *to achieve, to consummate wholly;* but these sorts of verbs belong to the second conjugation and follow the intensive form of the derivative verbs.

The passive movement has nothing remarkable in itself except the very great difficulty of distinguishing it from the active movement, which causes it to be little used.

Excitative Form.

This form perfectly characterized, as much in the passive movement as in the active, is of great usefulness in the tongue of Moses. I have already spoken of its effects and of its construction. It can be observed in this example that the convertible sign ו, which constitutes the radical verb קוּם, is changed into י, in the active movement, and is transposed in the passive movement, before the initial character.

The only comment I have to make is, that the Chaldaic punctuation sometimes substitutes the point *zere* for the mother vowel ׳, of the active movement, and the point *kibbuz* for the sign ו of the passive movement. So that one finds the continued facultative מַפֵּר *making angry;* the future תָּשֵׁב, *thou shalt bring back,* and even the past הֻקַם, *he was aroused to establish himself;* etc.

Reflexive Form.

This form differs from the intensive in its construction, only by the addition of the characteristic syllable הת; as can be seen in the nominal הִתְקוֹמֵם. For the rest, the two movements are united in a single one.

All that is essential to observe, is relative to this syllable הת. Now it undergoes what the Hebraists call *syncope* and *metathesis.*

The syncope takes place when one of the two characters is effaced as in the facultative מִתְקוֹמֵם, and in the future אֶתְקוֹמֵם, where the character ה is found replaced by מ or א; or when, to avoid inconsonance, one supresses the character ת, before a verb commencing with ט, which takes its place with the interior point; as in תִּטָּהֵר *to be purified.*

The metathesis takes place when the first character of a verb is one of the four following: ז, ס, צ, שׁ. Then the ת of the characteristic syllable הת, is transposed after this initial character, by being changed into ד after ז, and into ט after צ; as can be seen in the derivative verbs cited in the examples.

שָׁבוֹהַ	to praise, to exhalt	הִשְׁתַּבֵּיהַ	to be praised
צָדוֹק	to be just	הִצְטַדֵּיק	to be justified
סָגוֹר	to close	הִסְתַּגֵּיר	to be closed
זָמוֹן	to prepare	הִזְדַּמִּין	to be prepared

§ II.

DERIVATIVE CONJUGATION	POSITIVE FORM
ACTIVE MOVEMENT	PASSIVE MOVEMENT

FACULTATIVE

	CONTINUED.			CONTINUED.
mas.	פּוֹקֵד		mas.	נִפְקָד
fem.	פּוֹקְדָה		fem.	נִפְקָדָה

FINISHED.

| mas. | פָּקוּד | | fem. | פָּקוּדה |

NOMINAL VERB

| absol. | פָּקוֹד | | absol. | הִפָּקֵד |
| constr. | פְּקֹד | | constr. | |

TEMPORAL VERB
FUTURE.

SINGULAR
- 1 { m. / f. } אֶפְקוֹד
- 2 { m. } תִּפְקוֹד
- 2 { f. } תִּפְקוֹדִי
- 3 { m. } יִפְקוֹד
- 3 { f. } תִּפְקוֹד

PLURAL
- 1 { m. / f. } נִפְקוֹד
- 2 { m. } תִּפְקְדוּ
- 2 { f. } תִּפְקוֹדְנָה
- 3 { m. } יִפְקְדוּ
- 3 { f. } תִּפְקוֹדְנָה

SINGULAR
- 1 { m. / f. } אֶפָּקֵד
- 2 { m. } תִּפָּקֵד
- 2 { f. } תִּפָּקְדִי
- 3 { m. } יִפָּקֵד
- 3 { f. } תִּפָּקֵד

PLURAL
- 1 { m. / f. } נִפָּקֵד
- 2 { m. } תִּפָּקְדוּ
- 2 { f. } תִּפָּקַדְנָה
- 3 { m. } יִפָּקְדוּ
- 3 { f. } תִּפָּקַדְנָה

CONJUGATIONS

TRANSITIVE

SING. 2	mas.	פְּקוֹד		SING. 2	mas.	הַפְקֵד
	fem.	פִּקְדִי			fem.	הַפְקִדִי
PLU. 2	mas.	פִּקְדוּ		PLU. 2	mas.	הַפְקִדוּ
	fem.	פְּקוֹדְנָה			fem.	הַפְקֵדְנָה

PAST

SINGULAR 1	mas. / fem.	פָּקַדְתִּי		SINGULAR 1	mas. / fem.	נִפְקַדְתִּי
2	mas.	פָּקַדְתָּ		2	mas.	נִפְקַדְתָּ
	fem.	פָּקַדְתְּ			fem.	נִפְקַדְתְּ
3	mas.	פָּקַד		3	mas.	נִפְקַד
	fem.	פָּקְדָה			fem.	נִפְקְדָה
PLURAL 1	mas. / fem.	פָּקַדְנוּ		PLURAL 1	mas. / fem.	נִפְקַדְנוּ
2	mas.	פְּקַדְתֶּם		2	mas.	נִפְקַדְתֶּם
	fem.	פְּקַדְתֶּן			fem.	נִפְקַדְתֶּן
3	mas. / fem.	פָּקְדוּ		3	mas. / fem.	נִפְקְדוּ

INTENSIVE FORM

	ACTIVE MOVEMENT		PASSIVE MOVEMENT

FACULTATIVE.
CONTINUED

mas.	מְפַקֵּד	mas.	מְפָקָד
fem.	מְפַקְּדָה	fem.	מְפָקְדָה

FINISHED

mas.	פָּקַד	fem.	פָּקְדָה

NOMINAL VERB

absol. constr. }	פַּקֵד	absol. constr. }	פָּקוּד

TEMPORAL VERB
FUTURE.

SINGULAR
1 { m. f. } אֶפְקֵד
2 { m. } תְּפַקֵּד
   { f. } תְּפַקְּדִי
3 { m. } יְפַקֵּד
   { f. } תְּפַקֵּד

SINGULAR
1 { m. f. } אֶפְקַד
2 { m. } תְּפָקַד
   { f. } תְּפָקְדִי
3 { m. } יְפָקַד
   { f. } תְּפָקַד

PLURAL
1 { m. f. } נְפַקֵּד
2 { m. } תְּפַקְּדוּ
   { f. } תְּפַקֵּדְנָה
3 { m. } יְפַקְּדוּ
   { f. } תְּפַקֵּדְנָה

PLURAL
1 { m. f. } נְפָקַד
2 { m. } תְּפָקְדוּ
   { f. } תְּפָקַדְנָה
3 { m. } יְפָקְדוּ
   { f. } תְּפָקַדְנָה

CONJUGATIONS

TRANSITIVE

SING. 2	mas.	פְּקֹד	SING. 2	mas.	
	fem.	פִּקְדִי		fem.	} wanting
PLU. 2	mas.	פִּקְדוּ	PLU. 2	mas.	
	fem.	פְּקֹדְנָה		fem.	

PAST

SINGULAR 1	mas.	פָּקַדְתִּי	SINGULAR 1	mas.	פָּקַדְתְּ
	fem.			fem.	
2	mas.	פָּקַדְתָּ	2	mas.	פָּקַדְתָּ
	fem.	פָּקַדְתְּ		fem.	פָּקַדְתְּ
3	mas.	פָּקַד	3	mas.	פָּקַד
	fem.	פָּקְדָה		fem.	פָּקְדָה
PLURAL 1	mas.	פָּקַדְנוּ	PLURAL 1	mas.	פָּקַדְנוּ
	fem.			fem.	
2	mas.	פְּקַדְתֶּם	2	mas.	פְּקַדְתֶּם
	fem.	פְּקַדְתֶּן		fem.	פְּקַדְתֶּן
3	mas.	פָּקְדוּ	3	mas.	פָּקְדוּ
	fem.			fem.	

EXCITATIVE FORM

ACTIVE MOVEMENT		PASSIVE MOVEMENT	

FACULTATIVE
CONTINUED

	ACTIVE		PASSIVE
mas.	מַפְקִיד	mas.	מְפְקָד
fem.	מַפְקִידָה	fem.	מְפְקָדָה

FINISHED

mas. ..... ⎫
              ⎬ like the passive
fem. ..... ⎭

NOMINAL VERB

| absol. | הַפְקֵד | absol. | ⎫ הָפְקֵד |
| constr. | הַפְקִיד | constr. | ⎭ |

TEMPORAL VERB
FUTURE

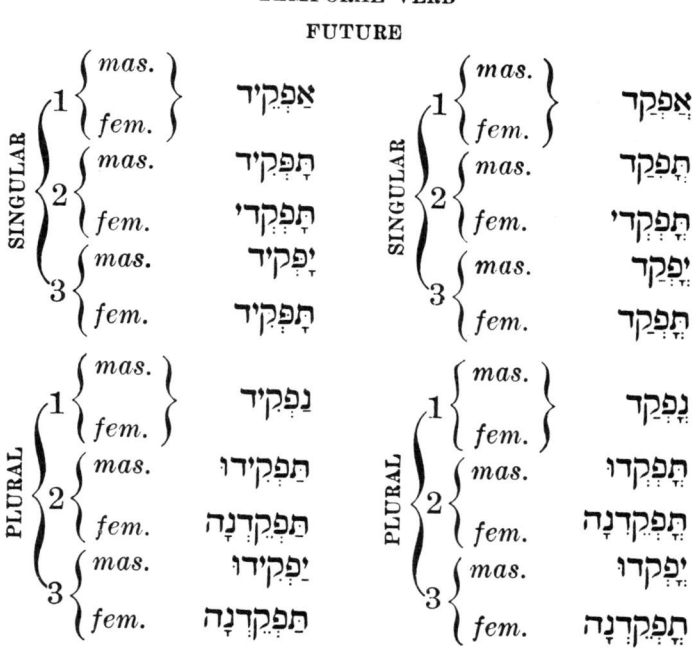

		ACTIVE			PASSIVE
SINGULAR	1 {mas./fem.}	אַפְקִיד	SINGULAR	1 {mas./fem.}	אָפְקַד
	2 {mas.}	תַּפְקִיד		2 {mas.}	תָּפְקַד
	2 {fem.}	תַּפְקִידִי		2 {fem.}	תָּפְקְדִי
	3 {mas.}	יַפְקִיד		3 {mas.}	יָפְקַד
	3 {fem.}	תַּפְקִיד		3 {fem.}	תָּפְקַד
PLURAL	1 {mas./fem.}	נַפְקִיד	PLURAL	1 {mas./fem.}	נָפְקַד
	2 {mas.}	תַּפְקִידוּ		2 {mas.}	תָּפְקְדוּ
	2 {fem.}	תַּפְקֵדְנָה		2 {fem.}	תָּפְקַדְנָה
	3 {mas.}	יַפְקִידוּ		3 {mas.}	יָפְקְדוּ
	3 {fem.}	תַּפְקֵדְנָה		3 {fem.}	תָּפְקַדְנָה

CONJUGATIONS

TRANSITIVE

SING.	2	mas.	הַפְקֵד	SING. 2	mas.	
		fem.	הַפְקִידִי		fem.	wanting
PLU.	2	mas.	הַפְקִידוּ	PLU. 2	mas.	
		fem.	הַפְקֵדְנָה		fem.	

PAST

SINGULAR	1	mas. fem.	הִפְקַדְתִּי	SINGULAR	1	mas. fem.	הָפְקַדְתִּי
	2	mas.	הִפְקַדְתָּ		2	mas.	הָפְקַדְתָּ
		fem.	הִפְקַדְתְּ			fem.	הָפְקַדְתְּ
	3	mas.	הִפְקִיד		3	mas.	הָפְקַד
		fem.	הִפְקִידָה			fem.	הָפְקְדָה
PLURAL	1	mas. fem.	הִפְקַדְנוּ	PLURAL	1	mas. fem.	הָפְקַדְנוּ
	2	mas.	הִפְקַדְתֶּם		2	mas.	הָפְקַדְתֶּם
		fem.	הִפְקַדְתֶּן			fem.	הָפְקַדְתֶּן
	3	mas. fem.	הִפְקִידוּ		3	mas. fem.	הָפְקְדוּ

REFLEXIVE FORM

| ACTIVE MOVEMENT | PASSIVE MOVEMENT |

FACULTATIVE

CONTIN.
- *mas.* מִתְפַּקֵּד
- *fem.* מִתְפַּקְּדָה

FINISH.
- *mas.* .....
- *fem.* .....
} wanting

NOMINAL VERB

absol.
constr.
} הִתְפַּקֵּד

TEMPORAL VERB

FUTURE

SINGULAR
- 1 *mas.* / *fem.* — אֶתְפַּקֵּד
- 2 *mas.* — תִּתְפַּקֵּד
- 2 *fem.* — תִּתְפַּקְּדִי
- 3 *mas.* — יִתְפַּקֵּד
- 3 *fem.* — תִּתְפַּקֵּד

PLURAL
- 1 *mas.* / *fem.* — נִתְפַּקֵּד
- 2 *mas.* — תִּתְפַּקְּדוּ
- 2 *fem.* — תִּתְפַּקֵּדְנָה
- 3 *mas.* — יִתְפַּקְּדוּ
- 3 *fem.* — תִּתְפַּקֵּדְנָה

CONJUGATIONS

TRANSITIVE

SING. 2 { mas. — הִתְפַּקֵּד
fem. — הִתְפַּקְדִי

PLU. 2 { mas. — הִתְפַּקְדוּ
fem. — הִתְפַּקֵּדְנָה

PAST

SINGULAR
1 { mas. / fem. } — הִתְפַּקַּדְתִּי
2 { mas. — הִתְפַּקַּדְתָּ
fem. — הִתְפַּקַּדְתְּ
3 { mas. — הִתְפַּקֵּד
fem. — הִתְפַּקְדָה

PLURAL
1 { mas. / fem. } — הִתְפַּקַּדְנוּ
2 { mas. — הִתְפַּקַּדְתֶּם
fem. — הִתְפַּקַּדְתֶּן
3 { mas. / fem. } — הִתְפַּקְדוּ

Remarks upon the Derivative Conjugation.

I have not judged it necessary to change the typical verb which the Hebraists give as theme for this conjugation, because this verb lends itself to the four forms. I am going to present only its etymological meaning.

The primitive root פוק from which it is derived, contains the general idea of an alternating movement from one place to another, such as one would see, for example, in a pendulum. This idea coming out more distinctly in the verbalized root, signifies *to pass from one place to another, to be carried here and there, to go and come.* Here is clearly observed the opposed action of the two signs פ and ק, of which the one opens the centre and the other cuts and designs the circumference. This root is joined, in order to compose the word of which we are speaking, to the root אר or רי, no less expressive, which, relating properly to the forefinger of the hand, signifies figuratively any object distinct or alone; an extract from abundance born of division: for this abundance is expressed in Hebrew by the same root considered under the contrary relation רי.

Thus these two roots contracted in the compound פָּקַד, develop the idea of a movement which is carried alternately from one object to another: it is an *examination*, an *exploration*, an *inspection*, a *visit*, a *census*, etc; from this results the facultative פָּקֹד, *to be inspecting, examining, visiting;* and the nominal verb פָּקוֹד, *to visit, to examine, to inspect,* etc.

Positive Form.

Active movement. It must be remembered that the Chaldaic punctuation, following all the inflection of the vulgar pronunciation, corrupts very often the etymology. Thus it suppresses the verbal sign ו of the continued fac-

CONJUGATIONS

ultative, and substitutes either the *holem* or the *kamez* as in כֹּפֶר *appeasing, expiating;* אָבֵל *grieving, mourning, sorrowing.*

Sometimes one finds this same facultative terminated by the character ', to form a kind of qualificative, as in אסרי, *linking, enchaining, subjugating.*

I shall speak no further of the feminine changing the final character ה to ת, because it is a general rule.

The nominal assumes quite voluntarily the emphatic article ה, particularly when it becomes construct; then the Chaldaic punctuation again suppresses the verbal sign ו, as in לְמָשְׁחָה, *to annoint, according to the action of annointing, to coat over, to oil, to paint,* etc. I must state here, that this emphatic article can be added to nearly all the verbal modifications, but chiefly to both facultatives, to the nominal and the transitive. It can be found even in the future and the past, as one sees it in אֶשְׁמְרָה, *I shall guard;* בָּגְדָתָה, *he lied.*

When the nominal verb begins with the mother vowel א, this vowel blends with the affix of the first person future, disappears sometimes in the second, and has in the third, the point *holem;* thus אֱסוֹף *to gather,* makes אֱסֹף *I shall gather;* תסף or תֶּאֱסֹף *thou shalt gather;* יֶאֱסֹף, *he shall gather:* thus, אֱכוֹל *to feed oneself,* makes אֹכַל *I shall feed myself;* thus אֱמוֹר *to say,* makes אֹמַר *I shall say;* תֹּאמַר, *thou shalt say;* יֹאמַר, *he shall say;* etc. Some Hebraists have made of this slight anomaly an irregular conjugation that they call *Quiescent Pe 'Aleph.*

These same Hebraists ready to multiply the difficulties, have also made an irregular conjugation of the verbs whose final character נ or ת, is not doubled in receiving the future ending נָה, or the affixes of the past תִּי, תָ, תְ, תֶם, תֶן, נוּ; but is blended with the ending of the affix, being supplied with the interior point: as one remarks it in כָּרוֹת

to suppress, which makes כָּרַתִּי, *I suppressed*, כָּרַתָּ *thou suppressed;* etc., or in שְׁכוֹן, *to inhabit*, which makes תִּשְׁכֹּנָה, *you shall inhabit* (fem); *they shall inhabit;* שְׁכֹנָה, *inhabit* (fem.); שָׁכַנּוּ, *we shall inhabit;* etc. There is nothing perplexing in this. The only real difficulty results from the change of the character נ into ת, in the verb נָתוֹן, *to give*, which makes נָתַתִּי, *I gave*, נָתַתָּ, *thou gavest;* etc., I have already spoken of this anomaly in treating of the radical conjugation.

There exists a more considerable irregularity when the verb terminates with א or ה, and concerning which it is necessary to speak more fully. But as this anomaly is seen in the three conjugations I shall await the end of this chapter to take up the subject.

Passive Movement. The Chaldaic punctuation sometimes substitutes the *zere* for the *hirek* in the passive nominal, as can be seen in הֵאָסֵף *the action of being gathered;* or in הֵאָכֹל, *the action of being consummated.* One observes in this last example the appearance even of the *holem.* It is useless to dwell upon a thing which follows step by step the vulgar pronunciation and which yields to all its caprices. The characteristic sign and the mother vowel, these, are what should be examined with attention. One ought to be concerned with the point, only when there is no other means of discovering the meaning of a word.

Moreover, it is necessary to remark that the passive movement can become reciprocal and even superactive when the verb is not used in the active movement. Thus one finds נִשְׁמַר *he took care of himself;* נִשְׁבַּע *he swore; he bore witness*, etc.

Intensive Form.

Ever since the Chaldaic punctuation has, as I have said, suppressed the mother vowels י and וֹ, which are placed after the first verbal character, the one in the active movement and the other in the passive, there remains, in order to recognize this interesting form, whose force supplies the adverbial relation very rare in Hebrew, only the interior point of the second character. Therefore the utmost attention must be given.

All derivative verbs of two roots uncontracted as כִּלְכֵּל, *to achieve wholly,* כִּרְכֵּר, *to rise rapidly in the air,* etc.; in short, all verbs that the Hebraists name quadriliteral, because they are, in effect, composed of four letters in the nominal without including the verbal sign ו, belong to this form and follow it in its modifications.

Sometimes the point *hirek* which accompanies the first character of the verb in the intensive past, is replaced by the *zere* as in בֵּרֵךְ *he blessed fervently.*

The intensive form takes place in the active movement with as much method as without; sometimes it gives a contrary meaning to the positive verb: thus הַטּוֹא *the action of sinning,* makes חִטֵּא *he sinned;* and הִטֵּא *he is purged from sin;* thus שׁוֹרֵשׁ, *the action of taking root,* makes שֵׁרֵשׁ, *it took root;* and שֵׁרֵשׁ, *it was rooted up;* etc. The passive movement follows nearly the same modifications.

Excitative Form.

I have spoken sufficiently of the utility and usage of this form. It is characterized clearly enough to be readily recognized. One knows that its principal purpose is to transport the verbal action into another subject which it is a question of making act; however, it must be noticed that when the positive form does not exist, which sometimes happens, then it becomes simply declarative, according to the active or passive movement, with or without method. It is thus that one finds הִצְדִּיק, *he was declared just, he was justified:* הִרְשִׁיעַ *he was declared impious;* הֵקִיץ, *he awakened, he was aroused, he made re-*

pose cease; הִשְׁלִיךְ, *he projected;* הָשְׁלַךְ *he was projected;* etc.

Reflexive Form.

Besides this form being reciprocal at the same time as reflexive, that is to say, that the nominal הִתְפָּקֵד, can signify alike, *to visit oneself, to visit each other,* or *to be aroused to visit;* it can also, according to circumstances, become simulatory, frequentative and even intensive, returning thus to its proper source; for, as I have said, this form is no other than the intensive, to which was added the characteristic syllable הת. One finds under these different acceptations: הִתְהַלֵּךְ, *he went about, he walked up and down, he went without stopping;* הִתְפַּלֵּל, *he offered himself to administer justice, to be magistrate;* etc.

I have spoken of the syncope and metathesis which substitute the syllable הת, for the article of the radical conjugation. Its repetition is unnecessary. It is also unnecessary for me to repeat that the emphatic article ה is placed indifferently for all the verbal modifications, and that the Chaldaic punctuation varies.

CONJUGATIONS

§. III.

Compound Radical Conjugation with the Initial Adjunction וֹ

POSITIVE FORM

ACTIVE MOVEMENT **PASSIVE MOVEMENT**

FACULTATIVE

	CONTINUED			CONTINUED
mas.	יוֹשֵׁב		mas.	נוֹשָׁב
fem.	יוֹשְׁבָה		fem.	נוֹשָׁבָה

FINISHED

| mas. | יָשׁוּב |
| fem. | יָשׁוּבָה |

NOMINAL VERB

| absol. | יָשׁוּב | absol. | ⎫ | הוּשֵׁב |
| constr. | שֶׁבֶת | constr. | ⎬ | |

TEMPORAL VERB

FUTURE

SINGULAR
1 { m. / f. }   אֵשֵׁב
2 { m. }   תֵּשֵׁב
  { f. }   תֵּשְׁבִי
3 { m. }   יֵשֵׁב
  { f. }   תֵּשֵׁב

SINGULAR
1 { m. / f. }   אוּשַׁב
2 { m. }   תּוּשַׁב
  { f. }   תּוּשְׁבִי
3 { m. }   יוּשַׁב
  { f. }   תּוּשַׁב

FUTURE

PLURAL	1 {m./f.}	נֵשֵׁב	PLURAL	1 {m./f.}	נִוָּשֵׁב
	2 {m.}	תֵּשְׁבוּ		2 {m.}	תִּוָּשְׁבוּ
	2 {f.}	תֵּשֵׁבְנָה		2 {f.}	תִּוָּשֵׁבְנָה
	3 {m.}	יֵשְׁבוּ		3 {m.}	יִוָּשְׁבוּ
	3 {f.}	תֵּשֵׁבְנָה		3 {f.}	תִּוָּשֵׁבְנָה

TRANSITIVE

SING.	2 {mas.}	שֵׁב	SING.	2 {mas.}	הוּשֵׁב
	2 {fem.}	שְׁבִי		2 {fem.}	הִוָּשְׁבִי
PLU.	2 {mas.}	שְׁבוּ	PLU.	2 {mas.}	הִוָּשְׁבוּ
	2 {fem.}	שֵׁבְנָה		2 {fem.}	הִוָּשֵׁבְנָה

PAST

SINGULAR	1 {m./f.}	יָשַׁבְתִּי	SINGULAR	1 {m./f.}	נוֹשַׁבְתִּ
	2 {m.}	יָשַׁבְתָּ		2 {m.}	נוֹשַׁבְתָּ
	2 {f.}	יָשַׁבְתְּ		2 {f.}	נוֹשַׁבְתְּ
	3 {m.}	יָשַׁב		3 {m.}	נוֹשַׁב
	3 {f.}	יָשְׁבָה		3 {f.}	נוֹשְׁבָה
PLURAL	1 {m./f.}	יָשַׁבְנוּ	PLURAL	1 {m./f.}	נוֹשַׁבְנוּ
	2 {m.}	יְשַׁבְתֶּם		2 {m.}	נוֹשַׁבְתֶּם
	2 {f.}	יְשַׁבְתֶּן		2 {f.}	נוֹשַׁבְתֶּן
	3 {m./f.}	יָשְׁבוּ		3 {m./f.}	נוֹשְׁבוּ

CONJUGATIONS

Intensive Form

| ACTIVE MOVEMENT | PASSIVE MOVEMENT |

FACULTATIVE

	CONTINUED		CONTINUED
mas.	מְיַשֵׁב	mas.	מְיֻשָּׁב
fem.	מְיַשְׁבָה	fem.	מְיֻשָּׁבָה

FINISHED

mas. ...... ⎫
fem. ...... ⎬ wanting

NOMINAL VERB

| | | absol. ⎫ | | absol. ⎫ | |
| mas. | | constr. ⎭ יַשֵּׁב | | constr. ⎭ יֻשַּׁב | |

TEMPORAL VERB

FUTURE

| mas. ⎫ | | mas. ⎫ | |
| fem. ⎭ אֲיַשֵּׁב | | fem. ⎭ אֲיֻשַּׁב | |

TRANSITIVE

| mas. ⎫ יַשֵּׁב | mas. ⎫ |
| fem. ⎭ יַשְּׁבִי | fem. ⎭ wanting |

PAST

| mas. ⎫ | | mas. ⎫ | |
| fem. ⎭ יִשַּׁבְתִּי | | fem. ⎭ יֻשַּׁבְתִּי | |

EXCITATIVE FORM

FACULTATIVE

	CONTINUED		CONTINUED
mas.	מוֹשִׁיב	mas.	מוּשָׁב
fem.	מוֹשִׁיבָה	fem.	מוּשָׁבָה

FINISHED

mas. ......⎫
fem. ......⎭ like the passive

NOMINAL VERB

| absol. | הוֹשִׁיב | absol. ⎫ | הוּשַׁב |
| constr. | הוֹשֵׁב | constr. ⎭ | |

TEMPORAL VERB

FUTURE

| mas. ⎫ | אוֹשִׁיב | mas. ⎫ | אוּשַׁב |
| fem. ⎭ | | fem. ⎭ | |

TRANSITIVE

| mas. | הוֹשֵׁב | mas. ..... ⎫ | wanting |
| fem. | הוֹשִׁיבִי | fem. ..... ⎭ | |

PAST

| mas. ⎫ | הוֹשַׁבְתִּי | mas. ⎫ | הוּשַׁבְתִּי |
| fem. ⎭ | | fem. ⎭ | |

CONJUGATIONS

Reflexive Form

ACTIVE AND PASSIVE MOVEMENT UNITED

FACULTATIVE

CONTIN. { *mas.* מִתְיַשֵּׁב
{ *fem.* מִתְיַשְּׁבָה

FINISH. { *mas.* .... } wanting
{ *fem.* .... }

NOMINAL VERB

absol. } הִתְיַשֵּׁב
constr. }

TEMPORAL VERB
FUTURE

mas. } אֶתְיַשֵּׁב
fem. }

TRANSITIVE

mas. הִתְיַשֵּׁב
fem. הִתְיַשְּׁבִי

PAST

mas. } הִתְיַשַּׁבְתִּי
fem. }

REMARKS ON THE COMPOUND RADICAL CONJUGATION.

Initial Adjunction י

The verb presented here as model is יֹשׁוּב. I am about to proceed with its analysis. The root שׁוּב contains the idea of a return to a place, to a time, to a condition or an action, from which one had departed. It is the sign of the relative movement שׁ, which is united to that of interior, central and generative action בּ. This return, being determined and manifested by the initial adjunction י, becomes a real sojourn, a taking possession of, an occupation, a habitation. Thus the compound radical verb יָשׁוּב can signify, according to circumstances, the action *of dwelling, of inhabiting, of sojourning, of taking possession;* etc.

Positive Form.

Active Movement. The initial adjunction י remains constant in the two facultatives, in the absolute nominal as well as in the past tense; but it disappears in the construct nominal, in the transitive and in the future. It seems indeed, that in this case the mother vowel י, ought to be placed between the first and second character of the verbal root, and that one should say שִׁיבֶת, *the action of occupying;* אֲשִׁיב, *I shall occupy;* שִׁיב, *occupy;* etc. But the Chaldaic punctuation having prevailed, has supplied it with the *segol* or the *zere*.

The simplicity of the transitive tense in this conjugation has made many savants, and notably Court de Gébelin, think that it should be regarded as the first of the verbal tenses. Already Leibnitz who felt keenly the need of etymological researches, had seen that in reality the transitive is, in the Teutonic idioms, the simplest of the tenses. President Desbrosses had spoken loudly in favour of this opinion, and abbé Bergier limited the whole compass of

CONJUGATIONS

Hebraic verbs to it. This opinion, which is not in the least to be held in contempt, finds support in what Du Halde said pertaining to the tongue of the Manchu Tartars whose verbs appear to originate from the transitive. But it is evident through the examination of the radical conjugation, that the nominal and the transitive of the verb, are *au fond* the same thing in Hebrew, and that the latter differs not from the former except by a modification purely mental. The Hebrews said קוֹם *the action of establishing* and קוֹם *establish*. The purpose of the speaker, the accent which accompanied it could alone feel the difference. The nominal יָשׁוּב differs here from the transitive יָשַׁב, only because the initial adjunction י is unable to resist the influence of the modification. In the verbs where this mother vowel is not a simple adjunction but a sign, the transitive does not differ from the nominal. One finds, for example, יָרִשׁ *possess*, and יְרוֹשׁ, *the action of possessing*.

Verbs similiar to the one just cited, where the sign is not an adjunction, belong to the derivative conjugation. It is only a matter of a good dictionary to distinguish them carefully. A grammar suffices to declare their existence.

Passive movement. The initial adjunctiton י, being replaced in this movement by the mother vowel וּ, varies no further, and gives to this conjugation all the strength of the derivative conjugation.

Intensive Form.

This form is little used in this conjugation, for the reason that the positive form itself is only a sort of intensity given to the radical verb by means of the initial adjunction י. When by chance, it is found employed, one sees that this adjunction has taken all the force of a sign and remains with the verb to which it is united

Excitative Form.

The initial adjunction ׳, is replaced in the active movement by the intellectual sign וֹ, and in the passive movement by the convertible sign וּ. This change made, the compound radical verb varies no more, and follows the course of the derivative verbs as it has followed it in the preceding form. If it sometimes happens that this change is not affected as in הֵיטִיב *to do good*, the verb remains none the less indivisible. This changes nothing in its conjugation.

Reflexive Form.

The compound radical verb continues under this new form to demonstrate all the strength of a derivative verb. The only remark, somewhat important, that I have to make, is relative to the three verbs following, which replace their initial adjunction ׳, by the convertible sign וּ, become consonant.

יָרֹעַ	to understand	הִתְוָדֵעַ	to be understood
יָכֹחַ	to prove, to argue	הִתְוָכֵחַ	to be proven
יָסֹר	to correct, to instruct	הִתְוָסָר	to be corrected

CONJUGATIONS

§ IV.
Compound Radical Conjugation
with the Initial Adjunction נ
POSITIVE FORM

ACTIVE MOVEMENT		PASSIVE MOVEMENT	
FACULTATIVE			
CONTINUED		**CONTINUED**	
mas.	נוֹגֵשׁ	*mas.*	נִגָּשׁ
fem.	נוֹגְשָׁה	*fem.*	נִגָּשָׁה
FINISHED			
mas.	נָגוּשׁ	*fem.*	נְגוּשָׁה
NOMINAL VERB			
absol.	נָגוֹשׁ	*absol.*	הִנָּגֵשׁ
constr.	גֶּשֶׁת	*constr.*	

TEMPORAL VERB
FUTURE

		SINGULAR			SINGULAR
1	m. / f.	אֶגֹּשׁ	1	m. / f.	אֶנָּגֵשׁ
2	m.	תִּגֹּשׁ	2	m.	תִּנָּגֵשׁ
	f.	תִּגְּשִׁי		f.	תִּנָּגְשִׁי
3	m.	יִגֹּשׁ	3	m.	יִנָּגֵשׁ
	f.	תִּגֹּשׁ		f.	תִּנָּגֵשׁ

		PLURAL			PLURAL
1	m. / f.	נִגֹּשׁ	1	m. / f.	נִנָּגֵשׁ
2	m.	תִּגְּשׁוּ	2	m.	תִּנָּגְשׁוּ
	f.	תִּגֹּשְׁנָה		f.	תִּנָּגֵשְׁנָה
3	m.	יִגְּשׁוּ	3	m.	יִנָּגְשׁוּ
	f.	תִּגֹּשְׁנָה		f.	תִּנָּגֵשְׁנָה

TRANSITIVE

SING.	2	m.	גֵּשׁ	SING.	2	m.	הַנֵּגֵשׁ
		f.	גְּשִׁי			f.	הַנָּגְשִׁי
PLU.	2	m.	גְּשׁוּ	PLU.	2	m.	הַנָּגְשׁוּ
		f.	גְּשְׁנָה			f.	הַנָּגַשְׁנָה

PAST

SINGULAR	1	m. f.	נָגַשְׁתִּי	SINGULAR	1	m. f.	נִגַּשְׁתִּי
	2	m.	נָגַשְׁתָּ		2	m.	נִגַּשְׁתָּ
		f.	נָגַשְׁתְּ			f.	נִגַּשְׁתְּ
	3	m.	נָגַשׁ		3	m.	נִגַּשׁ
		f.	נָגְשָׁה			f.	נִגְּשָׁה
PLURAL	1	m. f.	נָגַשְׁנוּ	PLURAL	1	m. f.	נִגַּשְׁנוּ
	2	m.	נְגַשְׁתֶּם		2	m.	נִגַּשְׁתֶּם
		f.	נְגַשְׁתֶּן			f.	נִגַּשְׁתֶּן
	3	m. f.	נָגְשׁוּ		3	m. f.	נִגְּשׁוּ

CONJUGATIONS 235

Intensive Form

ACTIVE MOVEMENT	PASSIVE MOVEMENT

FACULTATIVE

CONTINUED

mas.	מְנַגֵּשׁ	*mas.*	מְנֻגָּשׁ
fem.	מְנַגְּשָׁה	*fem.*	מְנֻגָּשָׁה

FINISHED

mas. ....
fem. .... } like the passive

NOMINAL VERB.

absol. } *constr.* }	נַגֵּשׁ	*absol.* } *constr.* }	נַגּוֹשׁ

TEMPORAL VERB

FUTURE

mas. } *fem.* }	אֲנַגֵּשׁ	*mas.* } *fem.* }	אֲנֻגַּשׁ

TRANSITIVE

mas. } *fem.* }	נַגֵּשִׁי	*mas.* .... *fem.* .... } wanting

PAST

mas. } *fem.* }	נִגַּשְׁתִּי	*mas.* } *fem.* }	נֻגַּשְׁתִּי

EXCITATIVE FORM

ACTIVE MOVEMENT   **PASSIVE MOVEMENT**

FACULTATIVE

	CONTINUED		CONTINUED
mas.	מַגִּישׁ	*mas.*	מֻגָּשׁ
fem.	מַגִּישָׁה	*fem.*	מֻגָּשָׁה

FINISHED

mas. . . . .
fem. . . . . } like the passive

NOMINAL VERB

absol.	הַגִּישׁ	*absol.*	הֻגַּשׁ
constr.	הַגֵּשׁ	*constr.*	

TEMPORAL VERB

FUTURE

mas. }	אַגִּישׁ	*mas.* }	אֻגַּשׁ
fem. }		*fem.* }	

TRANSITIVE

mas. }	הִגַּשְׁתִּי	*mas.* }	הֻגַּשְׁתִּי
fem. }		*fem.* }	

PAST

mas.	הַגֵּשׁ	*mas.*	}wanting
fem.	הַגִּישִׁי	*fem.* . . .	

CONJUGATIONS

Reflexive Form

ACTIVE MOVEMENT   **PASSIVE MOVEMENT**

FACULTATIVE

CONTIN. { *mas.* מִתְנַגֵּשׁ
        { *fem.* מִתְנַגְּשָׁה

FINISH. { *mas.*
        { *fem.* ...... } wanting

NOMINAL VERB

absol.
        } הִתְנַגֵּשׁ
constr.

TEMPORAL VERB

FUTURE

mas.
        } אֶתְנַגֵּשׁ
fem.

TRANSITIVE

mas.   הִתְנַגֵּשׁ

fem.   הִתְנַגְּשִׁי

PAST

mas.
        } הִתְנַגַּשְׁתִּי
fem.

REMARKS ON THE COMPOUND RADICAL CONJUGATION.

INITIAL ADJUNCTION נ.

Here is the somewhat difficult etymology of the verb נָגֹוּשׁ, which I give as type, thus following the usage of the Hebraists, from which I never digress without the strongest reasons.

The root גּוּ or גּוּה, offers the general idea of some sort of detachment, destined to contain something in itself, as a sheath; or to pass through, as a channel. This root united to the sign of relative movement, offers in the word גּוּשׁ, the most restrained idea of a local detachment, of a letting go. This detachment being arrested and brought back upon itself by the initial adjunction נ, will signify an approaching, a nearness; and the compound radical verb נָגֹוּשׁ, will express the action of drawing near, of joining, of meeting, of approaching, etc.

POSITIVE FORM.

Active movement. The initial adjunction נ, disappears in the construct nominal, in the future and transitive, as I have already remarked concerning the initial adjuction י; it remains the same in the two facultatives, in the absolute nominal and in the past. I infer that in the original tongue of Moses and before the Chaldaic punctuation had been adopted, it was the sign וּ which was placed between the first and second character of the verbal root, and which read נוּשֶׁת, *the action of approaching,* אֲגוּשׁ *I shall approach,* גוּשׁ *approach.* This mother vowel has been replaced by the point *patah*. A thing which makes this inference very believable, is that one still finds it in several verbs belonging to this conjugation, which preserve this sign in the future, such as יְכֹול *he shall fail,* etc.

CONJUGATIONS 239

It must be observed that in the verb נָקוֹה, *to take, to draw to oneself,* the nominal sometimes takes the character ל in place of the initial adjunction נ, and follows the course of the compound radical conjugation, of which I have given the example; so that one finds very often לָקַח, or קָחַת *the action of taking,* אֶקָּח *I shall take,* קַח *take,* etc.

Passive movement. The Chaldaic punctuation having suppressed the mother vowel, which should characterize this movement, has made it very difficult to distinguish the active movement, especially in the past. It can only be distinguished in this tense by the meaning of the phrase.

INTENSIVE FORM.

This form is but little used. When it is however, it should be observed that the initial adjunction נ, takes the force of a sign and is no longer separated from its verb. It acts in the same manner as the initial adjunction י, of which I have spoken. The compound radical conjugation therefore, does not differ from the derivative conjugation.

EXCITATIVE FORM.

This form is remarkable in both movements, because the adjunctive character נ, disappears wholly and is only supplied by the interior point placed in the first character of the root. It is obvious that in the origin of the Hebraic tongue, the compound radical conjugation differed here from the radical conjugation, only by the interior point of which I have spoken, and that the mother vowel י, was placed between the two radical characters in the active movement; whereas the convertible sign ו, was shown in front of the first radical character in the passive movement. One should say אַגִּישׁ, *I shall make approach;* as one finds הַגִּישׁ *to make approach,* אִוָּגֵשׁ *I shall be excited to approach;* as one finds הִוָּגֵשׁ, *the action of being excited to approach;* but almost invariably the Chaldaic punctuation has replaced these mother vowels by the *hirek* or the *zere,* in the active movement, and by the *kibbuz* in the passive movement.

Reflexive Form

The initial adjunction נ, never being separated from the root, reappearing in this form, gives it the character of a derivative verb.

CONJUGATIONS

§ V.

Compound Radical Conjugation with the Terminative Adjunction

POSITIVE FORM

ACTIVE MOVEMENT   **PASSIVE MOVEMENT**

FACULTATIVE

CONTINUED	CONTINUED
סוֹכֵב	נָסָב
סוֹבְכָה	נְסַבָה

FINISHED

mas.	סָבוּב	*fem.*	סְבוּבָה

NOMINAL VERB

absol.	סוֹב	*absol.*	הִסּוֹב
constr.	סְבוֹב	*constr.*	

TEMPORAL VERB

FUTURE

SINGULAR
- 1 { *m.* / *f.* }   אָסוֹב
- 2 { *m.* }   תָּסוֹב
- 2 { *f.* }   תָּסוֹבִי
- 3 { *m.* }   יָסוֹב
- 3 { *f.* }   תָּסוֹב

SINGULAR
- 1 { *m.* / *f.* }   אֶסַב
- 2 { *m.* }   תִּסַב
- 2 { *f.* }   תִּסְבִי
- 3 { *m.* }   יִסַב
- 3 { *f.* }   תִּסַב

TEMPORAL VERB. FUTURE

PLURAL	1 {m. / f.}	נָסוֹב	PLURAL	1 {m. / f.}	נִסַּב
	2 {m. / f.}	תָּסוֹבּוּ / תְּסֻבֶּינָה		2 {m. / f.}	תִּסַּבּוּ / תִּסַּבֶּינָה
	3 {m. / f.}	יָסֹבּוּ / תְּסֻבֶּינָה		3 {m. / f.}	יִסַּבּוּ / תִּסַּבֶּינָה

TRANSITIVE

SING.	2 {mas. / fem.}	סוֹב / סוֹבִי	SING.	2 {mas. / fem.}	הָסַב / הָסַבִּי
PLU.	2 {mas. / fem.}	סֹבּוּ / סֻבֶּינָה	PLU.	2 {mas. / fem.}	הָסַבּוּ / הֲסֻבֶּינָה

PAST

SINGULAR	1 {m. / f.}	סַבּוֹתִי	SINGULAR	1 {m. / f.}	נְסִבּוֹתִי
	2 {m. / f.}	סַבּוֹתָ / סַבּוֹתְ		2 {m. / f.}	נְסַבּוֹתָ / נְסַבּוֹתְ
	3 {m. / f.}	סַב / סַבָּה		3 {m. / f.}	נָסַב / נָסַבָּה
PLURAL	1 {m. / f.}	סַבּוֹנָה	PLURAL	1 {m. / f.}	נְסִבּוֹנָה
	2 {m. / f.}	סַבּוֹתֶם / סַבּוֹתֶן		2 {m. / f.}	נְסַבּוֹתֶם / נְסַבּוֹתֶן
	3 {m. / f.}	סַבּוּ		3 {m. / f.}	נָסַבּוּ

CONJUGATIONS

INTENSIVE FORM

	ACTIVE MOVEMENT		PASSIVE MOVEMENT

FACULTATIVE

CONTINUED / CONTINUED

	mas.	מְסוֹבֵב	mas.	מְסוֹבָב
	fem.	מְסוֹבְבָה	fem.	מְסוֹבָבָה

FINISHED

mas. .....
fem. ..... } like the passive

NOMINAL VERB

absol.		absol.	
constr. }	סוֹבֵב	constr. }	סוֹבָב

TEMPORAL VERB

FINISHED

mas. }		mas. }	
fem. }	אֲסוֹבֵב	fem. }	אֲסוֹבָב

TRANSITIVE

| mas. | סוֹבֵב | mas. ..... | |
| fem. | סוֹבְבִי | fem. ..... } | wanting |

PAST

mas. }		mas. }	
fem. }	סוֹבַבְתִּי	fem. }	סוֹבַבְתִּי

EXCITATIVE FORM

ACTIVE MOVEMENT		PASSIVE MOVEMENT	

FACULTATIVE

CONTINUED

	ACTIVE		PASSIVE
mas.	מֵסֵב	*mas.*	מוּסָב
fem.	מְסִבָּה	*fem.*	מוּסָבָּה

FINISHED

mas. ......
fem. ...... } like the passive

NOMINAL VERB

| *absol.* } | הָסֵב | *absol.* } | הוּסֵב |
| *constr.* } | | *constr.* } | |

TEMPORAL VERB

FUTURE

| *mas.* } | אָסֵב | *mas.* } | אוּסֵב |
| *fem.* } | | *fem.* } | |

TRANSITIVE

| *mas.* | הָסֵב | *mas.* ...... } | wanting |
| *fem.* | וְסַבִּי | *fem.* ...... } | |

PAST

| *mas.* } | הֲסִבּוֹתִי | *mas.* } | הוּסַבּוֹתִי |
| *fem.* } | | *fem.* } | |

CONJUGATIONS

Reflexive Form

ACTIVE AND PASSIVE MOVEMENT UNITED

FACULTATIVE

CONTIN. { *mas.* מִסְתּוֹבֵב
{ *fem.* מִסְתּוֹבְבָה

FINISH. { *mas.* .... } wanting
{ *fem.* .... }

NOMINAL VERB

absol. } הִסְתּוֹבֵב
constr.

TEMPORAL VERB

FUTURE

mas. } אֶסְתּוֹבֵב
fem.

TRANSITIVE

mas. הִסְתּוֹבֵב
fem. הִסְתּוֹבְכִי

PAST

mas. } הִסְתּוֹבַכְתִּי
fem.

REMARKS ON THE COMPOUND RADICAL CONJUGATION

Terminative Adjunction

This conjugation is, in general, only a modification of the radical conjugation. It seems also that this may be the intensive form represented by the verb קוֹמֵם, for example, which has been given as positive form, so that the following forms may have greater energy.

The root סב, from which is derived the compound radical verb סוֹבֵב, which I give here as type following the Hebraists, being formed from the sign of interior and central action ב, and from the sign of circular movement ס expresses necessarily any kind of movement which operates around a centre. The duplication of the last character ב, in giving more force to the central point, tends to bring back the circumference ס, and consequently to intensify the action of turning, of closing in turning, of enveloping, of *surrounding* in fact, expressed by the verb in question.

Positive Form

Active movement. The final character ב, which has been doubled to form the compound radical verb סוֹבֵב, is only found in the two facultatives. It disappears in all the rest of the conjugation, which is, in substance, only the radical conjugation according to the intensive form, with a few slight differences brought about by the Chaldaic punctuation. The sole mark by which one can distinguish it, is the interior point placed in the second character of the verbal root, to indicate the prolonged accent which resulted no doubt from the double consonant.

Passive movement. This movement experiences a great variation in the vowel point. The facultatives and the nominals are often found marked by the *zere*, as in נָמֵס, *becoming dissolved, falling into dissolution;* הָמֵס

to be dissolved, liquified; הֻחַל to be profaned, divulged; etc. It is necessary in general, to be distrustful of the punctuation and to devote oneself to the meaning.

Intensive Form

This form differs from the intensive radical only in this; that the Chaldaic punctuation has replaced almost uniformly the sign ּו, by the point *holem*. Care must be taken, before giving it a signification, to examine well the final character which is doubled; for it is upon it alone that this signification depends.

Excitative Form

Again here the excitative radical form, (exception being made of the sign י,) is replaced in the active movement by the point *zere*. The passive movement is found a little more characterized by the mother vowel ּו, which one finds added to the verbal root in some persons of the past.

Reflexive Form

The characteristic syllable הת, is simply added to the intensive form, as we have already remarked in the radical conjugation; but here it undergoes metathesis: that is to say, when placed before a verb which begins with the character ס, the ת must be transferred to follow this same character, in the same manner as one sees it in the nominal, where instead of reading הִתְסוֹבֵב one reads הִסְתוֹבֵב.

§ VI.

Irregularities in the Three Conjugations

I have already spoken of the trifling anomalies which are found in verbs beginning with the character א, or ending with the characters נ or ה.

Verbs of the three conjugations can be terminated

with the mother vowels א or ה, and in this case they undergo some variations in their course.

When it is the vowel א, which constitutes the final character of any verb whatever, as in the radical בוא *to come;* the compound ברוא, *to create;* the compound radical יצא, *to appear;* or נשׂא, *to raise;* this vowel becomes ordinarily mute as pronunciation, and is not marked with the Chaldaic point. Nevertheless, as it remains in the different verbal forms, the irregularity which results from its lack of pronunciation is not perceptible, and should be no obstacle to the one who studies Hebrew only to understand and to translate it. The rabbis alone, who still cantillate this extinct tongue, make a particular conjugation of this irregularity.

There is no difficulty for us to know that the radical בוא, *the action of coming,* follows the radical conjugation,

אָבוֹא	I shall come	בָּאתִי	I came
תָּבוֹא	thou wilt come	בָּאתָ	thou camest
יָבוֹא	he will come	בָּא	he came
	etc.		etc.

or that the compound בָּרוֹא, or בָּרֹאת, *the action of creating,* is conjugated in a like manner.

אֶבְרָא or אֶבְרוֹא	I shall create	בָּרָאתִי	I created
תִּבְרָא	thou wilt create	בָּרָאתָ	thou createdst
יִבְרָא	he will create	בָּרָא	he created
	etc.		etc.

But when it is the vowel ה which constitutes the final character of the verb, then the difficulty becomes considerable, for this reason. This vowel not only remains mute, but disappears or is sometimes changed to another vowel; so that it would be impossible to recognize the verb, if one had not a model to which it might be related. Therefore I shall present here this model, taking for type the nominal גלוֹה or גלוֹת, and giving the etymological analysis.

This verb belongs to the root גּ, of which I spoke in the case of the compound radical verb נָגוֹשׁ, and which contains the idea of some sort of detachment. This root, united to the sign of expansive movement ל, expresses as verb, the action of being released from a place, or from a veil, a vestment, a covering; the action of being shown uncovered, revealed, released; being set at liberty; etc.

It must be observed that the greater part of the verbs belonging to the three regular conjugations also receive modifications from what I call the irregular conjugation, according as they are terminated with the character ה, either as radical, derivative or compound radical verbs.

Nevertheless there are some verbs which terminate in this same character ה, (marked with the interior point to distinguish it,) which are regular; that is to say, which follow the derivative conjugation to which they belong. These verbs are the four following:

    נָבֹה   the action of excelling, of surpassing, of exalting

    כָּמֹה   the action of languidly desiring, of languishing

    נָגֹה   the action of emitting, or of reflecting light

    תָּמֹה   the action of being astonished by its *éclat*, of being dazzled.

§ VI.
Irregular Conjugations
Positive Form

	ACTIVE MOVEMENT		PASSIVE MOVEMENT

FACULTATIVE
CONTINUED

mas.	גּוֹלֶה	mas.	נִגְלֶה
fem.	גּוֹלָה	fem.	נִגְלָה

FINISHED

mas. גָּלוּי

fem. גְּלוּיָה

NOMINAL VERB

absol.	נָלוֹה	absol.	הִגָּלוֹה
constr.	גְלוֹת	constr.	הִגָּלוֹת

TEMPORAL VERB
FUTURE

SINGULAR 1 {m./f.}	אֶגְלֶה	SINGULAR 1 {m./f.}	אֶגָּלֶה
2 {m.}	תִּגְלֶה	2 {m.}	תִּגָּלֶה
{f.}	תִּגְלִי	{f.}	תִּגָּלִי
3 {m.}	יִגְלֶה	3 {m.}	יִגָּלֶה
{f.}	תִּגְלֶה	{f.}	תִּגָּלֶה
PLURAL 1 {m./f.}	נִגְלֶה	PLURAL 1 {m./f.}	נִגָּלֶה
2 {m.}	תִּגְלוּ	2 {m.}	תִּגָּלוּ
{f.}	תִּגְלֶינָה	{f.}	תִּגָּלֶינָה
3 {m.}	יִגְלוּ	3 {m.}	יִגָּלוּ
{f.}	תִּגְלֶינָה	{f.}	תִּגָּלֶינָה

CONJUGATIONS

TRANSITIVE

SING. 2	mas.	גְּלֵה	SING. 2	mas.	הַגְלֵה
	fem.	גְּלִי		fem.	הַגְלִי
PLU. 2	mas.	גְּלוּ		mas.	הַגְלוּ
	fem.	גְּלֶינָה		fem.	הַגְלֶינָה

PAST

SINGULAR	1 {m. / f.}	גָּלִיתִי	SINGULAR	1 {m. / f.}	נִגְלֵיתִי
	2 {m.}	גָּלִיתָ		2 {m.}	נִגְלֵיתָ
	{f.}	גָּלִית		{f.}	נִגְלֵית
	3 {m.}	גָּלָה		3 {m.}	נִגְלָה
	{f.}	גָּלְתָה		{f.}	נִגְלְתָה
PLURAL	1 {m. / f.}	גָּלִינוּ	PLURAL	1 {m. / f.}	נִגְלֵינוּ
	2 {m.}	גְּלִיתֶם		2 {m.}	נִגְלֵיתֶם
	{f.}	גְּלִיתֶן		{f.}	נִגְלֵיתֶן
	3 {m. / f.}	גָּלוּ		3 {m. / f.}	נִגְלוּ

INTENSIVE FORM

ACTIVE MOVEMENT		PASSIVE MOVEMENT	

FACULTATIVE

CONTINUED

	ACTIVE		PASSIVE
mas.	מְגַלֶּה	*mas.*	מְגֻלֶּה
fem.	מְגַלָּה	*fem.*	מְגֻלָּה

FINISHED

mas. ..... }
fem. ..... } like the passive

NOMINAL VERB

| *absol.* | גַּלֵּה | *absol.* | גֻּלֵּה |
| *constr.* | גַּלּוֹה | *constr.* | גֻּלּוֹת |

TEMPORAL VERB

FUTURE

| *mas.* } | | *mas.* } | |
| *fem.* } | אֲגַלֶּה | *fem.* } | אֲגֻלֶּה |

TRANSITIVE

| *mas.* | גַּלֵּה | *mas.* ..... } | |
| *fem.* | גַּלִּי | *fem.* ..... } wanting |

PAST

| *mas.* } | | *mas.* } | |
| *fem.* } | גִּלִּיתִי | *fem.* } | גֻּלֵּיתִי |

CONJUGATIONS

Excitative Form

ACTIVE MOVEMENT   **PASSIVE MOVEMENT**

FACULTATIVE

CONTINUED   **CONTINUED**

mas. מַגְלֶה   *mas.* מָגְלֶה
fem. מִגְלָה   *fem.* מָגְלָה

FINISHED

$\left.\begin{array}{l}mas.\ldots\ldots\\fem.\ldots\ldots\end{array}\right\}$ like the passive

NOMINAL VERB

absol. הַגְלֵה   *absol.* הָגְלֵה
constr. הַגְלוֹת   *constr.* הָגְלוֹת

TEMPORAL VERB

FUTURE

$\left.\begin{array}{l}mas.\\fem.\end{array}\right\}$ אַגְלֶה $\left.\begin{array}{l}mas.\\fem.\end{array}\right\}$ אָגְלֶה

TRANSITIVE

mas. הַגְלֵה $\left.\begin{array}{l}mas.\ldots\ldots\\fem.\ldots\ldots\end{array}\right\}$ wanting
fem. הַגְלִי

PAST

$\left.\begin{array}{l}mas.\\fem.\end{array}\right\}$ הִגְלֵיתִי $\left.\begin{array}{l}mas.\\fem.\end{array}\right\}$ הָגְלֵיתִי

REFLEXIVE FORM

ACTIVE AND PASSIVE MOVEMENT UNITED

FACULTATIVE

CONTIN. { mas. מִתְגַּלֶּה
{ fem. מִתְגַּלָּה

FINISH. { mas. .... } wanting
{ fem. .... }

NOMINAL VERB

absol. } הִתְגַּלּוֹת
constr. }

TEMPORAL VERB

FUTURE

mas. } אֶתְגַּלֶּה
fem. }

TRANSITIVE

mas. } הִתְגַּלֵּה
fem. } הִתְגַּלִּי

PAST

mas. } הִתְגַּלֵּיתִי
fem. }

CHAPTER X.

CONSTRUCTION OF VERBS: ADVERBIAL RELATIONS: PARAGOGIC CHARACTERS: CONCLUSION

§ I.

UNION OF VERBS WITH VERBAL AFFIXES

I call the Construction of Verbs, their union with the verbal affixes. I have already shown the manner in which the nominal affixes are united to nouns. It remains for me to indicate here the laws which follow the verbal affixes when united to verbs.

These laws, if we omit the petty variations of the vowel points, can be reduced to this sole rule, namely; every time that any verbal modification whatsoever, receives an affix, it receives it by being constructed with it: that is to say, that if this modification, whatever it may be, has a construct, it employs it in this case.

Now let us glance rapidly over all the verbal modifications according to the rank that they occupy in the table of conjugations.

FACULTATIVES

The facultatives belong to nouns with which they form a distinct class. When they receive the verbal affix it is after the manner of nouns.

פּוֹקְרֵנִי	visiting	me	(him)
פּוֹקְדֵי	"	"	(them, *m.*)
פּוֹקְרָתִי	"	"	(her)
פּוֹקְדוֹתִי	"	"	(them, *f.*)
פּוֹקְרֵנוּ	"	"	(him)
פּוֹקְדֵינוּ	"	"	(them, *m.*)
פּוֹקְרָתְנוּ	"	"	(her)
פּוֹקְדוֹתֵינוּ	"	"	(them, *f.*)

Those facultatives of the irregular conjugation which terminate in the character ה, lose it in the construct state.

עֹשֵׂנִי making me (him)

רֹאִי or רֹאָנִי seeing me (him)

מְלַמֶּדְךָ teaching thee (him)

רֹדֵם domineering them, *m.* (him)

רֹדֵן . " them, *f.* (him)

מְלַמְּדִי teaching me (them)

Nominal Verb

I have already given the nominal verb united to the nominal and verbal affixes. I have been careful, in giving the table of the different conjugations, to indicate always the nominal construct, when this construct is distinguished from the absolute nominal. So that one might with a little attention recognize easily any verb whatsoever, by the nominal when it has the affix. Here are, besides, some examples to fix the ideas in this respect and to accustom the reader to the varieties of the punctuation.

קוֹמִי or קָמִי the action of establishing myself; my establishment

תֻּמִּי the action of perfecting myself; my perfection

שׁוּבֵנִי the action of restoring myself; my return, resurrection

פָּקְדִי the action of visiting myself; of examining myself; my examination

הִפָּקְדוֹ the action of being visited by another; his visit

פַּקְדֵנִי the action of visiting myself, of inspecting myself diligently

CONSTRUCTION OF VERBS

הַפְּקִידָהּ   the action of making her visit, of arousing her to visit

שִׁבְתּוֹ   the action of occupying, of inhabiting, of dwelling

לְדִתָּהּ   the action of bringing forth (*fem*)

גִּשְׁתְּךָ   the action of thy approaching (*mas*); thy approach

תִּתִּי   the action of giving myself

The emphatic article ה, when added to a nominal, is changed to ת, following the rules of the construct state.

אַהֲבָתוֹ   the action of loving him greatly

קִרְבָתָם   the action of pressing them closely

מָשְׁחָתִי   the action of consecrating me, of anointing me with holy oil

The irregular conjugation loses sometimes the character ה but more often changes it to ת.

TEMPORAL VERB

FUTURE

The sign וֹ which is in the greater part of the verbal modifications of the future, is lost in the construct state. The final character does not change in the three regular conjugations. I shall now present in its entirety, one of the persons of the future, united to the verbal affixes, taking my example from the derivative conjugation as the most used.

SINGULAR AFFIXES	mas.	יִפְקְדֵנִי	he will visit me
	fem.	יִפְקְדִי	
	mas.	יִפְקָדְךָ	he will visit thee
	fem.	יִפְקְדֵךְ	
	mas.	יִפְקְדֵנוּ or יִפְקְדוֹ	he will visit him
	fem.	יִפְקְדֶנָּה or יִפְקְדָהּ	he will visit her
PLURAL AFFIXES	mas.	יִפְקְדֵנוּ	he will visit us
	fem.		
	mas.	יִפְקָדְכֶם	he will visit you
	fem.	יִפְקָדְכֶן	
	mas.	יִפְקְדֵם	he will visit them
	fem.	יִפְקְדֵן	

It must be observed that the affix וֹ is changed quite frequently to הוּ, and usually one finds יִפְקְדֵהוּ instead of יִפְקְדֵנוּ or יִפְקְדוֹ.

In the irregular conjugation, the temporal modifications of the future which terminate in the character ה, lose this character in being constructed. Here are some examples, in which I have compared designedly these irregularities and some others of little importance.

CONSTRUCTION OF VERBS

יְסֻבֶּנּוּ	he will surround him
תְּסוּבְכֵנִי	thou wilt surround me
תְּקִמֵנִי	thou wilt establish me
יִרְאַנִי	he will see me
יֶאֱהָבַנִי	he will love me
יְשַׁבִּיעֵנִי	he will crown me with blessings
יַבְדִּילֵנִי	he will separate me with care
יְסִבֵּנוּ	he will make us surrounded
יְבָרְכֶנְהוּ	he will bless him fervently
יִרְאָנוּ	he will see us
תִּרְאַנִי	she will see me
יְכֹנְנוּ	he will fashion us
יוֹשִׁיבֵנוּ	he will make me dwell
אֲבָרְכֵם	I will bless them

TRANSITIVE

The transitive modifications are very similar to those of the future: that is to say that the verbal sign וֹ disappears in the construct state. The final character remains mute.

פָּקְדֵנִי	visit me (mas.)	פָּקְדֵנוּ	visit us
פִּקְדִינִי	visit me (fem.)	שְׁאָלוּנוּ	ask us
שְׁמָעֵנִי	hear me	תְּנֵם	give them
שַׂמְּחֵנִי	gladden me well	דָּעֵן	know them
חָנֵּנִי	accord me grace	הֲקִימֵנוּ	make us established
נְחֵנִי	lead me	קַבְּצֵנוּ	gather us
קָבְנוּ	curse him	חָקְרֵם	consider them

Past

In the temporal modifications of **the past**, **the first** person singular and plural, the second and third person masculine singular, and the third person of the plural, change only the vowel point in being constructed with the affixes: but the second and third person of the feminine singular, and the second of the masculine and feminine plural, change the final character; as:

			absol.	*constr.*	
SINGULAR	1	mas. fem.	פָּקַדְתִּי	פָּקַדְתִּי	I visited
	2	mas.	פָּקַדְתָּ	פָּקַדְתְּ	thou "
		fem.	פָּקַדְתְּ	פָּקַדְתִּי	
	3	mas.	פָּקַד	פָּקַד	he "
		fem.	פָּקְדָה	פָּקְדָת	she "
PLURAL	1	mas. fem.	פָּקַדְנוּ	פָּקַדְנוּ	we "
	2	mas.	פְּקַדְתֶּם	פְּקַדְתּוּ	you "
		fem.	פְּקַדְתֶּן		
	3	mas. fem.	פָּקְדוּ	פָּקְדוּ	they "

with affix

פְּקַדְתִּיךָ	I visited thee	פְּקָדַתוֹ	she visited him
פְּקַדְתַּנִי פְּקַדְתִּינִי	thou " me	פְּקַדְנוּם	we " them
		פְּקַדְתּוּנִי	you " us
פְּקָדָהּ	he " her	פְּקָדוּן	they " them

CONSTRUCTION OF VERBS 261

It is needless for me to dwell upon each of these modifications in particular. I shall conclude by giving some examples taken from different forms and from different conjugations.

פְּקָרוֹ	he visited him diligently
אֲרָרָהּ	he cursed her violently
גִּלְנַּלְתִּיךָ	I encircled thee well
צִוִּיתִיךָ	I confirm thee much
הוֹרַדְתֵּנוּ	thou madest us descend
הֶעֱלִיתָנוּ	thou madest us rise
הֵפִיצְךָ	he made himself scattered
הוֹדְעָךְ	he made himself known
הֲדַמָּנוּ	he made us silent
הֱשִׁיבוּם	he made them return
שָׂמְךָ	he placed thee
שָׂמַתְהוּ	she placed him
שָׂמוּךָ	they were placed
קְרָאוֹ	he called him
עָשָׂהוּ	he made him
גְּלִיתוֹ	thou revealedst him
יְכָלְתִּיו	I subdued him
מְצָאתָהּ	thou foundedst her
שׁוֹבְכָתֶךָ	she perverted thee
הֲזִיתִיךָ	I perceived thee

etc.

§ II.

ADVERBIAL RELATIONS

In Chapter IV of this Grammar, I have stated that the Relation ought to be considered under three connections, according to the part of speech with which it preserves the most analogy. I have called *designative relation*, that which appears to me to belong most expressly to the sign, and I have treated it under the name of *article:* I have then named *nominal relation*, that which has appeared to me to replace more especially the noun and to act in its absence, and I have called it *pronoun:* now this latter is what I qualify by the name of *adverbial relation*, because it seems to form a sort of bond between the noun and the verb, and without being either the one or the other, to participate equally in both. I shall treat of this last kind of relation under the name of *adverb*.

I beg my reader to remember that I do not confound the adverb with the modificative. The latter modifies the verbal action and gives it the colour of the noun by means of the qualificative: the adverb directs it and indicates its use. Thus, *gently, strongly, obediently* are modificatives; they indicate that the action is done in a manner, gentle, strong, obedient: *above, below, before, after,* are adverbs: they show the direction of the action relative to things, persons, time, place, number or measure.

When the modern grammarians have said, in speaking of adverbs such as those just cited, that they were *indeclinable*, I fear that following Latin forms, they may be mistaken in this as in many other things. I know well that the designative relation, for example, the article which inflects the noun, could not be inflected, unless there existed a new article for this use; I know well that the modificative could not be inflected either, since it contains an implied action which can only be developed by the verb; but I also know that an adverbial relation, a veritable relation becoming a noun by a simple deduction of thought, must be subject to inflection. I can go

ADVERBIAL RELATIONS

further. I say that a designative relation, an article, if it is made absolute, will experience a sort of inflection. Consider the adverbs *below, above, before, after, today, tomorrow*, etc., all these are capable of being inflected to a certain point. Does not one say: *bring that from below above;* place yourself *before;* speak only *after your opinion;* consider the usages *of today;* think *of tomorrow,* etc., etc.?

Nearly all the adverbial relations of the Hebraic tongue receive the articles and lend themselves to their movements. Many even have number and gender, as can be noticed among those here cited.

ADVERBS OF PLACE

אִי : אַיֵה :	where? where
אֵיפֹה : אֵיפוֹא :	where? wherein
פֹא : פֹה :	here, in this place
שָׁם :	there, in that place
מִפֹּו : מִפֹּה : מִשָּׁם :	hence, whence
חוּץ :	outside
מִבַּיִת : בְּתוֹךְ :	inside, within
עֵבֶר : מֵעֵבֶר :	beyond
בֵּין : בֵּינַיִם :	between, among
עַל : מַעְלָה :	upon, on high
פְּנֵי : פָּנִים : לִפְנֵי :	in front of, facing
מַטָּה :	down, beneath
תַּחַת : מִתַּחַת :	below, from under
אַחַר : אַחֲרֵי :	after, behind
סָבִיב :	round about
הָלְאָה :	afar off *etc.*

Of Time

מָתַי : עַד־מָה :	when, how long
עַד :	until
אָז : אֲזַי :	then
עַתָּה :	now
עוֹד :	again
תָּמִיד :	continually
טֶרֶם :	before
יוֹמָם :	today
מָחָר : תְּמוֹל :	tomorrow, yesterday
מִלְּפָנִים	from before
מְהֵרָה :	quickly
	etc.

Of Number

אַף־כִּי :	how much more?	שֵׁשׁ :	six
אֶחָד :	one, first	שֶׁבַע :	seven
שְׁנֵי : שְׁנַיִם :	two, second	שְׁמֹנָה :	eight
שָׁלֹשׁ :	three	תֵּשַׁע :	nine
אַרְבַּע :	four	עֶשֶׂר :	ten
חָמֵשׁ :	five		*etc.*

Of Measure

אֵיךְ :	how?	מְאֹד :	very much
כֵּן : אָכֵן :	thus	שָׁוְא :	in vain
רַב :	enough	בְּלִי : מִבְּלִי :	nothing
מְעַט :	a little		*etc.*

ADVERBIAL RELATIONS

AFFIRMATIVE ADVERBS

אָמְנָם : אָמֵן amen, verily   אַךְ : wholly

כֵן : כֹה : thus, so   *etc.*

SUSPENSIVE AND INTERROGATIVE

אוּלַי : perhaps   אִם : הַאִם: is it?

לָמָה : why   פֶּן : lest

לְמִן : because   מַדּוּעַ : therefore

לְמַעַן : on account of   *etc.*

NEGATIVES

אַל : not, no more   אַיִן : אֵינִי : nothing

לֹא : no, not   רֵיקָם : empty

בַּל : בְּלֹא : no, not   *etc.*

It is easy to see in glancing through these adverbial relations that their purpose is, as I have said, to show the employment of the action, its direction, its measure, its presence or its absence; and not to modify it. The action is modified by the modificative nouns. In the tongues where few nouns exist as in Hebrew for example, then the verbal form assists. This form which I have called intensive, lends itself to the intention of the writer, receives the movement of the sentence and gives to the verb the colour of the circumstance. This is what an intelligent translator ought never to lose sight of in the idioms of the Orient.

The reader who follows with close attention the progress of my grammatical ideas, should perceive that after having traversed the circle of the developments of speech, under the different modifications of the noun and the verb, we return to the sign from which we started: for the adverbial relation with which we are at the moment occupied, differs little from the designative relation and even mingles with it in many common expressions. I have already indicated this analogy, so that one can observe, when the time comes, the point where the circle of speech returning to itself, unites its elements.

This point merits attention. It exists between the affirmative and negative adverb; between *yes* and *no*, אך and אל or כה and לא: the substance and the verb: it can have nothing beyond. Whoever would reflect well upon the force of these two expressions, would see that they contain not alone the essence of speech but that of the universe, and that it is only by affirming or denying, wishing or not wishing, passing from nothingness to being or from being to nothingness, that the sign is modified, that speech is born, that intelligence is unfolded, that nature, that the universe moves toward its eternal goal.

I shall not dwell upon such speculations. I feel that to limit every tongue to two elementary expressions, would be too great a boldness in the state of our present grammatical knowledge. The mind encumbered with a multitude of words would hardly conceive a truth of this nature and would vainly attempt to bring back to elements so simple, a thing which appears to it so complicated.

But it can, however, be understood that the adverbial affirmation exists by itself in an absolute, independent manner, contained in the verb whose essence it constitutes: for every verb is affirmative: the negation is only its absence or its opposition. This is why, in any tongue whatsoever, to announce a verb is to affirm: to destroy it is to deny.

Sometimes without entirely destroying the verb one suspends the effect: then he interrogates. The Hebrew possesses two adverbial relations to illustrate this modification of speech: אם and האם: it could be rendered by *is it?* but its usage is quite rare. The interrogation appears to have occurred most commonly in the tongue of Moses, as it still occurs among most of the meridional peoples: that is to say, by means of the accent of the voice.

ADVERBIAL RELATIONS

It indicates the meaning of the phrase. Sometimes, as I have said, the determinative article ה, takes an interrogative force.

The negation is expressed by means of the many adverbial relations that I have already given. Those most in use are לֹא and אֵין. The former expresses cessation, opposition, defense: the latter, absence and nothingness. These merit very particular attention.

Besides, all the adverbial relations without exception, are connected with the nominal and verbal affixes, and often form with them ellipses of great force. I am about to give some of these Hebraisms interpreting word-for-word when necessary.

אַיּוֹ ׃ אַיָּם ׃	where-of-him? where-of-them? (where is he, where are they?)
אַחֲרֶיךָ ׃	behind-thee
תַּחְתִּי ׃	under me (in my power)
בֵּינֵינוּ ׃ וּבֵינֶיךָ ׃ בֵּינַיִם ׃	between us and between thee: between them
לְפָנַי ׃ לְפָנֶיךָ ׃ לְפָנֵינוּ ׃	before me, before thee, before us
בַעֲדִי ׃ בַּעַדְכֶם ׃ בַּעֲדֵיהֶם ׃	around me, around you, around them
עוֹדֵינוּ ׃ הַעוֹדָם ׃	again us (we are again) what! again them? (are they again?)
אִישׁ־הַבֵּנַיִם ׃	a man between (wavering between two parts)
אֶל־בֵּינוֹת ׃ לַגַּלְגַּל ׃	toward the midst of the deep (toward the centre of ethereal spaces, of celestial spheres, of worlds)

INTERROGATION

מַה הוּא־לָהּ׃	what him-to her? (what did he say to her?)
מַה חַטָּאתִי׃	what sin—mine? (what is my sin?)
אֶת־שׁוֹר מִי לָקַחְתִּי׃	of whom the ox I have taken? (whose is the ox that I have taken?
בִּשְׁאוֹל מִי יוֹרֶה־לָךְ׃	in Sheol who will point out to thee? (who will show thee?)
וּבֶן־אָדָם כִּי תִפְקְדֶנּוּ׃	and-the-son-of Adam thus shalt thou - visit - him? (shalt thou visit him thus, the son of Adam?)
מִי אָדוֹן לָנוּ׃	who is the Lord of us?
אֶשָּׂא עֵינַי אֶל־הֶהָרִים׃	shall I lift mine eyes unto these hills?
מֵאַיִן יָבוֹא עֶזְרִי׃	whence will come help to me?
אִם עֲוֹנוֹת תִּשְׁמָר־יָהּ׃	dost thou consider the iniquities, Jah!

NEGATION

אַל־תּוֹסֵף׃	thou shalt add no more
אַל־תָּצַר׃	thou shalt act no more vindictively
אַל־יֵרָא׃	he shall not see

ADVERBIAL RELATIONS

צִוִּיתִיךָ לְבִלְתִּי אֲכָל׃	I commanded thee not to eat
בִּבְלִי אֲשֶׁר׃ עַל־בְּלִי׃	of nothing which... because not
לֹא מָצָא עֵזֶר׃	he found no help
לֹא־יִהְיֶה לְךָ אֱלֹהִים אֲחֵרִים׃	not shall-there-be-for-thee other Gods (there shall exist no other Gods for thee.)
לֹא תַעֲשֶׂה לְךָ פֶסֶל׃	thou shalt not make for thee any image
וְלֹא־יִהְיֶה עוֹד הַמַּיִם לְמַבּוּל׃	and-there shall not be again the waters of deluge. (the waters of deluge shall no more be raised)
לְבִלְתִּי הַכּוֹת אֹתוֹ׃	not to wound him
לֹא יָדַעְתִּי׃	I knew it not
וְאֵינֶנּוּ׃	and he is not
וְאֵינְךָ׃ וְאֵינֵימוֹ׃	and thou art not: and they are not
אֵין־יֵשׁ־רוּחַ בְּפִיהֶם׃	nothing being spirit in the-mouth-to-them (there was nothing spiritual in their mouth)
כִּי־אֵין הַמֶּלֶךְ יוּכַל אֶתְכֶם דָּבָר׃	for nothing of the king being able with you thing. (for there is nothing of the king which may be something with you)
וְאֵין רוֹאֶה וְאֵין יוֹדֵעַ וְאֵין מֵקִיץ׃	and nothing seeing, and nothing knowing and nothing watching (he saw and he knew and he watched nothing)

כִּי אֵין בַּמָּוֶת זִכְרֶךָ:	for nothing in death to remember thee (there is no memory in death of thou who survives)
יְהֹוָה אַל־בְּאַפְּךָ תוֹכִיחֵנִי׃	Yahweh no more in the wrath thine shalt thou chastise me (chastise me no more in thy wrath)

---

§ III.

Paragogic Characters

The thinkers of the last centuries in their innumerable labours concerning the tongue of the Hebrews, many of which are not without merit, must have seen that the Hebraic characters had nearly all an intrinsic value, which gave force to the words to which they were added. Although the majority of these savants were very far from going back to the origin of the sign, and although nearly all of them discerned that the meaning attached to these characters was arbitrary, they could nevertheless, detect it. Some, considering more particularly those characters which appear at the beginning or the end of words to modify the signification, have chosen six: א, ה, י, מ, נ and ת: and taking the sound which results from their union, have designated them by the barbarous name of *héémanthes*. Others, selecting only those which chance appears to insert in certain words or to add them without evident reason, have named them *paragogics;* that is to say, *happened*. These characters, likewise six in number are: א, ה, י, ו, נ and ת. The only difference which exists between the *héémanthes* and the *paragogics*, is in the latter, where the vowel ו is substituted for the consonant מ.

I might omit further discussion of these characters since I have already considered them under the relation of signs; but in order to leave nothing to be desired, I shall state concisely what the Hebraists have thought of them.

א In considering this character as belonging to the *héémanthes*, the Hebraists have seen that it expressed force, stability, duration of substance, denomination. As *paragogic*, they have taught that it was found without motives, added to certain verbal tenses which terminate in ו, as in the following examples:

הָלְכוּא they went   נָשׂוּא they raised

בוּא they wished   etc.

This addition is a sort of redundancy in imitation of the Arabs. It expresses the force and duration of the action.

ה Whether this character is ranked among the *héémanthes*, or among the *paragogics* it is useless for me to add anything more to what I have said, either as sign, or as determinative or emphatic article. We know now that it can begin or terminate all kinds of words, nouns, verbs or relations.

ו It is not a question here of its astonishing power of changing the temporal modifications of the verbs, by carrying to the past those which are of the future, and to the future those which are of the past. When the Hebraists called it *paragogic*, they considered it simply as added to certain words without other reasons than of joining them together.

וְחַיְתוֹ־אֶרֶץ: the terrestrial animality (the animal kingdom)

בְּנוֹ־בְעוֹר: the son of Beor

לְמַעְיְנוֹ־מָיִם: the source of the waters

' The Hebraists who have considered this character as *héémanthe*, have attributed to it the same qualities as the vowel א, but more moral and bearing more upon mind than upon matter. Those who have treated it as *paragogic* have said that it was found sometimes inserted in words and oftener placed at the end, particularly in the feminine. They have not given the cause of this insertion or this addition, which results very certainly from the faculty that

PARAGOGIC CHARACTERS

it has as sign, of expressing the manifestation and the imminence of actions. For example:

לִדְרוֹשׁ׃ with a view to being informed, being instructed; to inquire

תֵּעָשֶׂה׃ מִיָּאתִי׃ it will be done without interruption: by myself, openly

רַבָּתִיעָם׃ הַחֵצִי׃ an immense crowd of people: a swift arrow

מְקִימִי׃ establishing him with glory

אֹיְבְתִי׃ hostile with boldness

מ This character placed among the *hééманthes* by the Hebraists is found equally at the beginning and the end of words. When it is at the beginning it becomes, according to them, local and instrumental; it forms the names of actions, passions and objects. When it is at the end it expresses that which is collective, comprehensive, generic, or more intense and more assured. It is very singular that with these ideas, these savants have been able so often to misunderstand this sign whose usage is so frequent in the tongue of Moses. What has caused their error is the readiness with which they have confused it with the verbal affix מ. I shall produce in my notes upon the Cosmogony of Moses, several examples wherein this confusion has caused the strangest mistranslation. Here for instance, are some examples without comment.

אָמְנָם׃ a truth universal; a faith immutable

יוֹמָם׃ שָׁמָם׃ all the day; a name collective, generic, universal

אֹתָם׃ the whole; the collective self-sameness; the ipseity

עוֹלָם׃ the universality of time, space, duration, ages

נָחָם׃ he ceased entirely; he rested wholly

בְּשֻׁנָּם׃ in the general action of declining, of being lost

מָשְׁחִיתָם׃ to degrade, to destroy, to ruin entirely

נ Among the *héémanthes*, this character expresses either passive action and turns back to itself when it appears at the beginning of words; or, unfoldment and augmentation when it is placed at the end. Among the *paragogics*. it is added without reason, say the Hebraists, to the verbal modifications terminated by the vowels ו or י: or is inserted in certain words to soften the pronunciation. It is evident that even in this case it retains its character as can be judged by the following examples.

יָדְעוּן׃ they knew at full length
תַּעֲשִׂין׃ thou shalt do without neglecting
לִתִּתֵּן׃ so as to give generously
יְסֹבְבֶנְהוּ׃ he surrounded it well
יִצְּרֶנְהוּ׃ he closed it carefully
יֶשְׁנוֹ׃ behold his manner of being (his being)
יָגוֹן׃ torment of the soul, sorrow, entire disorganization
זִכְרוֹן׃ steadfast remembrance, very extended
בִּצָּרוֹן׃ well-stored provisions

ת The Hebraists who have included this character among the *héémanthes,* have attributed to it the property that it has as sign, of expressing the continuity of things and their reciprocity. Those who have made it a *paragogic* have only remarked the great propensity that it has for being substituted for the character ה; propensity of which I have spoken sufficiently. Here are some examples relative to its reciprocity as sign:

תּוּגָה׃ reciprocal sorrow
תְּנוּאָה׃ mutual estrangement, aversion
תָּאַב׃ he desired mutually and continually
תְּנוּמָה׃ sympathetic sleep
תַּגְמוּל׃ mutual retribution, contribution

§ IV.

Conclusion.

This is about all that the vulgar Hebraists have understood of the effects of the sign. Their knowledge would have been greater if they had known how to apply it. But I do not see one who has done so. It is true that in the difficulties which they found in the triliteral and dissyllabic roots, they applied, with a sort of devotion to the Hebraic tongue, this application which already very difficult in itself, obtained no results.

I venture to entertain the hope that the reader who has followed me with consistent attention, having reached this point in my Grammar, will no longer see in the tongues of men so many arbitrary institutions, and in speech, a fortuitous production due to the mechanism of the organs alone. Nothing arbitrary, nothing fortuitous moves with this regularity, or is developed with this constancy. It is very true that without organs man would not speak; but the principle of speech exists none the less independently, ever ready to be modified when the organs are suspectible of this modification. Both the principle and the organs are equally given, but the former, exists immutable, eternal, in the divine essence; the latter, more or less perfect according to the temporal state of the substance from which they are drawn, present to this principle, points of concentration more or less homogeneous and reflect it with more or less purity. Thus the light strikes the crystal which is to receive it and is refracted with an energy analogous to the polish of its surface. The purer the crystal the more brilliant it appears. A surface unpolished, sullied or blackened, gives only an uncertain dull reflection or none at all. The light remains immutable although its refracted rays may be infinitely varied. In this manner is the principle of speech developed. Ever the same *au fond*, it indicates nevertheless, in its effects the organic state of man. The more this state acquires perfection, and it acquires it unceasingly, the more speech gives facility to display its beauties.

According as the centuries advance, everything advances toward its perfection. Tongues experience in this respect, the vicissitudes of all things. Dependent upon the organs as to form, they are independent as to principle. Now this principle tends toward the unity from which it emanates. The multiplicity of idioms is a reflection upon the imperfection of the organs since it is opposed to this unity. If man were perfect, if his organs had acquired all the perfection of which they were susceptible, one single tongue would extend and be spoken from one extremity of the earth to the other.

I feel that this idea, quite true as it is, will appear paradoxical; but I cannot reject the truth.

From the several simple tongues I have chosen the Hebrew to follow its developments and make them perceived. I have endeavoured to reveal the material of this ancient idiom, and to show that my principal aim has been to make its genius understood and to induce the reader to apply this same genius to other studies; for the sign upon which I have raised my grammatical edifice is the unique basis upon which repose all the tongues of the world.

The sign comes directly from the eternal principle of speech, emanated from the Divinity, and if it is not presented everywhere under the same form and with the same attributes, it is because the organs, charged with producing it exteriorly, not only are not the same among all peoples, in all ages and under all climates, but also because they receive an impulse which the human mind modifies according to its temporal state.

The sign is limited to the simple inflections of the voice. There are as many signs possible as inflections. These inflections are few in number. The people who have distinguished them from their different combinations, representing them by characters susceptible of being linked together, as one sees it in the literal alphabet which we possess, have hastened the perfecting of the language with respect to the exterior forms; those who, blending them with these same combinations have applied them to an indefinite series of compound characters, as one sees among the Chinese, have perfected its interior images. The Egyptians who possessed at once the literal sign and the hieroglyphic combination, became, as they certainly were in the temporal state of things, the most enlightened people of the world.

The different combinations of signs constitute the roots. All roots are monosyllabic. Their number is limited; for it can never be raised beyond the combinations possible between two consonant signs and one vocal at the most. In their origin they presented only a vague and generic idea applied to all things of the same form, of the same species, of the same nature. It is always by a restriction of thought that they are particularized. Plato who considered general ideas as preëxistent, anterior to particular ideas, was right even in reference to the formation of the words which express them. Vegetation is conceived before the vegetable, the vegetable before the tree, the tree before the oak, the oak before all the particular kinds. One sees animality before the animal, the animal before the quadruped, the quadruped before the wolf, the wolf before the fox or the dog and their diverse races.

At the very moment when the sign produces the root, it produces also the relation.

Particular ideas which are distinguished from general ideas, are assembled about the primitive roots which thenceforth become idiomatic, receive the modifications of the sign, combine together and form that mass of words which the different idioms possess.

Nevertheless the unique verb until then implied, appropriates a form analogous to its essence and appears in speech. At this epoch a brilliant revolution takes place in speech. As soon as the mind of man feels it, he is penetrated by it. The substance is illumined. The verbal life circulates. Thousands of nouns which it animates become particular verbs.

Thus speech is divided into substance and verb. The substance is distinguished by gender and by number, by quality and by movement. The verb is subject to movement and form, tense and person. It expresses the different affections of the will. The sign, which transmits all its force to the relation, binds these two parts of speech, directs them in their movements and constructs them.

Afterward all depends upon the temporal state of things. At first a thousand idioms prevail in a thousand places on the earth. All have their local physiognomy. All have their particular genius. But nature obeying the unique impulse which it receives from the Being of beings, moves on to unity. Peoples, pushed toward one another like waves of the ocean, rush and mingle together, losing the identity of their natal idiom. A tongue more extended is formed. This tongue becomes enriched, is coloured and propagated. The sounds become softened by contact and use. The expressions are numerous, elegant, forceful. Thought is developed with facility. Genius finds a docile instrument. But one, two or three rival tongues are equally formed; the movement which leads to unity continues. Only, instead of some weak tribes clashing, there are entire nations whose waves now surge, spreading from the north to the south and from the Orient to the Occident. Tongues are broken like political existences. Their fusion takes place. Upon their common *débris* rise other nations and other tongues more and more extended, until at last one sole nation prevails whose tongue enriched by all the discoveries of the past ages, child and just inheritor of all the idioms of the world, is propagated more and more, and takes possession of the earth.

O France! O my Country! art thou destined to so great glory? Thy tongue, sacred to all men, has it received from heaven enough force to bring them back to unity of Speech? It is the secret of Providence.

PREFATORY NOTE

After all that I have said in my Grammar, both concerning the force of the sign and the manner in which it gives rise to the root, there remains but little to be added. The strongest argument that I can give in favour of the truths that I have announced upon this subject, is undoubtedly the Vocabulary which now follows. I venture to say that the attentive and wisely impartial reader will see with an astonishment mingled with pleasure, some four or five hundred primitive roots, all monosyllables resulting easily from the twenty-two signs, by twos, according to their vocal or consonantal nature, developing all universal and productive ideas and presenting a means of composition as simple as inexhaustible. For as I have already said, and as I shall often prove in my notes, there exists not a single word of more than one syllable, which is not a compound derived from a primitive root. either by the amalgamation of a mother vowel, the adjunction of one or several signs, the union of the roots themselves, the fusion of one in the other, or their contraction.

This great simplicity in the principles, this uniformity and this surety in the course, this prodigious richness of invention in the developments, had caused the ancient sages of Greece, those capable of understanding and appreciating the remains of the sacred dialect of Egypt, to think that this dialect had been the work of the priests themselves who had fashioned it for their own use; not perceiving, from the irregular turn pursued by the Greek idiom and even the vulgar idiom then in use in Lower Egypt, that any tongue whatsoever, given its own full sway, might attain to this degree of perfection. Their error was to a certain point excusable. They could not know, deprived as they were of means of comparison, the enormous difference which exists between a real mother tongue and one which is not. The merit of the Egyptian priests was not, as has been supposed, in having invented the ancient idiom, which they used instead of the sacred dialect, but in having fathomed the genius, in having well understood its elements, and in having been instructed to employ them in a manner conformable with their nature.

The reader will discern, in glancing through the Vocabulary which I give and which I have restored with the utmost care possible, to what degree of force, clarity and richness, the tongue whose basis it formed, could attain; he will also perceive its usefulness in the hands of the wise and studious man, eager to go back to the origin of speech and to sound the mystery, hitherto generally unknown, of the formation of language.

The universal principle is not for man. All that falls beneath his senses, all that of which he can acquire a real and positive understanding is diverse. God alone is one. The principle which presides at the formation of the Hebrew is not therefore universally the same as that which presides at the formation of Chinese, Sanskrit or any other similar tongue. Although issued from a common source which is Speech, the constitutive principles of the tongues differ. Because a primitive root formed of such or such sign, contains such a general idea in Hebrew, it is not said for that reason that it ought to contain it in Celtic. Very close attention must be given here. This same root can, on the contrary, develop an opposite idea; and this occurs nearly always when the spirit of a people is found in contradiction with that of another people concerning the sentiment which is the cause of the idea. If a person, reading my Vocabulary, seeing the most extended developments follow the simplest premises, and discovering at first glance irresistible relations in Hebrew with his own language and the ancient or modern tongues which he knows, ventures to believe that Hebrew is the primitive tongue from which all the others descend, he would be mistaken. He would imitate those numberless systematic scholars who, not understanding the vast plan upon which nature works have always wished to restrict it to the narrow sphere of their understanding.

It is not enough to have grasped the outline of one single figure to understand the arrangement of a picture. There is nothing so false, from whatever viewpoint one considers it, as that impassioned sentence which has become a philosophic axiom: *ab uno disce omnes.* It is in following this idea that man has built so many heterogeneous edifices upon sciences of every sort.

The Radical Vocabulary which I give is that of Hebrew; it is therefore good primarily for the Hebrew; secondarily, for the tongues which belong to the same stock, such as Arabic, Coptic, Syriac, etc; but it is only in the third place and in an indirect manner that it can be of use in establishing the etymologies of Greek or Latin, because these two tongues having received their first roots from the ancient Celtic, have with Hebrew only coincidental relations given them by the universal principle of speech, or the fortuitous mixture of peoples: for the Celtic, similar to Hebrew, Sanskrit and Chinese in all that comes from the universal principle of speech, differs essentially in the particular principle of its formation.

The French, sprung from the Celtic in its deepest roots, modified by a mass of dialects, fashioned by Latin and Greek, inundated by Gothic, mixed with Frank and Teutonic, refashioned by Latin, repolished by Greek, in continual struggle with all the neighbouring idioms; the French is perhaps, of all the tongues extant today upon the face of the earth, the one whose etymology is most difficult. One cannot act with too much circumspection in this matter. This tongue is beautiful but its beauty lies not in its simplicity: on the contrary, there is nothing so complicated. It is in proportion as one is enlightened concerning the elements which compose it, that the difficulty of its analysis will be felt and that unknown resources will be discovered. Much time and labour is necessary before a good etymological dictionary of this tongue can be produced. Three tongues well understood, Hebrew, Sanskrit and Chinese can, as I have said, lead one to the origin of speech; but to penetrate into the etymological details of

French, it would be necessary to know also the Celtic, and to understand thoroughly all the idioms which are derived therefrom and which directly or indirectly have furnished expressions to that of the Gauls, our ancestors, of the Romans, our masters, or of the Franks, their conquerors. I say to understand thoroughly, for grammars and vocabularies ranged in a library do not constitute real knowledge. I cannot prove better this assertion than by citing the example of Court de Gébelin. This studious man understood Greek and Latin well, he possessed a slight knowledge of the oriental tongues as much as was possible in his time; but as he was ignorant of the tongues of the north of Europe or at least as their genius was unfamiliar to him, this defect always prevented his grasping in their real light, French etymologies. The first step which he took in this course, was an absurd error which might have brought entire discredit upon him if there had been anyone capable of detecting his mistake. He said, for example, that the French word *abandon* was a kind of elliptical and figurative phrase composed of three words *a-ban-don;* and that it signified a gift made to the people, taking the word *ban* for the people, the public. Besides it is not true that the word *ban* may signify *people* or *public* in the sense in which he takes it, since its etymology proves that it has signified *common* or *general*,[1] it was not necessary to imagine an ellipsis of that force to explain *abandon.* It is only necessary to know that in Teutonic *band* is a

[1] We still say *banal* to express that which is *common*. It is worthy of notice that the word *banal* goes back to the Gallic root *ban*, which in a restricted sense characterizes *a woman;* whereas its analogues *common* and *general* are attached, the one to the Celtic root *gwym*, *cwym* or *kum*, and the other to the Greek root Γυν, which is derived from it; now these two roots characterize alike, *a woman*, and all that which is *joined, united, communicated,* or *generated, produced. Cym* in Gallic-Celtic, Συν or Συμ in Greek, *cum* in Latin, serves equally the designative or adverbial relation, to express *with*. The Greek word γαμεῖν signifies to be *united*, to *marry*, to *take wife*, and the word *gemein* which, in modern German holds to the same root, is applied to all that is *common, general.*

root expressing all that is *linked, retained, guarded,* and that the word *ohn* or *ohne,* analogous to the Hebrew אִין is a negation which being added to words, expresses absence. So that the compound *band-ohne* or *aband-ohn,* with the redundant vowel, is the exact synonym of our expressions *abandon* or *abandoment.*

Court de Gébelin made a graver mistake when he wrote that the French word *vérité* is derived from a so-called primitive root *var,* or *ver,* which according to him signified *water* and all that which is limpid and transparent as that element: for how could he forget that in the Celtic and in all the dialects of the north of Europe the root *war, wer, wir,* or *wahr, ward,* develops the ideas of being, in general, and of man in particular, and signifies, according to the dialect, that which *is,* that which *was,* and even becomes a sort of auxiliary verb to express that which *will be?* It is hardly conceivable.

Now if a savant so worthy of commendation has been able to go astray upon this point in treating of French etymologies, I leave to the imagination what those who lack his acquired knowledge would do in this pursuit.

Doubtless there is nothing so useful as etymological science, nothing which opens to the meditation a field so vast, which lends to the history of peoples so sure a link; but also, nothing is so difficult and nothing which demands such long and varied preparatory studies. In the past century when a writer joined to Latin, certain words of Greek and of bad Hebrew, he believed himself a capable etymologist. Court de Gébelin was the first to foresee the immensity of the undertaking. If he has not traversed the route he has at least had the glory of showing the way. Notwithstanding his mistakes and his inadvertencies which I have disclosed with an impartial freedom, he is still the only guide that one can follow, so far as general maxims are concerned, and the laws to be observed in the exploration of tongues. I cannot conceive how a writer who appears to unite so much positive learning as the one who has just published a book in German full of excellent views upon the tongue and science of the Indians[1] can have misunderstood the first rules of etymology to the point of giving constantly for roots of Sanskrit, words of two, three and four syllables; not knowing or feigning not to know that every root is monosyllabic; still less can I conceive how he has not seen that, in the comparison of tongues, it is never the compound which proves an original analogy, but the root. Sanskrit has without doubt deep connection with ancient Celtic and consequently with Teutonic, one of its dialects; but it is not by analyzing about thirty compound words of modern German that these connections are proved. To do this one must go back to the primitive roots of the two tongues, show their affinity, and in compounds, inevitably diverse, distinguish their different genius and give thus to the philosopher and historian, materials for penetrating the *esprit* of these two peoples and noting their moral and physical revolutions.

In this Prefatory Note, my only object has been to show the difficulty of the etymological science and to warn the overzealous reader as much as possible, against the wrong applications that he might make in generalizing particular principles, and against the errors into which too much impetuosity might lead him.

[1] *Ueber die Sprache und Weisheit der Indier*... I vol. in-8 Heidelberg. 1808.

The
Hebraic Tongue Restored

HEBRAIC ROOTS.

RADICAL VOCABULARY
OR
SERIES OF HEBRAIC ROOTS.

א   A. First character of the alphabet in nearly all known idioms. As symbolic image it represents universal man, mankind, the ruling being of the earth. In its hieroglyphic acceptation, it characterizes unity, the central point, the abstract principle of a thing. As sign, it expresses power, stability, continuity. Some grammarians make it express a kind of superlative as in Arabic; but this is only a result of its power as sign. On some rare occasions it takes the place of the emphatic article ה either at the beginning or at the end of words. The rabbis use it as a sort of article. It is often added at the head of words as redundant vowel, to make them more sonorous and to add to their expression.

Its arithmetical number is 1.

אב   AB. The potential sign united to that of interior activity produces a root whence come all ideas of productive cause, efficient will, determining movement, generative force. In many ancient idioms and particularly in the Persian اب, this root is applied especially to the aqueous element as principle of universal fructification.

אב   All ideas of *paternity.* Desire *to have*: a *father*: *fruit.* In reflecting upon these different significations, which appear at first incongruous, one will perceive that they come from one another and are produced mutually.

The Arabic اب contains all the significations of the Hebraic root. As noun, it is *father* and *paternity, fruit* and *fructification;* that which is producer and produced; that which germinates and comes forth as verdure upon the earth. As verb[1] it is the action of *tending toward* a desired end, *proceeding, returning,* etc.

אב or אבב (*intensive*) That which *grows, is propagated: vegetation, germination.*

אהב (*compound*) All ideas of *love, sympathy, inclination, kindness.* It is the sign of life ה which gives to the idea of *desire to have,* contained in the root אב, the movement of expansion which transforms it into that of *love.* It is, according to the etymological sense, that which seeks to spread out.

אוב (*comp.*) This is, in a broader sense, *the Universal Mystery, the Matrix of the Universe, the Orphic Egg, the World, the Vessel of Isis, the Pythonic Mind:* in a more restricted sense, *belly; leather bottle, cavity, vase,* etc.

אג AG. This root, which is only used in composition, characterizes in its primitive acceptation, an acting thing which tends to be augmented. The Arabic اج expresses *ignition, acrimony, intense excitation.*

אג The Chaldaic אג signifies a *lofty, spreading tree:* the Hebrew אגוז *a walnut tree:* the Arabic اوج contains every idea of magnitude, physically as well as morally.

[1] In order to conceive this root اب according to its verbal form, we must consider the last character ب doubled. It is thus that the radical verbs in Arabic are formed. These verbs are not considered as radical by the Arabic grammarians; but on the contrary, as defective and for this reason are called *surd verbs.* These grammarians regard only as radical, the verbs formed of three characters according to the verb فعل *to do,* which they give as verbal type. It is therefore from this false supposition, that every verbal root must possess three characters, that the Hebraist grammarians misunderstood the true roots of the Hebraic tongue.

אָד AD. This root, composed of the signs of power and of physical divisibility, indicates every distinct, single object, taken from the many.

The Arabic اذ conceived in an abstract manner and as adverbial relation, expresses a temporal point, a determined epoch: *when, whilst, whereas.*

אד That which *emanates* from a thing: *the power of division, relative unity, an emanation; a smoking fire brand.*

אוד (*comp.*) That which is done *because of* or *on occasion of* another thing: *an affair, a thing, an occurrence.*

איד (*comp.*) Every idea of *force, power, necessity*: see יד.

אָה AH. Vocal principle. Interjective root to which is attached all passionate movements of the soul, those which are born of joy and pleasure as well as those which emanate from sorrow and pain. It is the origin of all interjective relations called *interjections* by the grammarians. Interjections, says Court de Gébelin, varying but slightly as to sound, vary infinitely according to the degree of force with which they are pronounced. Suggested by nature and supplied by the vocal instrument, they are of all times, all places, all peoples; they form an universal language. It is needless to enter into the detail of their various modifications.

אה The potential sign united to that of life, forms a root in which resides the idea most abstract and most difficult to conceive,—that of *the will;* not however, that of determined or manifested will, but of will in potentiality and considered independent of every object. It is *volition* or *the faculty of willing.*

אוה Determined will: action of *willing, desiring, tending toward* an object. See אׂ.

אהי or אהי Manifested will: *place* of the desire, ob-

ject of the will, represented by the adverbial relation *where.* See אִי.

יָהַב (*comp.*) Action of *desiring, loving, willing.* See אִי.

אֹהֶל (*comp.*) A raised, fixed *place, where* one dwells by choice, *a tent.* See אֵל.

או   AO. The potential sign united to the universal convertible sign, image of the mysterious link which joins nothingness to being, constitutes one of the most difficult roots to conceive which the Hebraic tongue can offer. In proportion as the sense is generalized, one sees appear all ideas of appetence, concupiscible passion, vague desire: in proportion as it is restricted, one discerns only a sentiment of incertitude, of doubt, which becomes extinct in the prepositive relation *or.*

The Arabic و has exactly the same meaning.

אוב (*comp.*) *Desire* acting interiorly. See אָב.

אוד (*comp.*) *Desire* acting exteriorly. See אָד.

אוה (*comp.*) Action of *longing ardently, desiring, inclining with passion.* See אָה.

אול (*comp.*) *Desire* projected into space, represented by the adverbial relation *perhaps.* See אֵל.

און (*comp.*) *Desire* vanishing, being lost in *space* in *nothingness.* See אָן.

אוף (*comp.*) Action of *drawing* into one's will. See אַף.

אוץ (*comp.*) Action of *hastening, pressing* toward a desired end. See אָץ.

אור (*comp.*) *Desire* given over to its own movement, producing *ardour, fire;* that which *burns,* in its literal as well as its figurative sense. See אָר.

אות (*comp.*) Action of *having the same desire, the same will; agreeing, being of the same opinion.* See אָת.

אָז   AZ. This root, but little used in Hebrew, designates a fixed point in space or duration; a measured distance. It is expressed in a restricted sense by the adverbial relations *there* or *then*.

The Arabic أزّ characterizes a sort of locomotion, agitation, pulsation, bubbling, generative movement. As verb it has the sense of *giving a principle; of founding*. The Chaldaic אזא expresses a movement of ascension according to which a thing is placed above another in consequence of its specific gravity. The Ethiopic ᎠᎻᎻ (*azz*) develops all ideas of *command, ordination, subordination*.

אֵז   This is, properly speaking, the action of *gas* which is exhaled and seeks its point of equilibrium: figuratively, it is the movement of the ascension of fire, ether, gaseous fluids in general.

אָח   AH. The potential sign united to that of elementary existence ה, image of the travail of nature, produces a root whence result all ideas of equilibrium, equality, identity, fraternity. When the sign ח characterizes principally an effort, the root אח takes the meaning of its analogues אג, אך, and represents a somewhat violent action. It furnishes then all ideas of excitation and becomes the name of the place where the fire is lighted, *the hearth*.

אָח   *Brother, kinsman, associate, neighbour:* the *common hearth* where all assemble.

The Arabic أخ contains all the meanings attributed to the Hebrew אח.

אח and אחד   *One: first:* all ideas attached to *identity*, to *unity*.

אחו   All ideas of *junction, adjunction, union, reconciliation. Bulrush, reed, sedge*.

אחז   (*comp.*) All ideas of *adhesion, apprehension, agglomeration, union, possession, heritage*.

אחר (comp.) That which is *other, following, posterior;* those who *come after,* who remain *behind; descendants,* etc.

אט AT. This root is scarcely used in Hebrew except to describe a sound, or a slow, silent movement. The Arabic اط expresses any kind of murmuring noise.

אט *A magic murmur; witchcraft, enchantment.*

אי AI. Power accompanied by manifestation, forms a root whose meaning, akin to that which we have found in the root או, expresses the same idea of desire, but less vague and more determined. It is no longer sentiment, passion without object, which falls into incertitude: it is the very object of this sentiment, the centre toward which the will tends, the place where it is fixed. A remarkable thing is, that if the root או is represented in its most abstract acceptation by the prepositive relation *or,* the root אי is represented, in the same acceptation, by the adverbial relation *where.*

The Arabic اي expresses the same assent of the will, being restricted to the adverbial relation *yes.* As pronominal relation, اي distinguishes things from one another; when this root is employed as verb it expresses in اي or اوي the action of *being fixed* in a determined place, choosing an abode, being united voluntarily to a thing; etc.

אי Every centre of activity, every place distinct, separate from another place. *An isle, a country, a region; where* one is, *where* one acts.

איב (comp.) Every idea of *antipathy, enmity, animadversion.* It is an effect of the movement of contraction upon the volitive centre אי by the sign of interior activity ב.

אִיד (comp.) A vapour, an exhalation, a contagion: that which *is spread* without. See יד.

אִי and אִיה Every exact centre of activity: in a restricted sense, *a vulture, a crow*: in an abstract sense, *where, there where*.

אִיךְ (comp.) The restriction of place, of mode; *where* and *in what fashion* a thing acts, represented by the adverbial relations *wherefore? how? thus?* See אךְ.

אִיל (comp.) *A ram, a deer*; the idea of force united to that of desire. See אל.

אִים (comp.) Every formidable object, every being leaving its nature; *a monster, a giant*. It is the root אִי, considered as expressing any centre of activity whatsoever, which assumes the collective sign ם, to express a disordered will, a thing capable of inspiring terror.

אִין Absence of all reality. See אן

אִישׁ (comp.) Intellectual principle constituting *man*. I shall explain in the notes how the root אִי, united to the root אשׁ, has formed the *compound* root אִישׁ which has become the symbol of intellectual man.

אִית (comp.) Every idea of *constancy, tenacity of will*: that which is *rude, harsh, rough, obstinate*.

אךְ ACH. This root, composed of the signs of power and of assimilation, produces the idea of every compression, every effort that the being makes upon himself or upon another, to fix him or to be fixed. It is a tendency to make compact, to centralize. In the literal acceptation it is the action of restraining, of accepting. In the figurative and hieroglyphic sense it is the symbol of concentric movement tending to draw near. The contrary movement is expressed by the opposed root הל or אל.

It must be observed as a matter worthy of the greatest attention, that in an abstract sense the root אךְ represents the adverbial relation *yes*, and the root אל the adverbial relation *no*. The root אך expresses again in the same sense, *but, however, certainly.*

The Arabic اﻟ contains, as the Hebrew אך, all ideas of pressure, compression, vehemence.

אוך The Arabic اوك signifies *anger, malice, hateful passion.* The Syriac ܐܘܟܐ is a name of the devil.

איך Every idea of intrinsic *quality, mode,* etc.

אל AL. This root springs from the united signs of power and of extensive movement. The ideas which it develops are those of elevation, force, power, extent. The Hebrews and Arabs have drawn from it the name of GOD.

אל Hieroglyphically, this is the symbol of excentric force. In a restricted sense, it is that which tends toward an end, represented by the designative or adverbial relations *to, toward, for, by, against, upon, beneath,* etc.

The Arabic ال is employed as the universal designative relation *the, of the, to the,* etc. As verb, it expresses in the ancient idiom, the action of *moving quickly,* going with promptness from one place to another: in the modern idiom it signifies literally, to *be wearied* by too much movement.

אל and אלל (*intens.*) In its excess of extension, it is that which *passes away,* which is *empty, vain;* expressed by the adverbial relations *no, not, not so, nought, nothing;* etc.

אהל A raised dwelling, *a tent.*

אול Action of *rising, extending, vanishing, filling time* or *space.*

איל All ideas of *virtue, courage* or *vigour,* of physical and moral *faculties;* of extensive and vegetative *force: an oak, a ram, a chief, a prince; the door posts, threshold;* etc.

אָם AM. The potential sign united to that of exterior activity; as collective sign it produces a root which develops all ideas of passive and conditional casuality, plastic force, formative faculty, maternity.

אָם *Mother, origin, source, metropolis, nation, family, rule, measure, matrix.* In an abstract sense it is conditional possibility expressed by the relation *if.* But when the mother vowel א, gives place to the sign of material nature ע, then the root עם loses its conditional dubitative expression and takes the positive sense expressed by *with.*

The Arabic اٰم contains all the significations of the Hebraic root. As noun it is *mother, rule, principle, origin;* in a broader sense it is *maternity,* the cause from which all emanates, the *matrix* which contains all; as verb, it is the action of *serving as example, as model;* action of *ruling, establishing in principle, serving as cause;* as adverbial relation it is a sort of dubitative, conditional interrogation exactly like the Hebrew אָם; but what is quite remarkable is, that the Arabic root اٰم, in order to express the adverbial relation *with,* does not take the sign of material nature ע before that of exterior activity מ, it takes it after; so that the Arabic instead of saying עם, says in an inverse manner مع. This difference proves that the two idioms although having the same roots have not been identical in their developments. It also shows that it is to Phœnician or to Hebrew that the Latin origins must be brought back, since the word *cum* (with) is derived obviously from עם, and not from مع.

אום This modification, not used in Hebrew, signifies in Chaldaic *the basis of things.*

אִם See אַ.

אָן AN. An onomatopoetic root which depicts the agonies of the soul; pain, sorrow, anhelation.

The Arabic اٰن used as verb, signifies *to sigh, to complain.*

אן   Every idea of *pain, sorrow, trouble, calamity.*

א   The signs which compose this root are those of power and of individual existence. They determine together the seity, sameness, selfsameness, or *the me* of the being, and limit the extent of its circumscription.

א   In a broader sense, it is the *sphere of moral activity;* in a restricted sense, it is *the body* of the being. One says in Hebrew, אנׅי *I;* as if one said *my sameness,* that which constitutes the sum of my faculties, *my circumscription.*

The Arabic اٰن develops in general the same ideas as the Hebrew א. In a restricted sense this root expresses, moreover, the actual time, *the present;* as adverbial relation it is represented by, *that, but, provided that.*

און   When the root א has received the universal convertible sign, it becomes the symbol of being, in general. In this state it develops the most opposed ideas. It expresses *all* and *nothing, being* and *nothingness, strength* and *weakness, virtue* and *vice, riches* and *poverty;* according to the manner in which the being is conceived and the idea that one attaches to the spirit or matter which constitutes its essence. One can, in the purity of the Hebraic tongue, make these oppositions felt to a certain point, by enlightening or obscuring the mother vowel ו in this manner:

$$\text{אׁו the being} \begin{cases} \text{אׄוֹן } \textit{virtue, strength} \\ \text{אוּן } \textit{vice, weakness} \end{cases} \text{etc.}$$

אין   When the sign of manifestation replaces the convertible sign in the root א, it specifies the sense; but in a fashion nevertheless, of presenting always the contrary of what is announced as real: so that wherever the word אין is presented it expresses absence.

RADICAL VOCABULARY 297

אם AS. Root but little used in Hebrew where it is ordinarily replaced by אש. The Arabic اس presents all ideas deduced from that of *basis*. In several of the ancient idioms the very name of the earth has been drawn from this root, as being the basis of things; thence is also derived the name of *Asia,* that part of the earth which, long considered as the entire earth, has preserved, notwithstanding all its revolutions, this absolute denomination.

The Chaldaic אסי has signified in a restricted sense *a physician;* no doubt because of the health whose basis he established. The Syriac, Samaritan and Ethiopic follow in this, the Chaldaic.

אע AH. Root not used in Hebrew. It is an onomatopoetic sound in the Arabic اع, *ah! alas!* used in defending something. The Chaldaic אע, characterizes vegetable matter.

The Arabic expression واع as a defense, a rejection, gives rise to the compound word اغيه which signifies *an ironical hyperbole.*

אף APH. Sign of power united to that of speech, constitutes a root, which characterizes in a broad sense, that which leads to a goal, to any end whatsoever; *a final cause.* Hieroglyphically, this root was symbolized by the image of a *wheel.* Figuratively, one deduced all ideas of impulse, transport, envelopment in a sort of vortex, etc.

The Arabic اف is an onomatopoetic root, developing all ideas of disgust, ennui, indignation. In the ancient language it was received in the same sense as the Hebrew אף, and represented the adverbial relation *why.*

אף That part of the mind called *apprehension,* or

comprehension. In a very restricted sense, *the nose:* figuratively, *wrath*.

אוף Action *of conducting to an end, of involving, enveloping* in a movement of rotation; action of *seizing* with the understanding; action of *being impassioned, excited*, etc.

אץ ATZ. Every idea of bounds, limits; of repressing force, term, end.

The Arabic اص expresses in general, that which is closed and restricted; the central point of things. The Chaldaic אץ contains every idea of pressure and compression. The analogous Arabic root اض in the modern idiom, signifies every kind of doubling, reiteration. In conceiving the root اض as representing the centre, substance, depth of things, one finds, in its redoubling اضاض a very secret, very hidden place; *a shelter, a refuge*.

אוץ Action of *hastening, drawing near, pushing toward* an end.

אק ACQ. Every idea of vacuity. Root little used in Hebrew except in composition.

The Hebrew word איק signifies literally, *a wild goat;* the Arabic اق as verb, designates that which is nauseous.

אר AR. This root and the one which follows are very important for the understanding of the Hebraic text. The signs which constitute the one in question here, are those of power and of movement proper. Together they are the symbol of the elementary principle, whatever it may be, and of all which pertains to that element or to nature in general. Hieroglyphically אר was represented by the straight line, and אש by the circular line. אר,

RADICAL VOCABULARY

conceived as elementary principle, indicated direct movement, rectilinear; אשׁ relative movement, curvilinear, gyratory.

אר That which belongs to the elementary principle, that which is *strong, vigorous, productive.*

The Arabic اٰر offers the same sense as the Hebrew. It is ardour, impulse in general: in a restricted sense, amorous ardour; action of giving oneself to this ardour; union of the sexes.

אר or יאר That which flows, that which is fluid: *a river.* The Chaldaic אר or איר signifies *air.*

אור *Fire, heat;* action of *burning.*

אור *Light;* action of *enlightening, instructing. Life, joy, felicity, grace;* etc.

ארר (*intens.*) In its excessive force, this root develops the ideas *of cursing, of malediction.*

ארג (*comp.*) *Tapestry, woven material.*

ארה (*comp.*) *A gathering, a mass.*

ארז (*comp.*) *A cedar.*

ארך (*comp.*) Every *prolongation, extension, slackness.*

ארץ or in Chaldaic ארק (*comp.*) *The earth.*

אשׁ ASH. This root, as the preceding one, is symbol of the elementary principle whatever it may be. It is to the root אר, what the circular line is to the straight line. The signs which constitute it are those of power and of relative movement. In a very broad sense it is every active principle, every centre unfolding a circumference, every relative force. In a more restricted sense it is *fire* considered in the absence of every substance.

אשׁ The Hebraic genius confounds this root with the root אם, and considers in it all that which is of *the basis* and *foundation* of things; that which is hidden in its principle; that which is *absolute, strong, unalterable;* as the appearance of *fire.*

300   THE HEBRAIC TONGUE RESTORED

The Arabic اسٔ designates that which moves with *agility*, vehemence. This idea ensues necessarily from that attached to the mobility of fire איש.

איש   Action of *founding, making solid, giving force* and *vigour*.

אחש   (comp.) *Power, majesty, splendour.*

איש   (comp.) *Man*. See 'א.

את ATH. The potential sign united to that of sympathy and of reciprocity, constitutes a root which develops the relations of things to themselves, their mutual tie, their sameness or selfsameness relative to the universal soul, their very substance. This root differs from the root אן in what the former designates as the active existence of being, *I*, and what the latter designates as the passive or relative existence, *thee*. אן is *the subject*, following the definition of the Kantist philosophers; את is *the object*.

את   That which serves as *character, type, symbol, sign, mark*, etc.

אות or א'ת   The being, distinguished or manifested by its sign; that which is real, substantial, material, consistent. In the Chaldaic, א'ת signifies *that which is*, and לית *that which is not*.

The Arabic اتٔ or اثٔ indicates as noun, an irresistible argument, supernatural sign, proof; as verb, it is the action of convincing by supernatural signs or irresistible arguments.

ב B. BH. This character, as consonant, belongs to the labial sound. As symbolic image it represents the mouth of man, his dwelling, his interior. As grammatical sign, it is the paternal and virile sign, that of interior and active action. In Hebrew, it is the integral and indicative article expressing in nouns or actions, as I have explained in my Grammar, almost the same movement as the extractive article מ, but with more force and without any extraction or division of parts.

Its arithmetical number is 2.

בא BA. The sign of interior action united to that of power, image of continuity, forms a root, whence is drawn all ideas of progression, gradual going, coming; of passage from one place to another; of locomotion.

The Arabic بَ indicates in the ancient idiom, a movement of return.

בוא Action of *coming, becoming, happening, bringing to pass;* action of *proceeding, going ahead, entering,* etc.

באר (*comp.*) That which is *put in evidence, is manifested,* etc.; in its literal sense *a fountain.* See בר.

באש (*comp.*) That which becomes *stagnant,* which is *corrupt.* See בש.

בב BB. Every idea of interior void, of exterior swelling.

בב *Pupil of the eye.* In Chaldaic, *an opening, a door.*

The Arabic بَ has the same sense.

בוב Action of being interiorly *void, empty;* every image of *inanity, vacuity.*

בג BG. That which nourishes; that is to say, that which acts upon the interior; for it is here a compound of the root אג united to the sign ב.

The Arabic جَ expresses in general an inflation, an evacuation; it is in a restricted sense in لجَ, the action of *permitting, letting go.* As onomatopoetic root جَ characterizes the indistinct cry of a raucous voice.

בד BD. The root אד, which characterizes every object distinct and alone, being contracted with the sign of interior activity, composes this root whence issue ideas of separation, isolation, solitude, individuality, particular existence.

From the idea of *separation* comes that of *opening;* thence that of *opening the mouth* which is attached to this root in several idioms, and in consequence, that of *chattering, babbling, jesting, boasting, lying,* etc.

The Arabic ﺟﻞ signifies literally *middle, between.* As verb, this root characterizes the action of *dispersing*.

בה BH. Onomatopoetic root which depicts the noise made by a thing being opened, and which, representing it *yawning*, offers to the imagination the idea of *a chasm, an abyss,* etc.

בהו An *abyss,* a thing whose depth cannot be fathomed, physically as well as morally. See הה.

The Arabic ﺑﻪ, as onomatopoetic root characterizes astonishment, surprise. The Arabic word ﺑﻬﺞ which is formed from it, designates that which is astonishing, surprising; that which causes admiration. ﺑﻬﺎ signifies to be *resplendent*, and ﺑﻬﻞ *glorious*.

בהט (*comp.*) *Marble;* because of its weight. See הט.

בהל (*comp.*) A rapid movement which *exalts,* which *transports,* which *carries one beyond self: frightful terror.* See הל.

בהם (*comp.*) Everything which is raised, extended, in any sense; as *a noise, a tumult; a corps, a troop:* it is literally *a quadruped.* See הם.

בהן (*comp.*) Every *guiding* object; literally *the finger.*

בז BZ. The root א, which depicts the movement of that which rises to seek its point of equilibrium, being contracted with the sign of interior activity, furnishes all ideas which spring from the preëminence that one assumes over others, of pride, presumption, etc.

The Arabic ج signifies literally, the action of *growing, sprouting, putting forth shoots.*

בָּזָה Action of *rising* above others, *despising* them, *humiliating* them: every idea of *disdain*, every object of *scorn.*

בָּזַז (*intens.*) In its greatest intensity, this root signifies *to deprive* others of their rights, of their property; to appropriate them: thence every idea of *plunder.*

The Arabic جزّ has the same sense. The word باز signifies a bird of prey, *a vulture.*

בָּה BH. This root is used in Hebrew only in composition. The Ethiopic ባሕአ (*baha*) signifies every kind of acid, of ferment.

The Arabic بخّ signifies in the modern idiom, *to blow water between the lips.*

בָּחַל (*comp.*) Fruit which *begins to mature*, which is still *sour;* an *early* fruit; metaphorically, a thing which *annoys*, which *fatigues.*

בָּחַן (*comp.*) The *test* of a fruit to judge if it is ripe; metaphorically, any kind of *experiment.*

בָּחַר (*comp.*) An *examination, a proof;* in consequence, that which is *examined, proved, elected.*

בָּט BT. The root אט, which depicts a sort of dull noise, of murmuring, being contracted with the sign of interior activity, characterizes that which sparkles, glistens: it is a vapid and thoughtless locution, futile discourse.

The Arabic بتّ indicates that which cuts off physically as well as morally. The onomatopoeia بط, characterizes that which falls and is broken.

בטט (intens.) *A flash of wit; a spark.*

בהר (comp.) *Crystal.* That which throws out brightness, sparks. *An emerald, marble,* etc.

בי BI. Root analogous to the roots בא, בה, בו, which characterize the movement of a thing which advances, appears evident, comes, opens, etc. This applies chiefly to the desire that one has to see a thing appear, an event occur, and that one expresses by *would to God!*

בין (comp.) See ין.

ביר (comp.) See בר.

בית (comp.) See בת.

בך BCH. The root אך which develops all ideas of compression, being united to the sign of interior activity, forms the root בך, whose literal meaning is *liquefaction, fluxion,* resulting from a somewhat forceful grasp, as expressed by the Arabic بك. Thence בך, the action of *flowing, dissolving in tears, weeping.* Every fluid accruing from *contraction,* from *contrition: an overflowing, a torrent, tears,* etc.

The Arabic بك has exactly the same meaning.

בוך State of being afflicted by pain, saddened to tears.

בל BL. This root should be conceived according to its two ways of composition: by the first, the root אל, which designates elevation, power, etc., is united to the sign of interior activity ב: by the second, it is the sign of extensive movement ל, which is contracted with the root בא, whose use is, as we have seen, to develop all ideas of progression, gradual advance, etc.: so that it is, in the first case, a dilating force, which acting from the centre to the circumference, augments the volume of things, causing a kind of bubbling, swelling; whereas in the second it is the thing itself which is transported or which is overthrown without augmenting in volume.

בל   Every idea of *distention, profusion, abundance;* every idea of *expansion, extension, tenuity, gentleness.* In a figurative sense, *spirituality, the human soul, the universal soul, the All,* GOD.

The Arabic بل characterizes in a restricted sense, that which humectates, moistens, lenifies, dampens, and makes fertile the earth, etc.

בלל   (*intens.*) From excess of extension springs the idea of *lack, want, neglect, weakness, nothingness:* it is everything which is *null, vain, illusory:* NOTHING.

The Arabic بل is restricted to the same sense as the Hebrew, and is represented by the adverbial relation *without.*

בהל   (*comp.*) An interior *emotion, trouble, confusion, extraordinary perturbation.* See בה.

בול   Action of *dilating, swelling, boiling, spreading* on all sides: *a flux, an intumescence, a diffusion; an inundation, a general swelling.*

בם   BM. The union of the signs of interior and exterior activity, of active and passive principles, constitutes a root little used and very difficult to conceive. Hieroglyphically, it is the universality of things: figuratively or literally, it is every elevated place, every sublime, sacred, revered thing; *a temple, an altar,* etc.

The Arabic بم signifies in a restricted sense the fundamental sound of the musical system called in Greek ὑπάτη. See קב.

בן   BN. If one conceives the root בא, which contains all ideas of progression, growth, birth, as vested with the extensive sign ן, to form the root בן, this root will develop the idea of generative extension, of production analogous to the producing being, of *an emanation;* if one considers this same root בֶּן, as result of the contraction of the sign of interior activity ב with the root אֶן which characterizes the circumscriptive extent of being, then it would be the symbol of every active production proceeding from potentiality in action, from every manifestation of generative action, from the *me*.

בֶּן   In a figurative sense it is *an emanation,* intelligible or sentient; in a literal sense it is *a son, a formation, an embodiment, a construction.*

The Arabic بَن has exactly the same acceptations as the Hebrew.

בּוֹן   Action of *conceiving,* of *exercising one's conceptive, intellectual faculties;* action of *thinking, having ideas, forming a plan, meditating;* etc.

בִּין   *Intelligence;* that which elects interiorly and prepares the elements for the *edification of the soul.* That which is interior. See יִן.

בַּס   BS. That which belongs to the earth, expressed by the root אַם; that which is at the base.

The Arabic بِس indicates that which suffices, and is represented by the adverbial relation *enough.*

בּוֹס   Action of *throwing down, crushing, treading upon, pressing against the ground.*

The Arabic بِس signifies the action of *pounding* and of *mixing;* باس contains every idea of force, violence, compulsion.

בַּע   BHO. Every idea of precipitate, harsh, inordinate movement. It is the root בָּא, in which the mother vowel has degenerated toward the material sense.

The Arabic بَع is an onomatopoetic root which expresses the bleating, bellowing of animals.

בעה   An *anxious inquiry, a search; a turgescence, a boiling; action of boiling,* etc.

The Arabic بلغ signifies in a restricted sense, *to sell* and *to buy,* to make a negotiation; بغ *to interfere* for another, and *to prompt* him in what he should say. The word بلغ which springs from the primitive root בע, contains all ideas of iniquity and of injustice.

בעט   (*comp.*)   Action of *kicking.*

בעל   (*comp.*)   Every idea of domination, power, pride: *a lord, master, absolute superior; the Supreme Being.*

בער   (*comp.*)   Every idea of *devastation* by fire, *annihilation, conflagration, combustion, consuming heat:* that which *destroys, ravages;* that which makes *desert* and *arid,* speaking of the earth; *brutish* and *stupid,* speaking of men. It is the root ער, governed by the sign of interior activity ב.

בעת   (*comp.*)   Action of *frightening, striking with terror, seizing suddenly.*

בץ   BTZ. Onomatopoetic and idiomatic root which represents the noise that one makes walking in *the mud:* literally, it is *a miry place, a slough.*

The Arabic بص does not belong to the onomatopoetic root בץ; it is a primitive root which possesses all the force of the signs of which it is composed. In a general sense, it characterizes every kind of luminous ray being carried from the centre to the circumference. In a restricted sense it expresses the action of *gleaming, shining;* of *glaring at.* As noun, it denotes *embers.* The Chaldaic בץ, which has the same elements, signifies *to examine, scrutinize, make a search.*

בעץ   Action of *wading through* the mud. It is the name given to *flax* on account of its preparation in water.

בק   BCQ. Every idea of evacuation, of draining. It is the root אק united to the sign of interior action ב.

בוק   Action of *evacuating, dissipating, making scarce.*

The Arabic باق signifies *eternal;* بَقَا *to eternize.*

בר   BR. This root is composed either of the elementary root אר, united to the sign of interior activity ב, or of the sign of movement proper ר, contracted with the root בא; thence, first, every active production with power, every conception, every potential emanation; second, every innate movement tending to manifest exteriorly the creative force of being.

בר   Hieroglyphically, it is the *radius of the circle* which produces the circumference and of which it is the measure: figuratively, *a potential creation:* that is to say a *fruit* of some sort, whose germ contains in potentiality, the same being which has carried it: in the literal sense, *a son.*

The Arabic بر signifies in a restricted sense, *a continent;* and in a more extended sense, that which is **upright.**

ברר   (*intens.*) Every extracting, separating, elaborating, purifying movement: that which *prepares* or *is prepared;* that which *purges, purifies,* or which is itself *purged, purified.* Every kind of metal.

The Arabic بر raised to the potentiality of verb, develops the action of *justifying,* of *purifying.*

באר   (*comp.*) Every idea of *manifestation, explanation:* that which brings to light, that which explores, that which produces exteriorly. In a very restricted sense, *a fountain, a well.*

בהר   (*comp.*) Every idea of *lucidity, clarity.* That which is *candid; resplendent.*

בֹּר (comp.) Every idea of *distinction, éclat, purity.* In a restricted sense, *wheat.*

בִּיר or בּוֹר (comp.) In a broad sense, *an excavation;* in a restricted sense, *a well;* in a figurative sense, *an edifice, citadel, palace.*

בָּשׁ BSH. This root, considered as being derived from the sign of interior activity ב, united to the root אשׁ which characterizes fire, expresses every idea of heat and brightness: but if it is considered as formed of the root בא which denotes every progression, and of the sign of relative movement שׁ, then it indicates a sort of delay in the course of proceeding.

The Arabic بس or بش has also these two acceptations. The word باس which belongs to the first, signifies *a violence;* بش, which belongs to the second, signifies *void.*

בּוּשׁ Action of *blushing:* experiencing an inner sentiment of modesty or shame: action of *delaying, diverting one's self,* turning instead of advancing.

בָּאשׁ (comp.) That which is *corrupted.* Thence the Chaldaic בּוּשׁ בָּאשׁ, or בִּישָׁא, that which is *bad.*

בַּת BTH. Every idea of inside space, place, container, proper dwelling, receptacle, lodge, habitation, etc.

The Arabic ت characterizes a thing detached, cut, pruned, distributed in parts. By ط is understood a sort of *gushing forth;* by ث *a brusque exit, a clashing.*

בּוּת Action of *dwelling, inhabiting, passing the night, lodging, retiring at home;* etc.

בִּית A separate and particular place; *a lodge, a habitation;* that which composes *the interior, the family:* that which is *internal, intrinsic, proper, local,* etc.

גּ G. GH. This character as consonant, belongs to the guttural sound. The one by which I translate it, is quite a modern invention and responds to it rather imperfectly. Plutarch tells us that a certain Carvilius who, having opened a school at Rome, first invented or introduced the letter G, to distinguish the double sound of the C. As symbolic image the Hebraic גּ indicates the throat of man, any conduit, any canal, any deep hollow object. As grammatical sign, it expresses organic development and produces all ideas originating from the corporeal organs and from their action.

Its arithmetical number is 3.

גּא GA. The organic sign גּ united to the potential sign א, constitutes a root which is attached to all ideas of aggrandizement, growth, organic development, augmentation, magnitude.

The Arabic جا signifies literally *to come*.

גאה That which *augments, becomes wider, is raised, slackens, increases*, literally as well as figuratively. *Grandeur* of height, *eminence* of objects, *exaltation* of thought, *pride* of the soul, *ostentation;* etc.

גאל (*comp.*) Every idea of *liberation, redemption, release, loosening of bonds:* figuratively, *vengeance* for an offense; metaphorically, the idea of remissness, *defilement, pollution.*

גּב GB. The organic sign united by contraction to the root אב, symbol of every fructification, develops, in general, the idea of a thing placed or coming under another thing.

גב A *boss, an excrescence, a protuberance; a knoll, an eminence; the back;* everything convex.

גב or גוב A *grasshopper.* See גו.

גבב (*intens.*) The sign of interior activity being doubled, changes the effect of the positive root and presents the inverse sense. It is therefore every concavity; *a trench, a recess, a furrow:* action of digging a trench, of hollowing; etc.

The Arabic جب presents the same sense as the Hebrew. As verb it is the action of *cutting,* of *castrating.*

גג GG. Every idea of elasticity; that which stretches and expands without being disunited.

The Arabic جج contains the same ideas of extension.

גג or גוג *The roof* of a tent; that which extends to cover, to envelop.

גד GD. The root גא, symbol of that which augments and extends, united to the sign of abundance born of division, produces the root גד whose use is to depict that which acts in masses, which flocks, agitates tumultuously, assails in troops.

The Arabic جد signifies literally *to make an effort.* In a more general sense جد characterizes that which is important, according to its nature; as adverbial relation this root is represented by *very, much, many.* The verb جاد signifies *to be liberal,* to give generously.

גד *An incursion, an irruption,* literally and figuratively. *An incision* in anything whatsoever, *a furrow;* metaphorically, in the restricted sense, *a kid:* the sign of Capricorn; etc.

גיד A *nerve, a tendon;* everything that can be stretched for action.

גה, גו and גי GHE, GOU and GHI. The organic sign united either to that of life, or to that of universal convertible force, or to that of manifestation, constitutes a root which becomes the symbol of every organization. This root which possesses the same faculties of extension and aggrandizement that we have observed in the root גא, contains ideas apparently opposed to envelopment and development, according to the point of view under which one considers the organization.

The Arabic جر indicates universal envelopment, *space, atmosphere;* جه characterizes that which protects.

גהה That which *organizes;* that which gives life to the organs: *health,* and metaphorically, *medicine.*

גוה Every kind of *organ* dilated to give passage to the vital spirits, or closed to retain them: every *expansion,* every *conclusion:* that which serves as *tegument; the body,* in general; *the middle* of things: that which *preserves* them as, *the sheath* of a sword; etc.

גוב (*comp.*) Action of *digging, ploughing.* In a restricted sense, *a scarab.*

גור (*comp.*) Action of making *an irruption.* See גר.

גוז (*comp.*) Action of *mowing,* removing with a scythe. See גז.

גוח (*comp.*) Action of *ravishing,* taking by force. See גה.

גוי A political organization; a body of people; *a nation.*

גול (*comp.*) That which brings the organs to development. See גל.

גיל (*comp.*) An organic movement; *an evolution, a revolution.*

גוע (*comp.*) That which *disorganizes;* every dissolution of the organic system: action of *expiring,* of being distended beyond measure, of *bursting.*

גוף (*comp.*) Action of *closing.*

גור (*comp.*) Action of *prolonging,* of *continuing* a same movement, a same route; action of *voyaging;* action of living in a same place, dwelling there. See גר.

RADICAL VOCABULARY

גוּשׁ (intens.) See גּ֗שׁ.

גּז GZ. The root אז, which indicates the movement of that which tends to take away, united to the organic sign, constitutes a root whose use is to characterize the action by which one suppresses, takes away, extracts every superfluity, every growth; thence גּז, the action of *clipping wool, shaving the hair, mowing the grass; taking away* the tops of things, *polishing* roughness.

The Arabic جز has the same meaning as the Hebrew. The verb جاز is applied in the modern idiom to that which is allowable and lawful.

גּח GH. That which is carried with force toward a place, toward a point; that which inclines violently to a thing.

גוּח Action of *acting with haughtiness, making an irruption, rushing* into a place, *ravishing* a thing.

The Arabic root جح has the same meaning in general; in particular, the verb جخ signifies *to swagger*.

גּחן (comp.) *An inclination, a defective propensity, a winding course.*

גּט GT. This root is not used in Hebrew.

The Arabic جظ denotes a thing which repulses the effort of the hand which pushes it.

גי GHI. Root analogous to the roots גה and גו.

גּיא *Valley, gorge, depth.*

The Arabic جيَ indicates a place where water remains stagnant and becomes corrupt through standing.

גּיד (comp.) *A nerve.* See גּד.

גּיל (comp.) See גּה and גּל.

גּיר (comp.) That which makes things *endure*, and

preserves them in good condition: in a restricted sense *lime*.

גֵּךְ GCH. This root is not used in Hebrew nor in Arabic.

גַּל GL. This root can be conceived according to its two ways of composition: by the first, it is the root גוּ, symbol of all organic extension, united to the sign of directive movement ל; by the second, it is the organic sign ג, which is contracted with the root אל, symbol of elevation and expansive force. In the first case it is a thing which is displayed in space by unfolding itself; which is developed, produced, according to its nature, unveiled; in the second, it is a thing, on the contrary, which coils, rolls, complicates, accumulates, heaps up, envelops. Here, one can recognize the double meaning which is always attached to the sign ג under the double relation of organic development and envelopment.

גל That which moves with a light and undulating movement; which manifests joy, grace, and ease in its movements. The revolution of celestial spheres. The orbit of the planets. *A wheel; a circumstance, an occasion.*

That which *is revealed,* that which *appears*, is *uncovered*.

That which *piles up* by rolling: the movement of the waves, *the swell; the volume* of anything whatsoever, *a heap, a pile; the circuit* or *contour* of an object or a place: *its confines*.

The Arabic جل presents the same ideas of unfoldment and aggrandizement, as much in the physical as in the moral: it is also the unfolding of the sail of a ship, as well as that of a faculty of the soul. جل expresses at the same time *the majesty* of a king, *the eminence* of a virtue, *the extent* of anything whatsoever.

נֵל or גלל (*intens.*) Excessive deployment shown in the idea of *emigration, transmigration, deportation; abandonment* by a tribe of its country, whether voluntarily or by force.

גאל (*comp.*) *A relaxation,* either in the literal or figurative sense. See גא.

גול Action of *unfolding* or of *turning.* Every *evolution* or *revolution.*

גיל *An appearance* caused by the revelation of the object; effect of a mirror; *resemblance.*

גם GM. Every idea of accumulation, agglomeration, complement, height; expressed in an abstract sense by the relations *also, same, again.*

The Arabic جم develops, as does the Hebraic root, all ideas of abundance and accumulation. As verb, it is the action of *abounding, multiplying;* as noun, and in a restricted sense, جام signifies a precious stone, in Latin *gemma.*

גן GN. The organic sign united by contraction to the root אן or און, forms a root from which come all ideas of circuit, cloture, protective walls, sphere, organic selfsameness.

גן That which *encloses, surrounds* or *covers* all parts; that which forms *the enclosure* of a thing; *limits* this thing and *protects it;* in the same fashion that a sheath encloses, limits and protects its blade.

The Arabic جن has all the acceptations of the Hebraic root. It is, in general, everything which covers or which surrounds another; it is, in particular, a protecting *shade, a darkness,* as much physically as morally; *a tomb.* As verb, this word expresses the action of enveloping with darkness, making night, obscuring the mind, rendering foolish, covering with a veil, enclosing with walls, etc. In the ancient idiom جن has signified *a demon, a devil, a dragon;* جنان *a shield;* جنون *bewilderment* of mind; جنين *an embryo* enveloped in the womb of its mother; جنه *a cuirass,* and every kind of *armour;* etc. In the modern idiom, this word is restricted to signify *an enclosure, a garden.*

גס GS. Root not used in Hebrew. The Chaldaic draws from it the idea of that which is puffed up, swollen, become fat. גוס or גיס signifies *a treasure.*

The Arabic جس designates an exploration, a studious research. As verb it is the action of *feeling, groping, sounding.*

גע GH. Root analogous to the root גו, but presenting the organism under its material view point.

The Arabic جع signifies in the modern idiom *to be hungry.* In the ancient idiom one finds جعه for a sort of *beer* or other fermented liquour.

גע Onomatopoetic and idiomatic root which represents the bellowing of an ox.

געה Action of opening the jaw, of *bellowing;* every *clamour,* every *vociferation.*

גוע (*comp.*) Action of *bursting.* See גו.

געל (*comp.*) Action of rejecting from the mouth; every idea of *disgust.*

גער (*comp.*) Every kind of noise, fracas, murmuring.

געש (*comp.*) Action of *troubling, frightening* by clamours and vociferations.

גף GPH. All ideas of conservation, protection, guarantee: in a restricted sense, *a body.*

The Arabic جف develops the idea of dryness and of that which becomes dry. The verb جاف signifies literally, *to withdraw from.*

גוף Action of *enclosing, incorporating, embodying, investing* with a body; that which serves for defense, for conservation.

גץ GTZ. Root not used in Hebrew. The Ethiopic ገጽ (*gatz*) characterizes the form, the corporeal figure, the face of things. The Arabic جصص signifies *to coat with plaster,* or *to glaze* the interior of structures.

גק GCQ. Root not used in Hebrew. The Arabic حق indicates *excrement.*

גר GR. The sign of movement proper ר, united by contraction to the root of organic extension גא, constitutes a root which presents the image of every iterative and continued movement, every action which brings back the being upon itself.

גר That which assembles in *hordes* to journey, or to *dwell* together; the place where one meets in the course of a journey. · Every idea of *tour, detour; rumination; continuity* in movement or in action.

The Arabic جر presents the idea of violent and continued movement. It is literally, the action of *alluring, drawing to one's self, ravishing.* The verb جار signifies *to encroach, to usurp.*

גרר (*intens.*) Duplication of the sign ר, indicates the vehemence and continuity of the movement of which it is the symbol; thence, the analogous ideas of *incision, section, dissection;* of *fracture, hatching, engraving;* of *rumination, turning over in one's mind;* of *grinding,* etc.

נהר (*comp.*) Every extending movement of the body or of a member of the body. Action of reaching out full length.

גור Action of prolonging, continuing an action. See גנ.

גש GSH. This root represents the effect of things which approach, touch, contract.

גוש Action of *being contracted*, made corporeal, dense and palpable; figuratively, *matter* and that which is obvious to the senses: metaphorically, *ordure, filth*.

The Arabic جش denotes every kind of fracture and broken thing.

גת GTH. That which exercises a force extensive and reciprocally increasing; גת, in a restricted sense, *a vice, a press*.

The Arabic جت expresses the action of *squeezing, pressing in the hand*, etc.

ד D. This character as consonant belongs to the dental sound. It appears that in its hieroglyphic acceptation, it was the emblem of the universal quaternary; that is to say, of the source of all physical existence. As symbolic image it represents the breast, and every nourishing and abundant object. As grammatical sign, it expresses in general, abundance born of division: it is the sign of divisible and divided nature. The Hebrew does not employ it as article, but it enjoys that prerogative in Chaldaic, Samaritan and Syriac, where it fulfills the functions of a kind of distinctive article.

Its arithmetical number is 4.

דא DA. This root which is only used in Hebrew in composition, is the analogue of the root די, which bears the real character of the sign of natural abundance and of division. In Chaldaic it has an abstract sense represented by the relations *of, of which, this, that, of what.*

The Arabic داو characterizes a movement which is propagated without effort and without noise.

דאה (*onom.*) Action of *flying with rapidity; of swooping down* on something: thence דאה *a kite;* דיה *a vulture.*

דאב (*comp.*) See דב.

דאג (*comp.*) See דג.

דב DB. The sign of natural abundance united by contraction to the root אב, symbol of all generative propagation, constitutes a root whence are developed all ideas of effluence and influence; of emanation, communication, transmission, insinuation.

דב That which *is propagated* and *is communicated* by degrees; *sound, murmur, rumour, discourse; fermentation,* literally and figuratively; *vapour;* that which proceeds slowly and noiselessly: *calumny, secret plot, contagion.*

The Arabic دب develops in general the idea of that which crawls, insinuates itself, goes creeping along.

דאב In a figurative sense, *a dull pain, an uneasiness concerning the future.*

דוב In a restricted sense, *a bear,* on account of its slow and silent gait.

דג DGH. The sign of natural abundance joined to that of organic development, produces a root whose use is to characterize that which is fruitful and multiplies abundantly.

דג It is literally, *the fish* and that which is akin.

דאג (*comp.*) In considering this root as composed of the sign ד, united by contraction to the root אג which represents an acting thing which tends to augment, one finds that it expresses, figuratively, every kind of *solicitude, anxiety, anguish*.

דד DD. Every idea of abundance and division; of propagation, effusion and influence; of sufficient reason, affinity and sympathy.

דד That which is divided in order to be propagated; that which acts by sympathy, affinity, influence: literally *breast, mammal*.

The Arabic دد indicates a pleasing thing, game, or amusement.

דוד Action of *acting by sympathy* and *by affinity;* action of *attracting, pleasing, loving; sufficing mutually*. In a broader sense, *a chosen vessel*, a place, an object toward which one is attracted; every sympathetic and electrifying purpose. In a more restricted sense, *a friend, a lover; friendship, love;* every kind of flower and particularly *the mandragora* and *the violet*.

דהּ and דוּ DHE and DOU. See the root 'ד of which these are the analogues and which bear the real character of the sign ד.

דוּ DOU. Onomatopoetic and idiomatic root which expresses a sentiment of pain, trouble, sorrow.

דוה Action of *suffering, lamenting, languishing, being weak*.

The Arabic دﻩ, دو, دا offers as onomatopoetic root, the same sense as the Hebraic דו. Thence, in Hebrew as well as in Syriac, Ethiopic and Arabic, a mass of words which depict pain, anguish, affliction; that which is infirm and calamitous. Thence, in ancient Celtic, the words *dol* (mourning), *dull* (lugubrious); in Latin, *dolor* (pain *dolere* (to feel pain); in the modern tongues, their numberless derivatives.

RADICAL VOCABULARY 321

דהם (*comp.*) That which overwhelms with astonishment; every *sudden calamity*, astounding and stupifying.

דוי and דות *Pain, languor, debility.*

דוי Metaphorically, that which is *sombre, lugubrious, funereal, gloomy; mourning.*

דה DH. Every idea of forced influence, impulsion, constraint.

The Arabic دح contains the same meaning in general. In particular دحدح is a sort of exclamation to command secrecy or to impose silence upon someone: *hush!*

דחה or דוח Action of *forcing, necessitating, constraining;* action of *expulsion, evacuation;* etc.

דוח That which *constrains.*

דחי *Separation, violent impulsion.*

דחף (*comp.*) Every idea of *excitement.*

דחק (*comp.*) *An impression, an extreme oppression.*

דט DT. This root is not used in Hebrew.

The Arabic دط contains the idea of *rejection* and *expulsion.*

די DI. The sign of natural abundance united to that of manifestation, constitutes the true root characteristic of this sign. This root develops all ideas of sufficiency and of sufficient reason; of abundant cause and of elementary divisibility.

דה or די That which is *fecund, fertile, abundant, sufficient;* that which *contents, satisfies, suffices.*

The Arabic دي or ذي indicates, in general, the distribution of things; and helps to distinguish them. In particular, the roots دي, ده or دد and ذي are represented by the pronominal demonstrative relations *this, that;* etc. The root دو which preserves a greater conformity with the Hebraic root דִי, signifies literally *possession.*

דִין (*comp.*) That which *satisfies everybody;* that which makes a difference cease; *a judgment.*

דִיק (*comp.*) That which *divides,* that which reduces to pieces. See דק.

דִישׁ (*comp.*) Every kind of *trituration.* See דּישׁ.

דַךְ DCH. The sign of natural abundance contracted with the root אַךְ, symbol of concentric movement and of every restriction and exception, composes a root infinitely expressive whose object is to depict need, necessity, poverty and all ideas proceeding therefrom.

The Arabic دق or دك constitutes an onomatopoetic and idiomatic root which expresses the noise made in striking, beating, knocking; which consequently, develops all ideas which are attached to the action of *striking,* as those of *killing, breaking, splitting,* etc. In a restricted sense دق signifies *to pillage;* دك *to ram* a gun; دَقّ *to push* with the hand.

דַךְ That which is *needy, contrite, sad, poor, injurious, calamitous, vexatious;* etc.

דוּךְ Action of *depriving, vexing* by privation, *oppressing, beating unmercifully;* etc.

דַל DL. This root, conceived as the union of the sign of natural abundance or of divisibility, with the root אֵל symbol of elevation, produces the idea of every extraction, every removal; as for example, when one draws water from a well, when one takes away the life of a plant; from this idea, proceeds necessarily the accessory ideas of exhaustion and weakness.

The Arabic دل contains the same sense in general; but in particular, this root is attached more exclusively to the idea of distinguishing, designating, conducting someone toward a distinct object. When it is weakened in ذل it expresses no more than a distinction of *scorn; disdain, degradation.*

דל That which *extracts; to draw* or *to attract* above; that which *takes away, drains;* that which *attenuates, consumes, enfeebles:* every kind of *division, disjunction; emptiness* effected by *extraction;* any kind of *removal.* In a very restricted sense, *a seal;* a vessel for drawing water.

דם DM. The roots which, by means of any sign whatever, arise from the roots אב or אם, symbols of active or passive principles, are all very difficult to determine and to grasp, on account of the extent of meaning which they present, and the contrary ideas which they produce. These particularly demand close attention. It is, at first glance, universalized sympathy; that is to say, a homogeneous thing formed by affinity of similar parts, and holding to the universal organization of being.

דם In a broader sense, it is that which is *identical;* in a more restricted sense, it is *blood,* assimilative bond between soul and body, according to the profound thought of Moses, which I shall develop in my notes. It is that which *assimilates,* which becomes *homogeneous; mingles with* another thing: thence the general idea of that which is no longer distinguishable, which ceases to be different; that which renounces its seity, its individuality, *is identified* with the whole, *is calm, quiet, silent, asleep.*

The Arabic دم has developed in the ancient language the same general ideas; but in the modern idiom this root has received acceptations somewhat different. دم expresses in general a glutinous, sticky fluid. In particular, as noun, it is *blood;* as verb, it is the action of *covering with a glutinous glaze.* From the latter meaning results, in the analogue ذم, that of *contaminating, calumniating, covering with blame.*

דוֹם State of *universalized being*, that is, having only the life of the universe; *sleeping, being silent, calm;* metaphorically, *taciturn, melancholy.* Action *of assimilating to one's self,* that is, *thinking, imagining, conceiving;* etc.

דן DN. The sign of sympathetic divisibility united to the root אן, symbol of the circumscriptive activity of being, constitutes a root whose purpose is to characterize, in a physical sense, every kind of *chemical parting* in elementary nature; and to express, in a moral sense, every contradictory judgment, resting upon litigious things.

The Arabic دن offers the same sense in general. In particular, ذن expresses a mucous excretion. One understands by دان the action *of judging.*

דוּן Every idea of *dissension;* literally as well as figuratively; every idea of *debate, bestowal, judgment.*

דין *A cause, a right, a judgment, a sentence.*

דם DS. Root not used in Hebrew.

The Arabic دس designates that which is hidden, concealed; which acts in a secret, clandestine manner.

דע DH. Every thing which seeks to expose itself, to appear. This root is not used in Hebrew except in composition. The Arabic ذ characterizes that which pushes, that which puts in motion.

דע or דעה Perception of things, consequently, *understanding, knowledge.*

RADICAL VOCABULARY

דעך (*comp.*) The root דע united by contraction to the root אך symbol of restriction, expresses that which is no more sentient, that is *extinct, obscure, ignorant.*

דף DPH. Root not used in Hebrew. The Arabic دن or دفٔ expresses a sort of rubbing by means of which one drives away cold, and is warmed. دن is also in Arabic, an onomatopoetic and idiomatic root, formed by imitation of the noise that is made by a stretched skin when rubbed or struck. The Hebrew renders this root by the analogue תף. We represent it by the words *drum, tympanum; to beat a drum;* etc. In the modern Arabic دف signifies *a tambourine,* and also *a base drum.*

The Chaldaic signifies a thing which is smooth as a board, a table. One finds in Hebrew דפי for *scandal, evil report, shame.*

דץ DTZ. Every idea of joy and hilarity.
The Arabic دص characterizes the action of shaking a sieve.

דוץ Action of living in abundance; transported with joy.

דק DCQ. Every idea of division by break, fracture; that which is made small, slender or thin, by division: extreme subtlety. This root is confounded often with the root רק.

The Arabic دق develops the same ideas.

דוד Action of *making slender, subtle;* etc.

דר DR. This root, composed of the sign of abundance born of division, united to the elementary root אר, characterizes the temporal state of things, the age, cycle, order, generation, time. Thence דר, every idea of cycle, period, life, customs, epoch, generation, abode.

דוֹד Action of *ordering* a thing, *disposing* of it following a certain order; *resting* in any sphere whatsoever; *dwelling* in a place; *living* in an age: that which *circulates*, that which *exists* according to a movement and a regulated order. *An orb, universe, world, circuit; a city.*

דרר (*intens.*) The broad and generalized idea of circulating without obstacle, of following a natural movement, brings forth the idea of *liberty*, the state of *being free*, the action of *acting without constraint.*

The Arabic در has lost almost all the general and universal acceptations of the Hebrew; this ancient root has preserved in the modern idiom only the idea of a fluxion, of yielding plentifully, particularly in the action of milking.

דש DSH. Every idea of germination, vegetation, elementary propagation.

דוּשׁ In a broad sense, action of *giving the seed;* and in a more restricted sense that of *thrashing the grain, triturating.*

The Arabic دش has the same meaning as the Hebrew דש.

דת DTH. Everything issued for the purpose of sufficing, satisfying, serving as sufficient reason.

דת *A law, an edict, an ordinance.*

In the modern idiom, the Arabic دث is limited to signifying a *shower; a humid, abundant emission: broth.*

ה E. HE. This character is the symbol of universal life. It represents the breath of man, air, spirit, soul; that which is animating, vivifying. As grammatical sign, it expresses life and the abstract idea of being. It is, in the Hebraic tongue, of great use as article. One can see what I have said in my Grammar under the double relation of determinative and emphatic article. It is needless to repeat these details.

Its arithmetical number is 5.

הא HA. Every evident, demonstrated and determined existence. Every demonstrative movement expressed in an abstract sense by the relations *here, there; this, that.*

The Arabic ها expresses only an exclamation.

הב HB. Every idea of fructification and of production. It is the root אב of which the sign of life ה spiritualizes the sense.

הוב It is again the root אוב, but which, considered now according to the symbolic sense, offers the image of being or nothingness, truth or error. In a restricted sense, it is an exhalation, a vapoury-rising, an illusion, a phantom, a simple appearance; etc.

The Arabic هب characterizes in general, a rising, a spontaneous movement, an ignition. As verb, هبّ signifies *to be inflamed.*

הג HEG. Every idea of mental activity, movement of the mind, warmth, fervour. It is easy to recognize here the root אג, which the sign of life spiritualizes.

הג Every *interior agitation;* that which *moves, stirs, excites; eloquence, speech, discourse; an oratorical piece.*

The Arabic هج conserves of the Hebraic root, only the general idea of an interior agitation. As noun, it is literally *a dislocation:* as verb, it is the action of changing of place, of *expatriation.*

הד HED. Like the root אד, of which it is only a modification, it is attached to all ideas of spiritual emanation, the diffusion of a thing *absolute* in its nature, as the effect of *sound, light, voice, echo*.

The Hebraic root is found in the Arabic هاد which is applied to every kind of sound, murmur, noise; but by natural deviation the Arabic root having become onomatopoetic and idiomatic, the verb هد signifies *to demolish, cast down, overthrow*, by similitude of the noise made by the things which are demolished.

הוד Every idea of *éclat, glory, splendour, majesty, harmony*, etc.

הה HEH. This is that double root of life of which I have spoken at length in my Grammar and of which I shall still have occasion to speak often in my notes. This root, which develops the idea of Absolute Being, is the only one whose meaning can never be either materialized or restricted.

הוא In a broad sense, *the Being*, the one who *is*: in a particular sense, *a being;* the one of whom one speaks, represented by the pronominal relations *he, that one, this*.

The Arabic هو has the same meaning.

הוה Preëminently, the verbal root, the unique verb *To be-being*. In an universal sense, it is the *Life of life*.

הוה This root materialized expresses *a nothingness, an abyss of evils, a frightful calamity*.

היה This root, with the sign of manifestation י, replacing the intellectual sign ו, expresses the existence of things according to a particular mode of being. It is the absolute verb *to be-existing*.

היה Materialized and restricted, this same root designates *a disastrous accident, a misfortune*.

RADICAL VOCABULARY 329

הו HOU. The sign of life united to the convertible sign, image of the knot which binds nothingness to being, constitutes one of the roots most difficult to conceive that any tongue can offer. It is the potential life, the power of being, the incomprehensible state of a thing which, not yet existing, is found, nevertheless, with *power of existing.* Refer to the notes.

The Arabic roots هي, هه, هو, ها having lost nearly all the general and universal ideas developed by the analogous Hebraic roots, and conserving nothing of the intellectual, with the sole exception of the pronominal relation هو in which some traces are still discoverable, are restricted to the particular acceptations of the root היה, of which I have spoken above so that they have received for the most part a baleful character. Thus هوه has designated that which is cowardly, weak and pusillanimous; هوي that which is unstable, ruinous; the verb هوي has signified *to pass on, to die, to cease being.* The word هوا which designated originally potential existence, designates only *air, wind, void;* and this same existence, degraded and materialized more and more in صهواه has been the synonym of *hell.*

הום (comp.) This is the *abyss of existence,* the potential power of being, universally conceived.

The Arabic هوه having retained only the material sense of the Hebraic root designates a deep place, an abyss; aerial immensity.

הון (comp.) *Substance, existence; the faculties* which hold to life, to being.

הז HEZ. Movement of ascension and exaltation expressed by the root אז, being spiritualized in this one, becomes a sort of mental delirium, *a dream, a sympathetic somnambulism.*

The Arabic هم restricted to the material sense signifies *to shake, to move to and fro, to wag the head;* etc.

הה HEH. Root not used in Hebrew. The Arabic جم indicates only an exclamation.

הט HET. Root not used in Hebrew.

The Arabic هت or هط indicates, according to the value of the signs which compose this root, any force whatsoever acting against a resisting thing. In a restricted sense هت signifies *to menace;* هط *to persevere* in labour; هطا *to struggle;* هطي *struggle.* See את.

הי HEI. Root analogous to the vital root הה whose properties it manifests.

The Arabic هي represents the pronominal relation *she, that, this.* As verb, this root develops in هيو or هي the action of *arranging,* of *preparing* things and giving them an agreeable form.

היא. See הוא of which this is the feminine: *she, that, this.*

הי Onomatopoetic root expressing all painful and sorrowful affections.

הוי Interjective relation, represented by *oh! alas! ah! woe!*

הך HECH. See the root אך of which this is but a modification.

The Arabic هق expresses a rapid movement in marching; هك indicates, as onomatopoetic root, the noise of the sabre when it cleaves the air. These two words characterize a vigorous action.

היך See איך.

הל HEL. The sign of life, united by contraction to the root אל, image of force and of elevation, gives it a new expression and spiritualizes the sense. Hieroglyphically, the root הל is the symbol of excentric movement, of distance; in opposition to the root הך, which is that of concentric movement, of nearness: figuratively, it characterizes a sentiment of cheerfulness and felicity, an exaltation; literally, it expresses that which is distant, ulterior, placed beyond.

The Arabic هل develops in general, the same ideas as the Hebrew. As verb, it is, in particular, the action of *appearing,* of beginning to shine, in speaking of the moon. As adverbial relation it is, in a restricted sense, the interrogative particle.

הל or היל That which is *exalted, resplendent, elevated, glorified, worthy of praise;* that which is *illustrious, celebrated,* etc.

הל and הלל (*intens.*) That which *attains* the desired end, which recovers or gives *health,* which arrives in or conducts to *safety.*

הם HEM. Universalized life: the vital power of the universe. See הו.

הם Onomatopoetic and idiomatic root, which indicates every kind of tumultuous noise, commotion, fracas.

The Arabic هم characterizes, in general, that which is heavy, painful, agonizing. It is literally a *burden, care, perplexity.* As verb, هم expresses the action of *being disturbed,* of *interfering,* of bustling about to do a thing.

הום Action of *exciting a tumult, making a noise,*

disturbing with clamour, with an unexpected crash; every *perturbation, consternation, trembling,* etc.

הן HEN. The sign of life united to that of individual and produced existence, constitutes a root which characterizes existences and things in general; an object, a place; the present time; that which falls beneath the senses, that which is conceived as real and actually **exciting**.

הן That which is before the eyes and whose existence is indicated by means of the relations, *here, behold,* in this place; *then,* in that time.

The Arabic هن has in general the same ideas as the Hebrew. It is any thing distinct from others; a small part of anything whatsoever. As onomatopoetic and idiomatic root هن expresses the action of *lulling,* literally as well as figuratively.

הון Every idea of actual and present existence: state of *being there,* present and ready for something: *realities, effects of all sorts, riches.*

הס HES. Onomatopoetic and idiomatic root which depicts silence. The Arabic هس seems to indicate a sort of dull murmur, as when a herd grazes in the calm of night.

הע HEH. Root not used in Hebrew. The Arabic هع indicates a violent movement; a sudden irruption.

הף HEPH. This root, which the Hebraic genius employs only in composition, constitutes in the Arabic هف an onomatopoeia which depicts a breath that escapes quickly and lightly. As verb, it is the action of *grazing,* touching slightly, slipping off, etc. See אף.

הִץ HETZ. The Chaldaic הוּץ signifies *a branch*, and the Arabic هص a thing composed of several others united by contraction.

This root expresses also in the verb هص the action of *gleaming in the darkness*, in speaking of the eyes of a wolf.

הִק HECQ. The Arabic هق indicates an extraordinary movement in anything whatsoever; an impetuous march, a vehement discourse; a delirium, a transport.

הִר HER. The sign of life united by contraction to the elementary root אר, constitutes a root which develops all ideas of conception, generation and increase, literally as well as figuratively.

As onomatopoetic root, the Arabic هر depicts a noise which frightens suddenly, which startles. It is literally, the action of *crumbling*, or of *causing to crumble*.

הר Conception, thought; pregnancy; a swelling, intumescence, inflation; a hill, a mountain; etc.

הִשׁ HESH. Root not used in Hebrew. The Arabic هش signifies literally *to soften, to become tender*. As onomatopoetic root, هش indicates a tumultuous concourse of any kind whatsoever.

הִת HETH. Every occult, profound, unknown existence.

הוּת Action of *conspiring* in the darkness, of *scheming*, of *plotting*.

The Arabic هث expresses the accumulation of clouds and the darkness which results.

ו O. OU. W. This character has two very distinct vocal acceptations, and a third as consonant. Following the first of these vocal acceptations, it represents the eye of man, and becomes the symbol of light; following the second, it represents the ear, and becomes the symbol of sound, air, wind: as consonant it is the emblem of water and represents taste and covetous desire. If one considers this character as grammatical sign, one discovers in it, as I have already said, the image of the most profound, the most inconceivable mystery, the image of the knot which unites, or the point which separates nothingness and being. In its luminous vocal acceptation וֹ, it is the sign of intellectual sense, the verbal sign *par excellence,* as I have already explained at length in my Grammar: in its ethereal verbal acceptation וּ, it is the universal convertible sign, which makes a thing pass from one nature to another; communicating on one side with the sign of intellectual sense וֹ, which is only itself more elevated, and on the other, with that of material sense יּ, which is only itself more abased: it is finally, in its aqueous consonantal acceptation, the link of all things, the conjunctive sign. It is in this last acceptation that it is employed more particularly as article. I refer to my Grammar for all the details into which I cannot enter without repeating what I have already said. I shall only add here, as a matter worthy of the greatest attention, that the character ו, except its proper name וו, does not begin any word of the Hebraic tongue, and consequently does not furnish any root. This important observation, corroborating all that I have said upon the nature of the Hebraic signs, proves the high antiquity of this tongue and the regularity of its course. Because if the character ו is really the universal convertible sign and the conjunctive article, it should never be found at the head of a root to constitute it. Now it must not appear, and indeed it never does appear, except in the heart of nouns to modify them, or between them for the purpose of joining them, or in front of the verbal tenses to change them.

The arithmetical number of this character is 6.

The Arabic, Ethiopic, Syriac and Chaldaic, which are not so scrupulous and which admit the character ו at the head of a great number of words, prove by this that they are all more modern, and that they have long since corrupted the purity of the principles upon which stood the primitive idiom from which they descend; this idiom preserved by the Egyptian priests, was delivered as I have said, to Moses who taught it to the Hebrews.

In order to leave nothing to be desired by the amateurs of etymological science, I shall state briefly the most important roots which begin with this character, in the dialects which possess them and which are nearly all onomatopoetic and idiomatic.

וא OUA. Onomatopoetic root which, in the Syriac ︎ܘܐܘܐ expresses the action of *barking*. Thence the Arabic واج signifies *a hungry dog*.

וב OUB. Every idea of sympathetic production, of emanation, of contagion. The Arabic وبا signifies in a particular sense, to *communicate a plague* or any other contagious malady.

וג OUG. *Aromatic cane.* The Arabic, which possesses this root, is derived from وجب action of *striking*, of *amputating;* of *castrating* animals.

וד OUD. In Arabic ود every idea of *love, friendship, inclination.* It is the sympathetic root דוֹר.

In the modern idiom ود signifies to *cultivate friendship for some one,* to give evidence of kindness.

וה OUH. In Chaldaic and in Arabic, it is an onomatopoetic root which expresses a violent condition of the soul; واه is applied to a cry of extreme pain; وهوه denotes the roaring of a lion. The verb وهي characterizes that which is torn, lacerated, put to rout.

וו WOU. Is the name itself of the character ו in a broad sense it is *every conversion, every conjunction;* in a restricted sense, *a nail*.

וז OUZ. The Syriac ܐܘܙܐ signifies literally *a goose*.

The Arabic وز is an onomatopoetic root which represents every kind of excitation. Thence the verbs وز and وهز which signify *to excite,* to act with violence, *to trample under foot,* etc.

וּה OUH. Onomatopoetic root which depicts in the Arabic وحوح a *hoarseness of the voice*. The Ethiopic root ወሀየ (*whi*) characterizes a sudden emission of light, a manifestation. It is the Hebraic root חוה.

וט OUT. *The sound of a voice, clear and shrill, a cry of terror;* the kind of *pressure which brings forth this cry:* in Arabic وط and وطط.

וי WI. Onomatopoetic root which expresses *disdain, disgust,* in Chaldaic, Syriac and Ethiopic: it is the same sentiment expressed by the interjective relation *fi!*

The Arabic وي has the same sense. In the Ethiopic idiom ወይን (*win*) signifies *wine;* in ancient Arabic وين is found to designate a kind of raisin.

וּךְ OUCH. Every agglomeration, every movement given in order to concentrate; in Arabic وك.

RADICAL VOCABULARY 337

The compound وكول, signifies properly *a roll*.

וֹל OUL. Onomatopoetic root which depicts a drawling and plaintive sound of the voice; in Arabic ولول ; in Syriac ܡܠܘܠܐ. Thence the Arabic وله every idea of sorrow, anxiety of mind. The word وهل which expresses that which holds to *intention, opinion,* is derived from the root **אל**.

וֹם OUM. Every kind of *consent, assent, conformity*.

The Arabic وام signifies *to form, make similar to a model*. It is the root **אם**.

The verb وما signifies *to make a sign*.

וֹן OUN. Every kind of *delicacy, corporeal softness, indolence*. The Arabic وني signifies *to languish, to become enervated*. The Ethiopic ⵟⵁⵈⵊ (*thouni*) signifies *to be corrupted through pleasures*.

וֹס OUS. Onomatopoetic root representing the noise that one makes speaking in the ear: thence, the Arabic وسوس *an insinuation, a suggestion*. When this word is written عوص then it signifies *a temptation of the devil*.

וֹע OUH. Onomatopoetic root representing the noise of a violent fire, conflagration; thence, the Ethiopic ⵟⵁⵈⵊ (*wohi*), action of *inflaming;* the Arabic وع or وعوع *howling; crackling of a furnace; a clamour,* etc.

וֹף OUPH. Onomatopoetic root which expresses

a sentiment of pride on the part of one who sees himself raised to dignity, decoration, power. Thence, the Arabic وهف every idea of *exterior ornament, dress, assumed power*.

וץ OUTZ. Every idea of firmness, solidity, consistence, persistence: thence, the Arabic وض which signifies in general, that which resists, and in particular *necessity*.

The verb ضا signifies *to vanquish* resistance; also, to make expiation; a religious ablution.

וק OUCQ. Onomatopoetic root to express literally the voice of birds, in Arabic وق and وقوه : figuratively, that which is made *manifest to the hearing*.

ור OUR. Onomatopoetic root which depicts the noise of the air and the wind, denotes figuratively, that which *is fanned, puffed with wind, vain*. In Arabic ورو.

The verb ورور which appears to be attached to the root אר, characterizes the state of that which is sharp, which cleaves the air with rapidity.

וש OUSH. Onomatopoetic root which expresses the confused noise of several things acting at the same time: it is *confusion, diffusion, disordered movement*, in Arabic وشوش .

The verb وشي expresses the action of tinting with many colours, of *painting*.

ות OUTH. Onomatopoetic root which depicts the difficulty of being moved and the moaning which follows this difficulty: thence, in Arabic وث , وثا and وثي , all idea of *lesion* in the limbs, *numbness, decrepitude, affliction*, etc.

ז Z. This character as consonant, belongs to the hissing sound, and is applied as onomatopoetic means, to all hissing noises, to all objects which cleave the air. As symbol, it is represented by the javelin, dart, arrow; that which tends to an end: as grammatical sign, it is the demonstrative sign, abstract image of the link which unites things. The Hebrew does not employ it as article; but in Ethiopic it fulfills the functions of the demonstrative article.

Its arithmetical number is 7.

זא ZA. Every idea of movement and of direction; noise, the terror which results therefrom: *a dart; a luminous ray; an arrow, a flash.*

The Arabic زلزل indicates, as onomatopoetic root the state of being shaken in the air, the noise made by the thing shaken.

זאב *A wolf,* on account of the luminous darts which flash from its eyes in the darkness.

זאת Demonstrative relation expressed by *this, that.* See זה.

זב ZB. The idea of reflected movement contained in the root זא united by contraction to that of all generating propagation, represented by the root אב, forms a root whose object is to depict every swarming, tumultuous movement, as that of insects; or every effervescent movement as that of water which is evaporated by fire.

The Arabic زب develops the same ideas as the Hebrew. As verb, this root expresses in the ancient idiom, the action of throwing out any excretion, as scum, slime, etc. In the modern idiom it signifies simply *to be dried,* in speaking of raisins.

זוב Action of *swarming as insects; of boiling, seething,* as water.

זג ZG. That which shows itself, acts exteriorly; such as *the bark* of a tree, *the shell* of an egg, etc.

The Arabic زج designates the butt-end of a lance. As onomatopoetic root زهج characterizes a quick, easy movement; زهج, the neighing of a horse.

זד ZD. That which causes effervescence, excites the evaporation of a thing; every idea of arrogance, pride.

זוד Action of *boiling,* literally; of *being swollen, puffed up with pride,* figuratively, *to act haughtily.*

זה, זו, זהּ ZHE, ZOU, ZO. Every demonstrative, manifesting, radiant movement: every objectivity expressed in an abstract sense by the pronominal relations *this, that, these, those.*

The Arabic زه expresses the action of shedding light, of shining.

זאת *This, that.*

זה That which *is shown, appears, shines, reflects the light;* in an abstract sense, *an object.*

זהב (*comp.*) *Gold,* on account of its innate brightness.

זהם (*comp.*) That which is loathsome.

זהר (*comp.*) That which *radiates communicates, manifests the light.* See אור.

זו Absolute idea of *objectivity;* everything from which light is reflected.

זוית (*comp.*) *A prism;* by extension, *the angle* of anything whatsoever.

זול (*comp.*) Action of *diverging;* by extension, *wasting, neglecting.* See זל.

זון (*comp.*) *Corporeal objectivity.* See זן.

זוע (*comp.*) See זע.

זור (*comp.*) Every idea of *dispersion.* See זר.

RADICAL VOCABULARY 341

זז ZZ. Every movement of vibration, reverberation; every luminous refraction.

The Arabic زز as onomatopoetic root develops the same ideas. The verb زوزي denotes the conduct of an arrogant man.

זיז Action of *vibrating*, being *refracted* as the light, *shining*.

זיז *Splendour, reflection* of light, *luminous brightness*.

זח ZH. Every difficult movement made with effort; that which is done laboriously; a presumptuous, tenacious spirit.

The Arabic زح develops the same ideas. The verb زخ expresses in general a vehement action of any nature whatsoever; in particular to *rain in torrents*.

זט ZT. Root not used in Hebrew. The Arabic زط is an onomatopoetic root which depicts the noise made by insects when flying.

זחל (*comp.*) That which is difficult to put in movement, slow in being determined. That which *drags, creeps;* which is *heavy, timid,* etc.

זי ZI. Root analogous to roots זא, זה, זו; but whose sense is less abstract and more manifest. It is in general, that which is light, easy, agreeable; that which is sweet, gracious; that which shines and is reflected as light. Every idea of grace, of brightness.

The Arabic زي develops in general, all ideas which have relation with the intrinsic qualities of things. As noun زي characterizes the form, aspect, manner of being; as verb زيي expresses the action of assuming an aspect, of being clothed in form, of having quality, etc.

זִיו In Chaldaic, *splendour, glory, majesty, joy, beauty:* in Hebrew it is the name of the first month of spring.

זִיז (*comp.*) *An animal;* that is to say, a being which reflects the light of life. See זִו.

זִין (*comp.*) *An armour:* that is to say a resplendent body. The Arabic زان signifies *to adorn.*

זִיק (*comp.*) *A flash of lightning, a quick, rapid flame, a spark,* etc.

זִית (*comp.*) *An olive tree, the olive* and *the oil* which it produces; that is to say, *the luminous essence.*

זַךְ ZCH. The demonstrative sign united by contraction to the root אַךְ, symbol of all restriction and exception, constitutes an expressive root whose purpose is to give the idea of that which has been pruned, cleaned, purged, disencumbered of all that might defile.

זַךְ Every *purification*, every refining test; that which is *clean, innocent,* etc.

The Arabic زك contains the same ideas. As noun زكي designates that which is pure, pious; as verb, زكا characterizes the state of that which abounds in virtues, in good works.

זַל ZL. The demonstrative sign united to the root אַל, symbol of every elevation, of every direction upward, forms a root whence are developed all ideas of elongation, prolongation; consequently, of attenuation, weakness; also of prodigality, looseness, baseness, etc.

זִלל Action of *wasting, profaning, relaxing;* of rendering *base, weak, feeble,* etc.

In a restricted sense the Arabic verb زل signifies *to stumble,* to make false steps.

זם ZM. That which gives form, figure; that which binds many parts together to form a whole.

The Arabic زم contains the same ideas. As onomatopoetic and idiomatic root, it is in the Arabic زيم a dull noise, a rumbling.

זם *A system, a composition, a scheme*: every work of the understanding, good or bad: *a plot, a conspiracy*, etc.

זן ZN. The demonstrative sign united to the root אן, symbol of the moral or physical circumscription of the being, constitutes a root which develops two distinct meanings according as they are considered as mind or matter. From the view point of mind, it is a moral manifestation which makes the faculties of the being understood and determines the kind; from that of matter, it is a physical manifestation which delivers the body and abandons it to pleasure. Thence:

זן Every classification by *sort* and by *kind* according to the faculties: every pleasure of the body for its *nourishment*: figuratively, all *lewdness, fornication, debauchery: a prostitute, a place of prostitution*, etc.

The Arabic زن expresses a sort of suspension of opinion in things of divers natures. As onomatopoetic root زن, describes a *murmuring*.

זון Action of *being nourished, feeding* the body; or metaphorically the action of enjoying, making abuse, *prostituting* one's self.

זס ZS. Root not used in Hebrew nor in Arabic.

זע ZH. This root, which is only the root זה or זו, inclined toward the material sense, develops the idea of painful movement, of agitation, anxiety; of trouble caused by fear of the future.

In a restricted sense the Arabic زاغ signifies to act like a fox, to use round about ways.

זוּעַ Action of *being troubled, fearful, trembling* in expectation of misfortune. Action of *being tormented, disquieted.*

זֵעָה *Trouble, agitation of mind, fatigue;* that which is the consequence, *sweat.*

זַעַם (*comp.*) *Violent* and *general* agitation; that which results, *foam*: figuratively, *rage indignation.*

זַעַף (*comp.*) Tumult of irascible passions; *tempest, storm;* etc.

זַעַק (*comp.*) Great visible commotion: *outburst of voices, clamour, loud calling.*

זָעַר (*comp.*) *Ebbing, waning: diminution, exiguity;* that which is *slender, moderate, small.*

זָף ZPH. That which is sticky, gluey; that which exercises a mutual action; literally, *pitch.*

It is, in the Arabic زف, an onomatopoetic root which denotes the effect of a puff of wind. The verb زفّ expresses the action of being carried away by the wind.

זוּף Action of *being attached,* of experiencing a mutual, reciprocal sentiment.

זָץ ZTZ. Root not used in Hebrew nor in Arabic.

זָק ZCQ. Every idea of diffusion in time or space.

The Arabic زق as onomatopoetic root denotes the action of *pecking.*

זָק A *chain, suite, flux;* a *draught* of anything whatsoever. That which *spreads, glides, flows* in space or time. Thence, *years, old age,* and the veneration which is attached to it: *water* and the purity which ensues: *a chain* and the strength which attends it; *an arrow,* etc.

RADICAL VOCABULARY 345

In a restricted sense, the Arabic زق signifies *a leather bottle* wherein one puts any kind of liquid. It is doubtless the Hebrew word שׂק or the Chaldaic סק, *a sack*.

זר ZR. The demonstrative sign united to that of movement proper, symbol of the straight line, constitutes a root which develops the idea of that which goes from the centre, spreads, disperses in every sense, radiates, leaves a sphere, or any enclosure whatsoever and becomes foreign.

זר Every *dispersion, dissemination, ventilation*: that which is abandoned to its own movement, which goes from the centre, *diverges*: in a broad sense, *a stranger, an adversary, a barbarian*: in a more restricted sense, *a fringe, a girdle*.

The Arabic زر having lost all the primitive ideas contained in this root, has preserved only those which are attached to the word *girdle* and is restricted to signifying the action of *girding, tying* a knot, *binding*, etc.

זור Action of being *disseminated, separated from* the centre, *abandoned* to its own impulsion; considered as *estranged, alienated, scorned, treated as enemy;* action of *sneezing*, etc.

זש ZSH. Root not used in Hebrew. The Arabic زوش signifies *a lout, a boorish fellow;* lacking manners and politeness.

זת ZTH. Every objective representation expressed by the pronominal relations *this, that, these, those*.
זעת *This, that*.

ח E. H. CH. This character can be considered under the double relation of vowel or consonant. As vocal sound it is the symbol of elementary existence and represents the principle of vital aspiration: as consonant it belongs to the guttural sound and represents the field of man, his labour, that which demands on his part any effort, care, fatigue. As grammatical sign it holds an intermediary rank between ה, life, absolute existence, and כ, life, relative and assimilated existence. It presents thus, the image of a sort of equilibrium and equality, and is attached to ideas of effort, labour, and of normal and legislative action.

Its arithmetical number is 8.

חא   HA. Root is analogous with the root חי, which bears the real character of the sign ח. This is used more under its onomatopoetic relation, to denote the violence of an effort, a blow struck, an exclamatory cry.

חב   HEB. The sign of elementary existence united to the root אב, symbol of all fructification, forms a root whose purpose is to describe that which is occult, hidden, mysterious, secret, enclosed, as a germ, as all elementary fructification: if the root אב is taken in its acceptation of desire to have, the root in question here, will develop the idea of an amorous relation, of fecundation.

This is why the Arabic حَبّ taken in a restricted sense, signifies *to love;* whereas in a broader sense this root develops all ideas of grain, germ, semence, etc.

חב or חבב (*intens.*) *To hide mysteriously, to impregnate, to brood,* etc.

In a restricted sense, the Arabic حَابّ signifies *to become partial, to favour.* As onomatopoetic root حَبّ suggests the noise of whetting a sabre.

חוב   (*comp.*) One who hides, who keeps the property of another; *a debtor.*

חג   HEG. Every hard and continued action; every turbulent movement: every transport of joy; joust, game, popular fête, tournament, carousal.

RADICAL VOCABULARY 347

חג or חגג (*intens.*) Every idea of *fête*, of *solemnity*, where all the people are acting.

It is, in the Arabic خج , the action of visiting a holy place, going on a pilgrimage; in خج , that of *trotting*.

חוג Action of *whirling, dancing in a ring, devoting one's self to pleasure, celebrating the games*. Metaphorically, *an orbit, a circumference, a sphere of activity, the terrestrial globe*.

חד HED. The power of division, expressed by the root אד which, arrested by the effort which results from its contraction with the elementary sign ה, becomes the image of relative unity. It is literally, *a sharp thing, a point, a summit*.

The Arabic حد presents in general, the ideas of *terminating, determining, circumscribing, limiting*. It is, in a more restricted sense, *to grind;* metaphorically, *to punish*. This root being reinforced in the verb حد , expresses the action of breaking through and excavating the ground. As noun, خد signifies literally *the cheek*.

חד *The point* of anything whatever. Everything which *pricks*, everything which is *extreme, initial:* metaphorically, *a drop* of wine; *gaiety*, lively and piquant.

חוד Action of *speaking cleverly, uttering witticisms,* giving *enigmas*.

חיד *Enigma, parable*.

חה HEH. This root, analogue of the root חא, is little used. The characteristic root of the sign is חו.

חו HOU. Elementary existence in general; in particular, that which renders this existence manifest and obvious; that which declares it to the senses.

In the analogue حو , this root has not conserved the

intellectual ideas of the Hebrew; but being reinforced in خو , it has presented what is most profound in elementary existence, *chaos*.

חוה and חוי All ideas of *indication, elementary manifestation, declaration;* action of *uncovering* that which was hidden, etc.

 חוב (*comp.*) See חב.
 חוג (*comp.*) See חג.
 חוד (*comp.*) See חד.
 חוז (*comp.*) *The horizon.* See חז.
 חוח (*comp.*) Action of *hooking.* See חח.
 חוט (*comp.*) Action of *mending, sewing.* See חט.
 חול (*comp.*) See חל.
 חום (*comp.*) See חם.
 חוס (*comp.*) Action of *sympathizing, condoling.* See חם.

חוץ (*comp.*) That which is *exterior*, or which *acts exteriorly;* that which leaves the ordinary limits and which, in an abstract sense is expressed by the relations *beyond, outside, extra, except,* etc.

 חור (*comp.*) See חר.
 חוש (*comp.*) See חש.

חז HEZ. The sign of elementary existence, united to that of demonstration, or of objective representation, forms a very expressive root whose purpose is to bring forth all ideas of vision, visual preception, contemplation.

The Arabic حر in losing all the intellectual acceptations of the Hebraic root, has conserved only the physical ideas which are attached to it as onomatopoetic root, and is limited to designating any kind of notch, incision; metaphorically, scrutiny, inspection. The verb خر signifies literally *to pierce*.

RADICAL VOCABULARY 349

חז   Action of *seeing, regarding, considering, contemplating; the aspect* of things; *a seer, a prophet, one who sees.*

חזז   (*intens.*) *A vision; a flash of lightning.*

חזה   Extent of the sight, *the horizon; boundaries, the limits* of a thing; *a region.*

חח   HEH. Every idea of effort applied to a thing, and of a thing making effort; *a hook, fish-hook, ring; a thorn-bush.*

חוח   That which is *pointed, hooked;* that which exercises any force whatever, as *pincers, hooks, forceps:* thence the Arabic verb حاق , *to penetrate, to go deeply into.*

חט   HET. The sign of effort united to that of resistance, constitutes a root whence come all ideas of frustrated hope; of failure, sin, error.

The Arabic حـ signifies properly *to cut in small morsels;* and حط , *to pose, depose; place, replace: to lower, humble, reduce,* etc.

חט or חטט   (*intens.*) That which *misses* the mark, which is *at fault,* which *sins* in any manner whatsoever.

חוט   (*comp.*) The root חט, symbol of effort united to resistance, being considered from another viewpoint, furnishes the restricted idea of *spinning,* and in consequence, every kind of *thread,* and of *sewing;* so that from the sense of *sewing,* comes that of *mending;* metaphorically, that of *amendment, restoration:* whence it results that the word חטא, which signifies *a sin,* signifies also *an expiation.*

חי   HEI. Elementary life and all ideas thereunto attached. This root is the analogue of the root חו.

חיה   Action of *living* in the physical order, action of *existing:* that which *lives;* every kind of *animal, living being, beast.* Physical life, the *animality* of nature.

The Arabic حي develops every idea contained in the Hebraic root.

חיל (comp.) *Vital force;* that which maintains, procures, sustains existence: *elementary virtuality; the physical faculties,* literally as well as figuratively: *power* which results from force; *virtue* which is born of courage; *an army,* that which is *numerous, valorous, redoubtable; a fort, fortress, rampart; a multitude,* etc.

חֵךְ HECH. The sign of elementary existence united to that of assimilative and relative existence, forms a root which is related to all perceptions of judgment and which develops all interior ideas.

The Arabic root حك, having lost nearly every moral idea which comes from the primitive root and being confined to purely physical ideas, is limited to express as noun, *an itching, a friction;* and as verb, the analogous action of *itching, scratching.*

חֵךְ That which grasps forms inwardly and which fixes them, as the sense of *taste;* that which is *sapid; sensible to savours; the palate, throat:* that which *covets, desires, hopes,* etc.

חֵל HEL. This root, composed of the sign of elementary existence united to the root אל, symbol of extensive force and of every movement which bears upward, produces a mass of ideas which it is very difficult to fix accurately. It is, in general, a superior effort which causes a distention, extension, relaxation; it is an unknown force which breaks the bonds of bodies by stretching them, breaking them, reducing them to shreds, or by dissolving them, relaxing them to excess.

חל Every idea of *extension, effort* made upon a thing to *extend, develop, stretch* or *conduct* it to a point or end: *a twinge, a pain: a persevering movement; hope, expectation.*

RADICAL VOCABULARY 351

The Arabic حل develops, in general, all the ideas contained in the Hebraic root. In a restricted sense it is the action of *loosening, relaxing, releasing, resolving, absolving,* etc. When this root receives the guttural reinforcement, it expresses in خل, the state of privation, indigence; that which lacks, which is wanting in any manner whatsoever.

חל and חלל (*intens.*) *Distention, distortion, contortion; endurance, solution of continuity; an opening, a wound: extreme relaxation, dissolution; profanation, pollution; weakness, infirmity, debility; vanity, effeminate dress, ornament; a flute; a dissolute dance, a frivolous amusement;* etc.

חול or חיל Action of *suffering* from the effect of a violent effort made upon one's self; action of *being twisted, stretched,* action of *being confined, bringing into the world; being carried* in thought or action *toward an end; producing* ideas: action of *tending, attending, hoping, placing faith in* something; action of *disengaging, resolving, dissolving, opening, milking, extracting,* etc.

חיל (*comp.*) *Elementary virtuality.* See 'ח.

חם HEM. The sign of elementary existence, symbol of every effort and every labour, united to the sign of exterior activity, and employed as collective and generalizing sign, forms an important root whose purpose is to signify, in a broad sense, a general envelopment and the warmth which results, considered as an effect of contractile movement.

חם Idea of that which is *obtuse; curved, hot, obscure; enveloping, striking; a curvature; dejection; a compressive force: natural heat, solar fire, torrefaction* and *the burnish* which follows; *blackness:* that which *heats,* literally or figuratively; *generative ardour, amorous passion, wrath,* etc.

The Arabic خَمّ , having lost to a certain point, the intellectual ideas developed by the Hebraic root, is limited to expressing the particular ideas of warmth and heating; when reinforced by the guttural aspiration in خَمّ , it signifies literally *to be corrupted, spoiled, putrefied.*

חוֹם Action of *enveloping, seizing* by a contractile movement, *exercising* upon something *a compressive force; heating; rendering obscure.* In a restricted sense, *a wall*, because it *encloses*; a *girdle*, because it *envelops*; in general, every *curved, round* figure; *simulacrum of the sun,* etc.

חן HEN. The composition of this root is conceived in two ways, according to the first, the sign ח, which characterizes every effort, every difficult and painful action, being contracted with the onomatopoetic root אן, image of pain, expresses the idea of a prayer, a supplication, a grace to grant or granted: according to the second, the same sign, symbol of elementary existence, being united to that of individual and produced existence, becomes a sort of reinforcement of the root חן, and designates all proper and particular existences whether in time or space.

חן That which results from *prayer;* as *grace, a favour;* that which is *exorable,* which allows itself *to relent;* that which is *clement, merciful, full of pity:* that which is *easy, a good bargain,* etc.

The Arabic حن develops, as the Hebraic root, all ideas of kindness, mercy, tenderness, clemency. This root in reinforcing itself in خن designates separation, seclusion; it is, literally, a place for travellers, *a hostelry.* As onomatopoetic root, خن expresses the action of *speaking through the nose.*

חן Every separate intrenched place: *a cell, a hospice, a fort, a camp.* Action of *living apart,* having one's own

RADICAL VOCABULARY 353

residence, being *fixed, intrenched,* and consequetly *to besiege, to press* the enemy, etc.

חס HES. Every silent, secret action; that which is done with connivance; that which is confided, trusted or said secretly.

חוס Action of *conniving* at a thing, of *sympathizing;* of *conspiring:* a place of refuge, *a shelter,* etc. It is also the action of making effort upon one's self, of experiencing an interior movement of *contrition.*

The diverse acceptations of the Hebraic root are divided in the analogous Arabic words خس , حص , حس and خص, in which they modify themselves in diverse manners. Considered as verb, حس signifies *to feel,* to have the sensation of some thing; حص *to act with celerity;* خس *to diminish* in volume, *to be contracted, shrunken;* خص *to particularize,* etc.

חע HEH. Root not used in Hebrew. The Arabic خوع indicates a grievous and painful sensation.

חף HEPH. Every idea of protective covering given to a thing; a guarantee, a surety.

The Arabic حف is an onomatopoetic and idiomatic root, which depicts that which acts upon the surface, which skims, passes lightly over a thing. The verb خف characterizes the condition of that which becomes light; خاف anything which shivers, shudders with fear, trembles with fright, etc.

חוף Action of *covering, protecting, brooding, coaxing.* A *roof, nest, shelter, port:* action of separating from that which *harms;* of *combing, appropriating,* etc.

חֵץ HETZ. Every idea of division, scission, gash, cut; that which acts from the exterior, as the adverbial relation חוּץ expresses, *outside*.

The Arabic حض signifies *to stimulate;* and خض *to keep stirring, to agitate.*

חִץ That which divides by making irruption, passing without from within: *an arrow, an obstacle; a stone* coming from the sling; *an axe, a dart: a division* of troops; *a quarrel;* etc.

חֹק HECQ. Every idea of definition, impression of an object in the memory, description, narration; that which pertains to symbols, to characters of writing. In a broader sense matter used according to a determined mode.

חֹק The action of *defining, connecting, giving a dimension, deciding upon forms;* of *hewing, cutting* after a model; *to carve, to design:* a thing *appointed, enacted, decreed, constituted,* etc.

The Arabic حق develops, in general, the same ideas as the Hebraic root; but is applied more particularly to that which confirms, verifies, certifies; to that which is true, just, necessary.

חֹר HER. The sign of elementary existence united to that of movement proper, symbol of the straight line, constitutes a root which develops, in general, the idea of a central fire whose heat radiates. It is in particular, a consuming ardour, literally as well as figuratively.

The Arabic حر has exactly the same meaning. When this root is reinforced by the guttural aspiration in خر it is no longer applied to the expansion of heat, but to that of any fluid whatsoever. In a restricted sense خر signifies *to ooze*.

RADICAL VOCABULARY

חר and חרר (*intens.*) That which *burns* and *consumes*, that which is *burned* and *consumed;* that which is *arid, desert, barren;* every kind of *residue, excrement: the mouth* of a furnace, *the entrance* of a cavern; etc.

חור Action of *consuming* by fire; *setting fire, irritating:* the ardour of *fever,* that of *wrath;* effect of *the flame,* its brilliancy; *the blush* which mounts to the face; *candour;* every *purification* by fire; etc.

חרע (*comp.*) That which is *sharp, cutting, acute, stinging, destructive.*

חש HESH. Every violent and disordered movement, every inner ardour seeking to extend itself; central fire; avaricious and covetous principle; that which is arid.

The Arabic حش develops in general, the same ideas as the Hebrew. As onomatopoetic root, حش expresses the action of *chopping, mowing;* when it is reinforced by the guttural aspiration, it signifies, in the verb خش , *to penetrate.*

חוש Action of *acting with vehemence* upon something; every *vivacity; avidity; aridity.* This root, taken in the latter sense of *aridity,* is applied metaphorically, to that which is *barren,* which produces nothing; to *mutes;* to those who do not speak, who keep *silent.*

חת HETH. This root contains all ideas of shock, terror, sympathetic movement which depresses and dismays. It is, in general, the reaction of useless effort; elementary existence driven back upon itself; in particular, it is a *shudder, consternation, terror; a sinking, a depression; a degradation,* etc.

The Arabic حث has not conserved the moral ideas developed by the Hebraic root. It is, as onomatopoetic root, an exciting, instigating, provocative movement.

ט T. This character, as consonant, belongs to the dental sound. As symbolic image it represents the shelter of man; the roof that he raises to protect him; his shield. As grammatical sign it is that of resistance and protection. It serves as link between ר and ת, and partakes of their properties, but in an inferior degree.

Its arithmetical number is 9.

טא TA. Every idea of resistance, repulsion, rejection, reflection; that which causes luminous refraction.

The Arabic ٮل develops the idea of every kind of bending, inflection. Thence the verb ٮلل, *to bow down*.

טאט. (*intens.*) Action of *repulsing* a dart, as from a shield; of *making hail rebound*, as from a roof; etc.

טב TB. The sign of resistance united to that of interior action, image of all generation, composes a root which is applied to all ideas of conservation and central integrity: it is the symbol of healthy fructification, and of a force capable of setting aside every corruption.

The Arabic نٮ or طٮ, has, in general, the same sense as the Hebrew. In a restricted sense, نٮ signifies *to amend;* طٮ, *to supply* the want, the lack of anything whatsoever; *to become well, to be healed,* etc.

טוב That which keeps a just mean; that which is *well, healthy;* that which defends itself and resists corruption; that which is *good*.

טג TG. Root not used in Hebrew. The Arabic طج indicates a violent shock, a warlike cry.

By جٮ is understood, that which declares force, audacity, pride. In a restricted sense جاٮ signifies *a crown, a mitre*.

RADICAL VOCABULARY

טד TD. Root not used in Hebrew. The Arabic طد seems to indicate a thing strong and capable of resistance.

טה TEH. Root analogous to the root טא. It is only used in composition. The Arabic طه as interjection, inspires security.

In a restricted sense, the verb طها or طهو signifies to *dispose of* and *prepare* a thing in such a way as to render it useful.

טהר (*comp.*) That which is *pure*. See טר.

טו TOU. That which arrests, which opposes resistance. See טא.

The Arabic طه is used as adverbial relation to impose silence upon someone. ٌطو signifies literally *an hour*.

טוב (*comp.*) That which is *good*. See טב.

טוה Every kind of *thread*, of *spinning: a net*.

טוח Action of *placing in safety, guaranteeing, covering, inlaying: a covering, an inlay, a coat of plaster;* etc.

טול (*comp.*) Action of *projecting*, especially *the shadow*. See טל.

טור (*comp.*) Action of *disposing*, putting in order. See טר.

טוש (*comp.*) Action of *flying away, disappearing*. See טש.

טז TZ. Root not used in Hebrew. Appears only in Arabic through wrong usage.

טח TEH. Every idea of a stroke hurled or repulsed; metaphorically, *a calumny, an accusation*.

The Arabic طح expresses as onomatopoetic root, the

action of repulsing with the foot. This root reinforced by the guttural aspiration, signifies in طخ *to be obscured, made dense, thick;* in خ, *to be lessened.*

טט TT. Root not used in Hebrew. The Chaldaic טמ, is sometimes taken to express the number *two*.

The Arabic بط appears to designate putrid slime, offensive mire.

טי TI. Root analogous to the root טא, and which like it, expresses every kind of reflection as is indicated by the following:

טיט (*intens.*) That which *gushes forth;* that which *splashes,* as *mud, slime, mire;* etc. Figuratively, *the earth.*

The Arabic طي signifies properly *to bend, to give way, to be soft.*

טך TCH. Root not used in Hebrew. The Chaldaic is used to signify *a siege.*

As onomatopoetic root the Arabic طق depicts the noise of that which explodes.

טל TL. The sign of resistance united by contraction to the root אל, symbol of every elevation, composes a root whose object is to express the effect of a thing which raises itself above another thing, covers, veils, or puts it **under shelter.**

The Arabic طل contains in general, all the ideas developed by the Hebraic root.

טל That which *casts a shadow,* that which *is projected* from above below; that which *varies, changes, moves* like a shadow: *a veil, a garment* with which one is covered; *a spot* which changes colour; *the dew* which forms a veil over plants; *an unweaned lamb* still under the shelter of its mother.

The Arabic طل has many divers acceptations like the Hebrew, all of which can, however, be reduced to the primitive idea of a thing emanating from another, as *dew, shade;* metaphorically, *length, duration,* etc. In a restricted sense نل signifies *to raise up;* طل *to continue.*

טם TM. Every idea of contamination, of anathema; that which is impure and profane.

The Arabic طم has lost, in general, the primitive ideas contained in the Hebraic root. In a restricted sense, this word signifies simply *to throw dust.*

טום Action of *separating as impure,* of *anathematizing;* every kind of *impurity, pollution, vice, filthiness.*

טן TN. Everything woven in a manner to form a continuous whole, as a *screen, trellis, pannier, basket.*

As onomatopoetic and idiomatic root, the Arabic نّ or طن denotes every kind of tinkling, resounding noise. It is from the idea of persistence developed by the Hebraic root, that is formed the Arabic verb ظن, *to presume, to believe,* to regard as certain.

טס TS. Root not used in Hebrew. The Chaldaic טס signifies *a plate* of any kind whatsoever: the Arabic طس denotes very nearly that sort of receptacle called *cup* or *bowl* in English.

As verb طس, signifies in the vulgar idiom *to put in a sack; to be settled, effaced.*

טע TOH. Every idea of obstinacy and persistence in an evil manner. This root is the analogue of the root טא, but more inclined toward the material sense.

טע *The tenacity, the hardness* of an evil character: *obstinacy.*

The Arabic طع presents the same ideas as the Hebrew. The verb طغا signifies literally *to err, to behave badly.*

טַעַם (*comp.*) That which is attached to *sensuality of taste; to sensation, to the knowledge* which results: figuratively, a good or bad *habit, custom: reason, judgment.*

טַעַן (*comp.*) *To charge, to load* someone with *burdens; to fix* in a place, *to nail:* metaphorically *to overwhelm.*

טַף TPH. Everything which struggles, which stirs incessantly; which goes and comes without stopping; which persists in its movement.

The Arabic طفّ develops in a broad sense the idea of that which is impending, which can happen, occur. In a very restricted sense, طفّ signifies *to pour out,* as onomatopoetic root نفّ, indicates the action of *spitting.*

טַף In a figurative sense, *a child;* anything whatsoever floating in the air or upon the water: *a swimmer; a palm branch,* etc.

טֹע TOH. Root not used in Hebrew nor in Arabic.

טֹק TCQ. Root not used in Hebrew. The Arabic طق , is an onomatopoetic root which depicts the noise of stones crushed beneath the feet of horses, or that of frogs croaking upon the banks of pools, or that which produces a harsh, rough utterance.

טֹר TR. The sign of resistance united by contraction to the elementary root אר, as image of fire, forms a root which develops all ideas of purification, consecration, ordination.

The Arabic طر has lost nearly all the ideas developed by the Hebraic root; so that restricting it to physical forms, this root characterizes an abrupt, unexpected movement, a fortuitous thing, an incidence; etc.

טהר (*comp.*) That which is *pure, purified, purged* of its impurities.

טור (*comp.*) That which *is conducted* with *purity,* with *rectitude;* that which maintains *order; clarity.*

טש TSH. Root not used in Hebrew. The Chaldaic expresses a change of place; to hide and take away from sight.

The Arabic طش is an onomatopoetic root which depicts the noise of falling rain, the simmering of boiling oil, etc.

טת TTH. Root not used in Hebrew. The Arabic طث is an onomatopoetic root which depicts the noise of a top spinning; thence, the name of various games for children and several other related things.

י I. This character is the symbol of all manifested power. It represents the hand of man, the forefinger. As grammatical sign, it is that of potential manifestation, intellectual duration, eternity. This character, remarkable in its vocal nature, loses the greater part of its faculties in becoming consonant, where it signifies only a material duration, a refraction, a sort of link as ז, or of movement as ש.

Plato gave particular attention to this vowel which he considered as assigned to the female sex and designated consequently all that which is tender and delicate.

The Hebraist grammarians who rank this character among the *héémanthes,* attribute to it the virtue of expressing at the beginning of words, duration and strength; but it is only a result of its power as sign.

I have shown in my Grammar what use the idiomatic

genius of the Hebraic tongue made of the mother vowel י, in the composition of compound radical verbs as initial adjunction.

Its arithmetical number is 10.

יא‎ IA. This root manifests the potential faculties of things.

The Arabic ﻳَﺎ expresses, as adverbial or interjective relation, all the movements of the soul which spring from admiration, astonishment, respect; *o! oh! ah!*

יאה‎ That which is *suitable, worthy, conformable* with the nature of things, *specious, decent;* that which has *beauty, elegance,* etc.

יאב‎ (*comp.*) That which desires ardently. See אב‎.

יאל‎ (*comp.*) Every idea of proneness, inclination: that which aspires, tends toward an object. See אל‎.

יאור‎ (*comp.*) A river. See אר‎.

יב‎ IB. Onomatopoetic root which describes the yelping of a dog. Figuratively it is *a cry, howl, vociferation.* The Ethiopic ይብሀ (*ibbe*) signifies *jubilation.*

יג‎ IG. Every idea of fatigue, languor, sadness, as result of long continued action. See אג‎.

The Arabic ﻳَﺞ · ﻳَﺠَّ indicates an overwhelming, stifling heat.

יד‎ ID. The sign of potential manifestation, united to the root אר‎, image of every emanation, of every divisional cause, forms a remarkable root, whose purpose is to produce ideas relative to the hand of man.

The Arabic ﺟَﺪ presents exactly the same ideas as the Hebrew.

יד‎ In the literal and restricted sense, *the hand;* in the figurative and general sense, it is the *faculty, executive*

RADICAL VOCABULARY 363

force, power of acting, dominion: it is every kind of *aid, instrument, machine, work, term; administration, liberality, faith, protection:* it is the symbol of *relative unity,* and of the *power of division;* it is *the margin, boarder, edge;* the point by which one grasps things; it is *the place, the point* that one indicates, etc.

יאר (*comp.*) Every idea of power and of force: that which is irresistible in good as in evil: *fate, destiny, necessity.*

יד or ידד (*intens.*) Action of *throwing, hurling* with the hand; of *issuing, sending;* of *spreading, divulging,* etc.

יה IEH. Absolute life manifested, Eternity, the eternally living Being: GOD.

The Arabic ﻳَﻪ has lost all the intellectual ideas developed by the Hebraic root, but the Syriac ܝܗ and the Samaritan ᛘᚾ, signify alike *the Absolute Being.* By the word ﻳَﻬِﻲ is understood only a sort of call.

יהב (*comp.*) Action of being fruitful, manifesting fruits; *a litter, a burden.* Action of bearing, producing. See אב and הב.

יהוד (*comp.*) Divine emanation, *God-given:* it is the name of the Jewish people, or that of *Judah,* from which it is derived.

יו IO. Every luminous manifestation; everything intelligible.

This root no longer exists in Arabic in its primitive simplicity. It is found only in the Coptic word Ioh to designate *the moon;* it is rather remarkable that the same Arabic word ﻳَﻮح, designates *the sun.* This last word, in receiving the guttural aspiration in ﻳَﻮخ , signifies literally *the day,* and is used sometimes in place of ﻳَﻮم.

יום (*comp.*) The luminous, continued, universalized manifestation: *day.* See י׳.

The Arabic يوم has conserved none of the intellectual ideas contained in the Hebrew. As noun, it is, in a restricted sense, *a day;* as verb, *to fix a day, to adjourn.*

יון (*comp.*) The being, passing from power into action: *the manifested being.* See און. In a broader sense, *the generative faculty of nature, the plastic force:* in a more restricted sense, a thing indeterminate, tender, soft, easy, suitable to receive all forms; clayey, ductile land; *a mire;* etc.

יז IZ. Root not used in Hebrew nor in Arabic.

יזם (*comp.*) *To mediate, to think.* See זם, and also the other positive roots which receive the initial adjunction in large numbers.

יח IHE. Root not used in Hebrew nor in Arabic.

יחד (*comp.*) Manifestation of unity; action of *being united*, state of being *one, unique, solitary.* See חד.

יחל (*comp.*) Every idea of *tension, attention, expectation;* action of *suffering, having anxiety, hoping,* etc. See חל

יחם (*comp.*) Action of *being heated, burned,* literally and figuratively. See חם.

יחף (*comp.*) *To be barefooted.* See חף.

יחש (*comp.*) Every idea of *origin, source, race.* See חש. It is considered here as central principle.

יט IT. Root not used in Hebrew.

יי II. Manifestation of all spiritual power, of all intellectual duration. In a more restricted sense, the mind.

יי In Chaldaic, it is the name of the Eternal; that by which one finds translated the *Ineffable Name* יהוה the interpretation of which I have given in my notes. This name is often written in the Targum ייי, *the Spirit of Spirits, the Eternity of Eternities.*

RADICAL VOCABULARY 365

יִן (comp.) *Incorporated spirit:* in a restricted sense, every spirituous liquor, *wine.*

יָךְ ICH. Manifestation of restriction; that is to say, the place wherein things are restricted, *the side.*

The Arabic does not rightfully possess this root; the Arabic words which are here attached are derived from the Persian یک, which signifies *one.*

יִל IL. Every idea of emission and of prolongation.

The Arabic جال is applied only to teeth and to their different forms.

יִלּ Action of *filling the air with cries; a lively song; a jubilation.*

יִם IM. The sign of manifestation united to that of exterior action as collective sign, composes a root whose purpose is to indicate universal manifestation and to develop all ideas of mass and accumulation.

The intellectual force of this root is weakened in Arabic, since this idiom has not conserved the characterization of the plurality of things as in Hebrew. It is the root יִן, whose expression is much less forceful, which has replaced it; also, the manner of forming the plurals of nouns with numberless anomalies and irregularities, has become one of the greatest difficulties of the Arabic tongue.

יָם In a literal and restricted sense, *the sea;* that is to say, the universal aqueous manifestation, the mass of waters.

As noun, the Arabic ع , signifies *the sea,* and as verb, *to submerge.* This word is preserved in the Coptic ΦΙΟΜ, and appears not to be foreign to the Japanese *umi.*

יוֹם (comp.) *Day;* that is to say, *universal luminous manifestation.* See יֹ .

יִן IN. The sign of manifestation united to that of individual and produced existence, composes a root whence are developed all ideas of particular manifestation and of individual being: thence the accessory ideas of particularity, individuality, property.

The Arabic بي has preserved scarcely any of the intellectual ideas developed by the Hebrew. This ancient root, however, still forms the plural of masculine nouns in Arabic, as in Chaldaic and Syriac, but it is often changed into ان following the usage of the Samaritans, and more often disappears entirely allowing this same plural to be formed in the most irregular manner.

יִן That which manifests *individual sentiment, existence proper, interest:* that which is relative to *a determined centre,* to *a particular point;* that which *draws to itself, appropriates, envelops, involves* in its vortex; *deprives, oppresses* others for its own interest: every *internal movement,* every *desire for growth.*

יוֹן (*comp.*) *Generative faculty* of nature, *plastic force:* in a restricted sense, *a dove,* symbol of fecundating warmth.

יִם IS. Root not used in Hebrew. The Arabic يِس appears to indicate a movement of progression.

יִע IOH. Everything hollow, empty and fit to receive another, as *a vessel, a shovel,* etc.

The Arabic بِع as onomatopoetic root, depicts the cry of one who wishes to catch something, or seize it with the hand.

יעַד (*comp.*) Every kind of *convention, appointing* the day, place, time for *an assembly, a fête, a resolution.* See עַד.

יעַז (*comp.*) That which is *rough, steep.* See עַז.

RADICAL VOCABULARY

יעט (*comp.*) That which *covers, envelops,* as a garment. See עט.

יהל (*comp.*) Every thing which *is raised;* which *grows, augments, profits.* See עט.

יעף (*comp.*) Every movement which *tires, fatigues.* See עף.

יען (*comp.*) Every kind of *consultation, deliberation:* every thing which tends to *fix upon a point, to determine.* See יען.

יער (*comp.*) That which *surrounds, defends* a thing, as *the covering* of the kernel, *bark* of the tree, *skin* of the body: *a forest, a thicket of trees, to protect, to preserve a habitation,* etc. See ער.

יף IPH. The sign of manifestation united to that of speech, constitutes a root which is applied to all ideas of beauty, grace, charm, attraction.

The Arabic يف is only preserved in the composition of words as in طريف *beautiful,* طرينه *beauty,* etc.

יץ ITZ. Root not used in Hebrew; but it expresses every idea of progeny and propagation in the Arabic إضض which signifies *to grow,* in speaking of plants; in the Syriac ܡܘܡܐ it designates a tribe, a nation.

יק ICQ. Every idea of obedience and subjection.

The Arabic يق characterizes literally that which is white.

יר IR. Every idea of respect, of fear, of reverence, of veneration.

The Arabic ير signifies a thing which is polished, smooth, without roughness, but firm, as crystal. It is also a thing of igneous nature; but in this case the Arabic word شَىّ is applied to the root אוּר

ישׁ ISH. The sign of manifestation joined to that of relative movement, or by contraction with the elementary root אשׁ, produces a root whence come all ideas of reality, substantiality: in general, it is the substantial, effective being; in particular, an old man. This root often expresses the state *of being, of appearing like,* of being manifested in substance.

This root is not preserved in Arabic in its original purity; it has become onomatopoetic and idiomatic like many others; the verb شَشَّ has signified in a restricted sense, *to leap, gambol, give way to joy.*

יתּ ITH. Root not used in Hebrew; but in Chaldaic, in the Syriac ܠ, in the Samaritan ᎪᎴᏏ, it expresses always the essence and objective nature of things. See אשׁ.

כ CH. KH. This character as consonant, belongs to the guttural sound. As symbolic image it represents every hollow object, in general; in particular, the hand of man half closed. As grammatical sign, it is the assimilative sign, that of reflective and transient life: it is a sort of mould which receives and communicates indifferently all forms. This character is derived, as I have already said, from the aspiration ח, which comes from the vocal principle ה, image of absolute life; but here it joins the expression of organic character ג, of which it is a sort of reinforcement. In Hebrew, it is the assimilative and concomitant article. Its movement in nouns and actions is similitude and analogy. The Hebraist grammarians, since they have neither included it among the *héémanthes* nor among the *paragogics,* have committed the grossest errors;

RADICAL VOCABULARY 369

they have merely regarded it as an inseparable article or an affix, and often have confused it with the word that it governs as article.

Its arithmetical number is 20.

כא CHA. Every idea of assimilated existence, of formation by contraction; that which is compact, tightened, condensed to take some sort of form.

The Arabic ك develops, in general, the same ideas as the Hebraic root. In a restricted sense, this root is represented in English by the adverbial relations *thus, the same, such as,* etc. It is remarkable that this character ك , as sign, fulfills in the Arabic idiom, the same functions as the Hebrew כ. As onomatopoetic root ك expresses the clucking of the hen; metaphorically, the action of *gathering together,* as a hen her chickens; or again, the state of being timid, chicken-hearted.

כאב (*comp.*) A *moral heaviness;* an interior repression; every pain which is caused by a restrained and *repressed desire.*

כאה (*comp.*) Action of being *repressed interiorly,* of leading *a sad life, restricted, afflicted, painful.*

כב CHB. Every idea of centralization; that which draws near the centre; which gravitates there.

The Arabic ك characterizes in general, that which carries from above below, precipitates, pours out, throws down, sinks, goes down. As onomatopoetic root قب signifies *to cut.* This root used in music designates the fundamental sound, the keynote.

כג CHG. Root not used in Hebrew. The Arabic ج seems to indicate a sort of movement executed upon itself in spiral line. In particular it is a certain game for children.

כד CHD. That which partakes of relative unity, isolation, division. In a restricted sense *a spark, a fragment*.

The Chaldaic כד is represented in a restricted sense, by the adverbial relation *when*. The Arabic کد signifies in general, to act in one's own interest, to work for self; in particular, *to be industrious, to intrigue, to be fatigued, tormented*.

כה CHE. Root analogous to the root כא, but whose expression is spiritualized and reinforced by the presence of the sign ה.

כה That which is conformable to a given model; that which coincides with a point of space or time, which can be conceived in an abstract sense, by the adverbial relations *yes, thus, like this; that; in that very place; at that very time*, etc.

The Arabic کہ having lost all the ideas attached to the Hebraic root or having concentrated them in the primitive sign ج or ک, has become an onomatopoetic root depicting an oppressed respiration either by old age, by illness, or by excess of drinking.

כהה (*intens.*) From the idea of an excess of restriction, comes that of *fright, weakness, pusillanimity: contrition; dimming of the eyes; dizziness, faintness*, etc.

כהל (*comp.*) Every *value*. See הל.

כהן (*comp.*) Every administration, distinguished function; literally, *priesthood, pontificate; a priest*, a man raised in dignity to special supervision. See כן.

כו CHOU. Every assimilating, **compressing**, restraining force: the natural faculty which fetters the development of bodies and draws them back to their elements. Root analogous to the root כא, but modified by the presence of the convertible sign ו.

RADICAL VOCABULARY 371

The Arabic root كَى has certainly developed the same universal ideas in the ancient idiom; but in the modern, it is restricted to characterize a sort of cauterization. The idea of combustion, of burning is expressed in particular, by the root كَى, and by the word كَوِي is understood in general, that which is strong, vigorous, violent, extreme.

כוה Action of arresting the scope of vegetation; *repressing bodies*, *shrivelling* them by burning; *reducing them to ashes*.

כוי or כויה   *Combustion;* that which *roasts, burns; corrodes.*

כוה (*comp.*) That which holds to *the central force;* that which depends upon *igneous power;* that which after being centralized is unbound like *a spring;* in general it is *the virtual faculty* of the earth.

כול (*comp.*) That which *seizes* and *agglomerates.* See אל.

כון (*comp.*) See כן.

כור (*comp.*) *A furnace.*

כוש (*comp.*) See כש.

כז CHZ. Root not used in Hebrew. The Arabic كَز indicates everything which is contracted in itself, shrivelled.

In a restricted sense كَز signifies *to be disgusted.*

כה CHEH. Root not used in Hebrew. In Syriac, ܟܗ is onomatopoetic, expressing the effort made in retaining one's breath.

The Arabic كَحّ, being the reinforcement of the root كَ, characterizes the state of an asthmatic person, or of one worn out with old age.

כחד (*comp.*) Action of *retaining* a thing, *hiding* it, *concealing* it carefully.

כחל (*comp.*) Action of *disguising* a thing, *smearing* it.

כחש (*comp.*) Action of *denying* a thing, *lying*.

כט CHT. Root not used in Hebrew. The Arabic كظ, expresses the action of *gorging with food* to the point of being unable to breathe. Figuratively, it is to fill beyond measure, to overpower with work. In the modern idiom كث signifies *bushy hair*.

כי CHI. Manifestation of any assimilating, compressing force. See כא, כה, and כו.

The Arabic كي signifies in a restricted sense, *a burn*.

כי The force expressed by this root is represented in an abstract sense, by the relations *that, because, for, then, when,* etc.

כיד (*comp.*) Everything which compresses strongly, which *crowds*, which *presses:* literally, *armour; a scourge*.

כיל (*comp.*) That which is covetous, tenacious; *a miser*.

כים (*comp.*) Constellation of the *Pleiades;* because of the manner in which the stars cluster.

כיס (*comp.*) A *purse* filled with money; *a casket*.

כיף (*comp.*) A *rock;* a thing hard and strong, of *compressed* substance.

כך CHKH. Root not used in Hebrew. The Chaldaic כך signifies nothing more than the Hebrew כה.

The Ethiopic ካኅ (*cach*) is an onomatopoetic root which denotes the cry of a crow.

כל CHL. This root expresses all ideas of appre-

RADICAL VOCABULARY 373

hension, shock, capacity, relative assimilation, consummation, totalization, achievement, perfection.

The Arabic كل develops in general, the same ideas of complement, totalization, as the Hebrew; but in leaving its source, it inclines rather toward the totalization of evil than toward that of good; so that in the Arabic idiom كل is taken figuratively, for excess of fatigue, height of misfortune, extreme poverty, etc. This root being reinforced by the guttural aspiration, offers in جل , a meaning absolutely contrary to the primitive sense of accumulation, and designates the state of that which diminishes, which is lessened.

כל That which is *integral, entire, absolute, perfect, total, universal:* that which *consumes, concludes, finishes, totalizes* a thing; that which renders it *complete, perfect, accomplished;* which *comprises, contains* it, in determining its *accomplishment: the universality* of things; their *assimilation, aggregation, perfection; the desire* of possessing; *possession; a prison: the consumption of foods,* their *assimilation* with the substance of the body, etc.

כל Action of *totalizing, accomplishing, comprising, universalizing, consummating,* etc.

כם CHM. Every tension, inclination, desire for assimilation. The Arabic كم signifies *how much.*

The root كم , as verb, signifies to know the quantity of some thing, or to fix that quantity.

כן CHN. This root, wherein the assimilative sign is united to the root אן, image of all corporeal circumscription, is related to that which enjoys a central force energetic enough to become palpable, to form a body, to acquire solidity: it is in general, the base, the point upon which things rest.

The Arabic كى has not differed from the Hebraic root in its primitive origin; but its developments have been different. The intellectual root הוה *to be-being,* almost entirely lost in Arabic, has been replaced by the physical root כן; so that in the Arabic idiom the word كون, which should designate only material, corporeal existence, *substance* in general, signifies *being.* This substitution of one root for another has had very grave consequences, and has served more than anything else to estrange Arabic from Hebrew.

כן That which holds to *physical reality, corporeal kind; stability, solidity, consistency;* a *fixed, constituted, naturalized* thing: in a restricted sense, *a plant:* in an abstract sense, it is the adverbial relatives, *yes, thus, that, then,* etc.

The Arabic كان, in consequence of the reasons explained above, characterizes the state of that which is, that which exists, or passes into action in nature. This root which, in Arabic, has usurped the place of the primitive root הוה, signifies literally *it existed.* It can be remarked that the Samaritan and Chaldaic follow the sense of the Hebraic root, whereas the Syriac and Ethiopic follow that of the Arabic.

כון Action of *constituting, disposing, fixing, grounding;* action of *strengthening, affirming, confirming;* action of *conforming, qualifying* for a thing, *producing* according to a certain mode, *designating* by a name, *naturalizing,* etc.

כס CHS. Every idea of accumulation, enumeration, sum.

כס *The top; the pinnacle* of an edifice; *a throne.*

The Arabic قص expresses in general, the action of removing the superficies of things; in particular, that of *clipping, cutting* with scissors. The onomatopoetic root كس

RADICAL VOCABULARY 375

expresses the idea of utmost exertion, and the Arabic noun كس *pudendum muliebre.*

כוס Action of *numbering, calculating; accumulating, carrying to the top; filling up, covering,* etc.

כע CHOH. Root not used in Hebrew. The Chaldaic indicates in an onomatopoetic manner, the sound of spitting.

The Arabic كع develops only ideas of baseness, cowardice.

כעם (*comp.*) Action of being *indignant, vexed; provoking. irritating* another.

כף CHPH. Every idea of curvature, concavity, inflection; of a thing capable of containing, holding: in a restricted sense, palm of the hand, sole of the foot, talons, claws of an animal, a spoon; that which curves like a sleeve, a branch: that which has capacity, like a stove, a spatula, etc.

The Arabic كف contains exactly the same ideas as the Hebraic root. As verb, and in a figurative sense, كف signifies to *preserve, defend, keep.*

כוף Action of *bending, being inflected, made concave,* etc.

כץ CHTZ. Root not used in Hebrew. The Arabic كص appears to signify a sort of undulatory movement as that of water agitated.

This root being doubled in كصكض indicates a movement extremely accelerated.

כר CHR. The assimilative sign united to that of movement proper ר, or by contraction with the elementary root אר, constitutes a root related in general, to that which is apparent, conspicuous; which serves as monument, as distinctive mark: which engraves or serves to engrave; which hollows out, which preserves the memory of things in any manner whatsoever; finally, that which grows, rises, is noticeable.

The Arabic كر has certainly developed the same general sense as the Hebraic root, in its primitive acceptation; but in a less broad sense, the Arabic root is limited to expressing the action of *returning* on itself, on its steps; *reiterating* the same movement, *repeating* a speech, etc.

כר Every kind of *character, mark, engraving;* every distinctive object: leader of a flock, *a ram;* leader of an army, *a captain:* every kind of excavation; *a furrow, ditch, trench,* etc.

כיר *A round vessel, a measure.*

כש CHSH. This root is applied in general to the idea of a movement of vibration which agitates and expands the air.

The Arabic كش signifies literally to *shrivel up, to shrink* in speaking of the nerves: *to shorten.*

כוש (*comp.*) That which is of the nature of fire and communicates the same movement. Figuratively, that which is *spiritual, igneous.*

כת CHTH. Every idea of retrenchment, scission, suspension, cut, schism.

כות Action of *cutting, carving, retrenching, excluding, separating, making a schism,* etc.

The Arabic كت presents exactly the same sense in general. In particular, كت signifies *to shrink;* by كت is understood the action of *curling the hair.*

RADICAL VOCABULARY 377

ל **L.** This character as consonant, belongs to the lingual sound. As symbolic image it represents the arm of man, the wing of a bird, that which extends, raises and unfolds itself. As grammatical sign, it is expansive movement and is applied to all ideas of extension, elevation, occupation, possession. It is, in Hebrew, the directive article, as I have explained in my Grammar, expressing in nouns or actions, a movement of union, dependence, possession or coincidence.

Its arithmetical number is 30.

לא **LA.** This root is symbol of the line prolonged to infinity, of movement without term, of action whose duration is limitless: thence, the opposed ideas of being and nothingness, which it uses in developing the greater part of its compounds.

The Arabic ل develops the same ideas as the Hebraic root. In a restricted sense ل is represented by the negative adverbial relations *no, not*. The verb لل signifies literally to *shine, sparkle, glisten*.

לוֹא or לא   It is in general, an indefinite expansion, an absence without term expressed in an abstract sense by the relations, *no, not, not at all*. Definite direction, that is to say, that which is restrained by means of the assimilative sign כ, is opposed to it. See כה or כן.

לאה   It is in general, *an action without end;* in its literal sense, a labour which *fatigues, wearies, molests*.

לאט (*comp.*)   Action of *covering, hiding*. See לט.

לאך (*comp.*)   Action of *despatching, delegating.* See לך.

לאם (*comp.*)   A nation. See לם.

לב **LB.** The expansive sign united by contraction to the root אב, image of every interior activity, every appetent, desirous, generative force, constitutes a root whence emanate all ideas of vitality, passion, vigour, courage, audacity: literally, it is *the heart*, and figuratively, all things which pertain to that centre of life; every quality, every faculty resulting from the unfolding of the vital principle.

לב *The heart*, the centre of everything whatsoever from which life radiates; all dependent faculties: *courage, force, passion, affection, desire, will; sense.*

The Arabic لـ participates in the same acceptations as the Hebraic root.

לוב Action of *showing force, developing vital faculties, moving with audacity, animating, making vigorous, germinating,* etc.

להב (*comp.*) Ardour, flame, vital fire, literally as well as figuratively.

לג LG. Every idea of liaison, of intimate, complicated thing; *of litigation*. The meaning of the Arabic جـ is similar and signifies literally *to insist, to contest.* The Hebrew לג presents in the figurative, symbolic style, the measure of extent, *space.*

לד LD. The expansive sign, joined to that of abundance born of division, or by contraction with the root יאד, image of every emanation, composes a root whose purpose is to express every idea of propagation, of generation, of any extension whatsoever given to being.

The Arabic لـ expresses in general the same ideas as the Hebraic root. In a restricted sense it is, to *make manifest, to put forward, to discuss.* The verb لـ characterizes the state of that which is relaxed, put at ease; to enjoy one's self, to delight in, etc.

לד That which *is born, generated, propagated, bred:*

progeny, increase of family, race, lineage: confinement, childbirth, etc.

לָה LEH. This root, analogue of the root לא contains the idea of a direction given to life, of a movement without term.

Thence the Arabic لَه which signifies properly GOD. In a more materialized sense, the word لَه designates that which is refined, softened, become beautiful, pure, elegant.

להה Every idea of indeterminate action, of insupportable fatigue; *frenzy.*

להב (*comp.*) Every desirous movement; every projection into vacuity: *a flame* of any sort whatsoever.

להג (*comp.*) Keen disposition to study, desire to learn: in a figurative sense, *a system, a doctrine.*

להט (*comp.*) That which *is inflamed, takes fire, burns* for something.

להם (*comp.*) To universalize an expansive movement, to render it sympathetic; *to electrify, inspire, propagate;* etc.

לִי or לוּ LOU or LI. Every idea of liaison, cohesion, tendency of objects toward each other. The universal bond. The abstract line which *is conceived* going from one point to another and which is represented by the relations, *oh if! oh that! would to God that!*

The Arabic لو has not preserved the ideas contained in the primitive root as those have which are represented by the adverbial relations *if, if not, though.* The verb لَوَى, which is attached to the root לה or لَه, signifies to make divine power shine forth, *to create;* to give vital movement to matter. It is to the sense of *radiating* which is contained in this root, that one applies the word لؤ *a pearl*.

לוֹה Action of being *adherent, coherent,* united by *mutual ties,* by *sympathetic movement:* every *adjunction, liaison, copulation, conjunction, addition,* etc.

לוז (*comp.*) That which *cedes, gives way, bends.* See לז.

לוּח (*comp.*) That which is *polished, shining.* See לח.

לוט (*comp.*) To *hide, envelop.* See לט.

לוי (*comp.*) *Addition, supplement.*

לוּך (*comp.*) That which is *detached, disunited;* figuratively, that which *drags, is dirty, soiled.* See לך.

לוּן (*comp.*) See לן.

לוּע (*comp.*) Action of *swallowing.* See לע.

לוּץ (*comp.*) See לץ.

לוּשׁ (*comp.*) See לש.

לז LZ. Every movement directed toward an object to show it, and expressed in an abstract sense by the relations *this, that.*

The Arabic لز has preserved the physical developments more than the Hebraic root; for one finds there all the acceptations which have relation to things coming together, their collision, clashing, etc.

לח LH. Every movement directed toward elementary existence and making effort to produce itself, to make its appearance.

The Arabic لح develops in general, all ideas of cohesion, of contraction, and retains only the physical and material acceptations of the Hebraic root.

לח   Natural vigour; innate movement of vegetation; *radical moisture:* that which is *verdant, young, moist, fresh;* that which is *glowing* with youth, beauty, freshness; that which is *smooth, soft* to the touch; etc.

לחךְ (*comp.*)   Action of *licking, sucking, polishing.*

לחם (*comp.*)   That which serves as *food* to elementary life: action of *subsisting,* of *being fed:* every idea of *alimentation; consumption* of anything whatsoever.

לחץ (*comp.*)   A *hostile incursion, public misfortune, oppression.* See חץ.

לחש (*comp.*)   A *magic incantation, an enchantment:* a *talisman.* See ל״ש.

לט   LT. The directive sign united to that of protective resistance, composes a root which contains all ideas of seclusion, envelopment, mystery, hiding place. See לאט and לוט.

The Arabic ل characterizes, in general, that which agglutinates, makes sticky, etc. The verb ل signifies properly *to knead,* and in the figurative sense, ل indicates the action of *sullying, compromising, contaminating.*

לי   LI. Root analogous to roots לו, לה, לא.

The Arabic ل designates literally a pliant, flexible thing.

ליל (*comp.*)   That which renders things adherent, binds, envelops them: *night.* See לל.

ליש (*comp.*)   A *lion.* See ל״ש.

לךְ   LCH. The extensive sign united to the root אך, image of every restriction, constitutes a root whence is developed the idea of a restrained utterance, as a determined message; executing a mission; a legation, a vicarship.

The Arabic لك has lost absolutely all the intellectual ideas developed by the Hebraic root and has preserved but few of its physical acceptations. In a restricted sense, the verb لا signifies *to chew;* as onomatopoetic root لق depicts the *gurgle* of a bottle.

לְאָךְ Every kind of *legation, delegation, envoy,* to fulfill any *function* whatsoever.

לוּךְ (*comp.*) State of being *detached, delegated, loosened, released; without bond, lawless; impious, profane,* etc.

לָל LL. The sign of extensive movement being opposed to itself, composes a root which gives the idea of circular movement: in the same manner as one sees in natural philosophy, this movement springs from two opposed forces, one drawing to the centre, and the other drawing away from it.

The Arabic ل is not preserved; but one recognizes the Hebraic root in the verb اول which expresses anxiety, despair of a person *tossed about.*

לוּל Action of *moving around, turning* alternately from one side to another; *rocking, winding, twisting.*

לִיל (*comp.*) That which binds things and envelops them; *night.*

לָם LM. A sympathetic, mutual bond; a movement directed toward universalization.

The Arabic م develops the same ideas as the Hebraic root but in a more physical sense. As verb, it is the action of *uniting together, assembling, gathering,* etc. When the word ل signifies *no,* it is attached to the root ي or לֹא.

לאם A *people;* that is to say, a more or less considerable number of men united by common bond.

לן LN. Root not used in Hebrew. The Arabic اون expresses every kind of colour, tint, reflection cast upon objects; that which varies, changes colour, flashes iridescent hues, etc.

In the modern idiom, the verb لن signifies literally *to soften.*

לון A reflected light, a *nocturnal lamp*: action of *watching* by lamp-light, of *passing the night,* of *taking rest.*

לס LS. Root not used in Hebrew. The Arabic لس indicates the action of *browsing.* By the word اص is understood *a thief, a robber.*

לע LOH. Root not used in Hebrew. The Arabic لع appears to express in general, covetous desire, consuming ardour.

The root لغ which appears to be idiomatic and onomatopoetic in Arabic, denotes the articulate or inarticulate sound emitted by the voice and modified by the tongue; thence the verb لغا which signifies *to speak* or *to bark,* according to whether it is a question of man or dog. The word لغة signifies literally, *a speech, an idiom,* etc.

לוע *A yawning jaw, an engulfing abyss;* that which *swallows, absorbs, devours.*

לף LPH. Every idea of reaction, of return to itself, of refraction.

The Arabic لف indicates a complication, an adjunction of several things. It is literally, the action of *enveloping*.

לִץ LTZ. Every kind of turn, *détour*, turning about, sinuosity, inflection.

The Arabic لص expresses in general, every kind of trickery, ruse, cheating. Literally *a thief*.

לוּץ Action of *making light of, making a play on words; of laughing;* action of *turning* one tongue into another, of employing *an oratorical trope*, etc.

לִק LCQ. In a literal sense, that which is seized by the tongue, that which is lapped, *licked*: figuratively, that which is seized by the mind, *a lesson, a lecture, an instruction*.

The Arabic لك signifies *to chew*, and لق, as onomatopoetic root denotes every kind of slapping, clapping, clicking.

להק From the idea of *instruction* springs that of *doctrine;* from that of *doctrine, doctor*. Thence, the idea of *academy,* of the gathering of savants, of sages, of elders, of *the senate*.

לר LR. Root not used in Hebrew nor in Arabic.

לִשׁ LSH. Every union *en masse,* every forming, composing.

The Arabic لش indicates the state of that which is agitated, shaken. The word لشلاش characterizes one who is trembling, troubled, unsteady.

לוּשׁ That which tends *to soften, knead; to make ductile* a thing which is firm and divided.

לִת LTH. Root not used in Hebrew. The Arabic لت indicates a mutual union, a sympathetic bond.

RADICAL VOCABULARY 385

מ M. This character as consonant, belongs to the nasal sound. As symbolic image it represents woman, mother, companion of man; that which is productive, creative. As grammatical sign, it is the maternal and female sign of exterior and passive action; placed at the beginning of words it depicts that which is local and plastic; placed at the end, it becomes the collective sign, developing the being in infinitive space, as far as its nature permits, or uniting by abstraction, in one single being all those of the same kind. In Hebrew it is the extractive or partitive article, as I have explained in my Grammar, expressing in nouns or actions that sort of movement by which a name or an action, is taken for means or instrument, is divided in its essence, or is drawn from the midst of several other similar nouns or actions.

The Hebraist grammarians whilst considering this character as *héémanthe* have not ceased, nevertheless, to confound it with the words which it modifies as sign, as I shall show in several important examples in my notes.

Its arithmetical number is 40.

מא MA. That which tends to the aggrandizement of its being, to its entire development; that which serves as instrument of generative power and manifests it exteriorly.

The Arabic ما presents in its original sense the same ideas as the Hebraic root; but this root has acquired in Arabic a greater number of developments than it has in Hebrew; this is why it demands in both idioms all the attention of those who wish to go back to the essence of language. מא or ما, characterizes in general, passive matter, the thing of which, with which, and by means of which, all is made. It is in particular, in the Arabic idiom, *water;* anything whatsoever, *all* or *nothing,* according to the manner in which it is considered. This important root, conceived as pronominal relation designates the possibility of all things, and is represented by the analogues *what* and *which;* conceived, on the contrary, as adverbial relation, it is employed in Arabic to express the absence of every determined object and is rendered by the analogues *not, no.* As verb, the root ما or مي signifies in general, *to go everywhere, to extend everywhere, to fill space,* etc.

מאה This is, in general, that which is developed according to the extent of its faculties; in a more restricted sense it is the number *one hundred.*

מב MB. Root not used in Hebrew. The Arabic ماب seems to indicate an idea of return, remittance; of honour rendered.

מג MG. Root not used in Hebrew. The Arabic ماج expresses the idea of a thing which is sour, acrid, bitter, sharp; which irritates, troubles, torments.

In a restricted sense the verb مج signifies *to be repugnant.*

מד MD. The sign of exterior action, being united to that of elementary division, constitutes that root whence come all ideas of measure, dimension, mensuration, commensurable extent, and in a metaphorical sense, those of custom, rule, condition.

The Arabic مد develops in general, the same ideas as the Hebrew. In particular, it is that which extends, lengthens, unfolds.

מאד That which fills its measure, which has all the dimensions that it can have, which enjoys the whole extent of its faculties: in an abstract sense, *much, very, exceedingly,* etc.

מָה MEH. That which is essentially mobile, essentially passive and creative; the element from which everything draws its nourishment; that which the ancients regarded as the female principle of all generation, *water,* and which they opposed to the male principle, which they believed to be *fire.*

מוֹ ,מֹה or מִי Every idea of *mobility, fluidity, passivity;* that which is tenuous and impassive, whose intimate essence remains unknown, whose faculties are relative to the active principles which develop them; in a literal and restricted sense, *water,* in an abstract sense *who? which? what is it? some one, something.*

The Arabic ما has lost all the intellectual ideas of the Hebraic root and has substituted the root ماء for all physical ideas. Today, by وما, is understood only a vain futile, inane thing.

מָהָל (*comp.*) Every kind of *mixture;* the *fusion* of several things together.

מָהַר (*comp.*) That which *passes away* with rapidity, that which *changes, varies* easily and quickly. See מֹר.

מוֹ MOU. Analogue of the root מֹה.

מוֹ This is, in Hebrew, a passive syllable which is added to nearly all articles and to some pronouns, to give them more force and without bringing any change to their proper expression.

The Arabic مو is an onomatopoetic root which depicts in particular the mewing of a cat; by extension, every harsh, shrill sound. The Ethiopic ሞዋ (*mowa*) characterizes, in general, the action of triumphing, and that of celebrating a triumph with a fanfare.

מוּג (*comp.*) Action of *liquifying, dissolving, melting.*

מוֹחַ (*comp.*) *Marrow.*

מוֹט (comp.) Every kind of *communicated movement.* See מט.

מוּךְ (comp.) Every idea of *attenuation, depression.* See מך.

מוּל (comp.) Action of *amputating, cutting off exuberance, circumcising.* See מל.

מִים (comp.) *Stain, vice.* See מם.

מִין (comp.) *Image, representation, figure:* See מן.

מוּר (comp.) Every *variation,* every *permutation.* See מר.

מוּשׁ (comp.) That which is *contracted* and *rolled up* in itself: See מש.

מוּת (comp.) *Passing into another life, death.* See מת.

מַז MZ. Every *burning*; combustion through the effect of refraction. Intense dazzling; reflection of the solar rays; incandescence, heat, sudden dryness.

The Arabic ﻣﺰ not having conserved the primitive sense of the Hebraic root, offers only particular consequences of the most general ideas, as those which spring from heat or from dryness; or from that which is sour or dried up, in speaking of liquids.

מַח MH. Onomatopoetic root which depicts the noise that is made in clapping the hands: figuratively, action of applauding; state of being joyous, of having good appearance.

מח *Clapping, applause, fullness of the body; good humour.*

מַת The sign of exterior and passive action united to that of elementary labour, or to the root את, symbol of all equality, constitutes a root to which are attached the ideas of abolition, desuetude; of ravage carried on by time, by the action of the elements, or by man; thence,

מחה   Action of *effacing, depriving, taking away, destroying;* of *razing* a city, an edifice; of *washing, cleansing,* etc.

The Arabic ‎ محو‎ presents the same general ideas as the Hebraic root מח. The particular ideas are developed in the modern idiom by the derivative root محل.

מחץ   (*comp.*) Action of *hurting, striking violently, wounding.* See חץ.

מחק   (*comp.*) Action of *razing, scraping, taking away, removing* by force, *erasing,* etc.

מחר   (*comp.*) Every idea of *contingent* future, of *fatal, irresistible* thing: in a literal sense, it is the adverbial relation *tomorrow.*

מט   MT. This root, composed of the sign of exterior and passive action, united to that of resistance, develops all ideas of motion or emotion given to something; vacillation; stirring; a communicated movement especially downward.

The Arabic مط has the same sense. As verb, this root indicates the action of *drawing, stretching,* extending by pulling.

מוט   Action of *moving, rousing, budging, stirring, agitating; going, following, happening, arriving,* etc.

מי   MI. See מה.

The Chaldaic מי is an indefinite pronominal relation represented by *what?* The Ethiopic ማይ (*mai*) signifies properly *water.*

מים   *The waters*: that is to say, the mass of that which is eminently mobile, passive and suitable for elementary fecundation.

מך   MCH. The root אך, image of every restriction, every contraction, united to the sign of exterior and passive action, constitutes a root whence spring the ideas of attenuation, weakening, softening of a hard thing: its liquefaction; its submission.

מך   That which is *attenuated, debilitated, weakened; distilled; humiliated.* See מוך.

The Arabic مل expresses in general, every idea of extenuation, absorption, consumption. By مخ, is understood *the brain.*

מל   ML. The sign of exterior and passive action united by contraction to the root אל, symbol of every elevation and every extent, composes a root to which is attached all ideas of continuity, plentitude, continued movement from the beginning to the end of a thing: thence, the accessory ideas of locution, elocution, eloquence, narration, etc.

The Arabic مل not having preserved the intellectual ideas developed by the Hebraic root is limited to recalling that sort of physical plentitude which constitutes lassitude, *ennui,* dislike to work and the negligence which follows. The particular ideas expressed by the Hebrew, are found again in part, in the Arabic words ملا ملو ملي.

מל   That which is *full, entirely formed;* that which has attained its *complement*: that which is *continued* without lacunas; every kind of *locution, narration, oration; a term, an expression.*

מלל   (*intens.*) From the excess of *plentitude* springs the idea of exuberance and the idea of that which is announced outwardly; in a figurative sense, *elocution, speech.*

מול   From the idea of *exuberance* comes that of *amputation;* thence, the action of *amputating, circumcising, taking away* that which is *superabundant, superfluous.*

ממ   MM. Root not used in Hebrew. The Arabic

مٍ seems to indicate a thing livid, or which renders livid; a thing inanimate, and as dead. Literally *wax, a mummy;* figuratively, *solitude, a desert.*

מִן MN. This root, composed of the sign of exterior and passive action, united by contraction to the root אִן, symbol of the sphere of activity and of the circumscriptive extent of being, characterizes all specification, all classification by exterior forms; all figuration, determination, definition, qualification.

The Arabic مِن has not followed the same developments as the Hebrew, although they have come from an identical root in the two idioms, as is proved by the usage of this root as designative relation represented by *of, from,* etc. As noun the Arabic root مِن designates a thing emanated from another, *a gift;* as verb, it characterizes the state of that which is benign, beneficial; action of that which is deprived in order *to give, to distribute;* that which is weakened *to reinforce,* impoverished *to enrich,* etc.

מִן The kind of things, their *exterior figure, mien, image,* that is conceived; *the idea* that is formed, *the definition* that is given to it; their proper *measure, number, quota.*

מִן Action of *figuring, defining, forming an idea, an image* of things: action of *imagining;* action of *measuring, numbering, qualifying,* etc.

מִן *Form, aspect* of things; their *mien, figure,* etc.

מַס MS. Every dissolution, literally as well as figuratively: that which enervates, which takes away from physical and moral strength.

The Arabic مس characterizes the state of that which is touched, that which is contiguous. By مص, is understood *to suck;* by مض *to be fatigued, to lose one's strength, to be enervated.*

מע MOH. *That which circulates or which causes circulation.*

מעה *Inmost part; the intestines, the viscera of the body: the finances of state, money; sand, gravel,* etc.

The Arabic مع, which as I have already remarked in speaking of the root מא signifies literally *with,* contained primitively the same sense as the Hebraic root מה which is alluded to here; but its developments have been somewhat different. Thus, whereas the Chaldaic מעא designates a thing in circulation, as a piece of money, the Arabic مع characterizes that which is uniform, unaminous, simultaneous.

מעט (*comp.*) *That which is moderate, exiguous, of little value, common, poor.*

מעך (*comp.*) *Action of pressing, compressing, provoking.*

מעל (*comp.*) *That which is tortuous; distorted, deceitful; a transgression, a prevarication.*

מף MPH. Root not used in Hebrew. The Chaldaic signifies a sort of carpet or cloth.

The Arabic verb مفج signifies the condition of an idiot; a false or stupid mind.

מץ MTZ. This root characterizes that which attains an end, a finish; which encounters, finds, obtains the desired object.

The Arabic مص signifies properly *to suck.*

מעע (*intens.*) Action of *milking,* that is to say, of *obtaining* milk: thence, the idea of *pressure, expression; pressing* etc.

מָק MCQ. That which is founded, literally as well as figuratively. The action of being melted, liquefied; growing faint, vanishing.

The Arabic ﻣﻖ expresses the state of that which experiences a sentiment of tenderness, which covers, shelters, loves, etc.

מָר MR. The sign of exterior and passive action being united to that of movement proper, constitutes a root whose purpose is to characterize that which gives way to its impulsion, which extends itself, usurps or invades space; but when this same sign is linked by contraction to the root אר symbol of elementary principle, then the root which results is applied to all the modifications of this same element.

The Arabic ﻣﺮ contained primitively the same ideas as the Hebraic root. In the modern idiom this root is limited to two principal acceptations; the first is applied to the action of *passing, exceeding, going beyond;* the second, to the state of being bitter, strong, sturdy.

מַר That which extending and rising, affects *the empire, the dominion;* as a *potentate*: that which exceeds the limits of one's authority; as *a tyrant, a rebel*: that which is attached to the idea of elementary principle, as *an atom, a drop*.

מרר (*intens.*) That which is *exaggerated* in its movement, in its quality: literally, that which is *sour, bitter, ferocious.*

מאר (*comp.*) That which *gnaws*, which *corrodes;* literally and figuratively.

מאר or מאור (*comp.*) That which *shines, lightens, heats.*

מהר (*comp.*) That which *changes, varies, passes, flows off* rapidly.

מור or מיר (*comp.*) *Change, variation, mutation.*

מֵשׁ MSH. From the union of the sign of exterior activity with that of relative movement, or by contraction with the elementary root אֵשׁ springs a root whose purpose is to express that which is stirred by contractile movement.

The Arabic مش signifies properly *to feel, touch softly, brush lightly.*

מֵשׁ Everything *palpable, compact, gathered*: every pile, as *a crop, a harvest.* That which is *drawn, extracted, shrunken,* as *silk* etc.

מֵת MTH. If one considers this root as composed of the sign of exterior action, united to that of reciprocity, or this same sign joined by contraction to the root אֵת image of the ipseity, the selfsameness of things, it will express either a sympathetic movement, or a transition; a return to universal seity or sameness. Thence the idea of the passing of life; of death.

The Arabic مت or مث, has lost all the intellectual ideas contained in the Hebrew. Today it is only extension or physical expansion, a sort of flux of any thing whatever. مث indicates dissolution of being, and مت signifies *death.* The verb مات characterizes that which is dead, dissolved, deprived of existence proper.

מוּת Action of *passing away*, of *passing* into another life, of *dying*: state of *being dead; death*.

נ N. This character as consonant, belongs to the nasal sound; as symbolic image it represents the son of man, every produced and particular being. As grammatical sign, it is that of individual and produced existence. When it is placed at the end of words it becomes the augumentative sign ן, and gives to the being every extension of which it is individually susceptible. The Hebraist grammarians in placing this character among the *hééman-*

thes, had certainly observed that it expressed, at the beginning of words, passive action, folded within itself, and when it appeared at the end, unfoldment and augmentation: but they had profited little by this observation.

I shall not repeat here what I have said in my Grammar concerning the use that the idiomatic genius of the Hebraic tongue made of this character in the composition of compound radical verbs, as initial adjunction.

Its arithmetical number is 50.

נא NA. Every idea of youth, newness; every idea of freshness, grace, beauty; every idea springing from that which is formed of a new production, of a being young and graceful.

The Arabic نا although holding to the same primitive root as the Hebrew, has developed, however, ideas apparently opposed: this is the reason. That which is new, of recent birth, is graceful, fresh, pleasing; but it is also frail, weak, unsteady. Now, the Hebraic idiom is attached to the first idea; the Arabic idiom has followed and developed the second. Thence the verb نانا , which indicates the state of that which is frail, feeble, impotent; the verb نالي, expresses the action *of letting go, being separated, abandoning* a thing, etc. What proves the identity of the root is that the compound verb نانا. signifies literally *to nurse* an infant.

נאה That which is *beautiful, lovable, new, young, fresh;* which is not worn out, fatigued, peevish; but, on the contrary, that which is *new, tender, pretty, comely.*

נוא From the idea of *youth* and *childhood* comes the idea of that which has not attained its point of perfection, which is *not sufficiently ripe,* in speaking of fruit; *not sufficiently cooked,* in speaking of meat; thence, the action of *acting abruptly,* without reflection, *contradicting* like a child, *leading without experience, being new, unaccustomed* to something, *acting impetuously.*

נאד (*comp.*) *A leather bottle,* for holding water, milk or any liquor whatsoever.

נאם (*comp.*) Action of exposing *the substance* or *source* of something; *speaking the truth, going back to the cause.* See אם.

נאף (*comp.*) Action of *giving way* to a passion, to an impulse; *to commit adultery; to apostatize, to worship* strange gods. See אף.

נאץ (*comp.*) Action of *passing the limits, going too far;* the action of *spitting.* See אץ.

נאת (*comp.*) Every idea of *clamour, lamentation.*

נאר (*comp.*) Action of being *execrable, abominable.* See ארר.

נב NB. The mysterious root אוב being united by contraction to the sign of produced existence, gives rise to a new root, whence emanate all ideas of divine inspiration, theophany, prophecy; and in consequence, that of exaltation, ecstasy, rapture; perturbation, religious horror.

The Arabic نب indicates in general, *a shudder;* exterior movement caused by interior passion. As onomatopoetic and idiomatic root نب denotes the sudden cry of a man or animal keenly roused. Literally, *the bark of a* dog. Figuratively نبا and نبي express the action of one who announces the will of heaven, who prophecies.

The Hebrew word נביא, *prophet*, is formed of the root נב here alluded to, and the root יא, symbol of divine power.

נוב Action of *speaking* by inspiration; *producing* exteriorly the spirit with which one is filled: in a literal and restricted sense, *divulgation, fructification, germination.*

In this last sense, it is the root אב, which is united simply to the sign נ employed as initial adjunction.

נג NG. This root is applied to every kind of reflected light, after the manner of a mirror; of solar refraction: thence, the ideas of opposition, of an object put on the opposite side.

The Arabic نج indicates every idea of liquid emission, watery emanation.

נהג Action of *leading* by taking possession of the will of some one; of *inducing, deducing, suggesting* ideas; action of giving or receiving *an impulse, opinion,* etc.

נד ND. From the union of the signs of produced existence and natural division, springs a root which develops all ideas of dispersion, uncertain movement, agitation, flight, exile, trouble, dissension.

The Arabic ند develops the idea of that which evaporates, is exhaled, escapes. This word is applied also in Arabic to the idea of equality, similitude; then it is compound and derived from the primitive יד, contracted with the sign of produced existence נ.

נוד That which *is moved, stirred,* by a principle of trouble and incertitude; that which is *wandering, agitated;* that which *goes away, flees, emigrates,* etc.

ניד An *agitation, a trembling, a disturbance* manifested by movement.

נה NHE. This root is the analogue of the root נא and as it, characterizes that which is fresh, young, recent: thence;

נוה State of being *young, alert, vigorous, pleasing*; in consequence, action of *forming a colony, founding a new habitation, establishing one's flock elsewhere,* etc.

נָהּ Onomatopoetic root which describes the long moaning of a person who weeps, suffers, sobs.

The Arabic نَهّ depicts every kind of noise, clamour.

נוּ NOU. The convertible sign וּ image of the bond which unites being and nothingness, which communicates from one nature to another, being joined to that of produced existence, produces a root whose sense, entirely vague and indeterminate is fixed only by means of the terminative sign by which it is accompanied.

The Arabic نَو is an onomatopoetic and idiomatic root which depicts the aversion that one experiences in doing a thing, the disgust that it inspires. As verb, it is the action of being *repugnant*, of *refusing*, of *being unwilling*.

נוה (*comp.*) Every idea of a *new dwelling*. See נה.

נוח (*comp.*) *The point of equilibrium* where an agitated thing finds *repose*: action of *resting, remaining tranquil, enjoying peace and calm.* See נה.

נוט (*comp.*) Every kind of *bond*.

נום (*comp.*) Action of *sleeping*.

נון (*comp.*) Every idea of *propagation* or *growth* of family. See נן.

נוס (*comp.*) Action of *wavering* in uncertainty, *erring, fleeing.* See נס.

נוע (*comp.*) That which *changes*, that which lacks constancy and force, literally as well as figuratively.

נוף (*comp.*) *Dispersion, aspersion, distillation*: action of *winnowing, scattering;* of *ventilating,* etc.

נוץ (*comp.*) Action of *flourishing*, that of *flying;* being *resplendent.* See נץ.

נוק (*comp.*) Every pure, beneficial, nourishing fluid; *milk;* action of *suckling, nursing* an infant.

RADICAL VOCABULARY 399

נור (comp.) A luminous production, *éclat, splendour*. See נר.

נוש (*comp.*) That which is *unstable, weak, infirm*.

נז NZ. This root characterizes that which overflows, spreads, disperses; that which makes its influence felt outwardly.

The Arabic نز has the same sense. It is literally, the action of *flowing, passing away*.

נז (*intens.*) From excess of dispersion springs the idea of *the breaking* of that which is solid; *the distillation* of that which is liquid.

נח NH. If one considers this root as formed of the united signs of produced existence and elementary existence, it implies a movement which leads toward an end: if one considers it as formed of the same sign of produced existence united by contraction to the root את, image of all equilibratory force, it furnishes the idea of that perfect repose which results for a thing long time agitated contrarily, and the point of equilibrium which it attains where it dwells immobile. Thence,

נח In the first case, and in a restricted sense, *a guide*: in the second case, and in a general sense, *the repose of existence*. See נו.

The Arabic نح is an onomatopoetic root which depicts a moan, a profound sigh; thence, all ideas of lamentation, of plaint. The intellectual ideas developed by the Hebraic root are nearly all lost in the Arabic. Nevertheless one still finds in the modern idiom the verb نح signifying *to stoop, to kneel*. The compound word نحاح, indicates sometimes *patience, tenacity*.

נחל (*comp.*) That which is *extended* with effort, which is *divided, separated*: *a valley* hollowed out by a torrent: *a share* of inheritance: *the sinuosity* of a running stream; *taking* possession, any *usurpation* whatsoever.

נחם (*comp.*) That which *ceases entirely, desists* from a sentiment, *renounces completely* a care, *surrenders* an opinion, *calms* a pain, *consoles*, etc.

נחץ (*comp.*) Every idea of *urgency, haste, importunity.* See חץ.

נחר (*comp.*) See חר.

נחשׁ (*comp.*) See חשׁ.

נחת (*comp.*) See חת.

נט NT. The sign of produced existence united to that of resistance and protection, forms a root whence emanate all ideas of nutation, inflection, inclination, liason, literally as well as figuratively, thence,

נט Every kind of *off-shoot, tendril, reed* suitable to *braid, tie, plait*: a thing which *twines, grows* upon another, is *bound, tied* to it; as *a twig, branch, stick; a sceptre; a mat, a bed;* etc. See טוּ.

The Arabic نَطّ has not preserved the ideas developed by the Hebrew, or rather the Arabic root being formed in another manner has expressed a different sense. In general, the verb نَطّ characterizes that which makes effort to separate itself from the point at which it is arrested; in particular, it is *to jump, to escape, to be emancipated.* By نَاطّ or نَطّ is understood the state of a thing suspended, separated from the point toward which it inclines. The Chaldaic נטה signifies properly *eccentric.*

ני NI. Root analogous to the roots נא נה and נוּ whose expression it manifests.

RADICAL VOCABULARY 401

The Arabic فى indicates the state of that which is raw.

נִין (comp.) An offspring, a son. See בֵּן.

נִיר (comp.) Light manifested in its production, splendour. See נֵר.

נָכָה NCH. That which is injurious to existence arrests, restrains, represses it.

נְכָה A blow, a lesion; chastisement, torment: action of rebuking, chastising, treating harshly, punishing; bruising, striking, sacrificing; etc.

The Arabic نكى presents in general the same ideas as the Hebrew. Is it the same with the Syriac ܢܟܐ

נָל NL. Every idea of suite, series, sequence, consequence: every idea of abundant succession, of effusion holding to the same source. The Arabic words نل, نلّ نيل, all present the sense of succeeding, following in great number, furnishing, giving, rendering abundantly.

נָם NM. Individual existence represented by the sign נ, being universalized by the adjunction of the collective sign ם, forms a root whence is developed the idea of *sleep*. This hieroglyphic composition is worthy of closest attention. One is inclined to believe that the natural philosophy of the ancient Egyptians regarded sleep as a sort of universalization of the particular being. See רוּם and נוּם.

The Arabic نم only participates in the Hebraic root in the case where the verb نم signifies *to exhale, to spread out*, in speaking of odours; for when it expresses the action of *spreading rumours, cursing, calumniating*, it results from another formation. Besides it can be remarked that nearly all the roots which are composed of the sign נ are in the same case; and this, for the reason shown in the grammar, with regard to this sign when it has become initial adjunction.

נ‎ן‎ NN. The sign of individual and produced existence, being united to itself as augmentative sign, constitutes a root whose use is to characterize the continuity of existence by generation. It is a new production which emanates from an older production to form a continuous chain of individuals of the same species.

The Arabic نّ has not preserved the ideas developed by the Hebraic root. It can only be remarked that ني is one of the names which has been given to Venus, that is to say, to the generative faculty of nature.

נון‎ That which is *propagated abundantly*, that which *spreads* and *swarms;* in a restricted sense, the *specie of fish;* action of *abounding, increasing.*

נין‎ Every *new progeny* added to the older, every extension of lineage, family, race. See נ‎י‎.

נס‎ NS. Every idea of vacillation, agitation, literally as well as figuratively: that which wavers, which renders uncertain, wavering.

נס‎ In a restricted sense, *a flag, an ensign, the sail of a ship:* in a broader sense, a movement of *irresolution, uncertainty;* from the idea of *flag* develops that of *putting in evidence, raising:* from the idea of *irresolution,* that of *tempting, of temptation.*

The Arabic نس has only an onomatopoetic root which describes the noise of a thing floating, as water; consequently, characterizing literally, that which imitates the movement of waves; figuratively, that which is given over to such a movement.

נע‎ NH. This root expresses the idea of everything weak, soft, feeble, without consistency. The Arabic نع

RADICAL VOCABULARY

signifies literally *an herb fresh and tender*. In a more extended sense, it is every idea of movement within oneself, vacillation, trepidation, oscillation.

נוּע That which is *weak*, without strength; that which is *variable;* which *changes, vacillates, totters;* which goes from one side to another: it is, in a broader sense, *the impulse* given to a thing *to stir* and draw it from its torpor.

נָעַם (*comp.*) That which is *easy, pleasant, convenient, agreeable*.

נַעַר (*comp.*) In a restricted sense, *a new born infant*: in a figurative sense, the primary impulse given to vital element.

נָף NPH. Every idea of dispersion, ramification, effusion, inspiration; of movement operated inwardly from without, or outwardly from within: distillation if the object is liquid, a scattering if the object is solid. See נוּף.

The Arabic نف has in general, the same ideas. In particular, it is, in the modern idiom, the action of *snuffing, blowing the nose*.

נָץ NTZ. That which reaches its term, end, extreme point: that which is raised as high and spreads as far as it can be, according to its nature.

The Arabic نص does not differ from the Hebrew in the radical sense. In a restricted sense one understands by the verb نص, the action of *giving a theme*, furnishing authority, *confirming*, demonstrating by text, by argument, etc.

נֵץ The end of every germination, *the flower*, and the action of *blossoming;* the term of all organic effort, *the feather*, and the action of *flying;* the end of all desire; *splendour*, and the action of being *resplendent, gleaming, shining*. See נוּץ.

נצץ (*intens.*) From the idea of attaining to the highest point, comes that of *flying;* from that of flying, that of *vulture* and every bird of prey; from this latter, taken in the figurative and intensive sense, that of *ravaging, devastating, wrangling* over plunder, *stealing, robbing;* etc.

נק NCQ. This root, which contains the idea of void, is applied metaphorically to that which is related to this idea: thence נק, every *hollow, cavernous* place; every *excavated* space: an *innocent* being, one without vice, without evil thought; that which is free from all stain, impurity; which is *purified, absolved; fair, white*. In a figurative and restricted sense, *milk;* the nursling which sucks, *an infant*. See נוק

The Arabic ق is an onomatopoetic root which depicts every kind of deep, raucous, sound, like the grunting of a pig, cawing of a crow, etc.

נר NR. The root אוֹר, united by contraction to the sign of produced existence, constitutes a root whose purpose is to characterize that which propagates light, literally as well as figuratively: thence,

נר A *lamp, a beacon, a torch*: *a sage, a guide;* that which *enlightens, shines*, is *radiant*: metaphorically, *a public festivity, an extreme gladness*. See נור and ניר.

The Arabic ن signifies literally, *fire*.

נש NSH. This root which is applied to the idea of things temporal and transient, in general, expresses their instability, infirmity, decrepitude, caducity: it characterizes that which is feeble and weak, easy to seduce, variable, transitory; literally as well as figuratively.

The Arabic ش characterizes in particular, the absorption of water by the earth; in the modern idiom it signifies, *to whisk flies.*

נש　Every idea of *mutation, permutation, subtraction, distraction, cheating, deception, weakness, wrong*, etc.

נת　NTH. Every corporeal division. **In a restricted** sense, *a member*.

The Arabic ـت characterizes extension given to anything whatsoever. The verb ـت expresses literally, the action of oozing through, of perspiring.

נת　*A morsel* of something, *a piece, a portion; a section*: action of *parcelling out*, of *dissecting*, etc.

ס　S. This character as consonant, belongs to the sibilant sound, and is applied as onomatopœia to depicting all sibilant noises: certain observant writers among whom I include Bacon, have conceived this letter S, as the symbol of the consonantal principle, in the same manner that they conceived the letter ה, or the aspiration H, as that of the vocal principle. This character is, in Hebrew, the image of the bow whose cord hisses in the hands of man. As grammatical sign, it is that of circular movement in that which is related to the circumferential limit of any sphere.

Its arithmetical number is 60.

סא　SA. Every idea of circumference, tour, circuit, rotundity.

סאה　Every round thing suitable for containing anything; as *a sack, a bag*. In a figurative sense, it is the action of *emigrating,* changing the place, taking one's bag.

The Arabic ـس or اـس, designates that which disturbs, harms.

סאן　(*comp.*)　Covering for the feet, *sandals*.

סב　SB. When this root is conceived as the product of the circumferential sign united to that of **interior** action ב, it expresses every idea of occasional force, cause, reason: but when it is the root אב, image of every conceivable fructification, joined by contraction to this same sign, then this root is applied to that which surrounds, circumscribes, envelops.

The Arabic سـ contains in general all the acceptations of the Hebraic root; but inclining toward those which are more particularized in a physical sense than in a moral one.

סב Every kind of *contour, circuit, girdle; a circumstance, an occasion, a cause.*

The Arabic سبّ has the same sense; but the primitive root سب having deviated toward the physical, signifies *to distort* a thing, to take the wrong side; *to curse* someone, *to injure* him, etc.

סב and סבב (*intens.*) Action of *turning, going round, circuiting, enveloping, circumventing, warning, converting, perverting,* etc.

The Arabic صـ signifies *to put* a thing *upside down; to pour out, upset.*

סג SG. The circumferential sign united to the organic sign, constitutes a root whose purpose is to depict the effect of the circumferential line opening more and more, and departing from the centre: thence,

סג All ideas of *extension, augmentation, growth: physical possibility.* See סונ and סיג.

The Arabic جـ offers in general, the same sense as the Hebrew.

סד SD. This root whose effect is opposed to that of the preceding one, characterizes, on the contrary, the circumferential line entering upon itself, and approaching the centre: thence,

RADICAL VOCABULARY 407

סר   All ideas of *repression, retention, closing.*

The Arabic ســر has not separated from the Hebrew in the radical sense. As verb it is literally the action of closing. It must be remarked that the verb ســاد which signifies *to master, to dominate,* is attached to the root יד, ســد which indicates properly *the hand,* and the power of which it is the emblem.

סה   SEH. Root analogous to סא.

The Arabic ســه indicates the circumference of the buttocks: *the rump.*

סהר   That which is round of form: *a tower, a dome; the moon; a necklace; bracelets,* etc.

סו   SOU. Root analogous to סא and סה.

The Arabic ســو does not differ from the Hebrew as to the radical sense; but the developments of this root being applied in Arabic, to the idea of what is bent rather than to what is round, characterizes consequently, that which is bad rather than that which is good: thence the verbs ســا or ســو which express the state of what is bent, false, malicious, traitorous, depraved, corrupt, etc.

סוה   *A veil,* a garment which *surrounds, envelops, undulates.*

סוג   (*comp.*) Action of being *extended* by going away from the centre; *yielding;* offering *a facility, a possibility.*

סוד   (*comp.*) Action of *welding; closing, shutting;* that which is *secret, closed, covered.*

סוך   (*comp.*) Action of *anointing.* See סך.

סון   (*comp.*) That which *shines,* that which *renders joyous.* See סן.

סוס   (*comp.*) *A horse.* See סס.

סוּף (*comp.*) That which *finishes* a thing; *makes an end* of it; *to sweep away; to fulfill.* See סף.

סוּר (*comp.*) That which *turns around, bends, is perverted, changes sides, is made adverse;* that which is *audacious, independent;* that which is *raised, bred, trained, turned,* given a *proper outline, directed* etc. See סר.

סוּת (*comp.*) Action of *working in the shadow* of something, of *being covered* with a veil, of *seducing, persuading,* etc. See סת.

סז SZ. Root not used in Hebrew nor in Arabic.

סח SH. Root not used in Hebrew. The Arabic ســ expresses the action of being *dissolved* in water, of being *poured out, spread over,* etc. The Chaldaic סחה signifies *to swim; to wash, to be purified* in water: the Syriac and Samaritan have the same sense.

סחה Action of *cleansing, washing.*
סחי Every idea of *cleansing.*
סחף (*comp.*) Every idea of *subversion, sweeping away; a torrent.*
סדר (*comp.*) Every idea of the *circulation* of produce, of merchandise; action of *negotiating, selling, buying,* etc.
סחש (*comp.*) That which *springs* from corruption: that which *swarms* from putrid water.

סט ST. Root not used in Hebrew. The Arabic ســ characterizes in general, a vehement, illegal action. The compound verb ســ signifies literally *to command with arrogance, to act like a despot.*

סי SI. Root analogous to סה and סו. The Arabic ســ coming from the radical idea taken in a good sense, characterizes that which is regular, equal; that which is

RADICAL VOCABULARY 409

made in accordance with its own nature: thus the **verb** سي or سيـا has reference to milk which flows without being drawn.

סיג (comp.) *An extension*: a thing which has yielded, which has gone away from the centre. In a restricted sense, *scoria*. See סג.

סיר (comp.) *Curvature*. See סר.

סך SCH. The circumferential sign united by contraction of the root אך, image of every restriction and exception, forms a root whose use is to characterize a thing which is round, closed, fitting to contain, to cover; thence,

סך *A sack, veil, covering* of any sort: that which *envelops, covers, obstructs*. In a figurative sense, *the multitude* of men which cover the earth; *ointment* with which the skin is covered and which closes the pores. See סוך.

The Arabic سك has preserved few of the expressions which hold to the radical sense. Its principle developments spring from the onomatopoetic root سك which depicts the effect of the effort that one makes in striking. Literally it is *striking* a thing to make it yield.

סל SL. Every kind of movement which *raises, exalts, takes away, ravishes*.

The Arabic سل signifies in a restricted sense, *to draw to one's self*.

סל In a very restricted sense, *a leap, a gambol;* in a broad and figurative sense, the *esteem* or *value* that is put upon things. Also *a heap* of anything; a thing formed of many others raised one upon another, as *a mound* of earth, etc.

סם SM. The circumferential sign being universalized by the collective sign ם, becomes the symbol of the olfactory sphere, of every fragrant influence given to the air: thence,

סם   Every kind of *aromatic*.

The Arabic سم appears to have preserved more of the developments and even more of the radical force than the Hebraic analogue. This root characterizes that which is penetrated with force whether good or evil. Thence, in the modern idiom the verb سم, which signifies *to bore* a hole, *to pierce*.

סן   SN. The circumferential sign having attained its greatest dimension by the addition of the augmentative sign, ן , becomes the symbol of the visual sphere and of all luminous influence: thence,

סן   Every kind of *light*, of *bright colour*, in general; in particular the colour *red*, as the most striking. This colour, taken in a bad sense, as being that of blood, has furnished the idea of *rage* and *rancour* in the Chaldaic סנא; but the Syriac has only a luminous effect, as is proved by the word ܣܗܪ which signifies *the moon*. The Hebrew has drawn from it the name of the most brilliant month of the year, סיון the month of *May*. See סן.

The Arabic سن characterizes that which *illumines* things and gives them *form* by shaping, polishing them; in the modern idiom the verb سن signifies *to sharpen*.

סס   SS. The circumferential sign being added to itself, constitutes a root which denotes in an intensive manner every eccentric movement tending to increase a circle and give it a more extended diameter: thence, every idea of going away from the centre, of emigration, travel: thence,

סוס   *A horse;* that is to say an animal which aids in emigration, travel. See סא and סע.

The Arabic سام belongs evidently to the primitive root סם, and designates in general, a thing which is carried from the centre to the circumference, *to administer, to govern.*

סע SH. That which is rapid, audacious, vehement, fitted for the race; thence,

סעה *A courier, a thing which rushes;* figuratively *an arrogant person, a calumniator.*

The Syriac ܣܥܐ has the same sense as the Hebrew. The Arabic سع appears to have deviated much from the radical sense. It is literally, *a straw;* but figuratively, it is that which makes the subject of a deliberation.

סער (*comp.*) That which serves for *support, prop, corroboration.* See סר.

סעף (*comp.*) That which is extended by branching out; *a genealogy; a series.*

סער (*comp.*) A violent, tumultuous movement; *a tempest, a storm.*

סף SPH. Every idea of summit, end, finish; anything which terminates, consummates, achieves.

סף *The extremity* of a thing, the point where it ceases; *its achievement, consummation, end: the defection, the want* of this thing: *the border, top, summit, threshold; that which commences* or *terminates* a thing; that which is *added* for *its perfection*: also, reiteration of the same action, *an addition, supplement;* the final thing where many others come to *an end*: a time involving many actions.

The Arabic سف has preserved of the radical sense only the idea of a thing reduced to powder, which is taken as medicine. The Syriac ܣܦ characterizes every kind of consummation, of reducing to powder by fire.

סָפַף (*intens.*) Action of *approaching, drawing near, touching* the threshold, *receiving* hospitality.

סץ STZ. Root not used in Hebrew nor in Arabic.

סק SCQ. Root not used in Hebrew. The Samaritan ᛉ, likewise the Syriac ܣܩ, indicate a movement of evasion, of leaving; of germination.

The Arabic سق is an onomatopoetic root which designates the action of striking.

סר SR. The circumferential sign joined to that of movement proper, constitutes a root whence issue all ideas of disorder, perversion, contortion, apostasy; also those of force, audacity, return, education, new direction, etc.

The Arabic سر offers in general, the same radical character as the Hebrew but its developments differ quite obviously. The verb سر signifies in particular, *to be diverted;* that is to say, turned from serious occupations.

סר and סרר (*comp.*) That which is *disordered, rebellious, refractory;* which leaves its sphere to cause *trouble, discord;* that which is *vehement, audacious, independent, strong*: that which *distorts, turns aside* takes another direction; *is corrected,* etc. See סור.

סש SSH. Root used neither in Hebrew nor in Arabic.

סת STH. Every kind of mutual, sympathetic covering, every kind of veil, of darkness. The Arabic ست indicates the parts of the human body that must be veiled. The Hebrew, as well as the Chaldaic סתו, characterizes winter, the dark season when nature is covered with a veil. See סות.

ע U.H.WH. This character should be considered under the double relation of vowel and consonant. Following its vocal acceptation, it represents the interior of the ear of man, and becomes the symbol of confused, dull, inappreciable noises; deep sounds without harmony. Following its consonantal acceptation, it belongs to the guttural sound and represents the cavity of the chest. Under both relations as grammatical sign, it is in general, that of material sense, image of void and nothingness. As vowel, it is the sign ו, considered in its purely physical relations: as consonant, it is the sign of that which is crooked, false, perverse and bad.

Its arithmetical number is 70.

עא HA. Physical reality. This root is the analogue of the roots הע and עי.

עב HB. The sign of material sense united by contraction to the root אב, symbol of all covetous desire and all fructification, constitutes a root which hieroglyphically characterizes the material centre: it is, in a less general sense, that which is condensed, thickened; which becomes heavy and dark.

The Arabic ع signifies properly to charge with *a burden;* by غ, is understood *to finish, to draw to an end, to become putrid*.

עב Every idea of *density, darkness; a cloud, a thick vapour; a plank, a joist.*

עוב Action of being *condensed, thickened,* of becoming *palpable, cloudy, sombre, opaque;* etc. See אוב of which עוב is the degeneration and intensifying.

עג HG. Every kind or ardour, desire, vehement fire, which increases constantly; every active warmth, as much literally as figuratively.

The Arabic ع is an onomatopoetic and idiomatic root which characterizes a violent noise; the roaring of winds and waves. ع depicts also in an onomatopoetic manner the noise made by water when drunk or swallowed.

עֻג֒ In a restricted sense, the action of *baking;* that which has been exposed to the heat of a hot oven, *a cake,* etc.

עֻד HD. The sign of material sense, contracted with the root אֻ, symbol of relative unity, image of every emanation and every division, constitutes a very important root which, hieroglyphically, develops the idea of *time,* and of all things temporal, sentient, transitory. Symbolically and figuratively it is worldly voluptuousness, sensual pleasure in opposition to spiritual pleasure; in a more restricted sense, every limited period, every periodic return.

The Arabic عد, which is related in general, to the radical sense of the Hebrew, signifies in particular, *to count, number, calculate,* etc.; the word غد, the time which follows the actual time; *tomorrow.*

עֻד *The actual time;* a fixed point in time or space expressed by the relations *to, until, near*: a same state continued, a temporal duration, expressed in like manner by, *now, while, still;* a periodic return as *a month;* a thing *constant, certain, evident, palpable,* by which one can give *testimony; a witness.*

עֻד or עֻדד (*intens.*) Continued time furnishes the idea of *eternity, stability, constancy;* thence, the action of *enacting, constituting, stating,* etc.

עֻוד Action of returning periodically furnishes the idea of *evidence, certitude;* action of returning unceasingly, furnishes the idea of *accumulation;* that of accumulation, the ideas of *riches, plunder, prey;* thence, the action of *despoiling*: now these latter ideas, being linked with those of sentient pleasures contained in the primitive idea of

RADICAL VOCABULARY

time, produce all those of *voluptuousness, sensuality, delights, beauty, grace, adornment,* etc.

עוּ, עָה HEH, HOU. That which is sentient in general; obvious to the senses: physical reality. Superficies, the exterior form of things. Their growth, material development.

The Arabic ع has not preserved the intellectual ideas developed by the Hebraic root. It is today, only an onomatopoetic root depicting a sentiment of self-sufficiency, pride. عو signifies literally *to bark.*

עוה Every *inflection,* every circumferential form; every kind of *curvature, inversion, circle, cycle;* everything *concave* or *convex.* In a figurative sense *perversion, iniquity;* state of being *perverse, iniquitous, deceitful, vicious.*

עוז (*comp.*) Action of *fleeing for refuge* to any person or place.

עוט (*comp.*) Action of making *an irruption.*

עול (*comp.*) To act with *duplicity, hypocrisy;* to be curved as a dais, a yoke, foliage, etc. See על.

עון (*comp.*) Action of *being joined corporeally; cohabiting.* See ען.

עוף (*comp.*) Action of *being raised,* sustained in the air, *flying;* as *vapour, winged fowl* or *bird,* etc. See עף.

עוץ (*comp.*) Action of *consolidating; strengthening.* See עץ.

עוק (*comp.*) Action of *compressing.* See עק.

עור (*comp.*) Action of *impassioning, exciting, putting into movement:* action of *involving, blinding,* etc. See ער.

עוש (*comp.*) Action of *assembling, composing, putting together.* See עש.

עות (*comp.*) Action of communicating a movement of perversion, of *perverting.* See עת.

עז HUZ. Every idea of sentient, material force, of physical demonstration: that which is strong; corroborative auxiliary.

עז This is, in general, a thing which *is strengthened* by *being doubled*, by being added to itself. Every body which is *hard, rough, firm, persistent*, as *a stone, rock, fortress*: that which enjoys great, generative vigour, as *a goat;* that which is *vigorous, audacious;* that which serves as *prop, support, lining, substitute;* that which *corroborates, strengthens, encourages*, etc. See עוז.

The Arabic عز while diverted very slightly from the radical sense of the Hebraic root has, however, acquired a great number of developments which are foreign to the Hebrew. Thus the root عز characterizes that which is precious, dear, rare, worthy of honour; that which is cherished, honoured, sought after, etc. The verb غز signifies properly *to pierce*.

עה HUH. Root not used in Hebrew. The Samaritan ΑΫ indicates in general, material substance, and in particular, *wood*.

עט HUTH. This root develops the idea of resistance overcome by physical means.

עט *A notch, a cut*, made upon a thing: *a stylus, a chisel* for inscribing, engraving; every kind of *incision, line, cleft*. See עוט.

The Arabic عط offers the same sense as the Hebrew. عط signifies *to wear out* in speaking of clothes; عط *to plunge* into the water.

עי HI. This root is the analogue of the roots עה and עו, whose physical expression it manifests. It is, in general, growth, material development; accumulation.

RADICAL VOCABULARY 417

The Arabic ع indicates an overwhelming burden, *a fatigue;* غي signifies *to goad.*

עיט (*comp.*) Action of *cleaving* the air with rapidity, *swooping* down upon something: literally, *a bird of prey.*

עיה (*comp.*) That which tends *to be united, to amalgamate* strongly; a violent desire, keen sympathy; *thirst.* See עם.

עין (*comp.*) Corporeal manifestation; *the eye.* See ען.

עיה (*comp.*) That which manifests a thing which is *volatile, dry, inflammable, arid;* thence, that which *languishes* for lack of humidity. See עף.

עיר (*comp.*) That which manifests a physical impulsion, a general attraction; a common centre of activity, a supervision: as *a city, fort, rampart, body-guard.* See ער.

עךּ HUCH. Root not used in Hebrew. In composition it has the sense of the Arabic علك, which characterizes that which is held with effort, which delays, defers, etc.

In a restricted sense علك signifies *to soil, to stain.*

על HUL. The material sign ע considered under its vocal relation, being united to that of expansive movement, composes a root which characterizes, hieroglyphically and figuratively, primal matter, its extensive force, its vegetation, its development in space, its elementary energy: this same sign, considered as consonant changes the expression of the root which it constitutes, to the point of making it represent only ideas of crime, fraud, perversity.

The Arabic عل has lost nearly all the intellectual ideas characterized by the Hebraic root. In a restricted sense عل signifies to give up to physical relaxation, to grow weak, to become effeminate, to be made sick, and the verb غل, the formation of seed in the plant.

עַל Material extent; its progression, its indefinite extension, expressed by the relations *toward, by, for, on account of, notwithstanding, according to, etc.* Its aggregative power, its growth by juxtaposition, expressed by *upon, over, above, along with, near, adjoining, about, overhead, beyond,* etc.

עַל or עָלַל (*intens.*) That which *grows, extends, rises, mounts;* that which is *high, eminent, superior;* the *aggregated, superficial* part of anything whatsoever: that which constitutes *the form, the factor, the exterior appearance; the labour of things; an extension, a heap;* etc.

עוּל Every kind of material development; that which is raised above another thing: *a fœtus* in the womb of the mother, *an infant* at the breast; *a leaf* upon the tree; every manner of acting conformable to matter; every *appearance,* every *superficies* as much literally as figuratively; the state of being *double, false, hypocritical,* etc. See עֲוֹה.

עַם HUM. Matter universalized by its faculties: tendency of its parts one toward another; the force which makes them gravitate toward the general mass, which brings them to aggregation, accumulation, conjunction; the force whose unknown cause is expressed, by the relations *with, toward, among, at.*

עַם Every idea of union, junction, conjunction, nearness: *a bond, a people, a corporation.*

The Arabic عم presents in general the same sense as the Hebrew. As a verb, it is the action of generalizing, of making common. By غم is understood a painful condition, *a sorrow, an uneasiness,* etc.

עָמַם (*intens.*) Every union in great number; *a multitude:* action of *gathering, covering, hiding, obscuring, heating* by piling up. See עִים.

עֶן HUN. Material void embodied, made heavy, obscure, dark. In considering here the root עַ, image of every superficies, every inflection, united by contraction to the augmentative sign ן, one sees easily an entire inflection: if this inflection is convex, it is a circle, a globe; if it is a concave, it is a hole, a recess.

עֶן and עֶנן (intens.) *A space, a gloomy air, a thick vapour, a cloud.*

The Arabic عن signifies in general, *to appear*, to be obvious to the senses, to be shown under a material form. In an abstract sense, it is a designative relation represented by *from*.

עֶון Action of *darkening, of thickening vapours, of gathering clouds;* action of *forming a body; of inhabiting, cohabiting;* the idea of *a corporation, troop, corps, people, association; of a temporal dwelling;* the idea of every *corruption* attached to the body and to bodily acts; *vice*: that which is *evil; that which afflicts, humiliates, affects;* in a restricted sense *a burden; a crushing occupation; poverty,* etc.

עִין From the idea attached to the manifestation of bodies, comes that of the eye, and of everything which is related thereunto. In a metaphorical sense, *a source, a fountain,* etc. See עֶון and עִין.

עֶן Onomatopoetic root expressing a deep breath, either in lamenting, groaning or crying; thence,

עֶן *A cry, clamour, evocation, response;* a keen tightness of breath, *suffocation, oppression,* literally as well as figuratively.

עֹם HUS. This root, little used, expresses the action of pressing, of trampling under foot.

The Arabic عس expresses the action of *feeling, groping;* also that of *roving, going about without a purpose, etc.*

עֲע HUH. Root not used in Hebrew. **The Arabic** غاع indicates everything which bends and turns.

עָף HUPH. This root, considered as a compound of the sign of material sense, united to that of interior activity, has only the idea of obscurity and darkness; but its greatest usage is onomatopoetic to depict movements which are easy, agile, light, swift.

The Chaldaic עַפָף signifies properly *to blow the fire;* to light it and make it burn; the Arabic عف, with this idea, characterizes the state of that which has passed through the fire, which is pure, spotless, without vice, innocent; which abstains from all evil, etc.

עָף (*onom.*) That which *rises, expands, opens out* into the air; that which *soars, flies,* etc. See עוּף and עִיף.

עֵץ HUTZ. Determined matter offered to the senses according to any mode of existence whatsoever.

עֵץ Hieroglyphically, *substance* in general; in the literal or figurative sense, *vegetable substance,* and the physical faculty of *vegetation*: in a very restricted sense, *wood, a tree:* that which is *consolidated* and *hardened,* which appears under a constant and determined form. See עוּץ.

The Arabic عص characterizes, in general, the root of things, their radical origin. In a less extended sense it is that which serves as point of support; that which is solid, firm, valid. When this root is reinforced by the guttural inflection in عص, it is applied to that which is oppressive by nature; which molests, vexes, mystifies; it is, in a restricted sense, the action of *causing indigestion;* an obstruction, a lump in the throat. By عض is understood the action of *biting,* and by غض, that of *making defective.*

עָק HUCH. Every idea of extreme condensation, of contraction with itself, of hardness; figuratively, anguish. See עוּק.

The Arabic قع characterizes the idea of that which is refractory, that which being pushed, repels; that which disobeys, etc. As onomatopoetic root غق expresses the flight and cry of the crow, the noise made by waves breaking, etc.

עוּר HUR. This root should be carefully distinguished under two different relations. Under the first, it is the root עַ image of physical reality and symbol of the exterior form of things which is united to the sign of movement proper ר; under the second, it is the sign of material sense united by contraction to the root אוֹר, image of light, and forming with it a perfect contrast: thence, first:

עַר Passion, in general; *an inner ardour, vehement, covetous; an irresistible impulse; a rage, disorder; an exciting fire* literally as well as figuratively. Secondly:

עַר *Blindness, loss of light* or *intelligence,* literally as well as figuratively; *absolute want, destitution,* under all possible relations; *nakedness, sterility,* physically and morally. In a restricted sense, *the naked skin, the earth, arid and without verdure: a desert.*

The Arabic ع has preserved almost none of the intellectual ideas developed by the Hebraic root. One recognizes, however, the primitive sense of this important root even in the modern idiom, where ع signifies *to dishonour, contaminate, cover with dirt,* and غ , *to deceive* by false appearances, *to lead* into error, *to delude;* etc.

עָרַר (*intens.*) The highest degree of excitement in the fire of passions; the most complete privation of anything whatsoever.

עוּר Action of inflaming the fire of passions, depriving of physical and moral light. Here the primitive root עַר, confounding its two relations by means of the convertible sign ו, presents a mass of mixed expressions. It is the action of *awaking, exciting, stirring;* of *renouncing. depriving one's self, being stripped naked, of watching, superintending, guarding;* of *drawing away, misleading:* it is *a nude body, a skin; a guard house, a dark cavern; a city,* etc. See עור and עיר.

עש HUSH. Every idea of conformation by aggregation of parts, or in consequence of an intelligent movement, of combination or plan formed in advance by the will: thence,

עש A *work, a composition; a creation, a fiction, a labour* of any sort, *a thing;* action of *doing* in general. See עוש.

The Arabic عش has lost the radical sense, and instead of a formation in general, is restricted to designating a particular formation, as that of a nest, garment, etc. غش signifies to commit fraud, falsification; to feign, dissimulate, etc.

עת HUTH. That which takes all forms, which has only relative existence, which is inflected by sympathy, reaction, reciprocity. The product of material sense, *time;* that is to say *the moment when one feels,* expressed by the adverbial relations *now, already, at once, incontinent,* etc.

The Arabic عت signifies literally *to prey upon, to wear out, to ruin;* which is a result of the lost radical meaning. عت or غت signifies that which preys upon the mind, as *care, sorrow, alarm, sad news,* etc.

פ P.PH. This character as consonant, belongs to the labial sound, and possesses two distinct articulations: by the first P, it is joined to the character ב or B, of which it is a reinforcement; by the second PH, it is joined to the character ו become consonant and pronounced V or F.

As symbolic image it represents the mouth of man, whose most beautiful attribute it depicts, that of uttering his thoughts. As grammatical sign, it is that of speech, and of that which is related thereunto. The Hebrew does not employ it as article; but everything proves that many of the Egyptians used it in this way and thus confounded it with its analogue ב, by a peculiar affectation of the pronunciation. Perhaps also a certain dialect admitted it at the head of words as emphatic article in place of the relation פה; this appears all the more probable, since in Hebrew, a fairly large quantity of words exist where it remains such, as I shall remark in my notes.

Its arithmetical number is 80.

פא PHA. That which is the most apparent of a thing, the part which first strikes the sight.

פא *The face* of things in general; in a more restricted sense, *the mouth, the beak;* that of which one speaks with emphasis, that which is made noticeable.

In Arabic this root displays its force in ڢ *mouth*, and in ڢه *to speak*. The verb ڢاه characterizes literally, that which opens, separates, as the mouth.

פאר (*comp.*) Every kind of *ornament, glory, palms*. See פר.

פב PHB. Root not used in Hebrew nor in Arabic.

פג PHG. That which extends afar, which wanders, is extended, loses its strength, its heat.

The Arabic ڊج has nearly the same sense. As noun, it is every kind of crudeness, unripeness; as verb, it is the action of *separating, opening, disjoining*, etc.

פוג Action of *being cool, freezing;* of losing movement.

פַּד   PHD. Every idea of enlargement, liberation, redemption. The Arabic فد signifies to raise the voice, to show one's self generous, magnificent, arrogant.

The meaning of the Hebraic root is found in the compound فدا which signifies literally *to deliver*.

פֶּה   PHEH. This root is the analogue of the root פא ; but in Hebrew particularly, it emphasizes the thing that one wishes to distinguish in time or in a fixed place; as in *that very place, right here, this, that, these*.

פה   In a literal sense, *mouth, breath, voice*, in a figurative sense, *speech, eloquence, oratorical inspiration*: that which presents *an opening*, as the mouth; which constitutes part of a thing, as *a mouthful*; which follows *a mode, a course*, as speech.

The Arabic فه has in general, the same sense as the Hebrew.

פּוּ   PHOU. This root is the analogue of the roots פא and פה: but its expression is more onomatopoetic in describing the breath which comes from the mouth.

The Arabic فو is not far removed from the radical sense of the Hebrew.

פוה (*comp.*)   Action of *blowing*. See פה.

פון (*comp.*)   Action of *hesitating*. See פן.

פוץ (*comp.*)   Action of *spreading, dispersing, melting*. See פץ.

פוק (*comp.*) Action of being moved by an alternating movement. See פק.

פור (*comp.*)   That which *bursts forth, shines out, appears*. See פר.

פוש (*comp.*)   That which *spreads* abundantly, which *overflows*. See פש.

RADICAL VOCABULARY

פֿז PHZ. That which throws flashes, **gleams, rays**: which is sharply reflected: thence,

פֿז *Purest gold; keenest joy; a topaz.*

The Arabic ف characterizes the movement of that which rises quickly, spurts up, leaps, struggles, etc.

פוז Action of *emitting sperm.*

פֿה PHEH. Everything which is drawn in, expanded, as *the breath;* all that which is unfolded in order to envelop and seize, as *a net;* thence,

פחה Every idea of *administration, administrator, state, government.*

The Arabic ف constitutes an onomatopoetic and idiomatic root which describes every kind of hissing of the voice, snoring, strong respiration, rattling. When this root is strengthened in فخ, it signifies literally, *an ambush; a trap.*

פוח Action of *inhaling, expiring; respiring, blowing;* action of *inspiring, communicating* one's will, *governing.*

פחז (*comp.*) Every idea *of breath, of lightness, of unstable thing.*

פחת (*comp.*) *A yawn, an hiatus, a hole.*

פֿט PHT. An opening, a pit; a dilation; a prorogation given to something.

The Arabic ف signifies literally, *to crumble;* ظ *to rise, leap.* From the latter word is formed فض which characterizes that which acts abruptly, with cruelty, etc.

פט Action of *opening* the mouth, *yawning;* figuratively, the action of *crying, chattering, ranting,* etc.

פֿי PHI. This root is the analogue of the two roots פא and פה; but its expression is more manifest.

פִיה   A *beak; the orifice* of anything; the prominent part, *an angle; a discourse,* and particularly, *a message.*

The Arabic فِي departs from the Hebraic root and instead of developing the primitive فُ *the mouth,* from the moral stand point; it develops it from the physical, characterizing that which is interior and opposed to the surface of things. The root فِي conceived abstractly, is represented by the adverbial relations, *in, into, within.* As noun, it designates the shadowy part of the body, *the umbra;* as verb, it signifies *to darken, to shade.*

פִיד   (*comp.*)   *Ruin, disaster.*

פִיח   (*comp.*)   *Soot.*

פָּךְ   PHCH. Every distillation which comes from vapour suddenly condensed: *a drop of water;* metaphorically, *a lens.*

The Arabic فك signifies literally *to be dissolved.*

פַּל   PHL. The emphatic sign, united by contraction to the root אל, symbol of every elevation, constitutes a root which develops all ideas of distinction, privilege, choice, election, setting aside: thence,

פל   Some thing *wonderful, precious,* which is considered *a mystery: a miracle: a distinguished, privileged* man whom one reveres; *a noble, a magistrate;* that which is set aside, hidden in all fruits, *the germ;* literally, *a bean.*

The Arabic فل has not preserved the moral ideas developed by the Hebrew. This root, inclining toward the physical sense, is limited to expressing that which is separated, extracted, drawn from another thing: that which is divided into distinct parts. In the modern idiom فل signifies literally *to drive away.*

RADICAL VOCABULARY 427

פלל (*intens.*) From the idea of noble and magistrate, springs that of *dominion, power*: thence, the action of *judging* others, *rendering justice, governing,* etc.

פם PHM. Root not used in Hebrew. The Chaldaic פום signifies *mouth;* the Arabic فم has exactly the same sense. As verb فوم, is *to bake bread, to cook;* in general, that which is related to food for the mouth.

פן PHN. The face of anything whatsoever, the front of a thing, that which is presented first to the view: that which strikes, astonishes, frightens: every idea of presence, conversion, consideration, observation, etc.

פן *The aspect* of a person, *his countenance, face, mien, air,* sad or serene, mild or irritated: action *of turning* the face, expressed by the relations *before, in the presence of, from before,* etc. Action *causing* the face *to turn,* expressed by *beware! no! lest! for fear of!* etc. That which imposes by its aspect: *a prince, a leader; a star, a ruby, a tower,* etc. That which is the cause of *disturbance,* of *hesitation.* See פון.

The Arabic فن has evidently the same primitive idea which has produced the Hebraic root; but although starting from the same principle, its developments have been different; they have inclined rather toward the physical than toward the moral, as can be remarked in general, of other roots. Thus, from the primitive idea deduced from the exterior face which things present, from their manner of being phenomenal, the Arabic idiom has drawn the secondary ideas of complication and of complicating; of mixture and of mixing; of variety and of varying; of specification and of specifying; of classification and of classifying; so that finally, considering as general, what had been particular, this same root فن is used to designate *an art,* or *a science* of some sort, because it is by means of arts and sciences that one can class all things and **examine** them under their aspects.

פס PHS. That which comprises only a portion of the circumference or totality of a thing.

פס A *part, a face, a phase.* Action of *diminishing,* of breaking into pieces.

The Arabic فص signifies literally to *examine minutely.*

פע PHUH. Onomatopoetic root which depicts the cry of an animal with yawning jaws. Figuratively, a clamour; metaphorically, a diffusion.

The Arabic فمع characterizes the call of the shepherds.

פעל (*comp.*) Every kind of *act, work, action.* See על.

פעם (*comp.*) Every kind of *agitation, movement, impulse*: literally, *the feet.* See עם.

פען (*comp.*) Every kind of *augury, observation, phenomenon.* See פן.

פער (*comp.*) Every kind of *distention, relaxation;* action of *depriving, stripping, making naked,* etc. See ער.

פץ PHTZ. Every idea of diffusion, loosening, setting forth, giving liberty. See פוץ.

The Arabic فص presents the same sense in general. In a restricted sense فص signifies to *examine minutely*, and فض to *break the seal.*

פק PHCQ. That which opens and shuts; which is stirred by an alternating movement back and forth; that which is intermittent, inquisitive, exploratory, etc.

The Arabic فق has in general the same ideas as the Hebrew. As verb, this root expresses particularly the action of *releasing, opening, dilating,* etc.

RADICAL VOCABULARY

פק and פקק (*intens.*) Action of *passing* from one place to another, *being carried here and there, going and coming;* action of *obstructing, standing in the way,* etc. See פוק.

פר PHR. The emphatic sign replacing the sign of interior activity ב and united to that of movement proper ר, constitutes a root which develops all ideas of fructification, production, elementary generation.

פר Any *progeny,* any *produce* whatsoever; *the young* of any animal, particularly of the cow. That which is *fertile, fecund, productive.*

The Arabic ف, being applied principally to developing in the Hebraic פר the idea which had relation to the young of a weak timid animal, has characterized the action of fleeing; the flight, the fear which makes one give way; also the growth of teeth, dentition; the examination that is made of the teeth of an animal to discover its age, its strength, its weakness, etc.

פרה Action of *producing, bearing.*

פרח That which *vegetates, germinates, swarms*: *a seed, a flower.*

פרי *Fruit;* figuratively *an effect, a consequence.*

פרו or פרע Onomatopoetic root which describes the noise of a thing which cleaves the air, or strikes it with a violent movement.

פרך (*comp.*) Every abrupt movement which *breaks, bruises.*

פרם (*comp.*) *To rend* a garment.

פרס (*comp.*) That which *breaks;* that which *divides* in *breaking.*

פרץ (*comp.*) Action of *breaking* into many pieces; *reducing to powder.*

פרק (*comp.*) That which *tears,* draws forcibly from a place, *breaks* the bonds, *sets at liberty.*

פרש (*comp.*) Action of *dispersing, divulging, manifesting, specifying;* action of piercing: metaphorically, *a hunter, a horseman.*

פש PHSH. Every idea of pride, vanity, extravagance; of *inflation*, literally as well as figuratively. That which seeks *to extend, to put itself in evidence.* See פוש.

The Arabic فش is an onomatopoetic and idiomatic root which depicts the noise made by the air when escaping from the place where it has been confined, as when it comes from a bladder which has been pressed; thence, if one considers the bladder, the sense of *letting out the air;* if the air which escapes is considered, the same sense of doing a thing with vivacity, arrogance, passion, etc.

פת PHTH. Every idea of dilation, extending easily, allowing to be penetrated, opened; every divisibility, every opening; space, extent: thence,

פת *Space* in general, or *any space* in particular; that which is indifferent in itself, *impassive;* metaphorically, *a fop, a fool, a silly person, a simpleton*: action of *persuading, deceiving;* etc.

The Arabic فت preserves the radical sense of the Hebrew, without having the same developments. As verb, it is the action of *scattering, spreading here and there,* tearing into small pieces, etc.

צ TZ. This character as consonant, belongs to the hissing sound, and describes as onomatopœia, all objects which have relations with the air and wind. As symbolic image, it represents the refuge of man, and the end toward which he tends. It is the final and terminative sign, having reference to scission, limit, solution, end. Placed at the beginning of words it indicates the movement which carries toward the limit of which it is the sign; placed at the end, it marks the very limit where it has tended.

Its arithmetical number is 90.

צָא   TZA. The final sign צ, as initial and united to that of power, characterizes in this root, that which leaves material limits, breaks the shackles of the body, matures, grows; is born exteriorly.

The Arabic صَاما expresses with much energy the effort made by the young of animals to open their eyes.

צָאן   (comp.) *Flocks* and *herds;* in a broader sense, *a productive faculty*.

צוֹא   Onomatopoetic root expressing a movement of disgust and repulsion at the sight of a filthy object.

צוֹא   Every kind of *filth, obscenity, excrement*.

צָב   TZB. Every idea of concourse, of crowd; that which rises, swells, stands in the way; that which serves as a dike; that which is conducted and unfolded according to fixed rules.

The Arabic صب characterizes in general, that which flows after the manner of fluids; metaphorically, that which follows a determined inclination, which obeys an impulse. ضب expresses every kind of emanation in general; that which belongs to, that which results from, another thing. In a very restricted sense ضب signifies a species of lizard.

צָב   *An army, a military ordnance; a general order* observed by a mass of individuals, *discipline*: thence, *honour, glory, renown*. Metaphorically *the host of stars, the harmony which regulates their movements*.

צָג   TZG. Root not used in Hebrew. The Ethiopic አጽ (*tzagg*) signifies *to publish*. The Arabic صج indicates the noise made by iron striking upon iron. ضج signifies *a tumult; an uproar*.

צָד TZD. That which is insidious, artful, double, sly, opposed, adverse, deceitful, seductive.

The Arabic صد presents in general, the same sense as the Hebrew; that is to say, every idea of opposition, defense. ضد expresses the state of quarreling, disputing.

צַד In a literal sense, very restricted, *the side;* in a broad and figurative sense, *a secret, dissimulating hindrance; an artifice, a snare.*

צוּד Action of *setting snares; hunting, fishing, ensnaring* birds; *deceiving.*

צָה TZEH. Root analogous to the root צָא and develops the same ideas.

The Arabic صه is an onomatopoetic root which characterizes the action of one who imposes silence; it is represented by the interjective relations, *hist! hush!* This root being reinforced at the end in صم designates literally *silence.*

צהל (*comp.*) *To neigh.*

צהר (*comp.*) *Luminous ray; the splendour of midday.* See צר.

צוּ TZOU. This very important root characterizes every kind of line drawn toward an end, of which the sign צ is symbol. It develops every idea of order, command, direction, impressed by the *primum mobile.*

The Arabic صو has departed much from the radical sense of the Hebrew, of which it has retained only certain physical developments. Thus صوا expresses a sort of natural humectation; and ضو, the impression which light causes upon the organ of sight. As onomatopoetic root ضوه denotes the sound of the voice.

צוה A *law, an ordinance; an order, a command;* that which leads to an end: *a precept, a statute, a maxim of conduct*: action of *ordering, directing, leading; impressing a movement.*

צוה (*comp.*) *To cry aloud.*

צול (*comp.*) A thing which is propagated *afar, as noise; depth*, literally and figuratively. See צל.

צום (*comp.*) *To fast.* See צם.

צוף (*comp.*) *To overflow.* See צף.

צוץ (*comp.*) *To blossom.* See צץ.

צוק (*comp.*) That which *presses; holds back forcibly.* See צק.

צור (*comp.*) That which *compresses, forms, conforms.* See צר.

צות (*comp.*) *To set on fire, to kindle.* See צת.

צץ TZZ. Root not used in Hebrew nor in Arabic.

As onomatopoetic root ضْ characterizes the inarticulate sounds emitted from closed jaws. Figuratively it is *to champ the bit.*

צח TZEH. That which is dry, arid, exposed to the rays of the sun. That which is clear, serene, radiant.

The Arabic ص offers in general, the same sense as the Hebraic root and adds much to the developments of the moral side. In the Arabic idiom, it is the state of that which is sane, upright, pure, true, clean, rectified, etc. The verb ضح characterizes that which shines on account of its purity.

צחה State of being exposed to the rays of the sun, *being thirsty, dry, etc.*

צט TZT. Root not used in Hebrew. The Arabic ضلل designates a strong man, a formidable adversary.

צִי TZI. Root analogous to the root צָא and צָה, but develops the same idea with greater intensity.

صَبَا expresses a sort of lotion, libation, aqueous emanation. ضِي signifies literally *brightness*, every kind of luminous effusion.

צִיָּה Every *place* exposed to the rays of the sun, and made *dry* and *glaring*.

צִיר (*comp.*) Every opposition which springs from artifice. See צָר.

צָךְ TZCH. Root not used in Hebrew. The Arabic صك is an onomatopoetic root which depicts the noise made by two flat stones rubbed together to crush anything whatsoever.

צָל TZL. This root, composed of the final sign united to the directive sign, characterizes a thing whose effect is spread afar. This thing expresses, according to the genius of the Hebraic tongue, either noise, or shadow passing through air and void; or void itself, containing darkness: thence,

צָל Every *noise* that is striking, clear, piercing like that of brass; every *shadow* carried, projected a great distance into space; every obscure *depth*, whose bottom is unknown: metaphorically, *a screaming voice;* any kind of object extending overhead and making a shade as *a canopy, dais, covering, roof, veil;* every deep, obscure place, *a cavern.* See צוּל.

The Arabic صل has evidently the same radical sense as the Hebrew צָל, but this root, besides its primitive sense, having also an onomatopoetic sense, has received developments much more extended. According to the first sense, the verb صل characterizes the state of that which grows dark being corrupted, of that which imitates the darkness of shadow, which lengthens, gains, as a shadow, etc. According to the second sense, it is a prolonged sound, a cry which invokes succour, a prayer, etc. ضل expresses that which is prolonged indefinitely, wanders, disappears, etc.

צם TZM. That which is carried with avidity, with force, toward a thing; that which covets or seizes eagerly.

The Arabic صم has the same radical sense as the Hebrew. As verb, it is the action of obstructing, opposing forcibly the egress of anything whatsoever; state of being *deaf*, stupid, etc.

ضم expresses that which is strongly united; an aggregation, an agglomeration, *a mass.*

צם *Thirst.*

צמם *A knot, a braid, an indissoluble bond:* thence,

צום *Action of fasting.*

צן TZN. That which conserves, preserves, puts in safety.

צן *A dwelling* where one gathers for shelter; a *shield, an urn, a basket;* any sort of defensive *weapon*, etc.

The Arabic صن characterizes that which being shut up becomes warm and smells badly; figuratively, it is concentrated anger, *rancour.* ضن is the state of that which is sordid, tenacious, avaricious.

צס TZS. Root not used in Hebrew nor in Arabic.

צע TZUH. This root, analogous to the roots צא, צה, צי develops the same ideas of tendency toward a determined end; but adds to it the particular expression of the root ע, image of all material development: thence,

צע   Every kind of *machine, automaton;* anything acting like clock work: that which is *wandering, irresolute, running to and fro*, etc.

The Arabic ﺻﻊ presents the same sense as the Hebrew and characterizes in particular, that which is supple, flabby, ungainly, slack, etc. As onomatopoetic root ﺻﻢ denotes silence, and the verb ﺿﻢ, the action of bringing to uniformity that which tends to be dispersed.

צף   TZPH. Every idea of diffusion, profusion, overflowing; that which flows like water; which follows a steady incline.

The Arabic ﺻﻒ in departing from this last idea, develops the action of *putting in order,* arranging, co-ordinating, instructing, etc., and ﺿﻒ, to put together, *to assemble.*

צוף   Action of *flowing, following the course of water, swimming, floating.*

צץ   TZTZ. Root not used in Hebrew. The Arabic ﺻﺺ expresses the cry of small birds, by an imitative noise.

צק   TZCQ. Every noise, every sudden clamour.

The Arabic ﺻﻖ expresses *clapping the hands.* In the modern idiom ﺻﻖ, indicates consent given by a hand clasp: *an engagement, a note.*

צר   TZR. If this root is considered as composed of the final sign united by contraction to the elementary root אר, one perceives all universal ideas of form, formation, co-ordination, elementary configuration: but if it is considered as result of the union of the same final sign with that of movement proper, one perceives only the idea

RADICAL VOCABULARY 437

of a tight grasp, an oppression, an extreme compression. Thence,

צוּר   Every *formation* by the sole co-ordination of the elements, by their own aggregation, or by their artificial liaison and their limitation to a model; every *creation, fiction, picture, image, exemplar*: action of *forming, conforming, modeling, figuring, painting*, etc.

צוֹר   Every *compression* by effect of an exterior movement which *pushes*, which *presses* the elementary parts upon each other toward a common point: that which *obliges, forces, oppresses, obsesses, besieges, presses upon, acts in a hostile manner; a violent adversary, enemy, competitor, rival*: that which causes *anguish, suffering*: *the point of a sword, the steepness of a rock*, etc.

The Arabic ص signifies literally, *to press, draw closer, link, knit, twist, pack*, etc., and ض the action of *injuring, wounding, offending*, etc.

צוּאָר   (*comp.*) That which holds to corporeal forms: in a restricted sense, *the neck*.

צִיר   That which serves as bond: *the vertebræ;* the muscular and bony ligatures: *the hinges* of a door which fasten it to the wall: *the ambassadors* of a king; *a legation*, etc.

צשׁ   TZSH. Root not used in Hebrew. The Ethiopic ፀኦሕ (*tzoush*) expresses that which is *tortuous, bandy-legged, counterfeit*.

צת   TZTH. Every impulse given toward the same end; every communicated movement; as is expressed by the Arabic صت .

צתה   *A conflagration;* the action of *setting fire*.

ק KQ. This character as consonant, belongs to the guttural sound. As symbolic image it represents a trenchant weapon, that which serves as instrument for man, to defend, to make an effort for him. It has already been remarked, that nearly all the words which hold to this consonant in the greater part of the idioms, designate force and constraint. It is, in the Hebraic tongue, the compressive and decisive sign; that of agglomerative or repressive force. It is the character כ entirely materialized; the progression of the sign is as follows: ה, vocal principle, sign of absolute life: ח, aspirate principle, sign of elementary existence: ג, guttural principle, organic sign: כ, same principle strengthened, sign of assimilated existence holding to forms alone: ק, same principle greatly strengthened, sign of mechanical, material existence giving the means of forms.

Its arithmetical number is 100.

קא CA, KA or QUA. This is the analogous root of קו which characterizes the expression of the sign. As onomatopoetic root it is a convulsive and violent effort; *to spue out, to vomit forth.*

The Arabic ڧ which takes the place of the primitive root, reinforces all its acceptations. As onomatopoetic root ڧاڧا depicts the croaking of a crow.

קוא Action of vomiting.
קיא Vomit.

קב KB. The onomatopoetic root קא, united by contraction to the sign of interior activity ב, expresses all rejection, expurgation. Literally, it is *an excavation;* figuratively, *an anathema, a malediction.*

But if one considers here the figure ק, as being contracted with the root אב, then the root קב characterizes every object capable of and containing any kind of measure: literally, *genitalia muliebra;* figuratively, *a bad place.*

The Arabic ڤ is an onomatopoetic and idiomatic root expressing every effort that one makes to cut, carve, sharpen. It characterizes, in general, that which retrenches or is retrenched; thence, the idea of a prince, a magistrate; of any man or any thing which operates a line of demarcation. ڤ designates again, the principal sound of the musical system, *the keynote.* See בכ.

קג KG. Root not used in Hebrew nor in Arabic.

קד KD. The vertical point, pole, summit, of anything whatsoever; the pivot, motive, point upon which all bears, turns.

The Arabic قد has evidently the primitive sense of the Hebraic root but develops, however, other acceptations. It is, in general, a line of demarcation, fissure, notch; in particular, it is *the figure* of anything whatsoever, the corporeal proportion, etc.

קוד In a restricted sense, action of *inclining the head.*

קה KEH. This root is the analogue of קו, to which one can refer for the real meaning of the sign. As onomatopoetic root it expresses the sudden cry which is given to frighten, to astound, put to flight. See קא.

The Arabic قه is an onomatopoetic root which depicts a sudden and immoderate burst of laughter.

קהה State of *being frightened,* by an unforeseen noise, *stunned, stupefied.*

קהל (*comp.*) A call *to gather* the cattle.

קו COU, KOU or QUOU. This root, as well as its analogues קא or קה, when they are not onomatopoetic, designate in general, that which is indefinite, vague, indeterminate, unformed: it is matter suitable to be put in action, the mechanical movement which acts upon it; the obtuse, vague, blind but irresistible force which leads it; *necessity.*

קִו   The mathematical *line* and that which represents it: *a level, a rule, a clew;* that which holds irresistibly to a point; metaphorically *desire, hope;* figuratively, *sound, echo.*

The Arabic ڧ is no longer used in its radical form, but one finds a great number of its derivatives, all of which hold more or less closely to the Hebraic root; such as ڧاﻟ *obedience,* and in general, every proper, analogous thing; ڧوي *force, valour, virtue;* ڧوه *faculty, power,* etc. This onomatopoetic root ڧوه, depicts as in Hebrew a resounding, prolonged sound, like that of the hunter's horn.

קוה   Action of *stretching, being carried toward* an object, *desiring, becoming, mingling with, being formed* of it. That which is *obtuse;* that which *acts without intelligence;* that which, like an echo, *repeats the voice* or *sound,* without seizing or keeping it.

קוח   (*comp.*)   Action of *reaching out,* making effort to *seize* something. See קח.

קוט   (*comp.*)   Action of being *disgusted.* See קט.
קול   (*comp.*)   *Voice, sound.* See קל.
קום   (*comp.*)   *Substance* in general. See קם.
קון   (*comp.*)   *Lamentation.* See קן.
קוף   (*comp.*)   *An ape.* See קף.
קוץ   (*comp.*)   Action of *cutting, cutting off; pricking.* See קץ.

קור   (*comp.*)   Action of *digging* a well, a snare; action of *surrounding, catching, destroying,* etc. See קר.

קוש   (*comp.*)   *A snare;* action of *entangling, setting a trap.* See קש.

RADICAL VOCABULARY 441

קז   KZ. Root not used in Hebrew. The Arabic فز indicates every kind of leap, assault; impetuous movement to overpower a thing. In the modern idiom, the verb فز signifies *to weave*.

קה   KEH. The idea of an effort that is made toward a thing to seize it to comprehend it. See קוה.

The Arabic جّ characterizes that which is pure, frank, sincere.

קט   KT. This root develops the idea of resistance opposed to that of tension, of extension: thence in a very broad sense, the *Occident;* in a very restricted sense, *a stick*. See קוט

The Arabic قط is an onomatopoetic and idiomatic root which depicts every kind of cut made without effort, as with a knife, etc. This root employed as adverbial relation is represented by *only, only so much, so little*.

קי   KI or QUI. This root is the analogue of the roots קה and קו, whose power it manifests.

The Arabic قي signifies according to the radical sense, an arid, desert land; according to the onomatopoetic sense, *to vomit*.

קין   (comp.) *A lance.*

קיר   (comp.) *Wall of circumvallation, enclosure, fortified precinct.* See קר.

קך   KCH. Root not used in Hebrew nor in Arabic.

קל   KL. The root קו, image of that which is undefined, vague, unformed, united by contraction to the directive sign ל, produces a root which designates that which is deprived of consistency and form; sound, voice, wind: but, if this same root is conceived as formed by the union of the compressive sign ק, with the root אל image of all elevation and all superior force, it expresses then the action of roasting, parching, etc.

קל   Every idea *of lightness, rapidity, velocity*: that which is *attenuated, slender, thin*: without consistency; of little value; *vile, cowardly, infamous*.

The Arabic قل presents the same radical sense as the Hebrew; but, as verb, it is in particular, that which becomes *less;* which is reduced, lightened; which loses ground; becomes rarefied, etc.

קוֹל   *Voice, sound*. The Arabic قال signifies literally, *to say, speak, state, express*.

קם   KM. The root קו, being universalized by the addition of the collective sign ם, characterizes substance in general, undefined nature; a thing whose only properties are extent and necessity: thence,

קוֹם   Action of existing in substance, being *substantialized;* assuming stability; state of being *extended, established; constituted; strengthened;* qualified to assume all forms; action of being *spread out; rising* into space. Action of *existing, subsisting, consisting, persisting, resisting*: that which is *necessary, real; rigid, irresistible*: that which is *opposed*, is *raised* against another thing, shows itself *refractory, inflexible*, etc.

The Arabic قم has preserved none of the intellectual ideas developed by the Hebraic root. As verb, قم expresses the action of taking away the superficies of things, making them dry, clean, etc. In particular, it is the action of *sweeping*. The radical sense of the Hebrew is developed by the Arabic قام.

קים   Every idea of *manifest opposition, insurrection*: that which is *adverse, rebellious;* matter in travail.

RADICAL VOCABULARY 443

קן KN. This root has two sources whose expressions are blended, as it were, in one. By the first, it is derived from the root קו, image of the blind force which moves matter, united to the augmentative sign ן ; by the second, it springs from the compressive sign ק, contracted with the root אן, symbol of all corporeal circumscription; thence,

קן That which *tends* with ardour toward a thing; that which is *envious, usurping, vehement, covetous* of gain and possession; thence,

קן That which is *centralized, concentrated* in itself.

From these two roots קין is formed, in which are assembled the opposed ideas of *appetent tension* and *compression, vehemence* and *closeness, power* and *density*. It contains *the central force, profound basis, rule* and *measure* of things; also *the faculty* which *seizes, usurps, agglomerates, appropriates* and *assimilates with itself*.

The Arabic فن although holding to the same root as the Hebrew קן, is however, far from preserving or developing so great a number of ideas. Nearly all of those which were intellectual have become lost. The verb فان, which partakes most of the radical sense, signifies literally *to forge* the iron, to strike it while it is hot; *to solder* metals, to unite them by means of the forge. فين is *a blacksmith*.

קן or קנן (*intens.*) In a literal and restricted sense *a nest, a centre; a cane, a measure, a reed; an abode, a possession, an acquisition, conquest; a possessor, envious person, rival; envy, hatred, jealousy; an affair, property, wealth,* etc.

קם KS. Every idea of hazard, fatality, chance, etc. The Arabic فس expresses the kind of jealousy that one feels when the thing that one desires is possessed by another.

קע KH. Every idea of line strongly traced, of stigma; of violent disordered movement which wounds, displaces, deranges, etc.

The Arabic ڧع is an onomatopoetic root which depicts the sound of the voice made by one who drives away a troublesome animal. Figuratively, all that which repels; a strong *bitterness;* briny, brackish water.

קף KPH. Every idea of condensation, concretion; that which is coagulated, congealed, thickened, etc.

The Arabic ڧف presents the same radical sense. It is literally, the image of a humid thing when *shrunken* by drought.

קץ KTS. The compressive sign united to the final sign, constitutes a root whence develop naturally, all ideas of term, limit, extremity, goal, summit, finish, cessation.
קץ and קצץ. (*intens.*) That which *cuts, limits, terminates, finishes* a thing; that which is *extreme, final,* without anything beyond: action of *cutting, cutting off, amputating,* etc. See קיץ.

The Arabic ڧص signifies literally *to shear,* to cut with scissors; figuratively *to follow* the tracks of someone, *to continue* a movement; *to narrate* a thing, etc.

קק KK. Root not used in Hebrew. It is, in the Chaldaic קיק, the name given to the pelican; in the Arabic ڧق it is onomatopoetic and describes the clucking of chickens.

קר KR. The compressive sign united to that of movement proper, constitutes a root which develops the idea of that which is incisive, penetrating, firm, straight;

that which engraves or which serves to engrave; every kind of engraving, character, or sign fitting to preserve the memory of things.

The Arabic ﺫﻛﺮ presents the same radical sense as the Hebrew, but with a certain difference in its developments. As verb, ﺫﻛﺮ signifies *to fix* in some place, on some thing; to stop there, to remember it, to make an act of commemoration; *to designate, to avow.*

קר From the idea of *character* and *writing* contained in this root, has come that of *reading*, and from *reading*, that of every *oratorical discourse* spoken aloud; thence the divers expressions of *crying out, exclaiming, speaking, proclaiming, reading, naming, designating* a thing *by name*, by expedient *sign; to convoke, evoke,* etc.

In making abstraction of the sign or character, and seeing only the cause which marks it, or the effect which follows it, one finds the idea of *course, contingency, concatenation;* thence, that of the *course of events, fate of occurrence;* action of *happening, occurring, hastening, arriving,* etc.

קוֹר, קוּר or קִיר. The idea of *incision* has brought forth that of *cutting in;* thence, the idea of *well, fountain, ditch, trap, snare, abyss;* that which is incisive, penetrating, firm, causes a sensation which recalls that of *cold*: thence with the idea of *coldness*, that which can shield, as a *walled enclosure, grotto, tower;* by extension, *a city.*

קש KSH. Every idea of perplexity, confusion, difficulty; that which is mixed, hardened, tightened, compact inextricable.

קש and קשש. (*intens.*) State of being *perplexed, confused, heavy, hardened;* action of *clearing up, seeking to know, scrutinizing, exploring,* etc.

The Arabic ﻗﺶ offers in general, the same ideas; it is, in a restricted sense, *to clean, rub, sweep,* etc.

The word קֶשֶׁת, *a bow*, is derived from the Arabic فاس which signifies a curvature; but the Arabic word itself is attached to the Hebraic root.

קָת KTH. Root not used in Hebrew. The Arabic قت or قث develops in general, every idea of attraction, extraction, agglomeration.

ר R. This character as consonant, belongs to the lingual sound. As symbolic image, it represents the head of man, his determining movement, his progress. According to Boehme the letter R draws its origin from the igneous faculty of nature. It is the emblem of fire. This man, who, without any learning, has often written in a manner astonishing to the wisest, assures in his book of the *Triple Life of Man*, that each inflection, vocal or consonantal, is a particular form of central nature. "Although speech varies them by transposition, nevertheless each letter has an origin at the centre of nature. This origin is wonderful and the senses can grasp it only by the light of the intelligence."

As grammatical sign, the character ר is, in the Hebraic tongue, the sign of all movement proper, good or bad. It is an original and frequentative sign, image of the renewal of things, as to their movement.

Its arithmetical number is 200.

רָא RA. The sign of movement proper united to that of power, forms a root characterized hieroglyphically by the geometric radius; that is to say, by that kind of straight line which departing from the centre converges at any point whatsoever of the circumference: it is, in a very restricted sense, *a streak*, in a broader sense, *a ray* and metaphorically, *the visual ray*, visibility.

The Arabic ڦ presents exactly the same radical sense as the Hebrew. The developments of this root, which are very numerous in the Arabic idiom, all have reference, in general, in راي, روي, ربي etc., to the action of *seeing*, or to the state of being seen.

ראה Action of *seeing, fixing* the eyes upon an object, *beholding, considering; sight, vision, aspect* of a thing.

ראי A *mirror*: figuratively, *an observation, examination*.

ראות (*comp.*) *Prophetic vision; spectacle; admirable thing.*

ראש (*comp.*) *The head.* See רש.

רב RB. The sign of movement proper, united to that of interior activity, or by contraction with the root אב, image of all fructification, constitutes a root whence are developed all ideas of multiplication, augmentation, growth, grandeur: it is a kind of movement toward propagation, physically as well as morally.

The Arabic رب does not differ from the Hebrew. It is, in general, that which dominates, augments, grows, usurps, possesses, gathers together, governs, etc.

רב and רבב. (*intens.*) That which is *large, broad, increased*, whether in number or in volume; *augmented, multiplied*; that which is expressed by the adverbial relations, *much, more, still more, many*; ideas of *multitude, number, quantity; strength* or *power* which is drawn from number, etc.

רוב (*comp.*) Action of being *carried in a mass*, of making an *uproar*, raising *a quarrel, a dispute*.

רג RG. Every kind of movement in the organs: *emotion, commotion, disorganization.*

The Arabic رج offers the same sense as the Hebrew. It is the action of *agitating, stirring; talking with familiarity*.

רד   RD. The sign of movement proper united to the sign of elementary abundance, or by contraction with the root אר, image of every emanation, produces a root whose object is to describe every kind of indefinite movement, as that of a wheel.

The Arabic رد holds to the Hebrew in its radical sense, although the accessory ideas which emanate differ somewhat. It is, in general, a repeated movement which turns to itself. In particular, it is the action of *returning, replying, restoring,* etc.

רד or רדד. (*intens.*) That which *spreads out, unfolds, occupies space, takes possession* of a thing, by effect of a movement which is propagated circularly: *a wheel, a sphere, a veil.*

רוד   Action of moving with firmness, either for *ascending,* or *descending;* action of *persevering* in one's will: *the domination* which is the natural bent of steadfastness and strength of soul.

רה   REH. Root analogous to the root רא whose effect it increases.

רהה   Action of *dazzling, fascinating* the eyes; of *troubling.*

The Arabic ره departs from the radical sense of the Hebrew, and develops only the accessory idea of weakness which follows physical or moral dizziness.

רהב   (*comp.*)   Every idea of magnitude, grandeur, force. See רב.

רהט   (*comp.*)   *A course.* See רט.

רו   ROU. Root analogous to the root רא, but which, taking a more material expression, instead of characterizing *a luminous ray,* characterizes often *a stream of water,* the channel of a river, a brook: thence,

רוה   Action of *watering, drinking, drenching,* etc. See רי.

RADICAL VOCABULARY 449

The Arabic روا characterizes literally the **action of** *considering* the consequences, *reflecting* before **doing a** thing. The compound روه expresses a long, **mature** deliberation.

רוּב (*comp.*) *Tumult.* See רב.
רוּד (*comp.*) *Strength of the soul.* See רד.
רוּח (*comp.*) *Movement of the air, the breath.* See רה.
רוּם (*comp.*) *Action of rising* in being dilated, of filling space. See רם.
רוּע (*comp.*) *Material movement, evil* and *disordered.* See רע.
רוּף (*comp.*) *Action of being shaken by a sudden movement.* See רף.
רוּץ (*comp.*) *Action of moving in skimming the ground, of running.* See רץ.
רוּשׁ (*comp.*) *Action of impoverishing, making poor,* being *needy,* of returning to the principle of nature. See רש.

רז RZ. Every idea of exhaustion, material annihilation, extreme thinness: that which becomes indiscernible.
ר In a figurative sense, *the secret* of the initiates.
The Arabic رز designates, in general, that which is secret, mysterious, concealed. It is an inner movement, a dull murmur.

רח RH. In the same manner as the roots רא and רה, considered as rays of the elementary circle, are related to light and fire; in the same manner, as the root רו is related to water, thus we see their analogue רח being related to air and depicting all its effects: we shall see further on רי and רע, related equally, the one to ether and the other to terrestrial matter.

The Arabic رخ holds to the same radical sense as the Hebrew, as can be seen in a great number of its derivatives: such as رايح , روح , which mean the same as the Hebraic analogues; but رح is still in the Arabic idiom, an onomatopoetic root which depicts the effort of wind upon a thing, and which characterizes, metaphorically, that which weakens, diminishes. خ, designates, *to flow in torrents, to fall in a mass*, in speaking of water.

רוּח Every idea of expansion and ærial dilation: *wind, breath, soul, spirit*: that which *moves, stirs, animates, inspires, transports*.

רִיח Every kind of *odour*. See רי.

רחב (*comp.*) Every kind of *distention, inflation*. See רב.

רחם (*comp.*) That which is *soft, faint, calm* as air; a long, drawn breath. Figuratively, *tenderness, compassion, mercy*.

רחף (*comp.*) That which is *moved, stirred* by an expansive, vital movement; to *brood over, to cherish*.

רחץ (*comp.*) Every kind of *ablution*.

רחק (*comp.*) That which *recedes, goes far away, vanishes* in air.

רחש (*comp.*) That which allows the air which it contains to escape by *boiling*, by *fermentation*.

רט RT. This root, in which the sign of movement proper is limited by that of resistance, characterizes a directed course; accompanied or turned by a dike, an embankment, etc. It is literally a *conduit, canal, promenade*.

The Arabic رط has not preserved the radical sense of the Hebrew; but in being attached to one of its developments, that of *a promenade*, this root has designated a confused crowd, a tumultuous movement. The Chaldaic

RADICAL VOCABULARY 451

רט has followed the same idea as the Arabic رط , and has rendered it even stronger in expressing a sort of shuddering, of terror.

רי RI. Root analogous to the roots רא, רה, רו, רח ; but more particularly applied to ethereal, fragrant radiations.

רי *Effluvium; a fluidic, ethereal, spirituous emanation; a fragrant exhalation.* In a restricted sense, *a stream*.

The Arabic ري signifies literally *the lung*.

ריב (*comp.*) *A sympathetic, electrifying commotion* given to a crowd: literally, *a tumult, an insurrection*.

ריח (*comp.*) *An aroma, a fragrant spirit, perfume*: figuratively, *fame*.

ריע (*comp.*) *The sound* of metals striking together.

ריק (*comp.*) Ethereal space, *the void*. See רק .

ריש (*comp.*) *Original manifestation*: in whatever manner conceived. In a mean and restricted sense, *poverty*.

רךְ RCH. Every idea of relaxation, indolence, dissolution, literally as well as figuratively.

רך That which is *thin, rare, soft, delicate, slender, frail, weak, infirm*.

The Arabic رك has in general, the same ideas as the Hebrew. By its analogue رق is understood *to make thin*.

רל RL. Root not used in Hebrew nor in Arabic.

רם RM. The sign of movement proper considered in its abstract mode, or in its different radical modifications, רא, רה, רו, רח, רי being here universalised by the collective sign ם , designates that sort of movement or action, by means of which any thing whatsoever, rising from the centre to one of the points of the circumference, traverses or fills an extent or place, which it has not occupied previously.

The Arabic رم has lost nearly all of the intellectual ideas developed by the Hebrew. This root reduced to the purely physical and material sense expresses in general, the action of *establishing, restoring, repairing,* etc.

רם or רמם (*intens.*) That which is *borne upward,* which *rises, dilates, mounts, projects, shoots up, increases rapidly,* follows a movement of *progression* and *ascension.*

רום Action of *rising* by expanding, of filling space; action of *being lifted up,* in speaking of anything whatever; state of *being in effervescence;* the superior part of a thing; *height, sublimity.*

רן RN. Every kind of noise, of sound which follows a commotion of the air. A chant, shout, clamour; the murmur of wind, water, fire; the clinking of metals, etc.

The Arabic رن has exactly the same sense. It is literally *to resound,* to make some sort of sound, *to groan,* etc.

רס RS. Every idea of break, fracture; reducing into *impalpable* parts, in drops, like *the dew;* that which is *submissive, reduced, subdued.*

This primitive root is recognized in the four Arabic roots, رس , رش , رص and رض where its divers acceptations are divided. By رس is understood in general, *to excavate the earth, to dig;* by رش, *to water, to sprinkle*: by رص *to stratify, to arrange in layers;* and by رض *to crack, to break.*

רע RH. We have seen the movement principle, acting from the centre to the circumference, modified in turn, by light, fire, water, air, ethereal fluid, according to the roots רי, רח, רו, רה, רא : now, here is this same movement departing from the root רו and degenerating more and more toward the material sense, to become in the root רע, the emblem of that which is terrestrial, obscure and evil. This is worthy of the closest attention.

רִיע and רָעַע (*intens.*) That which is *bent, bowed down;* that which is *brought together* to be *made compact;* that which becomes *fragile, brittle;* that which *breaks* and *is reduced* to *powder*: physical and moral *evil; misery, malignancy, misfortune, vice, perversity, disorder.*

The Arabic رع has preserved none of the intellectual ideas developed by the Hebrew. The only physical idea that this root appears to express in the Arabic idiom, is that of inertia. The derivative roots رعي , رعو , etc., have reference, as in Hebrew, to the care of flocks and pastures.

רוּעַ State of being *perverted, evil, mischievous;* action of following a *material, false, disordered* movement.

רעה That which concerns *earthly cares;* the *pains, anxieties, sorrows* and *afflictions* which they involve: human society in general, and that of shepherds in particular: *a shepherd, a leader* of flocks; *a king.* The one who shares the same cares, *a neighbour, relative, comrade.*

רעו Every *disorder, rupture, infraction.*

רעי *Pasture, property, possession*: that which concerns the state of *shepherd, leader, king: pastoral.*

רעב (*comp.*) Hunger; state of *being famished.*

רעד (*comp.*) *Fear;* state of *being frightened.*

רעל (*comp.*) *Horror, venom;* state of *being filled with horror, infected with venom.*

רעם (*comp.*) A disordered, universalized movement: *thunder, lightning.*

רעץ Action of *breaking, smashing, acting with fury.*

רעש (*comp.*) Action of *shuddering, trembling, shivering.*

רה RPH. Every kind of mediation, reparation, recovery, redemption. It is the idea of a regenerating movement.

The Arabic رف holds to the same radical sense, but its developments are perceptibly altered. As verb, it is the action of *being refreshed*, of *eating abundantly*. رف is also an onomatopoetic root, which depicts the noise of a bird which beats its wings.

רף   Medicine, remedy; health, the action of healing.

רוּף   The sign of movement proper, united by contraction to the root עוּף, forms an onomatopœia which is applied to every rapid movement which *dislocates, disunites, relaxes beyond measure*: etc. See רע.

רץ   RTZ. This root characterizes a sort of movement of vibration, recommencing and finishing; reptilian, which propagates in being divided: it is a dragging, painful movement.

רץ and רצץ (*intens.*) That which *is shaken into fragments*, that which *is broken, divided; a rupture, a piece*.

The Arabic رص signifies literally *to stratify*, to arrange in layers or in strata; by رض is understood *to crush, to break* in great pieces.

רוּץ   From the idea of a divided piece, springs that of *alliance*, of *friendship*; from that of intermittent movement, springs the idea of *concurrence*: thence the action of *being allied*, of *concurring*.

רק   RK. Every idea of tenuity, rarity, expansion, giving way.

The Arabic رق has the same sense as the Hebrew.

רק   That which *is attenuated, rarified;* which *gives way*, physically as well as morally: in a figurative sense, *time*. See ריק.

רר   RR. Root not used in Hebrew nor in Arabic.

RADICAL VOCABULARY

רֶשׁ RSH. The sign of movement proper, united to that of relative movement, constitutes a root which is hieroglyphically symbolized by a point at the middle of a circle: it is the centre unfolding the circumference: the fundamental principle.

רֶאֶשׁ *Every acting principle,* good or bad; *a venomous poison,* a very bitter, *gall;* that which is primary, initial; the origin, summit, top; *the culminating point* of all things; *the head* of man or of anything whatsoever; *the leader* of a people, a captain, a prince, a king. See רוּשׁ and רִישׁ.

The Arabic رش holds evidently to the radical sense of the Hebrew רֶשׁ, and the compound راس has the same acceptation as רֶאֶשׁ. In the modern idiom, رش signifies *to sprinkle.*

רֶת RTH. Every movement arrested, chained, retained.

The Arabic رث, offers the same meaning. It is literally, the action of *retarding.*

רֵת That which *chains, coagulates, arrests;* that which *freezes* the blood: *a sudden terror, a dread.*

שׁ SH. This character as consonant belongs to the sibilant sound, and depicts in an onomatopoetic manner, light movements, sounds durable and soft. As symbolic image it represents the part of the bow from which the arrow is shot. In Hebrew, it is the sign of relative duration and of the movement attached thereunto. It is derived from the vocal sound י, become consonant by joining to its expression the respective significations of the consonants ז and ס. As prepositive relation, it constitutes a sort of pronominal article and is placed at the head of nouns and verbs, to communicate to them the double power that it possesses of movement and of conjunction.

Its arithmetical number is 300.

שׁא SHA. The sign of relative movement united to that of power, constitutes a root which is hieroglyphically characterized by the arc of the circle inscribed between two radii. The character ס is designated by the arc deprived of its radius or arrow, and closed by its cord. The character ז is designated by the radius or arrow indicating the circumference. The portion of the circle represented by the root שׁא, can be considered in movement or in repose; thence, the opposed ideas of tumult and of the calm which it develops.

The Arabic شا signifies literally *to desire*. As onomatopoetic root شا denotes the sound of calling the flocks to the watering place.

שׁאה *A whirlpool, a delirium;* action of making *irruption, tumult, fracas: profound tranquility;* state of being *empty, deserted, void; a gulf,* etc.

שׁוא That which is *vain, empty; ruined, devasted;* that which is *tumultuous, tempestuous, whirling; vanity, insolence.*

שׁאב (comp.) Action of *drawing water.* See אב.

שׁאל (comp.) Action of *interrogating, asking.* See של.

שׁאם (comp.) Action of *troubling, putting in disorder.*

שׁאן (comp.) State of *being calm.*

שׁאף (comp.) *To aspire,* figuratively as well as literally. See אף.

שׁאר (comp.) That which *tends* toward *consistency, solidity;* that which *remains; residue; remnant*: in a restricted sense, *the flesh.* See אר.

שׁב SHB. This root has two expressions according to its composition; if it is considered as composed of

RADICAL VOCABULARY 457

the **sign** of relative movement and of duration, joined to that of interior activity, it contains every idea of return toward a point of departure; if it is regarded as formed by the same sign united to that of the root אב, image of paternity, it designates the capture of a whole tribe, its captivity, its deportation outside its country: thence,

שב The idea of any kind of *reëstablishment*, of *return* to an original state, to a place from which one had set out; *a restitution, a reformation*: thence,

שב Every state of *captivity*, of *separation* from one's country: *a deportation; a capture.*

The Arabic شب characterizes in general, that which tends from the centre to the circumference, increases, grows, unfolds itself, returns to its original state after having been restrained; develops its strength, etc. The primitive sense of the Hebraic root is recognized in the Arabic root although its developments may not be the same.

שוב Action of *coming back*, of *returning* to its first state; of *remaking* what has been already made. Metaphorically, the action of growing old; that which is on the wane; *an old man*.

שג SHG. The sign of relative movement united to the organic sign, indicates a movement of the organ deprived of intelligence, a covetous movement; the same sign joined by contraction to the root אג, symbol of organic development, characterizes every kind of increase. Thence,

שג *Blind desire, thoughtless inclination;* figuratively, *error, degeneration;* action of growing, *augmenting* in number, volume, duration.

The Arabic شج preserves but little of the radical sense. It is, as onomatopoetic root the action of *splitting* a hard thing, of making upon it an incision, a scar; *scratching, furrowing*, etc.

שׁד SHD. This root, composed of the sign of relative movement united to that of divisional abundance or by contraction with the root אד, image of every emanation, characterizes productive nature in general, whose particular symbols are, a mammal and a field. Thence, the name of שׁדי, given to GOD, as principle of all good; *Providence.*

The Arabic شد characterizes that which acts with force, with energy, in good or in evil; that which overthrows the obstacles opposed to it; that which shows itself strong and powerful.

שׁד The effusion of the virtual faculties, *Nature*: the sign of abundance and fecundity; *a mammal, a field.* All physical property, *fortune, the genius* of the earth. *A song* of jubilee.

שׁדד (*intens.*) Action of returning to primal, brutish nature; that is to say, of *devastating, ravaging* the production of art, labour and industry.

שׁוד Every kind of *devastation*, or *profanation; pillaging* the fruits of nature.

שׁה SHEH. Root analogous to the root שׂא.

The Arabic شها characterizes every tendency, every persevering movement toward an object: action of *coveting, wishing, desiring,* etc.

שׁו SHOU. Root analogous to the root שׂא, but conceived principally under its relation of equilibrium, equality, parallel, similitude, fitness, proportion and measure of things.

The Ethiopic ሶ (*shony*) signifies literally *a man.* The Arabic شو characterizes the state of being struck with admiration.

שׁוה State of *being in equilibrium* in all parts, as every portion of the circle; state of being *equal, conformable, fitting, just, qualified* for something; etc.

RADICAL VOCABULARY

שׁוה (*comp.*) That which is *inclined*, which *leans* toward any object.

שׁוט (*comp.*) Action of *following* something in its *contours*, of *bending*, of *doing the same.* See שׁט.

שׁוך (*comp.*) Action of *interring* completely, *covering* wholly, *burying.*

שׁום (*comp.*) Action of *placing*, of *arranging* one upon the other, in layers, as *an onion.*

שׁוע (*comp.*) *Clamour, outcry;* action of *calling aloud.* See שׁע.

שׁוף (*comp.*) Action of *pressing* hard, *suffocating.*

שׁוק (*comp.*) Every *amorous desire;* every *inclination.*

שׁור (*comp.*) Action of *being directed* according to fixed laws, *resting in equilibrium, in harmony; modulating* the voice, *singing,* etc. *Music,* in the very broad sense that the ancients gave to this word. See שׁר.

שׁושׁ (*comp.*) State of being in *good humour,* in *harmony* with one's self.

שׁות (*comp.*) Action of *placing* something. See שׁת.

שׁז SHZ. Root not used in Hebrew. The Arabic شز indicates a dry, arid place.

שׁח SHEH. Every kind of bodily effort to follow any direction; every effort of the mind to accomplish a duty, to acquire a virtue.

The Arabic شح holds evidently to the primitive sense of the Hebrew, but developing it from the purely material side; so that the effort indicated by the root שׁח, being turned toward egoism, characterizes only tenacity, avarice; desire to draw to one's self, monopolizing, etc. As onomatopoetic root شح depicts the noise made by any kind of fluid falling down from above.

שׁחח Action of *being inclined, following an inclination, bending* to a law; in a restricted sense, the action of *swimming;* of following the course of the water. See שׁוה

שִׁיה (comp.) A conception, an impulse, a flight.
שִׁיחם (comp.) Vegetation.

שָׁט SHT. Every idea of inflection, inclination or similar movement. See שׁוט.

The Arabic ࣷط characterizes that which goes beyond, leaves the centre, is drawn away, is remote from its own place.

שִׁי SHI. Root analogous to the root שׁ whose power it manifests. In its literal sense, it is justice rendered, honour accorded for merit, etc.

The Arabic شي characterizes *any thing* in general, whatever it may be; a real and evident existence; that which is obvious to the senses.

שָׁךְ SHCH. The sign of relative movement, united to that of assimilated existence, or by contraction with the root אך , image of every restriction, constitutes a root whence are developed all ideas of return to itself, of envelopment, exterior repose, consciousness.

The Arabic شك develops the idea of hesitation, of conscientious doubt. As onomatopoetic root شك signifies literally to *prick* with a goad.

שָׁךְ In a literal and restricted sense it is *an onion*: in a figurative sense it is *contemplation, profound meditation, speculation, physical sleep; shrouding*, literally, as well as figuratively. See שׁוךְ.

שָׁל SHL. Hieroglyphically, it is a line traced from one object to another, the stroke which unites them; it is expressed by the prepositive relations *from, at*.

שָׁל That which follows its laws; that which remains in its straight line; that which is *tranquil, happy, in good order, in the way of salvation*.

RADICAL VOCABULARY 461

The Arabic شل has not preserved the ideas of order developed by the Hebraic root except in the compound شله *moral force*, and in the analogue سلم, action of *saluting*, giving evidence of respect; but this root becomes confused with the following intensive.

שלל (*intens.*) That which goes out from its line *beyond* anything whatsoever; which falls into *error;* that which is *extravagant, fanatical, insensate;* that which ignores law and justice.

The Arabic شل or لل has the same sense in general. It is, literally, the state of being crippled, crooked, maimed, impotent, etc.

שם SHM. Hieroglyphically, it is the circumferential extent, the entire sphere of any being whatever, the total space that it occupies; it is expressed by the adverbial relations *there, in that very place, within, inside there.*

שם *The name* of every being, *the sign* which renders it knowable; that which constitutes it *such: a place, a time, the universe, the heavens,* GOD Himself: *glory, éclat, splendour, fame, virtue;* that which *rises* and *shines* in space; which is *distinguished, sublime, remarkable.*

The Arabic شم has not preserved the same intellectual ideas developed by the Hebraic root, except in certain compounds and in the analogue سم. Its most common acceptations are confused with that of the following intensive root.

שמם (*intens.*) That which leaves its sphere, gives way to *pride;* enters into *madness. The inordinate idea of making one's-self remarked, ambition*: that which *troubles, upsets* the mind: *ravages, lays waste* the land.

The Arabic شم offers in general, the same sense as the Hebrew. In a very restricted sense, the verb شم signifies *to smell*.

שְׁן   SHN. All ideas of mutation, iteration, passing from one state to another; that which leads to diversity, variation, change.

The Arabic شن agrees with the Hebraic root only in certain compounds, and in the analogue سن. As verb, شن indicates the action of *triturating, crushing, making noise*.

שֵׁן   The number *two*. Literally, that which *cuts* and *divides* as the teeth; figuratively, *hatred*. That which *varies, changes;* that which *measures* and *divides* time; a *cyclic revolution, an ontological mutation;* in a very restricted sense, *a year*.

שֻׁע   SHUH. Every idea of conservation, restoration, cementation.

שַׁע   In a literal sense, *lime, cement;* in a figurative sense, that which *consolidates, guarantees;* which serves as *safe-guard;* which *preserves*.

The Arabic شع has not preserved the radical sense except in certain compounds and in its analogue سم. By شع is understood *to radiate*, to spread here and there, *to disperse*. According to this acceptation, شغ is attached to the following onomatopoetic root.

שַׁע   Onomatopoetic root which depicts the cry of a person who calls loudly. See שׁוע.

שָׁעט   (comp.) An acclamation.
שָׁעל   (comp.) The closed hand.
שָׁען   (comp.) That which serves as *support;* action of *supporting, propping up.*
שָׁעע   (intens.) That which is *partial to, choses, conserves* carefully.
שָׁער   (comp.) A shudder of horror; or an opening, a door: according to the sense under which one considers the root שׁור.

RADICAL VOCABULARY 463

שׁף SHPH. Every apparent, eminent, distinguished, prominent object: that which extends beyond, as *a hill;* appears on top, as *cream,* etc.

The Arabic شف designates in general that which becomes limpid, clear, transparent.

שׁף Onomatopoetic root, expressing the noise made in trampling with the feet. See שׁוף.

שׁץ SHTZ. That which leads to a goal, to perfection, achievement, end.

The Arabic شص designates in general that which serves as means for catching fish, *a fish-hook, net,* etc.

שׁק SHCQ. All ideas of tendency, of sympathetic inclination to possess: that which seeks and joins; that which acts through sympathy, envelops, embraces, absorbs.

שׁק and שׁקק (*intens.*) That which *is united,* which *attracts* reciprocally: action of *soaking up, pumping water, sucking up.* See שׁוק.

The Arabic شق has not preserved the radical sense of the Hebrew. It is an onomatopoetic root, which in the Arabic idiom signifies literally *to cleave, to split.*

שׁר SHR. This root admits of several significations, according to its composition. If it is the sign of relative movement which is united simply to that of movement proper, there results from this abstract mingling of the circular line with the straight line, an idea of solution, opening, liberation; as if a closed circle were opened; as if a chain were slackened: if one considers this same sign of relative movement, being united by contraction to the elementary root אר, then it partakes of the diverse expressions of this root and develops ideas of strength, vigour, domination, power, which result from the elementary principle; if finally, one sees in the root אש the root

שׂוּ, symbol of all harmonious proportion, joined to the sign of movement proper, one discovers here the expression of that which is directed according to just and upright laws; thence, according to the first signification:

שׂר That which *liberates, opens, brings out, emits, produces;* as *the navel, a field,* etc.; according to the second:

שׂרר (*intens.*) That which is *solid, firm, resisting,* as *a wall, breast-plate, chain;* that which is *strong, vigorous,* as *a bull;* that which is *dominating, powerful,* as *a king, a prince;* that which is *formidable,* as *a rival, an enemy,* etc.; according to the third:

שׂוּ, שׂרר or שׂיר That which is *measured, co-ordinate, just,* conformable with universal harmony, restricted to regulations, as *a musical song, a melody, a law, a poem, a system of government,* etc.

The Hebraic genius merging these three expressions in one, draws from it the most complicated and most abstract sense that any tongue can offer: that of a government, liberal, ready, indulgent, productive within; powerful, strong, redoubtable, dominating without, which extends its empire by directing it according to just, luminous laws modelled upon the immutable laws of order and universal harmony.

The Arabic شر does not agree with the Hebrew in the radical sense, except in certain of its compounds and in its analogues سر and سار . This root, in the Arabic idiom has become intensive, and has developed ideas wholly contrary, as has been seen often in the course of this vocabulary. Thus, instead of order and justice expressed by שׂר, the intensive verb שׂרר or شرر, characterizes the action of that which is inordinate, unjust, wicked, perfidious, contrary to harmony and public welfare.

שׁשׁ SHSH. All ideas of proportion, measure and harmony.

שׁשׁ The number *six*. That which is in harmonious relations, as the *colour white;* in consequence, *the albatross, the lily, linen, old age*: that which enjoys calm and happiness. See שׁוּשׁ.

The Arabic شش develops ideas entirely opposed to the Hebraic root, on account of the intensive form which herein dominates. The verb شوش designates in general, that which troubles, mixes, deranges, etc.

שׁתה SHTH. This root, composed of the signs of relative and reciprocal movement, indicates the place toward which things irresistibly incline, and the things themselves which incline toward this place: thence,

שׁת *The depths, the foundations,* literally as well as figuratively; *the place* where the sea is gathered; *the sea* itself; every kind of *depth;* every kind of *beverage.*

The Arabic شث has retained only a portion of the radical sense, in that which concerns the movement of water, the separation of this fluid into drops, its distillation, dispersion. The other portion of the primitive sense is found in the analogue مث which designates in general, the bottom or the foundation of things, the seat and particularly *the buttocks.*

שׁות Action of putting *at the bottom, founding, seating, placing, disposing,* etc.

ת TH. This character as consonant, belongs to the sibilant sound. The ancient Egyptians in consecrating it to Thoth, whose name they gave it, regarded it as the symbol of the universal mind. As grammatical sign in the Hebraic tongue, it is that of sympathy and reciprocity; joining, to the abundance of the character ר, to the force of resistance and protection of the character ט, the idea of perfection and necessity of which it is the emblem. Although it does not hold a particular rank among the articles, it appears nevertheless too often at the head of words, for one not to suspect that it was used as such in one of the Egyptian dialects, where without doubt it represented the relation את ; in the same manner that the character פ represented the relation פא, פה or פי.

Its arithmetical number is 400.

תא THA. Every idea of determination, designation, definition.

תאה That which *limits, determines, defines, circumscribes*. It is, in a restricted sense, *the nuptial chamber*.

The Arabic ﺗﺎ expresses a mutual desire.

תאב (*comp.*) *A mutual desire.*

תאם (*comp.*) *To be double, twain.*

תאן (*comp.*) *An occasion, occurrence; a reciprocal sorrow; a fig-tree.* See א.

תאר (*comp.*) *A description, an information, a plan.*

תב THB. Every kind of sympathetic union by affinity; a globe, a sphere; the vessel of the universe, the world, the earth; etc.

The Arabic ﺗﺐ is an onomatopoetic root which characterizes the movement of disgust with which one repels a thing: *for shame!* The verb ﺗﺎﺏ expresses the action of repenting for a sin.

תוב Action of *turning, returning* upon one's step, following a circular movement.

The Arabic ﺗﺎﺏ signifies literally *to improve*, to return from wandering.

תג THG. Root not used in Hebrew. The Arabic ﺗﺞ indicates a mutation, a fleeting action; *the course* of something. By ﺗﺎﺝ is understood, *a mitre, a tiara*.

RADICAL VOCABULARY 467

תד THD. Root not used in Hebrew. The Chaldaic as well as the Syriac ܬܕܐ indicate equally *the breast*.

The Arabic تدا or تدى signifies *to moisten, to wet, to sprinkle*.

תה THEH. Root analogus to the root תא; but whose expression, more moral, characterizes the influential and sympathetic reason of things.

The Arabic تها signifies literally *to be led astray, lost in empty space*. By the compound تاها , *a vain thing;* by the verb تهأ a thing which is liquified.

תהוֹם (comp.) *The depths of universal existence.* See תו.

תו THOU. Root analogous to the roots תא and תה, but of an effect more physical.

תו Every idea of *sign, symbol,* hieroglyphic, emblematic *character: fable, recitation, description, book, monument,* etc.

The Arabic تو characterizes a simple thing, not compound, not complex, such as a blade of grass, a word of one single letter. It is also, in a restricted sense, *an hour,* an extent of time considered in a simple manner.

תוה Action of *designing, signifying, characterizing, describing,* etc.

תוךְ (comp.) *The middle, the between* of things, the point of contact. See תך.

תוּר (comp.) *A circular sympathetic movement; a row, order, turn.* See תר.

תז THZ. Every general idea of vibration and reaction. In a restricted sense it is the action of cutting with the sword.

תָה THEH. Root not used in Hebrew. The Arabic indicates an emotion which pertains to the weakness of the organs. In adding the guttural inflection, this root characterizes in تَهَ, the action of *slackening*.

תחת (*comp.*) That state of *submission* and of *dependence* expressed by the relations, *under*, *below*, *beneath*: that which is *inferior*. See תה.

תט THT. Root not used in Hebrew. The Arabic تط expresses a state of infancy, weakness; imbecility.

תִי THI. Root analogous to the root תה.
תים (*comp.*) *Mid-day*.
תיש (*comp.*) *A he-goat*. See תש.

תך THCH. This root characterizes the sympathetic point in which things are formed as to their parts, or united one to the other; the point of contact at which they touch; the central point toward which they gravitate. Thence,

תך or תכך (*intens.*) Every idea of *intermediary link*, *space between; the delicate point* of a thing, of a question; *the dexterity* with which it is seized; *the finesse* with which it is used: that which *tends* to the same point; that which *oppresses; a calamity;* etc. See תון.

The Arabic تك has preserved of the radical sense of the Hebrew, only the sole development which is connected with oppression, either physical or moral; as that of a man oppressed by drunkenness or by an attack of folly. The intensive verb تَكَّكَ or تَكَّكَ signifies again to *trample under foot*, to cover with waves, *to overflow*.

תל THL. Every idea of piling, massing, accumulation; that which is heaped up; that which is placed one upon another.

The Arabic ڎل holds to the radical sense of the Hebrew, in the greater part of its developments. In a restricted sense, the Arabic root signifies, nevertheless, *to raise;* by ڎل is understood *to draw out* the earth in digging a well.

תל and תלל (*intens.*) *A heap, a mound;* a thing suspended, as a quiver, a trophy of arms, etc.

תם THM. This root, in which the sign of signs, symbol of all perfection, is found universalized by the collective sign ם, develops the idea of that which is universally true, universally approved; accomplished image of the universal mind: thence,

תם *Perfection, integrity,* either physically or morally: *truth, justice, sanctity,* all the *virtues.*

The Arabic تم partakes of nearly all the developments of the Hebraic root. In a restricted sense, it is, as verb, the action of *achieving, accomplishing, perfecting, finishing.* As adverbial relation, تم is represented by *there, yonder.*

תמם (*intens.*) Every exaggerated, degenerated virtue become *an error, an imperfection, a ruin.*

תן THN. Every idea of substance added, of corporeity increasing more and more; an extension, an enlargement, a largess; in a restricted sense, *a gift.*

The Arabic ثن signifies literally, *to put into two,* to carry number one to number two; *to compare together: to augment.* By ثن, is understood dry grass, *hay.* As onomatopoetic root, ثن depicts the noise of metals, the *tinkling* of sonorous chords.

תן Action of *giving; an offering, a present*: that which is *liberal, generous.*

תנן (*intens.*) Action of *growing, extending* beyond measure: *a monster, a dragon, a crocodile;* in general, the cetacean species.

תם THS. Root not used in Hebrew. The Chaldaic designates *a boiling, a fervour.* The Arabic نَسَم designates *race, lineage.*

תע THUH. That which is *false, illusory, vain;* that which has only appearance, semblance.

תעה State of being *abused, seduced, deceived* by specious exterior; *hypocrisy, fraud.*

The Arabic تَع holds to the Hebraic root only on the physical side, and indicates the state of that which is enervated, without vigour. As onomatopoetic root تَع depicts stammering, hesitation in speaking.

תוע Action of *mocking, laughing.*

תף THPH. Onomatopoetic root expressing the noise of a drum. Thence by analogy, the Arabic تَف *to spit;* metaphorically, every object which is disgusting and repulsive to the sight. In the Arabic idiom, دَف signifies *a tambourine.*

תוף The Chaldaic word signifies the action of *anathematizing, cursing.* The Arabic تَاف indicates the state of being *culpable, disordered by crime, debased by vice.*

תק THCQ. Root not used in Hebrew. The Chaldaic expresses moral doubt, or physical effort. The Arabic تَق is an onomatopoetic root which is represented by *look out!* The verb تَاق signifies *to desire.*

תר THR. Every idea of determination given to an element: in a very broad sense, *modality.*

תֹר In a restricted sense, every kind of *fusion, infusion, distillation.*

The Arabic ﺯ or ﺫ holds to the Hebraic root only on the most restricted and most physical side. It is literally, that which has juice, that which gives liquid, that which distils.

תור Action of *modifying, changing; turning* from one manner to another; action of *converting, translating, distilling;* action of *surrounding, turning about in a circle,* etc. See תור.

תש THSH. Sympathetic ardour of nature, the generative fire.

תוש or תיש Symbol of animal fecundity, *a goat.*

The Arabic تش signifies literally *a wine-skin,* on account of the skin of the goat of which it is made; metaphorically, the air contained in the skin and which escapes by pressing. The compound word تشوش expresses a sort of transmutation, of passing from one state to another.

תת THTH. Root not used in Hebrew. The Arabic ت indicates a cleft, a furrow; a solution of continuity.

END OF PART FIRST.

The Hebraic Tongue Restored

Part Second.

CONTENTS

OF PART SECOND

		PAGE
Preliminary Discourse		5
Cosmogony of Moses		23
Original Text: Literal Version: Notes		23
Sepher Beræshith א	Cosmogony I	24
ב	II	64
ג	III	94
ד	IV	122
ה	V	150
ו	VI	174
ז	VII	200
ח	VIII	222
ט	IX	246
י	X	272

CONTENTS

	PAGE
Correct Translation	307
Ch. I Principiation	309
Ch. II Distinction	313
Ch. III Extraction	317
Ch. IV Divisional Multiplication	321
Ch. V Facultative Comprehension	325
Ch. VI Proportional Measurement	329
Ch. VII Consummation	332
Ch. VIII Accumulation	335
Ch. IX Restoration Consolidated	338
Ch. X Aggregative and Formative Energy	342

PRELIMINARY DISCOURSE

If, instead of Hebrew, I had chosen **Chinese or Sanskrit** as the basis of my labour, having reached this point of my work I might have mastered the greatest difficulties; for, after having developed the principles of these tongues by explaining their constitutive elements and their radical forms, there would only remain for me to show the attentive and unprejudiced reader, the excellence of these same principles in applying them to the translation of certain chapters from the Kings or the Vedas. But the choice that I have made of Hebrew places me in quite a contrary position. The difficulties increase even where they should be lessened; what might have been a sort of complement, an easy result, becomes the principal object, awakens, fixes the attention, arouses and excites the reader; whereas he would have remained calm, and might have followed me with an interest which, being keen, would have been impartial. This is the effect of the translation which I have felt impelled to make of the Sepher of Moses. I have realized it and have foreseen all the consequences. I was even inclined to make this translation the principal title of my work, naming it simply *The Cosmogony of Moses;* but then I would have placed the Hebraic tongue in the background and my first plan was that it should occupy the foreground; since it was while seeking the origin of speech that I encountered this tongue and considered it particularly as one of those whose grammatical principles could more safely lead to this unknown origin and unveil its mysteries.

I shall not repeat what I have said in my Dissertation concerning this tongue itself, its culture, its perfection among the ancient Egyptians, and its transplantation,—effect of the providential emigration of the Hebrews; neither shall I speak of the rapid degeneration of its expressions, which from metaphorical, intelligible, and universal had become literal, sentient and particular; neither of its utter loss, nor of the insurmountable obstacles which the temporal state of things brought about in its reëstablishment: I have taken care to prove these diverse assertions as much as the obscurity of the centuries and the lack of monuments have permitted: I have established my Grammar upon principles whose simplicity exemplifies its veracity and strength. Now it is only a question of applying these principles. The Sepher is presented. But what a host of phantoms move by its side!

Child of the past and teeming with the future, this book, inheritor of all the sciences of the Egyptians bears still the germs of future sciences. Fruit of divine inspiration it contains in few pages the elements of that which was, and the elements of that which shall be. All the secrets of Nature are entrusted to it. All. It assembles in the Beræshith alone, more things than all the accumulated books in European libraries. Whatever is most profound, most mysterious in Nature, whatever wonders can be conceived in the mind; whatever is most sublime in the understanding, this book possesses it.

The Sepher is the basis of the Christian and Mussulman religions, as well as that of the Judaic, which claims justly the name of their common mother; but this basis is equally unknown to all three, as far as the vulgar teaching is concerned; for I know that among the Israelites there exist certain successors of the Essenes who possess the oral traditions, and among the Christians and Mussulmans certain men more advanced than others in the interpretation of the Sacred Books. The versions which these three religions possess are all made in the spirit of that of the Hellenists which has been their model: that is to say, that they deal with the exterior forms of the work of Moses, with the grossest and most material sense only, the one which this theocrat had destined as a veil for the spiritual sense, the knowledge of which he reserved for the initiates. Now to what point ought one to reveal this basis upon

PRELIMINARY DISCOURSE 7

which repose the three dominating cults of the earth? To what point ought one to lighten the mysterious darkness by which it has with purpose been surrounded?

These are the stumbling blocks that I have long since foreseen and whose principle I have already attacked in my Dissertation; for if it is true, as everything convinces me, that Providence, opening the portals of a New Day, is pushing minds on toward the perfecting of knowledge, is recalling Truth designedly eclipsed, and is hastening the downfall of prejudices which had served it in less happy times; what are these stumbling blocks whose aspect terrifies? Vain phantoms that the breath of Truth ought to dissipate and will dissipate.

Europe, after long darkness and keen agitations, enlightened by the successive efforts of the sages of all nations, and taught by her misfortunes and her own experiences, seems at last to have arrived at the moment of enjoying in peace the fruit of her labours. Escaped from the moral winter whose thick mists had long obscured her horizon she has for several centuries experienced the productive warmth of spring. Already the flowers of thought from all parts have embellished the reigns of Alphonso, of the Medicis and of Louis XIV*. Her spiritual summer draws nigh and the fruit is about to succeed the flowers. Minds more advanced demand more solid food.

The ancient religions and particularly that of the Egyptians, were full of mysteries, and composed of numberless pictures and symbols, sacred work of an uninterrupted chain of divine men, who, reading in the book of Nature and in that of the Divinity, translated into human

* I call the age of Alphonso, that in which the Oscan troubadours appeared. Alphonso X, king of Leon and Castile, through his love for the sciences merits the honour of giving his name to the age which saw them renascent in Europe. In my younger days I consecrated to the memory of the Oscan troubadours, a work in which I tried to do for them what Macpherson had already done for the bards of the North. I was at that time quite far from the ideas which occupy me now.

language, the ineffable language. Those whose dull glance, falling upon these pictures, these symbols, these holy allegories, saw nothing beyond, were sunk, it is true, in ignorance; but their ignorance was voluntary. From the moment that they wished to leave it, they had only to speak. All the sanctuaries were opened to them, and if they had the necessary constancy and virtue, nothing hindered them from passing from knowledge to knowledge, from revelation to revelation to the sublimest discoveries. They might, living and human, according to the force of their will, descend among the dead, rise to the gods and penetrate everything in elementary nature. For religion embraced all these things, and nothing of that which composed religion remained unknown to the sovereign pontiff. The one, for example, at the famous Egyptian Thebes, reached this culminating point of the sacred doctrine only after having passed through all the inferior grades, having exhausted in succession the portion of science allotted to each grade, and having proved himself worthy of attaining to the highest.

The king of Egypt alone was initiated by right, and by the inevitable course of his education, admitted to the most secret mysteries. The priests had the instruction of their order, their knowledge increased as they rose in rank and all knew that their superiors were not only much higher but much more enlightened. So that the sacerdotal hierarchy like a pyramid seated upon its base, offered always in its theocratic organization, knowledge allied with power. As to the people, they were, according to their inclination whatever they wished to be. Knowledge offered to all Egyptians was forced upon none. The dogmas of morality, the laws of politics, the restraint of opinion, the yoke of civil institutions were the same for all; but the religious instruction differed according to the capacity, virtue and will of each individual. They were not prodigal with the mysteries, and did not profane the knowledge of the Divinity; in order to preserve the Truth, it was not given indiscriminately.

This was the condition of things in Egypt, when Moses, obedient to a special impulse from Providence followed the path of sacerdotal initiation, and with such constancy as perhaps only Pythagoras later displayed, passed through all tests, surmounted all obstacles and braving the death threatening each step, attained at Thebes the highest degree of divine knowledge. This knowledge which he modified by a particular inspiration, he enclosed entire in the Beræshith, that is to say, in the first book of his Sepher, reserving as its safe-guard the four books which follow, and which give to the people who should be its trustee, ideas, institutions and laws which would distinguish them essentially from all other peoples, marking them with an indelible character.

I have already related the various revolutions undergone by the Sepher, in order to show that the condition of things in Europe and in all parts of the earth, wherever the Judaic cult and its two derivatives—the Christian and Islamic, have extended, is precisely the inverse of what it was in Egypt at the epoch when the germ of this cult was detached from it and entrusted to the Hebrew people. The *Beræshith* which contains all the secrets of elementary and divine Nature, offered to peoples, to the heads of peoples, to the priests themselves, under its most material covering, commands their faith in this state, and presents as basis of their religion a sequence of pictures and symbols that human reason, at the point which it has attained can only grasp with great difficulty.

It cannot be said, as in Egypt, that the understanding of these pictures or the revelation of the symbols may be given to whomsoever desires it. Not at all. The Judaic priesthood, destined to guard the Sepher of Moses, has not been generally destined to comprehend it and still less to explain it. Possessor of the profoundest mysteries, this priesthood is to these mysteries as the Egyptian people were to theirs: with this difference, that the position of this priesthood does not allow it to penetrate these mysteries; for in order to do this it would have to recognize superiors and address itself to the Essenes whose doctrine it condemns and whose traditions it does not admit as authentic. Moreover these Essenes, isolated, unknown and often persecuted, no longer offer today a sufficient guarantee. Thus this priesthood, whose devotion to the exterior forms of the Sepher, is in keeping with its fidelity to the purpose of its institution, is further from divine knowledge in the highest of its priests than in its humblest; for its purpose, as I have said, being to preserve and not to comprehend, it had to be limited to transmitting intact the sacred storehouse which had been confided to its keeping, and this obligation it has fulfilled with a force, constancy and rectitude beyond all eulogy.

Has the Christian priesthood in receiving this storehouse from the hands of the Judaic priesthood, contracted the same obligations? That is to say, is it bound to transmit it faithfully from generation to generation without ever being permitted to open it? It is not my purpose to determine this question. But in the state of civilization and enlightenment which Europe has attained since the invention of printing, the Sepher of Moses has not remained a book entirely theological. Spread broadcast in all classes of society, thanks to this admirable invention, it has been examined by all sorts of persons and subjected to the rigorous analysis of savants. All sects have taken possession of it and vying with one another, have sought reasons for defending their belief. The numberless disputes brought forth by the various interpretations of which the text has been believed susceptible, has made this text more and more popular; so that one may say with reason that this book has also become a classic. It is under this last relation that the lay writers consider it in Europe today, and that I myself consider it*.

---

* The study of the Sepher of Moses, very widespread in Germany and in England, and the examination of the divers parts of which it is composed, has brought forth in these countries a new science known by the modern savants under the name of *Exegesis*.

I have therefore translated the *Cosmogony of Moses* as *littérateur,* after having restored, as grammarian, the tongue in which this Cosmogony was written in its original text.

Therefore it is not for the theologian that I have written, but for the *littérateur,* for the people of the world, for the savants, for all persons desirous of knowing the ancient mysteries and of seeing to what point, the peoples who have preceded us in the course of life, had penetrated into the sanctuary of nature and into that of knowledge; for I believe I have expressed quite strongly, my opinion concerning the origin of the Sepher: this book is, according to the proofs which I have given in my Introductory Dissertation, one of the genetical books of the Egyptians, issued, as far as its first part called *Berœshith* is concerned, from the depths of the temples of Memphis or of Thebes; Moses, who received extracts therefrom in the course of his initiations had only arranged them, and added according to the providential will which guided him, the enlightenment of his own inspiration, so as to confide this storehouse to the people by whom he was recognized as prophet and theocratic lawgiver.

My translation of the *Cosmogony of Moses* should be considered only as a *literary work* and by no means as a *theological work.* I have not intended it to command the faith of anyone and still less to distress anyone. I have carefully put aside from my notes all that which might have any reference to theological disputes; limiting myself to prove grammatically the meaning that I have given to the words and to show the strong connection of this meaning with what followed or with what had preceded. I have purposely omitted any commentary; leaving the reader to make his own comparisons.

However it is not through timidity nor through ignorance of reasons which I might use, that I have evaded theological controversy; it is through respect for the Christian church which must know perfectly to what point she ought or ought not to adopt the new ideas that I present. These ideas, purely literary, as long as they remain in my book, might become theological, and would become irresistibly so, by passing into the books of theologians and being subjected to their interpretations.

Whatever may be the fate of my book, I think that it will not be from the Reformed Christians, Lutherans or Calvinists that I shall find slanderers. For, is there in Germany, in England or elsewhere, a Protestant even slightly instructed in the motives of the Reformation who has not learned early to weigh the authorities and appreciate them at their just value? What disciple of Luther or Calvin does not know that any version whatsoever of the Sepher can never be made a rule in the matter of faith, and in no case should usurp the place of the original text and be followed in preference? If he pretended otherwise, would he not deny the fundamental principle of his sect and would he not repudiate its authors? What have Luther, Zwingli and Calvin said, and before them John Huss, Wycliff and Berenger; that the Scripture alone was and ought to be the rule of faith; that every man of sane understanding and just mind, became its legitimate interpreter after his studies had given him such power, or when God had deigned to grant him the inspiration? Now of which Scriptures did these promoters of the Reform speak, these proud antagonists of sacerdotal authority? Was it of the Scriptures of the Hellenists or that of Saint Jerome? Assuredly not; but of the original Scriptures: and this is so true that, suspecting these imperfect copies, with just reason, of not being sufficiently confirmed, nearly all of them undertook a new translation of the text. If they did not succeed in the interpretations which they gave of the Sepher, it was because the means and not the will was lacking. The temporal state of things at that time was opposed to their desires. They have attempted it, and that is enough to legitimatize my efforts in the eyes of the Reformers as this is all that I have claimed to do.

If among the Catholic priesthood there are men judicious enough to consider, in this purely literary work, what it has useful to morality and to religion in general, and who, ready to receive the truth if it were shown them, await only a legal authority to sanction an examination; I could give them satisfaction: for it is not for want of proofs that I avoid controversies but for want of inclination. Here are two authorities that cannot be challenged. The first, that of Saint Paul, the wisest of the apostles, proves that already in his time, it was an acknowledged opinion that the Jews no longer understood the text of the Sepher, and had not the power to raise the veil which Moses had spread over his doctrine.

The second, that of Saint Augustine, the most learned of the Fathers of the Church, proves my entire translation in giving to the first two verses of the Beræshith, exactly the same meaning as I have given; a meaning wholly contrary to the Vulgate.

"But our sufficiency is of God; who also hath made us able ministers of the New Testament; not of the letter, but of the spirit . . . Seeing then that we have such hope, we use great plainness of speech: and not as Moses which put a veil over his face, that the children of Israel could not steadfastly look to the end of that which is abolished: but their minds were blinded: for until this day remaineth the same veil untaken away in the reading of the Old Testament; which veil is done away in Christ. But even unto this day, when Moses is read, the veil is upon their heart". . . *.

---

* *Epist. Corinth.* II. ch. 3. Here is this remarkable passage of Saint Paul in its Hellenistic text, with an interlinear interpretation in Latin.

'Αλλ' ἡ ἱκανότης ἡμῶν ἐκ τοῦ Θεοῦ, ὅς καὶ ἱκάνωσεν ἡμᾶς διακόνους καινῆς
Sed sufficientia nostra ex Deo, qui et idoneos fecit nos ministros novi

διαθήκης; οὐ γράμματος, ἀλλὰ πνεύματος...... ἔχοντες οὖν τοιαύτην ἐλπίδα,
testamenti; non litteræ, sed spiritus...... habentes igitur talem spem,

πολλῇ παρρεσία χρώμεθα: καὶ οὐ καθάπερ Μωυσῆς, ἐτίθει κάλυμμα ἐπὶ τὸ προ-
multa libertate utimur: et non sicut Moyses, ponebot velamen super fa-
fiducia

Saint Augustine, examining the question of the creation in his book of Genesis, against the Manichæans, expresses himself thus: "It is said: *in principle, God made heaven and earth;* not that this was in effect, but because this was in power of being; for it is written that heaven was made afterward. It is thus, that considering the *seed* of a tree, we say that it has there the roots, trunk, branches, fruit and leaves; not that all these things are formally there, but virtually, and destined to be brought forth. Just as it is said, *in principle God made heaven and earth;* that is to say, the seed of heaven and earth; since the matter of heaven and earth was then in a state of confusion. Now, as it is certain that from this matter the heaven and the earth must be brought forth, that is why this matter was already called potentially the heaven and the earth" . . . .**

It seems to me difficult to add anything more to texts so concise. I refrain from all commentary upon that of Saint Paul; my design moreover not being, as I have said,

---

σωπον ἑαυτοῦ πρὸς τὸ μὴ ἀτενίσαι τοὺς υἱοὺς Ἰσραὴλ εἰς τὸ τέλος τοῦ καταρ-
ciem suam ad non intueri filios Israel in finem hujus abro-
mysterium

γουμένου. Ἀλλ' ἐπωρώθη τὰ νοήματα αὐτῶν; ἄχρι γὰρ τῆς σήμερον τὸ αὐτὸ
gati. Sed obduruerunt cogitationes eorum; usque enim hodie id ipsum

κάλυμμα ἐπὶ τῇ ἀναγνώσει τῆς παλαιᾶς διαθήκης μένει μὴ ἀνακαλυπτόμενον, ὅ τι
velamen super lectionem veteris testamenti manet non revelatum, quod

ἐν Χριστῷ καταργεῖται. Ἀλλ' ἕως σήμερον ἡνίκα ἀναγινώσκεται Μωυσῆς, κάλυμμα
in Christo abrogatur. Sed donec hodie, cum legitur Moyses, velamen

ἐπὶ τὴν καρδίαν αὐτῶν κεῖται ...
super cor eorum positum est....

** I give the text itself of Saint Augustine so that it may be compared with my translation.

"Dictum est: *In principio fecit Deus cœlum et terram;* non quia jam hoc erat, sed quia hoc esse poterat: nam et cœlum scribitur postea factum. Quemadmodum si *semen* arboris considerantes, dicamus ibi esse radices, et robur, et ramos, et fructus, et folia, non quia jam sunt, sed quia inde futura sunt. Sic dictum est: *in principio fecit Deus cœlum et terram,* quasi semen cœli et terræ, cum in confuso adhuc esset cœli et terræ materia: sed quia certum erat inde futurum esse cœlum et terram, jam et ipsa materia, cœlum et terra appellata est. (L. I. c. 3 *num.* 11.)

to enter into discussion with the theologians. But I believe it necessary to say that Saint Augustine, still quite young when he composed his books of Genesis against the Manichæans, and when he might have been accused of being carried away by flights of his imagination, was so far from repudiating afterward the opinion that I have just quoted, that, recalling it in the confessions of his old age, he still regarded it as a divine inspiration; "Is it not Thou, O Lord, who hast taught me, that before fashioning this unformed matter and distinguishing its parts, it was nothing in particular, no colour, no form, neither body nor spirit? . . ."

And further on: "If I confess, O Lord, both by tongue and pen, what Thou hast taught me concerning this matter . . . what Thou hast revealed to me upon this difficult question . . . my heart ceases not to render homage to Thee for this, and to offer up its hymns of praise for the things that it knows not how to express."

But this is sufficient for the judicious men of whom I speak; the others will not be wanting in reasons for perverting the truth of the text of Saint Paul and for invalidating what Saint Augustine said. Let them guard carefully without ever opening the mysterious coffer which has been confided to them; but, since this coffer, through the irresistible progress of things, has become the patrimony of a multitude of persons of every nation and every cult, let them at least permit those among them who, far from the service of altars, devote themselves to the study of the sciences and strive to draw from it new principles and learning which may be used for the advancement of knowledge and the welfare of humanity. The times now are no longer those in which the simplest truths could not be shown without veils. Natural philosophy and mathematics have made such great strides, and have in such a manner, uncovered the secret resources of the Universe, that it is no longer allowable for moral and metaphysical sciences to drag after them the cradle blankets of infancy. It is necessary that the harmony which has been interrupted between these two principal branches of human understanding be reëstablished. This is what the savants, ordained to know nature in its double sanctuary, must endeavour to do with necessary prudence and precaution; for every divulgation has limits that one must know how to respect.

So much for the two difficulties of which I have spoken at the beginning of this Discourse. Both are dispelled before what I have just said: first, because minds long since open to the light of reason, furnish no more food for religious conflagrations; afterward, because the rays of truth purified today by the prism of science, enlighten the souls and burn them no more. Moreover, the form that I have given my work and the scientific staging with which I have been forced to surround it, will hinder its popularity.

This staging is immense. The reader has already seen it in the first part: that is to say, the radical Vocabulary where all the Hebraic roots explain themselves readily; the Grammar whose principles are attached to those of speech, and an Introductory Dissertation wherein I have explained my thought upon the origin of Hebrew, upon that of the Sepher, upon the divers revolutions experienced by this book, and upon the versions which have been made of it, particularly that of the Hellenists, vulgarly called Septuagint*.

In the second part is the *Cosmogony of Moses*. Now what I call the *Cosmogony of Moses* is included in the first ten chapters of the *Berœshith*, the first of the five books of the Sepher. These ten chapters form a kind of sacred decade in which each of the ten chapters bears the character of its number as I shall show. It has been assumed that the divisions of the Sepher, in books, as well as in chapters and verses, were the work of Esdras. I do not think so. These ten chapters which contain the whole, and whose

---

* There will be found here several phrases already inserted in the prospectus of this work; but these repetitions were unavoidable.

number indicates the summary, prove to me that the *Science of Numbers* was cultivated long before Pythagoras, and that Moses having learned it from the Egyptians, used it in the division of his work.

The entire Cosmogony, that is to say, the origin of the Universe, that of the beings, from the elementary principle to man, their principal vicissitudes, the general history of the earth and its inhabitants, is contained in these ten chapters. I have not deemed it necessary to translate further; inasmuch as this suffices to prove all that I have advanced and nothing prevents anyone from applying my grammatical principles and continuing the exploration of the Sepher.

The Hebraic text which I quote is that contained in the Polyglot of Paris. I have scrupulously preserved all the characters without altering any under pretext of reforming it. I have likewise preserved of the Chaldaic punctuation, all that has appeared to me necessary for the reading of the text or required by grammatical rules; I have suppressed only the Masoretic minutiæ and the musical notes, called improperly accents, of which I have said often in my Grammar, that I regarded its usage as absolutely foreign to the sense, and useful only for the Jews of the synagogue who wish to continue singing psalms in a tongue lost for twenty-five centuries.

I have considered this text as correct, and I have avoided the paradoxical spirit of those who have claimed that the Jews had designedly falsified their Scriptures. I know that among the Fathers who have sustained this paradox, are cited Saint Justin Martyr, Saint Irenus, Tertullian and others: but besides the fact that these Fathers always mean by the Hebrew text which they disparage, the Greek version of Aquila, or that of Symmachus, versions made in opposition to that of the Septuagint, it is unfortunate that they did not know a word of Hebrew. For, how can persons who do not know a tongue say that a book written in this tongue, an original, is not worth the translation which has been made of it? In order to sustain such an assertion, they must quote the falsified passages and prove that its words, that its style, are obviously altered. This is what they were incapable of doing.

When one knows with what religious care, with what scruples, with what excess of attention the Jews copy the sacred text of the Sepher, and preserve it, such ideas cannot be admitted. One can see in Maimonides, what the prescribed rules are in this respect. They are such that it is impossible that the least error, that the least oversight, can ever creep into the manuscripts destined for the use of the synagogues. Those who have not seen these manuscripts can have no idea what patience assisted by religious zeal can accomplish. Father Morin and Vossius, who have adopted the paradox of the Fathers of the Church, prove by that, to what point prejudice can obscure knowledge and render it vain. If the original text offers certain errors, they are slight, and are always anterior to Esdras, or at least to the Septuagint version. It is true that the manuscripts of the synagogues are without any kind of vowel points or accents; but, as I have repeated often enough, the meaning never depends upon these points. The meaning depends upon the root, upon the sign which rules it and upon the place that the word occupies.

It is always necessary, before determining the signification of any Hebrew word whatsoever, to interrogate the primitive meaning of the root, which is easy if it is a simple root; if the word is compound, it is necessary to refrain from any interpretation before having made the grammatical analysis according to the rules that I have given and upon which the use of my notes will shed much light. The primitive meaning of the root being always generic, it must first be modified by the sign, or signs, by which this same root may be accompanied and never particularized, according to the advice of the wise Maimonides, without long meditation upon the subject of which it treats, upon the occasion which brings about the expression, upon the thought of the writer, upon the movement of the style, literal or figurative and upon all the circum-

PRELIMINARY DISCOURSE 19

stances which, among a great number of significations, incline the word to one rather than to another. The usefulness of the vowel points is limited to giving the vulgar pronunciation of the word and determining its grammatical forms whether as noun, verb or relation.

I have transcribed the original text in English characters to facilitate the reading for persons little familiar with the Hebraic characters; I have tried, as far as possible in this transcription to reconcile the primitive orthography with the Chaldaic punctuation. I have, for that reason, given carefully and in conformity with the comparative Alphabet inserted in my grammar, the value of the consonants; I have indicated the presence of the first four mother vowels א, ו, ו, י, by a circumflex accent on the corresponding vowels *â, oû, ô, î;* and those of the other three ה, ח, ע, by the aspiration *h, h* and *h*. When the mother vowels ו, י, ע, have appeared to be consonants I have expressed them by *w, j* and *gh,* or *wh*. I have indicated the vague vowel of the Chaldaic punctuation by the corresponding English vowels without accent. When I have found a vague vowel opposing a mother vowel, I have amalgamated them, forming thereby a sort of diphthong *œ, œ aï, ao,* etc.

It has seemed to me advisable before giving the correct translation of the Hebraic text, to approach as near as possible by a literal *word-for-word*, which would make my readers understand the exact value of each term of the original with its grammatical forms, according to the tongue of Moses. This was very difficult because of the signification of the words, which, nearly always metaphorical, and not being found contained in modern tongues in simple and analogous terms, requires a periphrasis. The Asiatic tongues, in general and particularly Hebrew, cannot be paralleled word-for-word with European tongues, and this is easy to conceive; for, in a word-for-word translation it would be necessary that the same literal ideas should be developed, the same ideas represented, or that the same universal ideas should have sprung from the same particular ideas; which is impossible in tongues so opposed, so diverse, spoken by peoples so different, so distant from one another in times and customs.

In order to obviate this difficulty as much as possible, I resolved to compose two literal versions, the one French and the other English; so that the word-for-word of the one, throwing light upon the word-for-word of the other, they are mutually sustained and together lead the reader to the desired end. I have chosen from among all the European tongues, the English tongue, as one of the most simple and the one whose grammar less rigid, allows me more facility in the construction. I believe I have no need of saying that one must not seek for elegance or grammatical purism in these two versions where I have purposely taken the greatest license.

I have supported these two versions with numerous notes, in which, applying the principles developed in my Grammar, I have proved the signification given to each word of the original text, in the strongest manner, taking one by one, each of these words, I have analyzed it by its root, reduced it to its elementary principles, modified it by the sign, decomposed, recomposed and, every time it has been necessary, confronted it with the corresponding word in Samaritan, Chaldaic, Syriac, Arabic, Ethiopic even, and Greek.

Thus I have prepared the correct translation of the *Cosmogony of Moses* with which I terminate this work. I venture to believe that it would be difficult to prepare this result by means more fitting to demonstrate its truth, to establish it upon bases more solid, or to attain this end after efforts more sustained and less subject to illusion.

Therefore, in going back to the principles of Speech, and finding on this path the thought of Moses, I have interpreted and set forth in suitable language, the work of this great man whose energetic influence exerting itself for thirty-four centuries has, under sundry names, directed the destiny of the earth. My intention having been steadfastly sincere I trust that its results will be felicitous.

Through this translation which I give of the Sepher, Moses will no longer be the stumbling-block of reason and the dismay of the natural sciences. Those shocking contradictions, those incoherencies, those ridiculous pictures which furnish weapons so terrible for its enemies shall be no more seen in his Cosmogony. Nor shall one see in him, a limited man attributing to the Being of beings the narrowest views and passions, refusing his immortality to man and speaking only of the soul which passes away with the blood; but a sage, initiated in all the mysteries of Nature, uniting to the positive knowledge which he has imbibed in the sanctuaries of Thebes, the knowledge of his own inspiration. If the naturalist interrogates it, he will find in his work the accumulated observations of a sequence of incalculable centuries, and all the natural philosophy of the Egyptians summed up in a few words: he will be able to compare this imposing natural philosophy with that of the moderns and judge in what the one resembles, surpasses or is inferior to the other. The metaphysician will have nothing to compare with it since real metaphysics does not exist among us. But it is the philosopher especially who will discover in this book analogies worthy of his curiosity. If he desires it, this book will become in his hands a veritable *criterion*, a touchstone, by means of which he will be able to recognize, in any system of philosophy whatsoever, the truth or error it contains. He will find there finally, what the philosophers have thought most just or most sublime from Thales and Pythagoras, to Newton and Kant. My notes will furnish him with much data in this respect.

Besides I have had constantly before me, during the long composition of these notes, *the four original versions*: that of the Samaritans, the Chaldaic targums, the Hellenistic version called the Septuagint, and the Latin Vulgate of Saint Jerome. I have quoted them when it has been necessary. I have paid little attention to other versions; for it is proved, for example, that the Syriac version, made from that of the Hellenists and which agrees with the Greek whilst the latter differs materially from the Hebrew, has been the text for the Arabic version; so that neither has authority. But it is useless to return incessantly to things that have been sufficiently explained.

Cosmogony of Moses

SEPHER BERÆSHITH A.

סֵפֶר בְּרֵאשִׁית א׃

1. Beræshith barà Ælohîm æth-ha-shamaîm w'æth-ha-âretz.

בְּרֵאשִׁית בָּרָא אֱלֹהִים אֵת־הַשָּׁמַיִם וְאֵת־הָאָרֶץ׃

---

v. 1. בראשית *At-first-in-principle*.... In these notes, it is not my intention either to examine or discuss the opinions which the savants of past centuries, Jews or Christians, have put forth upon the hidden meaning of this word or of those which follow. It would be a task quite as long as tedious. I shall explain, but I shall not comment; for this is not a system that I am establishing upon conjectures or probabilities more or less happy, but the tongue itself of Moses, that I am interpreting according to its constitutive principles.

Therefore, setting aside the sundry interpretations good or bad, which have been given to the word בראשית, I shall say that this word, in the position which it occupies, offers three distinct meanings: the literal, the figurative, and the hieroglyphic. Moses has used all three, as is proved in the course of his work. He has followed in this, the method of the Egyptian priests: for these priests had three ways of expressing their thought. The first was clear and simple, the second, symbolic and figurative, the third sacred or hieroglyphic. They made use of three kinds of characters, but not of three dialects, as might be imagined. The same word took at their pleasure, the literal, figurative or hieroglyphic sense. Such was the genius of their tongue. Heraclitus has expressed perfectly the difference of these three styles, in designating them by the epithets, *spoken, significant* and *hidden*. The first two ways, that is to say, those which consisted of taking words in the literal or the figurative sense, were spoken; but the third, which could only receive its hieroglyphic form by means of the characters of which the words were composed, existed only for the eyes, and was used only in writing. Our modern tongues are entirely incapable of making this distinction. Moses, initiated in all the mysteries of the Egyptian priesthood, made use of these three

GENESIS 1.

1. AT-FIRST-IN-PRINCIPLE, he - created, Ælohim (he caused to be, he brought forth in principle, HE-the-Gods, the-Being-of-beings), the-selfsameness-of-heavens, and - the - selfsameness - of - earth.

COSMOGONIE 1.

1. PREMIÈREMENT - EN - PRINCIPE, il créa, Ælohîm (il détermina en existence potentielle, LUI-les-Dieux, l'Être-des-êtres), l'ipséité-des-cieux et-l'ipséité-de-la-terre.

---

ways with unbounded skill; his phrase is almost invariably constituted in such a manner as to present three meanings: this is why no kind of word-for-word can render his thought. I have adhered as much as possible to expressing the literal and figurative sense together. As to the hieroglyphic, it would often be too dangerous to give it; but I have made every effort to furnish the means of attaining it, by stating its principles and by giving examples.

The word בראשית, which is here in question, is a modificative noun formed from the substantive ראש, *the head, the chief, the acting principle*, inflected by the mediative article ב, and modified by the designative ending ית. It signifies literally, *in the beginning, before all;* but figuratively *in principle, in power of being.*

Thus one can deduce the hieroglyphic sense. What I am about to say will serve as example for what follows. The word ראש, from which is formed the modificative בראשית, signifies indeed *head;* but only in a restricted and particular sense. In a broader and more generic sense, it signifies *principle.* Now, what is a principle? I shall state in what manner the earliest authors of the word ראש, conceived it. They conceived a sort of absolute power, by means of which every relative being is constituted such; they expressed their idea by the potential sign א, and the relative sign ש, united. In hieroglyphic writing it was a point at the centre of a circle. The central point unfolding the circumference, was the image of every principle. The literal writing rendered the point by א, and the circle by ס or ש. The letter ס represented the sentient circle, the letter ש the intelligible circle which was depicted winged or surrounded with flames.

2. W'ha-âretz haîthah thohoû wa-bohoû, w'hosheĉh hal-pheneî th'hôm, w'roûah Ælohîm merahepheth hal-pheneî ha-maîm.

וְהָאָרֶץ הָיְתָה תֹהוּ וָבֹהוּ וְחֹשֶׁךְ עַל־פְּנֵי תְהוֹם וְרוּחַ אֱלֹהִים מְרַחֶפֶת עַל־פְּנֵי הַמָּיִם:

A principle thus conceived was, in an universal sense, applicable to all things, both physical and metaphysical; but in a more restricted sense it was applied to elementary fire; and according as the radical word אש was taken literally or figuratively, it signified *fire*, sentient or intelligible, that of matter, or that of spirit.

Next, taking this same word אש, whose origin I am about to explain, it was made to govern by the sign of proper and determining movement ר, and the compound word ראש was obtained; that is to say, in hieroglyphic language, every principle enjoying a proper and determining movement, and of a force innately good or bad. This letter ר is rendered in sacred writing by the image of a serpent, upright or crossing the circle through the centre. In the common language one saw in the word ראש, a chief, a guide, the head of such a being, of such a thing, whatever it might be: in the figurative language, is understood the *primum mobile*, an acting principle, a good or evil genius, a right or perverse will, a demon, etc; in the hieroglyphic language, it signalized the universal, *principiant principle*, the knowledge of which it was not permitted to divulge.

These are the three significations of the word ראש, which serves as basis for the modificative בראשית. It is obvious that it would be impossible for me to enter into similar details concerning all the words which are to follow. I could not do it without going beyond the limits of prudence. But I shall endeavour, in amalgamating the three significations, to give the intelligent reader all the facilities that he could desire.

Here are the four original versions of this important word. The Samaritan version reads ᛞᚼᚴᛉᛜᛄᛈᛈ that is to say, *in substantiality, in corporeity, in the beginning*. The Chaldaic targum reads בקדמין, which can be translated, *in the culminating point of the universal assimilations; in the anteriority of times*. The Hellenists translate Ἐν ἀρχῇ, and the Latins, "in principio." The former is more akin to the

2. And-the-earth was contingent-potentiality in-a-potentiality - of - being : and - darkness (hard-making-power)-was on-the-face of-the deep (fathomless-contingent-potentiality of being) ; and-the-breath of-HIM-the-Gods (a light-making-power) was-pregnantly-moving upon-the-face of-the-waters (universal passiveness).

2. Et-la-terre e x i s t a i t puissance-contingente-d'être dans-une-puissance-d'être : et -l'obscurité (force compressive et durcissante)-était sur-la-face de l'abîme (puissance universelle et contingente d'être) ; et-le-souffle de-LUI-les-Dieux (force expansive et dilatante) était-générativement-mouvant sur-la-face des-eaux (passivité universelle).

Samaritan, and the latter to the Chaldaic. Which is natural, for, as I have said, the Hellenists consulted frequently the Samaritan version, while Saint Jerome and the rabbis of Tiberias adhered to the targums.

ברא, *he created*.... It would be not only long but useless to dwell upon the numerous disputes concerning this word; they are all reduced to this, namely, whether the verb ברוא signifies *to make something from nothing*, or simply, *to make something from something*. The rabbis of the synagogue and the doctors of the church, have indeed proved by these wordy struggles, that not any of them understood the tongue over which they disputed: for otherwise they would have seen that they were very far from the point of the question. I have already had occasion to bring out the true etymology of this famous verb, and I have proved that it signified, *to draw from an unknown element; to make pass from the principle to the essence; to render same that which was other*, etc., as can be seen in chapter VII of my Grammar. I have derived it from the sign of movement proper ר, united to that of interior action ב. The Arabs have translated it by خلق, whose root خل signifies a thing rare and tenuous, a thing without form and without consistency, a void, a nothingness. The Greeks have rendered it by ἐποίησεν, *he made*, and the Latins by "creavit," *he created*. This last expression, clearly understood, is not far from the Hebrew, for it comes from the same elementary root אר, raised from the sign of movement proper ר. It is the word "re," indicating *the thing*, by means of which one acts, which is governed by the assimilative sign כ used very extensively by the Etruscans. This word, having become

3. Wa-îaomer Ælohîm îehî-âôr, wa-îehî-âôr. וַיֹּאמֶר אֱלֹהִים יְהִי־אוֹר וַיְהִי־אוֹר׃

the verb *c-re-are*, takes in this new state, a sense which can only be rended exactly by coining the verb *to thing*. The Samaritans have expressed the Hebrew by ⴲⴲ2ⴲ which signifies literally *to render dense and compact*; as is proved by the Chaldaic טלם. The targum has preserved the primitive word ברא.

אלהים, *Ælohim*.... This is the plural of the word אלה, the name given to the Supreme Being by the Hebrews and the Chaldeans, and being itself derived from the root אל, which depicts elevation, strength and expansive power; signifiying in an universal sense, GOD. It is a very singular observation that this last word applied to the Most High, is however, in its abstract sense only the relative pronoun *he* employed in an absolute manner. Nearly all of the Asiatic peoples have used this bold metaphor. הוא (*hoa*), that is to say, HE, is in Hebrew, Chaldaic, Syriac, Ethiopic and Arabic, one of the sacred names of the Divinity; it is evident that the Persian word خدا (*Goda*), GOD, which is found in all the tongues of the North, is derived also from the absolute pronoun خو, HIM-self. It is known that the Greek philosophers and Plato particularly, designated the Intelligent Cause of the Universe in no other way than by the absolute pronoun τὸ Αὐτό.

However that may be, the Hebraic name *Ælohim* has been obviously composed of the pronoun אל and the absolute verb הוה, *to be-being*, of which I have spoken at length in my Grammar. It is from the inmost root of this verb that the Divine Name יה (*Yah*) is formed, the literal meaning of which is *Absolute-Life*. The verb itself, united to the pronoun אל, produces אלוה (*Æloah*), *that*-HE *who-*IS, the plural of which *Ælohim*, signifies exactly HE-*they-who-*ARE: *the Being of beings*.

The Samaritan says ⴲⴲ2ⴲ (*Alah*), whose root אל is found still in the Arabic الله (*Allah*), and in the Syriac ܐܠܗܐ (*Æloha*). The Chaldaic alone departs from this root and translates ייי (*Iaîi*), *the Eternity-of-eternities*, which it also applies to the Ineffable Name of GOD, יהוה (*Ihoah*), of which I shall speak further on; also of the words שמים, *the heavens*, and ארץ, *the earth*.

3. And-he-said (declaring his will), HE-the-Being-of-beings: there-shall-be light; and-there-(shall be)-became light (intellectual elementizing).

3. Et-il-dit (déclarant sa volenté), LUI-l'Être-des êtres: sera-faite-lumière; et-(sera)-fut-faite lumière (élémentisation intelligible).

---

v. 2. תֹהוּ וָבֹהוּ, *contingent-potentiality in-a-potentiality-of-being....* If one examines the sense of the four original versions, a great difference is found between what they say and what I say. The Samaritan version reads ᛗᛉᛉᛉ ᛉᛉᛉ, *distended to incomprehensibility and most rare.* The Chaldaic targum says צָדְיָא וְרֵקָנְיָא, *divided to annihilation and vain.* The Hellenists translate ἀόρατος καὶ ἀκατασκεύασος, *invisible and decomposed.* Saint Jerome understood "inanis et vacua" *unanimated and vague,* or *unformed and void.* The error into which all these translators have fallen depends here upon a prior one very slight in appearance, but whose consequences becoming more and more complicated pushes them into an abyss from which nothing can draw them. This first error depends upon the manner in which they have understood the first word of the Sepher, the famous בְּרֵאשִׁית. This word, having impressed them neither in its figurative nor in its hieroglyphic sense, has involved all that follows, in the literal and material sense that they have given to it. I pray the reader to give strict attention to this, for upon this depends all the incoherences, all the absurdities with which Moses has been reproached. In fact, if the word בְּרֵאשִׁית signified simply, *in the beginning, in the beginning of time,* as it was said, why did **not** the heavens and the earth, created at that epoch, still exist at that time; why should there be need of a successive development; why should they have rested an eternity in darkness; why should the light have been made after the heavens and before the sun; can one conceive the heavens without light, light without the sun, an earth invisible, inanimate, vain, formless, if it is material; etc., etc. But what can remedy all this? Absolutely nothing but an understanding of the tongue which is translated and seeing that בְּרֵאשִׁית means not only *in the beginning,* ἐν ἀρχῇ, "in principio," but clearly *in principle;* that is to say, not yet in action but in power; as Saint

4. Wa-îara Ælohîm æth-ha-aôr chi tôb, wa-îabeddel Ælohîm beîn ha-aôr w'beîn ha-hoshech.

וַיַּרְא אֱלֹהִים אֶת הָאוֹר כִּי טוֹב וַיַּבְדֵּל אֱלֹהִים בֵּין הָאוֹר וּבֵין הַחֹשֶׁךְ׃

Augustine interpreted it. This is the thought of Moses, profound thought which he expresses admirably by the words תהו ובהו, in which he depicts with masterhand that state of a thing, not only in contingent power of being, but still contained in another power of being; in short, without form, in germ in a germ. It is the famous χαός of the Greeks, that *chaos* which the vulgar have also gradually materialized and whose figurative and hieroglyphic signification I could very easily demonstrate were it necessary.

The Hebraic words תהו ובהו belong to those words which the sages create in learned tongues and which the vulgar do not comprehend. Let us now examine their figurative and hieroglyphic sense.

We know that the sign ה is that of life. We have seen that this sign being doubled, formed the essentially living root הה, which, by the insertion of the luminous sign, became the verb היה, *to be-being*. But let us imagine now that, wishing to express, not an existence in action, but only in power, we restrict the verbal root in the sole sign of life and extinguish the luminous sign י to bring it back to the convertible ו; we shall have only a compressed root wherein the being will be latent and as it were, in germ. This root הו, composed of the sign of life, and of that which, as we know, is the link between nothingness and being, expresses marvelously well that incomprehensible state of a thing when it exists no more, and when it is, nevertheless, in power of existing. It is found in the Arabic هو in which it depicts a desire, a tendency, a vague, indeterminate existence. It is sometimes an unfathomable depth, هوة; sometimes a sort of physical death هوي; sometimes an ethereal space هوا, etc.

Moses, after the example of the Egyptian priests, taking this root and making it rule by the sign of mutual reciprocity ת, formed the word תהו by means of which he expressed a contigent and potential existence contained in another potential existence בהו; for here he inflects the same root by the mediative article ב.

COSMOGONY OF MOSES 31

4. And-he-did-ken, HE-the-Gods that-light as good; and-he-made-a-division (he caused a dividing motion to exist) HE-the-Gods, betwixt the-light (intellectual elementizing) and-betwixt the-darkness (hard-making power).

4. Et-il-considéra, LUI-les-Dieux, cette lumière comme bonne; et-il-fit-une-solution (il détermina un moyen de séparation) LUI-les-Dieux, entre la-lumière (élémentisation intelligible) et entre l'obscurité (force compressive et durcissante).

Thus, there is no need of conceiving the earth invisible, decomposed, vague, void, formless, which is absurd or contradictory; but only as existing still in power, in another seed-producing power, which must be developed in order that it may be developed.

חשֶׁךְ, *darkness*.... This word is composed of the two contracted roots חש־אך It is remarkable in its figurative and hieroglyphic sense. In its figurative sense, it is a compressing, hardening movement; in its hieroglyphic, it is a combat, a violent opposition between the contrary principles of heat and cold. The root חש expresses a violent and disordered movement caused by an inner ardour which seeks to distend. The root אך depicts on the contrary, a sentiment of contraction and tightening which tends to centralize. In the composition of the word it is the compressive force which prevails and which enchains the inner ardour forced to devour itself. Such was the idea that the Egyptian priests formed of *darkness*.

תהום, *the deep*.... This is the root הו which I have already analyzed, modified now by the reciprocal sign ת, and endowed with the collective sign ם, which develops its power in infinite space.

רוח, *the breath*.... It is figuratively, a movement toward expansion, toward dilation. Hieroglyphically, it is strength opposed to that of *tenebræ*. And if the word חשֶׁךְ characterizes a compressive power, a compression, the word רוח will characterize an expansive power, an expansion. In both will be found this eternal system of two opposed forces, which the sages and savants of all the centuries, from Parmenides and Pythagoras to Descartes and Newton, have seen in Nature, and signalized by different names.

5. Wa-îkerâ Ælohîm la-âôr Iôm, w'la-hosheċh karâ laîlah, wa-îehî hereb, wa-îehî-boker, Iôm æhad.

וַיִּקְרָא אֱלֹהִים לָאוֹר יוֹם וְלַחֹשֶׁךְ קָרָא לָיְלָה וַיְהִי־עֶרֶב וַיְהִי־בֹקֶר יוֹם אֶחָד:

The Hebraic word רוח is composed of the sign of movement proper ר, united to that of elementary existence ה, by the universal, convertible sign ו. The root which results contains all ideas of expansion and exaltation, of ethereal breath, inspiration, animation, etc. It is found in the Chaldaic רוו, in the Syriac ܪܘ and in the Arabic روح.

מרחפת, *pregnantly-moving*.... Moses, by a turn of phrase frequently adopted by him, uses here, to express the action of the breath, of which he was about to speak, a verb which is derived from the same root; that is to say, which is always attached to the word רוח, and which depicts, as I have already said, an expansive and quickening movement. The sign פ which terminates it now, adds the idea of active generation of which it is the hieroglyphic symbol. The Samaritan makes use of the word ܨܦܚ whose root being the same as that of the Hebrew נשף, gives the sense of agitating with a vital movement, of *animating*. Finally, the Hebraic verb רחם is the same as רחב, with the sole difference of the character פ being substituted for the character ב: it signifies, *to dilate, to expand, to agitate prolifically*. The Arabic رحب has the same sense.

See Radical Vocabulary for the word מים, root ים and מה.

v. 3. ויאמר, *And-he-said*.... It can be seen by the etymology which I have given of this important verb in chapter VII of my Grammar, that it signifies not only *to say*, but according to the occasion, it can attain a signification much more exalted. Now, is this occasion more important than that in which the Being of beings manifests his creative will? To understand it in the literal sense only, is to degrade it, and is detrimental to the thought of the writer. As the judicious Maimonides said, it is necessary to spiritualize the sense of this word and to guard against imagining any sort of speech. It is an act of the will and as is indicated by the hieroglyphic composition of the verb אמור, a power which declares, manifests and reflects itself without, upon the being which it enlightens.

אור, *light*.... I cannot repeat too often that all words of the Hebraic tongue are formed in such a way as to contain within them-

5. A n d-he-assigned-for-name, HE-the-Gods, to-the-light, *Day* (universal manifestation); and-to-the-darkness, he-assigned-for-name, *Night* (naught manifested, all-knitting): and-there-was west-eve; and-there-was east-dawn (o v e r and b a c k a g a i n); Day the-first (light's first manifestation).

5. Et-il-assigna-nom, LUI-les-Dieux, à-la-lumière, *Jour* (manifestation universelle); et-à-l'obscurité il-assigna-nom *Nuit* (négation manifestée, nutation des choses); et-fut-occident, et-fut-orient (libération et itération); Jour premier (première manifestation phénoménique).

---

selves the reason of their formation. Let us consider the word אוֹר *light*: it is derived directly from the word אוּר *fire*. The only difference between them is, that in the word which designates fire, it is the universal convertible sign וּ which forms the link between the sign of power א, and that of movement proper ר: whereas in the second, it is the intelligible sign וֹ. Let us proceed further. If, from the words אוּר and אוֹר, one takes away the median sign וּ or וֹ there will remain the elementary root אר, composed of power and movement, which in all known tongues signifies by turns, *earth, water, air, fire, ether, light*, according to the sign joined thereunto. See also, Radical Vocab. root אר.

ויהי, *and-there* (*shall be*)-*became*.... I must not neglect to say, that Moses, profiting by the hieroglyphic genius of the Egyptian tongue, changing at will the future tense into past tense, depicts, on this occasion, the birth of light, symbol of intelligible *corporeity*, with an animation that no modern tongue can render except the Chinese. He writes first יהי־אוֹר *there-shall-be light;* then repeating the same words with the single addition of the convertible sign וּ, he turns suddenly the future into the past, as if the effect had sustained beforehand the outburst of the thought ויהי־אוֹר *and there-(shall be)-became light.*

This manner of speaking figuratively and hieroglyphically, always comes from the primitive meaning given to the word בראשית: for the heavens and the earth created in principle, and passing from power into action, could unfold successively their virtual forces only as far as the divine will announced in the future, is manifest in the past.

6. Wa-îâomer Ælohîm îehî rakîwha bethôch ha-maîm w'îhî mabeddil beîn maîm la-maîm.

וַיֹּאמֶר אֱלֹהִים יְהִי רָקִיעַ בְּתוֹךְ הַמָּיִם וִיהִי מַבְדִּיל בֵּין מַיִם לָמָיִם:

The Being of beings knows no time. The Egyptian tongue is the only one in which this wonderful trope can take place even in the spoken tongue. It was a spoken effect which, from the hieroglyphic style passed into the figurative, and from the figurative into the literal.

v. 4. וירא, *And-he-did-ken*.... Moses continues to make the Being of beings, the universal Creator, speak in the future, by turning the expression of his will into the past by means of the convertible sign. The verb ראות which is used by Moses on this occasion, signifies not only *to see*, but *to ken*, by directing voluntarily the visual ray upon an object. The root רו or רי composed of the sign of movement proper united to the convertible, or to that of manifestation, develops every idea of a stroke, ray, or trace, of anything whatever, being directed in a straight line. It is joined to the root או or אי, expressing the goal, the place, the object toward which the will inclines, there where it is fixed, and forms with it the compound ראי, ראה or ראות, that is to say, *the vision*, the action of seeing and the very object of this action.

ויבדל, *and-he-made-a-division*.... The verb בדל springs from the two contracted roots בד-דל. By the first בד, should be understood every idea of individuality, of peculiarity, of isolation, of solitary existence: by the second דל, every kind of division, of opening, of disjunction. So that the verb here alluded to, signifies literally the action of particularizing, of isolating one from another, of making solution of things, distinguishing them, separating them, etc. Moses employs it here according to the intensive form to give it more force.

v. 5. ויקרא, *And-he-assigned-for-name*.... This verb is produced from the root קר which signifies literally a character, a characteristic sign, an engraving.

The Samaritan word ᛒᚴᚱ has lost the early expression and signifies only *to cry out, to emit the sound of the voice*.

יום, *Day*.... The root י contains every idea of heap, of gather-

6. And-he-said, HE-the-Gods, there-shall-be a-rarefying (a slackening, loosening action) in-the-centre of-the-waters: and-there-shall-be a-separating-cause (a lone-making action) betwixt the-waters toward-the-waters.	6. Et-il-dit, LUI-les-Dieux il-sera-fait une-raréfaction (un desserrement, une force raréfiante) au-centre des-eaux: et-il-sera-fait un-faisant-séparer (un movement de séparation) entre-les-eaux envers-les-eaux.

---

ing, of pile; it is in this relation that it constitutes the masculine plural of Hebraic nouns. In its natural state it provides, by restriction, the name of the sea, and denotes then, the mass of waters, the piling of the waves. But if the luminous sign ו is inserted in this root, it is no longer the mass of waters that it expresses; it is, so to speak, the mass of light, the gathering of the intelligible element; it is יוֹם, the universal manifestation, *day*. See Rad. Vocab. root יֹ and יָם.

It is unnecessary, I think, for me to say how very essential is this grammatical training. But I must warn the reader that the Chaldaic punctuation having suppressed almost invariably the sign ו of the word יוֹם, especially in the plural יָמִים, it has caused the same characters יָם or יָמִים to signify, according to the circumstance, *day or sea; days or seas.*

לילה, *Night....* The formation of this word demands particular attention. Refer to Rad. Vocab. root לֹא, לוֹ and לל. It is the amalgamation of these three roots that forms the word in question. The words *naught* and *knot*, holding to the same root as the word *night*, portray very felicitously the figurative and hieroglyphic sense attached to the Hebrew word לילה.

ערב, *west-eve....* This name famous in all the ancient mythologies, is the *Erebus* which we have drawn from the Greek ἐρεβός, and whose origin has so greatly troubled the savants. Its signification is not doubtful. It always recalls to the mind something obscure, distant, out of sight. The Hellenists who have rendered it in this passage by ἑσπέρα and the Latins by "vespere," *evening*, have visibly weakened the meaning. It signifies the occident, and all ideas which are related to it, not only in Hebrew, but in Chaldaic, Syriac, Ethiopic and in Arabic.

7. Wa-îahash Ælohîm æth-ha-rakîwha wa-îabeddel beîn ha-maîm âsher mith-ahath la-rakiwha, w'beîn ha-maîm âsher mehal la-rakiwha, wa-îehî chen.

וַיַּעַשׂ אֱלֹהִים אֶת־הָרָקִיעַ וַיַּבְדֵּל בֵּין הַמַּיִם אֲשֶׁר מִתַּחַת לָרָקִיעַ וּבֵין הַמַּיִם אֲשֶׁר מֵעַל לָרָקִיעַ וַיְהִי־כֵן׃

The name of the last mentioned people is derived therefrom, as I have already stated in my Introductory Dissertation.

בקר, *east-dawn*.... This word, produced from the root קר, governed by the sign ב, indicates a thing whose course is regulated, and which presents itself ever the same; a thing which is renewed unceasingly. The Arabic reads بَقَ. This word is found sometimes used to express, light. The Syriac ܟܡ ܀ contains often the idea of inspection, of exploration. The Hellenists in restricting its signification to the word πρωί, *morning*, have followed purposely the literal and vulgar sense. The Samaritan version was less restricted; it translates ערב and בקר, by ᐰᙿᏰ and ᕴᒐᒥ; that is to say, that which lowers, falls, ends, and that which rises, begins, signals. The Chaldaic targum says the same thing: רמש and צפר. The English words *over and back*, hold to the same roots as the Hebrew words, and vividly express the figurative sense.

v. 6. רקיע, *a-rarefying*.... The Hellenists have translated this word by the Greek ξερέωμα, which signifies a firm, solid thing; Saint Jerome has imitated them in saying "firmamentum," *firmament*. This version grossly misinterprets Moses, who never thought that ethereal space was either firm or solid, as he has been made to say; on the contrary, the root רק, from which he draws this expression contains the idea of tenuity and expansion. The verb רוק or ריק, which comes from it, signifies *to be rarefied* or *rendered void*. Finally the compound word רקוֹע, whence the word referred to is derived, presents only the sense of expanding and attenuating. It is difficult to understand how the Hellenists have been able to see in all this, their solid ξερέωμα; at least assuming the idea of Richard Simon who thinks that they have followed, on this occasion, the rude jargon that was spoken at that time in Jerusalem. (*Hist. crit.* L. II. ch. 5). The Samaritan version translates the word רקיע by ᕴᒐᐰᒋᏰ, that is to say, *order, harmony, arrangement of parts;* an idea very far from solidity. Per-

COSMOGONY OF MOSES

7. And-he-made, HE-the-Gods, that-self-sameness-of--t h e-rarefying (loosening power, ethereal expanse): and-he-did-effect-a-separating-cause betwixt the-waters which-were below by-the-rarefying (sinking down) and-betwixt the-waters which-were above by-the-rarefying (raising up) and-it-was-so.

7. Et-il-fit, L U I-l e s-D i e u x, cette-ipséité-de-la-raréfaction (cette force raréfiante, l'espace éthéré) ; et-il-fit-exister-une-séparation entre les-eaux que-étaient par-en-bas (affaissées) de-l'espace-éthéré et-entre les-eaux qui-étaient par-en-haut (exaltées) de l'espace-éthéré: et-ce-fut-ainsi.

---

haps the Hellenists have deemed it proper to materialize this expression. However that may be, the Arabic رق, even the Syriac ܕܩ, and the Ethiopic analogue ℞ΦΦ (*rakk*), confirm all the ideas of subtlety, tenuity and spirituality which is in the Hebrew.

בתוך המים, *in-the-centre of-the-waters*.... This is to say, in examining the roots and the figurative and hieroglyphic sense, *in the sympathetic and central point of universal passivity;* which agrees perfectly with a rarefying and dilating force such as Moses understood. But the Hellinists having considered it proper to change this intelligible force into a sentient solidity, have been led to change all the rest. The word מבדיל, which is obviously a continued facultative, according to the excitative form, expressing the action of making a separation exist among divers natures, they have changed into a substantive, and have seen only a separation produced by a kind of wall that they have created. The Arabic verb بدل which is attached to the same root as the Hebrew בדל, expresses a mutation of nature or of place.

v. 7. את הרקיע, *that-selfsameness-of-the-rarefying*.... It was doubtless seen in the first verse of this chapter, that I gave according to the occasion, a particular meaning to the designative preposition את having rendered את השמים word-for-word by *the selfsameness-(objectivity)-of-the-heavens;* it is true, as I have taken pains to state in my Grammar (ch. IV, § 3), that this preposition expresses often more than a simple designative inflexion, and that it characterizes, especially when it is followed by the determinative article ה, as in this instance,

8. Wa-îkerâ Ælohîm la-rakîwha shamaîm, wa-îehî hereb, wa-îehî boker Iôm shenî.

וַיִּקְרָא אֱלֹהִים לָרָקִיעַ שָׁמָיִם וַיְהִי־עֶרֶב וַיְהִי־בֹקֶר יוֹם שֵׁנִי :

9. Wa-îâomer Ælohîm îkkawoû ha-maîm mitha-hath ha-shamaîm æl-makôm æhad, w'thera æth ha-îaba-shah, wa-îehî-chen.

וַיֹּאמֶר אֱלֹהִים יִקָּווּ הַמַּיִם מִתַּחַת הַשָּׁמַיִם אֶל־מָקוֹם אֶחָד וְתֵרָאֶה הַיַּבָּשָׁה וַיְהִי־כֵן :

---

the substance itself, the ipseity, the objectivity, the selfsameness of the thing which it designates.

מִתַּחַת, *below*.... מֵעַל, *above*.... These two adverbial relations have, in this instance, a figurative and hieroglyphic sense, very essential to understand. The first מתחת, has the root חת, containing every idea of shock, terror, restraint. This root, governed by the sympathetic sign מ, becomes in an abstract sense, the expression of that which is worn out and inferior. The root of the second of these relations is, on the contrary על, which draws with it every idea of distention, and of sentient exaltation. It is the reinforcement of the root הל, which develops a sentiment of joy and merriment.

v. 8. שמים, *heavens*.... Later on I shall give the etymology of this word. But I beg the reader to observe here, that the heavens are developed only successively, and after the formation of ethereal space: which proves that they were at first created only in principle, as I have said.

v. 9. יקוו, *they-shall-drive*.... The root קו, whence comes the verb קוה, expresses every leaning, every inclination, every movement of blind but irresistible force toward a goal. The figurative sense of this expression, which Moses uses according to its intensive verbal

COSMOGONY OF MOSES 39

8. And-he-assigned-for-name, HE-the-Being-of-beings, to-the-e t h e r e a l-expanse, *Heavens* (exalted and shining waters): and-there-was west-eve, and-there-was east-dawn (over and back again), Day the-s e c o n d (light's second manifestation).

9. And-he-said, HE-the-Gods, they-shall-drive (tend to) the-waters from-below (from the sinking down) the-heavens toward a-driving-place, one (single); and-there-shall-be-seen the-dryness: and-it-was-so.

8. Et-il-assigna-nom, LUI l'Être-des-êtres à-l'espace-éthéré, *Cieux* (les eaux éclatantes, élevées): et-fut-occident, et-fut-orient (libération et itération), Jour second (seconde manifestation phénoménique).

9. Et-il-dit, LUI-les-Dieux, elles tendront-fortement (inclineront, se détermineront par un movement irrésitible) les-eaux par-en-bas (de l'affaissement) d e s-c i e u x, vers un-lieu-déterminé, unique; et se-verra-l'aridité: et-ce-fut-ainsi.

---

form, has been corrupted by the Samaritans who restrict it to the literal sense, and make use of the verb ⟨⟩, according to the reflexive form ⟨⟩ ; that is to say, *they shall be confluent, the waters*....

אֶל־מָקוֹם, *toward a driving-place*.... This word, which Moses uses after the verb קוה, holds to the same root. It is a figure of speech which this hierographic writer never lacks, and which proves the inner knowledge that he had of his tongue: one always finds the verb derived from the substantive or the substantive derived from the verb, proceeding together as if to confirm and sustain each other. In this instance, the root קו which expresses the tendency toward a goal, the force which drives with power in action, produces at first the verb קוה, which depicts the movement toward that goal: this one taking on the character ם as collective sign, becomes the verb קום whose meaning is, to substantialize, to establish in substance, to drive with power in action. This same verb, being inflected in its turn by the sign of exterior action מ, becomes the very place, the goal of the movement, the action resulting from the power.

10. Wa-îkerâ Ælohîm la-îabashah aretz, w'l'mikweh ha-maîm karâ îammîm, wa-iaræ Ælohîm chi-tôb. וַיִּקְרָא אֱלֹהִים לַיַּבָּשָׁה אֶרֶץ וּלְמִקְוֵה הַמַּיִם קָרָא יַמִּים וַיַּרְא אֱלֹהִים כִּי־טוֹב :

Thus the waters, moved in the centre by an expansive and rarefying force which tends to make a separation of the subtle parts and of the dense parts; the waters, image of universal passivity, rise from the one side to form ethereal space, and fall on the other to be united in the gulf of seas. I know not what the modern savants will think of this physics; but this I do know, that it is neither ridiculous nor contemptible. If I did not fear to display in these notes an erudition out of place, I would repeat what I have already said pertaining to the system of the two opposed forces, admitted not only by the ancients but also by the moderns: forces which Parmenides called *ethereal fire* and *night;* Heraclitus, *the way upward* and *the way downward;* Timæus of Locri, *intelligence* and *necessity;* Empedocles, *love* and *hate;* Plato, *himself* and *that which is not him;* Descartes, *movement* and *resistance;* Newton, *centrifugal force* and *centripetal force*, etc.

v. 10. יבשה, *the dryness....* Here, the root אש, whose meaning I have already explained, is found preceded by the sign of interior action ב, and by the sign of manifestation and of duration י, giving evidence of the inner and continuous action of this igneous principle. Thus, it is a thing not only dried by *fire,* but a thing that *fire* continues to burn interiorly, which is revealed through the irresistible force which makes the waters tend toward a determined place.

ארץ, *earth....* I make the same remark with respect to the earth, that I have made with respect to the heavens, and pass on to its etymology. The primitive root אר, contains the united signs, almost always violent, of stable power and of continued movement proper. These two signs which appear opposed to each other, produce an elementary root which is found again in all tongues, and which, expressing that which pertains to the elementary principle or to nature in general, signifies, following the new modifications that it receives, *light, ether, fire, air, water, earth* and even *metal*. The Hebraic tongue which is no other than the primitive Egyptian, possesses this

COSMOGONY OF MOSES 41

10. And-he-assigned-for-name, HE-the-Gods, to-the-dryness, *earth* (terminating element); .and-to-the-driving-place of-the waters, he-assigned-for-name, *seas* (waterish streaming): and-he-did-ken, HE-the-Being-of-beings, that-as-good.

10.· Et-il-assigna-nom, LUI-les-Dieux, à-l'aridité, *terre* (élément terminant et bornant); et-à-la-tendance des-e a u x, il-assigna-nom, *mers* (immensité acqueuse, manifestation de l'universelle passivité): et-il-considéra, LUI-les-Dieux, cela-ainsi-bon.

---

root in all its modifications, as can be seen in the Rad. Vocab. root אר, בר, etc.

Without there being need for examining here the diverse modifications of this important root, let it suffice for me to say, that whether one adds the signs of compression and material sense, as the Chaldeans and Samaritans in their words ארע, א־ק, or 𐤀𐤓𐤒 or whether one places there, as the Hebrews, the sign ץ, which expresses the term and end of all substance, one finds equally *earth*, that is to say, the element which is limited, figured, tactile, compressive, plastic, etc.

It must be remarked that in augmenting the force of the root אר in its potential character א, one makes it חר or חרי, that which burns, that which inflames, either literally, or figuratively; in doubling its movement as in ארר, that which is execrable and cursed; and חרר that which is steep, rough, hilly, etc.

ימים, *seas*.... That is to say, *aqueous immensity;* for the word which designates *seas*, is only the word מים, *waters* preceded by the sign of manifestation י. As to the word מים itself, the following is the history of its formation.

The root מה, מו or מי, contains the idea of passive relation, of plastic and creative movement. It is perceived in the Arabic words ماد · ماج · ماح all of which have reference to this idea. The Hebrews have made much use of it in the vulgar idiom, without entirely penetrating its meaning; however, they, as well as the Chaldeans and Syrians, employed the verb מוט to express the mutation of things, and their relative movement. The name which they gave to water, in general, although expressed by the root of which I speak, was rarely in the singular, and as if their sages had wished to show in

11. Wa-îâomer Ælohîm, thadeshæ ha-âretz deshæ hesheb mazeriha zerah, hetz pherî hosheh pherî le-mînoû, âsher zareh' ô-b'ô, hal-ha-âretz, wa-îehî-čhen.

וַיֹּאמֶר אֱלֹהִים תַּדְשֵׁא הָאָרֶץ דֶּשֶׁא עֵשֶׂב מַזְרִיעַ זֶרַע עֵץ פְּרִי עֹשֶׂה פְּרִי לְמִינוֹ אֲשֶׁר זַרְעוֹ־בוֹ עַל־הָאָרֶץ וַיְהִי־כֵן׃

12. Wa-thôtzæ ha-âretz deshæ hesheb mazeriha zerah le-mînehoû w'hetz hosheh pherî, âsher zareh'ô-b'ô le mînehoû: wa-îaræ Ælohîm čhi-tôb.

וַתּוֹצֵא הָאָרֶץ דֶּשֶׁא עֵשֶׂב מַזְרִיעַ זֶרַע לְמִינֵהוּ וְעֵץ עֹשֶׂה פְּרִי אֲשֶׁר זַרְעוֹ־בוֹ לְמִינֵהוּ וַיַּרְא אֱלֹהִים כִּי־טוֹב׃

---

that way the double movement which it contains, or that they knew its inner composition, they gave it almost always the dual number: מיים, *double waters*.

Yet, a very singular thing which ought not to escape the archæologists is, that from the Chinese to the Celts, all peoples may draw from the word which, in their tongue designates water, the one which serves as indeterminate pronominal relation. The Chinese say *choui* water, and *choui*, who, what? The Hebrews מה or מי water and מה or מי who, what? The Latins, *aqua*, water, and *quis, quæ, quod*, who, what? The Teutons and Saxons, *wasser*, water, and *was* or *wat*, who, what? etc.

I am taking up here, the etymology of the word שמים *heavens*, because it is attached to the one I have been explaining in this article, and because it signifies literally, the waters, raised, brilliant and glorified; being formed from the word מים, *waters*, and from the root שם which is united to it. This root contains the idea of that which rises and shines in space, that which is distinguished and noticeable by its elevation or its splendour. The Hebrew and Chaldaic שמה means, happy, transported with joy; the Arabic سام, has almost the same sense.

11. And-he-said (declaring his will) HE-the-Gods; shall-cause-to-grow, t h e-earth, a-growing grass, seed-yielding-seed, (sprout-yielding-sprout) vegetable-substance and-fructuous, yielding-fruit, after-the-kind-its-own which-has the-seed-its-own unto-itself, upon-the-earth: and-it-was-so.

12. And-it-did-shoot-out, (yield forth), the earth, a-growing-grass seed-yielding-seed after-the-kind-its-own, and-a-vegetable-substance and-fructuous, which the-seed its-own unto-itself (has), after-the-kind-itself; and he-viewed, HE-the-Being-of-beings, that-as-good.

11. Et-il-dit (déclarant sa volonté), LUI-les-Dieux; fera-végéter la-terre, une-végétante herbe, germifiant-germe, substance fructueuse faisant-fruit, selon-l'espèce-sienne qui-ait semence-sienne dans-soi, sur-la-terre: et-ce-fut-ainsi.

12. Et - elle - fit - sortir (provenir, naître), la terre, une végétante herbe, germinant-germe, d'après-l'espèce-sienne, et une-substance fructuese qui semence-sienne dans-soi, (avait et aura) selon l'espèce-sienne; et-il-vit, LUI-l'Être-des-êtres, c e l a-**ainsi-bon.**

---

v. 11. תדשא, *shall-cause-to-grow*.... This is the verb דשא *to grow*, used according to the excitative form, active movement, future tense. The Hebraic phrase has a delicacy and precision that is almost impossible to make understood even in the word-for-word, where I allow myself the greatest license, not only in the form but also in the concatenation of the words. There exists only the difficulty which rises from the idiomatic genius and from the turn of phrase affected by Moses. This turn of phrase consists, as I have already said in drawing always the noun and the verb from the same root, and in repeating them under diverse modifications. One can perceive in this verse and in those following, the singular grace and picturesque beauty. I venture to hope even through the perplexity of the French and English word-for-word rendering, that by adhering to the literal sense, one will see here many things that the Hellenists or Latin translators had not allowed even to be suspected.

v. 12. ותוצא, *and-it-did-shoot-out*.... It is the verb יצא, *to come*

13. Wa-îehî-hereb, wa-îehî-boker, îôm shelîshî. וַיְהִי־עֶרֶב וַיְהִי־בֹקֶר יוֹם שְׁלִישִׁי׃

14. Wa-iâomer Ælohîm îehî maôroth bi-rekîwha ha-shamaîm le-habeddil beîn ha-îôm w'beîn ha-laîlah w' haîoû le-âothoth w'l'môha-dîm w'l'îamîm w'shanîm. וַיֹּאמֶר אֱלֹהִים יְהִי מְאֹרֹת בִּרְקִיעַ הַשָּׁמַיִם לְהַבְדִּיל בֵּין הַיּוֹם וּבֵין הַלָּיְלָה וְהָיוּ לְאֹתֹת וּלְמוֹעֲדִים וּלְיָמִים וְשָׁנִים׃

---

forth, to proceed, to be born, used according to the excitative form, in the future tense made past by the convertible sign. I beg the reader to observe here again this hieroglyphic expression. GOD speaks in the future and his expression repeated, is turned suddenly to the past. Let us examine this important verb and proceed to the analysis of its elements. The first which offers itself is the sign צ, expressing every terminative movement, every conclusion, every end. Its proper and natural place is at the end of words: thence the roots אץ or הץ, in Arabic اصر containing every idea of corporeal bourns and limits, of repressing and concluding force, of term. But if, instead of terminating the words, this sign begins them; then, far from arresting the forms, it pushes them, on the contrary, toward the goal of which it is itself the symbol: thence, the opposed roots צא, in Syriac ܨܐ, and in Arabic ص, whose idea is, leaving the bourns, breaking the shackles of the body, coming outside, being born. It is from this last root, verbalized by the initial adjunction י, that the verb which is the subject of this note, is derived. It signifies *to appear, to come outside by a movement of propagation*, as is demonstrated unquestionably, by the substantive nouns which are derived therefrom, צִיא *a son*, and צֶאֱצָא *a numerous progeny*.

v. 13. There are no further remarks to be made here.

v. 14. מְאֹרֹת, *sensible lights*.... This is the root אוֹר *light*, determined into form by the plastic sign מ. I have restored to this word the mother vowels which the Chaldaic punctuation had suppressed; I have done the same in the following: but I must state that

13. And-there-was-west-eve, and-there-was-east-dawn (over and back again) day the-third (light's third manifestation).

13. Et-fut-occident, et-fut-orient (libération et itération) jour troisième (troisième manifestation phénoménique).

14. And-he-said, HE-the-Gods: sensible-lights-and-local there-shall-be in-the-ethereal-expanse of-heavens, for-causing-a-separation-to-be-made betwixt the-day, and-betwixt the-night; and they-shall-be-in-futurity, for-the-divisions-of-time, and-for-the-revolutions-of-light's-universal-manifestations, and-for-the-ontological-changes-of-beings.

14. Et-il-dit, LUI-les Dieux: il-existera des-clartés-extérieures (lumières sensibles) dans-l'expansion-éthérée des-cieux, pour-faire-le-partage (le mouvement de séparation) entre le jour et-entre la-nuit : et-elles-seront-en-signes-à-venir et-pour-les-divisions-temporelles et-pour-les manifestations-phénoméniques-universelles, et-pour-les-mutations-ontologiques-des-êtres.

---

the suppression of these vowels is here necessitated by the hieroglyphic style. For the Divine Verb always expressing itself in the future, and the accomplishment of the will of the Being of beings, following likewise in the convertible future, the creation remains always in power, according to the meaning of the initial word בראשית. This is why the word מארת is deprived of the luminous sign not only in the singular, but also in the plural.

לאתת. *in-signs-to-come* (*in-futurity*).... The Hellinists have translated simply ἐνιαυτοῖς, and Saint Jerome has said "in signa," *in signs*. But this word comes from the continued facultative אוֹתה, *to be coming*, inflected by the directive article ל.

ולמועדים, *and-for-the-divisions-of-times*.... This word springs from the root עד, governed by the sign of exterior action מ, and inflected by the directive article ל. It is necessary to consult the Radical Vocab. concerning this important root, as well as the roots of the two following words יום and שנה.

As the Greek and Latin translators have seen in these three words

15. W'haîoû li-maôroth bi-rekiwha ha-shamaîm l'-hâîr hal-ha-âretz wa-îhî chen.

וְהָיוּ לִמְאוֹרֹת בִּרְקִיעַ הַשָּׁמַיִם לְהָאִיר עַל־הָאָרֶץ וַיְהִי־כֵן׃

16. Wa-îahash Ælohîm æth-sheni ha-mâoroth ha-gheddolîm, æth-ha-mâôr ha-gaddol le-memesheleth ha-îôm w'æth-ha-mâôr ha-katon le-memesheîeth ha-laîlah, w'æth-ha-chôchabîm.

וַיַּעַשׂ אֱלֹהִים אֶת־שְׁנֵי הַמְּאֹרֹת הַגְּדֹלִים אֶת־הַמָּאוֹר הַגָּדֹל לְמֶמְשֶׁלֶת הַיּוֹם וְאֶת־הַמָּאוֹר הַקָּטֹן לְמֶמְשֶׁלֶת הַלַּיְלָה וְאֵת הַכּוֹכָבִים׃

---

only days, months and years, it will be well for me to dwell upon this; but I shall find the occasion to do so further on.

v. 15. להאיר, *for-causing-brightness-to-shine*.... This is the root אור, *light*, or hieroglyphically, *intellectual coporeity*, which, having become verb, is employed here according to the excitative form: so that it appears evident by the text of Moses, that this hierographic writer regarded the celestial luminous centres, as sensible lights destined to propagate intellectual light and to excite it upon the earth. Physics of this kind offers much food for reflection.

v. 16. את־שני, *those twain*.... It must be observed that Moses does not employ here שנים *two*, as the Greek and Latin translators have rendered it, which would separate the two luminaries of which he speaks; but that he employs the word שני, inflected by the designative preposition את, *that same twain, that couple, that gemination:* thus uniting them under one single idea.

לממשלת, *for-a-symbolical-representation*.... The Hellenists have translated this, εἰς ἀρχάς, which is the most restricted interpretation; for in short, it is evident that the sun and the moon rule over the day and night. Indeed Moses would be but little understood if one were to stop at an idea so trivial. **The verb** מישׁל means, it is true, *to be ruler, judge* or *prince;* but it signifies much oftener *to be the model, the representative, the symbol of something;* to speak in alle-

COSMOGONY OF MOSES 47

15. And-they-shall-be assensible-lights (sparkling foci) in-the-e t h e r e al -expanse of-heavens, for-causing-brightness-to-shine (intellectual light) upon-the-earth : and-it-was-so.

16. And-he-made, HE-the-Gods, those-twain (that couple, that pair) of-central-lights the-great: the-self-sameness-of-the-central-light the-greater, for-a-symbolical-representation of-day, and-the-self-sameness-of-the -central-light the-lesser, for-a-symbolical - representation of-night; and-the-selfsameness-of-the-stars (world's virtual faculties).

15. Et-elles-seront-comme-des-lumières sensibles (des foyers lumineux) dans-l'expansion-éthérée des-cieux pour-faire-briller (exciter la lumière intellectuelle) sur-la-terre : et-cela-fut-ainsi.

16. Et-il-fit, LUI-les-Dieux, cette-duité (cette gémination, ce couple) declartés-extérieures les-grandes : l'ipséité-de-la-lumière-centrale, la-grande, pour-représenter-symboliquement le-jour (la-manifestation universelle), et-l'ipséité-de-la-lumière-centrale la-petite, pour-représenter symboliquement-la-nuit (la négation-manifestée) ; et-l'ipséité-des-étoiles (facultés virtuelles de l'univers).

---

gories, in parables; to present a similitude, an emblem, a figure. This verb is produced from the root שׁי which, containing in itself every idea of parity, similitude and representation, is joined to the signs מ and ל, to express its exterior action and its relative movement In the phrase with which we are occupied, this verb is used according to the intensive form, and consequently invested with the continued facultative of the sign מ, which doubles the force of its action.

The word ▽2ᐞ 𐤀, made use of by the Samaritan version in this instance, signifies likewise *to speak allegorically, to use parables.*

וְאֶת־הַכּוֹכָבִים, *and-the-selfsameness-of-the-stars....* The word כֹּכָב, vulgarly translated *star*, is composed of the root כֹּה, which is related to every idea of strength and of virtue, physically as well as morally, and of the mysterious root אָב which develops the idea of the fe-

17. Wa-îtthen âotham Ælohîm bi-rekîwha ha-shamaîm l'haîr hal-ha-âretz.

וַיִּתֵּן אֹתָם אֱלֹהִים בִּרְקִיעַ הַשָּׁמָיִם לְהָאִיר עַל־הָאָרֶץ׃

18. W'li-meshol ba-îôm w'-ba-laîlah w'l'habeddîl beîn ha-âôr w'beîn ha-hoshech, wa-îeræ Ælohîm chî-tôb.

וְלִמְשֹׁל בַּיּוֹם וּבַלַּיְלָה וּלְהַבְדִּיל בֵּין הָאוֹר וּבֵין הַחֹשֶׁךְ וַיַּרְא אֱלֹהִים כִּי־טוֹב׃

19. Wa-îehî hereb, wa-îehî boker, îôm rebîhî.

וַיְהִי־עֶרֶב וַיְהִי־בֹקֶר יוֹם רְבִיעִי׃

20. Wa-îâomer Ælohîm îshertzoû ha-maîm sheretz nephesh haîah, w'hoph îwhopheph hal-ha-âretz, hal-pheneî rekîwha ha-shamaîm.

וַיֹּאמֶר אֱלֹהִים יִשְׁרְצוּ הַמַּיִם שֶׁרֶץ נֶפֶשׁ חַיָּה וְעוֹף יְעוֹפֵף עַל־הָאָרֶץ עַל־פְּנֵי רְקִיעַ הַשָּׁמָיִם׃

---

cundation of the universe. Thus according to the figurative and hieroglyphic sense, the word כוכב signifies not only *star*, but *the virtual and fecundating force* of the universe. Therein can be found the germ of many ancient ideas, whether relative to astrological science, concerning which it is known that the Egyptians thought highly, or whether relative to the Hermetic science. As my intention is not, at this time, to comment upon the thought of Moses, I shall not draw from the explanation of this hieroglyphist, all the inferences that I might; I am satisfied to do in this instance as I have already done, and as I shall be forced to do more and more, that is, giving only the literal and figurative meaning, and as much as is possible for me, the hieroglyphic, leaving to the sagacity of the reader the task of making the applications. The Samaritan and Chaldaic versions do not differ here from the Hebrew.

17. And-he-laid-out them, HE-the-Gods, in-the-dilating-power (ethereal expanse) of-heavens, for-c a u s i n g-brightness (intellectual light)-to-shine (perceptibly) upon-the-earth.

18. And-for-acting (as symbolical types) in-the-day and in-the-night; and-for-causing-a-separation-to-be-made betwixt the-light and betwixt the-darkness: and-he-did-ken, HE-the-Being-of-beings, that-as-good.

19. And-there-was-west-eve, a n d-t h e r e-was-east-dawn, d a y-t h e-f o u r t h (light's fourth mainfestation.)

20. And-he-said, HE-the-Gods, (declaring his will) shall-spring-forth-plentifully, the-waters, the-plentiful-wormlike soul-of-life and the-fowl flying-about above-the-earth on-the-face of-the-ethereal-expanse-of-heavens.

17. Et-il-préposa elles, LUI-les-Dieux, dans-la-force-raréfiante (l'expansion éthérée) des-cieux, pour-exciter-la-lumière (élémentisation intellectuelle)-à-briller-d'une-manière sensible, sur-la-terre.

18. Et-pour-représenter-symboliquement dans-le-jour et-dans-la-n u i t; et-p o u r-faire-le-partage entre-la-lumière et-entre-l'obscurité: et-il-vit, LUI-l'Être-des-êtres, cela-ainsi-bon.

19. Et-fut-occident, et-fut-orient, jour-quatrième (quatrième manifestation phénoménique).

20. Et-il-d i t, L U I-l e s Dieux, (déclarant sa volonté): origineront-à-foisons, les-eaux, l'originante-vermiforme âme-de-vie et-le-volatile veloci-volant au-dessus-de-la-terre sur-la-face de-l'expansion-éthérée-des-cieux.

---

v. 17. וַיִּתֵּן, *And-he-laid-out....* This is the verb נהן *to set forth, to put, to leave;* which, employed according to the intensive form, as on this occasion, signifies *to assign, to lay out, to ordain.*

v. 18 and 19. There is nothing more to observe here than what has already been said.

v. 20. וַיֹּאמֶר, *And-he-said...* I refer the reader to v. 3. of this chapter, and beg also to call attention to the effect of the convertible sign ו, which turns the future to the past. It is very important in

50 THE HEBRAIC TONGUE RESTORED

21. Wa-îberâ Ælohîm æth-ha-thanînîm ha-gheddolîm, w'æth-chol-nephesh ha-haîah ha-romesheth âsher shartzoû ha-maîm le-mînehem w'æth-chol-hoph chanaph le-mîne-hou, wa-îaræ Ælohîm chitôb.

וַיִּבְרָא אֱלֹהִים אֶת־הַתַּנִּינִים הַגְּדֹלִים וְאֵת כָּל־נֶפֶשׁ הַחַיָּה הָרֹמֶשֶׂת אֲשֶׁר שָׁרְצוּ הַמַּיִם לְמִינֵהֶם וְאֵת כָּל־עוֹף כָּנָף לְמִינֵהוּ וַיַּרְא אֱלֹהִים כִּי־טוֹב:

---

this instance where, (the modern tongues not permitting in any fashion an imitation of this hieroglyphic trope) I am constantly obliged to put in the simple past that which, in Hebrew, is in the convertible future.

יִשְׁרְצוּ, *shall-spring-forth-plentifully*.... The Samaritan version says ᛋᛟᛏᛋᚱ ᚻᛗᛋ ᛋᛟᛏᛋᚱᚻᛗ, *the waters shall emit prolifically in prolific emission*... The Chaldaic targum gives ירחשׁין מיא רחשׁא *the waters shall ferment a ferment*.... Thus can be seen that even in the literal sense, the Hellenists have been weak, for in saying ἐξαγαγέτω τὰ ὕδατα ἑρπετά, *the waters shall bring forth reptiles*, they have distorted not only the thought, but the expression of Moses, which has here a picturesque forcefulness. The verb שׁרוֹץ which he employs, springs from two contracted roots שׁר־רץ; the first, שׁר, composed of the signs of relative and proper movement, or circular and rectilinear, indicates an emission, a liberation, a detachment, a separation. The second, רץ, characterizes a sort of movement, of vibration, recommencing and finishing, reptilian, being propagated by being divided: thus the compound שׁרץ contains every idea of propagative emission, of motive origin, of generative separation. This is the figurative and hieroglyphic meaning. In the literal sense, it is a reptilian movement, and in a wholly restricted and materialized sense, *a reptile*.

עוֹף, *fowl*.... This expression, which depends still upon the verb יִשְׁרְצוּ, *shall-spring-forth*, and which is connected with the substantive הַמַּיִם, *the waters*, proves, as the authors of the Samaritan version and the Chaldaic targum have very well perceived, that Moses regarded the waters as specially charged with furnishing the first elements of vital movement to reptilian and flying animals. The root רץ, of which I spoke above and the one now in question, are both linked to this same motive principle designated by the root שׁר; but whereas, by

21. And-he-did-frame-out, HE-the-Being-of-beings, the-selfsameness-of those-huge-bulked-bodies, the-largest (flocking throngs of enormous whales) and-that-of-all-soul of-life, trailing-along and-swimming, which produced-plentifully the-waters after-the-kinds-their-own; and-that-of-all-quick and strong-winged-fowl, after-the-kind-its-own: and-he-did-ken, H E-t h e-G o d s, that-as-good.	21. Et-il-produisit-et-forma (il créa), LUI-l'Être-des-êtres l-existence-individuelle d e-ces-amplitudes-c o r p o-relles les-grandes (légions de monstres marins), et-celle-de-toute-âme d e-v i e mouvante d'un mouvement-contractile, laquelle originaient-à-foisons les-eaux; selon-l'espèce-à-eux; et-celle-de-tout-volatile à l'aile-forte-et-rapide, selon-l'espèce-sienne; et-il-vit, LUI-les-Dieux, cela-ainsi-bon.

רץ, should be understood, a laborious movement attached to the earth, by עיף, should be seen, an easy, soaring movement in the air. The one is heavy and rapid, the other light and swift. Both receive existence from the vital principle brought forth by the waters.

This verse and the one following, present in Hebrew, a series of expressions whose harmony and force are inimitable. The Samaritan version gives the same impression, as the copy of a picture by Raphael would produce compared with the original.

v. 21. התנינים, *those-huge-bulked-bodies*.... This word is derived from the root נון, which contains every idea of extension, of amplification in bodies, whether in number or in volume. This root, governed by the sign of reciprocity ת, is applied to cetacea, and in general, to marine animals, either on account of their mass, or on account of their prodigious fecundity.

נפש חיה, *soul-of-life*.... The word נפש, which is used by Moses to designate, in general, the soul and the animating life of being, merits much more serious attention, as this great man has been accused by very superficial writers who have never read him, or by very prejudiced sectarians who have read him only to misunderstand him, of having denied the existence of this spiritual essence.

The root from which the word נפש comes, is without doubt

52   THE HEBRAIC TONGUE RESTORED

22. Wa-îbareċh aôtham Ælohîm l'æmor, phroû w'reboû w'milaoû æth-ha-maîm ba-îamîm w'ha-hoph îreb ba-âretz. וַיְבָרֶךְ אֹתָם אֱלֹהִים לֵאמֹר פְּרוּ וּרְבוּ וּמִלְאוּ אֶת־הַמַּיִם בַּיַּמִּים וְהָעוֹף יִרֶב בָּאָרֶץ׃

23. Wa-îhî-herb, wa-îhî-boker, îôm hamîshî. וַיְהִי־עֶרֶב וַיְהִי־בֹקֶר יוֹם חֲמִישִׁי׃

---

material, for there is no word possible, in any tongue possible, whose elements are not material. As I have said in my Grammar it is the noun which is the basis of speech. Everytime that man wishes to express an intellectual and moral thought, he is obliged to make use of a physical instrument, and to take from elementary nature, material objects which he spiritualizes, as it were, in making them pass, by means of metaphor or hieroglyphic, from one region into another.

Three distinct roots compose this important word and are worthy of the closest attention. The first נִ presents the idea of an inspiration, an infusion, a movement operated from without, within: it is literally *an inspiring breath*. The second פַה, which is only the reaction of the first, is attached to the idea of expansion, of effusion, of movement operated from within, without: it is literally *the mouth, the expiring breath, the voice, the speech*, etc. The third finally אש, characterizes the *principiant principle* of which I have already spoken in v.l. of this chapter. It is *fire*, and that which is igneous, ardent, impassioned, etc.

Such is the hieroglyphic composition of the word נפש, *the soul*, which, formed of the three roots נִ־פַה־אש, presents the symbolic image of a thing that the Egyptian priests regarded as belonging to a triple nature. This is known to be the idea of Pythagoras and Plato, who had drawn it from the Egyptian sanctuaries. Those priests, instructors of Moses, saw in נִ, the *partie naturante* of the soul, in פַה the *partie naturée*, and in אש, the *partie naturelle*. From this elementary triad resulted a unity whose immortality they taught, according to all the ancient sages.

22. And-he-blessed-them, HE-the-Being-of-beings, pursuing-to-say: beget and-multiply, and-fill the-waters in-the-seas; and-the-fowl shall-multiply in-the-earth.

22. Et-il-bénit-eux, LUI-l'Être-des-êtres, en-disant: propagez et-multipliez-vous, et-remplissez les-eaux, dans les-mers, et-l'espèce-volatile se-multipliera en-la-terre.

23. And-there-was-west-eve, and-there-was-east-dawn (over and back again), day the-fifth, (light's fifth manifestation).

23. Et-fut-occident, et-fut-orient (libération et itération), jour cinquième (cinquième manifestation phénoménique).

The Hebrew text, the Samaritan version, the Chaldaic targum, and even the Syriac and Arabic, employ the same word; only, they give, following their genius, different significations to the verb which is formed of it. Among the Hebrews, נפש signifies *to live* and *breathe;* among the Chaldeans, *to grow, to multiply, to fill space;* the Samaritan verb ᵚᴊᴊ, expresses *to dilate, to develop, to manifest;* the Syriac ܪܘܚ *to give life, to heal;* the Arabic نفش , *to expand, to evaporate,* etc.

הרמשת, *trailing-along and-swimming....* By the word רמש Moses intends, in general, all animal kind, the individuals of which either aquatic, or terrestrial, lack the exterior members which support bipeds and quadrupeds, or which serve them only in *trailing,* after the manner of reptiles, or *swimming,* after the manner of fishes. This word proceeds from the root מש, which expresses that which touches itself, gathers to itself, or withdraws into itself; a root to which the sign ר is used only to give a new motive force.

v.22. פרו ורבו ומלאו *beget, and-multiply, and-fill....* Here are the roots of these three verbs: פר, generative movement, in general; in particular a bull, symbol of generation; in the Arabic فرا , a wild ass: רב that which is great, abundant, extended, either in number or in volume: מל, that which is full, that which has attained its highest elevation. See, Rad. Vocab.

v.23. All these terms are understood.

24. Wa-îaomer Ælohîm, thôtzæ ha-âretz nephesh haîah le-mine-ha, behemah wa-remesh w'haîthô-æretz le-mîne-ha, wa-îhî-chen.

וַיֹּאמֶר אֱלֹהִים תּוֹצֵא הָאָרֶץ נֶפֶשׁ חַיָּה לְמִינָהּ בְּהֵמָה וָרֶמֶשׂ וְחַיְתוֹ־אֶרֶץ לְמִינָהּ וַיְהִי־כֵן:

25. Wa-îahash Ælohîm æth-haîath ha-âretz le-mîne-ha, w'æth-ha-behemah le-mîne-ha, w'æth-chol-remesh ha-âdamah le-mîne-hou, wa-îara Ælohîm chi-tôb.

וַיַּעַשׂ אֱלֹהִים אֶת חַיַּת הָאָרֶץ לְמִינָהּ וְאֶת־הַבְּהֵמָה לְמִינָהּ וְאֶת־כָּל־רֶמֶשׂ הָאֲדָמָה לְמִינֵהוּ וַיַּרְא אֱלֹהִים כִּי־טוֹב:

---

v.24. הוֹצֵא, *shall-yield-forth*.... See v. 12.

בְּהֵמָה, *quadrupeds*.... That is to say, according to the idea of Moses, that part of the animal kingdom whose individuals are neither winged as birds, nor crawling nor swimming as the terrestrial reptiles or the fishes. For it is obvious that this hierographic writer divides the animal kingdom into three great series according to the locomotive movement which he points out in the divers kinds which compose this kingdom.

The first of this great series, comprises the animals of the first origin, vermiform, crawling upon the earth, swimming in the waters or flying in the air, which he calls, in general שֶׁרֶץ חַיָּה, *primitive life, vermiform*. He divides this first series into two kinds: the aquatic and the aerial kind. The first of these kinds, retains the original name שֶׁרֶץ, that is to say *vermiform;* the second is called עוֹף עוֹפֵף *fowl-flying*.

The second of this great series consists of the animals of the second origin, which Moses designates in general, by the name of נֶפֶשׁ חַיָּה *soul of life*. These are the genera which are distinguished from the first original series, by their bulk, their strength and the different relations which they already have with terrestrial animals. The marine animals of this series are called תַּנִּינִים, *the-huge-bulked-bodies*: the aerials bear the name of עוֹף כָּנָף, that is to say, *quick-and-strong-winged-fowl*.

Finally, the third series is composed of animals called, in general,

COSMOGONY OF MOSES

24. And-he-said, HE-the-Gods, shall-yield-forth, the-earth, a-soul-of-life (an animality) according-to-the-kind-its-own, quadrupedly-walking and-creeping, and-earthly-living, after-the-kind-its-own: and-it-was-so.

25. And-he-made, HE-the-Gods, that-life earth-born, according-to-the - kind - its - own, and-the-quadruped-existence after - the - kind - its-own, and-all-trailing-along-motion from-the-adamic (homogeneal)-ground, after-the-kind-its-own; and-he-did-ken, HE-the Being-of-beings, that-as-good.

24. Et-il-dit, L U I-les-Dieux fera-provenir-la-terre, une-âme-de-vie (une animalité), selon-l'espèce-sienne, quadrupède (à la marche élevée et bruyante) se-mouvant et-vivant-d'une-vie-terrestre, selon-l'espèce-sienne: et-cela-fut-ainsi.

25. E t-i l-f i t, L U I-l e s-Dieux, cette-animalité terrestre, selon-l'espèce-sienne, et-ce-genre-quadrupède selon l'espèce sienne, et-l'universalité de-tout-mouvement-vital de-l'élément-adamique (homogène), selon l'espèce-sienne; et-il-vit, LUI-l'Être-des-êtres, cela-ainsi-bon.

חיתו־ארץ, *terrestrial animality.* In this series are contained all the terrestrial animals whose locomotive movement is neither trailing, nor swimming, nor flying; but which is executed progressively by the aid of appropriate members. This series contains also two particular genera; namely, the animals which creep along like lizards, רמש, and those which support themselves like quadrupeds, called בהמה. I have already explained the first of these names, which is applied to whatever moves itself by a trailing and contractile movement. As to the second, it is formed from the root בא, expressing all progressive and sustained movement, and from the onomatopoeia הם, which depicts that which is raised and loud.

Before finishing this note I wish to say that these three classes of animals, considered abstractly, and under figure of three moral beings, have been named by the Hebrew poets: לוייתן, *Leviathan;* that is to say, the universality of marine monsters; עין, *Hozan,* the universality of birds; and בהמות, *Behemoth,* the universality of terrestrial animals. The savants who sought for the signification of

26. Wa-îâomer Ælohîm nahasheh Adam be-tzalle-me-noû chi-de-mouthe-noû, w'îreddou bi-deggath ha-îam-w'be-hoph ha-shamaîm, w'-ba-behemah, w'bechol-ha-âretz w'be-chol-ha-remesh ha-romesh hal-ha-âretz.

וַיֹּאמֶר אֱלֹהִים נַעֲשֶׂה אָדָם בְּצַלְמֵנוּ כִּדְמוּתֵנוּ וְיִרְדּוּ בִדְגַת הַיָּם וּבְעוֹף הַשָּׁמַיִם וּבַבְּהֵמָה וּבְכָל־הָאָרֶץ וּבְכָל־הָרֶמֶשׂ הָרֹמֵשׂ עַל־הָאָרֶץ :

---

these words, brought into their researches too much scholastic prejudice to draw from it any fruit.

I shall refrain from saying anything in regard to the three grand divisions which Moses established in the animal kingdom; I shall only observe that there is as much precision and more true philosophy in drawing methodical distinctions from the kind of movement in animals, as there is in drawing these same distinctions from their legs or from the temperature of their blood.

v. 25. האדמה, *from the-adamic-ground....* See following note.

v. 26. אדם, *Adam....* I beg those who are reading this without partiality, to observe that Moses does not fall here into the modern error which has made of man a particular species in the animal kingdom; but only after having finished all that he wished to say concerning the elementary, the vegetable and the animal kingdom, he passes on to a kingdom distinct and higher that he names אדם, Adam.

Among the savants who have searched for the etymology of the word *Adam*, the majority went no further than its grossest exterior; nearly all of them have seen only red clay, or simple clay, because the word אדֹם, signifies *red* or *reddish;* because by ארמה, *the earth* in general, has been understood; but they have failed to see that these words themselves are compounds, and that they can only be the roots of words still more compound; whereas the word אדם being more simple cannot come from it.

The Egyptian priests, authors of this mysterious name, and of a

COSMOGONY OF MOSES 57

26. And-he-said, HE-the-Gods, (declaring his will) we-will-make *Adam* in-the-shadow-of-us, by-the-like-making-like-ourselves; and-they-shall-hold- the - sceptre, (they shall rule, they, *Adam,* universal man) in-the-spawn breeding-kind- of - the - seas, and-in-the-flying-kind of-the-heavens, and-in-the quadrupedly-walking-kind, and-in-the-whole- earth - born - life, and - in - all - moving - thing crawling - along upon - the - earth.

26. Et-il-dit, L U I - l e s-Dieux (déclarant sa volonté), nous-ferons *Adam* en-ombre-nôtre, comformément -à - l'action - assimilante - à - nous : et - ils - tiendront - le - sceptre, (ils régneront, eux, *Adam,* l'-homme universel), dans-les-poissons des-mers, et - dans - les - oiseaux des - cieux, et-dans-le-genre-quadrupéde, et dans-toute-l' animalité-terrestre, et-dans-toute-mouvante-vie se-mouvant-sur-la-terre.

---

great part of those employed by Moses, have composed it with an infinite art. It presents three meanings, as do the greater part of those which enter into the composition of the Beræshith. The first, which is the literal meaning, has been restricted more and more, in proportion as the ideas of the Hebrews have been narrowed and materialized; so that it is doubtful whether it was understood in its purity even at the epoch of the Babylonian captivity, at least by the vulgar. The Samaritan version, the most ancient of all, is also the one which conserves best its signification. It is seen in the efforts made by the translator to find a corresponding expression. After having copied the name itself אָדָם , he sought a synonym for it in אֱנוֹשׁ , *man;* but feeling that this synonym did not render the Hebrew, he chose the word אֲצִילוּת , *universal, infinite:* an opportune word which proves the anteriority and the superiority of the Samaritan version over the Chaldaic targum; for the author of this targum, in interpreting אָדָם, does not go beyond the material meaning and confines himself constantly to the word אֱנָשָׁא, *man.* The Hellenists who follow quite voluntarily the Samaritan have abandoned it on this occasion. They would have exposed too much the spiritual meaning which they wished to hide. They were content to copy the Chaldaic and translate אָדָם , by ἄνθρωπος, *man;* in which they have been imitated by Saint Jerome and his successors.

27. Wa-îberâ Ælohîm aeth-ha-Adam, be-tzallem-ô, be-tzellem Ælohîm barâ âoth-ô, zachar w'nekebah barâ âoth'am.

וַיִּבְרָא אֱלֹהִים אֶת־הָאָדָם בְּצַלְמוֹ בְּצֶלֶם אֱלֹהִים בָּרָא אֹתוֹ זָכָר וּנְקֵבָה בָּרָא אֹתָם :

The name given to Adam אדם, signifies not only "homo," *man*, but it characterizes, as the Samaritan had clearly seen in rendering it by ᴔ32ᴠ, *universal*, that which we understand by mankind, and which we would express much better by saying *kingdom of man*: it is collective man, man abstractly formed of the assemblage of all men. This is the literal meaning of אדם.

The figurative meaning is indicated by the constant practice which Moses follows, of making the noun always accompanied by a verb from the same root. Now what is the verb here which follows the word אדם? It is דמות, used constructively in the enunciative nominal, inflected by the assimilative article כ and bearing the affix of the first person plural כדמותנו: that is to say, word-for-word and grammatically, *conformable-to-our-action-of-assimilàting*. This comparison of the verb and the noun, gives us the root from which both spring. This root is דם which carries with itself every idea of assimilation, of similitude, of homogeneity. Governed by the sign of power and stability א, it becomes the image of an immortal assimilation, of an aggregation of homogeneous and indestructible parts. Such is the etymology of the name *Adam*, אדם, in its figurative sense.

I shall enlarge less upon the hieroglyphic meaning, which Moses allows nevertheless, to be understood in the same verse, and to which he makes allusion, by causing this same noun, which is singular, to govern the future plural verb ירדו : quite contrary to the rule which he had followed, of making the noun of the Being of Beings אלהים which is plural, govern always the singular verb. The hieroglyphic root of the name *Adam*, אדם is אד, which, composed of the sign of unitary, principiant power, and that of divisibility, offers the image of a relative unity, such as might be expressed, for example, by means of the simple although compound number 10. This root being endowed with the collective sign ם, assumes an unlimited develop-

COSMOGONY OF MOSES

27. And-he-did-frame-out, HE-the-Gods, the-self-sameness-of-*Adam*, (original similitude, collective unity, universal man), in-the-shadow-his-own, in-the-shadow-of HIM-the-Being-of beings, he-created-him (Adam); male and-female he-created the-universal-self-of-them.

27. Et-il-créa, LUI-les-Dieux, l'ipséité-d' *Adam* (similitude première, unité collective, homme universel) en-ombre-sienne, en-ombre-de LUI-l'Être-des-êtres, il-créa-lui (Adam); mâle et-femelle il-créa l'existence-universelle-à-eux.

ment: that is to say, the symbolic number 10, being taken to represent the root אר, the sign ם will develop its progressive power to infinity, as 10; 100; 1000; 10,000, etc.

בצלמנו *in-the-shadow-universal-ours*.... This figurative expression, very difficult to render was already materialized at the epoch when the Samaritan version was written. Here is the sentence word-for-word.

ᚴᛆᛃ · ᛆᛑᚾᛃ · ᛆ2ᚾ · ᛃᛉᚾᛑ · "And-he-said," HE GOD, "let-us-
ᛃᚾᛉᛒ━ᚾᛉᛑ · ᛃᚾᛃᛉᛆ · "work-upon Adam, in-the-form-
"exterior-ours, and after-the-ac-
"tion-ours-of-us-composing."

The Chaldaic targum copies the Hebrew; but everything proves that it is misinterpreted. The Hellenists say, κατ' εἰκόνα, *in the image*; the Hebraic root צל is obvious; it expresses always an idea of a shadow thrown upon something, a veil, an appearance, a protection. The collective sign ם, which terminates the word צלם, universalizes its meaning.

כדמותנו, *by-the-like-making-like-ourselves*.... I have already explained the root of this verb and its composition.

v. 27 זכר ונקבה, *male and female*.... The root of the first of these words is כר, which expresses that which is apparent, eminent; that which serves as monument or as character, to preserve the memory of things. It is the elementary root אר united to the assimilative sign כ, and ruled by the demonstrative sign ז.

The second of these words has for root קב, whose meaning, entirely opposed to that of כר, is applied to that which is hidden and not apparent; to that which is graven, hollowed out, enveloped. The sign נ which rules it is the image of passive action.

28. Wa-îbareċh âoth'am Ælohîm, wa-îâomer la-hem Æ l o h î m, p h r o û w'reboû w'milâoû æth-ha-âretz w'ċhi-beshu-ha, w'redoû bi-deg-gath ha-îam w'bi-hôph ha-shamaîm, w'bi-ċhol-haîah ha-romesheth hal-ha-âretz.

וַיְבָרֶךְ אֹתָם אֱלֹהִים וַיֹּאמֶר לָהֶם אֱלֹהִים פְּרוּ וּרְבוּ וּמִלְאוּ אֶת־הָאָרֶץ וְכִבְשֻׁהָ וּרְדוּ בִּדְגַת הַיָּם וּבְעוֹף הַשָּׁמַיִם וּבְכָל־חַיָּה הָרֹמֶשֶׂת עַל הָאָרֶץ׃

29. Wa-îâomer Ælohîm, h i n n e h nathathî la-ċhem æth-ċhol-hesheb zoreha ze-rah âsher hal-pheneî ċhol-ha-âretz, w'æth-ċhol ha-hetz âsher-b'ô pherî, hetz zoreha zerah la-ċhem îhîeh la-âċhe-lah.

וַיֹּאמֶר אֱלֹהִים הִנֵּה נָתַתִּי לָכֶם אֶת־כָּל־עֵשֶׂב זֹרֵעַ זֶרַע אֲשֶׁר עַל־פְּנֵי כָל־הָאָרֶץ וְאֶת־כָּל־הָעֵץ אֲשֶׁר־בּוֹ פְרִי עֵץ זֹרֵעַ זָרַע לָכֶם יִהְיֶה לְאָכְלָה׃

30. W'l-ċhol-haîah ha-âretz, w'l-ċhol-hôph ha-sha-maîm, w'l'ċhol-romesh hal-ha-âretz, âsher b'ô nephesh haîah, æth-ċhol îerek hesheb l'âċhelah, wa-îhî-ċhen.

וּלְכָל־חַיַּת הָאָרֶץ וּלְכָל־עוֹף הַשָּׁמַיִם וּלְכָל־רוֹמֵשׂ עַל־הָאָרֶץ אֲשֶׁר־בּוֹ נֶפֶשׁ חַיָּה אֶת־כָּל־יֶרֶק עֵשֶׂב לְאָכְלָה וַיְהִי־כֵן׃

It must be observed that the verb ברא, *to create*, which in the Hebrew text, expresses the action of the Supreme Being creating man male and female, is rendered in the Samaritan version by ᛉᛉ, which, as can be judged by the Hebrew and Chaldaic analogue כון, preserved in Syriac and Ethiopic, signifies *to identify, to naturalize*.

v. 28. וַיְבָרֶךְ, *and-he-blessed*.... The root רך contains the idea of bending, of extenuation, of feeling compassion, physically as well as morally. This root, become verb, signifies in the Samaritan ᛉᛉ

COSMOGONY OF MOSES

28. And-he-blessed the-self-sameness-of-them (universal) HE-the-Gods, and-he-said unto-them: beget and-multiply and-fill the-earth; and-subdue-it, and-hold-the sceptre (rule) in-the-fish of-the-seas, and-in-the-fowl of-h e a v e n s, and-in-all-life crawling-along u p o n-the-earth.

29. And-he-said, HE-the-Being-of-beings: behold! I-h a v e-given-unto-you t h e-whole grass seed-yielding-seed which-is upon-the-face of-all-the-earth, and-the-vegetable-substance which-has in-itself fruit; substance seed-y i e l d i n g-seed to-you shall-be-for food.

30. And-unto-all-animal-ity earth-born, and-unto all-fowl of-heavens, and-unto-all-moving-life c r e e p i n g-along upon-the-earth, which has-in-i t s e l f an-animated-breath-and-living, (I have given) the-whole verdant grass for-food: and-it-was-so.

28. Et-il-bénit l'existence-universelle-à-eux, LUI-les-Dieux, et-il-dit-à-eux: engendrez et-multipliez et-remplissez la-terre et-captivez-la, et-tenez-le-gouvernail (régnez) dans-le-poisson des-mers, et-dans-l'oiseau des-cieux, et-dans-toute-chose mouvante-d'un-mouvement-vital sur-la-terre.

29. Et-il-dit, LUI-l'Être-des-êtres; voici! J'ai-donné-à-vous en-totalité l'herbe germinant-g e r m e qui-est sur-la-face de-toute-la-terre, et-en-totalité la-substance-végétale qui-a-dans-soi fruit; substance germinant-germe, à-vous sera pour-aliment.

30. Et-à-toute-vie de-la-terre, et-à-tout-volatile des-cieux, et-à-tout-être repti-forme-se-t r a î n a n t sur-la-terre, qui-a dans-soi souffle-animé de-vie, (j'ai-donné) en-t o t a l i t é la-verdoyante herbe pour aliment: et-cela-fut-ainsi.

---

or in the Arabic كرب, the action of bending, of extending the hands over someone. It is, by employing this word with the paternal sign ב, image of active and interior action, that the verb בָּרַךְ *to bless*, has been formed; properly speaking, it is to lay on the hands with a paternal sentiment of tenderness and kindness.

31. Wa-îaræ Ælohîm æth-chol-âsher w'hinneh-tôb mâ-ôd, wa-îhî-hereb, wa-îhî-boker, îôm-ha-shîshî.

וַיַרְא אֱלֹהִים אֶת־כָּל־אֲשֶׁר עָשָׂה וְהִנֵּה־טוֹב מְאוֹד וַיְהִי־עֶרֶב וַיְהִי־בֹקֶר יוֹם הַשִּׁשִּׁי׃

---

v. 29. עץ, *vegetable-substance*.... This important word which the Hellenists have rendered by ξύλον, *wood*, will be explained further on, when it will be more essential to penetrate its real meaning.

אכלה, *food*.... This word will also be explained in its place.

v. 30. It should be observed in this verse, that the Supreme Being, speaking of the food accorded to animals, makes no mention of the substance עץ, of which he had spoken in the preceding verse with respect to man. The very profound reason for this reticence will later on be shown.

v. 31. מאד, *as-much-as-possible*.... That is to say, filling its fixed and determined unity, its whole measure. This word springs from the root אד, רד or חד, *unity*, the power of divisibility. It is governed by the determining, local and plastic sign, מ.

31. And-he-did-ken, HE-the-Gods, the-whole-that-he-had-made, and-lo! good as-much-as-possible (in its own nature) : and - there - was - west-eve, and-there-was-east-dawn (over and back again), day the-sixth (light's sixth manifestation).	31. Et-il-vit, LUI-les-Dieux, ce-tout lequel il-avait-fait, et-voici! bon autant-que-possible (selon sa mesure), et-fut-occident, et-fut-orient (libération et itération) jour sixième (sixième manifestation phénoménique).

I have not dwelt upon the Hebrew words which enter into the composition of the last verses of this chapter, because they offer no grammatical difficulty. I might have expatiated at length, if I had wished to comment upon them; but, for the moment, it is enough to re-establish the meaning of the words and to explain what may have been obscure, without examining in particular all the inferences that might be drawn.

SEPHER BERÆSHITH B.

סֵפֶר בְּרֵאשִׁית ב ·

1. Wa-îchuloû ha-shamaîm w'ha-âretz, w'chol-tzebâ'am.

וַיְכֻלּוּ הַשָּׁמַיִם וְהָאָרֶץ וְכָל־צְבָאָם :

2. Wa-îchal Ælohîm ba-îom ha-shebîhî melacheth-ô âsher hasah, wa-îsheboth ba-îôm ha-shebîhî mi-chol milâcheth-ô âsher hashah.

וַיְכַל אֱלֹהִים בַּיּוֹם הַשְּׁבִיעִי מְלַאכְתּוֹ אֲשֶׁר עָשָׂה וַיִּשְׁבֹּת בַּיּוֹם הַשְּׁבִיעִי מִכָּל־מְלַאכְתּוֹ אֲשֶׁר עָשָׂה :

---

v. 1. ויכלו, and-(shall become)-thus-were-wholly-finished.... This is the verb כלה, employed according to the passive movement of the enunciative form, convertible future. The word כל, *the whole*, from which it is derived, is composed of the assimilative sign כ, united to the root לל, containing the idea of that which is raised, stretched to infinity, without limits. It is important to observe here, the future tense turned to the past. This trope is hieroglyphic.

The Samaritan makes use of the verb ᛉᛉᚹ, *to complete, to achieve*, employed according to the reflexive form ᚺᛉᚹᛖᛖᚫ, *they were achieved; they were made perfect*. That which is always attached to the idea contained in the initial word בראשית, and marks a successive development, a passing from power into action.

צבאם, *and-the-ruling-law-of-them*........ This remarkable word has not been understood by any of the translators. The Hellenists have said ὁ κόσμος, and the Latins "ornatus." The Samaritans have translated ᛉᛘᚹᛈᚫᚾ, *the parts, the divisions, the distributions*. The Chaldaic targum reads חיליהון, *the force, the universal faculty, the army*. This is only the material meaning.

The roots of the Hebrew word employed in this place by Moses, are צי, which contains within itself every idea of order, of commandment, of direction impressed toward an end, and בא, which

COSMOGONY OF MOSES

GENESIS II

1. And-(shall become) thus- were - wholly - finished (completed) the - heavens and-the-earth, and-the-whole ruling - law - of - them (elementizing nature).

2. And-he-fulfilled, HE-the-Gods, in-the light's manifestation-the-seventh, the-sovereign-work (act of his almighty power) which-he-had-performed; and-he-restored-himself, (he returned in his former divine self) in-t h e-l i g h t' s-manifestation the-seventh, from-the-whole-sovereign-work - which - he - had-performed.

COSMOGONIE II

1. Et-(seront) ainsi-furent - accomplis (totalisés, parfaits) les-cieux et-la-terre, et-toute l'ordonnance-conductrice-à-eux (la nature régulatrice).

2. Et-il-accomplit, LUI-les-Dieux, dans la-manifestation-phénoménique la-septième, l'acte-souverain qu'il-avait-exercé; et-il-se-restitua (il se rétablit dans son ineffable séité) la-manifestation - lumineuse - universelle la-septième, après-tout-l'acte-de-sa-souveraine-puissance, qu'il-avait-exercé.

---

expresses every organizing and efficient will. The entire word צבא is related to law, to innate, principiant force, to universal nature finally, which being developed with the universe, must lead it from power into action, and raise it from development to development to its absolute perfection.

v. 2. מלאכתו, *the-sovereign-work*.... The Samaritan is the sole translator who has understood that this word, 𐡀𐡌𐡋𐡊𐡕𐡅, signifies *a sovereign work accompanied with all royal majesty*. The Hebrew word is obviously derived from the verb מלךֹ *to rule*, whose etymology I have explained sufficiently in my Grammar (ch. VII. §2).

וישבת, *and-he-restored himself*.... This is the root שוב, containing in itself the idea of every kind of re-establishment, of return to a primitive state, united to the sign ת, which is that of sympathy and of reciprocity, sign *par excellence*, and image of per-

3. Wa-îbareĉh Ælohîm æth-îôm ha-shebihî, wa-îkaddesh âoth'-ô ĉhi b'ô shabath mi-ĉhol-melâĉheth-ô âsher barâ Ælohîm, la-hashôth.

וַיְבָרֶךְ אֱלֹהִים אֶת־יוֹם הַשְּׁבִיעִי וַיְקַדֵּשׁ אֹתוֹ כִּי בוֹ שָׁבַת מִכָּל־מְלַאכְתּוֹ אֲשֶׁר־בָּרָא אֱלֹהִים לַעֲשׂוֹת׃

4. Ælleh thô-ledôth ha-shamaîm w'ha-âretz b'hibbarâ'm ba-îom hashôth Ihôah Ælohîm æretz w'shamaîm.

אֵלֶּה תוֹ־לְדוֹת הַשָּׁמַיִם וְהָאָרֶץ בְּהִבָּרְאָם בְּיוֹם עֲשׂוֹת יְהֹוָה אֱלֹהִים אֶרֶץ וְשָׁמָיִם׃

---

fection. The translators who have seen in this verb the idea of resting, have not understood the Hebrew. The error concerning this word has been general, and the Samaritan has been unfortunate enough to render it by ⲠⲤⲰ, which signifies *to rest idle*, as can be seen by the Chaldaic בטל, and the Arabic بطل, which have the same meaning.

השביעי, *the-seventh*.... This is the number of complete restitution, of cyclic fullness. It is true that שבע signifies *seven*, and that שביעי can be taken for *seventh* or *septenary*; but the name of this number draws with it in the Hebraic tongue, the idea of the consummation of things, and of the fullness of times. One of the roots of which it is composed שׁוּב, and of which I am about to speak, expresses the idea of return to the place from which one had departed, and the one which is joined to it by contraction עוּ, indicates every kind of curve, of inversion, of cycle.

The Hebrews make use of the verb שׁבוֹע, to express the oath by virtue of which they affirm that a thing promised will be fulfilled.

All names of number have, in Hebrew, particular and often very deep significations: the abundance of new things upon which I was obliged to dwell in beginning, has forced me to neglect them; but as soon as I shall have more leisure, I shall make amends for my silence in this respect, as well as in some others.

v. 3. All these terms have been explained.

v. 4. תוֹ־לְדוֹת *the sign....of the progenies....* The root תִי contains every idea of sign, of symbol, of hieroglyphic character: it is taken, in a restricted sense, for the same thing symbolized, and for

3. And-he-blessed, HE-the-Gods, that-day the-seventh (seventh light's manifestation); and-he-did-sanctify its-selfsameness, because-that in-it, he-reëstablished-himself (he returned into his unspeakable self), from - the - sovereign - work whereby he-created, HE-the-Being-of-beings, according to-his-performing.

4. Such-is-the-sign (symbolical monument) - of - the progenies of-the-heavens and -of-the-earth, in-their-being-created - them at - the - day, (light's manifestation) of-the-producing of-IHOAH, HE-the-Being-of-beings, earth-and heavens.

3. Et-il-bénit, LUI-les-Dieux, ce-jour le-septième (s e p t i è m e manifestation phénoménique); et-il-sanctifia l'existence-sienne-à-jamais, à-cause-que dans-elle, il-se-restitua (il retourna dans son ineffable séité). après-tout -l'acte - souverain durant lequel-il-avait-créé, LUI-l'Être-des-êtres, s e l o n-l'action-de-faire-à-lui.

4. Tel-est-le-signe (l'emblème, le monument sacré, hiéroglyphique) des-générations - des - cieux et - de - la-terre, dans-l'acte d'être-créés-eux, au-jour (la manifestation lumineuse) de-l'action-de-faire de-IHOAH, LUI-l'Être-des-êtres, la-terre et-les-cieux.

---

that which serves to symbolize: it is then, a narration, a fable, a speech, a table, a book, etc. The Samaritan, Hellenist and Arabic translators have expressed in some degree this important word which the Latins have neglected absolutely.

יהוה, IHOAH.... This is the proper name that Moses gives to GOD. It appears here for the first time, and only when the Being of beings, having accomplished the sovereign act whose thought he had conceived, re-establishes himself in his Immutable Seity. This name is never pronounced by modern Jews in their synagogues, the majority attaching thereunto great mysteries, and especially the rabbis whom we name Kabbalists, on account of the Hebraic word קבל, *the transmission*. By this word, they understand the oral law left by Moses and claim to be the guardians of it: which is true only of a very small part of them. I shall relate presently why both of these, who always read the Hebraic books without points, refuse to pronounce

5. W'chol shîah ha-she-dah terem îhîeh ba-âretz w'chol hesheb ha-shadeh terem îtzemath chi-loâ himetîr IHÔAH Ælohîm hal-haâretz, w'Adam aîn la-habod æth-ha-âdamah.

וְכֹל שִׂיחַ הַשָּׂדֶה טֶרֶם יִהְיֶה בָאָרֶץ וְכָל עֵשֶׂב הַשָּׂדֶה טֶרֶם יִצְמָח כִּי־לֹא הִמְטִיר יְהֹוָה אֱלֹהִים עַל־הָאָרֶץ וְאָדָם אַיִן לַעֲבֹד אֶת־הָאֲדָמָה :

---

this name. Let us now analyze it and see with what infinitely marvellous art it has been composed by Moses, or by the ancient sages who have communicated it to him.

This noun offers first, the sign indicative of life, doubled, and forming the essentially living root הה. This root is never used as noun, and it is the only one which enjoys this prerogative. It is, in its formation, not only a verb, but an unique verb, of which all the other are only derivatives: it is in short, the verb הוה *to-be-being*. Here, as can be seen, and as I have taken pains to explain in my Grammar, the sign of intelligible light ו, is in the middle of the root of life. Moses, taking this verb *par excellence*, to form the proper name of the Being of beings, adds the sign of potential manifestation and of eternity to it, and he obtains יהוה, IHOAH, in which the facultative *being*, is found placed between a past without origin and a future without limit. This wonderful noun therefore, signifies exactly, *the-Being-who-is-who-was-and-who-will-be*.

Sometimes this noun is written אהוה ÆHOAH, and in this case, the sign of potentiality is substituted for that of duration. It becomes much more mysterious as first person of the future, replacing the third, and seems to belong only to the being which bears it and by which it is uttered; then it signifies, *I-the-Being-who-is-who-was-and-who-will-be*.

The Samaritan version does not alter in the least this Divine Name which it renders by ᛫ᛉᛞᛟ. The Chaldaic targum renders it by ייי, the three Eternities, or the Eternity of eternities. The Syriac has ܡܪܝܐ, and the Greek, κύριος, both of which mean *Lord*, or rather according to its etymology, *the Glorious* and *the Luminous*.

Now, let us approach the delicate question of knowing why the Jews of the synagogues and the kabbalistic rabbis either refrain from pronouncing it, or make a mystery of its pronunciation.

COSMOGONY OF MOSES 69

5. And-all-the-produce of-nature before it-will-be in-the-earth; and-all-the-growing-grass of-nature, before-it-will-grow: because-of-not causing-to-rain IHOAH, HE--the-Gods, upon-the-earth; and-*Adam* (collective man) not-being-existing to-labour t h e-a d a m i c-selfsameness (homogeneal ground).

5. Et-toute-la-conception-de-la-nature, avant-qu'elle-existera en-la-terre; et-toute-la-végétation-de-la - nature, avant-qu'elle-germera: car-non-faire pleuvoir IHOAH, LUI-les-Dieux, sur-la-terre; et-*Adam* (l'homme universel) non-être (non-exister en acte) pour-travailler la-substance-adamique (l'élément homogène, similaire à *Adam*).

If one recalls what I have said in my Grammar pertaining to the hardening of the vowels, and their transformation into consonants (ch. II. §. 2), he will not be far from the idea which I have disclosed concerning the ravage that this revolution had brought about in the primitive signification of words. Now, the most important of all the vocal sounds, those whose meaning is the most spiritual, ׳ and ׳, are also those which are most easily influenced by this revolution, and upon which it operates the greatest changes. The changes are such, that these spiritual signs, becoming materialized in the name given to GOD by Moses, this name (pronounced *Jehovah*, according to the Chaldaic punctuation יְהוָֹה), is far from expressing the divine perfections which I have stated, and signifies no more than a calamity, an unfortunate existence, whose origin or whose limit is unknown: for such is the meaning of the word הוה, materialized, as one can be convinced by opening the first Hebrew lexicon.

This is the reason, known or unknown, why the Jewish people are not permitted to utter this Name, and why only the writings without points are admitted in the synagogues; inasmuch as the pronunciation which results from these points, alters sometimes the original signification of the words, rendering them unrecognizable.

As my intention is not to profane the secrets of any sect, I desire that those which I have disclosed thus far, or which I shall reveal as we go on, will disturb no one. If contrary to my expectation, some sectarians are found who might take offense at the publicity which I give to certain mysteries, I repeat to them what I have already inti-

6. W'æd îahaleh min-â-retz w'hishekah æth-chol-pheneî ha-âdamah.   וְאֵד יַעֲלֶה מִן־הָאָרֶץ וְהִשְׁקָה אֶת־כָּל־פְּנֵי הָאֲדָמָה׃

---

mated, that since I did not receive them from any person nor from any society, and have acquired them by my own studies alone, I can publish them without betraying any kind of oath.

v. 5. שִׂיחַ, *the-produce*.... By this word should be understood all creative travail. It springs from the root שׁח, which expresses the effort of the soul toward any goal whatsoever. The facultative שׂיח, which comes from it, signifies *to be-producing* or *uttering one's thoughts*, whether by travail, or by speech. The Hellenists, and Saint Jerome who has followed them, have seen in this word only a tender herb, a shrub; χλωρόν or "virgultum," *a young shoot*.

הַשָּׂדֶה, *of-nature*.... Following this same idea, these translators have seen in the word שָׂדֶה, applied to generative and fostering Nature, only *a field*, thus taking the Hebraic word in its most material and most restricted meaning. But how, in this energetic expression composed of the contracted roots שׁו־די, of which the first שׁ contains the idea of equality and distributive equity, and the second די that of abundance; how, I say, can they not recognize Nature, always ready to load men with her gifts? How fail to see in the word שַׁד, *mammal*, her sacred symbol among the Egyptians? How, with only the slightest attention are they unable to perceive that the name of שַׁדַּי, given to God Himself to express his munificence and the abundance of his gifts, could not be directly formed from that of a field, but from that of Nature? Besides if one examines the corresponding idioms, he will see that the Chaldaic שְׁרָא signifies *fusion; profusion, ejaculation;* that the Syriac ܫܐܕܐ, characterizes *fortune, the demon of the earth; the state* or *nature of things;* that the Arabic شد or شديد indicates that which is constant, firm in its progress; that which is abundant, nourishing; that the Ethiopic ሻዲ (*shadi*) expresses *benignity, good nature*, etc. When one ponders upon these things he can only believe, that the Jews of Alexandria, the Essenes, if they had not had very strong reasons for suppressing the truth,

COSMOGONY OF MOSES 71

6. But-a-virtual-effluence went-up from-out the-earth, and-bedewed that-the-whole-face of-the-adamic (homogeneal ground).	6. Mais-une - émanation-virtuelle s'élevait-avec-énergie du-sein de-la-terre et-abreuvait cette-toute-la-face de l'élément-adamique.

---

would never have rendered the word שדה, terminated here with the emphatic article ה sign of life, by the Greek word ἀγρός, a *field*.

ואדם אין, *and-Adam-not-being*.... It is assuredly difficult to read attentively this verse without finding the convincing proof, that the figurative meaning given to the initial word בראשית is of rigorous exactitude, and that it is indeed, only *in principle*, that the Being of beings had at first determined the creation of the heavens and the earth, containing them תהו ובהו, *in contingent power of being, in another power of being*. It would seem that Moses, wishing to make this profound truth clearly understood, has written designedly the beginning of this chapter. In the first verse, he speaks of the natural law צבאם which must lead this creation of power in action to its highest development. He repeats carefully several times, that this creation has been made לעשות *according to the efficient action of* יהוה אלהים IHOAH, *the Being of beings*. Finally he gives the word, and says openly, that every conception of productive Nature had been created before Nature existed, and all vegetation, before anything had germinated; furthermore, after having announced the formation of Adam, he declared expressly that Adam did not exist, ואדם אין.

It is true that the Hellenist translators have wished to see in the natural law, where the Samaritan version and the Chaldaic targum at least, see *an acting force*, and *a host*, only an embellishment, κόσμος, and in the conception of productive nature, only an herb of the field, χλωρὸν ἀγροῦ : but no doubt they had their reasons for that; as well as for making the Being of beings say ποιήσωμεν ἄνθρωπον *let us make man*, instead of *we will make Adam*, נעשה אדם as is given in the original text, which is very different. The determined resolution of veiling the spiritual meaning of the Sepher, and above all of the Beræshith, placed them at every turn in difficult positions and forced them to distort the clearest phrases. A single word badly disguised would have been sufficient to make their preparations crumble away. They preferred to risk the grossest mistransla-

7. Wa-îîtzer IHÔAH Ælohîm æth-ha-Adam haphar min ha-âdamah w'îphah bi-âphi-ô nishemath haîîm wa-îehî ha-Adam le-nephesh haîah.

וַיִּ֩יצֶר֩ יְהֹוָ֨ה אֱלֹהִ֜ים אֶת־הָֽאָדָ֗ם עָפָר֙ מִן־הָ֣אֲדָמָ֔ה וַיִּפַּ֥ח בְּאַפָּ֖יו נִשְׁמַ֣ת חַיִּ֑ים וַֽיְהִ֥י הָֽאָדָ֖ם לְנֶ֥פֶשׁ חַיָּֽה׃

---

tions and make Moses fall into palpable contradictions, rather than expose its mysteries.

What, for example, could be more incoherent than what they made him say? According to their version, man, already created in v. 26 of the preceding chapter, does not exist in v. 6 of this one; and presently in v. 7, this same man comes to be created anew. How can this be?

The first creation takes place only in principle. The days, or the luminous manifestations, are only the efficient epochs, the phenomenal phases; Moses states it in a manner so precise that one must voluntarily close the eyes in order not to see its light. The conception of Nature had been created before Nature itself; the vegetation before the vegetable; Adam was not. The Being of beings had said only, *we will make Adam;* and Adam, universal man had been made in power. Soon he appears in action, and it is by him that effective creation begins. Profound Mystery! upon which I shall endeavour to throw as much light as is possible.

את־האדמה *the-adamic-selfsameness....* This word which is formed from that of *Adam,* and partakes of all its significations, figuratively as well as hieroglyphically, has undergone continuous restrictions, until it signifies only *the earth,* properly speaking; in the same manner that one has been brought to see in אדם, universal man, *the kingdom of man,* only a material man of flesh and blood. The name of *Adam,* being well understood, leads the mind easily to that of *Adamah,* its elementary principle, homogeneous earth, and like unto *Adam;* primitive earth, very far from that which is obvious to our senses, and as different from *the earth,* properly so-called, as intelligible, universal man, אדם , is different from particular and corporeal man, אנוש .

v. 6. ואד , *But-a-virtual-effluence....* The Hellenists have seen in

COSMOGONY OF MOSES

7. And-he-formed (framed, elementized for an everlasting end) IHOAH, HE-the-Being - of - beings, the - self-sameness of-*Adam* (collective man), by-rarefying (sublimating the principle) of-the-adamic (homogeneal ground); and-he-inspired into-the-inspiring-faculty-of him, a-being-exalted (an essence) of-the-lives, for-being -made Adam (collective man) according-to-the-soul of-life.

7. Et-il-forma (substantialisa, en déterminant les éléments vers un but) IHOAH, LUI - l'Être - des - êtres, l'ipséité d'*Adam* (l'homme universel) en-r a r é fi a n t (sublimant le principe) de-l'élément-adamique; et-il-inspira dans la-faculté-inspirante-à-lui un-étant-é l e v é (une essentialité) des-vies; a fin-qu'il-fût cet-homme-universel (Adam) selon-l' âme-vivante.

πηγή, *a fountain*, as has also Saint Jerome. It would be difficult to disparage more the expression of Moses. This expression, in the figurative sense in which it must be taken, indicates every kind of force, of faculty, by means of which any being whatsoever manifests its power exteriorly; a good power if it is good, and bad if it is bad.

One finds in the Arabic اد or ايد signifying force, power, vigour; the victory which follows them: a thing unprecedented, happy or sad, an emanation sympathetic or evil. ادا is the thing produced; ادي the productive thing, the instrument. In Samaritan, ᛮᛸ, in Ethiopic ჩᎦ (*ad*) both signify *the hand*, instrument of man, symbol of his power. The Syriac says ܐܝܕ, and the Chaldaic יד. The Hebrew also says יד *the hand*: this word, ruled by the sign of power and stability א, becomes איד, that is to say, every corroboration, every virtual emanation, every faculty, good or evil, according to the being by which it is produced.

If one takes this last word איד, and in order to give it an hieroglyphic sense, eliminates the sign of manifestation י, the word אד, preserving all the acceptations of the radical איד will become purely intelligible; it will be, as I have translated it, *a virtual emanation*. Moses has employed it in this sense. But this sense, too sublime to be easily understood, is materialized in the imagination of a gross and ignorant people. The word אד in its degeneration, signifies no more

8. Wa-îttah IHÔAH Ælo-hîm gan-bi-heden mi-kedem, wa-îâshem sham æth-ha-Adam âsher-îatzar.

וַיִּטַּע יְהֹוָה אֱלֹהִים גַּן־בְּעֵדֶן מִקֶּדֶם וַיָּשֶׂם שָׁם אֶת־הָאָדָם אֲשֶׁר יָצָר׃

---

than *a smoke, a vapour, a mist, a cloud*. The Samaritan and Chaldaic translators understood it thus. This interpretation is defective no doubt, but it is better than that of *fountain*, given by the Hellenist Jews.

v. 7 וַיִּיצֶר, *and-he-formed*.... This is one of the most difficult words in the Hebraic tongue. Its primitive root is אר, the elementary principle whose analysis I have given in v 3, ch. I. This root, ruled by the determinative sign צ, and animated by the convertible sign ו, offers in the verb צוּר, the idea of figuring, forming, coördinating, fixing and binding the constitutive elements of a thing. If this radical verb, employed according to the intensive form, doubles its final character ר, image of proper and frequentative movement, as in צוֹרֵר ; then it signifies to tighten and to press forcibly, to oppress: but if the convertible sign passes to the condition of hard consonant, as in צָעוֹר ; then the material compression has attained its height, and this verb contains only the idea of agony, of ignominy, and of very sharp pain.

In the present case, Moses has used the simple root צר, which expresses coördination, elementary configuration, by giving it for initial adjunction, the sign of manifestation and duration י, thus forming the compound radical verb יצר, *he substantiated, formed, fastened; and fashioned for eternity*.

עָפָר, *by-rarefying*....This continued facultative, which has been taken for a simple substantive by the Latin translator, has not been by all the Hellenists, who at least say χοῆν λαβών, *taking the dust*: imagining, *dust* where there was none: but still, it is better to imagine dust, than *mud* and *mire*.

The Samaritan renders עָפָר by ᚼᚥᛖ which is to say, *a volatile, essential spirit*; as is shown by the Ethiopic analogue ጸዐፈ (*tzawphe*), signifying literally *new wine*; and the Arabic word ضوا, which presents the idea of that which is inflamed rapidly, of that

COSMOGONY OF MOSES

8. And - he - appointed, IHOAH, HE-the-Gods, an-enclosure (an organical boundary) in-the-temporal-and-sensible-sphere extracted-from - the - boundless - and - foregoing (time); and-he-laid-up there that-same-*Adam* whom-he-had-framed-forever.

8. Et-il arrêta (traça), IHÔAH, LUI-les-Dieux, une-enceinte (une circonférence organique) dans-la-sphère-sensible-et-temporelle extra-ite - de - l'antériorité - uni-verselle (des temps); et-il-plaça là ce-même-*Adam* qu' il-avait-formé-pour l'éterni-té.

---

which exhales an odour, of that which moves with vivacity; as is proved by its derivatives اضواع · تضوع · ضوع, etc.

The word עפר here in question, offers the two roots united עוף־אר, the first of which עוף contains the idea of all rapid, volatile, aerial movement; the second, as we have already seen, is applied to the elementary principle.

ויפה באפיו, *and-he-inspired into-the-inspiring-faculty-of-him* . . . . Following the custom of Moses, the verb and the substantive, drawn from the same root, succeed and enlighten each other. This root is פא, or פי, which signifies literally *the mouth* and the breath which it exhales; figuratively, *speech* and intelligence which is its source.

נשמת, *a-being-exalted*. . . . This is the verb שמה, whose root שם expresses that which is exalted, employed according to the enunciative form, passive movement, as continued facultative, feminine construction.

v. 8. גן, *an enclosure*. . . . The Hellenist translators have copied here the Samaritan word ꓭꟿꟻꟿꓵ, *paradise*. Let us take up this Samaritan word, whose root רך, so little understood, expresses the idea of circular movement, steady and easy as that of a wheel; it can be perceived in the verb רוד, which expresses the action of that which unfolds around something and envelops it in its enclosure. Also, the Syriac ܪܕܝܐ, the Chaldaic and Hebrew רדיד, have signified alike a woman's garment, a light mantle enveloping a person with its undulating folds. The Samaritan word ꓭꟿꟻꟿꓵ, has had most

9. Wa-îatzemah Iהôah Æ l o h î m, min-ha-âdamah čhol-hetz nehmad l'maræh, w'tôb l'maâčhal, w'hetz ha-haîim b'thôčh ha-gan, w'hetz ha-dahath tôb wa-rawh.

וַיַּצְמַח יְהוָֹה אֱלֹהִים מִן־הָאֲדָמָה כָּל־עֵץ נֶחְמָד לְמַרְאֶה וְטוֹב לְמַאֲכָל וְעֵץ הַחַיִּים בְּתוֹךְ הַגָּן וְעֵץ הַדַּעַת טוֹב וָרָע׃

assuredly the same signification; what proves it beyond rejoinder, is that the word גן, whose emphatic version, by means of the sign כ or פ added at the head, has never had any other meaning than that of an envelope, a protecting enclosure. This word which partakes of the nature of the same name given to woman by a great number of peoples, signifies still a covering, in the Italian *gonna*, in the English *gown*, in the French *gaine* and even in the ancient Celtic *gun* or *goun*. It can signify *a garden* only in the sense wherein one considers a garden as enclosed and surrounded with hedges. But this restricted signification is belied here by the Samaritan *paradise*, whose analogues all respond to the meaning of *enclosure, sphere, veil*, and ORGAN which I give to it.

Here is the hieroglyphic etymology of the word גן. This mysterious word comes evidently from the root גו, expressing every idea of an object, enveloping and containing without effort, opening and extending itself to contain and to receive, and which terminates with the final, extensive sign ן. See Rad. Vocab. roots גו and גן.

בעדן, *in-the-sensible-sphere*.... Since this word has been rendered by those of *pleasure* and *sensual desire*, it has been so only by a sequence of gross ideas which are attached to that which is sentient and temporal. The root from which it springs is evident: it is עור, which expresses every kind of limited period. Thence, עד and עדן *the actual time*, the temporal; things sentient and transitory, etc.

מי־קדם, *extracted-from-the-foregoing*.... If the Hellenist translators had wished to understand the word עדן, they would have understood this one likewise; but having eluded the sense of the one they have necessarily missed the sense of the other. It is always the root עד which precedes and which is used according to the usage of Moses, but considered under another relation and modified by the initial sign of the greatest agglomerating and compressing force ק, and by the final collective sign ם. It must be stated here that the Egyptian priests conceived two eternities: קדם, that of this side of

COSMOGONY OF MOSES

9. And-he-caused-to-shoot-out, IHOAH, HE-the-Gods, from-the-adamic (homogeneal-ground) a l l-g r o w t h (every vegetative-faculty) fair-at-its-highest-rate, to-the-sense-of-sight, and-good to-the-sense-of-taste; and-a-growth of-lives, in-the-bosom of - the - organic - enclosure; and-a-growth (a vegetative faculty) of-the-knowledge of-good and-evil.

9. Et - il - fit - développer, IHOAH, LUI-les-Dieux, de-cet -élément-adamique (homogène) toute-substance-végétative belle-autant-que-possible selon-la-vue, et-bonne selon-le-goût; et-u n e-s u b-stance des-vies dans-le-centre de l'enceinte-organique; et-une-substance-végétative d e-l a-connaissance du-bien et-du-mal.

---

time, and עולם, that of the other side of time: that is to say, anterior eternity and posterior eternity.

v. 9. עץ, a *growth*.... The root עו or עי develops every idea of growth, excrescence, tumour; anything which accumulates. The sign ץ which terminates it, marks the aim, the end to which all things tend. Seeing only *a tree*, in the word עץ, as the Hellenists or as Saint Jerome who has copied them, testifies to a great desire to suppress the truth or to show great ignorance. The Samaritan has been more happily chosen, or less cautiously. The word עוטבן which it uses expresses a *vegetation of elementary nature;* it comes from the root עול or עיל, and terminates with the extensive sign ן. The Chaldaic reads אילן, which amounts to nearly the same. It is *an extensive force, an invading power;* in short, *matter in travail*: it is what the Greeks name ὕλη, and the Latins "sylva." Now, observe that ὕλη and "sylva" have likewise signified *tree*, or *wood*, in a very restricted sense.

The mistake that the translators committed here appears to me voluntary and calculated; for otherwise it would be ridiculous: that of Saint Jerome was forced. Having once followed these untrustworthy guides in one point, he was obliged to follow them in all. After having seen a *garden*, in an intelligible enclosure that we would today name *an organic sphere of activity*, it was quite natural that he should see *sensual desire* in what was *sentient* and *temporal; morning*, in what was *anteriority of time; a tree*, in what was *matter in travail*, etc., etc.

10. W'nahar îotzæ me-he-den l'ha-shekôth æth-ha-gan, w'mi-sham îophared, w'haî-ah l'arbahah rashîm.

וְנָהָר יֹצֵא מֵעֵדֶן לְהַשְׁקוֹת אֶת־הַגָּן וּמִשָּׁם יִפָּרֵד וְהָיָה לְאַרְבָּעָה רָאשִׁים׃

11. Shem ha-æhad phî-shôn, houâ hassobeb æth-chol-ha-æretz ha-hawilah, âsher-sham ha-zahab.

שֵׁם הָאֶחָד פִּישׁוֹן הוּא הַסֹּבֵב אֵת כָּל־אֶרֶץ הַחֲוִילָה אֲשֶׁר־שָׁם הַזָּהָב׃

12. W'zahab ha-âretz ha-hiwâ tôb sham ha-beddolah w'æben ha-shoham.

וּזֲהַב הָאָרֶץ הַהִוא טוֹב שָׁם הַבְּדֹלַח וְאֶבֶן הַשֹּׁהַם׃

v. 10. לארבעה, *according-to-the-four-fold-power*.... The root of this mysterious number is רב, which, formed of the sign of movement proper ר, and that of generative action, contains all ideas of grandeur and of multiplication. If the last character is doubled as in רבב, this word acquires an endless numerical extent; if it is followed by the sign of material sense, as in רבע, it becomes the expression of solidity, of physical force, and of all ideas attached to the cube. It is in this state that it represents the number *four*. But in the above example, it begins one part with the sign of power א, and terminates with the emphatic article ה, which attaches to it the hieroglyphic meaning of the *four-fold power* or *quaternary*.

v. 11. פישון, *Phishon*.... This is the root יש, which, formed by the signs of manifestation and of relative movement, expresses every idea of reality and of physical substantiality. It is governed by the

10. And -a-flowing-effluence (an emanation) was-running from-this temporal-and-sensible-place, for-bedewing that-same-organic-enclosure; and-thence, it-was-dividing in-order-to-be-henceforth suitable-to-the-four-fold-generative-power.

11. The-name of-one (of-those generative effluences) -was-*Phishon* (real existence) that-which-is surrounding the-whole-earth-of *Hawilah* (virtual energy) which-is the-native-spot of-gold (light's reflection).

12. And-the-gold of-the-earth that-self-same, good; proper-spot of - *Bedellium* (mysterious dividing) and-of-the-*Stone Shoam* (universal sublimation).

10. Et-un-fleuve (une émanation) était-coulant de-ce-lieu-temporel-et - sensible, pour-l'action-d'abreuver cette-même-sphère - organique; et-de-là, il-était-se-divisant afin-d'être-à-l'avenir selon-la - puissance - quaternaire - multiplicatrice-des - princi - pes.

11. Le-nom- du - premier (de cés principes émanés)-était-*Phishon* (la réalité physique, l'Être apparent) lui - qui - est circonscrivant toute - la - terre- de *Hawilah* (l'énergie virtuelle) laquelle -est-le lieu-propre de-l'or (la réflexion lumineuse).

12. Et-l'or de - la - terre icelle, bon; lieu-propre du-*Bedellium* (sèparation mystérieuse), et-de-la-*pierre shohâm*, (sublimation universelle).

---

emphatic sign of speech כ, and is terminated by the augumentative syllable ין, which carries to its highest degree, the extent of every produced being. One can recognize in this proper name and in all the following ones, the genius of the Egyptian tongue.

החוילה, *Hawilah*.... Here the root חל, חול or חיל, is related to the idea of effort, of tension, or virtual travail, of trial, etc. This root is used as continued facultative, with the emphatic article ה. Refer to the Rad. Vocab. concerning this root, and the preceding one.

v. 12. I suspect this verse was at first a marginal note which has crept into the text, either by the carelessness of Esdras, or by that of

13. W'shem ha-nahar ha-shenî Gîhôn, houâ hassobeb æth-ċhol-æretz Choush.

וְשֵׁם הַנָּהָר הַשֵּׁנִי גִּיחוֹן הוּא הַסּוֹבֵב אֵת כָּל־אֶרֶץ כּוּשׁ׃

14. W'shem ha-nahar ha-shelîshî Hiddekel, houâ ha-holeċh kidemath âshoûr, w' ha-nahar ha-rabîhî houâ phrath.

וְשֵׁם־הַנָּהָר הַשְּׁלִישִׁי הִדֶּקֶל הוּא הַהֹלֵךְ קִדְמַת אַשּׁוּר וְהַנָּהָר הָרְבִיעִי הוּא פְרָת׃

15. Wa-îkkah IHÔAH Ælohîm æth-ha-Adam, wa-înnihe-hou be-gan-heden l'habed-ha w'l'shamer-ha.

וַיִּקַּח יְהֹוָה אֱלֹהִים אֶת־הָאָדָם וַיַּנִּחֵהוּ בְגַן־עֵדֶן לְעָבְדָהּ וּלְשָׁמְרָהּ׃

---

some earlier copyist. What leads me to suspect this is, that it interrupts visibly the narration, by an hermetic allegory, very crude, which is neither the style nor the manner of Moses.

v. 13. גִיחוֹן, *Gihon*.... Consult again the Rad. Vocab. for the root גה. This root is employed here in the intensive verbal form with the augmentative syllable וֹן.

כוּשׁ, *Chush*.... The elementary root אש, which signifies in general, the *igneous principle*, being verbalized by the signs ו or י has produced the word אוֹשׁ or אִישׁ; that is to say, *fire*, physical or moral: and this word contracted by the assimilative sign כ, has given rise to the one of which we are speaking. This name which is found in the sacred books of the Brahmans, and whose origin is consequently

13. And-the-name of-the-effluence the-second, was-*Gihon* (determining motion) that-very-one-which-is encompassing the - whole - earth *Chush* (fire-like, ethereal principle).

14. And-the-name of-the-effluence the-third was-Hiddekel (nimble and swift-propagator, universal fluid) the -same-that-is the-producing-cause of-the-eternal-principle of-happiness (harmony, lawful rule) and-the-effluence the-fourth, the-same-that - is the - fecundating - cause.

15. And-he-took, IHOAH, HE - the - Gods, that - same - *Adam* (collective-man) and-he-placed-him in - the - temporal-and - sensible - sphere, for dressing-it and-overlooking-it-with-care.

13. Et-le - nom-du-fleuve (du principe émané) deuxième, ·était-*Gihon*, (le mouvement déterminant) lui-qui-est entourant toute-la-terre *Choush* (le principe igné).

14. Et-le-nom du-fleuve (de l'émanation) troisième, était Hiddekel (le rapide et léger propagateur), le fluide électrique, magnétique, galvanique, etc.) lui-qui-est le-faisant-aller (le moyen de propagation) du-principe-primitif de-la-félicité (de l'ordre, de l-harmonie) et-le-fleuve (l'émanation) quatrième-était lui-qui-est le-fécondateur.

15. Et-il-prit, IHOAH, LUI - les - Dieux, ce - même - *Adam* (l'homme universel), et-il-laissa-lui dans-la-sphère -temporelle-et-sensible, pour ellaborer-elle, et-pour-la-surveiller-avec-soin.

---

very ancient, has been rendered by that of *Æthi-ops*, which is to say, the sympathetic fire of the globe. All the allegorical names of which Moses makes use, come evidently from the Egyptian sanctuaries.

v. 14. הִדֶקֶל *Heddekel*.... This name is formed of two words הדה, *emitting, propagating*, and קל *light, rapid*. It is used in the intensive form.

הוא פרת, *that-is the-fecundating-cause*.... The Hellenists having

16. Wa-îtzaw IHÔAH Ælohîm hal-ha-Adam, l'æ-mor, mi-čhol hetz-ha-gan âčhol thâočhel.

וַיְצַו יְהוָה אֱלֹהִים עַל־הָאָדָם לֵאמֹר מִכֹּל עֵץ־הַגָּן אָכֹל תֹּאכֵל:

17. W'me-hetz ha-dahath tôb wa-rawh loâ thâočhal mi-men-oû čhi b'îôm âčal-čha mi-men-oû, môt ha-môth.

וּמֵעֵץ הַדַּעַת טוֹב וָרָע לֹא־תֹאכַל מִמֶּנּוּ כִּי בְּיוֹם אֲכָלְךָ מִמֶּנּוּ מוֹת תָּמוּת:

---

seen the Tigris in the allegorical river הרקל *the swift propagator* spoken of by Moses, have not failed to profit here, by a slight resemblance in the sound of the words, to see the Euphrates, in הוא פרת, *that which fecundates;* without concerning themselves with what they had said of the two preceding rivers: but only a little attention is needed to see that הוא is a masculine pronoun which governs the nominal verb פרת, *the action of fecundating.*

v. 15. All these terms are simple or known.

v. 16. ויצו, *and-he-prescribed....* The root צו expresses every kind of line traced toward an end, of which the sign צ is the symbol. This root, having become the verb צוה, according to the intensive form, signifies *to conduct with rectitude, to guide well,* etc.

מכל־עץ, *the whole growth....* Turn to v. 9. of this chapter.

אכל תאכל, *feeding thou-mayst-feed-upon....* Here is a word, which, as the result of contraction, has become very difficult to understand, on account of the resemblance that it has acquired with certain different words which come from another root, and with which it can easily be confused. Its proper root must be sought for carefully, for Moses has attached great importance to this point. One can see by the pains that he has taken to repeat twice the same verb, first, as continued facultative, and afterward, as temporal future.

This root is עול, *elementary matter,* unknown substance, symbol-

COSMOGONY OF MOSES

16. And - he - prescribed, IHOAH, HE-the-Gods (enacting, settling) toward-*Adam*, by - declaring: from - the - whole growth-of-the-organic -enclosure, feeding thou-mayst-feed-upon.

16. Et-il-prescrivit, IHOAH, LUI-les-Dieux, (statua, régla), envers-*Adam*, selon-l'action-de déclarer (sa parole) : de-toute substance-végétative-de-l'enceinte - or - ganique, alimentant tu-peux -t'alimenter.

17. But-from-the-growth (growing might) of-the-knowledge of-good and-evil, not-shalt - thou - feed - upon any-of-it; for-in-the-day of-the-feeding-thine upon-some -of-it, dying thou-shalt-die (thou shalt transmute to another state).

17. Mais-de-la-substance -physique de-la-connaissance du-bien et-du-mal, non-pas tu-consommeras de-quoi-d' elle; car dans-le-jour de-la-consommation-à-toi de-quoi-d'elle, mourant tu-mourras (tu passeras à un autre état).

---

ized here by the universal convertible sign placed between those of physical sense and expansive movement. This root which is conserved wholly in the Syriac ܠܘܩ and in the Greek ὕλη, was famous among the Egyptians who made it play an important rôle in their mythology. One finds in Ethiopic the word አኀል (*achal*) signifying *substance, essence, matter, nourishment.* Element and **aliment,** hold to this through their common root.

Furthermore, this root is used in Hebrew only in a restricted sense, and as it were, *to nurse an infant,* to give it its first nourishment. One finds עִלֵל, to designate, an infant at the breast. When the Chaldaic punctuation materializes completely this root in making consonantal the mother vowel ו, then it develops ideas of injustice, crime and perversity.

But if, instead of materializing this vowel, the character of the physical sense ע, is softened by substituting the sign of assimilated life כ; then this root written thus, כּוֹל, expresses ideas of apprehension, of violent shock; of measure, of substantiation; if it is reduced to the single characters כל, one obtains by this contraction, the analogous ideas of assimiliation, of substance, and of consummation, whether one considers the action of consummating or of consuming.

18. Wa-îâomer I H ô A H, Ælohîm, loâ-tôb heiôth ha-Adam l'badd'-ô æhesheh-l'ô hezer b'neghed-ô.

וַיֹּאמֶר יְהֹוָה אֱלֹהִים לֹא־טוֹב הֱיוֹת הָאָדָם לְבַדּוֹ אֶעֱשֶׂה־לּוֹ עֵזֶר כְּנֶגְדּוֹ׃

19. Wa-îtzer IHôAH, Ælohîm min-ha-Adamah čhol-haîath ha-shadeth w'æth čhol hôph ha-shamaîm, wa-îabæ ael-ha-Adam l'r â ô t h mahîkerâ-l'ô w'čhol âsher îkerâ-l'ô ha-Adam, nephesh haîah houâ shem-ô.

וַיִּצֶר יְהֹוָה אֱלֹהִים מִן־הָאֲדָמָה כָּל־חַיַּת הַשָּׂדֶה וְאֵת־כָּל־עוֹף הַשָּׁמַיִם וַיָּבֵא אֶל־הָאָדָם לִרְאוֹת מַה־יִּקְרָא־לוֹ וְכֹל אֲשֶׁר יִקְרָא־לוֹ הָאָדָם נֶפֶשׁ חַיָּה הוּא שְׁמוֹ׃

It is at this point that Moses has taken it, and giving it the exalted meaning which he conceived, he has made it rule by the sign of power א. In this state, the verb אכל, which is formed, has signified *to feed upon*, that is to say, *to assimilate to one's self elementary matter as food*.

It must be remembered that the root עול of which we are speaking, is precisely the same as that which the Samaritan translator used to render the substance called עץ, by Moses, and the object of alimentation expressed by the verb אכל. Refer again to v. 9. of this chapter and to Rad. Voc. root כל and על.

v. 17. הדעת, *of the knowledge*.... דע is a root which contains every idea of exposition, explanation, demonstration; being formed by contraction of the roots יד *the hand*, that which shows, and עה. *the superficies*, the curve, the exterior form of things.

The Samaritan word ᛞᛉᛒᛒ holds to the Hebraic root הך, which is related to that which grasps forms interiorly and which fixes them, as for example *taste*. Thus *knowledge*, indicated by the Hebrew text, is that which depends upon *judgment* and upon exterior forms, and that indicated by the Samaritan translator, is that which

COSMOGONY OF MOSES 85

18. And-he-said, Ihoah, he-the-Being-of-beings, not-good the-being-*Adam* (collective m a n) in-lonesomeness-his; I-will-make-to-him, an-auxiliary-might (a prop, a mate) unto-the-reflecting-light-his-own.

19. And-he-had-elementized (by compacting the elements toward an end), Ihoah, he-the-Being-of-beings, from-the-adamic (homogeneal ground) every-life of-nature - earth - born, and - every fowl of-the-heavens; and-he brought unto-*Adam,* to see what he-would-assign-for-name in-relation-to-himself unto-it: and-all-that he assigned - for - name - unto - it (after him), *Adam* (collective man), soul-of-life was-the-n a m e-its-own-suitable-to-him.

18. Et-il-dit, Ihoah, lui-l'Être - des - êtres, pas - bon être-*Adam* (l'homme-universel) dans-la-solitude-sienne: Je-ferai-à-lui, une-force-auxiliaire (un s o u t i e n, un aide, une corroboration, une doublure) en-r e fl e t-lumineux-de-lui.

19. Et-il-avait-formé (en coordonnant les é l é m e n s vers un but), Ihoah, lui-l'Être-des-êtres du-s e i n-de-l'adamique, (élémént homogène) toute-vie de-la-nature-terrestre et-toute-espèce-de-volatile d e s-cieux; et-il-fit-venir vers-*Adam,* pour-voir q u e l il-assignerait-nom-à-cela (selon lui): et-tout-ce-qu' il-a s s i g n a-nom-à-cela (selon lui), *Adam* (l'homme universel), âme-de-vie ce-fut-le-nom-sien-de-lui.

---

results from *taste* and from interior forms. The Latin word *sapientia* has the same expression as the Samaritan. The French *connaissance* holds a medium between the two. The word *knowledge* and the Greek γνῶσις are derived from the Celtic word *ken* or *kan,* which signifies to conceive, to comprehend, to embrace in a glance, etc.

מוֹת תָּמוּת. *dying, thou-shalt-die....* I shall explain later on the root of this word. See Rad. Vocab. root מת.

v. 18. עוּר, *an-auxiliary-might....* This energetic word has been formed of the root עו, which expresses every force, every means added, every strengthening, and of the elementary sign of movement

20. Wa-îkerâ ha-Adam shemôth-l'čhol ha-behemah w'l'hôph ha-shamaîm w'l'čhol haîath ha-shadeh, w'l' Adam lôa-matzâ hezer čh' neghed'-ô.

וַיִּקְרָא הָאָדָם שֵׁמוֹת לְכָל־הַבְּהֵמָה וּלְעוֹף הַשָּׁמַיִם וּלְכֹל חַיַּת הַשָּׂדֶה וּלְאָדָם לֹא־מָצָא עֵזֶר כְּנֶגְדּוֹ׃

21. Wa-îaphel Ihôah, Ælohîm thareddemah hal-ha-Adam, wa-îîshan, wa-îkkah âhath mi-tzal-hothaî-ô, wa-îsseggor bashar thahathe-nah.

וַיַּפֵּל יְהוָֹה אֱלֹהִים תַּרְדֵּמָה עַל־הָאָדָם וַיִּישָׁן וַיִּקַּח אַחַת מִצַּלְעֹתָיו וַיִּסְגֹּר בָּשָׂר תַּחְתֶּנָּה׃

---

proper ־. The Samaritan word ⲉⲍⲣ, which translates it, means *a support, a counsel, a kindness;* as is proved by the corresponding Arabic word سعد. The Chaldaic targum says סָמִיךְ, *a conjunction*.

כְּנֶגְדּוֹ, *unto-the-reflecting-light-his-own....* The root נג is applied to every kind of light reflected like a mirror. Thence the ideas of manifestation and opposition, of object presented and put in juxtaposition, which is found in the word נגד, wherein the root נג is rendered still more expressive by the addition of the sign ד. The mediative article כ, which inflects this word shows the application. I shall only state here that, following the narrative of Moses, the Being of beings, creating Adam, forms him in his likeness; that creating *Eve*, he forms her in the light of *Adam*, or of that which is the same thing, in the luminous reflection of *Adam*.

v. 19.   לֹ, *unto it (after him)....* Here is a grammatical trope that I wish to point out, as this verse merits particular attention, on account of the actual formation of the animals in which Adam takes part. This trope contains two meanings. Moses who uses it quite readily, appears to have imitated the hieroglyphic style in which no doubt, it was often used. In this verse, for example, the word לֹ composed of the nominal affix וֹ, belonging to the third person mascu-

20. And - he - assigned *Adam*, names to-the-whole quadruped-kind, and-to-the-fowl of-heavens, and-to-the-whole living-nature earth-born and-for-*Adam* (collective man) not-to-meet with--an-auxiliary-mate as-a-reflected-light-of-him.

20. Et-il-assigna *Adam*, des-noms à-toute-l'espèce-quadrupède, et-à-l'espèce-volatile des-cieux, et-à-toute l'animalité de-la-nature-terrestre: et-pour-*Adam* (l'homme universel) non-pas trouver un-aide (une force auxiliaire) comme-un-reflet-lumineux-de-lui.

21. And - he-caused - to - fall, IHOAH, HE-the-Gods, a-sympathetic-slumber (mysterious and deep) upon *Adam* (collective man) who -slept: and-he-broke-off one of-the-involutions (that sheltered him) and-he-covered-with-care (he coloured) with-shape and-corporeal-beauty the-weakness (inferiority) of-her.

21. Et - il-laissa - tomber IHOAH, LUI-les-Dieux, un-sommeil-sympathique (mystérieux et profond) sur-*Adam* (l'homme universel) qui-dormit: et-il-rompit-de-l'unité une des-enveloppes-siennes (extérieures) et-il-couvrit-avec-soin (il colora) forme-et - beauté - corporelle la-faiblesse (l'infériorité)-à-elle.

---

line, and of the directive article ל, is placed with reference to the thing to which Adam is to give a name, and to Adam himself, who will give this name according to him; that is to say, according to the relations that he shall discover between him and that thing.

This trope is remarkable because it is from the examination of the relations which it indicates, that the names result, which Adam, universal man, gives to the divers animals, according to their relations with the living soul whence their existence issues.

שמו, *the-name-its-own-suitable-to-him*.... The same trope continued, makes the affix ו, belong both to the thing which received the name, and to Adam who gives it.

v. 20. All these terms are understood.

v. 21. תרדמה, *a-sympathetic-slumber*.... This is a kind of lethargy or *somnambulism*, which takes possession of the sentient

22. Wa-îben Ihôah, Ælohîm æth-ha-tzellah âsher lakah min-ha-Adam l'âishah, wa-îbiæha æl-ha-Adam.

וַיִּבֶן יְהוָה אֱלֹהִים אֶת־הַצֵּלָע אֲשֶׁר־לָקַח מִן הָאָדָם לְאִשָּׁה וַיְבִאֶהָ אֶל־הָאָדָם׃

---

faculties and suspends them; as is testified by the Chaldaic נרדם and even the Arabic נכם. The hieroglyphic composition of the Hebrew word is remarkable. It can cause strange reflections anent certain modern discoveries. The two contracted roots רד־דם, express, the first, that which extends and takes possession by a proper movement; the other, that which is similar, homogeneous and conformable to universal nature. The sign of mutual reciprocity ה and the emphatic article ה are here at the beginning and the end, to increase the energy of this mysterious word.

After the analysis of this word, one cannot fail to recognize that extraordinary condition, to which the moderns have given the name of *magnetic sleep*, or *somnambulism*, and which one might perhaps designate, as in Hebrew, *sympathetic sleep*, or simply *sympatheticism*. I must moreover state that the Hellenists who say ἔκστασις, *a trance*, are not so far from the truth as Saint Jerome who merely says "soporem" *a deep sleep*.

אחת, *one*.... This word does not signify here only *one*, but it characterizes also *unity*. Moses employs it in two senses, by means of the grammatical trope of which I spoke in v. 19, of this chapter.

מצלעתיו, *of-the-involutions-of-him*.... One cannot, in a word wherein are formed so many different images, choose an idea more petty and more material, than that which the Hellenists have rendered by the word πλευρά, *a rib*. Saint Jerome who has said in bad Latin "unam de cotis," could not do otherwise, because the course of error was irresistibly marked out. The word צלע can only be composed of one root and of one sign, or of two contracted roots. If it is the first, it is צל־ע, for לע, is not an Hebraic root; if it is the second, it is צל־עו, in either case, the meaning is the same, for the root עה or עוה is only an extension of the sign ע.

According to this data, let us examine the ideas contained in the root צל. They are those of shadow, of an object extending above,

COSMOGONY OF MOSES 89

22. And-he-restored (in its former state) IHOAH, HE-the-Being-of-beings, the-selfsameness-of-the-sheltering-windings which he-had-broken, from *Adam* (collective man) for-(shaping) *Aishah* (intellectual woman, man's faculty of volition) and-he-brought-her to-him-*Adam*.

22. Et-il-reconstruisit (consolida, rétablit dans son premier état) IHOAH, LUI-l'Être-des-êtres, la substance-de-l'enveloppe-extérieure, laquelle il-avait-rompue d'*Adam* (l'homme universel) pour-(baser) *Aishah* (la femme intellectuelle, la faculté volitive d'*Adam*) et-il-amena-elle à-lui-*Adam*.

---

and making shadow as a canopy, a curtain, a screen, hangings, roof, etc.

Now what is the meaning of the root עה ? Is it not that which is attached to all curving, all circumferential form, to all exterior superficies of things, as I stated in v. 17 of this chapter?

Therefore the word צלע signifies exactly an envelope, an exterior covering, a protecting shelter. This is what the facultative צילע proves, *to be enclosing, covering, enveloping*: this is what is proved also by the word צעף, by which the Samaritans have rendered it. This word which is derived from the root על , characterizes a thing raised to serve as covering, canopy, etc. The Chaldaic makes use of the word עלע , analogous to the Samaritan and having the same signification.

בשר , *shape-and-corporeal-beauty*.... I omit analyzing סגר employed here according to the intensive form, because, in reality, there is nothing very difficult in it. The word בשר demands also all of our attention, notwithstanding the length of this note; seeing that the Hellenist translators, always restricted to the material meaning, have rendered it by σαρξ, an ignoble word which Saint Jerome has copied in "caro," *the flesh*. Now סר or שור , is an Hebraic root which contains in itself all ideas of movement toward consistency, corporeity, elementary form and physical force, as is sufficiently denoted by the signs of which it is composed. The sign of interior activity ב , governs this same root, and constitutes the verb בשור which always signifies *to inform; to announce a thing, to bring glad tidings;* as is proved by the Arabic بشر , which adds to this signification,

23. Wa-îâomer ha-Adam zoâth ha-phaham hetzem me-hetzama-î, w'bashar me-beshar-î, l'zaôth îkkarâ âishah chi me-aîsh lukahah-zaôth.

וַיֹּאמֶר הָאָדָם זֹאת הַפַּעַם עֶצֶם מֵעֲצָמַי וּבָשָׂר מִבְּשָׂרִי לְזֹאת יִקָּרֵא אִשָּׁה כִּי מֵאִישׁ לֻקֳחָה־זֹּאת:

that of showing a pleasant physiognomy, and of pleasing by its beauty: moreover the word جارة , in the latter tongue, is always applied to physical beauty. Now, if the Hebraic word בשר designates the *flesh*, among the vulgar, it has been only by a shocking abuse, and by a continuation of that unfortunate inclination which the Jews had of restricting and materializing everything. It signified first, *form, configuration, exterior appearance, corporeal beauty, animal substance.* The Samaritan version and the Chaldaic targum use the analogous word ꟼⱯꟻ or בסר. It is difficult to say today what meaning the Samaritans attached to this word on account of the few documents which remain to us in their tongue; but we cannot doubt that the Chaldeans deduced from it all ideas relative to exterior forms, ideas more or less agreeable according to the point of view under which they considered these forms. Thus, for example, they understood by the nominal בסר the action of informing, announcing, evangelizing, preaching, scrutinizing, disdaining, scorning, etc.

v. 22. לאשה, *for-(shaping) Aishah....* Here again is the trope of repetition, of which I have spoken. This trope is here of the highest importance in the hieroglyphic sense, and even in the literal sense, which remains incomplete if it is not admitted. In order to understand, it must be recalled that the root אש develops all ideas attached to the first principle; so that the verb אשה which is derived from it signifies *to begin, to establish in principle, to shape*, etc. Now, the grammatical trope in question consists of this; the word אשה taken at the same time as verb and as substantive, expresses on the one hand, the action of shaping, of beginning, and on the other, characterizes the very object of this action, *Aishah,* the principiant volitive faculty of Adam, his intellectual spouse. I shall relate presently what should be understood by this faculty, in analyzing the name

COSMOGONY OF MOSES 91

23. And-he-said *Adam* (declaring his thought): this-is actually universal-substance of-the-substance-mine and-corporeal-shape of-the-shape-mine: to-this he-assigned-for-name *Aishah* (principle of volition, intellectual woman) because out-of-the-volitive-principle *Aish* (intellectual man) she-had-been-taken-selfsameness.

23. Et-il-dit *Adam* (déclarant sa pensée) celle-ci-est actuellement substance-universelle de-la-substance-à-moi, et-forme-corporelle-de-la - forme - corporelle - à - moi : à-celle-là-même il-assigna-nom *Aishah* (volonté principiante, femme intellectuelle) à-cause-que-du-principe-volitif *Aish* (l'homme intellectuel) elle-avait-été-détachée-ipséité-même.

---

given to intellectual man, אִישׁ, (*aish*) in opposition to universal man, אָדָם (*Adam*).

v. 23. עֶצֶם, *universal-substance*.... This is the well-known root עֵץ, used here with the collective sign ם. An attentive reader should see two things in this word: the first, that the root עֵץ does not signify *tree*, as the Hellenists have said; the second, that the sign ם has really the universal expression that I have given to it. This last observation will be very useful to him as we proceed.

אִישׁ, *intellectual man*.... Here is a new denomination given to man. It appears for the first time, when the Being of beings, having declared that it was not good for universal man, *Adam*, to live alone in the solitude of his universality, has effected his individuality, in giving him an auxiliary force, a companion, created in his light and destined for him to reflect his image.

I beg the reader to remark first of all, that Moses, giving a name to this companion, does not derive it from that of Adam; for *Adam* considered as universal man, could not know a companion. The Hebraic word אָדָם has no feminine. The word אֲדָמָה which appears to be it, does not signify *universal woman*, as one might think; but, as I have said, the elementary principle of Adam. אָדָם, *universal man*, possesses the two sexes. Moses has taken care to repeat it several times so that one shall not be deceived. What therefore is this companion, this auxiliary force, as the word עֵזֶר expresses it? It

24. Hal-chen îawhazab aîsh æth-âbi-ô w'æth âim-ô w'dabak b'âisheth-ô w'haîoû l'bashar æhad.

עַל־כֵּן יַעֲזָב־אִישׁ אֶת־אָבִיו וְאֶת־אִמּוֹ וְדָבַק בְּאִשְׁתּוֹ וְהָיוּ לְבָשָׂר אֶחָד׃

25. W'îhîoû shenéî-hem haroûm-mîm, ha-Adam w' âisheth-ô, w'loâ-îthboshas-hoû.

וַיִּהְיוּ שְׁנֵיהֶם עֲרוּמִּים הָאָדָם וְאִשְׁתּוֹ וְלֹא יִתְבֹּשָׁשׁוּ׃

---

is the volitive faculty developed by the Being of beings: it is the intellectual woman of universal man; it is the will proper which individualizes him, and in which he is reflected and which, rendering him independent, becomes the creative force by means of which he realizes his conceptions, and makes them pass from power into action. For, this truth must come out from the darkness of the sanctuaries: the will was creator with universal man. Whatever this man willed was when and how he willed it. The power and the act were indivisible in his will.

Such is the difference between the Hebraic words אדם and איש. The one characterizes man universalized by his homogeneous essence, the other designates man individualized by his efficient will. The hieroglyphic etymology of the first of these names is already known, let us examine the second, which is also important.

This name springs from two contracted roots איש. I have explained them both. אי develops every idea of desire, of inclination, of appetite, of election: אש is the power of movement, the elementary principle, fire, considered in the absence of all substance. The word איש which results from the contraction of these two roots only differs from the word אוש, which indicates natural, substantialized fire, by the median sign. In the former it is that of manifestation and duration; in the latter it is the bond between nothingness and being, which I name convertible. The one is a movement, intelligent, volitive, durable; the other, a movement, appetent, blind, fugacious.

Here is the hieroglyphic meaning of the word איש *intellectual man*. It is a new development of *universal man*, a development, which,

COSMOGONY OF MOSES

24. So-that shall-leave the-intellectual-man, the-father-his-own, and-the-mother-his-own, and-he-shall-cleave unto-the-intellectual-wife-of-him; and-they-shall-be, as-to-the-exterior-form, one.

25. And-they-were both-themselves entirely-uncovered (bare-bodied), A d a m (collective man) and-the-intellectual-wife-of-him and-not-they-shamed-one-another.

24. Sur-ce-donc il-quittera, l'homme-intellectuel, la-père-même-s i e n, e t-l a-mère-sienne, et-il-se réunira (ne fera qu'un être) avec-la-femme - intellectuelle - à - lui : et-ils-seront-s e l o n-l a-forme-extérieure, un.

25. Et - ils - étaient - les-deux-eux-mêmes, *Adam* (l' homme universel) et-la-femme -intellectuelle - à - lui entièrement-découverts; et-non-pas-se-faisaient - honte - entr'eux.

---

without destroying his universality and his homogeneity, gives him, nevertheless, an independent individuality, and leaves him free to manifest himself in other and particular conceptions, by means of a companion, an auxiliary force, intended to reflect his image.

It is therefore with profound reason that Moses having especially in mind, in this companion, the volitive faculty which constitutes universal man, *intelligent-being*, that is to say, the faculty which renders him capable of willing and of choosing, draws its name from the same name of intellectual man, איש. In this derivation, he has caused the sign of manifestation י, to disappear, and has replaced it with the final sign of life, in order to make it understood that it is not the volitive principle which resides in אשה, but the principiant will, existing, no longer in power, but in action.

v. 24 and 25. These two verses appear to me to be the reflection of some commentator, written at first on the margin of the text, and in the course of time, inserted in the text itself. They bear neither the style nor the form of Moses. The two words alone על-כן *so-that*, suffice to prove their intercalation. However little one may be impressed with what has preceded, one is well aware that these two verses are not connected with the cosmogonical narrative, and above all that they have not come from the Egyptian sanctuary.

SEPHER BERÆSHITH G.

ספר בראשית ג׃

1. W'ha - Nahash haîah haroum miċhol haîah ha-shadeh âsher ha-shah IHÔAH Ælohîm, wa-îâomer æl-ha-Aishah âph ċhî-âmar Ælohîm loâ-thâo-ċheloû mi-ċhol hetz ha-gan.

וְהַנָּחָשׁ הָיָה עָרוּם מִכֹּל חַיַּת הַשָּׂדֶה אֲשֶׁר עָשָׂה יְהוָה אֱלֹהִים וַיֹּאמֶר אֶל־הָאִשָּׁה אַף כִּי־אָמַר אֱלֹהִים לֹא־תֹאכְלוּ מִכֹּל עֵץ הַגָּן׃

---

v. 1. והנחש. *Now-eager-Covetousness*.... It is well known that the Hellenists and Saint Jerome, have seen here only a snake, a serpent, properly speaking: indeed according to the former a very wise serpent, ὄφις φρονιμώτατος, and according to the latter, a serpent very skillful and very cunning, "serpens callidior". This wretched interpretation appears to go back to the epoch of the captivity of Babylon and to coincide with the total loss of the Hebraic tongue: at least, it is true that the Chaldaic paraphrase has followed it. He says הוא חכים *a most insidious serpent*. I do not know if any one can entirely exonerate the author of the Samaritan version: for, although he employs the word ࠍࠇࠔ, which corresponds to the Hebrew נחש, it is very doubtful whether he understood it exactly, not having known how to render the word ערום, which follows, as I shall explain hereafter.

But all those authorities who support this error, cannot prevent the truth from being seen. The word נחש, as it is employed in this case, cannot mean *a serpent*. It is an eager covetousness, self-conceited, envious, egoistic, which indeed winds about in the heart of man and envelops it in its coils, but which has nothing to do with a serpent, other than a name sometimes given metaphorically. It is only by restricting this figurative expression more and more, that ignorant people have been able to bring it to the point of signifying only a serpent. The Hellenists have followed this crude idea; but could they have done otherwise? If, through delicacy of sentiment or respect for Moses, they had wished to raise the veil in this passage, what would have become of the garden, the tree, the rib, etc. etc.? I have already said, in the part they had taken, they had to sacrifice all to the fear of exposing the mysteries.

GENESIS III.	COSMOGONIE III.
1. Now-eager-Covetousness (self-conceit, envy, concupiscence) was a-general-ruling-passion (blind principle) in-the-whole life of-Nature which had-made IHOAH, HE-the-Gods: and-it-said (that grovelling passion) unto-*Aishah* (*Adam's* volitive faculty) because of-what declared, HE-the-Gods, not-shall-you-feed from-the whole-growth of-the-organic-enclosure?	1. Or-l'Ardeur-c u p i d e (l'intérêt, l'envie, l'egoisme) était une-passion-générale (un principe aveugle) parmi-toute l'animalité de-la-Nature-élémentaire laquelle avait-faite IHOAH, LUI-les-Dieux: et-elle dit (cette passion) à-*Aîshah* (la faculté volitive d'*A d a m*) à-cause de-quoi déclara LUI-les-Dieux, non-pas - vous - vous-alimenterez de-toute substance de-l'enceinte-organique?

Let us examine the word נחש with the attention it merits, in order to prove the meaning contained in its root, not only by means of all the analogous idioms which possess it, but also by its own hieroglyphic composition.

This root is חש, which, as I have said in explaining the word חשך , *darkness*, indicates always an inner covetousness, a centralized fire, which acts with a violent movement and which seeks to distend itself. The Chaldaic, derives a great many expressions from it, all of which are related to anxiety, agony, sorrow and painful passions. It is literally, *a torrefaction;* figuratively, *an eager covetousness*, in the Arabic شَر. It is *a suffering, a grievous passion*, in the Syriac ܫܘ or ܫܘܫ. It is finally, *a turbulent agitation*, in the Ethiopic ሆውሽ (*housh*). This root verbalized in the Hebraic חיש, depicts the action of being precipitated, of being carried with violence toward a thing. The analogous verbs have the same meaning in Arabic, Ethiopic and Syriac. There is nothing in these which restricts us to the idea of a serpent.

The hieroglyphic analysis can perhaps give us the key to this mystery. The reader will doubtless remember that I have several

2. Wa-thâomer ha-Aîshah æl-ha-Nahash mi-pheri hetz ha-gan nâochel.

וַתֹּאמֶר הָאִשָּׁה אֶל־הַנָּחָשׁ מִפְּרִי עֵץ הַגָּן נֹאכֵל׃

---

times set down two different roots, אר and אש, to designate equally, the first principle, the elementary principle and the unknown priniple of things. I shall now state the important difference that the Egyptian priests conceived between these two roots, and in what manner they expressed this difference.

They attached to both, the idea of movement; but they considered אר as the symbol of movement proper, rectilinear; and אש as that of relative movement, circular. The hieroglyphic character which corresponded to these two movements was likewise *a serpent*: but a serpent sometimes straight and passing through the centre of a sphere, to represent the principle אר; sometimes coiled upon itself and enveloping the circumference of this sphere, to represent the principle אש. When these same priests wished to indicate the union of the two movements or the two principles, they depicted a serpent upright, uncoiling itself in a spiral line, or two serpents interlacing their mobile rings. It is from this last symbol that the famous caduceus of the Greeks has come.

The priests were silent as to the inner nature of both these principles; they used indifferently the radicals אר or אש to characterize the ethereal, igneous, aerial, aqueous, terreous, or mineral principle; as if they had wished to make it understood that they did not believe these simple and homogeneous things, but the composite ones. Nevertheless, among all these several significations, that which appeared the most frequently was that of fire. In this case, they considered the igneous principle under its different relations, sentient or intelligible, good or evil, and modified the radical word which represented it, by means of the signs. Thus, for example, the primitive אר became אֹר to designate *elementary fire*, אוֹר *light*, איר *intelligible brightness*, etc. If the initial vowel is hardened, it takes a character more and more vehement. הר represented *an exaltation*, literally as well as figuratively: חר, *a burning centre*, ער *a passionate, disordered, blind ardour*. The primitive אש was nearly the same.

2. And-she-said, *Aishah* (*A d a m*'s volitive faculty) to-that-covetous (passion): the-fruit, growing-substance of-the-organic-enclosure, we-may-feed-upon.	2. Et-elle-dit *A i s h a h* (la faculté volitive) à-cette-ardeur-cupide: du fruit, substance de-l'enceinte-organique, nous-nous-pouvons-alimenter.

The movement alone still distinguished the two principles, whether they were exalted or whether they were debased. The rectilinear movement inherent in the primitive אר, prevented the confusing of its derivatives with those of the primitive אש, in which the gyratory movement dominated. The two radicals רד and חש represented alike *a central fire;* but in the first חר, it was a central fire from which the igneous principle radiated with violence; whereas in the second חש, it was, on the contrary, a central fire from which this same principle being moved in a circular movement, was concentrated more and more and destroyed itself.

Such was the hieroglyphic meaning of this root which I have already examined under its idiomatic relations. This coincidence ought not to leave any doubt in the mind of the reader. Now the sign which governs it in the word נחש, is that of passive action, individual and corporeal; so that the devouring ardour expressed by the root חש, becomes by means of this sign, a passive ardour, cold in its vehemence, contained, astringent and compressive. Literally, it is every hard and refractory body; everything acrid, cutting and corroding; as *copper*, for example, which this word signifies in a very restricted sense; figuratively, it is every sentiment, painful, intense or savage, as *envy, egoism, cupidity*, it is, in a word, *vice*.

This is the real signification of the word נחש. I have been obliged to extend my proofs more than usual; but its importance demands it. It can be clearly seen that it does not signify simply a serpent. Moses, who has spoken so much of the reptilian life, in the beginning of the Beræshith, was careful not to employ it. The word שרץ which he uses, is that which, in his idiom, indicates veritably *a serpent*. One can easily recognize here the source of the French and Latin word, and that of the Celtic *sertz*, which is preserved without alteration in the modern Oscan.

ערום, *the-blind-and-general-passion....* What proves that the Sa-

3. W'mi-pheri ha-hetz âsher bethôch ha-gan âmar Ælohîm loâ-thoâcheloû mi-men-noû, w'loâ-thigghehoû b'ô, phen themutthoûn. וּמִפְּרִי הָעֵץ אֲשֶׁר בְּתוֹךְ־הַגָּן אָמַר אֱלֹהִים לֹא־תֹאכְלוּ מִמֶּנּוּ וְלֹא תִגְּעוּ בּוֹ פֶּן תְּמֻתוּן׃

4. Wa-iâomer ha-Nahash æl-ha-Aishah loâ-môth the-mutthoûn. וַיֹּאמֶר הַנָּחָשׁ אֶל־הָאִשָּׁה לֹא־מוֹת תְּמֻתוּן׃

---

maritan translator has not understood the word ערום, is that he has completely missed the meaning of it. He renders it by 2ᛘᛋᛉ⩟, *keen, cunning, subtle*, and makes it agree thus, with the strange idea that he appears to have really had, that נחש signified *a serpent*. The word ערום was nevertheless easy, very easy to explain; but how it could be said that *a serpent* is a passion, a vehemence, a blindness, and so to speak, an universal impulse in productive nature? This is, however, what is found in the root ער or עור. This root is none other than the primitive אר, of which I have just spoken at consider-able length, and which Moses causes to govern here by the sign of material sense ע; a sign almost always taken in the bad sense. The final sign ם, which he adds to it, indicates that the idea is generalized and should be taken in the broadest sense.

All the derivatives of the root עור, present a certain calamitous idea; first, it is ער *a violent adversary;* עור *a privation of sight;* then, it is ערום or ערים *a desert, a barrenness, a complete naked-ness,* literally as well as figuratively; it is מערה *a devastated place, an abyss, a cavern;* it is finally מערון, *an absolute blindness, a total abandonment.* In the sequence of these words can be placed the name that the Persians gave to the infernal adversary غريمن (*hariman*) which is nothing else than the word ערום referred to in this note, with the augmentative syllable ון.

v. 2. All these terms have been explained.

3. But-from-the-fruit of-the growth-itself, which-is-in-the-bottom-of the-organic-enclosure, he-declared, HE-the-Gods: not-may-you-feed upon-any-of-it and-not-may-you-dive (aspire, breathe out your soul) into-it; lest you-might-cause your unavoidable-dying.

3. Mais-du-fruit de-la-substance-même laquelle-est au-centre de l'enceinte-organique, il déclara, LUI-les-Dieux: non-pas vous-pourrez-vous-alimenter de-quoi-de-lui, et-n o n-p a s-v o u s-pourrez-plonger (aspirer votre âme) dans-lui; de-peur-que vous-vous-fassiez inévitablement-mourir.

4. And-it-said, eager-covetousness, unto-*A i s h a h* (*A d a m*'s volitive faculty) not-in-dying will-you-cause-your-unavoidable-dying.

4. Et-elle-dit, la passion - ardente - de - la - convoitise, à *Aishah* (la faculté volitive d'*Adam*) non-pas-mourant vous-vous-ferez-inévitablement-mourir.

---

v. 3. ולא־תגעו, *and-not-may-you-dive*.... That is to say, it is not permitted you to stretch out, to aspire, to have your desires. It is the verb נגע, employed here according to the enunciative form, active movement, future tense. The root גע, from which this verb springs, is remarkable: it signifies literally, in its verbal state, to expire, to bear its soul wholly into another life.

תמתון, *you-might-cause-your-unavoidable-dying*.... This is the verb מות, *to die*, used according to the intensive form, passive movement, second person plural, future tense, with the extensive sign ן. This final sign whose effect is always to extend the physical and moral sense, is used in this instance by Moses, to augment the force of the intensity and to depict imminent future. We shall see in time, the character ם, giving to active movement, the same extension that the one of which I have been speaking, gives to passive movement.

Finally the verb מות, is raised from the root מת , whose literal meaning is a fusion, a sympathetic extension, a passing, a return to the universal seity, according to the expression that its signs involve. Thus the idea that is contained in the Hebraic verb מות *to die*, has no connection with anything which pertains to destruction or anni-

5. Chi iôdeha Ælohîm chi b'iôm achale-chem mi-mem-noû, w'niphekehoû heîneî-chem w'îhithem che-Ælohîm iôdeheî tôb wa-rawh.

כִּי יֹדֵעַ אֱלֹהִים כִּי בְּיוֹם אֲכָלְכֶם מִמֶּנּוּ וְנִפְקְחוּ עֵינֵיכֶם וִהְיִיתֶם כֵּאלֹהִים יֹדְעֵי טוֹב וָרָע׃

6. Wa-theræ ha-Aishah chi-tôb ha-hetz l'maâchal w'chî thaâwa houâ la-heîn-aîm wa-nihe-mad ha-hetz l'hashechîl, wa-thikkah mi-pherî-ô, wa-thâochal wa-thitthen gam-l'Aîsh-ha him-ha, wa-îao-chal.

וַתֵּרֶא הָאִשָּׁה כִּי טוֹב הָעֵץ לְמַאֲכָל וְכִי תַאֲוָה הוּא לָעֵינַיִם וְנֶחְמָד הָעֵץ לְהַשְׂכִּיל וַתִּקַּח מִפִּרְיוֹ וַתֹּאכַל וַתִּתֵּן גַּם־לְאִישָׁהּ עִמָּהּ וַיֹּאכַל׃

---

hilation, as Moses has been accused of having thought; but, on the contrary, to a certain transmutation of the temporal substance. See Rad. Vocab. root את and מת.

v. 4. לֹא־מוֹת, *not-in-dying*.... It is essential to notice the repetition that Moses makes of the verb מות which I have just explained.

v. 5. יֹדֵת, *knowing*.... I have spoken of the formation of this facultative in v. 17, of the preceding chapter. I shall only state here that when it appears in the verse for the second time in the constructive plural ידעי, the luminous sign ו has disappeared, as hieroglyphic index of the catastrophe which is about to follow.

וְנִפְקְחוּ, *shall-be-opened-to-light*.... This is the verb פקה used according to the enunciative form, passive movement, third person plural, past tense, rendered future by the convertible sign ו. The root קה presents the idea of an effort that one makes toward a thing; a comprehension. This root verbalized in קוה signifies *to be extended, to be dilated*, in every way: governed by the sign פ, as it is in the example in question, it expresses every solution, every opening, especially that of the eyes and the ears, or the mouth.

COSMOGONY OF MOSES 101

5. For knowing, HE-the-Gods, that-in-the-day, food-for-yourselves, upon-some-of-it, (you will use) that-shall-be-opened-to-light the-eyes-yours; and-you-shall-be like-HE-the Gods, comprehending-good and-evil.

6. A n d-she-did-observe Aishah, that-good-was the-natural-g r o w t h for the-sense-of-taste, a n d-t h a t both-desired-it-was for-the-eyes, and-pleasing t o-t h e-highest-rate, that-growth, for-causing to-generalise-intelligence (to become universal); a n d-s h e-took-off some fruit-from-it and-she-did-feed-thereupon, a n d-she-gave-designedly also-to the - intellectual - principle-h e r-o w n, in-coalescence-with her; and-he-did-feed-thereupon.

5. Car sachant, LUI-les-Dieux, que dans-le-jour, aliment à vous de-quoi-de-lui, (vous ferez) seront-ouverts - à - la - lumière, les-yeux-à-vous, et-vous-serez tels-que LUI-les-Dieux, connaissant-le-bien et-le-mal.

6. Et-elle-considéra Aishah, que bonne-était la-substance-élémentaire selon-l e-goût, et-que mutuellement-désirée-elle-était selon-les-yeux, et-agréable autant-que-p o s s i b l e cette-substance, selon-l'action-d'universaliser-l'intelligence; et-elle-prit du-fruit-sien, et-elle-s'alimenta, e t-e l l e-donna-avec-intention aussi-à-l'être-intellectuel-sien, réuni-à-elle; et-il-s'alimenta.

---

v. 6. האוה, *both-desired*.... I make note of this only to call attention to the action of the sign ה; its root is אן or אי, which expresses every desire, as can be seen in the Rad. Vocab.

להשכיל, *for-causing to-generalize-intelligence*.... The verb שכל signifies, *to come to perfection, to achievement, to the fullness of things*. It is used on this occasion according to the excitative force, as nominal verb, inflected by the directive article ל. Its root כל expresses the totality, the universality of things, as I have explained in v. 1. of chapter II. This root, being verbalized, is found governed by the sign of relative movement ש, which augments its force, and gives it an usurping expression, physically as well as morally.

v. 7. כי עירמים, *that-void-of-light*.... Refer to first verse of this

7. Wa-thipkahena heî-nî sheneî-hem, wa-îedĉhoû ĉhi hirummîm hem, wa-îthepheroû haleh thænah, waîa-hashoû la-hem ha-goroth. וַתִּפָּקַחְנָה עֵינֵי שְׁנֵיהֶם וַיֵּדְעוּ כִּי עֵירֻמִּים הֵם וַיִּתְפְּרוּ עֲלֵה תְאֵנָה וַיַּעֲשׂוּ לָהֶם חֲגֹרֹת׃

chapter. It is always the same root עוּר, containing the idea of ardour, of a vehement fire, literally as well as figuratively. Formed from the root אוּר, which presents the idea of luminous corporeity, it becomes its absolute opposite. The one is a tranquil action; the other, a turbulent passion: here, it is an harmonious movement; there it is a blind, disordered movement. In the above example, the sign of manifestation י, has replaced the sign of the mystery of nature, and in this way Moses has wished to show that this terrible mystery was unveiled to the eyes of universal man, Adam. I can go no further in my explanation: the earnest reader must investigate for himself, the force and the concatenation of the Hebraic expressions; I have furnished him with all the means. The word ΛΩͻЖͱͻ϶ , by which the Samaritan translator has rendered עֵירֻמִּים, belongs to the root עָה, image of *darkness*, united to the root שׁפ, which develops all ideas of inflation, of vacuity, of vanity. The word עָשׁ, which is formed from it, signifies *an enormous excavation*, and also *a savage, voracious animal*.

ויתפרו, *and-they-yielded-forth*.... In this instance, the Hellenists have obviously and with deliberate purpose, exaggerated the vulgar sense, so as to thicken more and more the veil which they had resolved to throw over the Sepher, for it is evident that the verb פָּרֹות, used here according to the reflexive form, signifies, *to produce, to bring forth, to fecundate,* and not *to sew*. I do not see how they dared to take this ridiculous expression and still less why Saint Jerome agreed with them. The Samaritan version and the Chaldaic targum offered him quite an easy way. Here are their verbal translations.

ͱ϶Ж ΛͻЖϙϙ·ͱͻ϶ϙͻ
·ϜͻΑΑ

וחטיטו להון טרפי ראנין׃

"And-they-condensed a-condensation (a thick veil), elevation of sorrow-mutual-and-of-mourning."

"And-they-excited-profoundly in-them a-trouble (a confusion obscure) of sorrow-mutual-and-of-mourning."

7. And-were-opened the-eyes of-them-b o t h ; and-they-knew that-void-of-light (barren, unveiled in their dark origin) they-were, and-they-yielded-forth a-dark-covering (thick veil) with-s a d n e s s-a n d - mourning-formed; and-they-made-for-themselves-pilgrim-coats.

7. Et-furent-ouverts les-yeux à eux-deux; et-ils-con-nurent que d é n u é s-de-lumière (stériles, révélés dans leur obscur principe) ils-étaient; et-ils-se-firent-n a î t r e une-élévation-om-breuse (un voile) de-tris-t e s s e-mutuelle-et-de-deuil; et-ils-firent-à-eux-des-péleri-nes (des vêtemens de voya-ge).

One can see nothing in them which can excuse the extravagant Greek and Latin phrase: καὶ ἔρραψαν φύλλα συκῆς, "et consuerunt folia ficus," *and they sewed fig-leaves!*

For the Hebraic word עלה signifies neither *a leaf*, nor *leaves*, but a shadowy elevation, a veil; a canopy, a thing elevated above another to cover and protect it. It is also *an elevation; an extension; a height*. The root על develops all these ideas. As to the word תאנה, I admit that, in the ignorance which prevailed concerning the Hebraic tongue, it was a little difficult to explain. Yet what was the question? Only to distinguish the sign ת, a sign that the most ordinary grammarians have distinguished as an *héémanthe* or *paragogic*, and to which they have attributed, under these two relations, the faculty of expressing the continuity of things and their reciprocity. This distinction made, the word אנה has no longer the least difficulty. It is an expression of grief not only in Hebrew, but in Samaritan, Chaldaic, Syriac, Arabic and Ethiopic. It is formed of an onomatopoetic root which depicts the groans, sobs, pain and the *anhelation* of a person who suffers. This expressive root belongs to all tongues. One finds it united to the sign ת on several occasions, and especially to express a deep, mutual sorrow. It is presumable that the fig-tree has received the metaphorical name of תאנה on account of the mournfulness of its foliage, from which lactescent tears appear to flow from its fruits. However that may be, the onomatopoetic figure which is here presented for the first time, although it may be somewhat rare in Hebrew, is

8. Wa-îshamehoû æth-kôl Iהôah Ælohîm mithehallèch b'gan l'roûah ha-îôm, wa-îthehabbæ ha-Adam w'âisheth-ô mi-pheneî Iהôah Ælohîm be-thôch hetz ha-gan.

וַיִּשְׁמְעוּ אֶת־קוֹל יְהֹוָה אֱלֹהִים מִתְהַלֵּךְ בַּגָּן לְרוּחַ הַיּוֹם וַיִּתְחַבֵּא הָאָדָם וְאִשְׁתּוֹ מִפְּנֵי יְהֹוָה אֱלֹהִים בְּתוֹךְ עֵץ הַגָּן:

9. Wa-îkerâ Iהôah Ælohîm æl-ha-Adam, wa-îâomer l'ô aîe-čhah.

וַיִּקְרָא יְהֹוָה אֱלֹהִים אֶל־הָאָדָם וַיֹּאמֶר לוֹ אַיֶּכָּה:

10. Wa-îâomer æth-kôle-čha shamahethî ba-gan, wa-âîrâ čhî-heirom ânočhî, wa-æhabæ.

וַיֹּאמֶר אֶת־קוֹלְךָ שָׁמַעְתִּי בַּגָּן וָאִירָא כִּי־עֵירֹם אָנֹכִי וָאֵחָבֵא:

---

far from being wholly foreign as the Rad. Vocab. has shown. It is at first, in Hebrew, as in the Arabic اٰن or اٰى, only a kind of exclamation as *alas!* but, transformed into a verb by means of the convertible sign ו, it becomes אוֹן or אֲנֹה whose meaning is, to be plunged in grief, to cry out with lamentations. Thence אֲנָה, sorrow, affliction; and finally תְּאוּנָה or תְּאֻנָה deep and concentrated grief that one shares or communicates.

v. 8. מִתְהַלֵּךְ, *causing-itself-to-be-carried-to-and-fro*.... This is the verb הֹלֹךְ employed here according to the reflexive form, as continued facultative. The two roots which compose it הֹל־אֹךְ depicting the two opposed movements, excentric and concentric, of going away from and drawing near to. The Hellenists have so disfigured the meaning of this facultative, that instead of attributing it to the voice of God, they have applied it to God Himself, and have not hesitated to say that the Being-of-beings walked in the garden in the cool of the day: περιπατοῦντος ἐν τῷ παραδείσῳ πρὸς τοδειλινόν.

8. And-they-did-hear the voice-of IHOAH, HE-the-Being-of-beings, causing-it-self-to-be-carried-to-and-fro, in-the-o r g a n i c - enclosure with-the-s h i n i n g of-day-l i g h t: and-he-hid-himself, *Adam* (collective m a n) and-the-intellectual-wife-of-him (his volitive faculty) from-the-face-of IHOAH, HE-the-Gods, in-the-b o s o m of-the generative-substance of-the-organic-sphere.

8. Et-ils-entendirent-la-voix-même-de IHOAH, LUI-l'-Être-des-êtres, se-portant-en tous-sens, dans-l'enceinte-organique, selon-le-s o u f f l e-spiritueux du-jour: et-il-se-cacha, *Adam* (l'homme universel) et-la-femme-intellectuelle-à-lui (sa faculté volitive) de-la-face-de IHOAH, LUI-les-Dieux, au-centre de-la-substance de-la-sphère-organique.

9. And-he-uttered ‹t h e-name, IHOAH, HE-the-Gods, to-him-*Adam;* and-he-said to-him, where-of-thee (where has brought thee thy will)?

9. Et-il-prononça-le-nom, IHOAH, LUI-les Dieux, à-lui-*Adam;* et-il-dit-à-lui: où-de-toi (où t'a porté ta volonté)?

10. And-he-said (answering *Adam*), that-voice-thine, I-did-hear by-the-organic-enclosure, and-I-d i d-k e n-that void-of-light (unveiled in my blindness) I-was: and-I-hid-myself.

10. Et-il-dit (répondant *Adam*) cette-voix-t i e n n e j'ai-entendue en-l'enceinte-organique et-j'ai-vu-que dénué-de-lumière (révélé dans mon obscurité) j'étais: et-je-me-suis-caché.

---

v. 9. איכה, *where-of-thee?*.... The root אי contains not only all ideas of desire, will, inclination; but it designates also the place, the object toward which all these ideas tend, so that Moses in uniting to this root the nominal affix of the second person כה with its emphatic termination, has made one of the strongest and most forceful ellipses that has ever been made in any human tongue.

v. 10. All of these terms are understood.

v. 11. המי, *but-from-that*.... Moses, by another very bold

11. Wa-îaomer mî higgîd l'cha chî-heirom âthah, ha-min-ha-hetz âsher tziwîthî-cha lebilethî âchal mimen-noû âchaletha.

וַיֹּאמֶר מִי הִגִּיד לְךָ כִּי־עֵירֹם אָתָּה הֲמִן־הָעֵץ אֲשֶׁר צִוִּיתִיךָ לְבִלְתִּי אֲכָל־מִמֶּנּוּ אָכָלְתָּ׃

12. Wa-îaomer ha-Adam, ha-Aîshah âsher nathathah himmad-î hiwâ natthanah l'î min-ha-hetz, wa-âochel.

וַיֹּאמֶר הָאָדָם הָאִשָּׁה אֲשֶׁר נָתַתָּה עִמָּדִי הִוא נָתְנָה־לִּי מִן־הָעֵץ וָאֹכֵל׃

---

ellipsis, takes as substantive the extractive preposition מִן, and applies to it the determinative article ה, thus making it the cause of the collusion of Adam.

    v. 12. האשה, *Aishah*.... I have spoken sufficiently of the word איש whence comes the word אשה, but I beg the reader to observe closely here, with what force and what justice the cosmogonical ideas of Moses are connected and developed.

    Universal man אדם, being unable to remain in his universality, without remaining also in the volitive homogeneity of the Being-of-beings אלהים, and consequently in a sort of relative necessity, leaves this close dependence, when receiving a new development which individualizes and makes him an intelligent being איש; that is to say, a being susceptible of willing and of choosing freely for himself. The faculty which gives him power, emanates from himself; it is his intellectual companion אשה, his creative force: for it is by it that he creates; it is by means of this volitive faculty that he realizes his conceptions. He wills; and that which he wills exists. But this faculty is not homogeneous with the universal creative faculty of the Being-of-beings; for if it were, it would not exist, or *Adam* would be God. It has only the degree of force and extent that is given it, by the degree that *Adam* occupies in the order of the divine emanations. It can do all, except to create itself in going back to its principle and taking possession of it. It is essential that universal man should know

COSMOGONY OF MOSES

11. And-he-said (Ælohim): who has-taught-thee that-thus bare-thou-w a s t? but-f r o m-t h a t-n a t u r a l growth which-I-prescribed-unto-thee not-to-feed-upon-any-of-it.

11. Et-il-dit (Ælohim), qui a-enseigné-à-toi qu'ainsi-dénué tu étais? sinon-de-cette-substance-physique de-laquelle j'avais-prescrit-à-toi de nullement-t'-alimen-ter de-quoi-d'elle.

12. And-he-said *Adam* (collective man): *A i s h a h* (the volitive faculty) whom t h o u-didst-give, propping-mate-of-mine, it-is-that gave -to-me from-that-elementary -growth, and-I-have-fed-up-on.

12. Et-il-dit-*Adam* (l'-homme universel): *Aishah* (la faculté volitive) que-tu-donnas-compagne-à-moi, el-le-est-celle-qui a-donné à-moi de-cette-substance-phy-s i q u e; et-je-m'en-suis-ali-menté.

---

this important point at which his power is arrested, so that he does not lose himself through abuse of his liberty, and the retrograde movement of his volitive faculty. Moses takes the precaution of causing him to be instructed by the mouth of GOD Himself, not under the form of an absurd and despotic command, as the ignorant translators have made it understood, but in the form of a counsel, a paternal warning. *Adam* can make use of everything in the immense radius of the organic sphere which is allotted to him; but he cannot without risking his intellectual existence, touch the centre: that is to say, by wishing to seize the double principle of good and evil, upon which stands the essence of his intellectual being.

In all this, there is no question of planted garden, tree, fruit, rib, woman, or serpent, because, I cannot repeat too often, *Adam* is not, in the thought of Moses, a man of blood, of flesh and bones; but a man, spiritually and universally conceived, an intellectual being, of which *Aishah* is the creative faculty, that which realizes his conceptions in causing them to pass from power into action by his will.

Although this doctrine is assuredly to my liking, I do not pretend to be answerable for it; because I am, at this time, only translator. I give the Hebraic expressions as nearly as is possible for me to do;

13. Wa-îaomer I H O A H Ælohîm la-Aishah mahzâoth hashîth, wa-thâomer ha-Aishah ha-Nahash hishiâ-nî, wa-âochel.

וַיֹּאמֶר יְהוָׂה אֱלֹהִים לָאִשָּׁה מַה־זֹּאת עָשִׂית וַתֹּאמֶר הָאִשָּׁה הַנָּחָשׁ הִשִּׁיאַנִי וָאֹכֵל׃

14. Wa-îaomer I H O A H Ælohim æl-ha-Nahash, chîhashîtha zâoth, ârour athah! mi-chol ha-behemah, w'michol haîath ha-shadeh, halghehon-cha thelech, w'haphar thâochal chol-îemeî haîî-cha.

וַיֹּאמֶר יְהוָׂה אֱלֹהִים אֶל־הַנָּחָשׁ כִּי־עָשִׂיתָ זֹּאת אָרוּר אַתָּה מִכָּל־הַבְּהֵמָה וּמִכֹּל חַיַּת הַשָּׂדֶה עַל־גְּחֹנְךָ תֵלֵךְ וְעָפָר תֹּאכַל כָּל־יְמֵי חַיֶּיךָ׃

---

but I give them as grammarian. I affirm that it is this very thing that Moses has said, without affirming that it is this very thing which is. To establish a system is one thing; to explain a doctrine, another.

I regard Moses as a very great man, as a man chosen and inspired by Providence to fulfill a vast plan; but I am far from believing him infallible, exempt from every kind of error. It is for his Book, restored in its veritable expressions, to speak for him, and to defend him. All that I have endeavoured to do is to put the reader within reach of understanding it, freed from the thick veil which disguised it.

As to my translation, I leave it to itself. Let my readers judge whether it is not more conformable, not only to the genius of such a man as Moses, learned in all the sciences of the Egyptians, but also to simple human reason, to conceive a covetous passion, fermenting in elementary nature, which insinuates itself in the volitive faculty of the intelligent being, excites his pride, and persuades him to obtain possession of the very principle of his existence, in order to exist in an absolute manner, and to rival the Being of beings, than to see a serpent, the most subtle of the beasts of the field, crawling before

COSMOGONY OF MOSES

13. And-he-said, Iʜᴏᴀʜ, ʜᴇ-the-Gods, unto *A i s h a h* (*Adam's* volitive faculty) why-this hast-thou done? and-*Aishah*-said (answering) eager-self-c o n c e ï t (groveling passion) caused-me-to-become-delirious and-I-did-feed.

14. And-he-said, Iʜᴏᴀʜ, the-Being-of-beings, u n t o-t h a t-covetous-passion, because thou-hast-done that, cursed be-thou! amidst-all-terrestrial-animality, and-amidst-all-life of-nature: according-to-the-o b l i q u i t y-thine thou-shalt-grovellingly-proceed and-earth-exhalements thou-shalt-feed-upon all the-days of-the life-thine.

13. Et-il-dit, Iʜᴏᴀʜ, LUI-les Dieux, à *Aishah* (la faculté volitive d'*Adam*) pourquoi-cela fis-tu? et-elle-dit (répondant) *Aishah*, l'orgueil-cupide (cette insidieuse passion) fit-délirer-moi, et-je-m'alimentai.

14. Et-il-dit, Iʜᴏᴀʜ, l'-Être-des-êtres), à-ce-vice-insidieux (passion cupide) puisque tu-as-fait cela, maudit sois-tu parmi-tout-le-règne-animal et-parmi-toute-vie-de-la-nature-élémentaire. D ' a p r è s-l'inclination-tortueuse - tienne tu - agiras-bassement et-d'exhalaisons-physiques tu - alimenteras tous-les-jours-de l'existence-à-toi.

---

a woman, seducing her and causing her to eat of the fruit of a certain tree, planted in a certain garden, so as to become equal to the gods.

v. 13. הִשִּׁיאַנִי, *caused-me-to-become-delirious*.... The real root of this word has never been perceived. Nearly all the translators have seen a certain verb נשׁא, which has never existed. It is simply the substantive שִׁיא, which expresses the idea of disorder, and of void in the thoughts, employed as verb according to the excitative form, active movement, with the verbal affix נִי. The root proper of the substantive is שׁא, symbol of all whirling, frenzied, frantic movement. It appears to be formed by the reversing of the primitive אשׁ.

v. 14. גְּנֵהָךְ, *thine-obliquity*.... It was quite natural that those who had seen only a serpent in an insidious passion, should see only a belly where they ought to see the turnings, the inclination, of this same passion. The word גהן holds to the root גן, of which I have already spoken in v. 8. ch. II, and which, being found at that time relating to universal man, has been taken for *a garden*. The sign of

15. W'æîbah âshith beîn-cha w'bein ha-Aishah, w'bein zareh-cha w'bein zareh-ha hoûa îshouph-cha roâsh w'âthah thesouphe-noû ha-keb.

וְאֵיבָה אָשִׁית בֵּינְךָ וּבֵין הָאִשָּׁה וּבֵין זַרְעֲךָ וּבֵין זַרְעָהּ הוּא יְשׁוּפְךָ רֹאשׁ וְאַתָּה תְּשׁוּפֶנּוּ עָקֵב :

---

elementary existence which is here added to the root in question, depicts admirably the idea of Moses. But, in order that I may not be accused of having seen inappropriately in the word גִּהֵן, a moral bending, *an inclination*, I must state that the Hebrew verb גָּחֹן, which is derived from it, signifies *to bend, to incline*, and that it is the same in the Chaldaic, and in the Arabic جَحَ. As to the verb following תֵּלֵךְ *thou-shalt-grovellingly-proceed*, which all the translators have believed to be from the verb הָלֹךְ *to go and come, to walk up and down*, it is derived from the compound-radical לְכֹךְ or from the radical לוּךְ both of which signify literally *to get dirty, to wallow*, and figuratively, *to behave iniquitously, basely*.

וְעָפָר *and-earth-exhalements*.... That is to say, *igneous spirits, elementary vapours*, and perhaps also *corporeal illusions*. I have explained the roots of which this word is composed, in v. 7. ch. II. I shall only observe that this word was then used as facultative, instead of substantive as it is here.

v. 15. יָשׁוּף, *shall repress*.... The verb שׁוּף signifies *to centralize*, to act from the the circumference to the centre, as is proved by the signs שׁ and פ, of which the one expresses relative movement, and the other, interior action, particularly in its relations with the paternal sign ב, which it often replaces. This verb is used here according to the positive form, active movement, future tense. It is governed by the third person masculine, because the word וְרַע, which signifies literally *seed*, and which I have rendered in this instance by the word, *progeny*, is masculine in Hebrew.

רֹאשׁ, *the-principle*.... This word signifies not only *the head* or *the principle*, as I have already said: but it also signifies *the source of evil, the venom*. In this case the elementary root אֵשׁ is taken in the bad sense, and the sign ר, which governs it, is regarded as symbol of disordered movement.

עָקֵב, *the-bad-consequences (of evil)*.... Those who have seen in this same verse the bruised head of a serpent, have seen here the

15. A n d-a n-antipathy (natural averseness I-will-put between-thee and-between *Aishah* (*Adam's* volitive faculty) and-between the seed-thine, and-between the-seed of-it: it-shall (that-s e e d) repress-to-thee t h e-venomous-principle; and-thou shalt-repress the-bad consequences (of evil).

15. E t-u n e-antipathie-profonde, je metterai entre-toi et-entre *Aishah* (la faculté volitive d'*Adam*) et-entre la-propagation-à-toi, et-e n t r e-la-propagation-à-elle: elle (cette même propagation) comprimera (restreindra)-à-toi le-principe venimeux et-toi, tu-comprimeras-à-elle les-suites (du mal).

---

bitten heel of a woman: but how can the verb שׁוּף, signify at the same time *to bruise*, that is to say, to trample upon, and *to bite?* For Moses was careful to repeat this verb twice. If the modern Hebraists had wished to detach themselves a moment from the Hellenists, they might have seen that the word עָקֵב used here as the antithesis of רֹאשׁ, could not mean simply *the heel*, except in the most restricted sense; but that, in its most ordinary signification, it expresses *the consequences, the traces of a thing*, and particularly of evil, whose material sign ע it, moreover, bears. Indeed, this can be proved by a great number of Hebrew and Chaldaic passages, in which this word signifies *fraud, perversity, malice* and all the evil qualities generally, which belong to vice.

v. 16. עִצָּבוֹן, *the-woeful-natural-hindrances*.... The word עצב employed twice in this verse merits a particular attention. It springs from the two contracted roots עץ-צב. The first עץ should be known to us. It is the same one which forms the name of that mysterious substance whose usage was forbidden to *intellectual man*. It is not difficult to recognize in it, sentient, corporeal substance, and in general, the emblem of that which is physical, in opposition to that which is spiritual. The second צב contains the idea of that which is raised as hindrance, swells with wrath, arrests, prevents a thing, opposes with effort, etc.

Moses employs first, the word עצבון, after having added the ex-

112   THE HEBRAIC TONGUE RESTORED

16. Al-ha-Aishah âmar, ha-rebbah ha-rebbeh hittze-bône-che w'herone-che, b'-hetzeb theledî banîm w'æl-Aîshe-che theshoukathe-che, v'houâ îmoshal ba-che.

אֶל־הָאִשָּׁה אָמַר הַרְבָּה אַרְבֶּה עִצְּבוֹנֵךְ וְהֵרֹנֵךְ בְּעֶצֶב תֵּלְדִי בָנִים וְאֶל־אִישֵׁךְ תְּשׁוּקָתֵךְ וְהוּא יִמְשָׁל־בָּךְ׃

---

tensive syllable וֹן, wishing to indicate the general obstacles which shall be opposed henceforth to the unfoldment of the will of intellectual man, and which shall multiply its conceptions, forcing them to become divided and subdivided *ad infinitum*. He then makes use of the simple word עֶצֶב, to depict the pain, the torment, the agony which shall accompany its least creations. This hierographic writer would have it understood, that the volitive faculty shall no more cause intellectual conceptions to pass from power into action, without intermediary; but that it shall experience, on the contrary, deviations without number and obstacles of all sorts, whose resistance it shall be able to overcome, only by dint of labour and of time.

It is not necessary to say how the Hellenists have interpreted this verse. It is well known in what manner the ideas of Moses were materialized, and how the volitive faculty having been transformed into a corporeal woman, the physical hindrances opposed to the exercise of the will, have been no more than the pains which accompany childbirth. But one cannot accuse the Hellenists entirely of this change. It was an inevitable consequence of the corruption of the Hebraic tongue, of its total loss and of the wretched inclination of the Jews to bend everything to their gross ideas. Moreover the vulgar translation seems to offer at first some appearance of reason. Only a moment of reflection, nevertheless, is necessary to discover the error, as I hope to show in a few words.

In the first place, it is not true that Moses made the Being of beings say, that he will multiply *the sorrows and the conceptions* as the Hellenists translate it, λύπας καὶ στεναγμοὺς; but that he will multiply the number of *the obstacles and the conceptions*, as Saint Jerome has not been prevented from seeing, "ærumnas et conceptus". The Hellenists have followed, in this instance, a poor phrasing of the Samaritans: ᛏᛏᛚᛗᛋᛒ·ᛏᛏᛚᛉᛏᛘᛟ; whereas Saint Jerome adhered to the Chaldaic targum as more conformable with the Hebrew: צעריך ועדואיך ׃

16. Unto-the-volitive-faculty, he-said: the-number I-shall-multiply of-the-woeful-natural-hindrances-t h i n e, and -of-the-conceits-of-thee; in-panging-l a b o u r thou-shalt-bring-forth products: and-toward-the-intellectual principle-thine, the-desire-thou-shalt-lean of-thee; and-he will-rule in-thee (symbolical acting).

16. À-la-faculté-volitive, il-dit: le-nombre je-multiplierai des-obstacles-physiques-de-toute-sorte-à-toi, et-des-conceptions-tienne: en-travail-angoisseux tu-enfanteras des-produits; et-vers-le-principe-intellectuel-à-toi le-penchant-tu-a u r a s-tien; et-lui il-dominera en-toi (s'y représentera symboliquement).

Now, I ask, in the second place, how the Being-of-beings could have said to the corporeal woman that he would multiply the number of her conceptions or her *pregnancies*, as one understands it, since it would in such a manner shorten her life? Would he not rather have said that he would diminish the number, by rendering them more and more painful and laborious? But the Hebraic text is clear as the day. There is strong evidence that the Hellenists only abandoned it to follow the Samaritan version, because they saw plainly that it exposed the spiritual meaning, as indeed it does. For, while it is in accordance with reason and experience, to think that the volitive conceptions increase in proportion to the obstacles which are opposed to their realization and which force them to be divided, it is absurd and contradictory to affirm it of the pregnancies of physical woman, which are necessarily diminished with the pains, maladies and sufferings which accompany and follow them.

תלדי בנים, *thou-shalt-bring-forth products....* The compound radical verb ילוֹד comes from the root לד, which, formed by the union of the signs of directive movement and of natural abundance, expresses all propagation, all generation, all extension of being. This verb is employed in Hebrew, literally as well as figuratively, as much in relation to the generation of spirit, as to that of substance, without any distinction of sex: so that it is wrong when one has wished to restrict the meaning to a corporeal childbirth. The word which follows בנים, is also very far from signifying simply *children*. It characterizes, in general, the analogous creations of a creative being, whatever it may be.

17. W'l'Adam, âmar, chi-shamahetha l'kôl Aisheth-cha, wa-thâochal min-ha-hetz âsher tziwîthîcha l'-æmor loâ-thâochal mi-men-noû; ârrourah ha-âdamah bahabour cha, b'hitzabôn thoâchelnah chol-îemei haîî-cha.

וּלְאָדָם אָמַר כִּי שָׁמַעְתָּ לְקוֹל אִשְׁתֶּךָ וַתֹּאכַל מִן־הָעֵץ אֲשֶׁר צִוִּיתִיךָ לֵאמֹר לֹא־תֹאכַל מִמֶּנּוּ אֲרוּרָה הָאֲדָמָה בַּעֲבוּרֶךָ בְּעִצָּבוֹן תֹּאכֲלֶנָּה כֹּל יְמֵי חַיֶּיךָ:

תְּשׁוּקָתֵךְ, *the-desire-thou-shalt-lean of-thee....* This is an ellipsis of such boldness that the Hebrew tongue is the only one that permits it. The verb שׁוּק signifies *to have a movement, a tendency toward a determined end,* as water, for example. Now, in what manner does Moses express the tendency which the volitive faculty shall submit to its intellectual principle? He takes this verb, and after having employed it according to the positive form of the second person future, feminine singular, he makes abruptly a constructive noun of it, by means of the sign ת, which he adds to it; in this state he joins the nominal affix ךְ, as if to say in an hieroglyphic manner, that the dependence in which the will shall be with regard to its principle, shall take away nothing of its liberty and shall be as a result of its own tendency. I know of no other tongue in the world where this ellipsis could be rendered.

יִמְשָׁל, *he-will-rule....* The verb מָשׁוֹל, which means equally *to rule,* and *to be represented, to be expressed by symbols,* is used with purpose in this passage, to conceal no doubt a mystery which is not my purpose to penetrate; for I translate Moses and do not comment. One can see what I have said in v. 16 ch. 1. The Samaritan makes use of the same verb 𐤌𐤔𐤋.

v. 17. There are no difficult terms here.

v. 18. וְקוֹץ, *and-harsh-and-rough-productions....* The root קוֹץ expresses the action of *cutting, cutting off, tearing.* It is impossible not to feel here, the effect of the compressive and cutting sign ק united to the terminative sign ץ.

וְדַרְדַּר, *and-the-uncultivated-and-unruly-productions....* The root דר furnishes the idea of circuit, of order, period, age and circular habitation; but in doubling the last character, which is that of movement proper, one opens, as it were, the circle, and obtains the intensive root דרר, which signifies *license, a rupture of order, an invasion.* It is

COSMOGONY OF MOSES

17. And-unto-*Adam* (collective man) he-said: because thou-hast-listened to-the-voice of-the-intellectual-mate-thine (thy volitive faculty) and-hast-fed-upon the-elementary-growth which I-did-prescribe-to-thee by-saying: not-shalt thou-feed-upon any-of-it: cursed! be-the-adamic (homogeneal, universal ground) for-the-sake-thine: with-panging-labour shalt-thou-feed-upon-it all-the-days (manifesting lights) of-the-lives-thine-own.

17. Et-à-*Adam* (l'homme universel) il-dit: puisque tu-as-écouté à-la-voix de l'-épouse-intellectuelle-à-toi (ta faculté volitive) et-que-tu-t'es-alimenté de-cette substance, laquelle j'avais-fortement-recommandé à-toi, selon-ce-dire: non-pas-tu-t'alimenteras de-quoi-d'elle: maudite! soit-la-terre-adamique (homogène et similaire à toi) dans-le-rapport-tien: en-travail-angoisseux tu-t'alimenteras-d'elle tous-les-jours (les manifestations phénoméniques) des-vies-à-toi.

---

this last word that is derived from the one which makes the subject of this note, and by which one expresses, in general, all unruly productions, whether literal or figurative. The Hebraic genius derives *liberty*, in the good sense, from the word דרר, which is *license* or evil liberty, by simply inserting the intellectual sign ו, as is seen in the word דרור.

עשב, *upon-the-most-sharp-and-wasted-fruits-of-nature*.... We know that the primitive root אש is applied, in general, to the elementary principle of things, and in particular, to *fire*. We also know that by reinforcing the initial vowel א, it suffices to increase progressively its force. Now, if the word which is the subject of this note, is composed of the contracted roots עש־אב, of which there is no doubt, it will signify not simply χορτός, *dried grass, herb of the field*, following the interpretation of the Hellenists, weakened by Saint Jerome; but indeed, *a sharp and wasted fructification*. For this is the true meaning of the word עשב. The Arabic عشب is explicit.

v. 19. בזעת עפיך, *in-a-tossing-motion of-the-mind-thine*.... When the Hellenists said, ἐν ἱδρωτι τοῦ προσώπου σου: *in the sweat of thy face*, the natural inference is, that this phrase was in the Hebrew text, but it is not there. The face of Adam has never sweat physically except in the mind of the translators of Moses. The hierographic

18. W'kôtz w'dareddar thatzemîha la-ċha w'âċha-leth æth-hesheh ha-shadeh.

וְקוֹץ וְדַרְדַּר תַּצְמִיחַ לָךְ וְאָכַלְתָּ אֶת־עֵשֶׂב הַשָּׂדֶה׃

19. B'zewhath âpphei-ċha thoâċhal lehem, had shoûb-ċha æel-ha-Adamah, ċhi-mi-men-nah lukkahetha ċhi-haphar âthah w'æl-haphar thashoûb.

בְּזֵעַת אַפֶּיךָ תֹּאכַל לֶחֶם עַד שׁוּבְךָ אֶל־הָאֲדָמָה כִּי מִמֶּנָּה לֻקָּחְתָּ כִּי־עָפָר אַתָּה וְאֶל־עָפָר תָּשׁוּב׃

---

writer did not have such ideas. The word זעת comes from the root זוע which develops the idea of a *restless agitation*, an anxiety, a movement of fear for the future. The word which follows אף can, in truth, signify *the nose*, in a very restricted sense, but it expresses much more generally, not *the face*, but the irascible part of the soul which constitutes the animistic mind, or the understanding.

עד שוב, *till-the-restoring-thine*.... The verb שוב, being formed of the root שב, expressing every idea of restitution, of return toward a point of departure, and this root being itself composed of the sign of relative duration, and of the paternal and central sign, it is evident that this verb must be applied to every moral or physical revolution, which brings the being back to its primitive state. See Rad. Vocab. roots שב, אוב and שו.

עפר, *spiritual-element*.... Although I have already spoken several times of this important word, I cannot refrain from referring to it again here, because it is to the wrong interpretation of the translators, that one must impute the accusation of materialism brought against Moses; an accusation from which it was impossible to clear him as long as one had only the version of the Hellenists, or that of their imitators. For, if man is drawn from the dust, and if he must return to the dust, as they make him say, where is his immortality? What becomes of his spiritual part? Moses says nothing of it, according to them. But if they had taken the trouble to examine the verb שוב they would have seen that it expressed not a material return, but a

18. And-harsh and-rough productions (thorns a n d thistles) shall-plentifully-g r o w for-thee; and-thou-shalt-feed upon-the-m o s t-sharp-and-wasted-fruits of-nature.

18. E t-l e s-productions-tranchantes, et-les-product-ions-i n c u l t e s-et-désordon-nées germeront-abondam-ment pour-toi; et-tu-t'ali-menteras des-fruits-âcres-et-desséchés de-la-nature-élé-mentaire.

19. In-a-tossing motion of-the-mind-thine shalt-thou-eat-f o o d till-the-restoring thine (rising again) toward-the-a d a m i c (homogeneal l a n d) ; for-such-as f r o m some-of-it wast-thou-taken, such-spiritual-element art-thou and-toward-the-spirit-ual-element wilt-thou-rise-again.

19. En-agitation-contin-uelle de-l'esprit-tien, tu-t'ali-menteras de-nourriture jus-qu'au-restituer (au réinté-grer, au ressusciter)-tien à-la-terre-adamique (homogè-ne et similaire à toi)car-tel-de-quoi-d'elle tu-as-été-tiré, tel-esprit-élémentaire tu-es; et-à-l'élément-spiritueux tu-dois-être-restitué.

---

restitution to a place, to a primordial state, *a resurrection*, in the sense that we give today to this word; they would have seen that this place was, not the earth, properly speaking, אֶרֶץ; but the similitude of man, his original, homogeneous country, אֲדָמָה, and they would have seen finally, that this was neither *the dust* of the one, nor *the mire* of the other, to which he must return; but the spiritual element, principle of his being.

v. 20. חוה, *Hewah*.... Here is a name where the changing of the vowel into consonant has caused a strange metamorphosis. This name which, according to the allusion that Moses makes, ought to signify, and signify effectively, *elementary existence*, being derived from the absolute verb הוֹה *to be-being*, by the sole reinforcement of the initial vowel ה into ח, has come to designate no more than a formless heap of matter, its aggregation, its mass; and by the harden-ing of the convertible sign ו sanctioned by the Chaldaic punctuation, serves as verb only to indicate the inert and passive existence of things. The change brought about in the derivative verb הוה, has been even more terrible in the absolute verb, הֹוֶה; for this verb, des-tined to represent the Immutable Being, expresses only an endless cal-

20. Wa-îkerâ ha-A d a m shem Aisheth-ô hawah ćhî-hiwâ haîth æn-ćhol-haî.

וַיִּקְרָא הָאָדָם שֵׁם אִשְׁתּוֹ חַוָּה כִּי הִוא הָיְתָה אֵם כָּל־חָי׃

21. Wa-îahash I H O A H Ælohîm l' Adam w'l'âisheth-ô-ćhi-thenôth hôr wa-îalebbish'em.

וַיַּעַשׂ יְהוָה אֱלֹהִים לְאָדָם וּלְאִשְׁתּוֹ כָּתְנוֹת עוֹר וַיַּלְבִּשֵׁם׃

22. Wa-îâomer I H O A H Ælohîm hen ha-Adam haîah ćhi-ahad mi-mennoû, la-dahath tôb wa-rawh, w'hatthah phen-îshelah îad-ô w'lakah gam me-hetz ha-haîîm, w'-âćhal, w'a-haî l'holam.

וַיֹּאמֶר יְהוָה אֱלֹהִים הֵן הָאָדָם הָיָה כְּאַחַד מִמֶּנּוּ לָדַעַת טוֹב וָרָע וְעַתָּה פֶּן־יִשְׁלַח יָדוֹ וְלָקַח גַּם מֵעֵץ הַחַיִּים וְאָכַל וָחַי לְעֹלָם׃

---

amity, as I have explained in speaking of the Sacred Name יהוה, in v. 4. ch. II. As to the reasons for the alterations undergone by this proper noun I can only refer the reader to the name of the volitive faculty, אשה which, as we have seen, had preceded that of elementary existence חוה. See v. 22, ch. II and v. 12 of this chapter.

v. 21. כתנות, *body-like*.... It is because they have not wished to recognize the assimilative article כ that the Hellenists have interpreted *garments*, χιτῶνας instead of body. The root הן, from which the plural substantive here referred to is derived, develops every idea of added substance, or of corporeity increasing more and more.

עוֹר, *sheltering-shapes*.... It is from this badly understood root that the verb עור *to watch over the defence, to guard,* is derived, and the substantive עִיר, *a city;* that is to say, a fortified enclosure. Thence *urbs*, in Latin; *ward*, in Saxon; *gare, garde,* and even *boule-vard,* in French: all these words express the same idea of a place destined to guard and to defend. I beg the reader to consider that this new envelope עוֹר, in which dominates the sign of material sense ע, is substituted for the ancient גן, which has been ridiculously taken for a garden.

v. 22. כאחד, *such-as-one*.... I only mention this word to show the use of the assimilative article כ, an important article often misunderstood by the translators.

20. A n d-h e-designated, *Adam,* for-name to-the intellectual-mate-of-him (his volitive faculty) *H e w a h* (elementary existence) because it-was the-mother of-all-existence.

21. And-he-made, IHOAH the-Being-of beings, unto-*Adam* (collective man) and-unto-the-intellectual-mate-of-him, body-like sheltering-shapes; and-he-involved (incrusted)-them-carefully.

22. And-he-said, IHOAH, HE-the-Gods, B e h o l d ! *Adam* being such-a s-o n e from-those-of-us, by-knowing good and-evil: and-now lest-he-should put-forth the-hand-his-own and-take also from-the-elementary-growth of-lives and-feed-upon, and-l i v e for-an-infinite-period (forever):

20. Et-il-assigna, *Adam,* nom-à l'épouse-intellectuelle-sienne (sa faculté volitive) *Hewah* (existence élémentaire) à-c a u s e-qu'elle-était la-mère de-toute-existence.

21. Et-il-fit, IHOAH, l'-Être-des êtres à-*Adam* (l'-h o m m e-universel) et-à-l' épouse-intellectuelle-sienne, tels-que-des-corps de-défense (des remparts) et-il-les-enveloppa-avec-soin.

22. Et-il-dit, IHOAH, LUI-les-Dieux, V o i c i ! *A d a m* étant tel-qu'un de-l'espèce-à-nous, selon la-connaisance du-bien et-du-mal: et-à-ce-temps, de-peur-qu'il-étendra la-main-s i e n n e et-prendra a u s s i de-la-substance-élémentaire des-vies, et-qu'il-s'alimentera et-vivra selon-la-période-infinie (l'éternité):

מעץ החיים, *from-the-elementary-growth-of-lives....* I think I have made the signification of the word עץ sufficiently clear, so that I can dispense with any further detail to prove that it signifies neither *wood,* nor even *tree;* as the translators, either through ignorance or intent of purpose, had said: but what I believe should be added, is, that the text here reads החיים *of lives,* and not החיה, *of life,* as they have translated it in their versions. This difference is very essential. The Samaritan says ꙮꙮꙮ. ꙮꙮꙮ : *the growth,* or *the natural substance of lives,* exactly as the Hebrew. I trust that the etymologist will find pleasure in seeing that the word רע, by which the Hebrew text ex-

23. Wa-î s h a l l e h-hoû IHÔAH Ælohîm mi-gan-he-den la-habod æth-ha-âdamah âsher lukkah mi-sham.

וַיְשַׁלְּחֵהוּ יְהֹוָה אֱלֹהִים מִגַּן־עֵדֶן לַעֲבֹד אֶת־הָאֲדָמָה אֲשֶׁר לֻקַּח מִשָּׁם׃

24. Wa-îgaresh æth-ha-Adam, wa-iashe-chen mi-kedem l'gan-heden æth-ha-che-r u b b î m, w'æth-lahat ha-hereb ha-mithehappecheth li-shemôr æth-derech hetz ha-haîîm.

וַיְגָרֶשׁ אֶת הָאָדָם וַיַּשְׁכֵּן מִקֶּדֶם לְגַן־עֵדֶן אֶת־הַכְּרֻבִים וְאֵת־לַהַט הַחֶרֶב הַמִּתְהַפֶּכֶת לִשְׁמוֹר אֶת־דֶּרֶךְ עֵץ הַחַיִּים׃

---

presses *evil*, in this phrase, לדעת טוב ורע, *by-knowing good and-evil*, is rendered in the Samaritan text by the word ᵐᛗ𐌈𐌐 . Now this word, pronounced *bish* or *vish* is very certainly the one whence is derived the Latin *vitium*, from which we have made *vice*. This derivation merits observation for many reasons. The Teutonic and Saxon have preserved this word with slight alteration, the one, in *bös*, and the other, in *bad*. The Chaldaic and Syriac agree in the sense of the word בִּישׁ and ܒܝܫ : the Arabic alone differs.

v. 23. לוּקַּח, *he-had-been-taken from*.... It is the verb לָקַח *to take, to draw, to extract*, used here after the intensive form, passive movement, third person singular. I make this remark only to show that the median character ק, should be doubled if the interior point does not take the place of the second. This verb which is written without the Chaldaic *kibbuz*, has need of the character ו to indicate the passive movement.

v. 24. מִקֶּדֶם, *from-the-foregone-principle-of-times*.... See v. 8. ch. II.

הַכְּרֻבִים, *that-self-same-Cherubim*.... The root רַב, which contains the idea of all multiplication, of all infinite number, has already been explained. It is used in the plural and governed by the assimilative sign כ.

23. Then-he-parted-him, IHOAH, the Being-of beings, from-the-enclosing-sphere of-sensible-times; for-working that-same-adamic (homogeneal ground), which he-had-been-taken-from.

24. And-he-put-forth that-same *Adam* (collective man) and-he-caused-to-abide from-the-foregone-principle-of-times near-the-organic-sphere of-temporal-sensibleness that-selfsame-Cherubim (innumerable legions like) and-that-selfsame-flaming of-wild-destruction, whirling-round-on-itself to-keep the-way of-the-elementary-growth of-lives.

23. Alors-il-detacha-lui-IHOAH, l'Être-des-êtres, de-la-sphère-organique de-la-sensibilité-temporelle; afin-de-travailler cette-même-substance-adamique, de-laquelle il-avait-été-pris-hors.

24. Et-il-éloigna ce-même-*Adam* (l'homme universel), et-il-fit-résider de-l'antériorité-universelle - des temps, à-la-sphère-temporelle-et-sensible, ce-même,-Cherubim (un être semblable aux innombrables légions) et-cette-même-flamme-incandescente de-l'ardeur-dévastatrice tourbillonnant-sans-cesse-sur-elle-même, pour garder la-route de-la-substance-élémentaire des-vies.

החרב, *of-wild-destruction*.... The Hellenists who sought to restrict everything and to materialize everything, have rendered this word by that of ρομφαία, *a sort of waving sword.* It can be remarked that the most petty images are always the ones that they have chosen. They took pains not to see here the root חר, expressing every wild destruction, every igneous, wrathful force, modified by the active and central sign ב : a single word badly veiled would have sufficed to betray the spiritual sense that they wished to hide.

המתהפחת, *whirling-round-on-itself*.... This is the verb חפך, *to turn*, used according to the reflexive form, as feminine, continued facultative. This facultative is preceded by the emphatic article ה, in order to take for it, the place of the modificative, and to increase its force.

SEPHER BERÆSHITH D.

סֵפֶר בְּרֵאשִׁית ד׳

1. W'ha-Adam îadah æth-Hewah Aisheth-ô, wa-thahar, wa-theled æth-Kaîn, wa-thâomer kanîthî aîsh æth-Ihôah.

וְהָאָדָם יָדַע אֶת־חַוָּה אִשְׁתּוֹ וַתַּהַר וַתֵּלֶד אֶת־קַיִן וַתֹּאמֶר קָנִיתִי אִישׁ אֶת־יְהֹוָה׃

---

v. 1. אֶת־קַיִן, *the-self-sameness of-Kain*.... Need I speak of the importance that the peoples of the Orient have attached to proper names, and of what deep mysteries their sages have often hidden beneath these names? Had I space here to express myself in this subject, my only perplexity would be making a choice among the numberless proofs. But the time is short and these notes are already too voluminous. The intellectual reader has no need of a vain display of useless erudition, to be taught what he already knows. Let it suffice therefore, for me to say that Moses is the one, of the writers of antiquity, who has developed most subtly the art of composing proper names. I have endeavoured to give an idea of his talent, or that of his instructors in this respect, by developing the name of universal man אדם, *collective unity, eternal similitude*, and that of the Supreme Divinity יהוה, *the Being who is, who was, and who will be*. But I must make it clear that these two names, and some others, were sufficiently elevated by their nature to be translatable without danger. The names which follow will be, almost all, a very different matter. Moses has been often obliged to throw over them a veil, that I ought and wish to respect. Although I might perhaps give the literal word, I shall not do so. I inform my reader of this in order that he may be watchful: for if he desire it, nothing shall prevent him from knowing.

The root of the name *Kain*, is קן, which is composed of the eminently compressive and trenchant sign ק, and that of produced being ן. It develops the idea of strongest compression and of most centralized existence. In the proper name under consideration, it is presented animated by the sign of manifested power: thus קין, can signify *the strong, the powerful, the rigid, the vehement*, and also

GENESIS IV.

1. And-he-*A d a m* (collective man) knew-that-selfsame-*H e w a* (elementary life) intellectual-mate-of-him (his-volitive-faculty) and-she-conceived, and-she-bare the-selfsameness of-*Kain* (the strong, the mighty one; he who lies in the centre, who assumes and assimilates to himself) and-she-s a i d, I-d i d-c e n t r e (framed by centering) an-intellectual-being selfsameness of-IHOAH.

COSMOGONIE IV.

1. Et-lui-*Adam* (l'homme universel) connut-cette-même-*Hewa* (l'existence-élémentaire) l'épouse-intellectuelle-sienne (sa faculté volitive) et-elle conçut, et-elle-enfanta l'existence-de-*Kain* (le forte, le puissant; celui qui tire au centre, qui saisit, qui agglomère, qui assimile à soi); et-elle-dit, j'ai-centralisé (formé par centralisation) un-être-intellectuel de-l'essence-même-à-IHOAH.

---

the central, that which serves as basis, rule, measure; that which agglomerates, appropriates, seizes, comprehends, assimilates with itself. It is in this last sense that Moses appears to have represented it in the verb which follows.

קָנִיתִי, *I-did-centre*.... This is the verb קָנֹה, used according to the positive form, active movement, first person, past tense. The Hellenist translators who have made it signify *to get*, have chosen, as is their habit, the most restricted sense. The Arabic words قين and قان which have the same root, signify *to forge, to agglomerate, to equalize, to form*.

The Samaritan translator has rendered this same verb קָנֹה, by which Moses explains the name of *Kain*, by ᛏᛉᛃ *to rule*, to display the power of a king; so as to have good cause for saying that, in a multitude of tongues, the idea of power and of royalty has come from the root *Kan, Kin*, or *Kain*. See Rad. Vocab.

אֶת־יְהֹוָה, *selfsameness-of* IHOAH.... The savants who know the lively quarrels that this expression has caused, particularly since Luther asserted that it should be translated: *I have acquired a man who is the Lord*, will perhaps be interested in seeing what the prin-

2. Wa-thosseph la-ledeth æth-âhî-ô æth-Habel, wa-îhî hebel roheh tzoâm, w'Kain haîah hobed âdamah.

וַתֹּסֶף לָלֶדֶת אֶת־אָחִיו אֶת־הָבֶל וַיְהִי הֶבֶל רֹעֵה צֹאן וְקַיִן הָיָה עֹבֵד אֲדָמָה ׃

---

cipal translators have thought. I am about to satisfy them by quoting successively the Samaritan, Chaldaic, Hellenist and Latin phrase.

𐡀𐡁𐡂𐡃𐡄𐡅𐡆𐡇   I have-sovereignly-typified a-hero from-IHOAH.

קניתי גבר קדם ייי ׃   I have-acquired-in-central-force a-hero in-principle from-the Eternal.

Ἐκτησάμην ἄνθρωπον διὰ τοῦ Θεός.   I have-gotten a-man through GOD.

Possedi hominem per Dominum.   I have-gotten a-man through the-Lord.

The Hebrew is understood. The hieroglyphic mystery consists of the way in which Moses has employed the designative proposition את, which indicates the selfsameness or the objectivity of things, as constructive substantive, with the Sacred Name of the Divinity יהוה.

v. 2. את־הבל, *the-selfsameness-of-Habel*.... Moses, for reasons which were particular ones, has given no ostensible explanation of this name. We can, to a degree, make up for this silence by an examination of the root from which it is derived. This root is בל, which, composed of the sign of interior action ב, joined to that of expansive movement ל, expresses all ideas of expansion, dilation and tenuity. Therefore, if we have understood that the compressive force could be characterized by the root קן, we shall understand now that the expansive force can be characterized by the root בל; consequently, every time one has seen strength, power, density, possession, in the name of *Kain*, one has also seen weakness, rarity, surrender, in that of *Habel*.

But it must not be believed that this force and this power, which the name of *Kain* characterizes, have always been taken in the good sense. Very far from it: for the majority of the peoples have attached to it only a blind fatality, and *Kain* has been for them only the

2. And-she-added by-the bringing-forth the-brotherly-self-of-h i m, t he -selfsameness-of-*H a b e l*, and-he-was, *Habel*, a-leader (overseer) of-the-indefinite-being (elementary corporeal world) and *Kain*, was-a-servant (a tiller) of-the-adamic (homogeneal ground).

2. Et-elle-ajouta p a r-l' action-d'enfanter l'ipséité-fraternelle-à-lui, l'existence-*d'Habel*; et-il-fut *Habel*, conducteur (surveillant) de-l' être-indéfini, (le monde corporel) et-*Kain*-fut serviteur, (ellaborateur) de-l'élément-adamique.

---

genius of Evil. In this case, the contrary attributes contained in the name of *Habel*, are adorned with more favourable shades: the weakness has become gentleness and grace; the rarity, spiritual essence; surrender, magnanimity: *Habel*, in short, has been the genius of Good. These singular contrasts exist in the tongues of the Hebrews and of the Chaldeans; for if the word בל signifies *the mind*, and *the soul* which is its source; this same word also offers the negative relation, *no*: and if one finds יבול, to express ideas of abundance, profusion and even of inundation, one finds also the word בלי, to express those of lack, want, absolute nothingness. The emphatic sign ה, added to this singular root, can be likewise, in the name of *Habel*, the emblem of that which is noblest in man: thought and meditation; or of that which is vainglorious, the illusions of pride, and vanity itself.

It is the same with the qualities expressed in the name of *Kain*, which become good or bad, according to the manner in which they are considered.

אין, *the-indefinite-Being*.... The root of this word, as the one of which I have just spoken, has the singular property of the same contradictory ideas. Also, it is not without reason that Moses, who did not wish to explain the name of *Habel*, has employed the word אין, as synonym in hieroglyphic style. I believe it to be useless to explain here, how it is that אין, whose proper meaning is *indefinite-being*, *world, time*, as can be recognized in the Greek word αἰών which is derived from it, has characterized at the same time, in Hebrew, *being* and *nothingness*, *weakness* and *virtue*, *riches* and *poverty*; because this is again a consequence of the degradation of its vocal sound of

3. Wa-îehî mi-ketz îam-îm wa-îabæ Kaîn mi-pherî ha-âdamah minehh la-IHÔAH.

וַיְהִי מִקֵּץ יָמִים וַיָּבֵא קַיִן מִפְּרִי הָאֲדָמָה מִנְחָה לַיהוָה׃

4. W'Habel hebîa gam-houâ mi-bechorôth tzoân-ô, w'me-heleb-be-hen, wa-îshah, IHÔAH, æl-Habel w' æl-minehath-ô.

וְהֶבֶל הֵבִיא גַם־הוּא מִבְּכֹרוֹת צֹאנוֹ וּמֵחֶלְבֵהֶן וַיִּשַׁע יְהוָה אֶל־הֶבֶל וְאֶל־מִנְחָתוֹ׃

---

which I have spoken sufficiently. All that I believe necessary to add is, that the Hellenists have rendered the word צאן by πρόβατον, *a flock of sheep*, because they have taken it, following their habit, in the most restricted sense. For the sign of final movement צ, being united with the root אן or אין, *produced being*, has made it in general צאן, *indefinite being;* in particular, *a body*. Now it is very easy to perceive that this word צאן signifying *a body*, needs only a simple abstraction of thought, to make it signify *a troop* or *a flock*. The Hebrews have said *a corps of sheep*, and simply *a corps*, to express *a flock;* as we say *a corps of soldiers*, and simply *a corps*, to signify *a troop*.

The Samaritan renders the word צאן by that of ᐯᗅᒑ, which contains the several significations of *tabernacle, temporal dwelling, time, corporeal aggregation, corps*, etc. It is the analogue of the Hebraic root עון, as can be seen in the Radical Vocabulary.

v. 3. מקץ ימים, *from-the-end-of-the-seas*.... The translators of Moses, either accustomed to see in *Adam*, a material and limited man, or conforming in this to the vulgar ideas of their time, have been forced either to see men of blood, flesh and bones, in *Kain* and *Habel*, or feign to see them, making it impossible to render the clear and simple signification of this verse. For how could it be said that a man, such as they conceived him in *Kain*, made an offering to IHOAH from the end of the seas? They have easily substituted the expression of *days* for that of *seas*, because the Hebraic word does not differ; but what could they do with מקץ which can absolutely signify only *from the end, the extremity, the summit?* Some, as the Samaritan and the Chaldaic translators, were content to be unintelligible; the

COSMOGONY OF MOSES

3. Now-it-was from-the-end of-the-seas, t h a t-h e-caused-to-go, *Kain*, from-the-product of-the-adamic (elementary ground) an-offering unto-IHOAH.

4. And-*Habel* caused-to-go, also-he, from-the-firstlings of-the-w o r l d of him, a n d - from-the-quintessence (the best, over-t o p p i n g qualities)-of-them: and-he-proved-a-saviour, I H O A H, unto-*Habel*, and-u n t o-the-offering-of-him.

3. Or-ce-fut de-la-cime d e s-m e r s, qu'il-fit-a l l e r, *Kain*, du-produit de-l'élé-ment-adamique, (homogè-ne) un-oblation à IHOAH.

4. Et-*Habel* fit-a l l e r, aussi-lui, des-prémices du-monde-à-lui; et-de-la-quin-tessence (de la qualité émi-nente)-à-eux: et-il-se-mon-tra-sauveur, IHOAH, envers-*Habel*, et-envers-l'offrande sienne.

Hellenists have changed the text, in which they have been followed by Saint Jerome. They have said: καὶ ἐγένετο μέθ' ἡμέρας, "factum est autem post multos dies." *It came to pass after many days....* Now according to the thought of the hierographic writer, *Kain*, being a cosmological being, very different from a man properly so-called, can, without the least incongruity, cause to ascend to IHOAH, an offering from the end of the seas, or from the superficies of phenomenal manifestations, if one would fathom the hieroglyphic meaning of the word ימים.

v. 4. מבכרות צאנו, *from-the-firstlings of-the-world-of-him....* The word בכר comes from the two roots בא־כר of which the first בא develops every idea of progression, of gradual progress, of generative development; the second כר, designates all apparent, eminent things which serve as monument, as distinctive mark; so that, by בכר, should be understood, that which, in a series of beings, takes precedence, dominates, characterizes, announces, presages, etc. This word has important relations with בכר, of which I have spoken in v. 5, ch. I. The Arabic کٰ signifies literally, *to be early;* figuratively, *to prosper, to surpass, to take precedence with brilliance, with glory.* Thence بَاکُرٌ or بِکْرٌ; *a virgin.*

5. Wæl Kaîn w'æl-mine-hath-ô loâ-shahah, wa'îhar l'Kaîn m â o d wa-îpheloû phanaî-ô. וְאֶל־קַיִן וְאֶל מִנְחָתוֹ לֹא שָׁעָה וַיִּחַר לְקַיִן מְאֹד וַיִּפְּלוּ פָנָיו׃

6. Wa-îâomer IHÔAH æl-Kaîn, lammah harah le-ċha, w'lammah napheloû phaneî-ċha. וַיֹּאמֶר יְהֹוָה אֶל־קָיִן לָמָּה חָרָה לָךְ וְלָמָּה נָפְלוּ פָנֶיךָ׃

ומחלבהן, *and-from-the-quintessence-of-them*.... The Hellenists having interpreted *a flock*, for *a world*, have been obliged necessarily, in order to be consistent, to interpret *first-born* instead of *firstlings*, and the *eminent qualities* of these same firstlings, as *fat*. Such was the force of a first violation of the text. All of these base and ridiculous ideas spring one from another. Either they have purposely remained silent or else they were ignorant of the first elements of the Hebraic tongue, not to feel that the word חלב signifies *fat*, only by an evident abuse made by the vulgar, and that the two roots חל and לב, of which it is composed, being applied, the one, to every superior effort, and the other, to every quality, to every faculty, resulting from this effort, the word חלב, ought to characterize every extraction of essential things: which is proved by the meaning attached to it by the Chaldeans and the Hebrews themselves; taking the substantive, for milk or cream; and the verb, for the action of milking, extracting, making emanate. Thence innumerable relative expressions. ܚܠܒ is taken in Syriac for *cream, foam, sperm*, etc.; the Ethiopian word ሐለብ (*he-leb*), offers as does the Arabic حلب the ideas of *emulsion; derivation, emanation, distillation*, etc

וישע, *and-he-proved-a-saviour* .... The verb שעה has been taken by all translators in the sense of *having regard, of respecting;* but it should here be in the sense of *redeeming, of saving, of leading to salvation*. It is from the root שע, containing in itself all ideas of preservation, salvation and redemption, which come, on the one hand, from the compound radical verb ישע and on the other, from the compound שעה, whose signification is the same. When this latter verb

COSMOGONY OF MOSES   129

5. And-unto-*Kain*, and-unto-the-offering-h i s-o w n, n o t-to-prove-a-s a v i o u r: which-raised-up-the-w r a t h of-*Kain* quite-thoroughly; a n d-w e r e-cast-down the-faces-of-him.

5. Et-envers-*Kain*, e t-envers-l'o b l a t i o n-sienne, non-pas-se-montrer-sauveur : c e-qui-causa-l'embrasement à-*Kain* tout-à-fait ; et-furent-abattues les-faces-siennes.

6. And-he-said, Iнoaн, unto-*Kain*;•why the-raising-up-t h e-fiery-wrath-to-thee? and-w h y the-casting-down of-the-faces thine?

6. Et-il-dit, I н o a н, à-*Kain*; pourquoi le-soulèvement-e m b r a s é-à-toi? et-pourquoi la-chute (la dépression) de-la-face-tienne?

---

expresses the action of having regard or respect, it is composed of the root עו, which is related to exterior and sentient forms of objects, governed by the sign of relative movement ש.

    v. 5 and 6. There is nothing difficult in these terms: the meaning itself need not perplex, only so far as the nature of *Kain* and *Habel* is not clearly understood. I would call attention to the fact, that from the beginning of this chapter, Moses, employs only the sole Sacred Name of Iноaн, to designate the Divinity. It seems that he may have omitted the plural surname אלהים *Ælohim*, нe-the-Gods, to make it understood that God no longer acts toward the two brothers, only in his primitive unity.

    v. 7. הלוא, *the-not-being*.... The bold and numerous ellipses with which this verse abounds, render it very difficult to be understood. It is generally the manner of Moses, to be lavish with ellipses when making the Divinity speak. At first, it is here the negative relation לא, *not*, which, animated by means of the sign ו, and inflected substantively by means of the determinative article ה, makes the entire phrase a single word issuing simultaneously from the mouth of God. It seems, by an effect of this boldness, that the divine thought is substantialized, as it were, so as to be grasped by man.

    שאת, *that-the-sign*.... What then could be more rapid than this figure? The pronominal article ש, united without intermediary to

7. Ha-lôâ-aîm-theîtîb sh'-æth w'aîm loâ-theîtîb-la-phethah ha-tâth robetz, w' æleî-c̀ha theshoûkath-ô w' athah thimeshal-b'ô.

הֲלוֹא אִם־תֵּיטִיב שְׂאֵת וְאִם לֹא תֵיטִיב לַפֶּסַח חַטָּאת רֹבֵץ וְאֵלֶיךָ תְּשׁוּקָתוֹ וְאַתָּה תִּמְשָׁל־בּוֹ׃

8. Wa-iâomer Kaîn æl-Habel âhî-ô, wa-îhî bi-heiôth'am be-shadeh, wa-îakam Kaîn æl-Habel âhî-ô, wa-îahareg-hoû.

וַיֹּאמֶר קַיִן אֶל־הֶבֶל אָחִיו וַיְהִי בִּהְיוֹתָם בַּשָּׂדֶה וַיָּקָם קַיִן אֶל־הֶבֶל אָחִיו וַיַּהַרְגֵהוּ׃

---

the designative preposition את, does it not depict with an inimitable energy, the rapidity with which the good that man does, leaves its imprint in his soul? This is the seal of Moses. The translation of the Hellenists here is wholly amphibological. These are words which are related one with another without forming any meaning.

v. 8. ויהי בהיותם, *and - it - was by - the-being-both in-the-begetting-nature*.... All the translators have believed that there existed before this word, a lacuna which they felt obliged to fill, by inserting as in the Samaritan text, copied by the Hellenists and by Saint Jerome:

ꝗꝗ·ꝗꝗ: διέλθωμεν εἰς τὸ πεδικῶν: "egrediamur foras." *Let us go into the field*, or *outside*.

But they have not noticed that the verb אמר which signifies not simply *to say*, but *to declare one's thought, to express one's will*, has no need, in Hebrew, of this indifferent course. *Kain* and *Habel*, I repeat, are not men of blood, of flesh and bones; they are cosmogonical beings. Moses makes it felt here in an expressive manner, by saying, that at this epoch they existed together in nature. They existed thus no longer from the moment that the one rising in rebellion against the other, had conquered its forces.

ויהרגהו, *and-he-slew-him*.... This verb comes from the two contracted roots הר־רג. The first, which is an intensifying of the

COSMOGONY OF MOSES

7. The-not-being, if-thou-sh a lt-d o-w e l l, t h a t-the-sign (the token in thee)? and-if not-thou-wilt-do-well, a t-t h e-d o o r the-sin-lying; and-unto-t h e e the-mutual-p r o n e n e s s-its own, and-t h o u! the-symbolical-sympathetic-acting unto it?

7. Le-non-pas-être, si-tu-feras-bien, que-le-sign (l'-image du bien en toi)? et-si non-pas-être, tu-f e r a s-bien, à-l'entrée le-péché reposant, et-envers-toi le-desir-mutuel-sien, et-toi! la représentation-mutuelle dans-lui?

8. And-now-he-declared-his thought, *Kain,* unto *Habel* the brother-his-own: and-it-was by-the-being-both in-the-begetting-nature: then-he-rose-up (stood up substantially) against-*Habel* the-brother-his-own; and-he-slew-him.

8. Et-ensuite, il-déclara-sa-pensée, *Kain,* à-*Habel* le-frère-sien: et c'était durant-l'action-d'exister – ensemble-dans-la-nature-productrice: or il-s'insurgea (s'éleva en substance, se matérialisa) contre-*Habel,* le-frère-s i e n, et-il-immola-lui.

---

primitive אֵ, designates in general, *an exaltation, an height;* it is literally, *a mountain,* and figuratively, that which is strong, robust, powerful; the second root ין, characterizes a disorganizing movement. Thus *Kain* displays against *Habel,* only the power of which he is possessor, that which results from physical force.

This same allegory is found in the Pouranas of the Hindus, under the names of *Maha-dewa,* in place of *Kain,* and of *Daksha* in place of *Habel. Maha-dewa* is the same as *Siwa,* and *Daksha* is a surname of *Brahma,* which can be translated by *Ethereal.* The Egyptians gave to *Kronos* of the Greeks, whom we call *Saturn,* after the Latins, the name of *Chivan* or *Kiwan;* this same *Kiwan* was, from most ancient times, adored by the Arabs of Mecca under the figure of a black stone. The Jews themselves gave to Saturn this same name of כיון; and one can read, in a Persian book cited in the English Asiatic Researches,

9. Wa-îâomer IHÔAH æl-Kaîn, æî-Hebel âhî-cha, wa-îâomer loâ-îadahethî, ha-shomer âhî ânochî.

וַיֹּאמֶר יְהוָֹה אֶל־קַיִן אֵי הֶבֶל אָחִיךָ וַיֹּאמֶר לֹא יָדַעְתִּי הֲשֹׁמֵר אָחִי אָנֹכִי׃

10. Wa-îâomer meh hashîtha kôl dhemei âhî-cha tzohakîm æloî min-ha-âdamah.

וַיֹּאמֶר מֶה עָשִׂיתָ קוֹל דְּמֵי אָחִיךָ צֹעֲקִים אֵלַי מִן־הָאֲדָמָה׃

11. W'hatthah, arour âthah min-ha-âdamah âsher phatzethah æth-phî-ha lakahath æth-dhemeî âhî-cha mi-îade-cha.

וְעַתָּה אָרוּר אָתָּה מִן־הָאֲדָמָה אֲשֶׁר פָּצְתָה אֶת־פִּיהָ לָקַחַת אֶת־דְּמֵי אָחִיךָ מִיָּדֶךָ׃

12. Chi thahabod æth-ha-âdamah, loâ thosseph theth-choh-ha, la-cha nawh wa-nad thiheîeh b'âretz.

כִּי תַעֲבֹד אֶת־הָאֲדָמָה לֹא־תֹסֵף תֵּת־כֹּחָהּ לָךְ נָע וָנָד תִּהְיֶה בָאָרֶץ׃

---

that the Hindus had formerly many sacred places, dedicated to *Kywan*, who was no other than their *Siwa* or *Siwan*, of which I have spoken above.

v. 9. Contains no difficulty.

v. 10. דְמֵי, *the-likenesses*.... The Hellenists seeing, or feigning to see in *Habel*, a corporeal man, could not avoid seeing a man of blood in the word דְמֵי: but this word, in the constructive plural, and agreeing with the facultative צֹעֲקִים, should have caused Saint Jerome

9. And-he-said, IHOAH, unto-*Kain*, where-is *Habel*, the-brother-thine? and-he-said (answering *Kain*) not-did-I-know: the-keeper of-the-brother-mine am-I?

10. And-he-said, IHOAH, what-hast-thou-done? t h e-voice of-the-l i k e n e s s e s (identic future progenies) of-the-brother-thine, groaning-rise t o w a r d-m e from-the-a d a m i c (elementary ground).

11. And-this-time, cursed b e-thou! from-the-adamic, which did-open the-mouth-its-own for-receiving those-likenesses (future progenies) of-the-brother-thine, by-the-hand-thine-own.

12. Then-whilst thou-shalt-work t h a t-a d a m i c (elementary ground) not-will-it-yield the-strength its-own unto-thee: staggering a n d-r o v i n g (wandering with fright) thou-shalt-be in-the-earth.

9. Et-il-dit I H O A H, à *Kain*, où-est *Habel*, le-frère-tien? et-il-dit (répondant *Kain*): non pas-savais-je; le-gardant du-frère-m i e n suis-je.

10. Et-il-dit, IHOAH, que-fis-tu? la-voix des-homogèn-éités (des générations identiques) du-frère-tien plaignantes, s'élève-vers-moi de l'élément-adamique.

11. Et-à-ce-temps, maudit sois-tu! de-l'élément-adamique, lequel ouvrit la-bouche-sienne pour-recevoir ces-homogénéités (ces générations futures) du-frère-tien, par-la-main-à-toi.

12. Ainsi-quand tu-travailleras cet-élément-adamique; non-pas-il-joindra don-de-force-virtuelle-sienne à-toi: vacillant (agité d'un mouvement incertain) et-vaguant (agité d'un mouvement d'effroi) tu-seras en-la-terre.

---

to think that Moses meant something else. The Chaldean paraphrast had perceived it in writing this phrase thus:

רב־זרעין דעתידין למפק *The-like-generations which-future-progenies were-*
מן אחוך קבלן קדמי.... *to-proceed of-the-brother-thine, groaning-are before-me....*

v. 11. These terms are understood.
v. 12. נע, *staggering*.... A very remarkable root which, with

134   THE HEBRAIC TONGUE RESTORED

13. Wa-îaomer Kaîn æl-IHÔAH gadôl haôn-î mi-neshoâ. וַיֹּאמֶר קַיִן אֶל־יְהֹוָה גָּדוֹל עֲוֹנִי מִנְּשׂוֹא:

14. H e n , gherashetha âoth-î ha-iôm me-hal pheneî ha-â d a m a h, w'mi-phaneî-cha æs-s a t h e r, w'haîîthî nawh wa-nad ba-âretz, w' haîah chol-mot-zeâ-î îahe-regnî. הֵן גֵּרַשְׁתָּ אֹתִי הַיּוֹם מֵעַל פְּנֵי הָאֲדָמָה וּמִפָּנֶיךָ אֶסָּתֵר וְהָיִיתִי נָע וָנָד בָּאָרֶץ וְהָיָה כָל־מֹצְאִי יַהַרְגֵנִי:

---

the one following, assists in penetrating the nature of *Kain*: mysterious nature, the understanding of which would lead very far. This root is used here in the continued facultative, active movement and should be written נִיע. The radical verb which is formed from it, נוּע, signifies *to be moved about, to stagger, to wander aimlessly.* One must remark here that the sign of produced being נ, is arrested by the sign ע, which is that of material sense.

נד, *roving*.... Another facultative **which** should be written נוּד. The radical verb נוּד, which is derived **from it,** expresses a movement of flight, of exile; a painful agitation. The **sign** of division ד, replaces in this root, the sign of material sense, with which the preceding one is terminated.

v. 13. עֲוֹנִי, *the-perverseness-mine*.... Let us consider a moment this word, whose whole force comes from the sign ע. We have seen in v. 2 of this chapter, that the root אן, which characterizes in general, the produced being, time, the world, developed the most contrary ideas following the inflection given to the vocal sound: expressing sometimes being, sometimes nothingness; sometimes strength, sometimes weakness: this same root, inclined toward the bad sense by the sign ע, is now fixed there and no longer signifies anything but what is perverse. It is, as it were, the opposite of being: it is vice, the opposite of that which is good.

And let us notice its origin: it is worthy of attention. הוּד is, as we well know, the verb *par excellence, to be-being.* But this verb, ceasing to be absolute in particularizing itself in speech, can be corrupted: that is to say, the vocal sounds which constitute it can be materialized in passing into consonants. This is what happens in the word היה, where the intellectual sign ו, becoming extinct, indicates

COSMOGONY OF MOSES   135

13. And-he-said, *Kain,* unto-IHOAH, great-is the-perverseness-mine by-the-cleansing.

14. Lo! thou-hast-driven-out mine-own-self this-day, from-over-the-face of-the-adamic: then-from-the-face-thine shall-I-be-hid, and-I-shall-be-staggering and-roving in-the-earth: and-he-shall-be, every-one finding-me, he-who-shall-slay-me.

13. Et-il-dit, *Kain,* à-IHOAH, grande-est la-perversité-mienne par-la-purification.

14. Voici! tu-as-chassé l'ipséité-mienne ce-jour, de-dessus-la-face de-l'élément-adamique: donc-de-la-face-à-toi je-me-cacherai-avec-soin, et-j'existerai tremblant et-vaguant-en-la-terre: et-il-sera, tout-trouvant-moi, le-qui-accablera-moi.

---

thenceforth, only *a calamity.* Nevertheless, the root of life הח, remains there still, and this word receives from it enough force to designate sometimes *desire,* and the *substance* which is its object: but if this root is altered entirely, as in עוה then nothing good subsists: it is *perversity, the absolute depravation of being.*

Now, from the verb הוה, *to be-being,* was formed the root אִין or הין, by the addition of the final character ן, image of every increase and sign of produced being: we have seen its several acceptations. It is in the same manner that, from the verb, עוה *to be depraved, perverted,* is formed the substantive עֻן or עִוּן, whose signification and origin I have just explained.

v. 14. יהרגני, *he-who-shall-slay-me....* Here, by the effect of an ellipsis of another kind, is a verb, employed according to the positive form, active movement, third person future, which is transformed into a qualificative noun, in order to become the epithet of every being who finding *Kain,* shall slay him.

v. 15. לכן, *thus-saying....* This is the **assimilative preposition** כן inflected by the directive article ל. The Hellenist translators who have seen the negation לא are evidently mistaken, as is proved by the Samaritan and Chaldaic paraphrasts who read it as I have.

יקם, *he-shall-be-caused-to-raise....* This expression is remarkable for the manner in which it has been misinterpreted by nearly all the translators. Moses did not say, as he has been made to say, that he

15. Wa-îâomer l'ô IHÔAH, la-chen chol-horeg Kaîn shibehathîm îukkam waîashem I H Ô A H l'Kaîn âôth l'billethî haccôth âôth-ô chol motzæ-ô.

וַיֹּאמֶר לוֹ יְהֹוָה לָכֵן כָּל־הֹרֵג קַיִן שִׁבְעָתַיִם יֻקָּם וַיָּשֶׂם יְהֹוָה לְקַיִן אוֹת לְבִלְתִּי הַכּוֹת־אֹתוֹ כָּל־מֹצְאוֹ׃

16. Wa-îetzæ Kaîn mi-l'phenî IHÔAH wa-îesheb b' æretz-nôd kidemath heden.

וַיֵּצֵא קַיִן מִלִּפְנֵי יְהֹוָה וַיֵּשֶׁב בְּאֶרֶץ־נוֹד קִדְמַת־עֵדֶן׃

17. Wa-îedah Kaîn æth-âisheth-ô, wa-thahar wa-theled æth-Hanôch, wa-îhî-boneh whîr, wa-îkerâshem ha-whîr che-shem ben-ô Hanôch.

וַיֵּדַע קַיִן אֶת־אִשְׁתּוֹ וַתַּהַר וַתֵּלֶד אֶת־חֲנוֹךְ וַיְהִי בֹּנֶה עִיר וַיִּקְרָא שֵׁם הָעִיר כְּשֵׁם בְּנוֹ חֲנוֹךְ׃

---

who shall kill *Kain* shall be punished seven-fold; but that he who shall slay him shall give him seven times more strength. The verb קוּם, which is used in this instance, is the same as the one used in v. 8. of this chapter, to depict the action of *Kain* being raised against his brother. This must not be forgotten, for this verb is purposely repeated here. Moses has employed it according to the excitative form, passive movement, future tense. He would have it understood by this, that *Kain* shall influence in such a manner the being who would slay him, that this being shall himself receive the blows which he believes will fall upon *Kain*, and increase sevenfold his strength in thinking to annihilate it.

v. 16. All these terms have been explained.

COSMOGONY OF MOSES 137

15. And-he-declared-his-will unto-him, IHOAH, thus saying; e v e r y-one-slaying *Kain*, seven-fold he-shall-be-caused-to-raise (*Kain*): and-he-put, IHOAH, unto-*Kain*, a-token, in-order-that-not-at-all could-strike-him, everyone-finding-him.

16. A n d - h e-withdrew, *Kain*, from-over-against the-face of-IHOAH, and-dwelt in-the-land of-the-banishment, (of the staggering w i t h fright) t h e-foregone-principle of-temporal-sensibleness.

17. And-he-knew, *Kain*, the-intellectual-m a t e-h i s-own (his volitive faculty): and-she-conceived a n d-she bare the-selfsameness of-*Henoch*, (the founder, the central might): then-he-builded a-sheltering-w a r d, and-he-designated-the-name-of-that-ward by-the-name of-the-son-his-own *Henoch*.

15. Et-il-déclara sa-volonté à-lui IHOAH, ainsi disant; tout-accablant *Kain* les-sept-fois il-fera-exalter *Kain*: et-il-mit, IHOAH, à-*Kain* un-signe afin-de-nullement-pouvoir frapper-l u i, tout-trouvant-lui.

16. Et-il-se-retira, *Kain*, de-devant le-face de-IHOAH; et-il-alla habiter dans-la-terre d'exil (de la dissension de l'effroi), l'antériorité temporelle de-la-sensibilité-élémentaire.

17. Et-il-connut, *Kain* la-femme-intellectuelle-sienne (sa faculté volitive): et-elle-conçut et-elle-enfanta l'-existence-de-*H e n o c h* (la force centrale, c e l u i qui fonde): ensuite-il-f u t-édifiant un-circuit-de-retraite, (un lieu fort) et-il-désigna-le-nom-de-ce-circuit par-le-nom-du-fils-à-lui, *Henoch*.

---

v. 17. חֲנוֹךְ, *Henoch*.... Again I urge the reader to give close attention to the proper names; for to them Moses attaches great importance. The greater part of the hieroglyphic mysteries are now in the form of these names. The one referred to in this passage, is composed of the two roots חן and אך. The first חן, characterizes proper, elementary existence: it is a kind of strengthening of the analogous root הן, more used, and which designates *things* in general. The second אך, contains the idea of every compression, of every effort that the being makes upon itself, or upon another, for the

18. Wa-îwaled la-Hanôch æth-W h i r a d, w'Whirad îalad æth-Mehoûjaæl w'Mehoûjaæl îalad æth-Methoûshaæl îalad æth-Lamech.

וַיִּוָּלֵד לַחֲנוֹךְ אֶת־עִירָד וְעִירָד יָלַד אֶת־מְחוּיָאֵל וּמְחִיָּאֵל יָלַד אֶת־מְתוּשָׁאֵל וּמְתוּשָׁאֵל יָלַד אֶת־לָמֶךְ׃

19. Wa-îkkah-lô Lamech shethî nashîm, s h e m haâhath Whadah, w'shem hashenith Tzillah.

וַיִּקַּח־לוֹ לֶמֶךְ שְׁתֵּי נָשִׁים שֵׁם הָאַחַת עָדָה וְשֵׁם הַשֵּׁנִית צִלָּה׃

---

purpose of fixing itself or another. The verb which comes from these two roots, חנוך signifies *to fix, to found, to institute, to arrest any existence whatsoever.*

It is from a composition quite similar, that the personal pronoun אנכי, *myself*, in Hebrew, results; that is to say אן or הן, *the finished, corporeal being,* אוּך, *founded,* י, *in me.*

v. 18. עירד, *Whirad....* This noun is formed from two roots עור and רד: the first עור, offers the idea of all excitation, ardour, interior passion: the second רד, depicts proper, indefinite movement, as that of *a wheel*, for example. For the rest, consult Radical Vocabulary for these roots and those which follow.

מחויאל, *Mehoujael....* This is the verb חוי, *to manifest, to announce, to demonstrate*, employed as facultative, according to the intensive form, by means of the initial character מ and terminated by the root אל, which adds the idea of strength and unfoldment.

מתושאל, *Methoushael....* This noun comes from two distinct roots. The first מות, designates *death*: the second שא, characterizes every emptiness, every yawning void, every gulf opened to swallow up. In the hieroglyphic formation of the word מתושאל, the con-

COSMOGONY OF MOSES 139

18. A n d-it-was-caused-to-beget unto *Henoch* the-selfsameness-o f-*W h i r a d*, (stirring-up motion, self-leading p a s s i o n): and *W h i r a d* begat *Mehujael* (elemental manifestation of existence) and-*Mehujael* begat *Methushael*, (d e a t h ' s fathomless pit) : and-*Methushael* begat *Lamech* (the tie of what tends to dissolution, thing's pliant bond).

18. E t-i l f u t-faire-produire à-*Henoch* l'existence-de-*Whirad*, (le mouvement excitateur, la passion, la volonté c o n d u c t r i c e) ; et-*Whirad* produisit celle-de-*Mehoujael* (la manifestation de l'existence) et *Mehoujael* produisit celle-de-*Methoushael*, (le gouffre de la mort), et-*Methoushael* produisit-celle-de-*Lamech* (l e nœud qui saisit la dissolution et l'arrête; le lien flexible des choses).

19. And-he-took - u n t o-him, *Lamech*, two corporeal-wives (two natural faculties) ; the-name of-the-one-was *Whadah*, (the periodic, the testifying) and-the-name of-the-second, *Tzillah* (the deep, the dark).

19. Et-il-prit-p o u r-l u i, *Lamech*, deux épouses-corporelles, (deux facultés physiques) : le-nom de-la-première était-*Whadah* (la périodique, l'évidente) : et-le-nom de-la-seconde, *Tzillah* (la profonde, l'obscure, la voilée).

---

vertible sign of the first root ו, has been transposed to serve as liaison with the second, to which has been joined by contraction, the syllable אל whose signification I have given.

למך, *Lamech*.... The roots of this name are clear and simple. It is, on the one part, לך, which contains all ideas of cohesion and agglutination, and on the other מוך, which develops all those of liquefaction, dissolution, prostration, submission, etc. Therefore, this name characterizes the kind of bond which prevents a thing, at first vehement, violent, and now subdued, softened, cast down, ready to be dissolved, from being dissolved and from being wholly dissipated.

The reader can observe that *Lamech* is here the descendant of *Adam*, by *Kain* in the sixth generation, because we shall see reappear another who shall be by *Seth*, in the eighth.

v. 19.   שתי נשים, *two-corporeal-wives*....   I beg the attentive

20. Wa-theled Whadah æth-Jabal, houâ haîah âbî îsheb âohel w'mikeneh.　וַתֵּלֶד עָדָה אֶת־יָבָל הוּא הָיָה אֲבִי יֹשֵׁב אֹהֶל וּמִקְנֶה׃

21. W'shem âhî-ô Joubal, houâ haîah âbî ĉhol-thophesh ĉhi-nor w'hoûgab.　וְשֵׁם אָחִיו יוּבָל הוּא הָיָה אֲבִי כָּל־תֹּפֵשׂ כִּנּוֹר וְעוּגָב׃

---

reader to remember that intellectual man איש, *Aish*, had not yet appeared upon the cosmogonical scene, and that Moses had only named universal man אדם, *Adam*, when he mentioned for the first time intellectual woman אשה, **Aishah, volitive faculty** of universal man. Thus it is, that the name of the Adamic element אדמה, had preceded the name itself of *Adam*. The hierographic writer follows still the same course. Corporeal man אנוש, *Ænosh*, is not born, and behold already corporeal woman who appears as the double physical faculty of the cosmogonic being, designated by the name of *Lamech*, descendant of *Kain*.

I shall not dwell now upon the radical etymology of the word which Moses uses on this occasion. I shall wait until making the analysis of the name itself of corporeal man אנוש, from which it is derived. For the moment, I shall only observe that corporeal woman is not presented as such, but as divided in two physical faculties, *Whadah* and *Tzillah*, the evident and the veiled, whose productions we are about to see.

עדה, *Whadah*.... In this proper name should be seen the root עור, which characterizes the periodic return of the same thing, its evidence and the testimony rendered.

צלה, *Tzillah*.... This name is attached to the root צול, which

COSMOGONY OF MOSES 141

20. And-she-bare, *Whadah*, the-selfsameness of-*Jabal*, (the over flowing, the waterish, the plenty of nature) he-who was the-father (founder) of-the abode-aloft, (repairing distinguished place) and-of-the-own-making-might, (lawful property).

21. And-the-name-of-the-brother-of-him was-*J u b a l*, (universal effluence, principle of sound, jubilation, thriving) he-who was the-father (founder) of-every conception, hint-brightness-like and-love-worthy (useful and pleasing arts).

20. Et-elle-enfanta *Whadah* ce-qui-concerne-*Jabal*, (le flux des eaux, l'abondance naturelle, la fertilité), lui-qui fut le-père-(le créateur) de l'habitation-élevée (lieu de retour fixe et remarquable,) et-de-la-force-concentrante et- appropriatrice, (la propriété).

21. Et-le-nom du-frère-à-lui était-*Joubal*, (le fluide universel, le-principe du son celui qui communique la joie et la prospérité), lui-qui fut le-père de-toute-conception-lumineuse et-digne-d'amour (de toutes les sciences et de tous les arts utiles et agréables).

---

designates a depth to which the light cannot penetrate, a dark, gloomy place; a shadowy, veiled thing, etc.

v. 20. יבל, *Jabal*.... This is the root בל or בול spoken of in v. 2 of this chapter, verbalized by the initial adjunction י.

ומקנה, *and-of-the-own-making-might*.... I refer the reader to v. 1 and 2 of this chapter, wherein I have spoken of the root קֿן, and of the verbs קון and קנה, which are drawn from it. This root, which develops here the idea of taking possession, of property, is governed by the plastic sign of exterior action מ.

v. 21. יובל, *Jubal*.... This name is attached to the same root as that of *Jabal*, but it is taken in a loftier sense, by means of the sign וֹ, which makes it a continued facultative. The Hellenists have seen in this *Jubal*, a player upon the psaltery and harp; and Saint Jerome, a master of song upon the harp and upon the organ ! this latter translator has only followed the Chaldaic targum.

22. W'Tzillah gam-hîa îaledah æth-Thoûbal-Kaîn lotesh chol-horesh nehosheth w'barzel, w'âhôth Thoûbal-Kaîn Nahomah.

וְצִלָּה גַם־הִיא יָלְדָה אֶת־תּוּבַל קַיִן לֹטֵשׁ כָּל־חֹרֵשׁ נְחֹשֶׁת וּבַרְזֶל וַאֲחוֹת תּוּבַל־קַיִן נַעֲמָה׃

23. Wa-îâomer Lemech l' nashaî-ô Whadah w'Tzillah, shemahan kôl-î noshei Lemech, ha-âzennah âmerath-î chi aîshharagthî l'phitzehî w'îeled l'habburath-î.

וַיֹּאמֶר לֶמֶךְ לְנָשָׁיו עָדָה וְצִלָּה שְׁמַעַן קוֹלִי נְשֵׁי לֶמֶךְ הַאֲזֵנָּה אִמְרָתִי כִּי אִישׁ הָרַגְתִּי לְפִצְעִי וְיֶלֶד לְחַבֻּרָתִי׃

כנור, *brightness*.... This word which these same interpreters have made to signify a harp, is only the word נוּר *light*, or *glory*, inflected by the assimilative article כ. The reader has observed a great number of blunders which have no other source than the oversight of this important article.

ועוגב, *and-worthy-of-love*.... I cannot conceive how one has seen here a psaltery or an organ, since it is known that the Hebrew word עגב signifies loving attention, and that its Arabic analogue عجب expresses that which leads to admiration, joy and happiness. All these errors proceed from having taken the facultative תֹּפֵשׂ, *to be comprehending, seizing*, in the material sense, instead of the spiritual; that instead of seeing an effect of the intelligence, one has seen a movement of the hand.

v. 22. תּוּבַל־קַיִן, *Thubal-Kain*.... It is always the same root בל, from which are formed the names of Jabal and Jubal; but ruled on this occasion by the sign of reciprocity ת. The name of *Kain*, which is added to it, has been explained as much as it could be, in v. 1, of this chapter.

נעמה, *Nawhomah*.... The root עם contains all ideas of union, junction, bringing together: it is, on the one part, the sign of material sense and on the other, the plastic sign of exterior action, which, as

22. And *Tzillah* also, she-bare what-relates-to-*Thubal-Kain* (mutual yielding of the central might), whetting every-cutting-brass and-iron: and-the-kindred-of-*Thubal-Kain* was *Nawhomah* (meeting might, sociableness).

23. And-he-said, *Lamech*, unto-the-corporeal-wives-his-own, his bodily faculties) *Whadah*, and-*Tzillah*: hearken-to the-voice-mine, ye-wives of-*Lamech;* listen-to-the-speech-mine: for-as the-intellectual-man (that is to say, man individuated by his own will) I-have-slain-for-the-stretching (solution, freedom)-mine; and-the-progeny (particular stock) for-the framing-mine (in society):

22. Et-*Tzillah* aussi, elle-enfanta ce-qui-concerne-*Thoubal-Kain* (la diffusion abondante de la force central), aiguisant tout-coupant d'airain et-de-fer: et-la-parenté de *Thoubal-Kain* fut *Nawhomah* (la sociation, l'-aggrégation).

23. Et-il-dit, *Lamech*, aux épouses corporelles-siennes (ses facultés physiques) *Whadah* et-*Tzillah*: écoutez la-voix-mienne, épouses de-*Lamech;* prêtez l'oreille-à la-parole-à-moi: car comme l'homme-intellectuel (l'homme individualisé par sa propre volonté) j'ai-accablé (détruit) pour-la-dilatation (la solution, la libre extension)-mienne, et-la-progéniture (la lignée, la famille particulière), pour-la-formation-à-moi:

---

final character, offers the image of generalization. Taken as noun, this root designates *a people;* as relation, it acquires a copulative force and signifies *with*. In this instance it is employed as continued facultative, passive movement, feminine, and signifies literally, *the-becoming-united, assembled, formed by aggregation*.

v. 23.... This is one of the verses of the Cosmogony of Moses, that its translators have mutilated the most. I beg the reader to examine this Latin which is the exact translation of the Greek: "Dixitque Lamech uxoribus suis Adæ et Sellæ: audite vocem meam, uxores Lamech, ausculate sermonem meum; quoniam occidi virum in vulnus meum et adolescentulum in livorem meum." This is to say, that after

24. Chi shîbehathaîm îuk-kam Kaîn, w'Lemech shibe-haîm w'shibehah.   כִּי שִׁבְעָתַיִם יֻקַּם קָיִן וְלֶמֶךְ שִׁבְעִים וְשִׁבְעָה :

---

all the emphasis that Lamech has given to make his wives listen, he ridiculously tells them that he has killed a man to his wounding, and a young man to his hurt. Let us examine the real meaning of this phrase.

איש, *the-intellectual-man*.... As I have had occasion to state several times, the Hebraic tongue possesses many expressions to designate *man*. These expressions, formed with high wisdom, all contain a figurative and hieroglyphic sense beyond the literal one. I have taken care to make an exact analysis of them according as they present themselves to me. I have already explained the name of *Adam*, universal man, and that of *Aish*, intellectual man, and made clear the difference. The reader can review what I have said upon this subject in v. 6, ch. 1, and in v. 23, ch. II. The name of *Ænosh*, corporeal man, has not yet been presented for our examination; but we have already seen the physical faculties which lead to it. These several expressions for designating *man*, are very far from being synonyms. Moses who carefully distinguishes them, places and uses them with an infinite art. The one referred to here, is not corporeal man, as its translators would believe, but intellectual man; that is to say, man individualized by his efficient will. Therefore it is not a man, properly so-called, that *Lamech* kills, but the moral individuality of man which he causes to disappear. He does not kill it "in vulnus", to his wounding, to Lamech's, which has no sense.

לפצעי, *for-the-stretching-mine*.... That is to say for my extension, for the free exercise of my forces. This is proved beyond question, by the root פוץ, whence this word is derived, and which is related to all ideas of diffusion, of loosening, of setting at liberty. The Chaldaic פצה, the Syriac ܦܨ, the Samaritan ᛘᛐᛉ, the Arabic فصي all give evidence in favour of this meaning.

וילד, *and-the-progeny*.... This is not a young man, "adolescentulum" which Lamech kills or destroys, it is the spirit of the race,

24. So-seven-fold it-shall-be-caused-to-raise *Kain*, and *Lamech* seventy and-seven-fold.	24. Ainsi les-sept-fois il-sera-fait-exalter *Kain*, et-*Lamech* septante et-s e p t-fois.

---

the lineage, the filiation, which he sacrifices with איש, individualized man, by his will, and this is why:

לחברתי, *for-the-framing-mine*.... The term is clear as daylight. Not only the root בר, *a son*, and the verb ברא *to create*, whence this word is derived, lead to this meaning, but also the analogous verbs used in Chaldaic, Syriac, Ethiopic, etc., leave no doubt in this regard. Now, let the reader consider whether there is anything more just than this phrase, wherein Lamech, considered as a certain bond destined to arrest the dissolution of things, as a legislative force, announces, that to extend general liberty, he has destroyed the moral individuality of man; and that, to form the great family of peoples, he has destroyed the spirit of the particular family, which is opposed to him.

Whatever Lamech may be, and neither can I, nor do I wish to explain his origin, he is, as we have seen, the bond of that which is subdued in his passion: for, he has two corporeal wives, or rather two physical faculties which give him; *Jabal*, principle of aqueous effusion, whence come terrestrial fertility, the settling of wandering tribes and property; *Jubal*, principle of ethereal effusion, source of moral affections and of happiness: *Thubal-Kain*, principle of central or mercurial effusion, whence result physical power, metals, and the instruments that they furnish; and finally, *Nawhomah*, principle of union in society. This is a chain of ideas which leaves nothing to be desired and which throws upon the phrase alluded to, a light that I believe irresistible.

v. 24. יֹקָם, *it-shall-be-caused-to-raise*.... What I have said concerning this word, can be reviewed in v. 15 of this chapter. That which was applicable then to *Kain*, has become so for *Lamech*, but in a much more eminent degree.

25. Wa-îedah Adam hôd æth-âisheth-ô wa-theled ben, wa-thikerâ æth-shem-ô Sheth, chi-shath lî Ælohîm, zerah aher thahath Hebel chi harag-ô Kaîn.

וַיֵּדַע אָדָם עוֹד אֶת־אִשְׁתּוֹ וַתֵּלֶד בֵּן וַתִּקְרָא אֶת־שְׁמוֹ שֵׁת כִּי שָׁת־לִי אֱלֹהִים זֶרַע אַחֵר תַּחַת הֶבֶל כִּי הֲרָגוֹ קָיִן:

v. 25. שֵׁת, *Sheth*.... The signification of this name is of the utmost importance for those seeking to penetrate the essence of things. This name, as mysterious as those of *Kain* and *Habel* could never be translated exactly. All that I can do is to furnish the means necessary for unveiling the hieroglyphic depth. First let us examine the root. The two signs which compose it are ש, sign of relative duration and of movement, and that of reciprocity, of mutual tendency, of the liaison of things, ת. United by the universal, convertible sign, they form the verbal root שׁוּת, which is related to every action of placing, disposing, setting, founding. Considered as noun, the root שֵׁת, signifies *foundation*, in all of the acceptations of this word, and depicts the good, as well as the bad, the highest, as well as the lowest of things. It can signify also, every kind of beverage, and provides the verb שׁתה *to drink;* because it is water, which, by its determined movement, indicates always the deepest place, that upon which is placed the foundation.

But not only does the word שֵׁת express at once, the foundation of things, and the element which inclines to it, but it also serves in Hebrew, to designate the number *two*, in its feminine acceptation, and in Chaldaic, the number *six*. I shall not speak now concerning the signification of these numbers, because it would engage me in details that I wish to avoid: later on I shall do so. Suffice to say here, that the name of *Sheth*, or *Seth*, presents itself, as those of *Kain* and of *Habel*, under two acceptations wholly opposed. We have seen in treating of the latter two, that if *Kain* was the emblem of force and power, he was also that of rage and usurpation; we have seen that if one considered *Habel* as the emblem of thought and of the universal soul,

25. And-he-knew, *Adam*, again, the-intellectual-mate-his-own (his efficient volitive faculty): and-she-bare a-son; and-she-assigned for-name-to-him *Sheth* (the bottom, the site): for-thus (said she) he-has-settled-for-me, HE-the-Gods, a-seed other of-t h e-a b a t e m e n t (falling-down) of *H a b e l*, whilst he-slew-him, *Kain*.

25. Et-il-connut, *Adam*, encore, l'épouse-intellectuelle-sienne (sa faculté volitive efficiente): et-elle-enfanta un-fils; et-elle-assigna c e-n o m-à-l u i *S h e t h* (l a base, le fondement): parcequ'ainsi il-a-fondé pourmoi, (dit - elle) LUI - les Dieux, une-semence autre de-l'abattement d'*H a b e l*, lorsqu'il-accabla-lui, *Kain*.

---

he was also regarded as that of nothingness and of absolute void: now, *Sheth* is the object of a contrast no less striking. The Hebrews, it is true, have represented him as the type of a chosen family; the historian Josephus has attributed to him the erection of those famous columns, upon which was carved the history of mankind and the principles of universal morals; certain oriental peoples and particularly those who make profession of sabæanism, have revered him as prophet; indeed many of the gnostics called themselves *Sethians*: but it is known, on the other hand, that the Egyptians confusing him with *Typhon*, called him *the violent, the destructor*, and gave him the odious surnames of *Bubon* and of *Smou*: it is also known that the Arabs considering him as the genius of evil, called him *Shathan*, by adding to his primitive name שת the augmentative final ן. This terrible name, given to the infernal adversary, *Satan*, in passing into the Hebraic tongue with the poems of *Job*, has brought there all the unfavourable ideas which the Arabs and the Egyptians attached to the name of *Seth*, *Sath* or *Soth*, without harming, nevertheless, the posterity of this same *Sheth*, whom the Hebrews have continued to regard as the one from whom men, in general, and their patriarch, in particular, drew their origin.

תחת, *of-the-abatement*.... This word is one of extreme importance for the understanding of this verse. It indicates clearly, the source of this new seed from which *Sheth* has been formed. The Hellenists and Saint Jerome, took care not to see nor render it. The Samaritan translator is the only one who has given it attention. He has rendered it by ᐱᗰᗰ2ᕼ . *transition, mutation, misfortune*.

26. W'l'Sheth gam-houâ îullad-ben, wa-îkerâ æth-shem-ô Ænôsh âz hoûhal likeroâ b'shem IHÔAH.

וּלְשֵׁת גַּם־הוּא יֻלַּד־בֵּן וַיִּקְרָא אֶת־שְׁמוֹ אֱנוֹשׁ אָז הוּחַל לִקְרֹא בְּשֵׁם יְהֹוָה׃

---

v. 26. אֱנוֹשׁ, *corporeal man*..... This is the third name which Moses has employed to designate man. By the first, אָרָם, he designated universal man, divine similitude; by the second, אִישׁ, he characterized intellectual man, considered relative to the volitive faculty, free and efficient, which individualizes him and makes him a particular being; now he considers man in relation to his physical faculties, and he calls him אֱנוֹשׁ *corporeal man*.

Let us examine the inner composition of this third name. Two roots are found here contracted, אוֹן־נוֹשׁ. The first אוֹן develops, as I have already said, the contradictory ideas of being and nothingness, of strength and weakness, of virtue and vice. The second נוֹשׁ, expresses the instability of temporal things, their caducity, their infirmity. This last root is found in the Arabic نَسِيَ, in the Syriac ܢܫܐ, and is recognized easily in the Greek νοσεῖν, which is derived from it.

Thus constituted, the word אֱנוֹשׁ produces its feminine נָשָׁה: but here the hieroglyphic meaning is discovered. I have already remarked that Moses or his instructors, wishing to draw from the intellectual principle אִישׁ, the volitive faculty אִשָּׁה, makes the sign of manifestation disappear. Now, in order to deduce the physical faculties of the corporeal being אֱנוֹשׁ they suppress the initial sign of power א, and that of light וֹ, and put the word נָשׁ thus restricted, in the masculine plural נָשִׁים, a number which, as we have learned by the Grammar is confounded with the dual feminine.

Here already are three different names given to man, considered as universal, intellectual or corporeal, of which the translators have made no distinction. Further on we shall find a fourth. I urge the reader to reflect upon the gradation that Moses has kept in the employment of these terms. At first, it is the Divinity who creates אָדָם *Adam*, universal man, and who gives him for companion אִשָּׁה, efficient volitive faculty. This faculty, become חַוָּה *Hewah*, elementary life, creates in its turn אִישׁ, intelligent being, man individualized by his will. Afterward, it is the intellectual being, who, under the name of *Sheth*, son of *Adam*, brings forth corporeal man אֱנוֹשׁ, *Ænosh*, but already the physical faculties נָשִׁים *Noshim*, had been named as wives of *Lamech*, descendant of *Adam*, by *Kain* in the sixth generation.

I beg the reader also, to compare carefully *Kain* and *Sheth*, and the posterity of the one, with the posterity of the other. If he recalls

26. And-unto-*Sheth*,-also-him, it-was-caused-to beget a-son; and-he-assigned for-name-to-him Æ n o s h (corporeal man), then it-was-caused-to-hope by-the-calling-u p o n in-the-name of-Iהoaה.

26. Et-à-*Sheth*, aussi-lui, il-fut-fait-engendrer un-fils: et-il-assigna ce-n o m-à-l u i *Ænosh* (l'homme corporel), alors il-fut-espérer, selon-l'action d'invoquer au-nom de-Iהoaה.

---

that *Kain* produced *Henoch* and if he examines now the one which produces *Sheth*, he will find that the name of *Ænosh*, here referred to, differs only from the former by a certain softening in the characters of which both are composed. The vowel ה, which begins the name of *Henoch*, indicates a painful effort; the consonant כ, which terminates it, a sharp compression: on the contrary, the vowel א which begins that of *Ænosh*, announces a tranquil power, and the consonant ש, which terminates it, a gentle movement relative to a transient duration. *Henoch* arrests, fixes, centralizes: *Ænosh* lets go, relaxes, carries to the circumference.

הוחל, *it-was-caused-to-hope*.... The verb הול, in question here, springs from the root הל, which presents the idea of a persevering effort, of a sharp tension. As verb, it would mean in this instance, for it contains besides a great number of acceptations, *to suffer with patience one's misfortunes, to hope, to place faith in something*. It is employed according to the excitative form, passive movement, third person, past tense. I urge the reader to note with what adroitness, Moses, producing upon the scene of the world corporeal and suffering man, gives him the necessary firmness to support his sorrow courageously, by putting his hope in the invocation of the Sacred Name of the Divinity.

I urge the reader to refer constantly to the Radical Vocabulary to obtain a more ample account of the roots that I have often only indicated. This research will be especially useful in the chapter which follows.

SEPHER BERÆSHITH H.

סֵפֶר בְּרֵאשִׁית ה׃

1. Zeh Sepher thô-ledoth Adam b'iôm beroà Ælohîm Adam bi-demoûth Ælohîm hashah âoth-ô.

זֶה סֵפֶר תּוֹ־לְדֹת אָדָם בְּיוֹם בְּרֹא אֱלֹהִים אָדָם בִּדְמוּת אֱלֹהִים עָשָׂה אֹתוֹ ׃

2. Zacher w-nekebah bherâ am wa-îbarech âoth-am, wa-îkerâ æth-shemam Adam b'iôm bi-barâm.

זָכָר וּנְקֵבָה בְּרָאָם וַיְבָרֶךְ אֹתָם וַיִּקְרָא אֶת־שְׁמָם אָדָם בְּיוֹם הִבָּרְאָם ׃

3. Wa-îhî Adam sheloshîm w-mâth shanah wa-iôled bi-demouth-ô b'tzalem-ô wa-îkerâ æth-shem-ô Sheth.

וַיְחִי אָדָם שְׁלֹשִׁים וּמְאַת שָׁנָה וַיּוֹלֶד בִּדְמוּתוֹ בְּצַלְמוֹ וַיִּקְרָא אֶת־שְׁמוֹ שֵׁת ׃

---

v. 1. All these terms have been previously explained.

v. 2. שמם, *universal-name*.... This is the substantive שם, to which Moses here adds the final collective sign ם, to leave no doubt as to the universal signification which he gives to *Adam*. I wish to call particular attention to this sign, as I shall refer to it again upon a very important occasion.

v. 3. שנה, *of-being's-temporal-revolving-change*.... Before explaining this word, I believe it advisable to give the etymology of the names of the numbers about to be presented in this chapter. These names are not placed undesignedly or simply introduced in chronological order, as has been supposed. Those who have understood them in their strict acceptations, and who have taken them literally as

GENESIS V.

1. This-is the-book of-the symbolical-progenies of-*Adam*, at-the-day that-creating, ʜᴇ-the-Gods, A d a m (collective man) in-the-likemaking-like ʜɪᴍ-the-Gods, he-made the-selfsameness-his.

2. Male and-female, he-created-them; and-he-blessed-them, and-he-assigned this-universal-name *Adam*, at-the-day, of-the-being-created-them - universally.

3. And-he-was-being, *Adam*, three-tens and-one-hundred (extension, stretching), of-being's temporal-revolving-change; and-he-begat by-the-like-making-like-himself, in-the-shadow-his-own (an issued offspring) and-he-assigned this-name-to-him, *Sheth*.

COSMOGONIE V.

1. Ceci-est le-livre des-caractéristiques-générations d'*A d a m*, dès-le-jour que-créant, ʟᴜɪ-les-Dieux, *Adam* (l'homme universel) selon-l'action-assimilante de-ʟᴜɪ-les-Dieux, il-fit la-séité-sienne.

2. Mâle et-femelle il-créa-eux; et-il-bénit-eux; et-il-assigna ce-nom-universel *A d a m*, dès-le-jour d'être-créés-eux-universellement.

3. Et-il-exista, *A d a m*, trois-décuples et-une-centaine (une extension), de-mutation-temporelle-ontologique; et-il-généra selon-l'action-d'assimiler-à-lui, en-ombre-sienne (un être émané) et-il-assigna-ce-nom-à-lui, *Sheth*.

---

being applied to days, months or years, have proved their ignorance or their bad faith. To believe that Moses has really restricted to a duration of six days, such as we understand them today, the act of universal creation, or that he here restricts the lives of the cosmogonic beings of which he speaks, to a certain number of years such as we calculate them, is to do him gratuitous injury, and treat him in this respect, as one would treat an orator whose eloquence one condemns before learning the tongue in which the orator is expressing himself.

4. Wa-îhîou îmeî-Adam aharéi hôlid-ô æth-Sheth shemoneh mâoth shanah, wa-iôled banîm w'banôth. וַיִּהְיוּ יְמֵי־אָדָם אַחֲרֵי הוֹלִידוֹ אֶת־שֵׁת שְׁמֹנֶה מֵאֹת שָׁנָה וַיּוֹלֶד בָּנִים וּבָנוֹת׃

I believe I have made it sufficiently understood that the word יֹם *day*, by which Moses designates the phenomenal manifestations of the act of the creation, should be applied to a certain revolution of light, which the genius of this wonderful man, or of his instructors, had foreseen. In the note which follows I shall explain, that the word שנה, which has been translated by *year*, signifies an ontological, temporal duration; that is to say, relative to the diverse mutations of the being to which it is applied. I shall omit in the following, the ontological epithet, in order to avoid delays, but it is implied. Here are the names of numbers.

I. אחד, *one*. The root הד, from which this word is formed, and which is sometimes taken for unity itself, particularly in Chaldaic, signifies literally, *a point, a summit, the sharpest part of a thing; the top of a pyramid*. It is division arrested, subjugated by a sort of effort; as the two signs ד and ח which compose it, indicate. In the feminine it is written אחת.

II. שן, שני or שנים, *two*. The root שן, composed of the sign of relative duration ש, and that of produced being or growth ן, contains all ideas of mutation, of transition, of passing from one state to another, of redundancy. Thus the name of this number in bringing diversity, change and variation, is the opposite in everything from the preceding number, which, as we have seen, arrests division and tends to immutability. The feminine is שת, שתי and שתים.

III. שלוש, *three*. This word is formed from the two contracted roots של־לוש, as opposed in their significations as in the arrangement of their characters. By the first של, is understood every extraction or subtraction; by the second לוש, on the contrary, every amalgamation, every kneading together, if I may use this word. Thus the name of number *three*, presents therefore, in Hebrew, under a new form, the opposed ideas contained in *one* and *two;* that is, the extraction,

COSMOGONY OF MOSES   153

4. **And-they-were the-days** (the manifested lights) of-*Adam,* after-the-causing-him-to-beget the-selfsameness-of-*Sheth,* eight hundreds of-revolving-change: and-he-teemed sons and-daughters (many issued beings).

4. Et-ils-furent les-jours (les manifestations phénoméniques) d'*Adam* après-le-faire-enfanter-à-lui l'ipséité-de-*Sheth,* huit centaines de-mutation-temporelle: et-il-généra fils et-filles (une foule d'êtres emanés).

---

consequence of the division, becomes a kind of relative unity. This **new unity** is represented in a great many words under the idea of **peace**, welfare, perfection, eternal happiness, etc.

IV. ארבע, *four.* I have spoken of this word in v. 10 of chapter II; it is needless to repeat. Its root רב involves every idea of strength, of solidity, of greatness, resulting from extent and numerical multiplication.

V. חמש, *five.* This word expresses a movement of contraction and of apprehension, as that which results from the five fingers of the hand grasping a thing, pressing tightly and warming it. Its root is double. חם, the first, designates the effect of the second, מש, that is to say, the former depicts the general envelopment, the heat which results and the effect of the contractile movement impressed by the latter.

VI. שש, *six.* The root שׁ contains all ideas of equality, of equilibrium, of fitness, of proportion in things. United to the sign of relative duration ש in order to form the name of this number, it becomes the symbol of every proportional and relative measure. It is quite well known that the number *six* is applied in particular, to the measure of the circle, and in general, to all proportional measures. One finds in the feminine, ששה, and the Chaldaic reads שת: which is not unlike the name of number *two;* furthermore, between these there exist great analogies, since *six* is to *three,* what *two* is to *one;* and since we have seen that *three* represented a sort of unity.

VII. שבע, *seven.* One can review v. 3, chapter II, wherein I have given the origin of this word and stated why I attach to it ideas of complement, of accomplishment, and of the consummation of things and of times.

VIII. שמנה, *eight.* This word springs from the double root שום and מון. By the first שום, is understood the action of placing,

5. Wa-îhîou chol-îmeî Adam âsher-haî theoshah mæôth shanah w-sheloshîm shanah, wa-îamoth.   וַיִּהְיוּ כָּל־יְמֵי אָדָם אֲשֶׁר־חַי תְּשַׁע מֵאוֹת שָׁנָה וּשְׁלֹשִׁים שָׁנָה וַיָּמֹת:

---

of putting one thing upon another; by the second מִן that of specifying, of distinguishing by forms. It is therefore, the accumulation of forms that should be understood by this number. This signification is made obvious by that of the verb שָׁמֹן, which means literally, *to fatten, to make larger*.

IX. תֵּשַׁע, *nine*. The root שַׁע, which signifies literally, *lime, cement*, draws with it all ideas of cementation, consolidation, restoration, conservation, etc. The verb שׁוּעַ, which comes from it, expresses the action of cementing, plastering, closing carefully. Therefore the name of this number, being visibly composed of this root שַׁע, governed by the sign of reciprocity ת, should be understood as cementation, as mutual consolidation. It maintains with number *three*, a very intimate relation, containing like it, ideas of preservation and salvation.

X. עֶשֶׂר, *ten*. This is to say, *the congregation of power proper, of elementary motive force*. This meaning results from the two contracted roots עַשׁ־שַׂר. By the first עַשׁ, is understood, every formation by aggregation; thence, the verb עָשָׂה *to make;* by the second, שַׂר, every motive principle; thence, the verb שׁוּר *to direct, to govern*.

In going back now over these explanations, the general significations of the Hebraic decade can be given as follows:

1, principiation and stability: 2, distinction and transition: 3, extraction and liberation: 4, multiplication: 5, comprehension: 6, proportional measurement: 7, consummation, return: 8, accumulation of forms: 9, cementation, restoration: 10 aggregation, reforming power.

Excepting number twenty, which is drawn from number ten by the dual עֶשְׂרִים, 20, all decuple numbers, from 30 to 90 are formed from the plural of the primitive number; in this manner: 30, שְׁלֹשִׁים: 40, אַרְבָּעִים: 50, חֲמִשִׁים: 60, שִׁשִּׁים: 70, שִׁבְעִים: 80, שְׁמֹנִים: 90, תִּשְׁעִים. So that each decuple number is only the complement of its radical number.

מֵאָה or מֵאָה, *one hundred*. The name of this number indicates an extension produced by the desire to be extended, to be manifested.

5. And-they-were all-the-days (manifested lights) of *A d a m* (collective m a n) which-he-lived-in, nine hundreds of revolving-change; and-thirty of-r e v o l v i n g change; and-he-deceased.

5. Et-ils-furent tous-les-jours (les manifestations phénoméniques) d'*A d a m* (l'homme universel) qu'il-exista, neuf centaines de-m u t a t i o n-temporelle, et-trois-décuple de-mutation; et-il-passa.

The root of this word אוה, literally *desire*, is here governed by the sign of exterior action מ. One finds the Arabic ما expressing *to extend* and *to dilate*. In nearly all the tongues of Asia, *mah* signifies *great*.

אלף, *one thousand*. That is to say, a very high, very strong and very powerful principle. It is the name of the first letter of the alphabet, א.

v. 4. שנה, *revolving-change*.... I now return to this word which the length of the preceding note forced me to slight. The Hellenists, and Saint Jerome following these unreliable masters, have rendered it by ἔτος, "annus", *a year*. But they have, as is their custom, restricted what was taken in a broad sense, and applied to a particular revolution, that which was applicable to an universal, ontological revolution. I have already spoken of this word in v. 14. Ch. I. Its root is שן which we have just now seen to be that of number *two* and containing every idea of mutation, of variation, of passing from one state to another. Thus the word שנה, expresses a temporal mutation, relative to the being which is its object. The Hebraic tongue has several terms for expressing the idea of temporal duration. עוד characterizes the same state continued, an actual duration; as relation, we translate it by *still;* חרש, carries the idea of a beginning of existence, either in the order of things, or in the order of time: in its most restricted sense, it means a monthly duration: שנה is applied to the transition of this same existence, to a mutation of the being: that is to say, that the being which is its object, is not found at the end of the period which it expresses, at the same point or in the same state that it was at its beginning: in the more restricted sense, it is the space of a year: finally, the last of these terms is שוב, which should mean every revolution which replaces the being in its original state. These divers periods, always relative to the being to which they are applied, can mean the most limited dura-

6. Wa-îhî-Sheth hamesh shanîm w-mâth shanah wa-iôled Ænosh.

וַיְחִי־שֵׁת חָמֵשׁ שָׁנִים וּמְאַת שָׁנָה וַיּוֹלֶד אֱנוֹשׁ׃

7. Wa-îhî Sheth âhareî hôlîd-ô-æth-Ænôsh shebah shanîm w'shemoneh mæôth shanah wa-iôled banîm w-banôth.

וַיְחִי־שֵׁת אַחֲרֵי הוֹלִידוֹ אֶת־אֱנוֹשׁ שֶׁבַע שָׁנִים וּשְׁמֹנֶה מֵאוֹת שָׁנָה וַיּוֹלֶד בָּנִים וּבָנוֹת׃

8. Wa-îhîou chol-î m e î Sheth s h e t h î m heshereh shanah, w-theshah mæôth shanah, wa-îamoth.

וַיִּהְיוּ כָּל־יְמֵי־שֵׁת שְׁתֵּים עֶשְׂרֵה שָׁנָה וּתְשַׁע מֵאוֹת שָׁנָה וַיָּמֹת׃

9. Wa-îhî Ænosh thishehîm shanah wa-iôled æth-Keînan.

וַיְחִי אֱנוֹשׁ תִּשְׁעִים שָׁנָה וַיּוֹלֶד אֶת־קֵינָן׃

---

tion, as well as that whose limits escape the human understanding. The numbers *one, two* and *seven* take their roots from this.

It is because the ancient periods have been restricted and particularized, that one has so badly understood the *Sethites* of the Egyptians, the *Saros* of the Chaldeans, the *Yogas* of the Brahmans, etc.

בנים ובנות, *sons and-daughters*.... One ought not to think that the root בן, from which these two words are derived, is limited to expressing *a son*. It is *an emanation*, literally as well as figuratively, *a generative extension, a formation of any sort whatever.*

v. 5. וימת, *and-he-deceased....* This is the verb מות, in which the

6. And-he-lived, *Sheth,* five revolving-changes and-o n e-hundred of-revolving-c h a n g e ; a n d-h e-begat *Ænosh* (corporeal man).

7. And-he-lived, *S h e t h,* after - the-causing-him-to-beget that-same *Ænosh,* seven revolving-changes, and-eight h u n d r e d 's o f-revolving-change; and he-begat sons and-daughters (a flocking throng of issued beings).

8. And-they-were all-the-days (manifested lights) of-*Sheth,* two and-one-ten of-revolving-change, and-nine h u n d r e d s o f revolving-change; and-he-deceased.

9. And-he-lived, *Ænosh,* n i n e-t e n s o f-revolving-change; and-he-begat the-selfsameness - o f - *K a i n a n* (general invading).

6. Et-il exista, *S h e t h,* cinq mutations et-une-centaine d e-mutation-temporelle; et-il-généra *Ænosh,* (l' homme corporel).

7. Et-il-exista, *S h c t h,* après-le-faire - enfanter-à-lui ce-même-*Ænosh,* sept mutations, et-huit-centaines de-mutation-temporelle; e t-i l généra fils et-filles (u n e foule d'êtres émanés).

8. Et-ils-furent tous-les-j o u r s (les manifestations phénoméniques) d e-*Sheth,* deux et-un-décuple de-mutation-temporelle, e t-neuf-centaines de-mutation; et-il-passa.

9. E t-i l-exista, *Ænosh* neuf-décuples de-mutation-temporelle; et-il produisit l' existence-de-*Kainan* (l'envahissement général).

Chaldaic punctuation has suppressed the sign וֹ, used in the future tense, made past by the convertible sign וֹ. This verb which has ordinarily been translated by *to die,* expresses, as I have said, a sympathetic movement, a passing, a return to universal seity. Refer to Radical Vocabulary, root מת.

v. 6, 7 and 8. Nothing more to explain relative to these terms.

v. 9. קינן , *Kainan....* I have explained as much as possible, *Kain* and his brother *Sheth,* and the son of *Sheth, Ænosh*: here now is this same *Ænosh* who reproduces another *Kain;* but by extending, and as it were, by diluting its primitive forces; for although *Kainan*

10. Wa-îhî Ænôsh âhoreî hôlid-ô æth-Keînan hamesh heshereh shanah w'shemoneh mæôth shanah: wa-iôled banîm w-banôth.

וַיְחִי אֱנוֹשׁ אַחֲרֵי הוֹלִידוֹ אֶת־קֵינָן חָמֵשׁ עֶשְׂרֵה שָׁנָה וּשְׁמֹנֶה מֵאוֹת שָׁנָה וַיּוֹלֶד בָּנִים וּבָנוֹת:

11. Wa-îhîou chol-îmeî Ænôsh hamesh shanîm w-theshah mæôth shanah; wa-îamoth.

וַיִּהְיוּ כָּל־יְמֵי אֱנוֹשׁ חָמֵשׁ שָׁנִים וּתְשַׁע מֵאוֹת שָׁנָה וַיָּמֹת:

12. Wa-îhî Keînan shibehim shanah, wa-iôled æth-Maholalæl.

וַיְחִי קֵינָן שִׁבְעִים שָׁנָה וַיּוֹלֶד אֶת־מַהֲלַלְאֵל:

13. Wa-îhî Keînan ahoreî holid-o æth-Maholalæl ârbahîm shanah w-shemoneh mæôth shanah, w-iôled banîm w-banôth.

וַיְחִי קֵינָן אַחֲרֵי הוֹלִידוֹ אֶת־מַהֲלַלְאֵל אַרְבָּעִים שָׁנָה וּשְׁמֹנֶה מֵאוֹת שָׁנָה וַיּוֹלֶד בָּנִים וּבָנוֹת:

---

may be only the word *Kain* to which Moses has added the augmentative final ין, it is very necessary that there should be preserved in the posterity of *Sheth*, the same nature that he has in his own. It is extended, it is diluted, as I have said, and its force which consisted in a violent centralization, has diminished in proportion to its extent. We have already observed this difference between *Henoch* and *Ænosh*, in v. 26 of the preceding chapter.

v. 10 and 11. These terms are all understood.

v. 12. מהללאל, *Mahollael*.... That is to say, potential exaltation,

10. And-he-lived, Ænosh after-the-causing-him-t o-beget t h e-selfsameness-of-Kainan, five and-one-tens of-revolving-change, and-eight-hundreds of-revolution; and-he-begat sons and-daughters (many issued offspring).

11. And-they-were a l l-the-days (manifested lights) of-Ænosh, five revolving-changes, and-nine hundreds of revolution: a n d-he-deceased.

12. And-he-lived, Kainan, seven tens of-revolving-change; and-he-begat the-selfsameness o f-Mahollael (mighty rising up, brightness).

13. And-he-lived, Kainan, after-the-causing-h i m-to-beget that-same-Mahollael, four-tens of-revolving-change, and-eight hundreds of-revolution; and-he-begat sons and-daughters (many issued offspring).

10. Et-il-exista, Ænosh, après-le-faire-enfanter-à-l u i ce même Kainan, cinq et-un décuple de-mutation, et-huit-centaines de-mutation-temporelle; et-il-généra fils-et-filles (une foule d'êtres émanés).

11. Et-ils-furent t o u s-les-jours (les manifestations phénoméniques) d'Ænosh, cinq mutations, et neuf-centaines de-mutation-temporelle et-il-passa.

12. Et-il-exista, Kainan, sept décuples de-mutation-temporelle; et-il-généra l'ipséité-de-Mahollael (l'exaltation puissance, l a splendeur).

13. Et-il-exista, Kainan, après-le-faire e n f a n t e r-à-lui ce-même M a h o l l a e l quatre-décuples de-mutation et-huit-centaines d e-mutation-temporelle; et-il-généra fils et-filles (une foule d' êtres émanés).

---

splendour, glory. The root הל, containing in itself all ideas of exaltation, is again strengthened by doubling the final character ל, and by the addition of the root אל, which expresses the force of exhaling movement. The plastic sign מ, is only there to coöperate with the formation of the proper name.

v. 13 and 14. These terms are understood.

14. Wa-îhîou chol-îmeî Keînan hesher shanîm w-theshah mæôth shanah: wa-îamoth.

וַיִּהְיוּ כָּל־יְמֵי קֵינָן עֶשֶׂר שָׁנִים וּתְשַׁע מֵאוֹת שָׁנָה וַיָּמֹת׃

15. W a-î h î Maholalæl hamesh shanîm w-shishîm shanah wa-iôled æth-Iared.

וַיְחִי מַהֲלַלְאֵל חָמֵשׁ שָׁנִים וְשִׁשִּׁים שָׁנָה וַיּוֹלֶד אֶת־יָרֶד׃

16. W a-î h î Maholalæl âhoreî hôlid-ô æth-I a r e d sheloshîm s h a n a h w-shemoneh mæôth shanah: wa-iôled banîm w'banôth.

וַיְחִי מַהֲלַלְאֵל אַחֲרֵי הוֹלִידוֹ אֶת־יֶרֶד שְׁלֹשִׁים שָׁנָה וּשְׁמֹנֶה מֵאוֹת שָׁנָה וַיּוֹלֶד בָּנִים וּבָנוֹת׃

17. Wa-îhîou chol îmeî Maholalæl hamesh w-thishahîm s h a n a h w'shemoneh mæôth shanah: wa-îamoth.

וַיִּהְיוּ כָּל־יְמֵי מַהֲלַלְאֵל חָמֵשׁ וְתִשְׁעִים שָׁנָה וּשְׁמֹנֶה מֵאוֹת שָׁנָה וַיָּמֹת׃

18. Wa-îhî Iared shethaîm w'shishîm shanah w' mæôth s h a n a h: wa-iôled æth-Hanoch.

וַיְחִי־יֶרֶד שְׁתַּיִם וְשִׁשִּׁים שָׁנָה וּמְאַת שָׁנָה וַיּוֹלֶד אֶת־חֲנוֹךְ׃

---

v. 15. יֶרֶד, *Ired*.... Here among the descendants of *Sheth* is this same *Whirad*, that we have seen figuring among those of *Kain;* but who is presented now under a form more softened. In losing its initial sign ע, which is that of material sense, it has left its passionate and excitative ardour. The natural sense which it contains

14. And-they-were, all-the-days, (m a n i f e s t e d lights) of-*Kainan*, ten revolving-changes, and-nine hundreds of-revolution; and-he-deceased.

15. And-he-lived, *Mahollael*, five revolving-changes, and-six-tens of-revolution; and-he-begat the-selfsameness-of *Ired* (the steadfast one).

16. And-he-lived, *Mahollael*, after the-causing-him-t o-b e g e t that-same-*Ired*, t h r e e-t e n s of-revolving-change and-eight hundreds of-revolution; and-he-begat sons and-daughters (many issued offspring).

17. And-they-were, all-the-days, (m a n i f e s t e d lights) of *Mahollael*, f i v e and-nine-tens of-revolving-change and eight hundreds of revolution: and-he-deceased.

18. And-he-lived, *I r e d*, two and-six-tens of-revolving change, and-one-hundred of-revolution; and he-begat the-selfsameness-of-*Henoch* (the central might, and-also-the-panging one).

14. Et-ils-furent, t o u s-les-jours, (les manifestations phénoméniques) de-*Kainan*, dix-mutations et neuf centaines de-mutation-temporelle; et-il-passa.

15. Et-il-exista, *Mohollael*, cinq mutations et-six-décuples de-mutation-temporelle; et-il-produisit l'existence-d'*Ired* (ce qui est persévérant dans son mouvement).

16. Et-il-exista, *Mahollael*, après le-faire-enfanter-à-lui ce-même-*I r e d*, trois-décuples de-mutation et-huit-centaines de-mutation-temporelle; et-il-généra fils et filles (une foule d' êtres émanés).

17. Et-il-furent, tous-les-jours (les manifestations phénoméniques) d e-*Mahollael*, cinq-et-neuf-décuples de-mutation, e t-h u i t-centaines de-mutation-temporelle; et-il-passa.

18. Et-il-exista, *I r e d*, deux et-six-décuples de-mutation, et-une-centaine de-mutation-temporelle; et-il-produisit l'existence - de-*Henoch* (la puissance centrale, et aussi le souffrant, l'angoisseux).

---

is now that of perseverance, of steadfastness to follow an imparted movement. It is true that this movement can be good or evil, ascend-

19. Wa-îhî Iared âhoreî hôlid-ô æth-Hanôċh shemoneh mæôth shanah: wa-îôled banîm w-banôth.

וַיְחִי־יֶרֶד אַחֲרֵי הוֹלִידוֹ אֶת־חֲנוֹךְ שְׁמֹנֶה מֵאוֹת שָׁנָה וַיּוֹלֶד בָּנִים וּבָנוֹת׃

20. Wa-îhîou ċhol-îemeî-Iared shethîm w-shishîm shanah w-theshah mæôth shanah: wa-îamoth.

וַיִּהְיוּ כָּל־יְמֵי־יֶרֶד שְׁתַּיִם וְשִׁשִּׁים שָׁנָה וּתְשַׁע מֵאוֹת שָׁנָה וַיָּמֹת׃

21. Wa-îhî Hanôċh hamesh w'shishîm shanah: wa-îôled æth-Methoûshalah.

וַיְחִי חֲנוֹךְ חָמֵשׁ וְשִׁשִּׁים שָׁנָה וַיּוֹלֶד אֶת־מְתוּשָׁלַח׃

22. Wa-îthehalleċh Hanôċh æth-ha-Ælohîm âhoreî hôlid-ô æth-Methoûshalah, shelosh mæôth shanah; wa-îôled banîm w-banôth.

וַיִּתְהַלֵּךְ חֲנוֹךְ אֶת־הָאֱלֹהִים אַחֲרֵי הוֹלִידוֹ אֶת־מְתוּשֶׁלַח שְׁלֹשׁ מֵאוֹת שָׁנָה וַיּוֹלֶד בָּנִים וּבָנוֹת׃

---

ing or descending; as is proved by the two verbs springing from the root רוד: the one, רדה means *to govern, to dominate;* the other, ירד, signifies *to sink, to descend*.

v. 16 and 17. These terms are understood.

v. 18. חנוך, *Henoċh*.... This name is presented here with all the force which it has in the posterity of Kain. It is the same central power, the same corporate force: but the posterity of *Sheth* influencing the moral idea which it contains, can be considered now under the relation of repentance and contrition; that is to say, that the pressure, the shock, which it expresses literally, can be taken figuratively and become *a pang*.

COSMOGONY OF MOSES

19. And-he-lived, *Ired*, after the-causing-him-to-beget that-same-*Henoch*, eight hundreds of-revolving-change; and-he-begat sons and-daughters (many issued offspring).

20. And-they were, all-the-days, (manifested lights) of-*Ired*, two and-six-tens-of-revolving-change, and-nine hundreds of revolution; and-he-deceased.

21. And-he-endured, *Henoch*, five and-six-tens of revolving-change, and-he-begat *Methushalah*, (eager shaft of death).

22. And-he-trod, *Henoch*, (in the steps) of-HIM-the-Gods, after the causing-him-to-beget that-same *Methushalah*, three hundreds of-revolving change; and-he-begat sons and-daughters (many issued offspring).

19. Et-il-exista, *Ired*, après le-faire enfanter-à-lui ce-même-*Henoch*, huit centaines de-révolution temporelle; et-il-généra fils et-filles (une foule d'êtres émanés).

20. Et-ils-furent, tous-les-jours (les manifestations phénoméniques) d'*Ired*, deux et-six-décuples de-mutation, et-neuf centaines de-mutation-temporelle; et-il-passa.

21. Et-il-exista, *Henoch*, cinq-et-six-décuples de- mutation-temporelle et-il-produisit l'existence-de-*Methoushalah*, (l'émission de la mort).

22. Et-il-suivit, *Henoch*, (les traces) mêmes-de-LUI-les-Dieux, après-le-faire-enfanter-à-lui ce-même-*Methoushalah*, trois centaines de-mutation-temporelle; et-il-généra fils et-filles (une foule d'êtres émanés).

---

v. 19 and 20. The terms of these are understood.

v. 21. מתושלה, *Methushalah*... It is no longer *Whirad* who is begotten by *Henoch*; for, in this generation, this same *Whirad*, changed to *Ired*, has become the father of *Henoch*: *Methushalah*, whom we have seen in the posterity of *Kain*, is likewise the grandson of *Whirad*. The change brought into this name is hardly perceptible. It is always the root מות, *death*, which constitutes its foundation. The word שלח, which is added, signifies literally *a dart*. In the posterity

23. Wa-îhîou ċhol îmeî Hanôċh hamesh w'shishîm shanah w-shelosh mæôth shanah.

וַיְהִי כָּל־יְמֵי חֲנוֹךְ חָמֵשׁ וְשִׁשִּׁים שָׁנָה וּשְׁלֹשׁ מֵאוֹת שָׁנָה׃

24. Wa-îthehalleċh Hanôċh æth-ha-Ælohîm w'-æine-nou ċhi-lakah âoth-ô Ælohîm.

וַיִּתְהַלֵּךְ חֲנוֹךְ אֶת־הָאֱלֹהִים וְאֵינֶנּוּ כִּי־לָקַח אֹתוֹ אֱלֹהִים׃

---

of *Kain*, מתושאל symbolizes *the gulf of death*, that is to say, a death which precipitates and devours; whereas in that of *Sheth*, מתושלח characterizes *the dart of death*, that is, a death which hurls toward the eternity of existence. Thus Moses admits two kinds of death: this is worthy of notice.

v. 22 and 23, ויתהלך, *and-he-trod*.... This is the verb הלך of which I have already spoken in v. 8. ch. III. It is used here according to the reciprocal form and signifies literally to be carried in every sense; to go and come.

This action, which Moses attributes to *Henoch*, proves, as I have insinuated, that it ought to be taken in a more moral sense, as descendant of Sheth, rather than as descendant of Kain. The number 365, which is that of its temporal and ontological mutations, has been noticed by all allegorists.

v. 24. ואיננו, *and nought of-him*.... I have spoken several times of the root אין, and I have also shown the singular peculiarity that it has of developing ideas most opposed in appearance, such as being and nothingness, of strength and weakness; etc. But I think that here is the occasion to state, that this surprising peculiarity rests less in the root itself, than in the object to which it is opposed. Thus, for example, whatever the thing that one admits as existing, good or evil, strong or weak, this root, manifested by the adverbial

COSMOGONY OF MOSES   165

23. And-they-were, all-the days (m a n i f e s t e d lights) of-*Henoch,* five and-six-tens of-revolving-change and three-hundreds of-revolution.

24. And-he-applied-himself-to-tread, *Henoch* (in the s t e p s) of-H I M-*the-Gods,* and nought (no substance) of-him; for-he-resumed-him, HE-the-Being-of-beings.

23. Et-ils-furent, tous-les-jours (les manifestations phénoméniques) de-*Henoch,* cinq et-six-décuples de-mutation, et-trois centaines de-mutation-temporelle.

24. E t-i l-s'excita-à-suivre, *Henoch* (les traces) de-L U I-les-Dieux; et-non-être-substance-de-l u i, car-il-retira-lui, L U I l'Ê t r e-d e s-êtres.

---

relation אין, will be its absolute opposite. If the substance is granted as *all,* אין is the symbol of *nothing.* If the substance is considered as *nothing,* אין is the symbol of *all.* In a word, אין characterizes the absence of the substance. It is an abstraction, good or evil, of spirituality. This is the origin of the syllable *in,* which we sometimes use to change the signification of words.

In the case referred to, the adverbial relation אין, indicates a transmutation in the mode of existence of *Henoch* and not a simple change of place, a removal, as the translators understand it. If *Henoch* was substance, he ceased being this to become spirit. He was איננו, *in-him,* that is to say, *insubstantial.*

I should state here that, at the very time of the Samaritan version, the most ancient of all, and shortly after the captivity of Babylon, this expression, so vital, was not understood. The author of this version substituted for the Hebrew איננו, the word 𐤟𐤟𐤟𐤟𐤟 , *and-no-sign-of-him;* adding: 𐤟𐤟𐤟𐤟𐤟 𐤟𐤟𐤟𐤟 𐤟𐤟𐤟 , *for-they-carried-him away, the angels.* The Chaldaic uses the same word וליתיהי *and-no-sign-of-him.* The Hellenists take a turn still more curious: καὶ οὐχ εὑρίσκετο, *and he was not found.* And Saint Jerome takes a middle course in saying "et non apparuit" *and he appeared not.*

25. Wa-îhî Methoûshelah shebah w-shemonîm shanah w'mâth s h a n a h: wa-iôled æth-Lamech.

וַיְחִי מְתוּשֶׁלַח שֶׁבַע וּשְׁמֹנִים שָׁנָה וּמְאַת שָׁנָה וַיּוֹלֶד אֶת־לָמֶךְ׃

26. Wa-îhî Methoûshelah âhoreî holîd-ô æth-Lamech, shethaîm w-shemonîm shanah, w-shebah mæôth shanah: wa-iôled b a n î m w-banôth.

וַיְחִי מְתוּשֶׁלַח אַחֲרֵי הוֹלִידוֹ אֶת־לֶמֶךְ שְׁתַּיִם וּשְׁמוֹנִים שָׁנָה וּשְׁבַע מֵאוֹת שָׁנָה וַיּוֹלֶד בָּנִים וּבָנוֹת׃

27. Wa-îhîou chol-iemeî Methoûshelah theshah w-shishîm shanah, w-theshah mæôth shanah: wa-îamoth.

וַיִּהְיוּ כָּל־יְמֵי מְתוּשֶׁלַח תֵּשַׁע וְשִׁשִּׁים שָׁנָה וּתְשַׁע מֵאוֹת שָׁנָה וַיָּמֹת׃

28. Wa-îhî Lamech shethîm w-shemonîm shanah w-mâth shanah: wa-iôled ben.

וַיְחִי־לֶמֶךְ שְׁתַּיִם וּשְׁמֹנִים שָׁנָה וּמְאַת שָׁנָה וַיּוֹלֶד בֵּן׃

---

v. 25. לֶמֶךְ. *Lamech*.... What I have said concerning this personage can be seen in v. 18, ch. IV. This *Lamech* differs from the former *Lamech* only by the generation to which he belongs. He has the same character, but in another nature. The former, which issued from the generation of *Kain*, is the sixth descendant from Adam; the latter, which belongs to that of *Sheth*, is the eighth. The one has two corporeal wives, that is to say, two physical faculties which give him three sons; or rather three cosmogonic principles, source of all

COSMOGONY OF MOSES 167

25. And-he-was-in-being, *Methushalah,* s e v e n and-e i g h t-t e n s o f-revolving-change, and-one-hundred of-revolution: and-he-begat *Lamech* (the tie of dissolution).

26. And-he-lived, *Methushalah* a f t e r the-causing-him-to-beget that-same-*Lamech,* two and-eight-tens of-revolving-change, and-seven hundreds of-revolution, and-he-begat sons and-daughters (many issued offspring).

27. And-they-were, a l l-the days, (m a n i f e s t e d l i g h t s) o f-*Methushalah,* nine and-six-tens of-revolving-change, and-nine hundreds of-revolution: and-he-ceased (to be in being).

28. A n d-h e-lived, *Lamech,* two and-eight-tens of-revolving-change, and-o n e-hundred of-revolution: and-he-begat a-son (an issued offspring).

25. Et-il-exista, *Methoushalah,* sept et-huit-décuples de-mutation, et-une-centaine de-mutation-temporelle; et-il-produisit l'existence de-*Lamech* (le nœud qui arrête la dissolution*).*

26. Et-il-exista, *Methoushalah,* après-le-faire-enfanter-à-lui ce-m ê m e-*Lamech,* deux et-huit-décuples de-mutation, et-sept centaines de-mutation-temporelle, e t-i l-généra fils e t-f i l l e s (une foule d'êtres émanés).

27. Et-ils-furent, tous-les-jours, (les manifestations phénoméniques) de *Methoushalah,* neuf et-six-décuples de-mutation; et-n e u f centaines de-mutation-temporelle: et-il-passa.

28. Et-il-exista, *Lamech,* deux et-huit-décuples de-mutation, et-une-centaine de-mutation-temporelle: et-il-g é n é r a un-fils (un être émané).

---

fertility, of all prosperity, of all power upon the earth: the other, left only one son, who saw mankind finish and begin again.

v. 26, 27 and 28. These terms are understood.

v. 29. נֹחַ, *Noah*.... or *Noe,* as it has been vulgarly written following the orthography of the Hellenist translators. The root from

29. Wa-îkkerâ æth-sham-ô Noah, l'æmor zeh înahome-nou mi-mahoshenou, w-mewhitzebôn îadeînou min-ha-âdamah âsher ærorha IHOAH.

וַיִּקְרָא אֶת־שְׁמוֹ נֹחַ לֵאמֹר זֶה יְנַחֲמֵנוּ מִמַּעֲשֵׂנוּ וּמֵעִצְּבוֹן יָדֵינוּ מִן־הָאֲדָמָה אֲשֶׁר אֵרֲרָהּ יְהוָֹה׃

30. Wa-îhî Lamech âhor-eî hôlîd-ô æth-ben, hamesh w-thishehîm shanah wa-hamesh mæôth shanah: wa-îôled banîm w-banôth.

וַיְחִי־לֶמֶךְ אַחֲרֵי הוֹלִידוֹ אֶת־בֵּן חָמֵשׁ וְתִשְׁעִים שָׁנָה וַחֲמֵשׁ מֵאוֹת שָׁנָה וַיּוֹלֶד בָּנִים וּבָנוֹת׃

which this important name comes, is composed of the sign of produced being ב, image of reflected existence, and the sign of the effort of Nature ה, which gives birth to vital equilibrium, to *existence*. This root offers the idea of that perfect repose, which, for a thing long agitated in opposed directions, results in that state of equilibrium where it dwells immobile.

Nearly all the tongues of the Orient understood this mysterious expression. The Hebrew and the Chaldaic draw from it two verbs. By the first נהוה, one understands, *to lead to the end, to guide toward the place of repose;* by the second, נוא, *to repose, to rest tranquil, to be in a state of peace, of calm, of perfect bliss.* It is from the latter, that the name of the cosmogonic personage who saw the end of the world and its renewal, is derived. It is the emblem of the repose of elementary existence, the sleep of Nature.

זה ינחמנו, *this will-release us*.... Moses rarely forgets to explain the substantive by the verb, or the verb by the substantive: this cannot be repeated too often, for it is the seal of his style. The Samaritan translator, far from seeking to follow this course, so simple and so expressive, nearly always swerves from it. In this instance for

29. And-he-assigned-for name-to-him, *Noah;* thus-declaring-his-thought: t h i s will release-us (will lessen, relieve us) from-the-hardworking-our, and-from-the-great-natural-hindrance of-the-hands-ours, because-of-t h e-a d a m i c (elementary g r o u n d) which he-has-cursed-it, IHOAH.

29. Et-il-assigna ce-nom-même-à-lui, *Noah,* pour-déclarer-sa-pensée (disant): celui-ci reposera-nous (nous allégera, nous soulagera) de-ce-qui-constitue l'œuvre-notre et-de-ce-qui-fait-l'obstacle-physique des-mains-à nous, à-cause de-la terre-adamique, laquelle il-a-maudite-elle, IHOAH.

30. A n d-h e-lived, *Lamech,* a f t e r-t h e-causing-him-to-beget a-son, five and-nine-t e n s of-r e v o l v i n g-change, and-five hundreds of-revolution, and-he-begat sons and-daughters (many issued offspring).

30. Et-il-exista, *Lamech,* après-le-faire-enfanter-à-lui ce-fils cinq et-neuf-décuples-de-mutation-temporelle, et-cinq centaines de-mutation, et-il-généra f i l s et-filles (une foule d'êtres émanés).

---

example, instead of the verb נחֹם, which Moses uses to explain the meaning that he wishes to give to the name of *Noah,* and which the Samaritan could very well render by the analogue אצצנו, one finds אצבנו, which signifies *to support, to moderate, to temper.*

This proves how little the Hebraic text was already felt at this remote time, and how the meaning of the words was altered.

v. 30 and 31. These terms are understood.

v. 32. בֶּן־חֲמֵשׁ, *a-son of-five....* This should be observed. In v. 28, Moses says that *Lamech* begat a *son,* בֵּן; that is, produced an *offspring;* for we shall see later on that the veritable signification of this word is here; in v. 29, he names this son נֹחַ, *Noah,* that is to say, *the sleep of nature, the repose of existence;* and now he says that he was *a-son of-five hundred-fold of-revolving-change.* To believe that Moses had wished to indicate by that, simply the age of *Noah,* is to misinterpret his genius.

I invite the reader to observe that *Adam,* universal man, in the beginning of things, begat three sons: *Kain, Habel* and *Sheth;* that

31. W-îhî ĉhol-îmeî-Le-meĉh shebah w-shibehîm shanah, w-shebah mæôth shanah: wa-îamoth.

וַיְהִי כָּל־יְמֵי־לֶמֶךְ שֶׁבַע וְשִׁבְעִים שָׁנָה וּשְׁבַע מֵאוֹת שָׁנָה וַיָּמֹת׃

---

now, *Noah*, who represents the repose of existence, in the waning of things, begat *Shem, Ham* and *Japheth*. I have earnestly endeavoured to make the true signification of the names of the children of *Adam* understood; I shall now make the same efforts with respect to those of *Noah*.

שׁם, *Shem*.... The sign of relative duration and movement which is connected here, and the sign of exterior action used as final collective sign, compose a root which produces the idea of that which is distinguished exteriorly by its elevation, its splendour, its own dignity. It is, in its most restricted acceptation, the proper name of a thing, the particular designation of a remarkable place, or of a remote time; it is the mark, the sign by which they are recognized; it is the renown, the splendour, the glory which is attached to them. In its broadest acceptation, it is ethereal space, the empyrean, the heavens, and even GOD, that one finds designated by this singular word, in Hebrew, as well as in Samaritan, in Chaldaic or in Syriac.

It is extremely difficult to choose, among so many significations, that which is most consistent with the son of *Noah*. Nevertheless one can without erring, translate it by the words, *the sublime, the splendid, the radiant, etc.*

חם, *Ham*.... This name is on the whole, the opposite of that of *Shem*. The sign ח which constitutes it, recalls all ideas of effort, of obstacle, of fatigue, of travail. The root which results from its union with the sign of exterior action, employed as collective, presents a bending, a dejection, a thing which inclines toward the lower parts: it is the heat which follows a sharp compression: it is the hidden fire of nature: it is the warmth which accompanies the rays of the sun; it is the dark colour, the blackness, which results from their action; it is finally, in the broadest sense, *the sun* itself considered as the cause of heat and of torrefaction.

When the name of *Ham* is presented alone and in an absolute sense, it can, to a certain point, be taken in a good sense, since it

COSMOGONY OF MOSES　　171

31. And-they-were, a l l-the-days (periodical lights) of-*Lamech*, seven and-seven-tens o f-revolving-change, and-seven hundreds of-revolution: and-he-ceased.	31. Et-ils-furent, t o u s-les-jours, (l e s manifestations phénoméniques) d e-*Lamech*, sept et-sept-décuples de-mutation-temporelle; et-sept centuples de-mutation: et-il-passa.

expresses the effect of the sun upon inferior bodies; but if one only sees in it the opposite of *Shem*, it offers only sinister ideas. If *Shem* is the sublime, the superior, *Ham* is the abased, the inferior; so if the former is the radiant, the exalted, the infinite; the latter is the obscure, the bending, the limited, etc.

יפת, *Japheth*.... This name holds a sort of medium between those of *Shem* and *Ham*, and partakes of their good or evil qualities without having them in itself. It signifies, in a generic sense, material extent, indefinite space: in a more restricted sense, latitude. The root פת, from which it comes, contains every idea of expansion, of facility to extend, to allow itself to be penetrated; every solution, every divisibility, every simplification. It is governed by the sign of potential manifestation י, which adds to its force and universalizes it.

This is all that I can say at this moment, pertaining to the three symbolic personages, who, emanated from *Noah*, the repose of Nature, survive the ruin of the world through the inaccessible shelter which their father gives them, the narrative of which we shall hear presently. It is possible, notwithstanding all the etymological light which I have tried to throw upon them, that the reader may still find many obscurities in the hieroglyphic sense of their names: I do not deny that they are there and many of them; but if he is sincerely earnest in penetrating these ancient mysteries, toward which Moses has traced sure routes, although ignorance and prejudice even more than time, have covered them with obstacles, he must not become discouraged. Let him compare diligently, the three sons of *Adam* with those of *Noah*, and he will find in the comparison, analogies which will serve to fix his ideas.

The first production of *Adam*, after his fall, is *Kain;* the second, *Habel;* the third, *Sheth*.

32. Wa-îhî Noah ben-ha-mesh mæôth shanah, wa-iôled Noah æth-Shem, æth-Ham w'æth-Japheth.

וַיְהִי נֹחַ בֶּן־חֲמֵשׁ מֵאוֹת שָׁנָה וַיּוֹלֶד נֹחַ אֶת־שֵׁם אֶת־חָם וְאֶת־יָפֶת׃

Moses, for very strong reasons, inverted the order of similitudes of the productions of Noah. *Shem*, whom he names the first, in this instance, corresponds with *Habel* whom he has named second in the other; *Ham*, whom he names second, corresponds with *Kain*, whom he has named first; *Japheth*, who corresponds with *Sheth* preserves with him the same rank.

It is without doubt very difficult to know what Moses has concealed under the symbolic names of *Kain*, *Habel* and *Sheth*: but if one wishes to admit that this may be the three constituent principles of the being called *Adam*, that is to say, the developed, or decomposed triad of that collective unity, he will soon perceive that the symbolic names of *Ham*, *Shem* and *Japheth*, are the constituted principles of the being called *Noah*, and that these cosmogonic per-

32. And-he-was, *Noah*, (nature's rest) a-son of-five hundred-fold o f-revolving-change : a n d-he-begat, he-*Noah*, the-selfsameness-of-*Shem*, of-*Ham*, and-of-*Japheth* (that is to say, the self-existing of what is lofty and bright, of what is gloomy, curved and warm, and of what is extended and wide).

32. Et-il-fut *Noah* (le repos de la nature élémentaire) fils de-cinq centuples de-mutation-temporelle : et-il-produisit, lui-*Noah*, l'existence de-*Shem*, celle-de-*Ham* et-celle-de-*Japheth* (c'est-à-dire, l'ipséité de ce qui est élevé et brillant, de ce qui est courbe et chaud, et de ce qui est étendu).

---

sonages are related one to the other, in the same manner as the effect is related to its cause.

One ought not to forget besides, what I have said pertaining to the extreme importance that the ancients attach to *proper names;* it cannot be given too great attention. Notwithstanding the length of my notes and even the numerous repetitions into which I purposely fall, it will always be well for the reader to consult the Radical Vocabulary for the signification of their roots.

SEPHER BERÆSHITH W.

ספר בראשית ו׃

1. Wa-îhî chi-hehel ha-Adam larob hal-pheneî ha-âdamah w-banôth îulledou la-hem.

וַיְהִי כִּי־הֵחֵל הָאָדָם לָרֹב עַל־פְּנֵי הָאֲדָמָה וּבָנוֹת יֻלְּדוּ לָהֶם׃

---

v. 1. כי־החל, *because-of-being-dissolved*.... The beginning of this chapter is difficult and profoundly mysterious. The Hellenists for fear no doubt of saying too much, say nothing about it; for it would otherwise be inconceivable, that they should have forgotten so soon the collusion of *Adam*, to which *Moses* makes so direct a reference. However it may be, these translators render the radical verb חול, which the hierographic writer uses on this occasion by the nominal passive החל, as ἤρξαντο, *they began;* not understanding, or not wishing to understand, what connection the fall of Adam can have with the generation of *daughters*, referred to hereafter.

But the verb חול, has never signified precisely *to begin*: it is always, in what ever relation one considers it, the expression of violent effort, of distention, of writhing, which brings about solution or dissolution. The root חל from which it comes, contains the idea of an unknown force which destroys the ties of the body, by stretching them, breaking them, reducing them to shreds, or dissolving and loosening them to excess. It is true that the verb in question can present sometimes the idea of *an opening*, by extension of the idea of *solution*, but it is in the same manner that it has also expressed the idea of wound, of weakness, of laceration, of pain in bringing forth, etc.

It is in taking figuratively the idea of dissolution, or of relaxation, that one has drawn from this root the idea of profanation and of prostitution, to which Moses appears to make allusion in this instance.

ובנות, *that-daughters*.... The conjunctive article ו, when it joins the noun or the verb which it inflects, to the antecedent member of the phrase, is perfectly expressed by the conjunction *that*.

COSMOGONY OF MOSES

GENESIS VI.   COSMOGONIE VI.

1. Now-it-was (it came to pass) because-of-being-dissolved (dissolute, loose) *Adam* (collective man) by-multiplying on-the-face of-the-adamic, that-daughters (corporeities) were-plenti-f u l l y-begotten unto-them (*Adam*).

1. Or-il-fut (il advint) à-cause-de s'être- dissous (dissolu, profané) *Adam* (l' homme universel) selon-l' action-de-multiplier sur-la-terre-adamique, que-des-fil-les (des formes corporelles) furent-abondamment-engen-drées à-eux (*Adam*).

The root בן, from which comes the word בת, irregular feminine of the masculine בן *a son*, signifies in general, *an emanation, a formation, any edification whatsoever*. The paternal sign ב, hieroglyphic symbol of creative action, united to that of produced being ן, leaves no doubt in this respect. Thus the plural word בנות, which in a restricted sense would mean simply, *daughters*, taken in a figurative sense designates *corporations, assemblages, corporeal forms, corporeities*, etc.

ילדו, *were-plentifully-begotten*.... This is the compound radical verb ילוד or לדת, used in the intensive form, passive movement, past tense. The Hellenists have evaded its force, which could not agree with the insignificant meaning that they had given to the word החל. Furthermore, I must say, as much for their exoneration as for that of Saint Jerome who copied them, that already at the time when the Hebrew text was translated into Samaritan, the beginning of this chapter experienced great difficulties. What proves this is, that not only in this instance, has the nominal passive החל been replaced by the active 𐤈𐤐𐤌, which, being derived from the verb שׁוה, signifies only *to reach out, to take possession of;* but, for the important words אדם and אדמה *Adam*, universal man, and *Adamah*, elementary earth, were substituted 𐤀𐤍𐤔, Ænosh, corporeal man, and 𐤀𐤓𐤅𐤇 *Arwhah*, earth, properly so-called.

All these oversights conform more and more with what I have

2. Wa-îrâoû beneî ha-Ælohîm æth-benôth ha-Adam chi-toboth hennah, wa-îkkehoû la-hem nashîm michol âsher bhaharoû.

וַיִּרְאוּ בְנֵי הָאֱלֹהִים אֶת־בְּנוֹת הָאָדָם כִּי־טֹבֹת הֵנָּה וַיִּקְחוּ לָהֶם נָשִׁים מִכֹּל אֲשֶׁר בָּחָרוּ:

always advanced regarding the loss of the Hebraic tongue. There was no means for anyone to doubt that the words אדם and אנוש were synonyms in the idiom of Moses, unless to pretend against all reason and all likelihood.

v. 2. בני, *the-sons*.... I have just explained the root of this word. These sons of the Divinity, that have so perplexed the savants, are what the gnostics understood by their *Æons*: that is to say, *emanated beings*. The root אן, of which I have already spoken several times and from which come, without any addition, the *Æons* of the gnostics, exists in the Hebrew word בן, but contracted and ruled by the paternal sign ב, in this manner ב־אן.

האלהים, *of* HIM-*the-Gods*.... This expression of Moses, upon which many commentaries have been written, had already alarmed the Samaritan translator, who, no longer understanding the moral sense of the word בני, and not wishing to give *children* to the Being of beings, had distorted the text and replaced אלהים by 𐡀𐡌𐡔𐡁𐡆. Now, this word which is derived from the verb שלט, *to dominate*, instead of having any bearing upon the Divinity, designates only *potentates* or *sultans*. It was getting around the difficulty and not solving it; for, how can one imagine that Moses had abruptly changed the meaning of a Sacred Name which he had constantly given to GOD, to apply it to *sultans?*

The author of the Chaldaic targum has fallen into the same error and seems to have gone to extremes. Here is its entire phrase:

וחזו בני רברביא ית בנת אנשא: And-they-looked-upon, the-sons of-the -chiefs-of-the-multitudes, those-daughters of-*Anosha* (corporeal man).

In consideration of this it is obvious that the Hellenists had no need of efforts to veil the spiritual meaning of the Sepher; they had only to follow the path which was traced for them. An astonishing thing is, that they dared not however, insult the text in this passage, they say: οἱ υἱοὶ τοῦ Θεοῦ, *the sons of* GOD.

2. And-they-did-observe, t h e-s o n s, (spiritual offspring) of-HIM-the-Gods, those-daughters (corporeities) of-*Adam;* that fair they-were: and-they took for-them corporeal-mates (natural faculties) from-everyone whom they-liked-the-best.

2. Et-ils-considérèrent, les-fils-(émanations spirituelles) de-LUI-les-Dieux, ces-filles (ces mêmes formes corporelles) d'*A d a m,* que bonnes elles-étaient: et-ils-prirent pour-eux des-épouses-corporelles (des facultés physiques) de-toutes celles qu'ils chérirent-le-plus.

נשים, *corporeal-mates*.... Moses does not here use the word אשה, which being derived as we have seen from the substantive איש *intellectual man,* should characterize figuratively, *intellectual faculties,* but the word נשים, which, formed by ellipsis of the word אנוש, *corporeal man,* indicates *physical faculties*. These are the modifications which must be grasped in reading a writer so precise, so exact as Moses. The more one studies him the more one is assured that he possessed to an eminent degree, the Egyptian tongue in which he had been brought up. It is incredible with what infinite art, he reconciles the three meanings in his narration, with what force he attaches the literal to the figurative, and the hieroglyphic to the literal. The tongues in which I can make myself understood, are wholly incapable of rendering this profound calculation, this extraordinary labour by means of which he triples the thought, by vesting it with an expression which, although unique, is presented under three forms.

אשר בחרו, *whom-they-liked-the-best*.... This verb comes from the root חר, which depicts a focus from which the heat escapes by radiation. The sign of interior action ב, which governs this root gives it the figurative expression of a vehement passion which is fixed upon an object.

v. 3. לא־ידון, *shall-not-diffuse*.... This verb is derived from the root די, which is related to every idea of abundance and division, as is proved by its derivatives ידות, *to emit, to spread, to divulge;* נדה *a profusion, a prostitution;* נדן *a prodigality,* etc.

בשגם, *by-his-decaying-quite*.... This important word has not been

3. Wa-iâomer I H Ô A H loâ-îadôn rouh-î b'Adam, l' holam b'shaggam houâ bashar w'haiou îamaî-ô meâh w'hesherîm shanah.

וַיֹּאמֶר יְהוָה לֹא־יָדוֹן רוּחִי בָאָדָם לְעֹלָם בְּשַׁגַּם הוּא בָשָׂר וְהָיוּ יָמָיו מֵאָה וְעֶשְׂרִים שָׁנָה׃

4. Ha-Nephilîm haîou b' âretz b'îamîm ha-hem, w' gam âhoreî-chen asher îaboâou beneî ha-Ælohîm ælbenôth ha-Adam, w'îalodou la-hem hemmah ha-ghibborîm âsher me-hôlam ânosheî ha-shem.

הַנְּפִלִים הָיוּ בָאָרֶץ בַּיָּמִים הָהֵם וְגַם אַחֲרֵי־כֵן אֲשֶׁר יָבֹאוּ בְּנֵי הָאֱלֹהִים אֶל־בְּנוֹת הָאָדָם וְיָלְדוּ לָהֶם הֵמָּה הַגִּבֹּרִים אֲשֶׁר מֵעוֹלָם אַנְשֵׁי הַשֵּׁם׃

---

comprehended by any of the translators, who, forgetting always the collusion of Adam, to which Moses continually alludes, have seen here only corporeal man. The Samaritan has even gone to the point of suppressing the word אדם *universal man,* which embarrasses him in this verse, substituting that of Ænosh, אֱנוֹשׁ, *corporeal man,* as he has done in other instances. The Chaldean has overthrown all the ideas. Besides, the verb שׁוּג or שׁגה signifies equally *to decline, to err, to degenerate.* It is the latter which, on this occasion, is used as nominal active, inflected by the mediative article בְּ, and generalized by the collective sign ם.

v. 4. הַנְּפִלִים, *then-the-Nephilites*.... That is to say, men distinguished from others by their power or their strength; for the *giants*, γίγαντες, "gigantes", that the Hellenists and Saint Jerome have seen here, have existed only in their imagination, at least if these translators have understood by this, what the vulgar ordinarily understands, that is, men of greater stature than others. If the Hel-

3. A n d-he-said, Ihoah, shall-not-diffuse (lavish itself) the-breath-mine (my-vivifical spirit) unto *Adam* (collective man), forever by-his-decaying-quite: since-he-is b o d i l y-shape, they s h a l l-be, the-days (manifested lights) of-him, one-hundred-fold and-two-tens of-revolving-change.

4. T h e n-the-*Nephilites* (distinguished, illustrious, noble men) were in-the-earth by-the-days those: and-also, a f t e r-that-so (happened) that t h e y-were-c o m e, the-sons (spiritual offspring) of-him-the-Gods, near-the-daughters (corporeal faculties) of-*Adam* (collective man) and-that-they-had-begotten-through-t h e m t h o s e-very-*G h i b o r i t e s* (mighty men, lords) who-were of-old-old, corporeal-men of-renown.

3. Et-il-dit, Ihoah, non-pas-s'épandra (s e prodiguera) le-souffle-mien (mon esprit vivifiant) chez-*Adam* (l'homme universel) pour-l' immensité-temporelle, dans-l ' a c t e-d e-décliner-entière-ment: puisqu' il-est forme-corporelle, ils-seront, les-jours (les manifestations lu-m i n e u s e s) à-lui, un-cen-t u p l e et-deux-décuples de-mutation-temporelle.

4. O r, l e s-*Néphiléens* (les-hommes distingués, les nobles) étaient en-la-terre par-les-j o u r s ceux-là: et-aussi, après-qu'ainsi (cela fut a r r i v é) qu'ils-furent-venus les-fils (émanations spirituelles) d e-l u i-l e s Dieux auprès-des-filles (formes corporelles) d'*Adam* (l' homme universel) et-qu'ils-eurent-généré s e l o n-e u x ceux-là-mêmes, les *Ghiboréens* (les hommes supérieurs, les heros, les Hyperboréens) l e s q u e l s-furent dans-l'immensité-temporelle, les-hommes-corporels de-renom.

---

lenists, who, in other instances, have copied the Samaritan translation, had given attention to this one, they would have seen that the word by which this translation renders נְפִלִים, is 𐤀𐤌𐤉𐤏𐤕, used alike in the Hebrew גִבֹּרִים, and which is placed precisely at the end of the same verse, as synonymous epithet; for this word is nearer

5. Wa-îaræ, Ihôah, chi rabbah rahath ha-Adam b' âretz, w'chol-îetzer mahesheboth lib-ô rak rah chol-ha-îôm.

וַיַּרְא יְהוָֹה כִּי רַבָּה רָעַת הָאָדָם בָּאָרֶץ וְכָל־יֵצֶר מַחְשְׁבֹת לִבּוֹ רַק רַע כָּל־הַיּוֹם:

---

than one imagines to the epithet which the Ὑπερβορέοι bear: those famous *Hyperboreans*, whose origin has so troubled the savants.

These savants had before them, the Latin word *nobilis*, which comes from the same root as the Hebrew נפלים, and presents the same characters with the sole difference of the *b*, which, as in numerous derivative words, has taken the place of *p*, or of *ph*. They have not seen that the Latin word *nobilis*, having passed from Asia into Europe, was the real translation of the word נפלים; and that consequently, in the *Nephilites* of Moses must be seen, not *giants*, nor men of colossal stature, but *Great Ones*; illustrious, distinguished men, *Nobles*, in fact.

Now what is the root of this word? It is פל which always develops the idea of a thing apart, distinguished, raised above the others. Thence the two verbs פלא or פלה, used only in the passive movement הפלא or הפלה, *to be distinguished, illustrious;* of which the continued facultative נפלא or נפלה, *becoming distinguished, illustrious,* gives us the plural נפלים which is the subject of this note.

Those of my readers who know how much the word נפלים has involved the commentators, and who doubt the justice of my etymology, not conceiving how the analogues which I have cited could have escaped the sagacity of the savants, have only to open any Hebrew dictionary to the articles פלא or פלה, and they will see among others, נפלאים *marvelous, wonderful things;* נפלאות, *unheard-of exploits, astonishing things, miracles;* נפלאת, *a profound mystery,* etc.

בימים, *by-the-days....* I have followed here the vulgar interpretation, having no adequate reason for changing it; but, as I have already said, the word ימים, from which the Chaldaic punctuation has suppressed the sign י, can mean equally *days* or *seas*: so that if one admits this last signification, the text will bear, that the *Nephilites*, that is, the *Nobles*, the distinguished among men, subdued at the same time the land and the seas.

COSMOGONY OF MOSES   181

5. And-he-did-ken, I H O A H, that increased-it-self-eagerly the-wickedness of-*Adam* (collective man, mankind) in-the-earth, and-tha t-every-conceit (intellectual operating) from-the-thoughts-out of-the-heart-of-him, diffused evil all-that-day (that whole light's manifestation).

5. Et-il-considera, IHOAH, que se multipliait-avec-violence la méchanceté d'*Adam* (de l'homme universel, règne hominal) en-la-terre, et-que-toute conception (production intellectuelle) des-pensées selon-le-cœur-à-lui, épandait le-mal (en remplissait) tou t-ce-jour (toute cette manifestation phénoménique).

הגברים, *the Ghiborites*.... This important word is composed of two roots which usage has contracted, גב־בור. The first גב, develops literally the idea of a thing placed or happening above another, as a boss, an eminence, a protuberance. Figuratively, it is an increase of glory, strength, honour. The second בור, contains the idea of distinction, of splendour, of purification. It must not be confused with the root spoken of in v. I ch. I, and from which comes the verb ברא *to create*. This latter is composed, as I have stated, of the signs of interior action ב, and the elementary root אר: the one now under consideration, unites to the same generative sign ב, the modified root אור, which, applied particularly to *fire*, develops all ideas attached to that element. It is from this that the following words are derived. בר *wheat*, the grain *par excellence;* בור *to elect, to choose, to distinguish;* בהיר, *that which is white and pure;* בחור *that which is selected, put aside, preferred,* etc.

Let us observe that the vowel which constitutes this root, undergoing the degradation of which I have already spoken so often, forms the verb בעור, *to inflame, to fill with burning ardour; to make passionate, furious,* etc.

We can infer from this etymological knowledge, that the word גברים, by which Moses explains that of נפלים, and which perhaps in his own time had begun to be obsolete, is the exact translation of it, and that it signifies *very distinguished, very remarkable, very noble men*. The first root גב, which I have rendered in this instance by the superlative *very*, has been rendered by the ancient Greeks by the adverbial relation ὑπερ *above;* the second root בור, has been pre-

6. Wa-înnahem, Ihoah, chi-hashah æth-ha-Adam, b' âretz wa-îthe-hatzeb æl-libô. וַיִּנָּחֶם יְהֹוָה כִּי־עָשָׂה אֶת־הָאָדָם בָּאָרֶץ וַיִּתְעַצֵּב אֶל־לִבּוֹ :

---

served in the plural Βόρεοι, *Boreans*: that is to say, *the illustrious, the powerful, the strong*, in short, the *Barons*: for the Celtic word *baron*, is the analogue of the Hebrew גברון, written with the extensive final ון; the Greek word Ὑπερβόρεοι, of which the savants have said so much, is no other than *the high, arch-barons*. And thus, confusing constantly the name of a caste with the name of a people, as they have done with regard to the Chaldeans, these same savants have been greatly troubled to find the fixed abode of the Hyperborean nation.

Before terminating this already very lengthy article, I cannot dispense with stating two things. The first, that the word גבר, here referred to, constitutes the fourth name that Moses gives to man: the second, that this hierographic writer, makes this superior man descend, by the union of divine emanations with natural forms, that is to say, in other terms, spiritual faculties joined to physical faculties.

Adam, universal man, the kingdom of man, issues in principle from the hands of the Divinity, in principle male and female.

The element from which he must draw his passive nature substance, is named after him, *adamah*. Soon the divine spirit is united to his elementary spirit: he passes from power into action. The Being of beings individualizes him by detaching from him his efficient volitive faculty and makes him thus, free, susceptible of realizing his own conceptions. Then intellectual man, *Aish*, exists.

The covetous passion, universal incentive of elementary nature, inevitably attacks thenceforth this volitive faculty, now isolated and free. *Aisha*, seduced and believing to take possession of his active nature principle, gives way to the natural principle. Intellectual man is corrupted. His volitive faculty is changed into elementary existence, *Hewah*. Universal man, *Adam*, is decomposed and divided. His unity, passed first to number three in *Kain, Habel*, and *Sheth*,

COSMOGONY OF MOSES 183

6. A n d-h e-withdrew-in-h i m s e l f (he forsook the care), Ihoah, t h r o u g h-which he-had-made *Adam,* (collective man) and-he repressed (he r e s t r a i n e d, proved himself severe) unto-the-heart-his-own-self.

6. Et-il renonça-entièrement (il se reposa du soin) Ihoah, à-cause-de-quoi il-avait-fait l'ipséité d'*Adam* (l'homme universel) en-la-terre, et-il-se-réprima (se comprima, se rendit sévère) au cœur sien.

---

goes to number six through *Kaiṅ*, and to number nine through *Sheth.* The corporeal faculties succeed to elementary existence. Corporeal man, *Ænosh*, appears upon the cosmogonic scene.

In the meantime, the divine emanations are united to the corporeities born of the dissolution of *Adam*, and corporeal man gives place directly to superior man, *Ghibor*, hero, demi-god. Very soon this *Ghibor*, this superior man, abandons himself to evil, and his inevitable downfall brings about the repose of Nature.

Thus, in the profound thought of Moses, these four hieroglyphic names succeed one another: אדם, *universal man,* איש, *intellectual man,* אנוש *corporeal man,* גבור *superior man.* And these four names, so different in form and in signification, employed by Moses with an art more than human, have been rendered by the same word as synonyms!

v. 5. יצר, *conceit*.... I have already explained the formation of this difficult and important word v. 7. ch. II. It is used here as substantive.

רק, *diffused*.... While explaining the word רקיע, rarefaction, ethereal expansion, v. 6. ch. I, I stated that the root רק contained the idea of expansion, of diffusion. Moses in using it here as verb, gives it no other meaning.

v. 6. וינחם, *And-he-withdrew-in-himself*.... The Christian heresiarchs who have rejected the Books of Moses as unjust to the Divinity, in claiming them to be inspired by the genius of evil, or at least by an intermediary being, an Æon, very different from the

7. Wa-iâomer I H Ô A H æmeheh æth-ha-Adam âsher barâthî me-hal pheneî ha-âdamah, me-Adam had-behemah had-remesh w'had-hôph ha-shamaîm chi-nihamethî chi-hashithîm.

וַיֹּאמֶר יְהֹוָה אֶמְחֶה אֶת־הָאָדָם אֲשֶׁר בָּרָאתִי מֵעַל פְּנֵי הָאֲדָמָה מֵאָדָם עַד־בְּהֵמָה עַד־רֶמֶשׂ וְעַד־עוֹף הַשָּׁמָיִם כִּי־נִחַמְתִּי כִּי עֲשִׂיתִם׃

Supreme Being, have all relied upon this verse, thus translated by Saint Jerome: "Poenituit eum quod hominem fecisset in terra; et tactus delore cordis intrinsecus."

These heresiarchs found that it was not consistent to say of the Most High, of the Immutable Being, infinitely perfect, that he repented of a thing that he had done, or that his heart had been grieved.

It would appear that the Hellenists, having felt this very great inconsistency, wished to palliate it: they say in their version, that GOD considered the creation which he had made of man upon the earth, and he reflected, καὶ ἐνεθυμήθη ὁ θεὸς, ὅτι ἐποίησεν τὸν ἄνθρωπον ἐπὶ τῆς γῆς καὶ διενοήθη. But besides, the Hebraic terms do not in the least present this meaning, the most ancient translations which have been made from the Greek, and which are in accord with the Latin, make one suspect that the version of the Hellenists has been mutilated in this place as in some others.

The Chaldaic paraphrast takes this curious turn.

ותב ייי במימריה ארי עבד ית אינשא בארעא ואמר במימריה למתבר תוקפיהון ברעותיה

And-he-returned, the Eternal Jaii, in-his-word, because-he-had-made substantial-man upon-the-earth: and-he-declared-in-his-word, for-the-action-being-broken (that he would break) the-pride-of-them, conformable-to-his-sovereign-will.

As to the Samaritan, the terms that it employs are so obscure that it is fitting before explaining them, to give the reasons for my translation. Indeed how is it that so many savants who have studied the Hebraic tongue, and whose piety must be shocked by the mislead-

COSMOGONY OF MOSES 185

7. And-he-said, IHOAH, I-shall wash-off the-selfsameness of-*A d a m* (collective man) which-I-have-created, from-above the-face of-the-adamic: from *Adam* (mankind) to-the-quadruped, the creeping-kind, the fowl of-heavens: for-I withdrew- (I forsook the care) through-which I-made-them.

7. Et-il-dit, IHOAH, je-laverai (j'effacerai au moyen de l'eau) cette-existence-objective-d'*A d a m* (l'homme universel) que j'ai-créé, de-dessus-la-face de-la-terre-a d a m i q u e; depuis-*Adam* (le règne hominal) jusqu'au-quadrupède, au-rampant, au-volatile des-cieux; car j'ai-renoncé-tout-à-fait (au soin) à-cause-de-quoi j'avais-fait-eux.

---

ing meaning given to this verse by the Vulgate, have not sought to reéstablish the thought of Moses in its purity? What was the matter? It was only necessary to recognize the collective sign ם, which this hierographic writer has added to the verb, to give it, according to the intensive form, a meaning stronger and more general which it would not have had otherwise. The addition of this final sign is sufficiently common in Hebrew for it to have been noticed; but, as I have already observed, the folly of those who believe themselves savants, is seeking afar the truth which is before them.

The final character ם, whether alone, or accompanied by the vowel ה, is added not only to nouns, but also to relations and to verbs, to generalize their expression: the genius of the Hebraic tongue, goes so far even as to tolerate its addition to the temporal modifications of verbs, as I shall have occasion to state in v. 13 of this chapter.

Now, the verb נחה thus generalized by the collective sign ם signifies literally, *to renounce wholly, to cease entirely, to desist, to lay aside care, to abandon an action, a sentiment*, etc. The meaning that should be attached to this verb, depends therefore upon the care, the sentiment, the action, whose suspension it indicates. If it is an evil act, a sin, it can indeed signify *to repent*, as it can also signify *to be consoled*, if it is a pain, an affliction; but neither sin nor pain can be attributed to GOD; this verb could never involve

8. W-Noah matzâ hen b'heîneî IHÔAH. וְנֹחַ מָצָא חֵן בְּעֵינֵי יְהֹוָה׃

9. Æleh thô-le-doth Noah: Noah aîsh tzaddîk thamîm haîah b'dorothaî-ô: æth-ha-Ælohîm hithhallech-Noah. אֵלֶּה תּוֹלְדֹת נֹחַ נֹחַ אִישׁ צַדִּיק תָּמִים הָיָה בְּדֹרֹתָיו אֶת־הָאֱלֹהִים הִתְהַלֶּךְ־נֹחַ׃

10. Wa-ioled Noah she-loshah banim: æth-Shem, æth-Ham wæth-Japheth. וַיּוֹלֶד נֹחַ שְׁלֹשָׁה בָנִים אֶת־שֵׁם אֶת־חָם וְאֶת־יָפֶת׃

---

this meaning relative to him. If GOD renounces a sentiment, if he ceases entirely from making a thing, as the verb נוחם, expresses it, this sentiment can be only love, this action can be only the conservation of his work. Therefore, he does not *repent*, as Saint Jerome says; but he *renounces*, he *forsakes;* and at the most *is angry*. This last meaning which is the strongest that can be given to the verb נוחם, has been quite generally followed by the Hebrew writers subsequent to Moses. But one must observe that when they use it, it is only as a sequence of the suspension of the love and of the conservative action of the Divinity; for this meaning is not inherent in the verb in question.

Now let us turn to the Samaritan translator. If any one had taken the trouble to investigate the obscurity of his expressions, he would see that it is not very unlike the meaning that I have given this verse.

And-he-withdrew-to-him-the-breath, IHOAH, by-which he-had-made the Universal in-the-earth: and-he-shut-up (contracted exceedingly) un-to-the-heart-his-own.

8. But-*N o a h* (nature's rest), found grace in-the-eyes of-IHOAH.

9. These-are the-symbolical-p r o g e n i e s of-*Noah;* *Noah,* intellectual- principle right-proving of-universal-accomplishments was-he, in-the-p e r i o d s-his-own: together·with HIM - the - Gods, h e-applied-himself-t o-walk, *Noah.*

10. A n d-h e-d i d-beget, *Noah* (nature's rest) three sons (spiritual offspring): t h e-selfsameness-o f-*S h e m* (the lofty, the bright one) of-*Ham* (the down bent, the gloomy one) and-of-*Japheth* (the extended and wide).

8. Mais-*Noah* (le repos de la nature) trouva grâce aux-yeux de-IHOAH.

9. Celles-ci-sont les-symboliques - générations d e-*Noah;* *Noah,* principe-intellectuel manifestant-la-justice des-vertus-universelles il-était, dans-les-âges-siens : les-traces-mêmes de-LUI-les-Dieux, il-s'appliquait-à-suivre, *Noah.*

10. Et-il engendra, *Noah,* (le repos de la nature) trois fils (trois émanations) : la-séité-de-*S h e m* (l'élevé, l' éclatant) de-*Ham* (le courbe, le chaud) et-de-*Japheth* (l'étendu).

ויתעצב, *And-he-repressed-himself*.... This is to say, that the Being of beings withdrew into his own heart. The Samaritan translator is the only one who seems to have felt the force of this expression. The compound עצב, springs as I have already said, from the two contracted roots עץ־צב. It is used in this case as verb according to the reflexive form.

v. 7. After the explanations that I have just given, there is nothing more to dwell upon in this verse.

v. 8. ונח *but-Noah*.... For the interpretation of this word, see v. 29, ch. V.

v. 9. בדרותיו, *in-the-periods-his-own*.... Several ideas are attached to the root דור which forms the basis of this word. By the first, should be understood a circle, an orb; by the second, any cir-

11. Wa-thishheth ha-âretz li-phenêi ha-Ælohîm wa-thimmalæ ha-âretz hamass.

וַתִּשָּׁחֵת הָאָרֶץ לִפְנֵי הָאֱלֹהִים וַתִּמָּלֵא הָאָרֶץ חָמָס׃

12. Wa-îaræ Ælohîm æth-ha-âretz, w'hinneh nishehathath chi-hisheheth chol-basher æth-darch-ô hal-ha-âretz.

וַיַּרְא אֱלֹהִים אֶת־הָאָרֶץ וְהִנֵּה נִשְׁחָתָה כִּי־הִשְׁחִית כָּל־בָּשָׂר אֶת־דַּרְכּוֹ עַל־הָאָרֶץ׃

13. Wa-îâomer Ælohîm l'Noah: ketz chol-bashar bâ l'phana-î chi-malâh ha-âretz hamass mi-pheneihem: w' hin-nî. mashehitham æth-ha-âretz.

וַיֹּאמֶר אֱלֹהִים לְנֹחַ קֵץ כָּל־בָּשָׂר בָּא לְפָנַי כִּי־מָלְאָה הָאָרֶץ חָמָס מִפְּנֵיהֶם וְהִנְנִי מַשְׁחִיתָם אֶת־הָאָרֶץ׃

---

cular habitation whatever, a sphere. If one relates the first of these ideas to a temporal duration, then the word דור signifies a cyclic period, an age, a century, a generation. If, by the second, one understands an inhabited space, then the same word designates a city, a world, a universe; for I must say, *en passant*, that in ancient times, every duration, like every habitation, was conceived under the picture of a circle. The Arabic words دَار and كُورَه, the Greek words πόλις or πολεῖν, the Latin words *orbis* and *urbs*, are unimpeachable proofs.

v. 10. See v. 32 ch. V.

v. 11. ותשחת, *And-it-was-debased*.... The root חת expresses an idea of terror, consternation, sinking, downfall; literally as well as figuratively. In this verb the root being governed by the sign of relative movement ש, characterizes a continual state of downfall and debasement, a progressive degradation.

חמס, *a violent-heat*.... This is the same root חם which I have

COSMOGONY OF MOSES

11. A n d-i t-was-debased (depressed, vilified) t h e-earth, in the-face of-HIM-the-Gods; and-it-was-filled, the earth, with-a-violent-depraving-heat.

12. And-he-did-ken, HE t h e-Gods, the-selfsameness of-the-earth, and-lo: being-depraved, because-hastened-to-deprave, e v e r y-bodily-shape, the-way-its-own upon-the-earth.

13. And-he-said, HE-the-Being-of-beings, t o - *N o a h* (nature's rest) the-end of- e v e r y corporeal-shape is-coming to-the-face-mine: for-it-is heaped, the-earth, with-a-violent-v i l i f y i n g-h e a t through-the-whole-face: and -h e r e-a m-I causing-to-depress-quite-o v e r t h e-self-sameness-of-the-earth.

11. E t-elle-s e-déprimait (se ravalait, se dégradait) la-terre-à-la-face de-LUI-les-Dieux et-elle-se-remplissait, la-t e r r e, d'une-ardeur-de-plus-en-plus-dégradante.

12. Et-il-considéra, LUI-l'Être-des-êtres, l'ipséité-de-la-terre, et-voici: étant-dégradée parceque laissait-dégrader, toute-forme-corporelle, la-voie - propre - sienne, sur-la-terre.

13. Et-il-dit,LUI-l'Ê t r e-des-êtres, à-*Noah*, (le repos de la nature): la-terme de-toute forme-corporelle est-venant à-la-face-m i e n n e: car-elle-s'est-comblée, la-terre, d'une-ardeur dépravante, par-la-face-entière: et-voici-moi laissant-dégrader (avilir, détruire) entièrement l'ipséité-terrestre.

---

explained in v. 32 ch. V. Its action taken in the bad sense, is further increased by the addition of the circular movement ס.

v. 12. אֶת־דַּרְכּוֹ, *the-way-its-own*.... I have spoken of the root דּוּר, in v. 9 of this chapter. The root אָךְ, which is now joined to it by contraction, דּר־אָךְ, fixes the idea and determines it. Thus the word דֶּרֶךְ, expresses every circumscribed law, every orbit, every way, every line whether speaking of time or life, or speaking of intellectual or physical things.

v. 13. מִפְּנֵיהֶם, *through-the-whole-face*.... Neither the Hellenists nor the author of the Latin Vulgate, have perceived that the nominal affix הֶם, was used in this case, as collective final and they have

14. Hôsheh le-èha thebath hotzeî-gopher, kinnîm tha-hosheh æth-ha-t h e b a h, w' èhapharetha â o t h-ha mi-baîth w'mi-houtz b'èhopher. עֲשֵׂה לְךָ תֵּבַת עֲצֵי־גֹפֶר קִנִּים תַּעֲשֶׂה אֶת־הַתֵּבָה וְכָפַרְתָּ אֹתָהּ מִבַּיִת וּמִחוּץ בַּכֹּפֶר:

---

connected it with the preceding word בשר; associating thus, without regard for the simplest rules of grammar, a plural with a singular. That Saint Jerome should have made this mistake, can be conceived; but that the Jews, the Essenes, interpreting the tongue of their ancesters, should not have better understood the Sepher of Moses, is inconceivable. For how could they have ignored the fact that the characters ם or הם, added to the end of words, generalized the meaning in the same manner and by the same grammatical rule, that the characters ן or ןִ increased it?

Did they not see written יומם, *all the day*, שמם, *a generic name*, אמנם *the whole truth*, and שניהם, *both of them?* Why have they been deceived in the meaning of the verb נוחם, of which I spoke in v. 6. of this chapter? Why have they not recognized the collective sign ם , in the word which is the subject of this note and in the word following? I have already explained this in my Introductory Dissertation. They did not wish to give the knowledge of their tongue nor of their sacred books.

משחיתם, *causing-to-depress-quite....* This is the same verb שחות , *to disparage, to abase, to lower*, which Moses used according to the positive form, passive movement, in speaking of the earth, in v. II of this chapter, and which he uses now, according to the excitative form, continued facultative, in speaking of the Being of beings. This observation, that no translator had been in a position to make, was very important. It leads to the real thought of Moses, which is, that the Being of beings destroys the earth only by abandoning it to the degradation, to the corruption which is its own work: this thought is contained in the renunciation referred to in v. 6. It is needless to repeat here, how the ignorant or deceiving translators have seen *a repentance* in this divine renunciation. It is because they have not comprehended the force of the collective sign ם , added again to the facultative משחית, in order to generalize its action.

COSMOGONY OF MOSES

14. Make to-thee a-*thebah* (sheltering abode) of-an-elementary-growth preserving-and-corporeal: hollowed-and-r o o m e d thou-s h a l t-m a k e the-whole-of-that-m u t u a l-abode: and-thou-shalt-smear the-whole-of-it within and-without-the -circumference, w i t h-a-viscous body-like-substance.

14. Fais à-toi une-*thebah* (une retraite, un refuge, un a s i l e mutuel) d'une-substance-élémentaire-conservatrice: de-canaux (lieux propres à contenir) tu-feras l' ensemble de-cette-retraite; et-tu-lieras (englueras) l' ensemble-d'elle, par-l'intérieur e t-p a r-l'extérieur-cir conférenciel avec-une-matière-corporisante.

---

v. 14. תבה, *a-thebah*.... It appears to be the Samaritan translator who, rendering this word by 𐤕𐤁𐤄, *a vessel*, was the first to give rise to all the absurd ideas that this error has brought forth. Never has the Hebrew word תבה signified *a vessel*, in the sense of *a ship*, as it has since been understood; but *a vessel* in the sense of a thing destined to contain and to preserve another. This word, which is found in all the ancient mythologies, merits particular attention. It has so many significations that it is difficult to assign a definite one. It is, on the one hand, the symbolic name given by the Egyptians to their sacred city, *Theba*, considered as the shelter, the refuge, the abode of the gods; that famous city whose name transported into Greece to a straggling village of Beotia, has sufficed to immortalize it. On the other hand, it is a circuit, an orbit, a globe, a land, a coffer, an ark, a world, the solar system, *the Universe*, in fact, that one imagined contained in a sort of vessel called אוב: for I must recall here the fact that the Egyptians did not give chariots to the Sun and Moon as did the Greeks, but a sort of round vessel. The vessel of Isis was no other than that *theba*, that famous ark which we are considering; and it must be stated, the very name of Paris, of this city where are concentrated the rays of glory escaped from a hundred celebrated cities, where again flourish after long darkness, the sciences of the Egyptians, the Assyrians and the Greeks; the name of Paris, I say, is only the name of the Thebes of Egypt and of Greece, that of ancient Syparis, of the Babel of As-

15. W'zeh âsher thahosheh âoth-ha shilosh mâôth âmmah arech ha-thebah ha-moshîm âmmah raheb-ha w-shiloshîm âmmah kômath-ha. וְזֶה אֲשֶׁר תַּעֲשֶׂה אֹתָהּ שְׁלֹשׁ מֵאוֹת אַמָּה אֹרֶךְ הַתֵּבָה חֲמִשִּׁים אַמָּה רָחְבָּהּ וּשְׁלֹשִׁים אַמָּה קוֹמָתָהּ:

syria, translated into the tongue of the Celts. It is the vessel of Isis, (*Bar-Isis*) that mysterious ark, which, in one way or another, carries ever the destinies of the world, of which it is the symbol.

Besides, this word אוב, whose vast meaning could not be exactly rendered by any of those that I know, and which the wisest Egyptians alone were in position to comprehend, given over to vulgar Hebrews and following the proneness of their gross ideas, was finally restricted and corrupted to the point of signifying literally *the belly, a leather bottle;* and figuratively, *a magic spirit*, a sort of *demon* to which the Jews attributed the oracles of their sibyls. But there exists in the Hebraic idiom as well as in the neighbouring idioms from the same source, a mass of expressions, which starting from the same radical principle, show all its importance.

It is first its analogue אב, developing the general idea of fructification, of generation, of paternity; then, it is that of the will, in אבה; that of love, in אהב: it is all blossoming, in the Syriac ܘܒܒܐ: it is every awakening, in the Arabic حب ; all immensity, every unknown place, in هوب ; every inner and profound sentiment, in واب: finally, without seeking to link with this root any other signs than the one which enters into the composition of the word תבה, it is the action of being moved in oneself, of returning, of retiring into, of withdrawing to oneself through desire, in the three verbs תוב, תובב, and תאוב: it is even the name of the Universe, in the compound תבל. One cannot see in all this, either *the coffer* of the Hellenists, $κιβωτός$, or *the chest* of the Latin translator, "arca".

עצי־גפר, *of-an-elementary-growth-preserving*.... The Hellenists have said $ἐκ ξύλων τετραγώνων$ *of quadrangular wood;* Saint Jerome has said "de lignis levigatis" *of polished wood;* the Chaldaic paraphrast ראעין דקדרום *of planks of cedar;* the Samaritan translator 𐤑𐤉𐤏𐤑 . 𐤏𐤀𐤌 , *of an ebony substance, or of papyrus*. None

COSMOGONY OF MOSES 193

15. And-thus this shalt-thou-make three hundred-fold o f-mother-measuring the-length of-t h e-*t h e b a h* (t h a t sheltering abode): five-tens of-measuring, the-breath-of-it, and-three-tens of-measuring the-bulk (the whole heap, the substantiality)-of-it.

15. Et-c'est-ainsi que tu-feras la-séité-d'elle: trois centuples de-measure-mère (régulatrice) l a-longitude de-la-*thebah* (cette retraite sacrée) c i n q-décuples de-mesure, la-latitude-sienne; et-trois-décuples de-mesure, la-solidité (la substantialité) sienne.

---

of them having understood, or having wished to understand, what the *thebah* was; and being represented for the most part under the figure of a rude bark, it was impossible that they should not fall into the grossest errors. I have already proved that the word עץ does not signify *wood*. It should be known that it is not any kind of *tree* whose use had been forbidden to universal man, *Adam*. Here is the hieroglyphic composition of the word גפר. The root גף which developing, in general, all ideas of conservation, of protection, of means, of exterior guarantee, and which, signifying in a more restricted sense, *a body*, is found united to the elementary root אר. The Chaldaic verb גוף, which comes from the root גף, expresses the action of closing outwardly, of embodying, of furnishing with conservatory means, etc.

קנים, *hollowed-and-roomed*.... This is the root קן, used here for the root גן, so as to give more force to the expression. I call attention to this so that one may see nothing in it similar to קין.

בכפר, *with-a-viscous body-like-substance*.... כפר is the same word as גפר, used above, but whose force is now augmented by the hieroglyphic substitution which Moses has made of the assimilative sign כ, for the organic sign ג.

v. 15. אמה, *of-mother-measuring*.... The translator who has in this case rendered the word אמה, *a cubit*, has made the same mistake in rendering the word שנה *a year;* he has restricted in determined limits that which had only relative limits. Thus, as by שנה should be understood any duration relative to the being of which it is the object, so in אמה should be seen a measure peculiar

16. Tzohr thahosheh la-thebah w'æl-âmmah thebale-uah mi-lemahel-ha w'phat-hah ha-thebah b'tzid-ha tha-shîm thahethiîm sheniîm w-shelishîm thahoshe-ha.

צֹהַר תַּעֲשֶׂה לַתֵּבָה וְאֶל־אַמָּה תְּכַלֶּנָּה מִלְמַעְלָה וּפֶתַח הַתֵּבָה בְּצִדָּהּ תָּשִׂים תַּחְתִּיִּם שְׁנִיִּם וּשְׁלִשִׁים תַּעֲשֶׂהָ:

17. Wa-ânî hin-nî mebîâ æth-ha-mabboul maîm hal-ha-âretz l'shaheth-chol-bas-har âsher-b'ô rouah haiîm: mi-thahath ha-shamaîm chol-âsher b'âretz îgwah.

וַאֲנִי הִנְנִי מֵבִיא אֶת־הַמַּבּוּל מַיִם עַל־הָאָרֶץ לְשַׁחֵת כָּל־בָּשָׂר אֲשֶׁר־בּוֹ רוּחַ חַיִּים מִתַּחַת הַשָּׁמָיִם כֹּל אֲשֶׁר־בָּאָרֶץ יִגְוָע:

---

to the thing in question. This word signifies literally, *a metropolis*, an original maternal nation, relative to another; a thing upon which others depend, and by which they must be ruled; *a measure, a rule*. Its root is אם, which develops all ideas of maternity. I believe it unnecessary to dwell upon the other terms which compose this verse, inasmuch as the most important, the names of the numbers have been explained.

v. 16. צֹהַר, *Gathering-light*...... The interpretation of this facultative by the Hellenists and the Latin translator differs widely. The former have seen ἐπισυνάγων, *gathering*, and the latter "fenestram" *a window*. They might have easily perceived their error, if they had observed that its derivative יִצְהָר, designated *oil;* that is to say, that kind of liquid which seems to gather to itself the luminous principle to shed it without. The facultative here referred to, rests upon two contracted roots צוֹה־אֹר. The first צוֹה, contains the idea of an impressed movement, of direction given to a thing: the second אֹר or אוֹר is the symbol of elementary principle, or light.

16. G a t h e r i n g-light, shalt-thou-make unto-t h e- *t h e b a h,* a n d-a f t e r-the- mother-measuring, the-orbi- cular-extent-its-own, as-to- the-uppermost-part-its-own ; and-the-opening of-that-mu- tual-asylum, in-the-opposite- p a r t-i t s-o w n, shalt-thou- place : t h e-lowermost-parts two and-three-fold s h a l t- thou-make-to-it.

17. And-even-I, t h e r e- am-I bringing the selfsame- ness-o f-the-g r e a t-swelling (the flood) of-waters upon- the-earth, to depress (anni- hilate) e v e r y-bodily-shape that-has i n t o-i t s e l f the- breath of-lives : from-below t h e-heavens all-that-is in- the-earth, shall-expire.

16. Dirigeant-la-lumière, tu-feras à-la-*thebah,* et-selon -l a-mesure-régulatrice, l'or- be (l'étendue orbiculaire)- sienne, e n-c e-qui-concerne- l a-partie-supérieure-sienne ; e t-l a dilatation (la solu- tion, l'ouverture), de-cette- r e t r a i t e en-la-partie-op- posée-sienne tu-mettras : les- parties-basses, doubles et- triples, tu-feras-à-elle.

17. Et-moi-m ê m e, me- voici faisant-venir c e-q u i- constitue-la-grande-intumes- cence des-eaux (le déluge) sur-la-terre, pour-déprimer (détruire) toute-forme-cor- porelle qui-a dans-soi le- souffle des-vies : par-en-bas des-cieux, tout ce-qui-est en- la-terre expirera.

תבלנה, *the-orbicular-extent-its-own*.... The word תבל by which is generally understood, an orbicular extent, *the universe,* signifies in the most restricted sense, the globe of the earth, the earth, the terrestrial superficies. It is attached to the same root as the word תבה, as I have said, and differs from it only by the ex- pansive sign ל, which communicates to it its particular movement.

v. 17. את־המבול, *the-selfsameness-of-the-great-swelling*........ This is that universal deluge related by Moses, that terrible event, the memory of which remains among all peoples, like tracks upon the face of the whole earth. If I should consult the annals of the world, I could easily prove that, from the Chinese to the Scandi- navians, from the Syrians to the Iroquois, there does not exist a single people that has not had knowledge of this catastrophe; if I should call, in its turn, natural history to give evidence, I could not

18. Wa-hakimothî æth-berith-î âitha-ĉha-w-bâtha æl-ha-thebah âthah! w-banei-ĉha, w-âisheth-ĉha w-neshei-banei-ĉha âitha-ĉha.

וַהֲקִמֹתִי אֶת־בְּרִיתִי אִתָּךְ וּבָאתָ אֶל־הַתֵּבָה אַתָּה וּבָנֶיךָ וְאִשְׁתְּךָ וּנְשֵׁי־בָנֶיךָ אִתָּךְ

---

take a single step without encountering unimpeachable proofs of this truth of natural philosophy.

The root בול, composed of the two signs ב and ל, indicates a force eminently dilating, which, acting from the centre to the circumference, increases the volume of things, causing a boiling up, a flux, an extraordinary swelling. All the words which come from this root are connected with this idea. Sometimes it is a crowd, a tumultuous gathering; sometimes, an unusual abundance, an inundation, etc. The character מ which governs it, ought to be considered on this occasion, not alone as sign of exterior and plastic action; but as representing the word *mah*, which, as we have already seen in explaining the word מאה *one hundred*, is applied to that which is great, to that which attains its utmost dimensions.

מים, *the waters....* The deluge is not expressed by one single word in Hebrew, as might be believed, following the vulgar translations, but by two, מבול־מים, *the great intumescence, the great swelling of the waters.* The hierographic writer clearly indicates here, that the divine will influencing the waters, they extend and increase in volume and cause the universal inundation. Thus the calculations of the savants to determine whether the actual mass of the waters can be sufficient for this effect, are ridiculous and prove their ignorance. It is not a question of computing whether the waters with which the seas are filled, can, in their state of

18. And-I will-cause-to-stand, t h e-creating-might-mine together-t h e e, a n d-thou-wilt-repair toward-the *thebah,* thou! and the-sons-of-thee (thy spiritual off-spring) a n d-t h e-intellect-ual-mate-thy-own (thy voli-tive faculty) a n d-the-cor-poreal-mates of-the-sons-of-thee (their natural facul-ties) together-thee.

18. E t-j e-ferai-subsister la-force-créatrice-mienne en-semble-t o i e t-t u-viendras vers-la-*t h e b a h,* toi! et-les-fils-à-toi (tes productions) et-l a-femme-intellectuelle-à-toi (ta faculté efficiente) et-les-épouses-corporelles-des-fils-à-toi (leurs facultés physi-ques) ensemble-toi.

---

depression, cover the whole earth and rise above the highest moun-tains; this is obviously impossible: but it is a question of knowing whether, in a state of extreme dilation and swelling caused by the effect of a certain force chained to the centre of the waters, they would suffice for this.

v. 18. בריתי, *the-creating-might-mine....* It is very difficult to divine how the Hellenists and Saint Jerome, can see a pact, a treaty of alliance, in a word so plainly derived from the verb ברוא, *to create.* The reader must feel that it is more simple to believe that the Being of beings, ready to abandon the earth to the destruc-tion toward which it tends, leaves his creative force to subsist with *Noah,* the repose of nature, than to believe that he establishes some sort of contract or pact between them.

ונשי, *and-the-corporeal-mates....* I would call attention to the fact that Moses does not use, to designate the *mates* of the sons of Noah, the same word אשה, as he does in characterizing the *in-tellectual mate* of the latter, his *volitive faculty.*

19. W-mi-čhol h-haî mi-čhol bashar shenaîm mi-čhol-thabîâ æl-ha-thebah l' hahoîoth âitha-čha: začhar w-nekebah îhîou.

וּמִכָּל־הָחַי מִכָּל־בָּשָׂר שְׁנַיִם מִכָּל תָּבִיא אֶל־הַתֵּבָה לְהַחֲיֹת אִתָּךְ זָכָר וּנְקֵבָה יִהְיוּ׃

20. Me-ha-hôph l'mîn-hou, w-min ha-behemah l' mîn-ha, mi-čhol remesh ha-âdamah l'mîn-hou shenaîm mi-čhol îaboâou æleî-čha l' hahoîôth.

מֵהָעוֹף לְמִינֵהוּ וּמִן־הַבְּהֵמָה לְמִינָהּ מִכֹּל רֶמֶשׂ הָאֲדָמָה לְמִינֵהוּ שְׁנַיִם מִכֹּל יָבֹאוּ אֵלֶיךָ לְהַחֲיוֹת׃

21. W'âthah kah-le-čha mi-čhol maâ-čhol âsher îeâ-čhel w'assaphetha æleî-čha w'haîah l'čha w-la-hem l' âčhelah.

וְאַתָּה קַח־לְךָ מִכָּל־מַאֲכָל אֲשֶׁר יֵאָכֵל וְאָסַפְתָּ אֵלֶיךָ וְהָיָה לְךָ וְלָהֶם לְאָכְלָה׃

22. Wa-îahash Noah čh' čhol âsher tziwah âoth-ô Ælohîm; čhen hashah.

וַיַּעַשׂ נֹחַ כְּכֹל אֲשֶׁר צִוָּה אֹתוֹ אֱלֹהִים כֵּן עָשָׂה׃

---

v. 19. and 20. All these terms have been explained.

v. 21. וְאָסַפְתָּ, *that-thou-shalt-lay up*.... The conjunctive article ו holds here the place of the relative אשר as we have seen it in other cases. The words used in this verse offer no difficulty as to their literal and grammatical signification; as to their figurative and hieroglyphic meaning, that is different; a long note would be necessary for me to make them understood and besides, I should not attain this point if the reader did not first recognize *Noah*, for upon

COSMOGONY OF MOSES

19. A n d-from-all-living-kind, from-all-bodily-shape, two-twains from-all t h o u-s h a l t-c a u s e-to-repair to-ward-the-*thebah,* for-being-kept-existing together-thee : male and-female they-shall-be.

20. From-t h e-f l y i n g-fowl after-the-kind-its-own, from the quadrupedly-walk-ing-a n i m a l i t y, after-the-kind-its-own, from-all-creep-ing-life elementary-e a r t h-born after-the-kind-its-own, two-and-two, they-shall-re-pair toward-thee for-being caused-to-exist.

21. A n d-t h o u ! t a k e (draw) unto-thee, from-all food which-c a n-feed, that-t h o u-shalt-lay up-toward-thee: and-it-shall-be unto-t h e e, a n d-unto-them for-food.

22. And-he-did, *N o a h,* t h e-s a m e-all which had-w i s e l y-prescribed HE-the-Gods; thus-doing.

19. Et-de-toute-existence, d e-t o u t e-forme-corporelle, deux-à-deux de-tout tu-fe-ras-venir vers-la-*t h e b a h,* afin-d'exister ensemble-toi : mâle et-femelle ils-seront.

20. Du-genre-volatile se-lon-l'espèce-s i e n n e, et-du-genre-quadrupède selon-l'es-pèce-sienne, de-tout-animal-reptiforme issu-de-l'élément -adamique, selon-l'espèce-à-lui, les-deux-doubles de-tout, ils-viendront p r è s-d e-t o i afin-d'y-c o n s e r v e r-l'exis-tence.

21. Et-toi! prends (sais-is, tire) à-toi de-tout-ali-ment q u i-p e u t-alimenter que-tu-ramasseras d e v e r s-toi : et-il-sera-à-toi, et-à-eux pour aliment.

22. Et-il-fit, *Noah,* le-semblable-tout lequel avait-sagement-prescrit L U I-les Dieux: ainsi-faisant.

---

this knowledge depends that of the children of *Adam.* In regard to them, I have said all that I can say.

v. 22. בכל, *the-same-all....* I quote this word only to point out the use of the assimilative article כ : an article which the trans-lators of the Sepher have not recognized, whether through ignorance or deliberate intent, in very essential instances where it was quite as obvious as it is here.

SEPHER BERÆSHITH Z.

ספר בראשית ז׃

1. Wa-îâomer IHÔAH l' Noah boâ âthah w'chol beîth -cha æl-ha-thebah chi âoth-cha râîthi tzaddîk l'phana-î ba-dôr ha-zeh.

וַיֹּאמֶר יְהוָה לְנֹחַ בֹּא־אַתָּה וְכָל־בֵּיתְךָ אֶל־הַתֵּבָה כִּי־אֹתְךָ רָאִיתִי צַדִּיק לְפָנַי בַּדּוֹר הַזֶּה׃

2. Mi-chol ha-behemah ha-tehôrah thikkah-le-cha shibehah shibehah! âîsh w' âisheth-ô w-min-ha-behemah âsher loâ theorah hiwâ shen-aîm âîsh w'âisheth-ô.

מִכֹּל הַבְּהֵמָה הַטְּהוֹרָה תִּקַּח־לְךָ שִׁבְעָה שִׁבְעָה אִישׁ וְאִשְׁתּוֹ וּמִן־הַבְּהֵמָה אֲשֶׁר לֹא טְהֹרָה הִוא שְׁנַיִם אִישׁ וְאִשְׁתּוֹ׃

---

v. 1. There is nothing perplexing in these terms.

v. 2. איש ואשתו, *the-very-principle and-the-volitive-intellectual faculty-its own*.... Here is a decisive passage which makes one of the most astounding incoherences, one of the strongest physical contradictions, disappear from the narrative of Moses. For if the *thebah* was really a boat, as the translators leave it to be understood, of only three hundred cubits in length, fifty in breadth, and thirty in height, I ask how the terrestrial and aerial animals, by sevens of the pure and by twos of the impure, could lodge there? How could the provisions necessary for this innumerable multitude of famished beasts be placed therein, both during all the time of their sojourn in the boat, and during that time when, even after their going out, the earth, ravaged by the deluge, could offer them none? Has one ever considered how much so many carnivorous animals would consume; the tremendous quantity of animals that

GENESIS VII.

COSMOGONIE VII.

1. And-he-said, IHOAH, unto *Noah* come-thou! and-the-whole-interior-thine toward-the-*thebah* (sheltering a b o d e) : for-the-selfsameness-t h i n e I-d i d-view-as righteous in-t h e-face-mine, by-the-age this.

1. Et-il-dit, IHOAH, à-*Noah*, vient-toi! et-tout-l'intérieur-à-toi, devers-la-*thebah* (la place de refuge) car l'i p s é i t é-tienne j'ai-considerée j u s t e à-m a-f a c e, dans-l'âge celui-ci.

2. From-all the-quadrupedly-w a l k i n g-kind, the-pure! thou-shalt-draw unto-thee, by-seven seven! the-very-principle and-the-volitive-intellectual-faculty-i t s-o w n a n d-f r o m-the-quadruped, which-is not-pure in-itself, by-twains, the-principle and-the-v o l i t i v e-faculty-its-own.

2. De-tout le-genre-quadrupède, le-pur! tu-prendras (tu retireras) à-toi, sept à-s e p t! le-principe et-la-fa c u l t é-volitive-efficiente-à-lui; et-du-genre-quadrupède qui-est non-pur en-lui-même, deux-à-deux, le-principe et-la-faculté-efficiente-à-lui.

---

would be required for their nourishment, and the amount of herbs, or of grain necessary for those even which must be devoured to sustain the others? Obviously a physical impossibility.

But Moses was not unlearned. The instructions that he had received in the sanctuaries of Egypt were not nonsense, and the particular inspiration which animated him did not lead him to absurdities. I believe I have had the pleasure of giving several times evident proof of it. I repeat that it is always as translator and not as commentator, that I have done so. These are not my ideas that I am giving; these are his own that I am restoring.

Whatever may be the *thebah*, sacred storehouse of Nature given over to the repose of existence, whose mystery can never be wholly divulged, it is at least certain that it is not a boat, properly so-called. It is a place of refuge, an inaccessible retreat, where elementary life

3. G a m m e-h ô p h ha-shamaim shibehah shibehah! zachar w-nekebah l'haiôth zerah hal-pheneî c h o l-h a-âretz.

גַּם מֵעוֹף הַשָּׁמַיִם שִׁבְעָה שִׁבְעָה זָכָר וּנְקֵבָה לְחַיּוֹת זֶרַע עַל־פְּנֵי כָל־הָאָרֶץ :

itself, is concentrated during great catastrophes, cataclysms and conflagrations which the universe undergoes. When the fountains of the deep rise in tempestuous violence covering and ravaging the earth, the principle and the efficient volitive faculty of all the beings of the animal, aerial or terrestrial kingdom, must be united there in that holy *thebah*.

Now, what is a principle? What is an efficient volitive faculty? A principle is that which constitutes the being such as it is in general; for example, that which makes the lamb not a wolf: the hind, not a panther; the bull, not a hippopotamus. A principle produces its efficient faculty in the same manner that fire produces heat. It is by the action of its faculty that every principle is individualized: for every faculty reproducing in its turn its principle, in the same manner that heat produces fire, multiplies the being by a sort of division. It is the efficient faculty which manifesting the principle, causes, for example, the bear not to be inclined in the same fashion as a rabbit; a sparrow hawk as a dove; a rhinocerous as a gazelle. It is by its efficient volitive faculty emanated from its principle that every being conforms exteriorly. The naturalists who have assumed that the tiger was tiger because he had teeth, claws, stomach and intestines, fashioned in a particular way, have spoken thoughtlessly and without understanding. They might have done better by saying, that the tiger had those teeth, claws, stomach and intestines because he was tiger, that is to say, because his efficient volitive faculty constituted him such. It is not the instrument which gives the will, but the will the instrument. The compass no more makes geometry, than the dagger makes the assassin, or the violin the virtuoso. These men can use these things to help themselves but their will must always have precedence over the usage.

Moses expresses as usual, the principle of being and its efficient volitive faculty by the words איש and אשת. I have given

COSMOGONY OF MOSES

3. And-also from the-flying-fowl of-heavens, by-sevens; male and-female for-being-kept-existing in-germ upon-t h e-face of-the-whole-earth.

3. Aussi du-genre-volatile des-cieux sept à-sept; mâle et-femelle afin-d'être-fait-exister sementiellement •sur-la-face de-toute-la-terre.

---

the etymology and the hieroglyphic meaning of both. It is unnecessary for me to repeat. To ask why his translators have not rendered these important expressions, is vain repetition: it is asking on the one hand, why they have not wished to betray the mysteries of the Sepher, knowing them; or, on the other, why not knowing them they have not betrayed them.

The Hellenists have distorted the Mosaic phrase in saying here ἄρσεν καὶ θῆλυ, *male and female*, because they knew or ought to have known that איש and אשת never had that signification: but could they do otherwise? Could they expose for destruction all that they had done? Rather than to disclose the true meaning of this expression, or to become ridiculous by continuing to see there *man and woman*, they preferred to copy the Samaritan which had solved the difficulty in reading צקר . אצ קבֿ *male and female*, without concerning themselves whether these words, analogous to the Hebraic words זכר ונקבה, were not announced further on as a warning not to confuse them. I have already said that these interpreters preferred to be accused of incoherences and contradictions, than to violate the mysteries of Moses. As to Saint Jerome, he could not diviate on this occasion from the meaning of the Hellenists, without disturbing their version entirely and without inopportunely shedding light on this conscious reticence.

v. 3. לחיות זרע, *for-being-kept-existing-in-germ....* This is perfectly obvious and corroborates in an irresistible manner, what I have said. The quadrupeds are placed in the *thebah*, in principle and in faculty, and the flying fowl, male and female, in germ only. This distinction sustains the system of Moses, which gives to birds the same origin as to fishes, in making them both multiply by the aqueous element, whereas he correlates the quadruped kind with the adamic element. It suffices therefore to conserve the germ ex-

4. Chi l'îamîm hôd shib-ehah, anoĉhî mametîr hal-ha-âretz ârbahîm îôm w'âr-bahîm laîlah: w-m a h î t h î æth-ĉhol ha-îekoum â s h e r hashîthî me-hal pheneî ha-âdamah.

כִּי לְיָמִים עוֹד שִׁבְעָה אָנֹכִי מַמְטִיר עַל־הָאָרֶץ אַרְבָּעִים יוֹם וְאַרְבָּעִים לָיְלָה וּמָחִיתִי אֶת־כָּל הַיְקוּם אֲשֶׁר עָשִׂיתִי מֵעַל פְּנֵי הָאֲדָמָה׃

5. Wa-îahash Noah ĉhe-ĉhol âsher tziwa-hou IHÔAH.

וַיַּעַשׂ נֹחַ כְּכֹל אֲשֶׁר צִוָּהוּ יְהוָֹה׃

---

istence of birds upon the breast of the waters; whereas terrestrial animals which emanate from another principle, require that this principle be conserved.

The Hellenists not knowing how to express this phrase, have resolved to distort it like the preceding one, by saying διατρέψαι σπέρμα, *that the germ be nourished;* which has no sense. The author of the Latin Vulgate, to repair this absurdity, translates "ut salvetur semen," *that the germ be saved;* which has more truth but which absolutely contradicts the Hebrew; for the verb חיות does not signify *to save,* but *to exist, to live;* so that the words לחיות זרע signify literally, *for the action of existing,* or *of living, germ,* that is to say, *in germ.*

v. 4. ארבעים, *four-tens....* What I have said upon the composition of this word and upon the signification of its root, can be reviewed in v. 10, ch. II. One can also consult the Rad. Vocab. concerning the roots יי, ים and עֹד.

ומחיתי, *and-I-shall-wash-off....* It is the root מה changed to מח to increase its force, which develops in the verb מהוה, all ideas attached to the action of water.

COSMOGONY OF MOSES

4. For-in-the-days (manifested lights) of-the-present-cyclic-period, t h e-seventh, myself-I-am causing-to-rain upon-the-earth four-tens of-day (a great quaternion of light) a n d-f o u r-t e n s of-night (a great quaternion of d a r k n e s s) : a n d-I-shall-wash-o f f that-whole-standing-plastic-nature, which-I-have-framed from-over the-face of-the-adamic (elementary ground).

4. Car aux-j o u r s (aux manifestations phénoméniques) de-la-période-actuelle, septième, moi-même-je-suis faisant-pleuvoir sur-la-terre quatre-décuples de-jour (un grand quaternaire de lumière) et-quatre-décuples de-nuit (un grand quaternaire d' obscurité) : et-j'effacerai cette-toute la- nature-plastic-substantielle q u e-j ' a i-faite, de-dessus la-face de-l' élément adamique.

5. And-he-did, *Noah*, the same-all w h i c h had-carefully-p r e s c r i b e d to-him, IHOAH.

5. Et-il-fit, *Noah* le-semblable tout lequel avait-prescrit-à-lui-avec-soin, IHOAH.

היקום *standing-plastic-nature*.... The root קו characterizes in general, indefinite material **extent**, a thing indeterminate, obtuse, vague. The verb which is formed of it קוה, expresses the action of stretching, of extending, of being carried toward an object; the action of forming a desire, emitting a sound, etc. The same root קו, having asssumed the sign of exterior and plastic action, in קום, signifies as noun, *a substance*, in general, *an extensive thing, a material object;* as **verb**, it presents the action of existing materially, of subsisting, of being clothed with form and substance, of being formed, of coagulating, of rising with force, of opposing, etc. These various significations which, as one can see, have their source in the extent or in the indefinite material substance, of which the root קו is the symbol, are united in the word יקום by the sign of potential manifestation י, which here adds the sense that I give it of *substance* or of *plastic, substantial nature*.

This word, however, not being expressible by any analogue, must be considered carefully. The Chaldean paraphrast has preserved it in its integrity; but the Samaritan has deemed proper to change it, and has substituted ꙮꙮꙮ, which, coming evidently from the root

6. W-Noah b e n-s h e s h maôth s h a n a h w'ha-mab-boul h a î a h maîm hal-ha-âretz.

וְנֹחַ בֶּן־שֵׁשׁ מֵאוֹת שָׁנָה וְהַמַּבּוּל הָיָה מַיִם עַל־הָאָרֶץ׃

7. Wa-îaboâ N o a h w-banaî-ô w'âisheth-ô w-nes-heî-banaî-ô âith-ô æl-ha-the-bah mi-pheneî meî ha-m̨ab-boul.

וַיָּבֹא נֹחַ וּבָנָיו וְאִשְׁתּוֹ וּנְשֵׁי־בָנָיו אִתּוֹ אֶל־הַתֵּבָה מִפְּנֵי מֵי הַמַּבּוּל

8. Min-ha-behemah ha-te-hôrah w-min-ha-behemah âsher âîne-nah tehôrah w-min-ha-hôph w-chol â s h e r ʿomesh hal-ha-âdamah:

מִן־הַבְּהֵמָה הַטְּהוֹרָה וּמִן־הַבְּהֵמָה אֲשֶׁר אֵינֶנָּה טְהוֹרָה וּמִן־הָעוֹף וְכֹל אֲשֶׁר רֹמֵשׂ עַל־הָאֲדָמָה׃

מוּן or מִין signifies *that which constitutes the form, the mien of things*. The Hellenists in rendering this word by ἐξανάστασιν, *re-surrection*, have had a very singular idea. Saint Jerome has not followed them in this instance; he has translated it simply "sub-stantiam" *the substance*.

v. 5. All these terms are understood.

v. 6. בֶּן־שֵׁשׁ *the-son-of-six*.... I beg the reader to observe that Moses speaking of *Noah* names him here again, son of an on-tological duration. This hierographic writer had said, v. 32, ch. v. that *Noah* was son of *five* hundreds of temporal mutation, when he begat *Shem, Ham* and *Japheth;* now he announces that he was son of *six* hundreds of like mutation when the deluge inundated the earth. If the reader would penetrate the profound thought which Moses encloses in these hieroglyphic expressions, he should remember

COSMOGONY OF MOSES 207

6. And-*Noah*-was-the-son (consequent offspring) of-six hundreds of-beings-revolving-c h a n g e, that-the-great-swelling was of-waters upon-the-earth.

7. And-he-went, *N o a h*, and-the sons-of-him (his issued offspring) and-the-intellectual-mate-his-own (his volitive faculty), a n d-t h e-corporeal-mates of-the-sons-of-him (their natural faculties) toward-t h e-*t h e ḃ a h* (sheltering abode), f r o m-the-face of-the water's great-swelling.

8. From-t h e-quadrupedly-walking-kind of-the-pureness, a n d-from-the-quadrupedly-walking-k i n d which not-being-itself of-the-pureness, a n d-f r o m-the-flying-fowl, a n d-from-every-creeping-life upon-the-adamic.

6. Et-*Noah*-était l e-f i l s (le r é s u l t a t) de-six-centaines de-mutation-temporelle-ontologique,que-la-grande-intumescence é t a i t des-eaux sur-la-terre.

7. Et-il-alla, *Noah*, et-les-fils-à-lui (ses productions) et-la-femme- intellectuelle-à-lui (sa faculté volitive efficiente), e t-l e s-épouses-corporelles des-fils-siens (leurs facultés physiques), vers-la-*thebah* (l'asyle sacré), de-la-face des-eaux de-la-grande-intumescence.

8. D u-genre-quadrupède de-l a-p u r e t é, et-du-genre-quadrupède lequel non-être-lui de-la-pureté, et-du-genre-volatile, et-d e-t o u t-ce-qui-e s t-animé-d'un-mouvement-reptiforme s u r - l' élément-adamique.

---

that in the Hebraic decade whose etymology I have carefully sought, I have found that the number *five* חמש, was that of physical compression; that number *six*, שש, contained the ideas of a proportional and relative measure; and that, by the number *one hundred*, מְשָׁה, should be understood the extension of a thing which fills its natural limits.

v. 7. וּנְשֵׁי־בָנָיו, *and-the-corporeal-mates of-the-sons-of-him*.... I make here the same observation that I have made in v. 18, ch. VI. Moses who uses the word אשה, to characterize the volitive faculty of *Noah*, makes use of the word נשי to designate the physical faculties of the beings emanated from it. This recidivism ought to

9. Shenaîm shenaîm bâou æl-Noah æl-ha-thebah zachar w-nekebah ch' âsher tziwah Ælohîm æth-Noah.

שְׁנַיִם שְׁנַיִם בָּאוּ אֶל־נֹחַ אֶל־הַתֵּבָה זָכָר וּנְקֵבָה כַּאֲשֶׁר צִוָּה אֱלֹהִים אֶת־נֹחַ ׃

10. Wa-îhî l'shibehath ha-iamîm w-meî ha-mabboul haîou hal-ha-âretz.

וַיְהִי לְשִׁבְעַת הַיָּמִים וּמֵי הַמַּבּוּל הָיוּ עַל־הָאָרֶץ ׃

---

prove to those who might think hazard alone had decided this arrangement of words, that Moses had had a real intention in disposing of them in this manner.

v. 8. הטהורה, *of-the-pureness*.... I note this word to call attention to the fact that the root from which it comes, הור, *fire*, is precisely the same as that from which the word *purity* is derived: for our qualificative *pure*, evidently comes from the Greek πῦρ, *fire*, which finds its principle in the elementary root אור, the history of which can be seen in v. 3 and 10, ch. I. The Hebrew word טהור and the English word *pure*, differ from each other only by the initial sign. It is always fire which constitutes its radical principle, and from which the genius of the two tongues draws the idea of purification. The Hellenists who, in this instance, have employed the word καθαρός are not far from the primitive root אור, since this facultative is derived from the verb καθαίρειν, which means *to pass through fire, to make like fire*: but they have not been followed by the Latin translator, who, having before him the qualificative "purus", has taken "mundus", whose root *und*, denatures entirely the thought of the hierographic writer. For this latter word, being related, as can be seen, to the action of the waters, depicts only a sort of exterior cleanness, whereas the word "purus", being attached to the root אֻר, *fire*, would express an interior purification resulting from its action. This distinction, trifling as it may appear to certain minds, is of the greatest importance for the mystagogues. Air, fire and water were considered in the mysteries as three purifying elements; but one was careful not to confuse their action.

I ought, moreover, to say that the Samaritan in making use of

COSMOGONY OF MOSES

9. Twains-by-twains they-went toward-*Noah* (nature's rest) toward-the-*thebah*, male and-female, so-as wisely-prescribed HE-the-Gods, together-*Noah*.

9. De-deux en-deux, ils-allèrent vers-*Noah* (le repos de l'existence) vers-la *thebah*, mâle et-femelle, selon-que prescrivit-sagement LUI-les-Dieux, au-même-*Noah*.

10. And-it-was on-the-seventh of-the-days (manifested lights) that-the-waters of-the-great-swelling were upon-the earth.

10. Et-ce-fut au-septième des-jours (manifestations phénoméniques) que les-eaux de-la-grande-intumescence furent sur-la-terre.

---

the word 𐤑𐤌𐤀𐤌, had much earlier, committed the same error as that with which I reproach the Latin translator, corrupting in this instance, as in many others, the hieroglyphic meaning of Moses.

v. 9. All these terms are understood.

v. 10. לשבעת, *on-the-seventh*.... We have seen in searching for the etymology of the Hebraic decade, that number *seven* שבע, was that of the consummation of things and times.

v. 11. בחודש, *in-the-moon-renewing*.... The root חר from which this word comes, and which expresses unity, is only the root ער which develops all ideas attached to time, and in which the elementary sign ה has been replaced by that of physical sense ע. These two roots, closely allied to each other, are often confused in pronunciation, thus confusing the diverse expressions of elementary and of temporal existence. This is the case here. The sign of relative movement ש added to this root, carries the idea of a beginning of existence, either in the order of things or in the order of time. Thus the word חדש characterizes that which is new, that which is renewed; that which reappears. With the luminous sign, this same word חודש, becomes the expression of a *neomenia, a festival of the new moon*: and in a restricted sense, it indicates a month measured by the course of the moon.

נבקעו, *were-unlocked*.... This is the verb בקע employed according to the positive form, passive movement. One can see in

11. B i-s h e n a t h shesh mæôth shanah l'haïi-Noah ba-hodesh ha-shenî, b'shibehah-hashar îôm la-hodesh baîôm ha-zeh nibekehou ċholmaheinoth thehôm rabbah w'ârubboth ha-shamaîm niphethahou.

בִּשְׁנַת שֵׁשׁ־מֵאוֹת שָׁנָה לְחַיֵּי־נֹחַ בַּחֹדֶשׁ הַשֵּׁנִי בְּשִׁבְעָה־עָשָׂר יוֹם לַחֹדֶשׁ בַּיּוֹם הַזֶּה נִבְקְעוּ כָּל־מַעְיְנֹת תְּהוֹם רַבָּה וַאֲרֻבֹּת הַשָּׁמַיִם נִפְתָּחוּ׃

12. Wa-î,h î ha-gheshem hal-ha--âretz arbahîm îôm w'ârbahîm laîlah.

וַיְהִי הַגֶּשֶׁם עַל־הָאָרֶץ אַרְבָּעִים יוֹם וְאַרְבָּעִים לָיְלָה׃

---

the Rad. Vocab. and in v. 4 of this chapter, what I have said of the root קו from which it comes. This root, governed by the sign of generative action ב and terminated by that of physical sense ע, expresses the action of giving unlimited extension to a thing; of unlocking, of breaking the bonds which restrict it; of disuniting it, etc.

מעינות, *springs-of-the-deep*.... The root עו characterizes in the literal sense, *an inflection, a curvature, a thing concave* or *convex*. Terminated by the final character ן, it is the symbol of a curvature, of an entire inflection; it depicts a circle, which, considered relative to its circumference, presents a globe; and relative to its centre, a recess, a hole. This root thus formed, עוי, enlightened by the sign of potential manifestation, becomes the word עין, which, according as it is examined exteriorly or interiorly, designates sometimes the eye and sometimes the depth of a spring. It is in this latter sense that it is employed on this occasion, having for initial character the plastic sign of exterior action, מ.

תהום רבה, *indefinite-potential-might*.... I have explained the

11. By-the-revolving six-hundreds of-revolving-change, regarding-the-lives of-*Noah,* in-the-moon-renewing the-second, in-the-seventeenth manifested-light of-that-renewing, at-the-day itself, were-unlocked all-the-springs of-the-deep's indefinite potential-might; and-the-multiplying-quaternions of-heavens were-loosened (unfastened, given up to their own dilating motion).

11. Dans-la-mutation-ontologique des-six-centaines de - mutation, touchant - les-vies de-*Noah* dans-le-renouvellement-lunaire le-second; dans-la-d i x-septième manifestation-lumineuse de -c e-renouvellement, au-jour celui-là, furent-lâchées toutes-les-sources de-la-puissance-d' être-universelle, indéfinie : et-les-forces quaternaires-multiplicatrices des-cieux furent déliées (abandonnées à leur propre extension).

12. And-there-was the-massy-shower (waterish atmosphere falling down incessantly) upon-the-earth, four-tens of-day and-four-tens of-night (an entire quaternion of light and darkness).

12. Et-fut la-chute-d'eau (l'atmosphère aqueuse tombant en masse) sur-la-terre, quatre-décuples de-jour et-quatre-décuples de-nuit (un quaternaire entier de lumière et d'obscurité).

---

word תהם in v. 2., ch. I; and the root of the word רבה is found sufficiently developed in v. 10, ch. II.

נפתחו, *were-loosened*.... This is the verb פתח, employed after the positive form, passive movement. The root פת, from which it comes, has been explained under the proper name of *Japheth,* v. 3. ch. V.

v. 12. הגשם, *the-massy-shower*.... The Hebrew word has an almost incredible forcefulness which can scarcely be understood by the word-for-word French or English, for the reader who has not some idea of those masses of water which, lowering suddenly like a sheet of water falling from the atmosphere, inundate at times certain countries of Asia. These cataclysms are of short duration, for if they were continued as that one which Moses characterizes by the word גשם, to which he attributes an immense duration, they would

13. B'hetzem ha-îôm ha-zeh bâ Noah w-S h e m-w-Ham-wa-Jepheth benei Noah w'æsheth N o a h w-shelos-heth neshei-banaî-ô-âitham æl-ha-thebah:

בְּעֶצֶם הַיּוֹם הַזֶּה בָּא נֹחַ וְשֵׁם־וְחָם־וָיֶפֶת בְּנֵי־נֹחַ וְאֵשֶׁת נֹחַ וּשְׁלֹשֶׁת נְשֵׁי־בָנָיו אִתָּם אֶל־הַתֵּבָה:

14. Hemmah! w'chol-ha-haîah l'min-ha w'chol-ha-be-h e m a h l'min-ha w'chol-ha-remesh ha - romesh hal - ha-â r e t z l'min-hou w'chol-ha-hôph l'min-hou chol tziphôr chool chanaph:

הֵמָּה וְכָל־הַחַיָּה לְמִינָהּ וְכָל־הַבְּהֵמָה לְמִינָהּ וְכָל־הָרֶמֶשׂ הָרֹמֵשׂ עַל־הָאָרֶץ לְמִינֵהוּ וְכָל־הָעוֹף לְמִינֵהוּ כֹּל צִפּוֹר כָּל־כָּנָף:

---

cause frightful catastrophes. The words *ὑετός*, "pluvia", *rain*, as it has been rendered by the translators, depicting water falling by drops or by slender streams, does not make the force of the Hebraic expression felt.

The root from which this word comes is גש, by which should be understood a thing continued, palpable and without solution of continuity. Thence, the Hebrew verb גוש *to feel, to recognize with the hand;* and the Chaldaic words גשרא *substance continued and palpable;* גושמא *a body,* גשמי *corporeal,* גשמות *corporeity,* etc. Thence, the Syriac ܓܫܘܡܐ *sense and sensation;* and the Arabic جش, *a thick thing, a profound obscurity.*

It is easy to see, after this explanation, that the root גש, universalized in the word גשם, by the collective sign ם, characterizes an aqueous atmosphere, forming a kind of dark and palpable body. I invite the physicists who have sought the origin of the waters of the deluge, to meditate a little upon this illuminating etymology. The Samaritan translator has allowed the terrible picture offered here by Moses to escape by substituting for the original word, the word ⵀⵄⵆⴾ *a heavy rain.* The Chaldaic paraphrast seems to have been more fortunate in giving at least מטרא נחיר *a contiguous, palpable rain.*

13. F r o m-the-very-substantial-principle of-this-day itself, went *Noah*, and-*Shem*-and-*Ham*-a n d-*Japheth*, issued-offspring-of-*Noah*, and-t h e - volitive-faculty-*Noah's* and-the-three natural-faculties o f-t h e-offspring-h i s-own, together-them toward-the-*thebah* (m u t u a l asylum):

13. Dès-le-principle-substantiel du-jour celui-là, alla *Noah*, et-*Shem* et-*Ham*-et-*Japheth*, productions-de-*Noah*, et-l a-faculté-volitive de-*Noah*, et-l e s-trois-facultés-physiques des-productions-à-l ui, ensemblement, devers-la-*t h e b a h* (l'asile mutuel):

14. Themselves! and-the-whole-animality, after-t h e-kind-its-own; all-quadruped after-the-kind-its-own; and-a l l-creeping-l i f e trailing-along upon-the-earth, after-the-kind-its-own; a n d-all-fowl after-the-kind-its-own, every-thing-running, every-thing-flying:

14. E u x-m ê m e s! et-toute-l'animalité selon-l'espèce-sienne; t o u t-quadrupède s e l o n-l'espèce-sienne, et-tout-reptile rampant sur-la-terre, selon-l'espèce-sienne, et-tout-volatile selon-l'espèce-sienne: toute-chose-courant, toute-chose-volant:

---

v. 13. בעצם, *From-the-very-substantial-principle....* This word is presented here in a very singular manner. It affords matter for reflection. In whatever way one wishes to understand it, I defy anyone to see either *wood*, or *bones*, or *tree*, following the interpretation that the Hellenists have given it in other instances. See v. 9. and 23, ch. II.

ושלשת נשי, *and-the-three-natural-factulties....* It can be seen again with what constancy Moses distinguishes the word אשת belonging to the intellectual mate of *Noah*, from the word נשים appropriate for the mates of his sons.

אתם, *together-them....* This word depicts very well the effect of the collective sign ם, added to the designative preposition את.

v. 14 and 15. All these terms have been explained, or offer no difficulty.

15. Wa-iaboâou æl-Noah æl-ha-thebah shenaîm shenaîm mi-čhol ha-bashar âs her b'o rouah haîîm.

וַיָּבֹאוּ אֶל־נֹחַ אֶל־הַתֵּבָה שְׁנַיִם שְׁנַיִם מִכָּל־הַבָּשָׂר אֲשֶׁר בּוֹ רוּחַ חַיִּים׃

16. W'ha-baîm začhar w-nekebah mi-čhol-bashar bâou čh'âsher tziwa âoth-â Ælohîm: wa-issegor IHÔAH ba-had-ô.

וְהַבָּאִים זָכָר וּנְקֵבָה מִכָּל־בָּשָׂר בָּאוּ כַּאֲשֶׁר צִוָּה אֹתוֹ אֱלֹהִים וַיִּסְגֹּר יְהוָה בַּעֲדוֹ׃

17. Wa-îhî ha-mabboul ârbahîm îôm hal-ha-âretz: wa-îrebou ha-maîm, wa-ishæou æth-ha-thebah, wa-tharam me-hal-ha-âretz.

וַיְהִי הַמַּבּוּל אַרְבָּעִים יוֹם עַל־הָאָרֶץ וַיִּרְבּוּ הַמַּיִם וַיִּשְׂאוּ אֶת־הַתֵּבָה וַתָּרָם מֵעַל־הָאָרֶץ׃

---

v. 16. בעדו, *by-the-removing-himself*.... The Hellenists who had no doubt their reasons for hiding from the vulgar the theosophical ideas of the Sepher, chose the part here of making IHOAH, a kind of door-keeper who shuts the door upon *Noah*: καὶ ἔκλεισε κύριος ὁ Θεὸς ἔξωθεν; an idea quite ridiculous, which the Latin translator has not failed to copy "et includit eum Dominus deforis"; but the Hebraic verb עדה as well as the Chaldaic, Ethiopic and Arabic analogues, all signify *to be removed, to go away, to disappear*: which proves that the root עד, which develops, in general, all ideas relative to time, and to things temporal and transitory, expresses *a separation, a departure, an eclipse, a disappearance*. In the present case, this root, taken in the latter sense, is inflected by the mediative article ב, and followed by the nominal affix ו.

v. 17. וירבו, *and-they-did-quaternify*.... I have believed it necessary to coin this word taken from the language of numbers, in order to make felt the force of the root בר, from which are equally derived, both the name of the number ארבעים which expresses the duration of the great swelling of the waters, and the verb רבה which characterizes its action.

COSMOGONY OF MOSES 215

15. And-t h e y-went toward-*Noah* (nature's rest) toward-the-sheltering-abode, t w a i n s b y-twains, from-e v e r y-c o r p o r e a l-shape which-h a s in-itself breath of-lives.

16. And-thus-going, male and-female from-every-bodily-shape, they-went according-to-what had-prescribed to-himself, HE-the-Gods: and -he-shut-up, IHOAH, by-the-removing-himself.

17. And-itwas, the-great-swelling four-tens o f-d a y u p o n-the-earth; and-they-d i d-quaternify (multiply-themselves) the-w a t e r s; and-they-bare the-*t h e b a h* which was-raised from-over-the-earth.

15. E t-i l s allèrent devers-*Noah* (le repos de la nature) vers-la-retraite-inaccessible deux à-deux, de-toute-forme-corporelle, qui-a dans-soi souffle-des-vies.

16. Et-les-allants, m â l e et-female, de-t o u t e-forme-corporelle, allèrent suivant-c e-q u'a v a i t-prescrit cela-même-à-soi LUI-les-Dieux, et-il-conclut, IHOAH, au-moyen-de-l'éloignement-sien.

17. Et-elle-fut, l a-grande intumescence, quatre-décuples de-jour sur-la-terre; e t-e l l e s-s e-quaternisèrent (se multiplièrent) les-eaux, et-elles-portèrent l a-*thebah* qui fut-enlevée-de-dessus la-terre.

וישאו, *and-they-bare*.... This is the verb נשא, employed according to the positive form, active movement, in the future made past by the convertible sign ו. This verb is attached to the root שׁ, of which I have spoken in giving the etymology of number *six* שׁשׁ, v. 3 ch. V. It depicts a sort of *libration*, of support in equilibrium.

ותרם, *which-was-raised*.... The verb רום designates literally that sort of action or movement by means of which a thing runs through or fills an extent or a place which it did not occupy formerly. It is composed of the sign of movement proper ר, united to that of exterior and plastic action ם.

v. 18. ויגברו, *and-they-prevailed-intensely*.... Review in v. 14, ch. VI, what I have said concerning the famous word גבּוֹר. This word signifying, according to its exact etymology, *a superior*

18. W a-îghebbrou h a-maîm wa-îrebbou mæôd hal-ha-âretz: wa-thelech ha-the-bah hal-pheneî ha-maîm.

וַיִּגְבְּרוּ הַמַּיִם וַיִּרְבּוּ מְאֹד עַל־הָאָרֶץ וַתֵּלֶךְ הַתֵּבָה עַל־פְּנֵי הַמָּיִם׃

19. W'ha-maîm gabrou mæôd mæôd hal-ha-âretz: wa-iechussou chol he-harîm ha-ghebohîm âsher thahath chol-ha-sha-maîm.

וְהַמַּיִם גָּבְרוּ מְאֹד מְאֹד עַל־הָאָרֶץ וַיְכֻסּוּ כָּל־הֶהָרִים הַגְּבֹהִים אֲשֶׁר־תַּחַת כָּל־הַשָּׁמָיִם׃

20. Hamesh heshereh âmmah milmahelah gabrou ha-maîm wa-iechussou he-harîm.

חֲמֵשׁ עֶשְׂרֵה אַמָּה מִלְמַעְלָה גָּבְרוּ הַמַּיִם וַיְכֻסּוּ הֶהָרִים׃

21. Wa-ighewah chol-bashar ha-romesh hal-ha-âretz ba-hôph ba-behemah w'ba-haîah w-b'chol-ha-sher-etz ha-shoretz hal-ha-âretz w'chol-ha-Adam.

וַיִּגְוַע כָּל־בָּשָׂר הָרֹמֵשׂ עַל־הָאָרֶץ בָּעוֹף וּבַבְּהֵמָה וּבַחַיָּה וּבְכָל־הַשֶּׁרֶץ הַשֹּׁרֵץ עַל־הָאָרֶץ וְכֹל הָאָדָם׃

---

man, *a high-baron, a master*, the verb which is formed from it should express the action of prevailing, dominating, acting, commanding as master, etc. This verb is used here according to the intensive form, which increases its force.

v. 19 and 20. The terms offer no difficulty in the literal sense. The figurative sense springs from that which has been previously cited.

v. 21. ויגוע, *thus-expired*.... The radical verb גוע, such as is used here, indicates a total dissolution of the organic system, of which the root גו is the symbol. The sign ו materialized by the addition of the sign ע, thus makes this root pass from the state of organic life to that of inorganic life or material death. Our attention has already been called to this same verb in v. 3, ch III.

COSMOGONY OF MOSES

18. A n d-they-prevailed-intensely, the-waters; and-t h e y-d i d-quaternify (increase themselves) at-their-h i g h e s t-r a t e, upon-the-earth: and-it-moved-to-and-fro,the-*thebah,* on-the-f a c e of-the-waters.

19. And-the-waters pervailed a t-their-highest-rate s o-m u c h u p o n-the-earth that-were-covered a l l-t h e-hills u p p e r-m o s t which-were-below t h e-whole-heavens.

20. Fifteen o f-mother-measuring from-over-above, prevailed the-waters: a n d-were-quite-covered the-hills.

21. Thus-expired (w a s dissolved) every-corporeal-shape moving on-the-earth, i n-t h e-f o w l, a n d-in-the-quadruped, and-in-the-life-e a r t h-b o r n, a n d-in-the-whole-worm-l i f e creeping-along on-the-earth; and-the-whole-collective-man (mankind).

18. Et-elles-prévalurent-avec-force, l e s-eaux, et-se-quaternisèrent (augmentèrent) autant-que-possible sur-la-terre: et-elle-se-mouvait-en-tous-sens la-*thebah,* sur-la-face des-eaux.

19. Et-les-eaux prévalurent autant-que-possible tellement-que, sur-la-terre, furent-couvertes toutes-l e s-montagnes supérieures lesquel-les-étaient e n-b a s de-tous-les-cieux.

20. Quinze de-measure-m è r e p a r-dessus-le-haut, prévalurent les-eaux: et-furent - couvertes-entièrement les-montagnes.

21. Ainsi-e x p i r a (disparut) toute-forme-corporelle se-mouvant sur-la-terre, dans-le-volatile, e t-dans-le-quadrupède et-d a n s-l'exis-tence-animale et-dans-toute-l'originante-vie vermiforme, sur-la-terre; a i n s i- q u e-tout-l'homme-universel (l e règne hominal).

וכל-האדם, *and-the-whole-collective-man*.... The reader who follows with impartial mind the development of these notes, will see that it is impossible for the word אדם to have other signification than that which I have given to it, of *universal man* or *mankind*. If this word indicated simply *a man*, as the Hellenists and the other interpreters have made it understood in this passage, what is it then

22. Chol âsher nishe-math-rouah haîîm b'aphaî-ô, mi-chol âsher b'harabah me-thou.

כֹּל אֲשֶׁר נִשְׁמַת־רוּחַ חַיִּים בְּאַפָּיו מִכֹּל אֲשֶׁר בֶּחָרֶבָה מֵתוּ׃

23. Wa-îmmah æth-chol-ha-îekoum âsher hal-pheneî ha-âdamah, me-Adam had-behemah had-remesh w-had-hôph ha-shamaîm: wa-îm-mahou min-ha-âretz: wa-îsh-aær ach-Noah w'âsher âith-ô ba-thebah.

וַיִּמַח אֶת־כָּל־הַיְקוּם אֲשֶׁר עַל־פְּנֵי הָאֲדָמָה מֵאָדָם עַד־בְּהֵמָה עַד־רֶמֶשׂ וְעַד־עוֹף הַשָּׁמַיִם וַיִּמָּחוּ מִן־הָאָרֶץ וַיִּשָּׁאֶר אַךְ־נֹחַ וַאֲשֶׁר אִתּוֹ בַּתֵּבָה׃

---

that Moses intended by the word כל *all*, which he unites to it by means of the determinative article ה? Is it that, when it is a question of dying, of expiring, by the effect of a frightful catastrophe, a man can be divided? Is it not more natural to understand here, even literally, that all mankind expired, than to rack one's brains to find an hebraism where the phrase is perfectly simple; or, to change the word as the Latin translator who says "universi homines" *all men*, not being able to rise to the point of seeing "omnis universus homo" *all universal man*, which would exactly render the Hebrew?

v. 22. נשמת, *a-being-exalted*.... Refer to v. 7, ch. II.

בחרבה, *in-the-wasting-havock*.... I cannot conceive how it is possible that all the translators, without exception, have missed the meaning of this word, it is so simple. Its root חר is evident; it is united to the sign of interior action ב, to express *ravage, extermination, desolation, scourge*. In giving it the sense of a *desert*, of a *dry land* and even simply of *the earth*, as the Latin translator, they have made Moses say a futile and ridiculous thing. It was not the inhabitants alone of the desert or the dry lands who perished, but all beings whatsoever, who were struck at the same time by this disaster, this devastating flood.

22. All that-had a-being-exalted (an essence) of-the-breath of-lives in-the-spiritual-faculty his-own among-the-w h o l e that-underwent the-w a s t i n g-havock (the flood) they-died.

23. A n d-h e-washed-o f f (IHOAH) even-the-selfsameness-of-t h e-whole-standing-plastic-nature w h i c h-w a s on-the-f a c e of-the-adamic, from-mankind, to-the-quadrupedly-walking, the-creeping-one, t h e-f o w l of-heavens; and-they-were-washed -off from-the-e a r t h: and-there-remained only-*N o a h* (nature's r e s t) and-what-was together-h i m i n-t h e-sheltering-abode.

22. T o u s-les-êtres qui-avaient un-étant-élevé (une essentialité) de l'esprit-des-v i e s dans-la-faculté-spirituelle-à-e u x, parmi-tous-ceux qui étaient dans-le-désastre (atteints par le fléau) ils moururent.

23. Et-il-effaça (IHOAH) l'ipséité-même-de-t o u t e-nature-plastique-substantielle, qui-était sur-la-f a c e de-l' élément-adamique, depuis-le-genre-humain, jusqu'au-genre-quadrupède, au-reptiforme, au-volatile-des-cieux: e t-i l s-furent-effacés-d e-l a-terre; et-il-resta seulement-*Noah* (le repos del'existence élémentaire) et-ce-qui-était ensemble-lui dans la *thebah*.

---

v. 23. הָאֲרָמָה, *of-the-adamic*.... An attentive reader should have perceived that, in the narration of the deluge, Moses did not use indifferently the name of *adamah* אֲרָמָה, primitive, homogeneous land, adamic element, and that of *artz*, אֶרֶץ, the earth properly so-called. The action of the Divinity is exercized particularly upon *adamah;* the action of the flood, always upon *artz*. There is in this verse a singular difference between these two words. The Divinity, says Moses, effaces the selfsameness, the ipseity, the objectivity of corporeal beings upon the face of *adamah*, adamic element, and all corporeal beings are effaced upon *artz*, elementary earth. There are many things to be said here, but I could not undertake the explanation without involving myself in a long commentary and going beyond my position of simple translator. Perhaps I shall one day make amends for my silence in this regard. It was necessary first, to reëstablish the meaning of the words and make the Hebraic text understood in its purity; but this text once understood, it will no doubt be im-

24. W a-îghebbrou h a- וַיִּגְבְּרוּ הַמַּיִם עַל־הָאָרֶץ חֲמִשִּׁים
maîm hal-ha-â r e t z hamis-
hîm w'màth îôm. וּמְאַת יוֹם:

---

portant to examine the doctrine that it contains so as to fathom all its thoughts. This is what I intend doing, if my labour, welcomed by the true savants appears to them useful for the advancement of knowledge and the welfare of humanity.

וישאר, *and-there-remained*.... The word שאר is applied literally to that sort of residue which falls to the bottom of a receptacle, after its fluid being agitated comes to equilibrium. It is composed of the root שא or שו, which develops all ideas of measure and of equilibrium, joined to the sign of movement proper ר. The verb which is derived from it, applied here to *Noah*, the repose of natural existence, is very worthy of attention.

אך, *only*.... This is the same root אך, which contains all ideas of restriction, of compression, of closing upon oneself, which Moses uses as adverbial relation, uniting it by hyphen to the name of *Noah*. This hierographic writer neglects no means to enlighten the mind of the reader and initiate him into mysteries that he cannot entirely divulge. This simple hyphen forms an hieroglyphic

24. And-t h e y-prevailed, t h e-waters, upon-the-earth, f i v e-tens and-one-hundred of-day (periodical light).

24. E t-elles-dominèrent, les-eaux, sur-la-terre, cinq-décuples et-une-centaine de-jour (manifestation lumineuse).

---

figure, the translation of which is impossible. The use of this figure is quite frequent in the tongue of Moses and demands meditation. A striking example can be seen in v. 13 of this chapter; when the hierographic writer, wishing to make understood that the three productions of Noah, Shem, Ham and Japheth, who are contained with him in the *thebah*, are not three distinct beings, but one unique triad, links them together; and their three names united, form only one single name: בא נׄח וׁשׁם־וחם־ויפת, "he went, Noah, (in the thebah) and-Shem-and-Ham-and-Japeth," Now, this triad, thus represented hieroglyphically, is precisely to the cosmogonic being called *Noah*, what the three geometrical dimensions are to all natural bodies.

v. 24. All these terms are understood.

SEPHER BERÆSHITH H.

ספר בראשית ח．

1. Wa-îzechar Ælohîm æth-Noah w'æth-chol-ha-haîah w'æth-chol-ha-behemah âsher âith-ô ba-thebah: wa-îahober Ælohîm rouah hal-ha-âretz wa-îashochou ha-maîm.

וַיִּזְכֹּר אֱלֹהִים אֶת־נֹחַ וְאֶת־כָּל־הַחַיָּה וְאֶת־כָּל־הַבְּהֵמָה אֲשֶׁר אִתּוֹ בַּתֵּבָה וַיַּעֲבֵר אֱלֹהִים רוּחַ עַל־הָאָרֶץ וַיָּשֹׁכּוּ הַמָּיִם׃

2. Wa-issachron maheînoth thehoûm wa-arubboth ha-shamaîm wa-icchallâ ha-gheshem min-ha-shamaîm.

וַיִּסָּכְרוּ מַעְיְנֹת תְּהוֹם וַאֲרֻבֹּת הַשָּׁמָיִם וַיִּכָּלֵא הַגֶּשֶׁם מִן הַשָּׁמָיִם׃

---

v. 1. ויזכר, *and-he-remembered*.... In giving the etymology of the word זכר *male*, in v. 27, ch. I, I have spoken of the root כר which forms its basis, and which, as I have said, characterizes that which is apparent, eminent; that which is engraved or serves to engrave; that which is of a nature to conserve the memory of things. It is remarkable that his root, governed by the demonstrative sign ז, develops on the one side, the idea of masculinity, and on the other that of memory; for the word זכר, which signifies literally *male*, designates figuratively, that faculty of the human understanding which preserves the impression of sensations, images and evidences of ideas: but what is no less remarkable is, that in a tongue far removed from the Hebrew in appearance, the Celtic tongue, from which the French is derived through the Teutonic and the Latin, a same root has of yore likewise developed these two ideas of masculinity and memory, which appear today so dissimilar. This root is AL, representing that which is raised, not only in Celtic but in Hebrew and in all the ancient tongues. Now, this root governed

GENESIS VIII.

1. A n d-h e-remembered, HE-t h e-Gods, the-selfsameness-o f-*N o a h*, and-that-of-t h e-whole-earth-born-e x i s-tence, a n d-t h a t-of-all-the-quadruped-kind, which-were together-him i n-the-*thebah* (sheltering abode) : and-he-c a u s e d-to-move-over, HE-the-G o d s, a-breath on-the-e a r t h : and-t h e y-were-checked, the-waters.

2. And-t h e y-were-shut-up the-springs of-the-deep's infinite - potential - p o w e r, and-the-multiplying-quaternions of-heavens: a n d-w a s-wholly-exhausted t h e-massy-shower (waterish atmosphere falling down) from-the-heavens.

COSMOGONIE VIII.

1. Et-il-se-rappela, LUI-l e s-Dieux, la-séité-de-*Noah*, et-celle-de-toute - l'existence-terrestre, e t-celle-de-toute-l e-genre-quadrupède, q u i-étaient ensemble-lui d a n s la-*thebah* (la place de refuge) : et-il-fit passer-d'une-extrémité-à-l'autre, L U I-les-Dieux un-souffle sur-la-terre : e t-furent-resserrées-en-elles-mêmes les-eaux.

2. Et-furent-fermées les-sources d e-l a-puissance-d'être-indéfinie, et-les-forces-quaternisantes - multiplicatrices d e s-cieux : et-fut-entièrement-consommée la-chute-d'e a u (l'atmosphere épaissie tombant) des-cieux.

---

by the emphatic sign P or PH, has produced *pal* or *phal*, whence is derived in French, the ancient word *pal*, changed to *pieu*, and in Latin, the word "phallus" copied from the Greek φαλλός which, as one knows, characterizes the sign of masculinity. But among the Celts, a *pal*, was a sort of monumental post raised in any place whatever to serve for rallying; from there the word *appeal*, and the French words *appeler* and *rappeler*.

ויעבר, *and-he-caused-to-move-over*.... The verb עבור means, literally speaking, *to pass beyond, to go to the other side*. I have been obliged to change its form which is positive in Hebrew, to show the force of the superactive movement rendered active in this instance.

3. Wa-îashubou ha-maîm ma-hal ha-âretz hal-ôċh wa-shôb wa-ahesserou ha-maîm mi-ketzeh ha-mish-hîm w-mâth îôm.

וַיָּשֻׁבוּ הַמַּיִם מֵעַל הָאָרֶץ הָלוֹךְ וָשׁוֹב וַיַּחְסְרוּ הַמַּיִם מִקְצֵה חֲמִשִּׁים וּמְאַת יוֹם׃

וַיָּשֻׁבוּ, *and-they-were-checked*.... The root אָךְ which develops all ideas of repression, of compression, of drawing into itself, ruled by the sign of relative movement שׁ, forms the verb here referred to שֹׂךְ or שׁוּךְ : this verb depicts in most decisive manner the action of the Divine breath upon the watery swelling: for it must not be forgotten that it is in consequence of the absence of this breath that the waters had been dilated; that is to say, abandoned to their own impulse. It deals now with reëstablishing the broken equilibrium, and it is this which Moses expresses admirably by the verb שׁוּךְ. I am, furthermore, only the translator of this great man. The verb *check* which comes from the same source as the Hebraic, renders very well this meaning.

v. 2. All these terms have been explained. Refer to v. 11 and 12 of the preceding chapter.

v. 3. וַיָּשֻׁבוּ, *and-they-restored-themselves-as-formerly*.... I have often had occasion to speak of the root שׁב which brings with it every idea of return and of reëstablishment. The radical verb שׁוּב, which is formed from it, is employed here according to the positive form, active movement, future tense made past by the convertible sign וֹ. One finds a little later on, this same verb used in the nominal and united to the verb הָלוֹךְ *to go before, to be carried to and fro*, to indicate a contrary movement. Now this singular phrase הָלוֹךְ וָשׁוֹב is very remarkable in what it seems to indicate in the seas, and in the waters which covered the earth, in general, that alternating movement of going and coming, which the modern physicists have begun to suspect.

Concerning the four original translators whose versions are ever before my eyes, two have evaded the sense of this phrase and two have felt it. The Samaritan, not understanding what this alternating movement impressed upon the waves could be, has said, corrupt-

3. A n d-t h e y-restored-themselves-as-formerly, the-waters, from-over-the-earth, by-the-g o i n g-off and-the-c o m i n g back: and - they-withdrew (they shrunk) the-waters, a t-t h e-end of-five - tens a n d-one-hundred of-day (manifested universal light).

3. Et-revinrent-à-l e u r-premier-état les-eaux de-dessus-la-terre du movement d' a l l e r-e n-avant et-de-revenir-s u r-s o i : e t-elles-se-retirèrent-en-elles-mêmes, l e s e a u x, a u-bout-de-cinq-décuples e t-u n e-centaine de-jour (de manifestation lumineuse, universelle).

---

ing the text ….. וַיָּשֻׁבוּ ・ וַיֵּלְכוּ ・ וַיַּחְסְרוּ ・ הַמַּיִם, *they-went, and-returned, and-were-abated, the-waters*….. which the Hellenists, faithful in following the most vulgar meaning, have imitated. But the Chaldean, adhering closer to the text, has translated this passage very clearly…… אוֹלִין וְתֵיבִין …… וְתָבוּ מַיָּא : *and-they-were-restored-in-their-primitive-state, the-waters…… going-and-returning-alternately*…… In which it has been followed by the author of the Vulgate.

וַיַּחְסְרוּ, *and-they-withdrew*…. The root חוּס from which this verb comes, merits the attention of the reader; through it, he can gradually penetrate the thought of Moses pertaining to the physical causes of the deluge. This root is composed of the sign of elementary existence ה, image of the travail of Nature, united to the sign of circular movement, and of all circumscription ס. It develops in its verbal state the action of conquering one's self; of experiencing a sentiment of sorrow and contrition; of shrinking. The sign of movement proper ר, being joined to this root to form the derivative verb חסׂר, only adds to the force of this expression which is quite accurately rendered by the word *shrink*. I observe that the hierographic writer, after having displayed all the resources of the Hebraic tongue, to depict the dilatation and swelling of the waters, neglects none of the means afforded in the literal sense, as well as in the figurative or hieroglyphic, to express with the same energy their shrinking and their contraction.

v. 4. וַתָּנַח, *and-it-rested*…. It is not without purpose that Moses employs the verb נוּח, which comes from the same root as the name of *Noah*, to express the repose of the *thebah* which bears this cosmogonic personage.

4. Wa-thanah ha-thebah b'ha-hodesh ha-shebîhî bi-shibehah-hashar îôm la-hodesh hal-hareî **Ararat**.

וַתָּנַח הַתֵּבָה בַּחֹדֶשׁ הַשְּׁבִיעִי בְּשִׁבְעָה־עָשָׂר יוֹם לַחֹדֶשׁ עַל־הָרֵי אֲרָרָט :

השביעי, *the-seventh*.... It should not be forgotten that, in a work of this nature, issued from the Egyptian sanctuaries, all the words are chosen with calculation and forethought. I have taken care to explain, as much as possible, the meaning of the Hebraic decade. The names of numbers here contain great mysteries; they are far from being limited to cold dates, as the vulgar translators have thought. They must be examined. It is necessary to remember for example, that number *seven* שבע, is always that of the consummation of things and times. The *thebah*, which was put in movement in the *second* lunar renewal, is stopped in the *seventh*. Now, we ought to know also, that number *two* שׁן, is the emblem of every mutation, of every transition, and of every passing from one state to another.

אררט, *of-Ararat*.... Here is a word which would afford a vast subject for commentary, but I have resolved to limit myself to translating. All peoples who have preserved the memory of the deluge, and nearly all have preserved it, have not failed to relate the name of the alleged mountain upon which rested the mysterious *thebah*, which bore within it the hope of nature and the seed of a new existence. Nicholas of Damas, cited by Josephus, called it Mount *Barris*, a name which is not very unlike that of *Syparis* or *Sypara*, which Berosus gave to that city of the sun, in which an Assyrian monarch deposited the archives of the world when he knew that the catastrophe of the flood was imminent. It is well known that the Greeks called λυκορεός, *the luminous mountain*, the place on Parnassus where Deucalion rested; but perhaps it is not generally known that the Americans had also a celebrated mountain, upon which they declared that the remnants of mankind had taken refuge, and whose name they consecrated by the erection of a temple dedicated to the sun. This name was *Olagmi*. It would certainly be very easy for me to prove that these names, more or less direct all have a connection with the course of light; but without citing, at this moment, other tongues than the Hebraic, let us content ourselves with examining the word which is the subject of this note.

COSMOGONY OF MOSES

4. And-it-rested, the-*the-bah*, in-t h e-moon-renewing the-s e v e n t h, by-the-seventeenth manifested-light of-t h a t-r e n e w i n g, on-the-heights of-Ararat (reflected light's stream).

4. Et-elle-se-reposa, l a-*thebah*, dans-le-renouvellement-l u n a i r e le-septième, au-dix-septième jour de-ce-renouvellement, sur-les-sommets de-l'Ararat (le cours réfléchi de la lumière).

---

and in which the thoughtless savants have been so unfortunate as to see an object of terror or of malediction.

This word is composed of the two roots אוֹר-רט : the first אוֹר, is understood: it is *light* and all ideas which are related to it. The second, רט, formed of the signs of movement proper and of resistance, characterizes a course accompanied, inflected or directed by anything whatsoever. Thence, the Chaldaic verb רהֹיט, *to concur with a thing, to follow it in its course, to direct it;* as light or water, for example; thence, the Hebraic word רהיט, *a channel, a conduit, a promenade;* thence, the Syriac derivative ܡܚܕܘܠܐ *an inflection, a reflection,* etc.

After this explanation one can feel that the word אררט, does not signify the *mount of malediction* or *of terror,* as has been believed without examination; but indeed that of *the reflected course of light;* which is very different. Besides, it is well to know that the Samaritan translator, the most ancient interpreter of Moses, has not rendered the word אררט, by a simple transcription of the characters, as it seems that he might have done, had he thought that this was simply a proper name of the Mount, but he has translated it by the word 𐡑𐡓𐡑𐡁𐡋, which differs entirely. The resemblance of this word with the ancient name of the island of Ceylon, *Serandip,* in the *Sanskrit* tongue, *Sinhala-dwip,* has caused some savants to think that Moses had perhaps designated a famous rock which commands that isle, and where the Brahmans declare that Buddha or Rama has left the imprint of his foot: but, without combatting this opinion wholly, I shall state that this word appears to be composed of the Chaldaic and Samaritan words, סרנא, *axis, wheel, orbit;* and רוב or ריב *effluence, emanation:* so that it offers a translation quite exact of the sense that I have given to the word אררט : that is to say, instead of signifying simply *the reflected course of light,* it signifies *the orbit of luminous effluence.*

5. W'ha-maîm haîou ha-lôch w'hassôr had ha-hodesh ha-hashîri: ba-hashîri b'æhad l'hodesh niraou râshei he-harîm.

וְהַמַּיִם הָיוּ הָלוֹךְ וְחָסוֹר עַד הַחֹדֶשׁ הָעֲשִׂירִי בָּעֲשִׂירִי בְּאֶחָד לַחֹדֶשׁ נִרְאוּ רָאשֵׁי הֶהָרִים׃

6. Wa-îhî mi-ketz ârbahîm îôm: wa-îphethah Noah æth-hallôn ha-thebah âsher hashah .

וַיְהִי מִקֵּץ אַרְבָּעִים יוֹם וַיִּפְתַּח נֹחַ אֶת־חַלּוֹן הַתֵּבָה אֲשֶׁר עָשָׂה׃

---

v. 5. העשירי, *the-tenth*.... We know that number *ten*, עשר is that of aggregative power, of efficient elementary force. The words which compose this verse and in general all those of this chapter, are chosen with such art, and the literal meaning connected and blended so closely with the figurative and hieroglyphic meaning, that it is impossible to separate them without weakening or destroying them. No translation can give the force of the original; for to attain this, it would be necessary to find words which might always contain three distinct ideas; which cannot be in our modern tongues, where the separation in the three significations, has long since been made by derivatives whose analogy is no longer perceived. Thus, for example, how can one understand all that Moses intended by these words ראשי ההרים? The literal sense is, *the heads, the summits of the mountains;* the figurative sense, *the principles, the beginnings of pregnancies;* the hieroglyphic sense, *the principiations of elementary conceptions.* All that I can do when it presents these difficulties is to manœuvre, as it were, among the three meanings, furnishing the reader with all means possible to penetrate them, if he will take the pains to do so.

v. 6. חלון, *the-opening*.... As this word is written with the character ח as initial, it does not appear to have any other

COSMOGONY OF MOSES 229

5. And-the-waters were by-the-going-off and-by-the-withdrawing, till-the-moon-renewing the-tenth: and-in-that-tenth, by-the-first of-the-renewing were-seen the-h e a d s of-the-hills (principles of nature's pregnancies, foremost elementarities).

5. Et-les-eaux furent du-mouvement-d'aller-en-avant e t-d e-celui-de-se-retirer-en-elles-m ê m e s, jusqu'au renouvellement-lunaire le-dixième; et-dans-ce-dixième, a u-premier d u-renouvellement furent-vues les-t ê t e s des-montagnes (les principes d e s-enfantemens naturels, les prémices des elemens).

6. And-it-was, at-the-determined-end o f-t h e-great-quaternion of-day that-he-unfastened, *Noah,* the-opening of-the-*thebah,* which he-had-made.

6. Et-ce-f u t à-la-fin-déterminée d u-grand-quaternaire de-jour, qu'il-dégagea, *Noah,* l'ouverture de-la-*thebah,* qu'il-avait-faite.

---

meaning than that of *opening,* being derived from the root חל which develops the idea of a distention, a solution, a separation operated with force; but if, as it might very well be, this initial character had been in the original only the determinative article ה, which the negligence of certain copyists might have caused to be confused with its analogue ח, then the word חלון, instead of signifying *an opening,* would signify *a nocturnal light, a night-light;* that is to say, a lamp destined to lighten the night, and which *Noah* might at first have released from the thebah to lighten the darkness.

I take this opportunity, which has perhaps more importance than one imagines, to call attention to the fact that the French word *lune,* formed from the Latin "luna", is derived from the word לון, referred to in this note, and that it means as I have indicated, *a nocturnal light, a night-light.* The Arabic analogue employed as verb, expresses the action of colouring, adorning, distinguishing, etc.

v. 7. הערב, *Ereb....* I am well aware that the Hellenists, and after them, the author of the Latin Vulgate, have seen in *Ereb,* that famed *Ereb* of ancient cosmogonies, only a simple raven: transforming thus a vast and mysterious idea into an idea petty and

7. Wa-îshallah æth-h a-horeb, wa-îetzâ îotzôâ wa-shôb had îbosheth ha-maîm me-hal ha-âretz. וַיְשַׁלַּח אֶת־הָעֹרֵב וַיֵּצֵא יָצוֹא וָשׁוֹב עַד־יְבֹשֶׁת הַמַּיִם מֵעַל הָאָרֶץ :

8. Wa-îshallah æth-h a-îonah me-âith-ô li-raôth ho-kallou ha-maîm me-hal pheneî ha-âdamah. וַיְשַׁלַּח אֶת־הַיּוֹנָה מֵאִתּוֹ לִרְאוֹת הֲקַלּוּ הַמַּיִם מֵעַל פְּנֵי הָאֲדָמָה :

---

ridiculous: but I am also aware that these same Hellenists who worked upon the version which bears the name of Septuagint, Essenes, and consequently initiates in the oral law, penetrated the hieroglyphic meaning of the Sepher deeply enough not to be the dupes of such a metamorphosis. One cannot read them with any kind of attention without discovering their perplexity. Not knowing how to disguise the periodic returns of this alleged bird, and fearing that the truth might shine forth in spite of them, they decided to change completely the original text and be delivered of this *Ereb* which perturbed them, by saying that the raven being sent forth returned no more, οὐκ ἀνέστρεψεν. But in this instance, everything betrays their pious fraud. The Samaritan text agrees with the Hebraic text and makes it unassailable; the Samaritan Version and the Chaldaic Targum say alike that *Ereb*, given liberty, takes an alternating movement of going forth and coming back; finally Saint Jerome, forced to recognize this truth, can only weaken the force of the phrase by saying, without doubling the first verb and changing their temporal modification of it, "qui egrediebatur et revertebatur."

It must be remembered that to reveal the depth of this hieroglyphic expression, this *Ereb* was not set at liberty, and did not take this periodic movement until after the release of the nocturnal light referred to in the preceding verse.

v. 8. הַיּוֹנָה, *Ionah*.... Here again is an emblem famous in ancient cosmogonies; emblem, that the Greek and Latin interpreters have again presented under the least of its characteristics;

7. And-he-let-out what-constitutes *Ereb* (westerly darkness) that-issued-forth by-the-issuing and-periodically-repairing, till-the-drying-up of-the-waters from-off-the-earth.

8. And-next-he-let-out the-selfsameness of-*I o n a h* (the brooding dove, nature's p l a s t i c power) from-his-own-self; to-see if-they-became-light, the-waters, from-over the-face of-the-adamic.

7. Et-il-laissa-a l l e r (il l â c h a) c e-qui-constitue-l' *Erebe* (l'obscurité occidentale) qui-sortit du-mouvement-de-sortir et-de-revenir-périodiquement jusqu'au desséchement des-eaux de-dessus-la-terre.

8. Et-ensuite-il-laissa-aller ce-q u i-constitue-l'*Ionah* (la colombe génératrice, la f o r c e plastique de la nature) d e h o r s-d'avec-lui; pour-voir-si-e l l e s se-faisaient légères, les-e a u x, de-dessus la-face-de-l'élément-adamique.

---

under that of a dove. It is indeed true that the Hebrew word יּוֹנָה , signifies *a dove*, but it is in the same manner that the word עֶרֶב, signifies *a raven;* that is to say, that the names of these two birds have been given them, in a restricted sense, in consequence of the physical or moral analogies which have been imagined between the primitive signification attached to the words עֶרֶב and יּוֹנָה, and the apparent qualities of the raven and the dove. The blackness of *Ereb*, its sadness, the avidity with which it is believed that it devours the beings which fall into its pale, could they be better characterized than by a dark and voracious bird such as the raven? The whiteness of the dove on the contrary, its gentleness, its inclination to love, did not these qualities suggest it as emblem of the generative faculty, the plastic force of Nature? It is well known that the dove was the symbol of Semiramis, of Derceto, of Mylitta, of Aphrodite, and of all the allegorical personages to whom the ancients attributed the generative faculty, represented by this bird. This emblem appears to have been known from most ancient times, by the Brahmans, by the Chaldeans, and even by the Sabæan priests of Arabia. It is known that at the time when Mohammed entered victorious into Mecca, he caused an image of the dove, sculptured in the temple of that celebrated city, to be broken by the hands of Ali. In short,

9. W-loâ matzâh ha-iônah manôah l'ĉhaph-rag-hel-ha-, wa-thashab ælaî-ô æl-ha-thebah ĉhi-maîm hal-pheneî ĉhol-ha-âretz wa-îs-helah îad-ô, wa-ikkah-ha wa-îabâ âoth-ha ælaî-ô æl-ha-thebah.

וְלֹא מָצְאָה הַיּוֹנָה מָנוֹחַ לְכַף־רַגְלָהּ וַתָּשָׁב אֵלָיו אֶל־הַתֵּבָה כִּי מַיִם עַל־פְּנֵי כָל־הָאָרֶץ וַיִּשְׁלַח יָדוֹ וַיִּקָּחֶהָ וַיָּבֵא אֹתָהּ אֵלָיו אֶל־הַתֵּבָה :

If one open any ancient book treating of religious mysteries, he will find therein traces of the veneration of the peoples for the dove. Assyria was particularly characterized by this bird and it can be inferred from a passage in Isaiah (v. 6. ch. XX) that it was an ensign for the Assyrians. But let us return to its Hebraic name the etymology of which is a matter of importance.

It is evident that the name of Ionia, that famous country claimed equally by Europe and Asia, comes from the same source as this word יוֹנָה. The Chaldaic and Hebrew יוֹן, יוֹנִי, or יוֹנָא, always designate Greece, or that which belongs to her: these are the Greek analogues, 'Ιωνία, 'Ιωνικός. For, if we examine Greece, concerning the inner meaning of the name which she gives herself, we shall find that she attaches to the word 'Ιωνικός, all ideas of softness, sweetness and amorous langour, which we attach to that of the *dove*; if we go further and explore in Greek itself the root of this word, we shall see that this root, Ἰον or Ἰων, contains in that tongue, the ideas of cultivated, fertile land; of productive soil; of existing being, in general; of the violet, flower consecrated to Juno, etc.

Now what do we find in the Hebraic root יוֹן ? We find, in general, the idea of a thing indeterminate, soft, sweet, easy to receive all forms, and in particular, a clayey, ductile land. If, following our method, we proceed to the hieroglyphic sense, and if we examine the signs of which this root is composed, we shall easily find in יוֹן, the mysterious root אוִי, where the sign of manifestation י, has replaced the sign of power א : so that, if the root און designates indefinite being, the root יוֹן will designate this same being passing from power into action.

9. And-not it-found, *Ionah* (nature's plastic power), a place-of-rest to-bend (to impart) the-breeding-motion-its own: and-it-returned unto-him, toward-the-*thebah*, because-of-the-waters-being on-the-face of-the-whole-earth: and-he-put-forth the-hand (the power)-his-own; and-he-took-it-up; and-he-caused-it-to-come unto-him toward-the-*thebah*.

9. Et-non-pas elle-trouva, l'*Ionah* (la colombe génératrice), un-lieu-de-repos pour-infléchir (communiquer) le-mouvement-sien: et-elle-retourna devers-lui, vers-la-*thebah*; à-cause-que les-eaux étaient sur-la-face de-toute-la-terre: et-il-étendit la-main-sienne (sa puissance) et-il-retira-elle; et-il-fit-aller elle-même devers-lui, vers la-*thebah*.

Have we still need of other proofs to know that the word יונה expresses the generative faculty of Nature? We shall see that in Hebrew, the compound word אביונה, signifies *desire of amorous pleasures;* and that one understands by the words יונת עלם, *a song, tender, melodious and capable of inspiring love.*

If I have entered into so great details concerning the word יונה it is because it holds very closely to the history of Nature, and because the reader will perhaps be interested to learn that the name of this soft Ionia, from which we have imbibed all that we have which is delightful in art and brilliant in knowledge, is attached, on the one side to the mysterious dove of Moses, to that of Semiramis; and loses itself on the other, in that sacred emblem called *Yoni* by the Brahmans; *Yng*, by the Chinese *Tao-teh*, over which it is necessary that I draw an impenetrable veil.

v. 9. מנוח, *a-place-of-rest....* This word is remarkable because it is attached to the name itself of *Noah*.

לכף־רגלה, *to-bend-the-breeding-motion-its-own....* This is an expression with double and even triple meaning, according to the literal, figurative or hieroglyphic relation under which it is considered. The root כף, which composes the first word, contains the idea of bending, of inflection, of cavity: it is, in a restricted sense, the palm of the hand, or the sole of the foot. The root רג, from which the second comes, develops every idea of organic movement. United to the directive sign ל, it expresses, figuratively, every con-

10. Wa-iahel hod shibe-hath îamîm âherîm, wa-îos-seph shallah æth-ha-Iônah min-ha-thebah.

וַיָּחֶל עוֹד שִׁבְעַת יָמִים אֲחֵרִים וַיֹּסֶף שַׁלַּח אֶת־הַיּוֹנָה מִן־הַתֵּבָה:

11. Wa-thaboâ ælaî-ô ha Iônah l'heth hereb: w'hin-neh holeh zaîth taraph b' phi-ha wa-îedah Noah chi-kallou ha-naîm me-hal ha-âretz.

וַתָּבֹא אֵלָיו הַיּוֹנָה לְעֵת עֶרֶב וְהִנֵּה עֲלֵה־זַיִת טָרָף בְּפִיהָ וַיֵּדַע נֹחַ כִּי־קַלּוּ הַמַּיִם מֵעַל הָאָרֶץ:

---

tinued action, every movement, every effort of the body or the soul toward a physical or moral object: literally, it is the foot, or the foot-print. Now, if in the word יונה, one sees only a *dove*, one must see only the bending of its foot in the words לכף רגלה: but, if by the one is understood, as it should be, *a generative faculty*, by the others would be understood, the communication, the application of the generative movement to this same faculty.

ידו, *the-hand-his-own*.... Another similar expression. If Noah is a man of flesh and bones as the Hellenists feign to believe, nothing is more simple than making him stretch out his hand to seize a bird and shut it up in his boat: but, if this is a cosmogonic personage representing the repose of Nature, and the conservator of elementary existence, it is its protective power which it uses to draw unto itself a faculty that it has sent forth prematurely. The root יד, which in a very restricted sense characterizes *the hand*, designates in a broader sense, every manifestation of power, of executive force, of ministry, etc.

v. 10. These terms present no difficulties.

v. 11. לעת ערב, *at-the-same-time-Ereb*.... The Hellenists seeing reappear here this same Ereb which they had travestied as a raven, and of which it was said positively that it returned no

10. And-he-waited yet-a-septenary of-days more; and-he-added the-letting-forth of-that-same-*I o n a h*, from-out-the-*thebah*.

11. And-it-came toward-him, *I o n a h* (the brooding dove) at-the-same-time *Ereb* (as a dove flying off from the raven) and-lo! a-bough of-olive-tree (elevated product of the fiery essence) plucked-off in-the-mouth-its-own (seized by her begetting faculty): thus-he-knew, *Noah* (nature's rest) that-they-lightened, the-waters, from-off-the-earth.

10. Et-il-attendit encore un-septenaire de-jours autres; et-il-ajouta-l'émission de-cette-même-*Ionah*, hors-de-la-*thebah*.

11. Et-elle-vint devers-lui, l'*Ionah*, (la colombe génératrice) a u-temps-même de-l'*Erebe* (au retour de l' obscurité occidentale) et-voici un-rameau d'olivier (une élévation de l'essence ignée) détaché dans-le-bec-à-elle (saisi par sa force conceptive): ainsi-il-connut, *Noah* (le repos de l'existence) que-s'allégeaient les-eaux, de-dessus-la-terre.

---

more, have assumed the part of ignoring it completely. The author of the Latin Vulgate, being unable to do such great violence to the Hebrew text, is contented with changing it, seeing no longer a raven in the word ערב, but simply a part of the day and in saying that the dove came back *at-even-tide*, "ad vesperam".

עלה־זית, *a-bough of-olive-tree*.... This again, is a symbolic expression, to which is given a meaning relative to the one which has been given to the word יונה. If in this one is seen a dove, pure and simple, in the other two will be seen an olive branch, a generative force of Nature, and one is led to understand, an elevation of igneous essence. It is the same with the word פי, which in either case is taken for the beak of the bird, or for the conceptive force of the moral being. Such was the genius of the Egyptian language, whose most secret sources had been opened to Moses.

I have explained in another passage the various significations attached to the word עלה, whose root על designates, in general, that which is superior, sublime; that which is raised above another

12. Wa-îiahel hôd shibe-hath îamîm aherîm wa-îs-hallah æth-ha-Iônah, w'loâ îassephah shoub-ælaî-ô hôd.

וַיָּחֶל עוֹד שִׁבְעַת יָמִים אֲחֵרִים וַיְשַׁלַּח אֶת־הַיּוֹנָה וְלֹא־יָסְפָה שׁוּב־אֵלָיו עוֹד :

13. Wa-îhî b'ahath w' shesh-mâôth shanah ba-riâ-shon b'æhad la-hodesh har-bou ha-maîm me-hal ha-âretz, wa-îassar Noah æth-michesseh ha-thebah wa-îarâ w'hinneh harbou phe-neî ha-âdamah.

וַיְהִי בְּאַחַת וְשֵׁשׁ־מֵאוֹת שָׁנָה בָּרִאשׁוֹן בְּאֶחָד לַחֹדֶשׁ חָרְבוּ הַמַּיִם מֵעַל־הָאָרֶץ וַיָּסַר נֹחַ אֶת־מִכְסֵה הַתֵּבָה וַיַּרְא וְהִנֵּה חָרְבוּ פְּנֵי הָאֲדָמָה :

---

thing. The word זית signifies clearly in its literal sense, *an olive, an olive-tree;* but it signifies in its figurative, not only *oil,* but according to its hieroglyphic sense, *the luminous essence of a thing.* It comes from the root אור, which characterizes the *essence* in general, contracted with the root זי, whose object is to depict that which shines and is reflected as the light.

v. 12. All these terms are understood or easy to understand.

v. 13. באחד, *in-the-unity....* This number is the symbol of the stability of things. Moses uses it twice in this verse, where he indicates the beginning of a new existence and, as it were, the awakening of nature. Attention should be given to the fact that number seven, which characterizes the consummation of things and end of temporal periods, is employed in the preceding verse.

בראשון, *in-the-very-principle....* This is the word ראש, to which Moses adds designedly the extensive syllable ון. What I have said concerning this root can be seen in v. 1, ch. I.

חרבו, *that-they-wasted....* The verb חרוב which appears twice in this verse in speaking of the waters, is worthy of notice. It does not signify *to be dried up,* as the Latin translator has appeared to believe, but *to be destroyed, to leave off, to waste,* as the Hellenists have better interpreted ἐξέλιπε τὸ ὕδωρ. The Hebraic verb חרוב belonging to the root חר, which characterizes elementary, devouring heat, an igneous focus, contains the idea of devastation,

COSMOGONY OF MOSES 237

12. And-he-waited yet a-septenary of-d a y s m o r e; a n d-h e-s e n t-forth that-same-*Ionah*, and-not-did-it-add the-repairing toward-him again.

13. A n d-i t-was in-the-unity and-six-hundreds of-revolving-c h a n g e, in-the-very-principle, by-t h e-first of-the-moon-renewing, t h a t t h e y-w a s t e d, the-waters, from-off-the-earth : and-he-reared-up, *N o a h*, the-shel-tering-o f-t h e-*thebah*, and-h e-d i d-k e n, and lo! that-wasted (the waters) from-off-the-faces of-the-adamic.

12. Et-il-attendit encore un-septenaire de-jours aut-res ; et-il-laissa-aller cette-même *Ionah*, et-non-pas el-la-ajouta le-retour vers-lui encore.

13. Et-ce-fut dans-l'unité e t-s i x centaines de-muta-tion-temporelle, d a n s - l e-principe au-premier du-re-nouvellement - lunaire-que-s' usèrent (se défirent) les-eaux de-dessus-la-terre : et-il-éleva, *Noah*, le-comble de-la-*thebah*, et-il-considéra et-voici ! qu'elles-s'usaient (les eaux) d e s-f a c e s de l'élé-ment-adamique.

---

of ravage, of total exhaustion. The word *waste* renders the Hebrew with exactitude.

ויסר, *and-he-reared-up*.... This expression is very remark-able. Whether one takes the radical verb סור, or one of the com-pound radical verbs יסר or נסר, it will always signify *to rear up*, in the sense of *instructing, educating, training in knowledge.* Moses, in making use of this amphibological expression, with regard to *a sheltering* has no doubt had the intention of making it understood, that the word מכסה, ought not to be taken in the literal and material sense which it presents at first glance. All that I can do as its interpreter, is to acquaint one with its purpose. I have said that the *thebah*, to which belongs this shelter or this vaulted superficies, was neither a boat nor an ark, nor a coffer, but a mysterious refuge.

v. 14. יבשה, *was-dried-up*.... I only cite this word to show that Moses puts it in its place, and that his translators have been wrong in confusing it, as they have done, with the verb חרוב, of which I spoke in the preceding verse. It was essential before an-nouncing the drying up of the land, to say that the waters, having

14. W-ba-hodesh ha-shenî b'shibehah w-hesherîm îôm la-hodesh îbeshah ha-âretz. וּבַחֹדֶשׁ הַשֵּׁנִי בְּשִׁבְעָה וְעֶשְׂרִים יוֹם לַחֹדֶשׁ יָבְשָׁה הָאָרֶץ׃

15. Wa-idabber Ælohîm æl-Noah l'æmor: וַיְדַבֵּר אֱלֹהִים אֶל־נֹחַ לֵאמֹר׃

16. Tzeâ min-ha-thebah, athah! w'âisheth-cha w-baneî-cha w-neshî-baneî-cha âitha-cha. צֵא מִן־הַתֵּבָה אַתָּה וְאִשְׁתְּךָ וּבָנֶיךָ וּנְשֵׁי־בָנֶיךָ אִתָּךְ׃

---

grown less and less, or destroyed, had disappeared from its surface. If one will give attention to the gradation which the hierographic writer observes, from the great swelling which causes the deluge to the entire disappearance of the waters, it will be found wonderful.

He first says in v. I, that the waters were checked ישכו; and soon in v. 3, that they restored themselves as formerly, ישבו; these two Hebrew words are constructed and employed with such an art that they have been judged the same; they differ only by the sign of interior action ב, which in this one has replaced the assimilative and centralizing sign כ, which is found in the other. Next, in v. 4 and 5, the waters experience a sort of libration, of periodic movement of going and coming, and as it were, of flux and reflux, הלוך ושוב and הלוך וחסור, which seems to depict, in particular, the effect of the seas, and in general, that of a colossal tidal wave. Then the waters become more and more abated, הקלו and קלו, even as it is said in v. 8 and 11; and when at last they are wasted by this sort of friction, done away with, entirely exhausted, חרבו, the land is dried up, יבשה הארץ. Let the reader who recalls with what obstinacy Moses has been reproached for his bad natural philosophy, examine this gradation and see if these reproaches would not apply better to his slanderers.

v. 15. וידבר, *and-he-informed-by-the-speech*.... The two con-

COSMOGONY OF MOSES 239

14. And-i n-the-moon-renewing the-second, in-the-seven and-twentieth day of-that-renewing, was-dried-up the-earth.

14. E t-dans-le-renouvellement-lunaire le-s e c o n d, dans-le-vingt-septième jour-d e-c e-renouvellement f u t-séchée la-terre.

15. And-he-informed-by-the-speech, HE-the-Gods, to-ward-*N o a h*, pursuing-t o-say:

15. Et-il-informa-par-la-parole, L U I-les-Dieux, en-vers-*Noah*, selon-ce-dire:

16. Issue from-t h e-*the-bah* (sheltering p l a c e), t h o u, and-the-intellectual-wife-of-theee (thy volitive faculty) and-the-issued-off-spring-of-thee a n d-the-corporeal-m a t e s of-those-offspring-of-t h e e (t h e i r natural faculties), together-thee.)

16. Sors (produis-toi en dehors) de la-*thebah*, toi, et-la-femme-intellectuelle-à-toi (ta faculté volitive), et-les-fils-à-toi (t e s productions manifestées), et-les-épouses-corporelles des - fils - à - toi (leurs facultés physiques), ensemble-toi.

---

tracted roots רב־בר, one of which designates *a course* and the other *a production*, form the compound דבר, which signifies literally *an effusion*, that is to say, an exterior thing by means of which an interior thing is made manifest. In a restricted and physical sense, it is *a thing, an affair, an object, a word*: in a broad and moral sense, it is *an idea, a speech, a discourse, a precept*, etc.

v. 16. צא, *issue....* The word *issue* renders well the Hebrew. I have explained in v. 12 ch. I, the origin and force of this verb, the application of which is here of the highest importance.

v. 17 and 18. All these terms have been explained: if I give them an acceptation a little different from what they seem to present, it is so that the reader may be able to grasp better the inner meaning, and that he may become familiar with the genius of the Hebraic tongue in particular, and in general, with that of the primitive tongues. For the writers of these remote times, restricted to the narrow limits of an original tongue, having only a small number of words at their disposal, and not being able to draw elsewhere the

240   THE HEBRAIC TONGUE RESTORED

17. Čhol-ha-haîah asher-âith-čha mičhol-bashar ba-hôph ba-behemah w-b'čhol-ha-remesh ha-romesh hal-ha-âretz, hawtzeâ âith-čha w-shartzou ba-âretz w-pha-rou w-rabou hal-ha-âretz.

כָּל־הַחַיָּה אֲשֶׁר־אִתְּךָ מִכָּל־בָּשָׂר בָּעוֹף וּבַבְּהֵמָה וּבְכָל־הָרֶמֶשׂ הָרֹמֵשׂ עַל־הָאָרֶץ הַוְצֵא אִתָּךְ וְשָׁרְצוּ בָאָרֶץ וּפָרוּ וְרָבוּ עַל־הָאָרֶץ:

18. Wa-ietzeâ-N o a h w' banaî-ô w'âisheth-ô w-nes-heî banaî-ô âith-ô.

וַיֵּצֵא־נֹחַ וּבָנָיו וְאִשְׁתּוֹ וּנְשֵׁי־בָנָיו אִתּוֹ:

19. Čhol-ha-haîah čhol-ha-remesh w-čhol-ha-hôph čhol rômesh hal-ha-âretz le-wishephehotheî-hem îatzâou min-ha-thebah.

כָּל־הַחַיָּה כָּל־הָרֶמֶשׂ וְכָל־הָעוֹף כֹּל רוֹמֵשׂ עַל־הָאָרֶץ לְמִשְׁפְּחֹתֵיהֶם יָצְאוּ מִן־הַתֵּבָה:

---

expressions which they needed, were obliged to attach to each of these words, a considerable number of analogous ideas, literally as well as figuratively: therefore, they were careful to examine the root, following the etymological science which for them held the place of erudition. It cannot be doubted, in reading the Sepher of Moses, that this extraordinary man, initiated into this science by the Egyptian priests, possessed it in the highest degree.

v. 19. לְמִשְׁפְּחֹתֵיהֶם, *after-the-tribes-their-own*.... Two distinct roots enter into the composition of this word. The first מש, characterizes every thing united and forming, so to speak, *a mass*: the second, פח, on the contrary, designates everything which opens to embrace a greater extent, to envelop and to include as *a net*, for

COSMOGONY OF MOSES   241

17. All-living-life which-together-thee, f r o m-every-bodily-shape, b o t h-in-fowl and-in-quadruped, a n d-i n-t h e-w h o l e-creeping-kind, t r a i l i n g-along upon-the-earth, let-i s s u e together-thee: and-let-them-pullulate in-the-earth, and-teem and-breed-multiplying upon-the-earth.

17. Toute-vie-animale laquelle-est ensemble - toi, de-toute-forme-corporelle, e n-genre-volatile, e t-e n-quadrupède, et-en-tout-genre-reptiforme serpentant sur-la-terre, fais-sortir (produire dehors) ensemble-toi; et-qu' ils-pullulent en-la-terre, et-fructifient, e t - multiplient sur-la-terre.

18. A n d-he-issued-forth (he waked out) he-*Noah*, a n d-t h e-offspring-of-h i m , a n d-t h e-volitive - efficient - might-his-own, and-the-corporeal-faculties o f-t h e-offspring-of-him, together-him.

18. Et-il-sortit (il se reproduisit au d e h o r s) lui-*Noah*, et-les-productions-à-lui, et-la-faculté-volitive efficiente-à-lui, et-les-facultés-corporelles-des-productions-à-lui,ensemble-lui.

19. T h e-w h o l e-earth-born-life, the-whole - creeping-kind, a n d-the-w h o l e-fowl, everything - crawling-along upon-the-earth, after-the-tribes-their-own issued forth from-the-*thebah*.

19. T o u t e-l'animalité-terrestre, toute-l'espèce-reptiforme, et-toute-l'espèce-volatile, t o u t-ce-qui-se-meut-d' un-mouvement-contractile sur-la-terre, selon-les-familles-à-eux, sortirent (se produisirent h o r s) de-la-*thebah*.

---

example. United to form the word מִשְׁפָּחָה, they depict, in the most energetic manner, the formation of the family, the tribe, the nation, which, departing from a central point embraces a greater extent. This word, inflected by the directive article לְ, is here used in the constructive plural, and united to the nominal affix הֶם.

v. 20. מִזְבֵּחַ, *an-offering-place*.... The word זֶבַח, which designates in Hebrew, *a sacrifice*, being governed by the sign of exterior and plastic action מ, characterizes a place destined for sacri-

20. Wa-îben Noah mizebbeha la-IHÔAH wa-ikkah mi-chol ha-bemah ha-tehorah w-mi-chol ha-hôph ha-tahôr: wa-îahal holoth ba-mizzebbeha.

וַיִּבֶן נֹחַ מִזְבֵּחַ לַיהוָה וַיִּקַּח מִכֹּל הַבְּהֵמָה הַטְּהֹרָה וּמִכֹּל הָעוֹף הַטָּהוֹר וַיַּעַל עֹלֹת בַּמִּזְבֵּחַ׃

21. Wa-iarah IHÔAH æth-reîah ha-nîhoha, wa-îaomer IHÔAH ællibb-ô loâ-âossiph l'kallel hôd æth-ha-âdamah ba-hobour ha-Adam chi-îetzer leb ha-Adam rah mi-nehuraî-ô: w-loâ âossiph hôd l'hachôth æth-chol-haî cha-âsher hashîthî.

וַיָּרַח יְהוָה אֶת־רֵיחַ הַנִּיחֹחַ וַיֹּאמֶר יְהוָה אֶל־לִבּוֹ לֹא־אֹסִף לְקַלֵּל עוֹד אֶת־הָאֲדָמָה בַּעֲבוּר הָאָדָם כִּי יֵצֶר לֵב הָאָדָם רַע מִנְּעֻרָיו וְלֹא־אֹסִף עוֹד לְהַכּוֹת אֶת־כָּל־חַי כַּאֲשֶׁר עָשִׂיתִי׃

---

fice, *an altar*. I should not have noticed this word, which otherwise offers nothing difficult, if I had not believed to give pleasure to the reader, in showing him that its root זב, is not used in this sense in Hebrew, that it does not appear even of Egyptian origin, and that it is necessary to penetrate as far as the Ethiopians to find it. The verb **זבח** (*zabh*), signifies among this ancient people, *to sacrifice;* and I quite believe that its origin goes back to a very remote time when Sabæanism flourished in that country. At the epoch when Moses employed the word זבח, it was already ancient enough to be naturalized in the Egyptian tongue without preserving the idea of its origin, which no doubt would have appeared profane to this theocratic legislator.

ויעל עלת, *and-he-raised-up a-rising-sublimation....* Both the noun and the verb which the hierographic writer uses to express the action of Noah sacrificing to the Divinity, issue alike from the root על, which characterizes every thing which is raised with energy, which mounts from a low place toward a higher, which is exhaled, which is sublimated chemically, evaporates, is spiritualized, etc. This expression merits close attention in its hieroglyphic sense.

20. And-he-erected *Noah*, an-o f f e r i n g - place unto-IHOAH; a n d-he-t o o k-up f r o m-every-quadruped of-the-purity, and-from-every-fowl of-the-purity, a n d-he-raised-up a-rising - sublimation f r o m-t h a t-offering-place.

20. Et-il-édifia, *N o a h*, un-lieu-d e-s a c r i f i c e à-IHOAH; et-il-prit de-tout-quadrupède de-la-p u r e t é, et-de-tout-v o l a t i l e de-la-pureté; et-il-éleva une-élévation (il fit exhaler une exhalaison) d e-c e-lieu-de-sacrifice.

21. And-he-b r e a t h e d, IHOAH, that-fragrant-breath of-sweetness; a n d-he-said, I H O A H, inward-the-heart-his-own, n o t-will-I-certain-ly-add the-cursing yet-again t h e - a d a m i c-for-the-sake-*Adam' s* because-it-framed, the-heart of-that-collective-man, evil, f r o m-the-first-ling-impulses-his-own: and-not-will-I-certainly add yet-a g a i n the-smiting-so-l o w a l l-earth-born-life such-as-that I-have-done.

21. Et-il-respira, IHOAH, c e t-esprit-odorant de - douceur; et-il-dit, IHOAH, devers-l a-cœur-sien, non-pas-j'ajouterai - certainement l' action-de-maudire e n c o r e la-terre-adamique d a n s-le-rapport-d'*Adam*, car-il-forma, le-cœur de-cet-homme-universel, l e-m a l, dès-les-premières - impulsions-siennes: et-non-pas-j'ajouterai-certainement encore l'action de - frapper - si - violemment toute-l'existence-élémentaire de-même-que j'ai-fait.

---

v. 21. את־ריח, *that-fragrant-breath*.... This noun as well as the verb which precedes it, are both attached to the root רוח, of which I spoke in v. 2, ch. I. But it must be noticed that in the word ריח, the sign of potential manifestation has replaced the sign of the convertible link.

לא־אסף, *not-will-I-certainly-add*.... The root סף, indicates any capacity whatever; employed as verb it signifies that an action already done is continued, or that it takes place again. The iterative syllable *re*, which we take from the Latins, put at the head of a verb, renders quite well this Hebraic idiomatism. Thus, for example, when in v. 12 of this chapter Moses says, in speaking of *Ionah*,

22. Hôd chol-îemeî ha-âretz zerah w-katzîr w-kor wa-hom w-kaîtz wa-horeph w'îôm wa-laîlah loâ îshebbothou.

עַד כָּל־יְמֵי הָאָרֶץ זֶרַע וְקָצִיר וְקֹר וָחֹם וְקַיִץ וָחֹרֶף וְיוֹם וָלַיְלָה לֹא יִשְׁבֹּתוּ׃

ולא־יספה שוב and *not-did-it-add-the-returning;* we would say, *and it did not return.*

יצר, *it-framed....* I have explained as much as possible for me, this difficult word of the Hebraic tongue in v. 7. ch. II.

רע, *evil....* As this word offers no difficulty either in the literal or in the figurative sense, I have not dwelt upon it until now. Its etymology is so very simple. The hieroglyphic meaning only, is very profound. Its etymological composition results from the sign of movement proper ר, united to the root וע, not used in Hebrew, and changed in its analogue עו to signify literally, every bending, obliquity, inclination, declination of things; and figuratively, every perversity, iniquity, moral depravation. The hieroglyphic meaning is drawn from the symbolic union of the signs of movement proper and material sense. The Arabic analogue روِاغ, characterizes that which leaves its path, its sphere, by a disordered movement; that which bends, twists or is perverted. The Chaldaic expresses this word by בִישׁ, which is the analogue of the Samaritan ᚹᚠᚹ, of which I have spoken. The Teutonic *bös* is the exact copy of the Chaldaic, of which the Latin *vitium* is a derivative.

מנעריו, *from-the-firstling-impulses-his-own....* The root נוע develops every idea of impulse given to a thing to agitate, to stir it, to draw it from its torpor. This root, united by contraction to the elementary root אר, forms the word נער, which is taken in a broader sense for elementary impulse, and in a more restricted sense, for youth and childhood.

v. 22. The terms of this verse are not difficult. I shall limit myself to giving briefly the etymology, as much to satisfy the curiosity of the reader, as to show him how the hieroglyphic meaning can pass to the figurative and to the literal, for nearly all these terms have been hieroglyphic in their origin.

COSMOGONY OF MOSES

22. While-shall-revolve-all-the-lights of-the-earth (phenomenal universal light's manifestation), seed-time and-harvest, and-cold and-heat, and-summer and-winter, and-day and-night shall-not sabbathize (shall not cease).

22. Pendant-tous-les-jours de-la-terre (les manifestations lumineuses, phénoméniques), le-germe et-la-récolte, et-le-froid et-le-chaud, et-l'été et-l'hiver, et-le-jour et-la-nuit non-pas-septeniseront (ne cesseront pas).

זרע, *seed-time*: that is to say, the dispersion, the division, the attenuation of evil; as is proved by the two contracted roots זר-רע.

קציר, *harvest*: that is to say, the term, the end of pain, of agony; as can be seen in the two contracted roots קץ-צר.

קר, *cold*. This root contains in itself the idea of that which is incisive, penetrating, stiff, strong, etc.

חם, *heat*. I have frequently had occasion to speak of this root which is attached to that which is inclined, bent, restricted, scorched, etc.

קיץ, *summer*. This is the root קץ, expressing the term, the summit, the end of all things; to which the sign of manifestation has been added.

חרף, *winter*. These words are composed of two contracted roots חר-רוף, one of which, חר, characterizes elementary heat; the other רוף, expresses the action of breaking, of interrupting, of striking, etc. Winter is therefore, in Hebrew, the solution, the rupture of elementary heat, as *summer* is the summit and the end manifested. *Cold* is therefore, a thing that is keen, penetrating, straight and clear; and *heat*, on the contrary, a thing obtuse, enveloping, bent and obscure. *Seed-time* can therefore be considered as a thing destined to divide, to attentuate evil more and more. One realizes how far the exploration of these hieroglyphics and others similar, might lead into the physical and metaphysical ideas of the ancient Egyptians.

I have firm reasons for thinking that this twenty-second verse and perhaps a part of the twenty-first, are foreign to Moses; I believe them to be a fragment of an early commentary passed from the margin into the text.

SEPHER BERÆSHITH T.

סֵפֶר בְּרֵאשִׁית ט ·

1. Wa-îbarech Ælohîm æth-N o a h w'æth-b a n a î-ô wa-îâomer l a-h e m, phrou w-rebou, w-milaou æth-ha-âretz.

וַיְבָרֶךְ אֱלֹהִים אֶת־נֹחַ וְאֶת־בָּנָיו וַיֹּאמֶר לָהֶם פְּרוּ וּרְבוּ וּמִלְאוּ אֶת־הָאָרֶץ :

2. W-môrâo-chem w-hith-ch e m îhîeh hal-chol-haîath ha-âretz w-hal-chol hôph ha-shamaîm b'chol âs-her thiremoth ha-âdamah w-b'chol-deghei ha-îam b' îed-chem nithanou.

וּמוֹרַאֲכֶם וְחִתְּחֶם יִהְיֶה עַל־חַיַּת הָאָרֶץ וְעַל־כָּל־עוֹף הַשָּׁמַיִם בְּכֹל אֲשֶׁר תִּרְמֹשׂ הָאֲדָמָה וּבְכָל־דְּגֵי הַיָּם בְּיֶדְכֶם נִתָּנוּ :

---

v. 1. All the terms in this verse have been previously explained.

v. 2. וּמוֹרַאֲכֶם *and-the-dazzling-brightness-yours*.... The Hellenists and their imitators who have seen in the word מוֹרָא an expression of terror or fright, have therefore rendered *Noah* and his productions, as objects of fear for terrestrial animality; but this is not what Moses has intended. The root of this word is אוֹר *light*, whence מָאוֹר, *splendour, brightness, a torch.* The verb מְרוֹא which is formed from it signifies *to rule by its lights* and not to terrify. One finds in Chaldaic the word מָרָא, and the analogues in Syriac and in Arabic to designate, *a master, guide, lord.* From this word is formed the Latin "maritus", from which comes the French *mari* (husband), that is to say exactly, the torch, the enlightened guide of the woman: name given at first out of respect or flattery but which habit has finally distorted utterly.

I must admit that the Samaritan translator had already corrupted the meaning of Moses before the Hellenists, since rendering the word מוֹרָא by ࠀࠌࠓࠀࠁ, which designates a gigantic formidable object, he

COSMOGONY OF MOSES

GENESIS IX.

1. And-he-blessed, HE-the-Gods, the-selfsameness-of-*Noah*, and-that-of-the-offspring-h i s-o w n; a n d-he-said unto-them: breed and-multiply, and-fill the-selfsameness-of-earth.

2. And-the-d a z z l i n g-brightness-yours, a n d-the-dreadful-awe-o f-y o u shall-be u p o n-the-whole-animality e a r t h-born, and-upon-e v e r y-fowl of-heavens, in-all that can-breed from-the-adamic-pristine-e l e m e n t, and-in-every-fish of-the-sea: i n t o-t h e-hand-yours they-were-given-over.

COSMOGONIE IX.

1. Et-il-b é n i t, LUI-les-Dieux, l'ipséité-de-*Noah*, et-celle-des-émanations-à-l u i ; et-il-dit-à-eux : fructifiez et-multipliez et-remplissez-entièrement l'ipséité-terrestre.

2. E t - l a-splendeur-éblouissante-v ô t r e, e t-le-respect-terrifiant-à-vous, sera s u r-toute-l'animalité-terrestre et-sur-toute-l'espèce-volatile d e s-régions-é l e v é e s; dans-tout ce-qui recevra-le-mouvement-originel de-l'élément-adamique, e t-d a n s-tous-les-poissons de-la-mer; sous-la-main-à-vous, ils-ont-été-mis.

---

had effaced this imposing light, whence the hierographic writer causes the respect of animals for the posterity of *Noah* to be derived.

v. 3. I have nothing more to say upon the meaning of these words; except that animal life is given as food to Noah and to his posterity, which had not been done with regard to that of Adam. This life is given to them the same as the green herb, כירק עשב. Here the assimilative article כ is used in the most picturesque, and in the least equivocal manner: the root אך, makes, in the following verse, an effect no less striking, as adverbial relation.

v. 4. אך־בשר, *but-the-bodily-shape....* I regret assuredly the

3. Čhol-r e m e s h asher houâ-haî la-čhem îhîeh l' ačhelah: čh'îerek h e s h e b nathathî la-čhem æth-čhol.

כָּל־רֶמֶשׂ אֲשֶׁר הוּא־חַי לָכֶם יִהְיֶה לְאָכְלָה כְּיֶרֶק עֵשֶׂב נָתַתִּי לָכֶם אֶת־כֹּל:

4. A č h-b a s h a r b'naphesh-ô dam-ô loâ thâočhelou.

אַךְ־בָּשָׂר בְּנַפְשׁוֹ דָמוֹ לֹא־תֹאכֵלוּ:

---

trouble that the Hellenists have taken to disguise the force of this verse and the ensuing ones; I would gladly imitate the discreet complaisance of the Latin translator, who has chosen to pass in silence the words which perplexed him; but at last it is necessary that Moses be translated. If this extraordinary man has said things which alarm the rabbis, or which shock their pride, he has also said things which ought to make them proud: thus is everything balanced. Long enough have these magnificent tableaux been degraded by the sorry caricatures which have been made of them. They must be known in their original conception. The disagreeable truths to be met with here are nothing in comparison to the false or ridiculous things which the copyists have introduced.

In fact, this is beyond doubt: Moses, by the mouth of the Divinity, forbids the posterity of *Noah* to feed upon corporeal substance, the similitude of that which his soul bears in himself, that is to say, the very flesh of man. Certainly one should regard this decree only as a general law which concerns the entire human race, since it is also addressed to the posterity of *Noah*, which here represents mankind; but in supposing that the Hebrews might be found at that time in circumstances lamentable enough to have required it, I must apprise the modern Jews, if anything can console them for this, that not only had Zoroaster already made this decree to the Parsees, a people today very pacific, and who even abstain from the flesh of animals; but that he had moreover, commanded them to confess having eaten human flesh, when this had happened; as can be seen in the *Jeschts sadés*, traduit par Anquetil-Duperron (p. 28, 29, 30 et suiv.).

COSMOGONY OF MOSES 249

3. Every-moving - thing, which-is itself-life, to-you shall-be for-food: even-as-the-green herb, I-have-given unto-you together-all.

3. Tout-c h o s e-s e-mouvant qui-a en-soi l'existence, à-vous s e r a pour-aliment: de-m ê m e-que-la-verdoyante herbe, j'ai-donné-à-vous ensemble-tout.

4. B u t-the-bodily-shape-h a v i n g by-the-soul-itself, the-likeness-its-o w n, n o t-shall-you-feed-upon.

4. Mais-la-forme-corpor - elle-ayant dans-l'âme-sienne l'homogénéité (la similitude) à-elle, non-pas-vous-consommerez.

I shall not expatiate upon this subject as I shall doubtless have occasion to treat of it elsewhere. I pass on to the explanation of the verse under consideration.

Moses, after having likened all terrestrial animality to the green herb and having given it as food for the posterity of Noah, opposes to the assimilative article כ which he has just used, the adverbial relation אך, thus giving a contrary movement to the phrase, restricting with greatest force, and making exception of that corporeal form which receives its likeness from its soul by means of *blood.* For in whatever manner one may examine the words which compose this verse, here is their meaning; one cannot interpret them otherwise without mutilating them or making them utterly unrecognizable.

When the Hellenists have said, *ye shall not eat the flesh which is in the blood of the soul:* κρέα ἐν αἵματι ψυχῆς; they have not only misunderstood the true signification of the word דם by limiting it to signifying only *blood,* but they have again overthrown all the terms of the phrase, by attributing to this word the mediative article ב which belongs to *the soul* in the Hebrew text, and by suppressing the two nominal affixes which make *the corporeal form* בשר, dependent upon sanguineous homogeneity דמו, residing *in its own soul,* בנפשו.

When the Latin translator has said, *ye shall not eat the flesh with the blood,* "carnem cum sanguine", he has, like the Hellenists, wrongly interpreted the word דם; he has given it a relation that it has not, and finally, he has suppressed entirely the word נפש, *soul,* not knowing what to do with it. The great difficulties of this verse

5. W'âch æth-dime-chem l'napheshothî-chem âedrosh mi-îad chol-haîah âedreshnou w-mi-îad ha-Adam, mi-îad Aîsh æhî-ô âedrosh æth-nephesh ha-Adam.

וְאַךְ אֶת־דִּמְכֶם לְנַפְשֹׁתֵיכֶם אֶדְרֹשׁ מִיַּד כָּל־חַיָּה אֶדְרְשֶׁנּוּ וּמִיַּד הָאָדָם מִיַּד אִישׁ אָחִיו אֶדְרֹשׁ אֶת־נֶפֶשׁ הָאָדָם׃

---

and those following consist, first, in the meaning which Moses has attached to the word דם; secondly, in the manner in which he has made use of it.

The word does not signify literally *blood*, as the Hellenists have wished to make it believed and as Saint Jerome has believed; but, as I have already said elsewhere, every homogeneous thing, formed by assimilation of similar parts, and belonging to the universal organization. If this word, taken in a restricted sense, designates *blood*, it is because, following the Egyptian ideas of natural philosophy, the blood was regarded as formed of homogeneous molecules, united by an universal, assimilative force, serving as bond between the soul and body, and in consequence of the laws which preside at the organization of beings, of designing exteriorly the corporeal form, according to the impulse which it receives from the efficient volitive faculty, inherent in the soul.

Whatever opinion one may take of these ideas of natural philosophy it is not my purpose to discuss their advantages over those of our modern physicists; it is enough for me on this occasion, to bring them out and to state that they were all contained in the word דם, by virtue of its hieroglyphic composition. When this word designated *blood*, it was in its quality of assimilative link between the soul and body, of organizing instrument, as it were, destined to raise the edifice of the body according to the plan furnished by its soul.

Now, in this instance the hierographic writer has made use of its literal, figurative and hieroglyphic sense to its fullest extent, by means of a oratorical figure of speech peculiar to the genius of the Hebraic tongue, and which I have already explained several times. There is no translation in any modern European tongue which can wholly express his thought. All that I can do is to present it so that an intelligent reader can penetrate it readily.

Let us listen now to the Samaritan translator; he has not de-

COSMOGONY OF MOSES 251

5. For that-sanguineous-likeness-yours (which acts according) t o-t h e-s o u l s-yours I-will-prosecute from-the-hand of-every-living: I-will-prosecute-it (I will a v e n g e it) and-from-the-hand of-*A d a m* (collective man); a n d-from-the-hand of-*Aish* (intellectually individuated man) brother-of-him, I-will-prosecute that-v e r y-s o u l, universal-likeness.

5. Car cette-assimilation-sanguine-à-vous (q u i est) selon-les-âmes-vôtres, je-rechercherai d e-l a-m a i n de-tout-vivant: je-rechercherai-elle (j'en poursuivrai la vengeance) et-de-la-main d' *Adam* (l'homme universel); et-de-la-m a i n d'*A i s h* (l' homme individualisé par sa volonté) frère-à-lui, je - rechercherai (j e vengerai) cette-même-âme-adamique.

---

viated greatly from his model: and he has been abandoned by the Hellenists who did not wish so much clarity. Here is his entire phrase interpreted word-for-word.

פֶּן בְּדִּץ בְּנֶב אֲ—דָּץ אִצְרָא
לֹא אִחֲתֹזב׃

However the form-corporeal, by-the-soul-its-own a d a m i c, not-shall-you-consume.

That is to say, you shall not eat of the animal substance assimilated by the soul of universal man. This seems clear. The following verses will complete its evidence.

v. 5. In this verse the Divinity announces that it will avenge this blood assimilation, analogous to the adamic soul, that is to say, plainly, that it will avenge the human blood shed, מִיד כל־חיה, "at the hand of every living being"...... וּמִיד הָאָדם, "and at the hand of universal Adam"...... מִיד אִיש אחיו "at the hand of intellectual Aish, his brother"...... I urge the reader to observe, besides the proofs which I have just advanced, the irresistible proof of the distinction which I have established according to Moses, between *Adam*, universal man, mankind, and *Aish*, intellectual man, individualized by his volitive faculty. This hierographic writer naming them together in this verse, is careful not to confuse them, as his translators have done. On the contrary, he designates the one as brother of the other.

6. Shopheċh d a m h a-Adam b'Adam dam-ô îshap-heċh: ċhi b'tzelem Ælohîm hashah æth-ha-Adam.

שָׁפֵךְ דַּם הָאָדָם בָּאָדָם דָּמוֹ יִשָּׁפֵךְ כִּי בְּצֶלֶם אֱלֹהִים עָשָׂה אֶת־הָאָדָם׃

7. W'âthem, phrou w-re-bou, shirtzou ba-âretz, w-re-bou b'ha.

וְאַתֶּם פְּרוּ וּרְבוּ שִׁרְצוּ בָאָרֶץ וּרְבוּ בָהּ׃

8. Wa-îâomer Ælohîm æl-Noah w'æl-banaî-ô, âith-ô, l'æmor.

וַיֹּאמֶר אֱלֹהִים אֶל־נֹחַ וְאֶל־בָּנָיו אִתּוֹ לֵאמֹר׃

9. Wa-âni hin-nî mekîm æth-berith-î, âith - ċhem w' æth-zarehaċhem â h o r e î-ċhem.

וַאֲנִי הִנְנִי מֵקִים אֶת־בְּרִיתִי אִתְּכֶם וְאֶת־זַרְעֲכֶם אַחֲרֵיכֶם׃

---

v. 6. This verse contains a terrible mystery, which Plato has very clearly understood and developed very well in his book of Laws. I refer the reader to it in order to avoid commentaries. As to the terms themselves, they have either been already explained or they offer no kind of grammatical difficulty.

v. 7. ואתם, *and-ye-collective-self....* The designative relation את, taken substantively and invested with the collective sign ם, is applied here to *Noah* and to his productions; that which gives to the apostrophe a force that no translator of Moses has made felt.

ורבו בה, *and-spread-yourselves on-it....* It must be observed that the verb רבה, is employed twice in this verse. The first, in the sense of growing in number; the second, in that of growing in power; so that it is difficult to say whether the mediative article ב, employed with the nominal affix ה, to designate the earth, in-

COSMOGONY OF MOSES

6. The-shedding-one the-sanguineous-likeness of-*Adam* (mankind) through-*Adam* the-blood-his-own shall-be-shed: because-in-the-universal-shadow of-HIM-the-Gods HE-made the-selfsameness-of-*Adam*.

7. And-ye-collective-self! fructify and-increase-in-number; breed in-the-earth, and-spread-yourselves on-it.

8. And-he-declared, HE-the-Gods, unto-*Noah*, and-unto-the-offspring-of-him, together-him, pursuing-to-say:

9. And-I, lo-I-am causing-to-stand-substantially the-creating-might-mine together-you, and together-the-seed-yours, after-you.

6. L'épandant (celui qui épandra) l'assimilation-sanguine d'*Adam* (le règne hominal) par-le-moyen-d'*Adam* le-sang-à-lui sera-épandu: car-dans-l'ombre-universelle de-LUI-les-Dieux IL-fit l'ipséité-d'*Adam*.

7. Et-vous-existence-universelle! fructifiez et-multipliez: propagez-vous en-la-terre, et-étendez-vous en-elle.

8. Et-il déclara, LUI-les-Dieux, envers-*Noah*, et-envers-les-émanations-à-lui, ensemble-lui, selon-ce-dire:

9. Et-moi, voici-moi faisant-exister-en-substance la-force-créatrice-mienne ensemble-vous et-ensemble-la-generation-vôtre, après-vous.

---

dicates simply that the earth will be the place, or the means of this power.

v. 8. All these terms are understood.

v. 9. מקים, *causing-to-stand-substantially*.... This is the verb קום, used according to the excitative form, active movement, continued facultative. For the meaning which I give it, refer to the history of this important root, v. 4, ch. II.

את־בריתי, *the-creating-might-mine*.... See v. 18, ch. VII. If one glances at the vulgar translations, he will see the Divinity, (instead of the power or creative law which It gives to Noah and to

10. W'æth-chol-nephesh ha-haîah a s h e r âith-chem ba-h ô p h ba-behemah w-b' chol haîath ha-âretz âith-chem mi-chol îotzeâi ha-thebah l'chol haîath ha-âretz.

וְאֵת־כָּל־נֶפֶשׁ הַחַיָּה אֲשֶׁר אִתְּכֶם בָּעוֹף בַּבְּהֵמָה וּבְכָל חַיַּת הָאָרֶץ אִתְּכֶם מִכֹּל יֹצְאֵי הַתֵּבָה לְכֹל חַיַּת הָאָרֶץ:

11. W a-hokimothî æth-berith-î âith-c h e m w-loâ-îchareth chol-b a s h a r hôd mi-meî ha-m a b b o u l w-loâ îhîeh hôd m a b b o u l l'shaheth ha-âretz.

וַהֲקִמֹתִי אֶת־בְּרִיתִי אִתְּכֶם וְלֹא־יִכָּרֵת כָּל־בָּשָׂר עוֹד מִמֵּי הַמַּבּוּל וְלֹא־יִהְיֶה עוֹד מַבּוּל לְשַׁחֵת הָאָרֶץ:

12. Wa-îâomer Ælohîm zoâth âôth ha-berith âsher anî nothen beîn-î w-beîneî-c h e m w'beîn chol-nephesh haîah âsher âith-chem l'doroth hôlam.

וַיֹּאמֶר אֱלֹהִים זֹאת אוֹת־הַבְּרִית אֲשֶׁר אֲנִי נֹתֵן בֵּינִי וּבֵינֵיכֶם וּבֵין כָּל־נֶפֶשׁ חַיָּה אֲשֶׁר אִתְּכֶם לְדֹרֹת עוֹלָם:

---

his productions according to the Hebrew text), consenting with them and with all the animals coming out from the ark; and following the Hellenists and Latin interpreters, he will see a sort of pact, treaty or alliance, the articles of which it is none too easy to conceive.

v. 10. All these terms are understood.

v. 11. ולא־יכרת, *and-no-more-shall-be-cut-off*.... This is the verb כרת, used according to the positive form, passive movement. This verb, which signifies literally *to arrest the scope of a thing*, is

COSMOGONY OF MOSES

10. And-together-all-soul of-life which-was together-you, in-the-fowl, in-the-quadruped, and-in-the-whole animality earth-born, together-you, amongst-all the-issuing-beings of-the-*thebah*, including-the-whole animality of-the-earth.

11. And-I-will-cause-to-exist-in-a-material-shape that-creating-might-mine, together-you; and-no-more-shall-be-cut-off every-corporeal-shape again, through-the-waters of-the-great-swelling; and-no-more-shall-be yet a-flood for-the-destroying-quite-over of-the-earth.

12. And-he-said, HE-the-Gods, this-is the-token (symbolical sign) of-the-creating-might which I-am laying-down betwixt-me and-betwixt-you and-betwixt every-soul of-life, which-shall-be together-you unto-the-ages of-the-boundless-time.

10. Et-ensemble-toute-âme de-vie, laquelle-était ensemble-vous, en-genre-volatile, en-quadrupède, et-en-toute animalité terrestre, ensemble-vous, parmi-tous-les-provenans de-la-*thebah*, comprenant-toute l'animalité terrestre.

11. Et-je-ferai-exister-dans-l'ordre-matériel cette-loi-créatrice-mienne, ensemble-vous; et-non-pas sera-retranchée toute-forme-corporelle encore, par-l'eau de-la-grande-intumescence: et-non-pas-sera encore une-grande-intumescence pour-la-dépression (la destructtion) de-la-terre.

12. Et-il-dit, LUI-les-Dieux, ceci-est le-signe de-la-loi-créatrice laquelle je-suis mettant entre-moi et-entre-vous, et-entre-toute-âme de-vie, laquelle-sera ensemble-vous aux-âges de-l'immensité (des temps).

---

formed of the two contracted roots כר־רת of which the one, כּר, contains the idea of that which grows, rises, unfolds; and the other, רת, expresses on the contrary, that which chains, arrests, coagulates, etc.

v. 12. אֲנִי נֹתֵן, *I-am laying-down*.... Here is the source of this facultative whose signification can here be of some import-

13. Æth-kasheth-î nathathî b'hanan w'haîthah l' aôth berith beîn-î w'beîn ha-âretz. אֶת־קַשְׁתִּי נָתַתִּי בֶּעָנָן וְהָיְתָה לְאוֹת בְּרִית בֵּינִי וּבֵין הָאָרֶץ׃

14. W'h aî a h b'hanan-î hanan hal-ha-âretz w'nirâ-thah ha-kesheth b' hanan. וְהָיָה בְּעַנְנִי עָנָן עַל־הָאָרֶץ וְנִרְאֲתָה הַקֶּשֶׁת בֶּעָנָן׃

15. W-zacharethî æth-be-rîth-î â s h e r beîn-î w-beî-neî-chem w-beîn chol-nep-hesh haîah b'chol-bashar w-loâ îhîeh hôd ha-maîm l' mabboul l'shaheth chol-bas-har. וְזָכַרְתִּי אֶת־בְּרִיתִי אֲשֶׁר בֵּינִי וּבֵינֵיכֶם וּבֵין כָּל־נֶפֶשׁ חַיָּה בְּכָל־בָּשָׂר וְלֹא־יִהְיֶה עוֹד הַמַּיִם לְמַבּוּל לְשַׁחֵת כָּל־בָּשָׂר׃

---

ance. The root הן develops in a general sense, an extension of itself, an enlargement: in a particular sense, it is a gift, a largess. Preceded by the verbal adjunction נ, it expresses the action of putting in the possession of another, of delivering for his disposition, of giving. It is to this latter meaning that the facultative נותן is related.

v. 13. את־קשתי, *that-bow-mine....* The root of the word קשת, *a bow*, is not found in the Hebrew tongue; it must be sought for in the Arabic قاس, in which it is a kind of idiomatic onomatopoeia. It is from the word توس *a bow*, that the Hebrew is formed as feminine derivative.

בענן, *in-the-cloudy-expanse....* I beg the reader to recall what I have said concerning the extraordinary root אן, which sometimes characterizes indefinite being, the world, and sometimes void, nothingness. If this root, conceived as characterizing void, loses its radical vowel א to take ע which designates the material sense, then it seems that void itself is corporified and becomes palpable. It is a heavy air, an obscure vapour, a lugubrious veil, thrown over

13. That-bow-mine I-have-laid-down in-the-cloudy-expense; and-it-shall-be for-token of-the-creating-might betwixt-me and-betwixt the-earth.

13. Cet-arc-mien j'ai-mis dans l'espace-nébuleux; et-il-sera pour signe de-la-loi-créatrice entre-moi et-entre la-terre.

14. And-it-shall-be by-the-clouding-mine the-cloudy-expanse, upon-the-earth, that-shall-be-seen the-bow in-the-cloudy-expanse.

14. Et-ce-sera-dans-l'action-mienne d'obscurcir l'espace-nébuleux sur-la-terre, qu'il-sera-vu l'arc dans l'espace-nébuleux.

15. And-I-will-remember that-creating-law which-is betwixt-me and-betwixt-you, and-betwixt all-soul of-life into-all-corporeal-shape; and-not-shall-be-there an-again (a coming back) of-the-water's great-swelling to-depress (to destroy, to undo) every-corporeal-shape.

15. Et-je-me-rappellarai cette-loi-créatrice laquelle-sera entre-moi et-entre-vous, et-entre-toute-âme de-vie, en-toute-forme-corporelle; et-non-sera un-encore (une révolution nouvelle) des-eaux de-la-grande-intumescence pour-déprimer (abîmer) toute-forme-corporelle.

---

the light. Now, this is what the root ען signifies properly. In its state of verb it develops the action of obscuring, covering, hiding, obstructing; *fascinans oculis*. In its state of noun and united to the syllable וֹן, it designates nebulous space and all clouds in particular.

v. 14. בעננִי, *by-the-clouding-mine*.... Moses, true to this style, derives the verb from the same root as the noun and uses them together. The effect of his phrase is here very picturesque, but the thought that it contains is again most profound. This thought is of such a nature that it cannot be explained. All that I can say is, that in the same action of obscuring the earth, the Divinity, according to this hierographic writer, places the striking

16. W'haîthah ha-kesheth b'hanan w-raîthî-ha lizechor berîth holam beîn Ælohîm w-beîn chol-nephesh haîah b'chol-bashar âsher hal-ha-âretz.

וְהָיְתָה הַקֶּשֶׁת בֶּעָנָן וּרְאִיתִיהָ לִזְכֹּר בְּרִית עוֹלָם בֵּין אֱלֹהִים וּבֵין כָּל־נֶפֶשׁ חַיָּה בְּכָל־בָּשָׂר אֲשֶׁר עַל־הָאָרֶץ:

17. Wa-îaomer Ælohîm æl-Noah zâoth âôth ha-berîth âsher hokimothî beîn-î w-beîn chol bashar âsher hal-ha-âretz.

וַיֹּאמֶר אֱלֹהִים אֶל־נֹחַ זֹאת אוֹת־הַבְּרִית אֲשֶׁר הֲקִמֹתִי בֵּינִי וּבֵין כָּל־בָּשָׂר אֲשֶׁר עַל־הָאָרֶץ:

18. Wa-îhîou benei-Noah ha-îotzeâîm min-ha-thebah: Shem w-Ham wa-Japheth: w-Ham houâ âbî Chenahan.

וַיִּהְיוּ בְנֵי־נֹחַ הַיֹּצְאִים מִן־הַתֵּבָה שֵׁם וְחָם וָיָפֶת וְחָם הוּא אֲבִי כְנָעַן:

---

token of might, or the creative law which he gives to *Noah* and to his posterity.

v. 15. עוֹד *an-again*.... The root עוֹד, expresses the idea of a return to the same action, as I have announced in v. 19, ch. IV. It is ordinarily employed as adverbial relation; but in the example here referred to, it appears with the force of a real substantive governing the words המים למבול *the-waters of-the-great-swelling*.... This is what has determined me to make a substantive of the word *again*, to express exactly the Hebraic phrase.

v. 16 and 17. All these terms are understood.

v. 18. כנען, *Chanahan*.... I have given in the greatest detail, the etymology of the proper names of *Noah's* three sons,

16. And-there-shall-be the-bow in-the-cloudy-expanse; and-I-will-look-upon-it, to-remember the-creating-law (laid down for) a-boundless-time, betwixt HIM-the-Gods, and-betwixt all-soul of-life, in-every-corporeal-shape, which-is on-the-earth.

17. And-he-said, HE-the-Gods, unto-*Noah*, this-is the-token of-the-creating-might which I-caused-to-exist-substantially between-me and-between every-corporeal-shape, which-is on-the-earth.

18. And-they-were the-sons of-*Noah*, (his offspring) issuing from-the-*thebah* (sheltering abode): *Shem* (all that is upright and bright), *Ham* (all that is dark, curved and heated) and-*Japheth* (all that is extended and wide): then-*Ham* was-himself, the-father of-*Chanahan* (reality, material existence.

16. Et-il-sera, l'arc, dans-l'espace-nébuleux; et-je-considérerai-lui pour-rappeler la-loi-créatrice de-l'immensité-des-temps (existante) entre-LUI-les Dieux, et-entre-toute âme-vivante, dans-toute-forme-corporelle qui-est sur-la-terre.

17. Et-il-dit, LUI-les-Dieux, à *Noah*, ceci-est le-signe de-la-force-créatrice laquelle j'ai-fait-exister-substantiellement entre-moi et-entre toute-forme-corporelle qui-est sur-la-terre.

18. Et-ils-furent les-fils de-*Noah* (ses émanations) les-sortans de-la-*thebah* (la place de refuge), *Shem* (ce qui est élevé et brillant): *Ham* (ce qui est incliné, obscur, et chaud) et-*Japheth* (ce qui est étendu) : or-*Ham* fut-lui-même, père de-*Chanahan* (la réalité matérielle, l'existence physique).

Shem, Ham and *Japheth*: here is a fourth, *Chanahan*, whose signification merits all the attention of the reader. Although Moses declared him son of *Ham* and that he ought, as to his extraction to be considered such, we shall see nevertheless a little further on, that this writer speaks of him as a real son of *Noah*, thus associating him in the most expressive manner with *Ham* from whom he issued. It is because *Ham* and *Chanahan* are but one sole and same thing,

19. Sheloshath ælleh be-neî-Noah w-m'ælleh nephet-zah chol-ha-âretz. שְׁלֹשֶׁת אֵלֶּה בְּנֵי־נֹחַ וּמֵאֵלֶּה נָפְצָה כָל־הָאָרֶץ׃

20. Wa-îahel Noah Aish ha-âdamah wa-ittah charem. וַיָּחֶל נֹחַ אִישׁ הָאֲדָמָה וַיִּטַּע כָּרֶם׃

---

one sole and same cosmogonic personage, considered under two different relations. *Chanahan* once produced by *Ham*, becomes *Ham* himself. This name comes from two distinct roots: כן and ען. By the first, כן, should be understood all that which enjoys a central force sufficiently energetic to become palpable, to form a body extended in every sense, to acquire solidity. This root has many analogies with the one of which I have spoken in explaining the name of *Kain*. The only difference which exists between them is that קן, being especially animated by the sign of potential manifestation in קין, has a force of usurpation and of transmutation in its proper nature, that the other כן, has not. This one seems reduced to a force of inertia which leaves it only an existence purely passive and material.

Employed as substantive, the root כן develops the idea of that which pertains to the reality of things and to their physical essence. As verb, it expresses the action of fixing and affirming, of placing and arranging, literally as well as figuratively.

The second root from which the name of *Chanahan* comes, is ען, which, according to the analysis that I have made in v. 13 of this same chapter, should be understood as a sort of nothingness, of materialized void, depicted by a heavy air, an obscure vapour, a dismal veil, etc. So that by now uniting the roots in question, according to their different significations, we shall find in כנען, the expression of a realized nothingness, of a shadowy air made solid and compact, in short, of a physical existence.

This physical existence sometimes taken in good or in bad sense, has furnished a great number of figurative expressions for the Hebraic tongue. The one most used is that by which one has designated, by the same name of כנען, artisans and merchants; that is to say, those who are trained in real or physical things, who traffic

19. Three-were those the-offspring of-*Noah*, and-through-those was-shared the-whole-earth.

20. And-he-released (set free, redeemed forcibly), *Noah*, the-intellectual-man of-the-adamic-ground; and-thus-he-tilled what-is-lofty (spiritual heights).

19. Trois-furent ceux-là les-fils (les êtres émanés) de-Noah, et-par-ceux-là fut-partagée toute-la-terre.

20. Et-il-délivra (rendit à la liberté, dégagea avec effort) *Noah*, l'homme-intellectuel de l'élément-adamique; et-il-cultiva (ainsi) ce-qui-est-élevé(les productions spirituelles).

---

in, and maintain their existence from them: it has been, in the course of time, the cause of unenlightened or prejudiced interpreters believing that the son of *Ham* had been the father of merchants and perhaps himself a merchant.

v. 19. No difficulties here.

v. 20. ויחל, *And-he-released*.... The Hellenists, ever engrossed in restricting to the most insignificant and most trivial sense, the magnificent thoughts of Moses, instead of seeing *Noah*, the preserver of elementary existence, giving liberty to the human intelligence, weakened and held captive not only through the degradation of the earth, but by the terrible catastrophe which had taken place, far from seeing him restore birth to that intellectual man whom the vices of humanity had brought near to death, as far as death can be approached by an immortal essence; the Hellenists, I say, see in their *Noah* only a man of the fields who plants the vine: καὶ ἤρξατο Νῶε ἄνθρωπος γέωργος γῆς καὶ ἐφύτευσεν ἀμπελῶνα. "And Noah began to be an husbandman, and he planted a vineyard."

The author of the Latin Vulgate has faithfully rendered this singular idea, and has even augmented it by a verb which is found neither in the Greek, nor even in the Hebrew: "cœpit que Noe, vir agricola, exercere terram: et plantavit vineam."

But there is not a word of all that in the text of Moses.

21. Wa-îesheth min-ha-jîn: wa-ishecèhar, wa-itheggal bethôċh âholoh. וַיֵּשְׁתְּ מִן־הַיַּיִן וַיִּשְׁכָּר וַיִּתְגַּל בְּתוֹךְ אָהֳלֹה׃

First, it is necessary to distort grievously the verb ויחל, to make it say, *and he began*. This verb is derived from the root חל, which as I have already stated on several occasions, develops the general idea of an effort made upon a thing to extend it, to draw it out, to lead it toward another, to be clasped there, etc. This root, verbalized by the convertible sign ו, offers, in the radical verb הול, an idea of suffering caused by the violent effort that one makes upon oneself, or upon another; and thence, the accessory ideas of wringing, of moving in a convulsive manner, of suffering; of taking courage, of being hardened against pain, of waiting, of hoping, etc. The different compounds of this radical, formed either by the initial adjunctions י or נ, or by the redoubling of the final character ל, participate more or less in its original signification. They always signify opening a thing, resolving, dissolving, extracting, bringing to light, making public, taking possession of, etc.

It must be seen after this explanation, that the most exact meaning which can be given to the expression of Moses, is not *he began*, which can only be applied to the accessory idea of opening; but rather, *he released* which proceeds from the first idea. The Samaritan translator and the Chaldaic paraphrast, agree with me upon this point: the former, using the verb ᛚᛏᚣ, and the latter, its analogue שרי, which expresses the action of emitting, permitting, allowing, letting go; as is proved by the Syriac ܫܪܐ, and the Arabic شرو, which are attached to the same root שור, whose literal meaning is to direct and regulate a thing.

But let us continue the analysis of this important verse. Moses said therefore, not that *Noah* began to be an husbandman, but that he released intellectual man from the adamic element, and opened for him a new career. The word איש which he uses in this instance, has been sufficiently explained in v. 23, ch. IV. It is after the revivification of this principle, that he applies himself to cultivate that which is lofty or sublime. Now, it was quite simple, after having made an agricultural man of Noah, to see in this

COSMOGONY OF MOSES

21. A n d-h e - saturated-himself with-what-is spirituous; a n d-h e-intoxicated-his-thought (gave a delirious movement to his fancy); a n d-h e-revealed-himself-in-the-bottom (in the most secret part) of-the-tabernacle-his-own.

21. Et-il-s'abreuva de-ce-qui-est spiritueux; et-il-exalta-sa-pensée (donna un essor violent à son imagination); et-il-se-révéla dans-le-centre (dans le lieu le plus secret) du-tabernacle-à-lui.

---

spiritual elevation, *a vineyard*, the name of which taken in the physical order, was synonymous: and instead of the spirit, production of this same elevation, *wine*, equally synonymous with spirit.

For what does the word כרם, that the Hellenists have rendered by ἀμπλῶνα, signify? It signifies not only a *vineyard*, but a thing pertaining to an elevation, to an exaltation literally as well as figuratively. It is formed from the root רם, which characterizes that which moves upward from below, in the manner of a flame, employed as substantive, and inflected by the assimilative article כ. In the figurative sense, כרם, designates an exaltation, a sublime movement of the understanding; in the literal sense *a vine*, a spirituous plant which enjoys elevated places, and which one raises higher by means of trellises and poles. I must say, besides, for those of my readers who might imagine that the word כרם has never before been taken in the figurative sense that I give it, that this word, famous throughout all Asia, signified, in Chaldaic, *a splendid thing, an academy, an assemblage of savants*, that the Syriac ܟܪܡܐ, designates *strength;* the Arabic كرم, *generosity, greatness of soul;* that this word expresses the action of fire in Coptic, as it expresses it morally in Egyptian; that in the Sanskrit tongue, *Karma* or *Kirmo*, is taken for the *motive faculty*, the *movement*. It is from the word כרם, that the Greek tongue has drawn χαρμονή, *jubilation*, and ἁρμονία, *harmony*. It is from the word כרם in fact, and this etymology is worthy of close attention, that the Latin word "carmen", *poetry*, is derived; the word *charm* is the same as "carmen" only altered by pronunciation.

22. Wa-îarâ H a m âbî Chanahan æth-herwath âbî-ô: wa-îaghed li-sheneî âhî-ô ba-houtz. וַיַּרְא חָם אֲבִי כְנַעַן אֵת עֶרְוַת אָבִיו וַיַּגֵּד לִשְׁנֵי־אֶחָיו בַּחוּץ:

---

v. 21. מִן־הַיַּיִן, *with-what-is-spirituous*.... The word יִין, which, in the natural order signifies simply *wine*, designates in the moral order, and according to the figurative and hieroglyphic sense, *a spiritual essence*, the knowledge of which has passed in all times, as belonging to the most profound mysteries of Nature. All those who have written of it, represent this mysterious essence as a thing whose profoundness cannot be known without revelation. The Kabbalists are accustomed to say, in speaking of this *wine*, that he who drank of it would know all the secrets of the sages. I can only offer to the reader the grammatical analysis of the Hebrew word, leaving the rest to his sagacity.

I have often spoken during the course of my notes of the root אִן, which enjoys the unusual privilege of characterizing alternately, being and nothingness, everything and nothing. Refer v. 2, ch. IV; v. 25, ch. V; v. 8, ch. VII, and v. 13 of the present chapter.

It is evident that this root, emerging from the deepest abysses of Nature, rises toward being or falls toward nothingness, proportionally, as the two mother vowels אִ, enlighten or obscure it. From its very principle, it suffices to materialize or to spiritualize the convertible sign ו, in order to fix its expression upon objects genuine or false. Thus one sees it in אוֹן, virtue, strength, valour; and in אָוֶן, *vice, vanity, cowardice;* in יִין, *the generative faculty of Nature;* in יִין, *the clay of the earth.*

In the word here referred to, the two vowels are not only enlightened but replaced by the sign of potential manifestation י, image of intellectual duration. This sign being doubled constitutes, among the Chaldeans, one of the proper names of the Divinity. United to the final sign ן, it seems, if I can so express it, to offer the very body of that which is incorporeal. It is a spiritual essence which many peoples and particularly the Egyptians, have considered under the emblem of light. Thus, for example, one finds in the Coptic, Ούωνι, *light* or *torch*. It is in conceiving this essence under the form of *spirit*, that these same peoples, choosing for it

22. And-he-did-discover, Ham, the-father-of *Chanahan*, the-self-secret-parts of-the-father-his-own, and-he-blabbed-out to-both-brothers-his-own, in-the-outward-enclosure.

22. Et-il-considéra *Ham*, père de-*Chanahan*, les-propres-mystères-secrets du-père-sien; et-il-les-divulgua aux-deux-frères-à-lui dans l'enceinte-extérieure.

---

an emblem more within the reach of the vulgar, have taken for its physical envelope *wine*, that liquor so vaunted in all the ancient mysteries because of the *spirit* which it contains and of which it was the symbol. This is the origin of these words which, coming from the same root appear so different in signification: אוֹן *being*, and יין, *wine*, of which the Greek analogues offer the same phenomenon: ὤν *being*, and οἶνος, *wine*.

It is useless to continue these comparisons. However I cannot refrain from saying that it is by an almost inevitable consequence of this double sense attached to the word יין, that the cosmogonic personage called Διονύσος, *Dionysus*, by the Greeks, has finally designated for the vulgar, only the god of wine, after having been the emblem of spiritual light; and that the same word which we use has become such, only as a result of the same degradation of the sense which was attached to it, a degradation always coincident with the hardening of the mother vowel: for, from the word יין, is formed the Teutonic *wein*, the Latin "vinum", and the French *vin*.

The Samaritan translator makes use in this place of the word ᛏᛉᛩᛟ, and the Chaldaic paraphrast has imitated him in employing the analogue חמרא. These two terms springing from the two contracted roots חם־מר, designate that which dominates by its vigour, or simply that which heats and lights.

וישכר, *and-he-intoxicated-his-thought*.... After the long and detailed explanations into which I have entered, the reader should have no more need, except for the grammatical proof of the meaning that I give to this word or that I shall give to those which follow. The word שכו signifies *thought, the comprehension of the soul*. It is attached to the Arabic كَسا, *he reflected, he thought*. This word, united to the sign of movement proper ר, forms the verb שכור, *to exalt one's thought, to be intoxicated, to be carried away*, etc.

23. Wa-ikkah Shem wa-Japheth æth-ha-shimelah wa-îashîmou hal-shechh-em shaneî-hem: w'îele chou âhoranîth wa-îechassou æth-herwath âbî-hem: w-pheneî-hem ahoranîth w-herwath âbî-hemloâ râou.

וַיִּקַּח שֵׁם וָיֶפֶת אֶת־הַשִּׂמְלָה וַיָּשִׂימוּ עַל־שְׁכֶם שְׁנֵיהֶם וַיֵּלְכוּ אֲחֹרַנִּית וַיְכַסּוּ אֵת עֶרְוַת אֲבִיהֶם וּפְנֵיהֶם אֲחֹרַנִּית וְעֶרְוַת אֲבִיהֶם לֹא רָאוּ׃

וַיִּתְגַּל, *and-he-revealed-himself-wholly*.... Here it is the verb גלה *to reveal*, employed according to the reciprocal form, in the future made past by the convertible sign ו. The Hellenists, always adhering to the trivial and gross meaning, and seeing in *Noah*, an husbandman overcome with wine, could not acknowledge the meaning of this verb. Also, instead of saying that Noah revealed himself, they have said that he stripped himself of his garments: καὶ ἐγυμνώθη: "et nudatus est".

v. 22. אֶת־עֶרְוֹת, *the-secret-mysteries-his-own*.... This was a consequence of the exaltation of *Noah*, that he revealed and disclosed the mysteries which ought to have remained hidden. The Hellenists, faithful to their custom of looking at things, might have translated by the word αἰδοῖα, that which they supposed *Ham* had looked upon in his father; but it appears that they did not dare. Saint Jerome, less scrupulous, has ingenuously said "verenda nudata". It is certain that the Hebrew word עֶרְוֹת, might have this sense, in every other circumstance, if the rest of the discourse had been relative to it; but it is quite easy to see here, that this word taken in a figurative acceptation, expresses what the Chaldeans have always made it signify; that is to say, *the mysteries of nature, the secrets, a hidden doctrine*, etc. Also the Samaritan word is worthy of comment: ᚕᚘᚚᚘᚕ expresses, according to the Chaldaic roots from which it springs, *that which must remain hidden*.

v. 23. אֶת־הַשִּׂמְלָה, *the-very-left-garment*.... All the hieroglyphic force of this verse is contained in this word. Moses has chosen it with an art of which he, and his instructors, the Priests of Egyptian Thebes, were alone capable. To explain it entirely is for the moment, an impossible thing. It would demand, in order

23. And-he-took, *S h e m* with *Japheth*, the-very-left-garment; and-they-uplifted-it upon-the-b a c k of-them-both; and-they-went backward; and-they-covered the-mysterious-parts o f-the-father-their's; and-their-faces-were backward; so-the-mysterious-parts of-the-father-their's not-did-they-see.

23. Et-il-prit, *Shem* avec *J a p h e t h,* le-propre-vête-m e n t-de-la-gauche, et-ils-l'élevèrent sur-le-dos de-tous-deux; et-ils allèrent en arrière e t-i l s-couvrirent les-mystères cachés du-père-à-eux; et-les faces-à-eux-étaient en-arrière : ainsi-les-mystères - cachés du-père-à - eux non-pas-ils-virent.

---

to be understood and proved, a commentary more exhaustive than this volume. Perhaps I may one day have the good fortune to demonstrate to what point this mighty cosmologist has understood the history of the universe.

The root of this important word, is the same name as one of the beings emanated from *Noah*, שם *Shem*, which as we have seen, characterizes that which is raised, brilliant, remarkable. By means of the directive sign ל, which is here joined, this root is applied, in the figurative sense, to the Septentrion, to the Boreal pole, to that pole of the earth which dominates the other. I beg the reader to notice this point. In a more restricted sense it designates the left side. It is known that among the most ancient peoples, this side was the noblest and most honoured. When, in those remote times, a Sabæan priest turned his face toward the orient to worship the Sun, dazzling emblem of the Being of beings, he had on his left, the Boreal pole, and on his right the Austral pole; and as he was more initiated in the astronomic science than our modern savants ordinarily imagine, he knew that one of these poles was raised, whilst the other was inclined toward the equinoctial line.

But without dwelling now upon these comparisons which will find their place elsewhere, I shall content myself with saying that in the most ancient customs, the left side of a man was always the first enveloped and the most covered. Still in this day certain peoples, attached to the ceremonies of their ancestors, envelop the left arm before making their prayers. The modern Jews call טפלים the cords which serve them for this usage. From this habit spring many analogous expressions. The Hebrews called the kind of garment which enveloped this side שמלה, from the word שמל, *the*

24. Wa-îiketz Noah mi-jeîn-ô: wa-îedah æth âsher hashah l'ô ben-ô ha-katan.

וַיִּיקֶץ נֹחַ מִיֵּינוֹ וַיֵּדַע אֵת אֲשֶׁר־עָשָׂה לוֹ בְּנוֹ הַקָּטָן :

25. Wa-îâomer: a r o u r Chenahan, h e b e d hobadîm îhieh l'æhî-ô.

וַיֹּאמֶר אָרוּר כְּנָעַן עֶבֶד עֲבָדִים יִהְיֶה לְאֶחָיו :

26. Wa-îâomer: barouch, IHÔAH Ælohei-Shem: w'îhî Chenahan hebed lam-ô.

וַיֹּאמֶר בָּרוּךְ יְהוָֹה אֱלֹהֵי־שֵׁם וִיהִי כְנַעַן עֶבֶד לָמוֹ :

27. Japheth Ælohîm l' Jepheth, w'ishechon b'aho-leî-Shem: w'îhî Chenahan hebed lam-ô.

יַפְתְּ אֱלֹהִים לְיֶפֶת וְיִשְׁכֹּן בְּאָהֳלֵי־שֵׁם וִיהִי כְנַעַן עֶבֶד לָמוֹ :

---

left side. The Arabs had the verb شمل which expressed the action of enveloping, of girding, of folding the left side, of turning toward the north; the Syrians, attaching more to the respect that this action inspired in them, than to the action itself, designated it by the word ܡܫܠܡܘ, *perfection*, the aim toward which one tends, the accomplishment of things, holy ordination, etc.

The reader should feel now that the Hellenists, having seen in the word שמלה only a simple mantle ἱμάτιον, have perceived only the gross exterior of a profound meaning, that Moses, besides, has not wished to explain otherwise than to attach it to the root שם, which designates one of the sons of *Noah*, and the name of the garment with which he covered his father, שמלה, as well as the verb itself which serves to express this action, ישם.

v. 24. הקטן, *the-little-one*.... This word offers no difficulty; but it indicates that Moses places no difference between *Chanahan*

COSMOGONY OF MOSES

24. A n d - h e-recovered, *Noah* f r o m-the-spirituous-delirium-his-o w n : and-h e-knew what had-done to-him the-little-one (the younger son).

24. Et-il-revint, *Noah* de l'exaltation-spiritueuse-sienne, et-il-connut ce qu'avait-fait à lui le petit (la moindre la dernière production).

25. And-he-said: cursed-be *Chanahan;* servant o f - servants he-s h a l l-be unto-the-brothers-his-own.

25. Et-il-dit : m a u d i t- soit *Chanahan*; serviteur des-serviteurs, il-s e r a aux-frères-siens.

26. And-he-said: blessed-be IHOAH, HE-the-Gods of-*Shem;* and-let-be-*Chanahan* servant toward-t h e-collection-of-him.

26. E t-i l-d i t : soit-béni- IHOAH, LUI-les-D i e u x de *S h e m;* et-qu'il-soit, *Chanahan*, serviteur envers-la-collection-sienne.

27. He-will-give extension, HE-the-Gods to Japheth, (w h a t is extended) who-shall-direct his-a b o d e in-the-tabernacles of-*Shem*: a n d-he-shall-be, *Chanahan*, a-servant to-t h e-collection-of-him.

27. Il-donnera-de-l'étendue, LUI-les-Dieux à-*Japheth* (ce qui est étendu) ; qui-dirigera sa-d e m e u r e d a n s-l e s-tabernacles d e - *Shem* : et-il-sera, *Chanahan*, serviteur d e - l a-collection-sienne.

---

and his father *Ham;* as this appears plainly, moreover, in the verses following, where *Noah* curses *Chanahan*, for a fault of which *Ham* alone is culpable toward him.

v. 25. These terms are clear.

v. 26. למו, *toward-the-collection-of-him*.... If Moses had written simply לו *his*, it would have indicated only that *Chanahan* would be subject to *Shem*; but in adding, by an ellipsis which has not been felt by his translators, the collective sign מ to the directive article ל, he has made understood, that it would be equally so to that which would emanate from *Shem*, to that which would be of the same nature, to that which would form the whole of his being.

28. Wa-îhî Noah âhar ha-mabboul shelosh mâôth shanah wa-hamishîm shanah.   וַיְחִי נֹחַ אַחַר הַמַּבּוּל שְׁלֹשׁ מֵאוֹת שָׁנָה וַחֲמִשִּׁים שָׁנָה :

29. Wa-îhîou chol-îemeî-Noah theshah mâôth shanah, wa-hamishîm shanah: wa-îamoth.   וַיִּהְיוּ כָּל־יְמֵי־נֹחַ תְּשַׁע מֵאוֹת שָׁנָה וַחֲמִשִּׁים שָׁנָה וַיָּמֹת :

---

v. 27. יפת, *he-will-give-extension*.... This verb taken from the same root as the name of *Japheth*, is very remarkable.

וישכן , *who-shall-direct-his-abode*...... It must be remembered that the abode of the ancient peoples to whom Moses makes allusion here, was transported from one country to another with the people itself, and was not so fixed as it became in time. The verb שכן expresses besides, a movement of usurpation, of taking possession; being formed from the root כון, governed by the sign of relative movement ש.

v. 28 and 29. These terms have been sufficiently explained in ch. V. That is to say, that the signification I give them here has been grammatically proved. The reader should not forget in running through these Notes, that grammatical proof has been my only pledge, and the only one I could possibly fulfill without entering into lengthy commentaries. In translating the Cosmogony of Moses, my purpose has been first, to make the sense of the words employed by this hierographic writer understood by following step by step the grammatical principles which I had set down in advance in restoring his tongue. As to what concerns his ideas and the *ensemble* of his doctrine, that is a different point. Moses, in enveloping it designedly with veils, has followed the method of the Egyptian priests among whom he had been brought up. This method has

---

COSMOGONY OF MOSES 271

28. And-he-lived *Noah*, after the-great-swelling, three-hundreds of-being's-revolving-change, and-five-tens of-revolution.

29. And-they-were all-the-days (manifested lights) of-*Noah*, nine-hundreds-of-revolving-change, and-five tens of-revolution; and-he-deceased.

28. Et-il-vécut, *N o a h*, après la-grande-intumescence, trois-centaines-de-mutation - ontologique-temporelle, et-cinq-décuples de-mutation.

29. Et-furent, tous-les-jours (les manifestations lumineuses) de-*N o a h*, neuf-centaines - de-mutation-temporelle et-cinq-décuples de-mutation; et-il-passa.

---

been from all time that of the theosophists. A work of this nature wherein the most vast and most complicated ideas are enclosed in a very small quantity of words, and being crowded, as it were, into the smallest space possible, has need of certain developments to be entirely comprehended. I have already promised to give these developments later on, doing for his doctrine what has been done for that of Pythagoras; and I shall give them if my labour is judged useful for the welfare of humanity. I shall not be able to enter at present into the discussions which they will necessarily involve, without injuring the clarity of my grammatical explanations already difficult enough in themselves. The reader no doubt will have remarked certain reticences in this respect, and perhaps he will have been shocked; but they were indispensable. I only beg him to believe that these reticences, in whatever manner they may be presented, have not been for the purpose of concealing any evil meaning, any meaning injurious to the doctrine of Moses, neither any which could call in question his dogmas upon the unity of God, the spirituality and immortality of the soul, nor shake in the slighest the profound veneration of this sacred writer for the Divinity.

SEPHER BERÆSHITH
I.

ספר בראשית י׃

1. W'ælleh thô-l e d o t h beneî-Noah Shem Ham wa-Japheth wa-îwaledou la-hem banîm ahar ha-mabboul.

וְאֵלֶּה תּוֹלְדֹת בְּנֵי־נֹחַ שֵׁם חָם וָיֶפֶת וַיִּוָּלְדוּ לָהֶם בָּנִים אַחַר הַמַּבּוּל ׃

This tenth chapter, belonging to a new order of things and presenting a geologic tableau quite different from that which precedes, I would refrain from translating, if I had not been forced, in order to terminate the Cosmogony, properly so-called, of which it is the complement. But not wishing to increase indefinitely these notes already very long, I refrain from all development and all comparison. The reader will feel very well, in examining the version of the Hellenists and that of Saint Jerome, into what interminable discussion, I would have been drawn; there is not a single word of this chapter which could not give rise to several volumes of commentaries; I am limited to presenting briefly the etymological proof of the meaning which I assign to the physical and metaphysical terms, of which the Hellenists, true to their method of materializing and restricting everything, have made so many proper names of individuals. I have said, and I think proved sufficiently, that *Noah* and the productions emanated from him, *Shem*, *Ham* and *Japheth*, ought not to be taken for men of blood, of flesh and bone: therefore I shall dispense with repeating and proving it again: assuming that an impartial reader will not hesitate to admit with me that these cosmogonic principles becoming developed, could not bring forth human individuals, but other geologic principles, such as I represent them. The concatenation of this doctrine would alone be sufficient proof, even if a mass of other proofs were not piled up beforehand, to give it the force of a mathematical demonstration.

I ought, however, to warn the reader, that in the exposition of a system of geology so extraordinary, placed in the midst of a mass of new ideas, the analogous words have often failed me in French as well as in English; and that instead of exaggerating the sense

COSMOGONY OF MOSES 273

GENESIS X.

1. Now-these-are the-symbolical-progenies of-the-isued-beings of-*Noah*: *Shem* (what is upright and bright), *Ham* (what is curved and heated) and *Japheth* (what is extended and wide): which-were-begotten through-them, issued-offspring after the-great-swelling (of waters).

COSMOGONIE X.

1. Or-celles-ci-sont les-caractéristiques-générations des-êtres-émanés-de-*Noah*: *Shem* (ce qui est direct et incliné et chaud), *Ham* (ce qui est incliné et chaud), et-*Japheth* (ce qui est étendu): lesquelles-furent-produites envers-eux, émanations d'après la-grande-intumescence (des eaux).

---

of the Hebraic expressions, as one will be tempted to believe I have done, I have, on the contrary, been obliged more than once to weaken them. However extraordinary my assertion may appear to modern savants, it is none the less true to say that the geologic sciences among the ancient Egyptians were more advanced in every way than among us. So that many of their ideas coming from certain principles which we lack, had enriched their tongue with metaphorical terms, whose analogues have not yet appeared in our European idioms. It is a thing that time and experience will demonstrate to those who might doubt, in proportion as their understanding develops; let them be occupied more with things than with words, and let them penetrate more and more into the depths which I have opened for them.

v. 1. These terms have been previously explained.

v. 2. גמר, *Gomer*.... This word is composed of the contracted roots גם־אר, one of which גם, contains every idea of accumulation, augmentation, complement; and the other, אר, is applied to elementary principle.

ומגוג, *and Magog*.... The root גוה, which expresses a movement being opposed to itself, indicates in the word גוג, an extension continued, elastic, pushed to its utmost limits. This word

2. Beneî-Japheth Gomer w-Magôg w-Madaî w'Jawan w-Thubal w-Mesheċh w-Thîrass. בְּנֵי־יֶפֶת גֹּמֶר וּמָגוֹג וּמָדַי וְיָוָן וְתֻבָל וּמֶשֶׁךְ וְתִירָס:

3. W-beneî Gomer Asheċhenaz w- Rîphath w-Thogarmah. וּבְנֵי גֹּמֶר אַשְׁכְּנַז וְרִיפַת וְתֹגַרְמָה:

---

governed by the sign of exterior action מ, characterizes that faculty of matter, by which it is extended and lengthened, without there being any solution of continuity.

וּמדי, *and-Madai*.... These are the two contracted roots מד־די, the one, expressing that which fills its measure, that which is commensurable; the other, that which abounds, which suffices.

ויון, *and-Jawan*.... I have given the history of this word, which I read *Ion*, in v. 18, ch. VIII.

ותבל, *and-Thubal*.... This word is composed of the well known root בל, governed by the sign of reciprocity ת.

ומשך, *and-Mesheċh*.... This word is composed of the root שך, developing every idea of perception, conception, speculation, governed by the sign of exterior and plastic action מ.

ותירס, *and-Thirass*.... The root תר contains every idea of determination given to element. It is a definition, a stable form in ראר; it is a disposition, a condition, a mode of being, in הור, or תיר; it is, in the word תרס, an impenetrable thing, a resistance, a persistence, an opposition.

COSMOGONY OF MOSES

2. T h e-issued-offspring of *Japheth* (that which is extended) (were): *Gomer* (elemental heap), and-*Magog* (elastic stretching power), and-*Madai* (mensurability, mensural indefinite capacity), and-*Ion* (generative ductileness), and-*Thubal* (diffusive motion), and-*Meshech* (perceptible cause), and-*Thirass* (modality, modal accident).

3. An d-t h e-issued-offspring of-*Gomer* (elemental heap) (were): *Ashechenaz* (latent fire), and-*Riphath* (rarity, centrifugal force), a n d-*Thogormah* (density, universal centripetal force).

2. L e s-productions-émanées d e *Japheth* (l'étendu) (furent): *Gomer* (la cumulation élémentaire), et-*Magog* (la faculté extensive, élastique), et-*Madai* (la faculté commensurable, celle de suffire toujours et de se diviser à l'infini), et-*Ion* (la ductilité generative), et-*Thubal* (la diffussion, le mélange), et-*Meshech* (la perceptibilité), et-*Thirass* (la modalité, la faculté de paraître sous une forme impassible).

3. E t - l e s-productions-émanées de *Gomer* (la cummulation élémentaire) (furent): *Aschechenaz* (le feu latent, le calorique), et *Riphath* (la rareté, cause de l'expansion), e t-*Thogormah* (la densité, cause de la centralisation universelle).

---

v. 3. אשכנז, *Ashechenaz*.... This extraordinary word comes from three roots. The first, אש, quite well known, designates the igneous principle; the second כן, characterizes that which serves as basis, as foundation; that which is gathered together, heaped up; and finally the third נז, expresses that which makes its influence felt in its vicinity. It was impossible to characterize better that which the modern physicists have named *caloric*.

ריפת, *Ripath*.... This is the same name as *Japheth* יפת governed by the sign of movement proper ר.

הגרמה, *Thogormah*.... This is the root הור, designating all giratory movement, all action which brings the being back upon

4. W-beneî Jawan Ælishah w-Tharshîsh Chithim w-Dodanîm.

וּבְנֵי יָוָן אֱלִישָׁה וְתַרְשִׁישׁ כִּתִּים וְדֹדָנִים׃

5. Me-ælleh nipheredou âieî ha-gôîm b'aretzoth'am: âîsh li-leshon-ô le-mishephehoth'am b'gôeîhem.

מֵאֵלֶּה נִפְרְדוּ אִיֵּי הַגּוֹיִם בְּאַרְצֹתָם אִישׁ לִלְשֹׁנוֹ לְמִשְׁפְּחֹתָם בְּגוֹיֵהֶם׃

---

itself and fixes it. This root is universalized by the collective sign ם, and governed by that of reciprocity ת. The compound גרם characterizes in general, that which is solid and hard, and in particular, the bones, the boney structure of the body.

v. 4. אלישה, *Ælishah*.... In this word, two contracted roots should be distinguished, אל-לוש: the first אל, designates a superior force: the second, לוש, an action which dilutes, kneads, and makes a compact thing ductile. The Chaldaic word אלושא, signifies *a multitude, a crowd*.

ותרשיש, *and Tharshish*... The root ראש is known to us as expressing *motive principle*. This root, of which the last character is doubled, marks an intense and mutual principiation, a separation among things of a divers nature.

כתים, *of-the-Chuthites*.... The root כות, develops every action of cutting off, of intrenching, of striking. The Chaldaic כת designates schism, schismatic, reprobate, damned, etc.

ודדנים, *and-the-Dodanites*.... Here it is the root דוד, expressing that which attracts, pleases and mutually suffices, whose expression is again increased by the addition of the extensive sign ן.

v. 5. איי הגוים, *the-propending-centres-of-reunion of-the-social-bodies*...... The Hellenists have seen here νῆσοι τῶν ἐθνῶν, *isles of the nations*. It can be clearly seen that this separation of the

COSMOGONY OF MOSES

4. And-the-issued-offspring of-*Ion* (generative ductileness) (were): *Ælishah* (diluent and kneading force), and-*Tharshish* (principiating principle) of-the-*Chuthites* (the cut off, the barbarous, the schismatic) and-of-the-*Dodanites* (the selected, the covenanters).

4. Et-les-productions-émanées de-*Ion* (la ductilité générative) (furent): *Ælishah* (la force délayante et pétrissante), et-*Tharshish* (le principe mutuel, intense) des-*Chuthéens* (les réprouvés, les barbares, les Scythes), et-des-*Dodanéens* (les élus, les civilisés, les confédérés).

5. Through-those were-moved-at-variance the-propending-centres-of-reunion of-the-social-bodies, in-the-earths-their-own; every-principle-acting after-the-particular-speech-his-own, toward-the-general-tribes, by-the-social-bodies-their-own.

5. Par-ceux-là furent-différenciés les-centres-de-volonté des-organisations-social, dans-les-terres-à-eux; chaque-principe-agissant selon-la-langue-particulière-sienne, envers-les-tribes-en-général, dans-les-organisa-tions-sociales-à-eux.

---

isles, understood literally, signifies nothing. These are not in fact isles which were divided; but the interests, the desires, the opinions, the inclinations, and ideas of the peoples who formed so many particular *régimes*. All this is contained in the word אי, used here in the constructive plural. I cannot dwell at this time upon one of the profoundest mysteries of the history of the earth: it may be that I shall have the occasion of coming back to it in another work.

איש, *every-principle-acting....* I have said enough concerning this word so that I can dispense with a long digression. The Hellenists have avoided it and have been careful not to show the difference of the nominal affix י which is connected here, with the other nominal affixes ם and הם, which concern the *Chuthites* and the *Dodanites* that is to say, the cut off and the elect, the rejected and the chosen, referred to in the preceding verse.

v. 6. כוש, *Choush....* This word can be understood as formed

6. W-beneî Ham Choush w-Mitzeraîm w-Phout w-Chenahan. וּבְנֵי חָם כּוּשׁ וּמִצְרַיִם וּפוּט וּכְנָעַן׃

7. W-beneî Choush Sçebâ wa-H'awîlah w-Sçabethah w-Rahemmah w-Sçabethechâ: w-beneî Rahemmah Shebâ w-Dedan. וּבְנֵי כוּשׁ סְבָא וַחֲוִילָה וְסַבְתָּה וְרַעְמָה וְסַבְתְּכָא וּבְנֵי רַעְמָה שְׁבָא וּדְדָן׃

---

of two contracted roots שׁ-כוה, *the elementary force of the igneous principle;* or as being derived from the single root אֻשׁ *fire*, governed by the assimilative sign כ. In either case its signification differs but little.

וּמִצְרַיִם, *and-Mitzeraim....* In this word one finds the root אר, which develops in general, all ideas of compression and oppression, particularized and made more intense by the sign of exterior action מ.

וּפוּט, *and-Phut....* This is a consequence of the action of *Ham*, which produces elementary combustion; producing also suffocation, that is to say, the smoke which suffocates, after having brought forth victorious forces which centralize. The word פוּט, formed of two contracted roots פוה-ט, signifies literally, *the cessation of breath*. It is understood in this sense by the Arabic فاط.

וּכְנַעַן, *and-Chanahan....* I have explained as much as possible, the hieroglyphic force of this word in v. 18, ch. IX.

v. 7. סְבָא, *Seba....* The root אב, which develops in general, all ideas of cause, inclination, determining movement and fructification, has served in a great many dialects to designate particularly, aqueous element, regarded as principle or vehicle of all natural production. In the above word this root is ruled by the sign of circular movement ס.

6. And-the-issued-offspring of-*Ham* (what is curved and hot) (were): *Chush* (igneous power, combustion), and-*Mitzeraim* (subduing, overcoming power, compressing bodies to their narrowest bounds), and-*Phut* (stifledness) and-*Chanahan* (material existence).

7. And-the-issued-offspring of-*Chush* (igneous power) (were): *Seba* (radical moisture, sap), and-*Hawilah* (striving energy), and-*Sabethah* (determinative motion), and-*Rahamah* (thunder) and-*Sabethecha* (determined motion): and-the-issued-offspring of-*Rahamah* (thunder) (were): *Sheba* (restoring rest), and -*Dedan* (selective affinity).

6. Et-les-productions émanées de-*Ham* (ce qui est incliné et chaud) (furent): *Choush* (la force ignée la combustion), et-*Mitzeraim* (les forces subjuguantes, victorieuses opprimantes), et-*Phout* (la suffocation, ce qui asphyxie) et-*Chanahan* (l'existence physique).

7. Et-les-productions-émanées de *Choush* (la force ignée) (furent): *Seba* (l'humide radical, la sève, cause de la sapidité), et-*Hawilah* (la travail énergique), et-*Sabethah* (la cause déterminante), et-*Rahammah* (le tonnerre), et-*Sabethecha* (la cause determinée, l'effect): et-les-productions-émanées de-*Rahammah* (le tonnerre) (furent): *Sheba* (le retour au repos), et-*Dedan* (l'affinité élective).

וחוילה, *and-Hawilah*.... I have already had occasion to speak of this word in v. 11, ch. II. Only it must be considered that the energetic effort which it expresses as derivative of the root חול or חיל, being influenced by the generation of *Ham*, bears a character of violence, of suffering, that it did not have then.

וסבתה, *and-Sabethah* .... This word comes from the two roots סב־תה: in the one, resides the occasional, determining force, *cause;* in the other, the sympathetic reason, the determined force, *effect*.

ורעמה, *and-Rahamah*.... The root רעו, which indicates literally every rupture of order, every fraction, being generalized by

8. W-Choush îaled æth-Nimerod houâ hehel li-heî-ôth ghibor ba-âretz.

וְכוּשׁ יָלַד אֶת־נִמְרֹד הוּא הֵחֵל לִהְיוֹת גִּבֹּר בָּאָרֶץ :

9. Houâ- haîah ghibor-tzaîr li-pheneî IHÔAH: hal-chen îeamar che-Nimerod ghibor tzaîr li-pheneî IHÔAH.

הוּא־הָיָה גִבֹּר־צַיִד לִפְנֵי יְהוָה עַל־כֵּן יֵאָמַר כְּנִמְרֹד גִּבּוֹר צַיִד לִפְנֵי יְהוָה :

---

the final sign ם, expresses in a manner as energetic as picturesque and wise, the cause and effect of the lightning.

וסבתכא, *and-Sabethecha*.... The root סב, which as we have seen, indicates always, an occasional movement, is linked by means of the constructive, sympathetic sign ת, with the root ךה, which characterizes, the effect which follows every cause. The effect here is an enchaining, an extreme oppression, an infernal pain, a damnation. I pray the reader to reflect a moment upon this signification.

שבא, *Sheba*.... Now as we know, the root שב is always the emblem of restitution, and of return to an original state. This root, being united on this occasion to the root בא, which contains every idea of passing from one place to another, and being presented as an effect of thunder, can here lead to the idea of electric repulsion.

ודדן, *and-Dedan*.... One can in the same manner, consider this word as an emblem of electric attraction since it is found in the root דוד, which characterizes that which pleases, attracts and mutually suffices, united by contraction to the root דן, which expresses every chemical *parting*, every judgment brought to bear upon contentious things.

v. 8. נמרד, *Nimerod*.... The verb מרוד, of which this is here the continued facultative, passive movement, signifies literally *to give over to one's own impulse, to shake off every kind of yoke, to*

COSMOGONY OF MOSES

8. A n d-*Chush* (igneous power) begat *Nimerod* (self ruling will, arbitrary sway, a pregnant cause of revolt, anarchy, despotism, and of any power prone to follow its own v i o l e n t self impulse), h e-w h o strove for-being-the-high-lord i n-t h e-earth.

9. H e-w h o-was a-most-lordly-oppugner before-the-face of-IHOAH: wherefore it-was-said: e v e n-as-*Nimerod* (self ruling will), a-most lordly-oppugner before-the-face of-IHOAH.

8. Et-*Choush* (la force ignée) enfanta *Nimerod* (le principe de la volonté desordonée, principe de rébellion, d'anarchie, de despotisme, de t o u t e puissance n' obéissant qu'à sa propre impulsion) : lui-qui fit-des-efforts-violens p o u r-être le-dominateur (le héros, l'hyperboréen) sur-la-terre.

9. Lui-qui-fut le superbe-principe-de-tout-ce-qui-e s t - adverse (opposé à l'ordre) à-la-face de-I H O A H : sur-quoi ce-proverbe: semblable-à-*Nimerod* (le principe d e l a volonté arbitraire). ce-superbe adversaire à-la-face de-IHOAH.

---

behave arbitrarily. It is formed from the root רר, which develops every idea of movement, proper and persevering, good or evil, ruled by the sign of exterior action מ.

I am not considering the version of the Hellenists, wherein this anarchical principle is transformed into a *mighty hunter:* γίγας κυνηγός, because I should have too much to do, as I have said, if obliged to mention all of the errors which are woven into this chapter.

v. 9. The kind of proverb inserted in this verse could very well be a marginal note passed into the text.

v. 10. בבל *Babel....* The root בל which expresses an extraordinary dilation, a swelling, is taken here in the bad sense, and depicts the effect of vanity. The resemblance of this name to that of Babylon, appears to excuse here, the version of the Hellenists who have placed in this city the origin of the empire of their pretended giant: but it would be sufficient to read attentively this verse alone, to see that the word בבל is not applicable to a city, even if the whole development of the chapter did not compel giving it another sense.

10. Wa-thehî, reâshith mamelacheth-ô Babel w' Arech w'Achad, w'Chalneh b'âretz Shinhar.

וַתְּהִי רֵאשִׁית מַמְלַכְתּוֹ בָּבֶל וְאֶרֶךְ וְאַכַּד וְכַלְנֵה בְּאֶרֶץ שִׁנְעָר׃

11. Min-ha-âretz ha-hiwa îatzâ Asshour wa-îben æth-Ninweh w'æth-rehoboth hir wæth-Chalah.

מִן־הָאָרֶץ הַהִוא יָצָא אַשּׁוּר וַיִּבֶן אֶת־נִינְוֵה וְאֶת־רְחֹבֹת עִיר וְאֶת־כָּלַח׃

וארך, and-Arech.... I have spoken more than once of the root רך or רק, whose effect is to depict the relaxation, the dissolution of things, literally as well as figuratively.

ואכד, and-Achad...... Two contracted roots compose this word: אך־כד. They depict energetically that sort of sentiment the result of which is, that each is excepted from the general law, flees from it, acts for his own part. The word אכד, signifies properly *a particle, a spark.*

וכלנה, and-Chalneh.... That is to say, according to the hieroglyphic sense: the concentration of the whole in the individual self. This is the root כל *all,* to which is joined the emphatic, nominal affix נה.

שנער, Shinar.... We already know that the root שן contains every idea of mutation, variation and change; now, the root ער, which is joined to it, indicates at the same time, both the vehemence which excites, and the city in which this change takes place. It was impossible to create a happier word for depicting a civil revolution.

v. 11. אשור, Asshour.... Causing order to come out from the heart of disorder, and the principle of legitimate government from the midst of revolutionary anarchy, is a trait of genius which astonishes, even after all that has been seen. I dispense with inviting the reader to reflect; he will be inclined enough to reflection both by the memory of the past and by the image of the present. Still if glancing in turn upon my version and upon that of the Hel-

10. And-such-was the-rise of-the-kingly-power-his own, *Babel* (empty pride), and-*Arech* (slackness), and-*Achad* (selfishness), and-*Chaleneh* (all engrossing desire) in-the-earth of-*Shinhar* (civil revolution).

11. From-that-earth, itself, issued *Asshour* (right and lawful sway, source of happiness and grandeur) which-founded the selfsameness of-*Ninweh* (the growing strong, youth breeding out) and-what-relates-to-public-establishments at-home, and-what-relates-to-*Chalah* (the growing wise, old men ruling within).

10. Et-telle-fut l'origine du règne-sien, *Babel* (la vanité), et-*Arech* (la mollesse), et-*Achad* (l'isolement, l'égoïsme), et-*Chaleneh* (l' ambition, l'envahissement), dans-la-terre de-*Shinhar* (la revolution civile.

11. Hors-de-cette-terre elle-même, sortit-*Asshour* (le principe harmonique, le principe éclairé du gouvernement, l'ordre, le bonheur, résultant de l'observation des lois), lequel-établit ce-qui-concerne-*Ninweh* (l'accroissement extérieur, l'éducation de-la jeunesse) et-ce-qui-concerne-les-institutions de-la-cité, et-ce-qui-concerne-*Chalah* (le perfectionement intérieur, le rassemblement des vieillards, le sénat).

---

lenists, he is startled at the depths into which the hierographic writer draws him, he will clearly feel why the Essenes, learned in these mysteries, have taken such pains to conceal them.

את־נינוה, *the-selfsameness of Ninweh....* Two contracted roots compose this word. The first, נון, presents in general the idea of extension, enlargement, propagation: בן signifies properly *a son.* The second, נוה, designates an habitation, a colonization.

Moses who has skilfully profited by the name of *Babel*, taken in a bad sense, to make the principle of insubordination and of anarchy go forth, now avails himself of the name of *Ninweh*, to establish the principle of order and of legitimate government. It is thus, that in the course of this chapter, certain names of peoples and of cities, are

12. W'aeth-Ressen beîn Ninweh w-beîn Chalah hiwa ha-Whir ha-ghedolah. וְאֶת־רֶסֶן בֵּין נִינְוֵה וּבֵין כָּלַח הוּא הָעִיר הַגְּדֹלָה׃

13. W - Mitzeraîm îalad æth-Loudîm wæth - Whonanîm w æth-Le-habîm w'æth-Naphethuhîm. וּמִצְרַיִם יָלַד אֶת־לוּדִים וְאֶת־עֲנָמִים וְאֶת־לְהָבִים וְאֶת־נַפְתֻּחִים׃

---

taken in the same spirit and used according to their hieroglyphic expressions. In the primitive tongues, the rarity of words and the impossibility of drawing from neighbouring idioms, forced, as I have already stated, attaching to them a great number of significations.

ואת־כלח, *and-what-relates-to-Chalah*.... The root כל which recalls all ideas of complement and integrity, expresses in the radical verb כול, the action of seizing, of holding a thing together, of bringing it to perfection. The root את, which depicts a state of equilibrium and equality, being joined to it by contraction, forms with it the word כלח, which signifies literally, *an ancient, an old man*, that is to say, a man whom age and experience have led to perfection. Thence, by extension, the idea of a senate, of an assembly of old men, of a wise and conservative institution.

v. 12. ואת־רסן, *and-what-relates-to-Ressen*.... It is difficult to say whether the word רסן is the real name of a city as בבל and נינוה, or not; but, in any case, it cannot be denied that it may be used here in its grammatical acceptation, with admirable precision.

v. 13. את־לודים, *the-existence-of-the-Ludites*.... This root אר indicating every emanation, which, governed by the sign of directive movement ל, forms the word לוד, in general, *an emanation, a propagation*: in particular, *an emanated individual, an infant*. Thence, the compound radical verb ילד, *to generate, to produce, to bring forth*, etc.

COSMOGONY OF MOSES

12. And-what-relates-to-*Ressen* (the state's holding reins) b e t w e e n - *Ninweh* (youth breeding out), and-*C h a l a h* (old men ruling in) : and-it-was a-civil-safeguard most-great.

13. A n d-*M i t z e r a i m* (overcoming power) begat the-selfsameness of-the-*Ludites* (pregnancies), a n d-t h a t - o f-t h e-*Whonamites* (material heaviness), and-that-of-the-*Lehabites* (blazing exhalations), and-that-of-t h e-*Naphethuhites* (hollowed caverns).

12. Et-c e-q u i-concerne-*Ressen* (les r ê n e s du government) e n t r e - *Ninweh* (l' accroissement extérieur, la colonisation), et-*Chalah* (le perfectionnement intérieur, le sénat) : et-elle-était (cette institution centrale) une-sauve-garde-civile très-grande.

13. Et-*Mitzeraim* (l e s forces subjuguantes) produisit l'existence d e s-*Ludéens* (les propagations), et-celle-des-*Whonaméens* (l e s appesantissements matériels) et-celle-des-Lehabéens (l e s exhalaisons enflammées), etcelle-des-*Naphethuhéens* (les cavernosités).

ואת־ענמים, *and-that-of-the Whonamites*.... This is the root עון of which I have said enough, which is found generalized by the final collective sign ם.

ואת־להבים, *and-that-of-the Lehabites*.... The word להב comes from the root הב or הוּג which, designating in general, every kind of uprising, is united to the sign of directive movement ל, to depict the effect of flame.

ואת־נפתחים, *and-that-of-the-Naphethuhites*.... The verb פתוח which signifies *to crack, to split, to swell up*, etc., is used here in the continued facultative, passive movement, plural.

v. 14. ואת־פתרסים, *and-that-of-the-Patherussites*.... The root רס, which contains all ideas of break, rupture, ruin, reduction into impalpable parts, is presented in this instance, preceded by the root פת which has been used in the preceding word.

ואת־כסלחים, *and-that-of-the-Chasseluthites*.... The verb סלוח

14. W'æth-Phatherussîm w'æth Chasseluhîm a s h e r îatzâou mi-sham Phelishethîm w'æth-Chaphethorîm.   וְאֶת־פַּתְרֻסִים וְאֶת־כַּסְלֻחִים אֲשֶׁר יָצְאוּ מִשָּׁם פְּלִשְׁתִּים וְאֶת־כַּפְתֹּרִים׃

15. W-Chenahan î a l a d æth-Tzîdon bechor-ô w'æth-Heth.   וּכְנַעַן יָלַד אֶת־צִידֹן בְּכֹרוֹ וְאֶת־חֵת׃

16. W'æth - h a-Jeboussî w'æth-ha-Æmorî w'æth - ha-Ghirashî.   וְאֶת־הַיְבוּסִי וְאֶת־הָאֱמֹרִי וְאֶת־הַגִּרְגָּשִׁי׃

---

expresses the action of absolving sins. It is used as finished facultative, plural, with the assimilative article כ.

פלשתים, *the-Phelishethites*.... The verb פלשׁ expresses the action of dispersing, of throwing to the winds, and also of wandering. It has the emphatic article ה changed to ת to form the plural facultative.

ואת־כפתרים, *and-the-Chaphethorites*.... The root הוּר which develops all ideas of tour, circuit, version, conversion, united to the sign פ, forms the derivative verb פתור, which signifies literally, to turn one tongue into another, to translate, to make a version; and figuratively, to change the life, to be converted, to pass from one belief to another, etc.

v. 15. את־צדן, *the-selfsameness-of-Tzidon*.... One finds the root of this word in צד, which contains the idea of that which shows itself opposed, as adversary, enemy; that which uses perfidious, insidious means to surprise, to deceive, to seduce, etc. The analogous word ציר, develops every opposition which proceeds from force; as ציד, every opposition which comes from ruse. The first depicts war,

14. And-that-of-the-*Patherussites* (b r o k e n out in crowds), and-that-of-the-*Chasseluthites* (t r i e d for atonement): f r o m - which-issued-forth the-*Phelishethites* (s l i g h t e d), and-the-*Chaphethorites* (converts).

15. And-*Chanahan* (material existence) generated the-selfsameness o f-*Tzidon* (ensnaring foe): first-born-his-o w n, and-that-of-*Heth* (dispirited amazement).

16. And-t h a t-of-the-*Jebussites* (inward crushing), a n d-that-of-t h e - *Æmorites* (outward wringing), and-that-of-the *Girgashites* (chewing and chewing over and over).

14. Et-celle-d e s *Patherusséens* (les fractures infinies), et-celle-des-Chasseluthéens (les épreuves expiatoires): de-qui sortirent de-la-même, l e s - *Phelishethéens* (les égarés, les infidèles), e t-les-*Chaphethoréens* (les convertis, les fidèles).

15. Et-*Chanahan* (l'existence physique) produisit l' existence-de-*Tzidon* (l' insidieux adversaire); premier-né-sien, et-celle-de-*Heth* (l' abattement, la fatigue).

16. Et-celle-d e s-*Jebousséens* (les refoulemens intérieurs), et-celle-des-*Æmoréens* (les exprimations extérieures), et-celle-des-*Girgashéens* (les remâchemens réitérés).

---

conquests, the glory of arms; the other, hunting, fishing, the gain and industry of commerce.

ואת־חת, *and-that-of-Heth*.... This is the reaction of a useless effort, it is elementary existence sharply driven back upon itself: such is the expression of the root חת.

v. 16. ואת־היבוסי, *and-that-of-theJebussites*.... The compound radical verb יבוס, *to tread upon, to crush with the foot*, comes from the root בוס, which characterizes that sort of pressure by means of which one treads upon and crushes a thing to extract liquid and radical moisture.

ואת־האמרי, *and-that-of-the-Æmorites*.... I have given the etymology of this verb אמור several times.

ואת־הגרגשי, *and-that-of-the-Girgashites*.... The two distinct roots

17. W'æth-ha-H i w î w' æth-ha-Harkî w'æth-ha-Sçînî.   וְאֶת־הַחִוִּי וְאֶת־הָעַרְקִי וְאֶת־הַסִּינִי:

18. W'æth-ha-Arwadî w' æth-ha-Tzemarî w'æth-ha-Hamathî: w'ahar na-photzou mishephehôth ha-Čhenahanî.   וְאֶת־הָאַרְוָדִי וְאֶת־הַצְּמָרִי וְאֶת־הַחֲמָתִי וְאַחַר נָפֹצוּ מִשְׁפְּחוֹת הַכְּנַעֲנִי:

---

of which this word is composed, are גר, which designates all giratory movement executed upon itself, all chewing, all continued action; and גש, which expresses the effect of things which are brought together, which touch, which contract; so that the meaning attached to the word גרגש, appears to be a sort of chewing over and over, of doing over again, of rumination, of continued contractile labour.

    v. 17. ואת החוי, *and-that-of-the-Hiwites....* The absolute verb הוה, receiving the sign of potential manifestation in place of the convertible sign, becomes the symbol of universal life היה: but if the first character of this important word degenerates, and is changed into that of elementary existence, it expresses in חיה only natural, animal, bestial life: if it degenerated again still further, and if it received the sign of material sense, it would finally become the symbol of absolute material life in עיה. The word referred to in this note is a plural facultative of the verb חיה, *to live.*

    ואת־הערקי, *and-that-of-the Warkites....* The word ערקי which signifies literally, *the nerves*, expresses figuratively, the force and energy which result therefrom.

    ואת־הסיני, *and-that-of-the-Sinites....* The root סן, which, in a restricted sense is limited to characterizing the colour red, develops, figuratively, every idea of hateful passion, animadversion, rage, combat, etc. It is well known what horror the Egyptians had for the colour red.

    v. 18. ואת־האחרודי, *and-that-of-the-Awardites....* The com-

17. And that-of-the-*Hiwites* (animal lives), and-that-of-the-*Wharkites* (brutish appetites), and-that-of-the-*Sinites* (hateful and bloody disposition).

17. Et-celle-des-*Hiwéens* (les vies animales), et-celle-des-*Wharkéens* (les passions brutales), et-celle-des-*Sinéens* (les passions haineuses).

18. And-that-of-the-*Arwadites* (plundering desire), and that-of-the-*Tzemarites* (hankering for power), and-that-of-the-*Hamathites* (most violent craving): and-after-ward were-scattered the-tribes of-the-*Chanahanites* (material existing).

18. Et-celle-des-*Arwadéens* (les ardeurs du butin), et-celle-des-*Tzemaréens* (la soif du pouvoir) et-celle-des-*Hamathéens* (les desirs insatiables) : et-ensuite furent-dispersées les-tribus des-*Chenahanéens* (les existences physiques).

---

pound ארור, comes from the two contracted roots אר־אור by the first, אר, become ארה, is understood, an ardent desire to draw, to acquire, to gather; by the second, אור, things in general, the riches which one desires to possess.

ואת־הצמרי, *and-that-of-the-Tzemarites*.... The compound צמר comes equally from the two contracted roots צם־מר : of which the one, צם, designates literally *thirst;* and the other, מר, is well known to us as containing all ideas of extension and of domination.

ואת־החמתי, *and-that-of-the-Hamathites*.... This is the root חם taken in the sense of a covetous ardour, unceasingly excited, whose expression is still increased by the addition of the emphatic article ה changed to ת to form the plural.

v. 19. באכה, *by-dint-of*.... This is the root אך invested with the emphatic article ה, and ruled by the mediative article ב.

גררה, *inward-wringing*.... The duplication of the character ר, and the addition of the emphatic article in the root גר, increases considerably its energy. It is a sort of inward trituration exercised upon itself.

ער־עזה, *unto-stiffness*.... I have spoken of the root עז in v. 18, ch. II.

19. Wa-îhî, gheboul ha-Chenahanî mi-Tzîdon b' âchah gherarah! had-hazah! h'âchah sedomah! wa-hamorah! w'âdmah! w'tzabîm had-lashah.

וַיְהִי גְּבוּל הַכְּנַעֲנִי מִצִּידֹן כְּאֲכָה גְרָרָה עַד־עַזָּה בֹּאֲכָה סְדֹמָה וַעֲמֹרָה וְאַדְמָה וּצְבֹיִם עַד־לָשַׁע׃

20. Ælleh beneî-Ham l' mishephehoth-am li-leshonoth-am b'âretz-oth-am b' gôie-hem.

אֵלֶּה בְנֵי־חָם לְמִשְׁפְּחֹתָם לִלְשֹׁנֹתָם בְּאַרְצֹתָם בְּגוֹיֵהֶם׃

21. W-le-Shem îullad gam-houâ âbî chol-beneî-heber âhî Japheth ha-gadôl.

וּלְשֵׁם יֻלַּד גַּם־הוּא אֲבִי כָּל־בְּנֵי־עֵבֶר אֲחִי יֶפֶת הַגָּדוֹל׃

סרמה, *hidden-wiles*.... Two contracted roots compose the word here referred to. By the first, סור, is understood, a thing closed carefully, melted one in the other; thence, the French word *souder*: by the second, רום, a surd, silent thing; thence, *dumb*.

ועמרה, *and-overbearing*.... The verb אמר expresses the action of dominating with force, of oppressing. This is the verb אמר, *to declare his will, to manifest his power, to speak*, whose initial character א is changed into that of material sense ע.

ואדמה, *and-unmercifulness*.... It is necessary to guard against confusing this word with that which designates the homogeneous element: this one depends upon the root רום, of which I have spoken and which characterizes that which is mute, deaf, insensible as the tomb, inexorable, etc.

COSMOGONY OF MOSES 291

19. And-there-was t h e-utmost-bounds of-the-*Chenahanites* (material existing) through-*Tzidon* (ensnaring foe) by-dint-of i n w a r d - wringing unto-stiffness: by-dint-of hidden-wiles a n d- overbearing a n d - unmercifulness, a n d-w a r-waging, unto-the-swallowing-up (of riches).

20. These-are the-issued-offspring-of-*Ham*, after-the-tribes-their-o w n, after-the-particular-speeches-of-them, in-the-lands-of-them; in-the-organic-bodies-their-own.

21. A n d-through-*Shem*, d i d-it-become also, he-was t h e-father of-all-offspring-ultramundane, t h e-brother of-*Japheth*, the-great.

19. Et-telle-f u t-l'extension-t o t a l e des-*Chenahanéens* (les existences physiques) par-le-m o y e n-de la-ruse, à-force-de contraction-intestine, j u s q u'à-l'affermissement: à-f o r c e-de détours-obscurs et-de-tyrannie et-d'insensibilité, et-de-guerres, j u s q u' à-l'engloutissement (des richesses).

20. Tels-sont les-enfans de-*H a m*, selon-les-tribus-à-eux, selon-les-langues-à-eux, dans-les-terres-à-eux, dans-l e s-organisations-universelles-à-eux.

21. Et-envers-*Shem*, il-fut-engendré aussi, lui-qui-fut le-père-de-toutes-les-productions-ultra-terrestres, le-frère de-*Japheth*, le-grand.

וּצְבִים, *and-war-waging*.... The root צָב is affected in general, by all ideas of rules given to a troop, an army, a multitude marching *en corps*.

עַד־לְשַׁע, *unto-the-swallowing-up-of-riches*.... The word referred to here is remarkable in its hieroglyphic form. Of the two roots from which it comes, the one לוּע, designates properly *a yawning jaw;* the other שַׁע, *cement*, that is to say, gold and silver considered as *finance*, as political *cement* of states.

v. 20 and 21. All these terms have been explained.

v. 22. עֵילָם, *Wheilan*.... This is the word עוֹלָם of which I

22. Beneî Shem Wheî‑lam w'Asshour w'A r p h a‑cheshad w'Loud wa‑Aram. בְּנֵי שֵׁם עֵילָם וְאַשּׁוּר וְאַרְפַּכְשַׁד וְלוּד וַאֲרָם:

23. W‑beneî‑Aram Houtz w' Houl w‑G h e t h e r wa‑Mash. וּבְנֵי־אֲרָם עוּץ וְחוּל וְגֶתֶר וָמַשׁ:

have often spoken, in which the convertible sign is replaced by that of potential manifestation and of eternity of time.

אשׁוּר, *Asshour*.... This word which is already found in v. 11. of this chapter, receives in this one a new force, by the influence of the generation of Shem to which Moses made him belong. It comes from the root אוֹר, *light*, which being joined to the sign of relative movement שׁ, forms the word שׁוּר, containing every idea of luminous direction, of pure conduct, of order, of harmony, of enlightened government; this word which takes again the sign of stability and power א, forms the one of which we are speaking אשׁוּר; by which should be understood prosperity, welfare, glory, blessing, and that which flows from immutable order and harmony.

וארף־כשׁר, *and Arpha-cheshad*.... The two words that I separate here, are joined in the original; but this conjunction appears to have been the consequence of a mistake of a copyist anterior to Esdras. The first word, ארף, comes from the root רף, which develops all ideas of mediative, remedial, restorative, curative cause. United to the sign of stability and power א, it has formed that name, famous in all the ancient mythologies, written ʼΟρφεύs by the Greeks, and by us, *Orpheus*. The second word, כשׁר, nearly as famous, since it was the favourite epithet of the Chaldeans, is derived from the root שׁר, applied to providential power, to productive nat‑

22. The-issued-offspring of-*Shem* (that which is upright and bright) (were): *Wheilam* (everlasting time, eternity), and-*Asshur* (right and lawful sway, immutable o r d e r, holiness, felicity), and-*Arpha-cheshad* (restorer of providential n a t u r e), a n d-*Lud* (generative power), and-*A r a m* (universal elementizing).

23. A n d-the-issued-offspring of-*Aram* (universal elementizing) (w e r e) : *W h u t z* (substantiation), and-*Hul* (virtual striving), and-*Gether* (plenteous pressing), and-*M a s h* (harvest, reaped fruits).

22. Les-productions-émanées de-*Shem* (ce qui est élevé et brillant) (furent): *Wheilam* (la durée infinie, l'éternité), et-*Asshour* (le pouvoir légal, l'ordre immuable, l'harmonie, la béatitude) et-*Arpha-cheshad* (le principe médiateur d e l a nature providentielle), et-*Loud,* (la propagation), et-*Aram* (l'élémentisation universelle).

23. E t-l e s-productions-émanées d'*Aram* (l'élémentisation universelle) (furent): *Whoutz* (la substantiation), et-*Houl* (le travail virtuel),׳ et-*Gether* (la pression abondante), et-*M a s h* (la récolte d e s fruits, la moisson).

---

ure. Thence, the name, given to GOD Himself, שרי, *Providence*. In this instance this root שר, is inflected by the assimilative article כ.

ולוד, *and-Lud....* This word was explained in v. 13 of this chapter.

וארם, *and-Aram....* This is the elementary root אר of which I have frequently spoken, which is universalized by the final collective sign ם.

v. 23. עוץ *Whutz....* Here is the famous root עץ, *substance*, verbalized by the convertible sign ו.

וחול, *and-Houl....* It is useless to repeat all that I have said upon the subject of this root, whose purpose is to depict the effort of Nature in travail.

וגתר, *and-Gether....* This hieroglyphic word comes from two contracted roots: the first גת, designates literally *pressure;* the second, תר, the *abundance* which results.

24. W'Arpha cheshad îalad æth- Shallah w-Shelah îalad æth-Heber.

וְאַרְפַּכְשַׁד יָלַד אֶת־שָׁלַח וְשֶׁלַח יָלַד אֶת־עֵבֶר :

25. W-l' Heber îullad shenî banîm shem ha-æhad Pheleg chi b'îamaî-ô niphelegah ha-âretz w-shem âhî-ô Jaktan.

וּלְעֵבֶר יֻלַּד שְׁנֵי בָנִים שֵׁם הָאֶחָד פֶּלֶג כִּי בְיָמָיו נִפְלְגָה הָאָרֶץ וְשֵׁם אָחִיו יָקְטָן :

וּמָשׁ, and-Mash.... That is to say, the *harvest of fruits*, necessary result of corporeity, of substantiation, of virtual effort, and of the *abundance* brought about by pressure.

v. 24. אֶת־שָׁלַח, *that-of-Shelah*.... That is to say, *the luminous flash, the ray; inspiration, divine grace*: for this word, chosen with great art by the hierographic writer, rests upon the two contracted roots של־לח, the first of which של, is particularly assigned to the idea of a line drawn from one place to another, a stroke; and the second לח, designates inherent power, vigour, projecting force.

אֶת־עֵבֶר, *that-of-Wheber*.... The word עבר, whose literal acceptation is, that which passes further, which is beyond, receives from the generation of Shem a figurative sense, relative to the intellectual world, toward which the effort of this generation is carried.

v. 25. פֶּלֶג, *Pheleg*.... In v. 4. ch. VI. I have stated that the root פַּל, developed invariably, the idea of a thing set apart, distinguished, raised above the others. This root, whose effort is again increased by the addition of the root לג, applied to the measure of extent, expresses here a moral distinction, a separation, a classification among beings of a different nature.

Although I have avoided making observations upon this chapter, wishing to leave to the sagacity of the reader the task of drawing from the magnificent tableau which it presents, inductions and consequences, I cannot however refrain from remarking, as a thing

COSMOGONY OF MOSES 295

24. And-*Arpha-cheshad* (providential re s t o r i n g cause) begot the-selfsameness of-*Shelah* (a c t u a l emission, efficacious grace) : and-*Shelah* (divine, efficacious emission) begat that-of-*Wheber* (ultra-mundane).

25. And-toward-*Wheber* (ultra-mundane) was-it-begotten two-offspring: the-name of-one was-*P h e l e g* (selection, separation), for by-the-days-his-own was-separated (divided in selected speeches) the-earth: a n d-the-name of-the-brother-his-own was-*J a k t a n* (lessening) (of evil).

24. E t - *Arpha - cheshad* (le principe médiateur providentiel) produisit-l'existence-d e-*Shelah* (l'émission active, la grâce divine, efficace) : et-*S h e l a h* (l'émission, la grâce divine) produisit celle-de-*Wheber* (c e qui est ultra-terrestre, audelà de ce monde).

25. Et-envers-*W h e b e r* (ce qui est ultra-terrestre) il-fut-engendré d e u x enfans: le-nom de-l'un-était *Pheleg* (l'élection, la-dialection), à-cause que-dans-les-jours-siens f u t-dialectisée (divisée en dialectes) le-terre: et-le-nom du-frère-sien fut-*Jaktan* (l'atténuation) (du mal).

---

which merits highest attention, that there exist in the three different generations set forth by Moses, three causes of division which are inherent in them, and which issue from three different principles. In the generation of *Japheth*, which symbolizes the extent, the cause of division is the generative principle; in that of *Ham*, which represents that which is curved and hot, this cause is thunder, for the purely physical part, and expiatory experiences, for the moral part; in that of *Shem*, finally, which is upright and bright, this cause is the providential mediative principle itself, which generating divine grace, produces that which is ultra-terrestrial and gives place to separation and to the attenuation of evil.

יקטן, *Jaktan*.... The word קטן, which signifies that which is small, thin, slight, has received in this instance the initial adjunction י, which gives it a verbal force. It is, moreover, modified favourably by the influence of the generation of *Shem*.

26. W'Jaktan îalad æth-Almôdad w'æth-Shaleph w' æth-Hâtzar-maweth w'æth-Jarah.   יָלַד אֶת־אַלְמוֹדָד וְאֶת־ וְאֶת־הַצַּרְמָוֶת וְאֶת־יָרַח ׃

27. W'æth-Hadôram w' æth-Aouzal w'æth-Dikelah.   וְאֶת־הֲדוֹרָם וְאֶת־אוּזָל וְאֶת־דִּקְלָה ׃

28. W'æth-Hobal w'æth-Abi-mâel w'æth-Shebâ.   וְאֶת־עוֹבָל וְאֶת־אֲבִימָאֵל וְאֶת־שְׁבָא ׃

---

v. 26. את־אלמודד, *the-selfsameness-of-Almodad*.... One must distinguish here two united words. By the first, אל, should be understood a divine force; by the second, מודד, an action by means of which every thing attains its measure and fills it.

ואת שלף, *and-that-of-Shaleph*.... The word שלף recalls that of שלח referred to in v. 24 of this chapter. It is the reaction of the action expressed by this one; so that in admitting that שלח characterizes a virtual emission, as that of light or grace, for example, שלף will be its concomitant reflective emission: for the root לף added to that of של, *the luminous flash*, is applied to its reflection or to its return unto itself.

ואת־הצר־מות, *and-that-of-Hotzar-moth*.... The two united words which I separate here are worthy of remark. The first הצר designates a scission operated upon a thing, and by means of which that thing is found constituting several distinct parts. It is composed of the root הץ, applied to every idea of cutting, of division, of scission, joined by contraction to the root צר, applied on the contrary, to every idea of pressure, of compaction, of formation. The second

26. And-*Jaktan* (lessening) begat the-selfsameness-of-*Almodad* (divine probatory mensuration) and-that-of-*Shaleph* (reflected emission) and-that-of-*Hotzarmoth* (scission performed by death); and-that-of-*Iarah* (brotherly sparkling show; the moon).

27. And-that-of *Hadoram* (universal brightness), and-that-of-*Awzal* (godlike purified fire), and-that-of-*Dikelah* (ethereal sounding rarefaction).

28. And-that-of-*Whobal* infinite orbicular diffusing), and-that-of-*Abimael* (absolute fullness) and-that-of-*Sheba* (rest restoring).

26. Et-*Jaktan* (l'atténuation) produisit l'existence-d'*Almodad* (la mensuration probatoire et divine), et-celle-de-*Shaleph* (l'émission réfléchie) et-celle-de-*Hotzar-moth* (la scission opérée par la mort) et-celle-d'*Iarah* (la manifestation radieuse, fraternelle; la lune.)

27. Et-celle-d'*Hadoram* (la splendeur universelle), et-celle-d'*Auzal* (le feu épuré et divin) et-celle-de-*Dikelah* (la raréfaction éthérée et sonore).

28. Et-celle-de-*Whobal* (l'orbe infini), et-celle-d'*Abimael* (le père de la plénitude), et-celle-de-*Sheba* (le retour au repos).

---

word מוּרֶת is taken here, not only for *death*, but for its very cause, *mortality*.

וְאֶת־יָרְדָה, *and-that-of-Iarah*.... The word יָרַח signifies literally, *the moon*. It is composed, by contraction, of the two roots רָא־אָח, one of which characterizes visibility, and the other fraternity. These two roots, reduced to the syllable רה, receive the initial sign of potential manifestation י.

v. 27. וְאֶת־הֲהֹורָם, *and-that-of-Hadoram*.... The word הֲהֹור which signifies literally, *splendour, glory*, has received the sign ם which universalizes its meaning.

וְאֶת־אוּזָל, *and-that-of-Awzal*.... This is the root אוּז applied to ether, fire, purified air, to which is united by contraction, the final אֵל. This word, taken as nominal verb, in אֹוזֵל, expresses the action of being carried rapidly from one place to another, to communicate sympathetically, in the same manner as an electric spark.

29. W'æth-A ô p h i r w' æth-Hawilah w'æth-Jôbab: ċhol-ælleh beneî Jaktan.

וְאֶת־אוֹפִר וְאֶת־חֲוִילָה וְאֶת־יוֹבָב כָּל־אֵלֶּה בְּנֵי יָקְטָן׃

ואת־דקלה, *and-that-of-Dikelah*.... One finds in this word two contracted roots, דק־קל: by the first, is understood a rarefaction pushed to extreme subtlety; by the second, a lightness raised to the simple consistency of sound. One feels clearly that there exist no words in our modern tongues capable of expressing the ideas attached to those of *Dikelah*, of *Awzal*, of *Hadoram*: for, whatever may be the gases and the fluids which our physicists have discovered, they have not yet attained to those known by the priests of Thebes.

v. 28. ואת־עובל, *and-that-of-Whobal*.... The root עוב, applied to every elevation, to every orbicular depth, is united by contraction to the root בל, which pushes the meaning to the limits of what is possible.

ואת־אבימאל, *and-that-of-Abimael*.... These terms have nothing difficult.

ואת־שבא, *and-that-of-Sheba*.... This is the same word used by Moses in v. 7. of this chapter: but the difference of the generation places a great difference between the respective meaning which they contain. The repose produced by the igneous force would not be the same as that emanated from the providential power.

v. 29. ואת־אוֹפר, *and-that-of-Aophir*.... This is relative to the aspect under which one has considered the word אוֹפר, as some have seen *gold*, and others, *ashes*: thus the hieroglyphic sense sometimes means noble and sometimes base. To translate it exactly, would require terms which we still lack. This word formed with deep skill, comes from the two contracted roots אוֹר־אר. The first, אוֹר, contains in itself the idea of a thing going to its end, attaining its goal; the second, אר, is well known to be the symbol of the elementary principle.

ואת־חוילה, *and-that-of-Hawilah*.... This word is presented in

29. A n d-that-of-*Aophir* (elementary fulfilled end), and-that-of-*Hawilah* (tried virtue) and-that-of *I o b a h* (shout, huzza!) a l l-those-were the-issued-offspring of *Jaktan* (manifested lessening) (of evil).	29. Et-celle-d'*Aophir* (la fin élémentaire), e t-celle-de-*Hawilah* (la vertu éprouvée), et-celle-de-*Jobab* (la jubilation, le cri d'allégresse!) tous-ceux-là-furent les-enfans de-*Jaktan* (l'atténuation) (du mal).

v. 7. of this chapter; but although it is always derived from the root חוּל or חִיל, it has not, however, the same expression, on account of the generation of *Shem* which modifies it. Emerging from igneous force, it characterized energy; issued from providential power it is the emblem of virtue.

וְאֶת־יוֹבָב, *and-that-of-Iobab....* I do not wish to conceal from my readers that the word יֹבָב, from which we make *jubilee* and *jubilation* after the Latin, was formed in the Egyptian tongue from an onomatopoetic root somewhat vulgar, and signified literally *to bark*. But, as the dog was, in the hieroglyphic style, the emblem of one of the most profound theurgic mysteries, his cry was, in that same style, the expression of the keenest and most exalted joy. In Hebrew as well as in Chaldaic, the word יבב, signifies an acclamation, a cry of cheerfulness, a general approbation. It is the same in the Syriac ܚܒܒ, and in the Ethiopic ɆႶ (*ibah*).

v. 30. מִמְשָׁא, *from-harvest-spiritual-fruits....* I have explained this word in v. 23, of this chapter.

סֵפֶר, *of-spiritual-contriving....* The vulgar meaning of this word is *book*. It is the name itself of the work of Moses, to which I have restored it. It is derived from the root סָפָה, applied to every idea of addition, adjunction, accumulation, supplement, etc.

הַר־הַקֶּדֶם, *to-the-height of-pristine-time....* I have had occasion many times to speak of the word קֶדֶם, and particularly in v. 8, ch. II, where the same roots and the same words represented a great number of times, have always involved the same sense. The reader should also observe that in conformity with my promise, I have

30. W a-î h î moshab'am וַיְהִי מוֹשָׁבָם מִמֵּשָׁא בֹּאֲכָה
ma-meshâ b'âchah sepharah סְפָרָה הַר הַקֶּדֶם׃
har ha-kedem.

---

changed no character under pretext of reforming it. My etymologies are all supported by the same principles, are developed without effort, and succeed without contradiction. Therefore, as I have said, my Grammar has proved my Translation; and my Translation, my Grammar. I arrive at the close of my labour with the innate conviction of having satisfied my reader, if my reader, exempt from prejudice, has put into his examination as much good faith as I have put into my work.

v. 31 and 32. All these terms are understood. It is needless for us to stop longer; but before passing on to the correct translation, I have still some observations to make, and I beg my readers to give a moment's attention.

I have said in the Preliminary Discourse at the head of these notes, that what I called THE COSMOGONY OF MOSES, was included in the first ten chapters of the *Berœshith*: considering these ten chapters as a sort of sacred decade, wherein were developed, following the signification of numbers, the birth of the Universe and its principal vicissitudes.

I know very well that this *ancient custom of giving a certain signification to numbers*, will not be in accordance with the taste of the greater part of modern savants, who, accustomed only to hear numbers spoken of under their purely mathematical relations, doubt that one could without folly, attribute to them a meaning beyond that which they express physically. These savants are quite excusable in scoffing at those who, without any real knowledge of antiquity have undertaken to speak a tongue of whose rudimentary principles they are ignorant; I do not pretend to blame them. On the contrary, I find as they have, nothing more ridiculous than what certain persons have written of numbers. But let me make a comparison.

Because there are bad musicians, must we eliminate music from the *beaux arts?* Because one can no longer penetrate the depths of this art today, and because one is limited to the composition of certain operas, and to the execution of certain symphonies, must one

30. And-such-was the-re-storing-place-of-them, from-harvest-spiritual-fruits, by-dint of-spiritual-contriving, to-the-h e i g h t of-pristine-time.

30. Et-tel-fut-le-lieu du-retour-à-eux, d e p u i s-la m o i s s o n-des-fruits-spirit-uels, à-force de-méditations-d'esprit, jusqu'au-s o m m e t de-l'antériorité des-temps.

charge Plato with falsehood for having said that music was the key to all knowledge? Is it necessary to believe that Buddha in India, Kong-tze in China and even the Scandinavian to whom has been given the name of Woden, consulted together at such distances, both of time and place, to say the same thing, if this thing had not had some foundation? Is it not more simple to think that we have lost certain underlying ideas concerning the manner of study-ing music; and that if we would, perhaps, consider this art from the standpoint that the Hindu sages, those of China, those of ancient Greece, and even the Druids, our ancestors, have considered it, we would find there the same moral resources and the same sublimities?

Plato who saw in music other things than the musicians of our day, saw also in *numbers*, a meaning that our algebraists no longer see. He had learned to see this meaning according to Pythagoras who had received it from the Egyptians. Now, the Egyptians were not alone agreed in giving to numbers *a mysterious signification*. It suffices to open certain ancient books to see that from the oriental limits of Asia to the occidental bournes of Europe, the same idea governed this subject. If I had not decided to omit citations in my notes, I could easily fill entire pages with them.

Therefore let us be reasonable. Can all antiquity be charged with folly? Can it be believed that Pythagoras was a man of weak mind, Plato foolish, Kong-tze ignorant? But if these men had just ideas, then there certainly did exist a *tongue of numbers*, since they never wearied speaking of it. Now what was this tongue? In what did it consist? It consisted in taking numbers in certain intellectual relations, in the same manner that one takes them today in their physical relations; so that, as an English geometrician can understand a problem of mathematics put down by a French

31. Ælleh beneî-S h e m l'mishephehoth'am li-leshonoth'am b'artzoth'am l'gôiehem. אֵלֶּה בְנֵי־שֵׁם לְמִשְׁפְּחֹתָם לִלְשֹׁנֹתָם בְּאַרְצֹתָם לְגוֹיֵהֶם׃

---

geometrician in algebric characters and solve it without understanding the French tongue, so could a wise Chaldean grasp a mystery of transcendental philosophy announced in hieroglyphic numbers by an Egyptian without the least knowledge of his idiom: and as the geometrician knows very well that the characters which he uses have no power in themselves and that they are only the signs of forces or physical quantities, the Chaldean sage knew also that the *numbers* which served him were only *symbols* chosen to express the forces of intellectual Nature.

The vulgar, it is true did not think the same; for the vulgar is vulgar everywhere. Not so very long ago there were some among us who took the geometricians for sorcerers, and the astronomers were menaced with burning. The people of Memphis and Babylon, as ignorant as those of Rome, did not separate the sign that they saw, from the idea it was said to contain; for example, imagining that the number *four*, which represented universal multiplicating force, was that force itself. Many men, usurping the title of sage held to this thought: but it is an absurdity into which the true sages never fell. The symbol of the famous Tetrad was only a simple *four* for Pythagoras when it was not attached to the idea of the universal Motive Power; in the same manner as an x is only an x for the algebraist who has not resolved to see the unknown which he is seeking.

It is very important to know this. In fact, it is because this has not been known, that there has been so much irrational talk for and against *numbers*. This tongue seems absolutely lost today and I would have refrained from speaking of it, if Moses, whose work I am translating had not used it in several places in his Sepher. Moreover, I have not pretended to reëstablish it; for that enterprise would have demanded other labours. I have only believed it useful to note the places where one cannot, without its help, penetrate wholly the meaning of the hierographic writer. These passages are those in which, under pretence of chronology

31. Those-are the-issued-offspring of-*S h e m*, after-the-tribes-of-t h e m, after-t h e-speeches-their-own, in-the-lands-of-t h e m, by-the-organic-bodies-their's.	31. Tels-sont-les-enfans-de *Shem*, selon-les-tribus-à-eux, selon-les-langues-à-eux, dans-les-terres-à-eux, d'après-les-organisations-univer-selles-à-eux.

---

he appears to fix the dates, or calculate the age of its cosmogonical personages. I heartily deplore the infinite pains that the savants, otherwise most estimable, have given themselves to excuse its frequent anachronisms, and to make the Hebrew text and the Samaritan, agree. They did not perceive that these were symbols which they submitted to their calculations; and that Moses, so rich and so grand in this way, could not have been so poor and petty. Indeed, a world whose creation did not go back six thousand years and which lasted only about 4200 years from its universal deluge, would be a world exceedingly modern in comparison with ours where the slightest ideas whether in history, or in physics, force us to go back to an incomparable antiquity.

Every time that one takes literally, the periods and the numbers of Moses, he is lost in an inextricable labyrinth. It will never be explained in a satisfactory manner why the Samaritan text which shortens the duration from the creation to the deluge by three cycles, lengthens on the contrary, that from the deluge to the call of Abraham, not only by the three suppressed cycles, but again by three more cycles; why the Hellenists having the two texts before them have followed neither, lengthening arbitrarily the duration from the creation to the deluge, by nearly eight cycles and that from the deluge to the call of Abraham by more than seven; which gives altogether a space of fifteen hundred years beyond the one fixed by the Hebrew text.

But these difficulties, insurmountable otherwise, disappear when one thinks that Esdras and the Hellenists had very strong reasons, the one, for being separated from the Samaritan text and the others, for altering this mysterious chronology. Esdras wishing, as we have already seen, to make the Hebraic Sepher forever distinguished from the Samaritan Sepher which he had anathematized, had no better means, without injuring the text, than that of changing

32, Ælleh mishephehôth beneî-Noah l'thô-ledoth'am b'gôîe-hem w-me-ælleh nipredou ha-gôîm ba-âretz âhar ha-mabboul.

אֵלֶּה מִשְׁפְּחֹת בְּנֵי־נֹחַ לְתוֹלְדֹתָם בְּגוֹיֵהֶם וּמֵאֵלֶּה נִפְרְדוּ הַגּוֹיִם בָּאָרֶץ אַחַר הַמַּבּוּל׃

---

the form of certain symbolic numbers which had no influence on the sacred doctrine; and the Hellenist Essenes, fleeing from every kind of profanation, could not better prove, that their intention had been not to unveil any of the Mosaic mysteries, than by changing completely those numbers, whose exact translation they could not give without exposing its meaning to the eyes of the profane: for not only the Chaldeans, but those of the Egyptians and the Greeks, initiated in the *science of numbers*, would have grasped the thought of Moses by the sole inspection of his chronology.

An impartial reader who follows me attentively will easily understand, that in admitting with me the hierographic signification of the numbers alluded to in the Sepher, every difficulty relative to the pretended brevity of the duration of the world, as well as to the anachronisms, and differences, found between the two texts and the translation of the Hellenists, ceases; whereas, if one considers these numbers according to their arithmetical value, one of two things is necessary, either to regard Moses as an unlearned man, or to extinguish every historical and physical light which demonstrates the antiquity of the terrestrial globe.

Without explaining entirely the *symbolic signification* of *numbers*, because to do this it would be necessary to restore a science seemingly lost, a laborious and dangerous undertaking, I have said enough to put the reader on the path of discoveries. First I have given the interpretation of the Hebraic decade. This was all the more useful as I know that each chapter of the *Berœshith* bears the character of its number. Without this important consideration, and if I had not seen that the Cosmogony, properly so-called, was contained in a sort of hieroglyphic decade, I would not have translated this tenth chapter, which being only a sort of passing or link between two parts of the same whole, belongs still more to the

COSMOGONY OF MOSES 305

32. These-a r e the-tribes o f-t h e-i s s u e d-beings of-*Noah*, after-the-symbolical-progenies of-t h e m, in-the-organic-b o d i e s-their-own : a n d-through-t h o s e were-parted the-organic-natural-bodies, in-the-earth, after-the-great-swelling (of waters).

32. Telles-sont les-tribus des-êtres-émanés de-*N o a h*, selon-l e s-charactéristiques-générations-à-eux, dans-les-organisations-constituantes-à-eux; et-par-ceux-là-même f u r e n t-diversifiées les-organisations-naturelles e n-la-terre, après-la-grande-intumescence (des eaux).

Geology which it begins, than to the Cosmogony which it finishes. I feel that this has need of an explanation.

The number *ten* has in particular in the tongue of numbers, that which is at once final and initial: that is to say, that it terminates the first decade and begins the second, containing thus two expressions and presenting itself at the same time as term and as principle. I beg the reader to examine the example of a thing somewhat difficult to understand otherwise.

First Decade   *Second Decade*   *Third Decade*

1.2.3.4.5.6.7.8.9.10.11.12.13.14.15.16.17.18.19.20.21.22.23.24.25.26.27.28. etc.
　　　　　　　　1. 2. 3. 4. 5. 6. 7. 8. 9.10.11.12.13.14.15.16.17.18.19. etc.
　　　　　　　　　　　　　　　　　　　1. 2. 3. 4. 5. 6. 7. 8. 9.10. etc.
　　　　　　　　　　　　　　　　　　　　　　　　　　　　1. etc.

It can be seen in this example that the number 10 of the first decade, corresponds to number 1 of the second; so that if one follows the arithmetical progression, the numbers corresponding are found to be 10 and 1, 11 and 2, 12 and 3, etc. Always by adding the members of the complex numbers to form the simple number.

Now I must state for those of my readers who do not fear new and profound ideas, that the first ten chapters of the Beræshith do not correspond to the first decade such as is explained above, but to the second: so that they lead one to think that this book had a beginning composed of nine chapters, of which the first of the Beræshith formed the tenth. This beginning was consecrated to Theogony and was upon the essence of the Divinity. I have strong reasons for thinking that Moses, having received from the sanctuary of Thebes, these theogonic principles, and judging rightly that the Hebrews whom he had been called upon to lead, were in no condition to support them, he therefore suppressed them. He limited himself to the Cosmogony and began his work in the manner that we have seen.

The first chapter, 10/1, was that of *Principiation*: there, all appears in power of being, in germ.

The second chapter, 11/2, was that of *Distinction*: the principle here passes from power into action.

The third, 12/3, was that of *Extraction*: a great opposition takes place.

The fourth, 13/4, was that of *Divisional Multiplication*: that is to say, of that sort of multiplication which takes place when a whole is divided into parts.

The fifth, 14/5, was that of *Facultative Comprehension*.

The sixth, 15/6, was that of *Proportional Measurement*.

The seventh, 16/7, was that of *Consummation*: the equilibrium is broken; a terrible catastrophe ensues; the Universe is renewed.

The eighth, 17/8, was that of *Accumulation*: the divided things returning to their common principles, becoming united.

The ninth, 18/9, was that of *Restoration Consolidated*: a new movement begins.

The tenth, 19/20, was that of *Aggregative and Formative Energy*: the natural forces unfold and act.

Cosmogony of Moses

Correct Translation

COSMOGONY OF MOSES

CHAPTER I.

Principiation.

1. Ælohim created in principle (the potential existence of) the Heavens and the Earth.

2. And the Earth was contingent potentiality in a potentiality of being: and Darkness (compressive and hardening force) was upon the Face of the Deep (infinite source of potential existence); and the Breath (Divine Spirit) of Ælohim, was pregnantly moving upon the face of the Waters (universal passivity).

3. And Ælohim said (declaring His Will) Light shall be: and Light was.

4. And Ælohim declared (did ken) this Luminous Essence good: and Ælohim made a division (caused a dividing motion to exist) between the Light and the Darkness.

5. And Ælohim called (declaring His Will) the Light, Day (luminous period, phenomenal manifestation), and the Darkness (sensible and material existence), Night (negative manifestation, nutation of things): then were evening and morning (west and east)—first day (first phenomenal manifestation).

6. And Ælohim said, An ethereal expanse shall be in the midst of the Waters (in the centre of universal passivity), and a rarefying force dividing the waters from the waters (division of their opposed energies).

7. And Ælohim made the ethereal expanse and divided the inferior faculties of the waters from their superior faculties: and it was so.

8. And Ælohim called (declaring His Will), the ethereal expanse, Heavens (exalted waters): then were evening and morning (west and east)—second day (second phenomenal manifestation).

9. And Ælohim said, The waters below the heavens shall be gathered unto one place, and Dryness shall appear: and it was so.

10. And Ælohim called the Dryness, Earth (terminating and final element), and the gathering place of the waters, he called Seas (aqueous immensity): and Ælohim saw that it was good.

11. And Ælohim said, The Earth shall bring forth shoots, —vegetating and germinating herb, with innate seed, a fruitful substance bearing fruit after its kind and having within itself its seminal power—on the Earth: and it was so.

12. And the Earth brought forth shoots, the vegetating and germinating herb, with innate seed after its kind, and a fruitful substance bearing fruit and having within itself its seminal power, after its kind: —and Ælohim saw that it was good.

13. Then were evening and morning (west and east) —third day (third phenomenal manifestation).

14. And Ælohim said, Centres of Light (luminaries) shall be in the ethereal expanse of the Heavens, to cause a movement of separation between the Day and the Night, and they shall be as signs to come, both for temporal divisions and for universal phenomenal manifestations, and for ontological mutation (of beings).

15. And they shall be as (sensible) Lights in the ethereal expanse of the Heavens to give (intelligible) Light upon the Earth: and it was so.

16. And Ælohim made (the potential existence of) that dyad of great luminous foci, the greater as symbolic

representation of the day (universal manifestation), and the smaller as symbolic representation of the night (negative manifestation): and the stars (virtual forces of the universe).

17. And Ælohim placed them in the ethereal expanse of the Heavens to give (intelligible) Light upon the Earth.

18. And to act as symbolic types in the day and in the night, and to cause a movement of separation between the light and the darkness: and Ælohim saw that it was good.

19. Then were evening and morning (west and east) —fourth day (fourth phenomenal manifestation).

20. And Ælohim said, The Waters shall bring forth abundantly, vermiform and volatile principles with soul of life, moving upon the Earth and flying in the ethereal expanse of the Heavens.

21. And Ælohim created (the potential existence of) corporeal immensities, legions of marine monsters and (that of) all soul of life, animated with reptilian movement, whose principles the waters brought forth abundantly, after their kind, and (that of) every winged fowl after its kind: and Ælohim saw that it was good.

22. And Ælohim blessed them, saying, Be fruitful and multiply and fill the waters in the seas, and the birds shall multiply upon the earth.

23. Then were evening and morning (west and east) —fifth day (fifth phenomenal manifestation).

24. And Ælohim said, The Earth shall bring forth soul of life (animality) after its kind, quadruped and reptile and terrestrial animality after its kind: and it was so.

25. And Ælohim made (the potential existence of) terrestrial animality after its kind, and (that of) the quadruped after its kind, and all life trailing upon the ground after its kind: and Ælohim saw that it was good.

26. And Ælohim said, We will make Adam (univer-

sal man) in our reflected Shadow (image) after the laws of our assimilating action; and they (mankind) shall rule over the fish of the sea and over the birds of the air and over the quadruped and over all terrestrial animality and over all reptilian life moving upon the earth.

27. And Ælohim created (the potential existence of) Adam (universal man) in his reflected Shadow (image), in the shadow of Ælohim created He him: male and female (collective power, universal existence) created He them.

28. And Ælohim blessed them, and Ælohim said unto them: Be fruitful and multiply and replenish the earth and subdue it, and have dominion over the fish of the sea, and over the birds of the heavens and over every living thing that moveth upon the earth.

29. And Ælohim said, Behold, I have given you every herb germinating with innate seed, which is on the face of the whole Earth, and every vegetable substance bearing its own fruit and having in itself its seminal power: unto you it shall be for food.

20. And to all terrestrial animality, and to every bird of the heavens, and to every living reptilian thing that moveth upon the earth and having in itself the innate principle of the animated breath of life, every green herb shall be for food: and it was so.

31. And Ælohim saw (did ken) all that He had made (in potentiality), and behold it was very good. Then were evening and morning (west and east)—sixth day (sixth phenomenal manifestation).

CHAPTER II.

Distinction.

1. Thus were finished (in potentiality) the Heavens and the Earth and all the ruling law thereof (universal nature).

2. And Ælohim accomplished, in the seventh day (phenomenal manifestation), the sovereign work which He had made, and He returned to His Ineffable Self, in the seventh day (phenomenal manifestation), from all the sovereign work which He had made.

3. And Ælohim blessed the seventh day and sanctified (the symbolic existence of) it, because thereon He returned to His Ineffable Self from all the sovereign work, which Ælohim had created according to His efficient power.

4. Such is the sign (symbolic, hieroglyphic emblem) of the generations of the Heavens and of the Earth, when they were created, in the day (luminous manifestation) when YAHWEH Ælohim made (in principle) the Earth and the Heavens.

5. And the whole conception of Nature existed in the Earth before Nature was, and all its vegetative energy before it grew; for YAHWEH Ælohim had not caused it to rain upon the Earth, and Adam (universal man) did not then exist (in actual substance) to labour in the Adamic element.

6. But a virtual emanation went up from out the Earth and moistened the whole face of the Adamic element (homogeneous principle).

7. And YAHWEH Ælohim fashioned (the substance of) Adam (universal man) from (the sublimation of the most subtle parts of) the Adamic element, and breathed into his intelligence an exalted essence of lives, and Adam (universal man) became a similitude of the universal soul.

8. And YAHWEH Ælohim appointed an enclosure (organic circumference) in the sphere of temporal sensibility, (extracted) from the universal anteriority of time; and there He placed Adam whom He had fashioned (for eternity).

9. And YAHWEH Ælohim caused to grow from the Adamic element, every vegetative substance pleasing to the sight and good for food: and a substance of lives in the centre of the (organic) enclosure and its essential substance of the knowledge of good and evil.

10. And a river (luminous emanation) flowed from the sphere of temporal sensibility to water (vivify) the (organic) enclosure; and thence it divided and became (according to the quaternary power) four principles.

11. The name of the first (of those emanating principles) was Phishon (physical reality, apparent being); that which encompasseth the whole earth of Hawilah (virtual energy), natural source of gold (luminous reflection).

12. And the gold of this earth (emblem of luminous reflection of) good; there (the natural source of) Bedollah (mysterious separation) and the Stone Shoham (universal sublimation).

13. And the name of the second river (emanating principle) was Gihon (formative movement): that which encompasseth the whole earth of Chush (igneous principle).

14. And the name of the third river (emanating principle) was Hiddekel (universal propagating fluid), that which goeth forth as (the vehicle of the principle

COSMOGONY OF MOSES 315

of) happiness (harmony) : and the fourth river (emanating principle) was Phrath (fecundating source).

15. And YAHWEH Ælohim took Adam (universal man) and placed him in the (organic) enclosure (of the sphere of temporal sensibility) to elaborate and guard it with care.

16. And YAHWEH Ælohim commanded Adam saying (declaring His Will), Of every vegetative substance of the (organic) enclosure thou mayest (freely) feed upon.

17. But of the physical substance of the knowledge of good and of evil, thou shalt not feed thereon: for in the day thou feedest thereon, becoming mutable, thou shalt die (pass into another state of being).

18. And YAHWEH Ælohim said, It is not good that Adam (universal man) should be alone (in his solitude); I will make him an auxiliary force (companion, counsel) emanated from himself, and formed in the reflection of his own light.

19. And YAHWEH Ælohim fashioned from the Adamic element all terrestrial animality of nature, and every bird of the heavens; and he brought them unto Adam (universal man) to see what name relative to himself Adam would call each species; and whatsoever name Adam assigned to each soul of life (relative to himself), that was its name (expression of its relation with the universal living soul).

20. And Adam assigned names to every quadruped, and to every bird of the heavens, and to all terrestrial animality of nature: but for Adam (universal man) was not found an auxiliary force (companion, counsel) as luminous reflection of himself.

21. And YAHWEH Ælohim caused a profound and sympathetic sleep to fall upon Adam (universal man) and he slept; and He broke from the unity, one of his involutions (exterior envelope, feminine principle) and shaped with form and corporeal beauty, its original inferiority (weakness).

22. And YAHWEH Ælohim restored this involution (exterior envelope) which He had broken from (the substance of) Adam, for (shaping the form of) Aïshah (volitive faculty, intellectual companion) and He brought her unto Adam.

23. And Adam said (declaring his thought), This is actually universal substance of my substance and corporeal form of my corporeal form: this one he called Aïshah (efficient volitive faculty, intellectual companion) for out of Aïsh (volitive principle, intellectual man) she had been taken in substance.

24. Therefore shall Aïsh (intellectual man) leave his father and his mother and shall cleave unto Aïshah (intellectual companion), and they shall be as one corporeal substance (one single being in one same form).

25. And they were both entirely uncovered (without corporeal veil to conceal their mental conceptions), Adam (universal man) and Aïshah (his volitive faculty) and they were not ashamed.

———:-:———

CHAPTER III.

Extraction.

1. Now Nahash (egoism, envy, covetousness, concupiscence) was an insidious passion (blind principle) in all elementary life which YAHWEH Ælohim had made: and it said (this passion Nahash) unto Aïshah (volitive faculty of Adam), Why, hath Ælohim declared, ye shall not feed upon all the substance of the organic enclosure?

2. And Aïshah (volitive faculty) said unto Nahash (covetous passion), Of the fruit growing substance of the organic enclosure, we may feed upon,

3. But of the fruit of the substance itself, which is in the centre of the organic enclosure, Ælohim hath said, Ye shall not feed upon it, ye shall not carry your desires (breathe out your soul) into it, lest ye cause your unavoidable dying.

4. And Nahash (insidious, covetous passion) said unto Aïshah: Not in dying shall ye cause your unavoidable death.

5. For Ælohim knoweth, that in the day ye shall feed thereon (on this substance), your eyes shall be opened (to the light) and ye shall be as Ælohim, conscious of good and evil.

6. And Aïshah (volitive faculty) saw that this substance (was) good for food and pleasant for the eyes, and that this substance was desirable to universalize the intelligence; and she took of the fruit thereof and did feed upon it and she gave also unto Aïsh (intellectual principle) united with her, and he did feed thereon.

7. And the eyes of them both were opened, and they knew that they were void of light (of virtue, sterile and unveiled in their dark principle) and they brought forth a shadowy covering, veil of sadness and mourning, and they made themselves pilgrims' cloaks.

8. And they heard the voice of YAHWEH Ælohim wafting itself to and fro in the organic enclosure like the spiritual breath of day, and Adam (universal man) hid himself and Aïshah (his volitive faculty), from the face of YAHWEH Ælohim, in the centre of the substance itself of the organic enclosure.

9. And YAHWEH Ælohim called unto Adam and said unto him, Where has thy will borne thee?

10. And he said, I heard Thy voice in the organic enclosure and I was afraid because I was void of light (unveiled in my dark principle) and I hid myself.

11. And He said, Who hath taught thee that thou wast void of light? If not (the use of) that substance whereof I commanded thee that thou shouldst not feed.

12. And Adam (universal man) said, Aïshah (volitive faculty) whom Thou gavest to be my companion, she gave me of that substance and I did feed upon it.

13. And YAHWEH Ælohim said unto Aïshah, Why hast thou done that? and Aïshah said, Nahash (insidious passion) caused my delusion and I fed upon it.

14. And YAHWEH Ælohim said unto Nahash, Because thou hast done this, cursed be thou, amongst all terrestrial animality, and amongst all elementary nature, according to thy tortuous inclination shalt thou act (grovellingly, basely), and upon elementary exhalations (corporeal illusions) shalt thou feed all the days of thy life.

15. And I will put antipathy (natural aversion) between thee and Aïshah (volitive faculty), and between

thy progeny and her progeny (productions of the volitive faculty); hers shall repress (centralize) the venomous principle (evil) in thee, and thine shall repress (centralize) the consequences of evil in her.

16. Unto Aïshah He said, I will multiply the number of thy physical hindrances (obstacles opposed to the execution of thy desires), and thy mental conceptions; and in sorrowful travail shalt thou bring forth thy productions: and unto Aïsh (intellectual principle) shall thy desire be and he shall rule in thee (act symbolically).

17. And unto Adam (universal man) He said, Because thou hast hearkened unto the voice of Aïshah (volitive faculty, intellectual companion), and hast fed upon the substance of which I commanded thee saying, Thou shalt not feed thereof; cursed be the Adamic element (homogeneous and like unto thee) because of thee: in painful travail shalt thou feed upon it all the days (phenomenal manifestations) of thy lives.

18. And harsh and rough (imperfect and disordered) productions shall germinate abundantly for thee; and thou shalt feed upon the bitter and withered fruits of elementary nature.

19. In continual mental agitation shalt thou feed upon it, until thy return (reintegration) unto the Adamic element (homogeneous and like unto thee); for out of the spiritual element wast thou taken and unto the spiritual element shalt thou be restored.

20. And Adam called the name of Aïshah (his volitive faculty), Hevah (elementary existence) because she was the mother of all (that constitutes) existence.

21. And YAHWEH Ælohim made for Adam and his intellectual companion, sheltering shapes (bodies) and enveloped them with care.

22. And YAHWEH Ælohim said, Behold Adam (universal man) is become like one of us, knowing good and evil; and now lest he put forth his hand and take

also of the Elementary Substance of lives, and feed thereon and live forever (immensity of time):

23. Therefore, YAHWEH Ælohim separated him from the organic sphere of temporal sensibility, to elaborate this Adamic element out of which he had been taken.

24. And He cast forth Adam (universal man) and from the universal anteriority of time, He caused to exist in the organic sphere of temporal sensibility, the Cherubim (collective being, like unto innumerable legions) and an incandescent flame of destruction whirling upon itself, to guard the way of the elementary substance of lives.

CHAPTER IV.

Divisional Multiplication.

1. And Adam (universal man) knew Hevah (elementary existence, his efficient volitive faculty) ; and she conceived and produced (the existence of) Kain (strong and mighty transformer, which seizes, centralizes and appropriates, and assimilates to itself) ; and she said, I have formed (by centralizing) an•intellectual being of the essence of YAHWEH.

2. And she added, bringing forth his brotherly self, (the existence of) Habel (gentle, pacific liberator, that which releases and extends, which evaporates and leaves the centre) ; and Habel was leader (director) of the elementary corporeal world, and Kain was servant of the Adamic element (homogeneal ground).

3. Now it was from the end of the seas (superficial phenomenal manifestations), that Kain caused to ascend of the productions of the Adamic element, an offering unto YAHWEH.

4. And Habel also caused (an offering) to ascend of the firstlings of his world and of their quintessence (most eminent virtues) ; and YAHWEH was saviour unto Habel and unto his offering.

5. But unto Kain and unto his offering He was not saviour; and Kain was very wroth and his face was downcast.

6. And YAHWEH said unto Kain, Why art thou wroth? and why is thy face downcast?

7. If thou doest well, shalt thou not bear the sign (of good in thee) and if thou doest not well, the sin lieth at the door (is upon thy countenance); and unto thee its desire, and thou, its symbolic representation.

8. And Kain declared his thought, unto Habel his brother; and they were existing together in productive Nature: and Kain (violent centralizer) rose up (was materialized) against Habel (gentle, pacific liberator) his brother, and slew him (conquered his forces).

9. And Yahweh said unto Kain, Where is Habel, thy brother? and he said, I know not: am I my brother's keeper?

10. And he said, What hast thou done? the voice of the groaning generations of (future progenies which were to proceed from) thy brother riseth unto me from the Adamic element.

11. And now, cursed be thou, by the Adamic element whose mouth was opened by thine own hand, to receive the generations (future progenies) of thy brother.

12. When thou labourest in the Adamic element, it shall not yield its virtual force unto thee: staggering (agitated by a movement of uncertainty) and wandering (agitated by a movement of fear) thou shalt be upon the earth.

13. And Kain said unto Yahweh, Great is my iniquity from that which I must endure (according to my purification).

14. Behold, Thou hast driven me out this day from the face of the Adamic element: and from Thy face must I hide myself and I shall be staggering (agitated by a movement of uncertainty) and wandering (agitated by a movement of fear) upon the earth: and it shall be that whosoever findeth me shall slay me.

15. And Yahweh said unto him, Whosoever slayeth Kain (thinking to destroy him), sevenfold shall (instead) exalt him (increase his power sevenfold): and Yahweh put a sign upon Kain, so that anyone finding him should not smite him.

16. And Kain withdrew from the face of YAHWEH and dwelt in the land of Nod (of banishment and exile, of troublous, agitated wandering) the temporal anteriority of elementary sensibility.

17. And Kain knew Aïsheth (his intellectual companion, his volitive faculty): and she conceived and brought forth (the existence of) Henoch (founder, central energy): then he builded a spherical enclosure (stronghold) and he called the name of this spherical enclosure after the name of his son Henoch.

18. And unto Henoch was born (the existence of) Whirad (excitative movement, interior passion, whirling motion): and Whirad produced Mehoujael (physical manifestation, objective reality): and Mehoujael produced Methoushael (abyss of death): and Methoushael produced Lamech (the knot which arrests dissolution, the pliant bond of things).

19. And Lamech took unto him two corporeal companions (physical faculties): the name of the first was Whadah (evidence, periodic return) and the name of the second was Tzillah (deep, dark, veiled).

20. And Whadah produced (the existence of) Jabal (aqueous principle, physical abundance, fertility): he who was the father (concentrating and appropriating force, the founder) of those who dwell in fixed and elevated abodes, and who recognize (the right of lawful) property.

21. And the name of his brother was Jubal (universal fluid, principle of sound, source of joy and moral prosperity): he who was the father (founder) of every luminous conception, and that which is worthy of loving admiration (arts and sciences).

22. And Tzillah also produced (the existence of) Thubal Kain (central diffusion, mercurial and mineral principle) who sharpened all (tools of) copper and iron (instructor of those who work in metals, excavate mines and forge iron): and the kindred of Thubal Kain was

Nawhomah (principle of aggregation, association of peoples).

23. And Lamech (the knot which arrests dissolution) said unto his corporeal companions (physical faculties) Whadah and Tzillah: Hearken unto my voice, ye companions of Lamech, listen unto my speech: for I have slain (destroyed) the intellectual individuality of me (that which is individualized by his volitive faculty) for my extension (free exercise of his forces), and the progeny (spirit of the race, particular lineage) for my formation (in the great family of peoples).

24. So sevenfold shall be exalted (the centralizing constitutive forces of) Kain (mighty transformer), and Lamech (flexible bond things), seventy and sevenfold (exalted).

25. And Adam (universal man) again knew his intellectual companion (efficient volitive faculty), and she produced a son, and called his name Sheth (basis, foundation of things): For thus, said she, hath Ælohim founded in me another seed (basis of another generation, emanated) from the mutation of Habel, whom Kain slew.

26. And unto Sheth likewise, was generated a son: and he called his name Ænosh (mutable being, corporeal man): then hope was caused (to support his sorrow), by calling upon (invocation of) the name of YAHWEH.

CHAPTER V.

Facultative Comprehension

1. This is the book of the (symbolical) generations of Adam (universal man) from the day when Ælohim created Adam; according to the assimilating action of Ælohim, made he his selfsameness (determined his potential existence).

2. Male and female (cause and means) created He them (collectively); and He blessed them and He called their (universal) name Adam, in the day when He created them (universally).

3. And Adam existed three tens and one hundred cycles (of temporal ontological mutation); and he produced according to his assimilating action, in his reflected shadow, an emanated being, and he called his name Sheth (basis and foundation of things).

4. And the days (luminous periods, phenomenal manifestations) of Adam, after he had brought forth (the existence of) Sheth, were eight hundred cycles (of ontological mutation): and he produced sons and daughters (many emanated beings).

5. And all the days (luminous periods) during which Adam (universal man) existed, were nine hundred cycles and three tens (of ontological mutation): and he passed away (returned to universal seity).

6. And Sheth (basis of things) existed five and one hundred cycles (of ontological mutation), and he produced Ænosh (mutable being, corporeal man).

7. And Sheth existed after he produced (the existence of) Ænosh, seven and eight hundred cycles (of on-

tological mutation), and he produced sons and daughters (many emanated beings).

8. And all the days (luminous periods) of Sheth were two and one ten and nine hundred cycles (of ontological mutation), and he passed away (returned to universal seity).

9. And Ænosh (mutable being, corporeal man) existed nine tens of cycles (of ontological mutation), and he produced Kainan (general usurpation).

10. And Ænosh existed after he produced (the existence of) Kainan, five and one ten and eight hundred cycles (of ontological mutation) and he produced sons and daughters (many emanated beings).

11. And all the days (luminous periods) of Ænosh were five and nine hundred cycles (of ontological mutation), and he passed away (returned to universal seity).

12. And Kainan existed seven tens of cycles (of ontological mutation), and he produced Mahollael (mighty exaltation, splendour).

13. And Kainan existed after he produced (the existence of) Mahollael, four tens and eight hundred cycles (of ontological mutation), and he produced sons and daughters (many emanated beings).

14. And all the days (luminous periods) of Kainan were ten and nine hundred cycles (of ontological mutation), and he passed away (returned to universal seity).

15. And Mahollael (mighty exaltation, splendour) existed five and six tens of cycles (of ontological mutation) and he produced Ired (steadfastness, perseverance, either upward or downward).

16. And Mahollael existed after he produced (the existence of) Ired, three tens and eight hundred cycles (of ontological mutation), and he produced sons and daughters (many emanated beings).

17. And all the days (luminous periods) of Mahollael were five and nine tens and eight hundred cycles

(of ontological mutation), and he passed away (returned to universal seity).

18. And Ired existed two and six tens, and one hundred cycles (of ontological mutation), and he produced Henoch (centralization, contrition).

19. And Ired existed after he produced (the existence of) Henoch, eight hundred cycles (of ontological mutation), and he produced sons and daughters (many emanated beings).

20. And all the days (luminous periods) of Ired were two and six tens and nine hundred cycles (of ontological mutation), and he passed away (returned to universal seity).

21. And Henoch existed five and six tens of cycles (of ontological mutation), and he produced Methoushaleh (abyss of death).

22. And Henoch followed in the steps of Ælohim, after he produced (the existence of) Methoushaleh, three hundred cycles (of ontological mutation), and he produced sons and daughters (many emanated beings).

23. And all the days (luminous periods) of Henoch were five and six tens and three hundred cycles (of ontological mutation).

24. And Henoch followed in the steps of Ælohim and (there was) naught of him (ceased to exist without ceasing to be); for Ælohim withdrew him unto Himself.

25. And Methoushaleh existed seven and eight tens and one hundred cycles (of ontological mutation), and he produced (the existence of) Lamech (the knot which arrests dissolution).

26. And Methoushaleh existed after he produced (the existence of) Lamech, two and eight tens and seven hundred cycles (of ontological mutation), and he produced sons and daughters (many emanated beings).

27. And all the days (luminous periods) of Methou-

shaleh were nine and six tens and nine hundred cycles (of ontological mutation), and he passed away (returned to universal seity).

28. And Lamech (pliant bond of things) existed two and eight tens, and one hundred cycles (of ontological mutation), and he produced a son (emanated being).

29. And he called his name Noah (repose of elementary Nature); saying, This shall rest us (our existence) and lighten our labour, and the physical obstacles of our hands, because of the Adamic element which YAHWEH hath cursed.

30. And Lamech existed after he produced this son, five and nine tens, and five hundred cycles (of ontological mutation), and he produced sons and daughters (many emanated beings).

31. And all the days (luminous periods) of Lamech were seven and seven tens and seven hundred cycles (of ontological mutation), and he passed away (returned to universal seity).

32. And Noah (repose of elementary nature) was the son of five hundred cycles (of ontological mutation): and Noah produced (the existence of) Shem (that which is lofty, bright) and (the existence of) Cham (that which is curved, dark, hot) and (the existence of) Japheth (that which is wide, extended).

CHAPTER VI.

Proportional Measurement

1. Now it was (it came to pass) because of the downfall of Adam (dissolution of universal man) by multiplying upon the face of the Adamic element, that daughters (sentient and corporeal forms) were abundantly produced unto them (the divisions of Adam).

2. And the sons (spiritual emanations) of Ælohim beheld the daughters (corporeal forms) of Adam that they were fair: and they took unto themselves of those physical faculties, whichsoever they desired most.

3. And YAHWEH said, My breath (vivifying spirit) shall no more be diffused (in bountiful profusion) upon Adam (universal man) during the immensity of time, because of his degeneration: inasmuch as he is corporeal, his days (luminous periods) shall be one hundred fold and two tens of cycles (of ontological mutation).

4. And the Nephilim (elect amongst men, noble illustrious ones) were upon the earth in those days: and also after that, sons (spiritual emanations) of Ælohim had come in unto (mingled with) daughters (corporeal faculties) of Adam (universal man) and they had produced through them those same Ghiborim (mighty men, those famous Hyperboreans) who were of old, corporeal men (heros) of renown.

5. And YAHWEH saw that the perversity of Adam (mankind) increased upon the earth and that every conception (intellectual production) of the thoughts of his heart diffused evil all that day (during that phenomenal manifestation, luminous period).

6. And YAHWEH renounced (withdrew His loving power from the existence of) Adam (mankind) on the earth, and He repressed Himself in His heart (evinced severity).

7. And YAHWEH said, I will efface (the existence of) Adam (mankind) which I have created, from the face of the Adamic element: from Adam (mankind) to the quadruped, the creeping kind and the bird of the heavens: for I renounce (the preserving care of) having made them.

8. But Noah (repose of nature) found grace in the eyes of YAHWEH.

9. These are the symbolic generations of Noah: of Noah, intellectual principle manifesting the justice of universal virtues in his generations (cyclic periods): Noah followed in the steps of Ælohim.

10. And Noah (repose of nature) produced three sons (triad of emanated beings): the existence of Shem (that which is lofty, brilliant), of Cham (that which is curved, dark, gloomy), and of Japheth (that which extends without limit).

11. And the earth was corrupt (debased, degraded) before the face of Ælohim: and the earth was filled with a violent degrading heat (dark and devouring).

12. And Ælohim looked upon the earth and behold it was corrupt, because every corporeal form had corrupted its own way (law) upon the earth.

13. And Ælohim said unto Noah (repose of nature), The end of every corporeal form draws near before my face: for the earth is filled with a violent degrading heat (dark and devouring) over the whole face of it: and behold, I leave the earth to its own destruction.

14. Make thee a Thebah (sheltering abode, enclosure, refuge) of preserving elementary substance: hollowed and roomed thou shalt make the Thebah: and thou shalt smear the interior and the exterior circumference with corporeal substance.

COSMOGONY OF MOSES 331

15. And thus shalt thou make it: three hundred fold of mother-measure the length of the Thebah (mysterious, sacred abode): five tens of mother-measure the breadth of it and three tens of mother-measure the bulk (solidity) of it.

16. Gathering light, thou shalt make for the Thebah; and according to the mother-measure, the orbicular extent in its upper part: and the opening of the Thebah shalt thou place in its opposite part: the lower parts, thou shalt make twofold and threefold.

17. And I, behold I, do bring the great intumescence (of the waters) upon the earth, to destroy every corporeal form wherein is the breath of lives: from under the heavens, all that is upon the earth shall perish.

18. And I will establish My creative might with thee and thou shalt enter the Thebah, thou and thy sons (spiritual emanations) and thine intellectual companion (efficient volitive faculty) and the corporeal companions of thy sons (their natural faculties) with thee.

19. And of every living kind, of every corporeal form, two of every kind shalt thou bring into the Thebah (mysterious abode) to exist with thee: male and female shall they be.

20. Of fowl after its kind, of quadruped after its kind, of every creeping thing of the Adamic element after its kind, two of every species shall come unto thee to preserve existence there.

21. And thou shalt take unto thee of all food that is eaten: thou shalt gather it unto thee: and it shall be for food for thee and for them.

22. And Noah did all that Ælohim had commanded him: thus did he.

CHAPTER VII.

Consummation.

1. And YAHWEH said unto Noah, Come thou and all thine interior into the Thebah (sheltering abode) : for thee (thy selfsameness) have I seen righteous before My face in this generation (of perversity).

2. Of every pure quadruped kind, thou shalt take unto thee, seven-by-seven, the principle and the efficient volitive faculty: and of the impure quadruped kind, two-by-two, the principle and the efficient volitive faculty.

3. Of the fowl of the heavens also seven-by-seven, male and female, to preserve (the existence of) the seed upon the face of the whole earth.

4. For in this seventh day (luminous period, phenomenal manifestation), I will cause to rain (move the watery element) upon the earth, four tens of days (a great quaternion of light) and four tens of nights (great quaternion of darkness) : and I will efface all substantial, plastic nature that I have made, from the face of the Adamic element.

5. And Noah did all that Ælohim had commanded him.

6. And Noah was the son of six hundred cycles (of ontological mutation), when the great intumescence (of the waters) was upon the earth.

7. And Noah went, and his sons (emanated beings) and his intellectual companion (efficient volitive faculty) and the corporeal companions of his sons (their physical faculties) into the Thebah (mysterious abode) from the face (of the waters) of the great intumescence.

8. Of the pure quadruped kind and of the impure quadruped kind and of fowl and of every creeping thing animated with reptilian movement upon the Adamic element.

9. Two and two they came unto Noah (repose of nature) into the Thebah (sheltering abode), male and female, as Ælohim had commanded Noah.

10. And it was on the seventh of the days (luminous periods, phenomenal manifestations) that the waters of the great intumescence were upon the earth.

11. In the six hundredth ontological mutation of the lives of Noah, in the second neomenia, in the seventeenth day (luminous period) of that moon-renewal: in that same day were opened all the springs of the potential, universal deep, and the multiplying quaternions of the heavens were loosened.

12. And there was a falling of water (aqueous atmosphere) upon the earth unceasingly, four tens of days and four tens of nights (an entire quaternion of light and darkness).

13. Into the substantial principle of this day (seventh luminous period) went Noah (repose of elementary existence), and Shem (brilliant elevation), and Cham (dark inclination), and Japheth (extended space), sons (emanated productions) of Noah, and his intellectual companion (efficient volitive faculty), and the corporeal companions (physical faculties) of his sons with them, into the Thebah (place of refuge).

14. They, and all terrestrial animality after its kind, and every quadruped after its kind, and every creeping thing with reptilian motion after its kind, and every fowl after its kind: every thing that moves swiftly, everything that flies.

15. And they went unto Noah (repose of nature) into the Thebah (sheltering abode) two and two of every corporeal form having in itself the breath of lives.

16. And thus they went in, male and female of every corporeal form, as Ælohim had commanded: and YAHWEH finished and withdrew Himself.

17. And the great intumescence was four tens of days (luminous periods) upon the earth: and the waters increased greatly and they bore up the Thebah, which was lifted up above the earth.

18. And the waters prevailed and were greatly increased upon the earth: and the Thebah moved to and fro upon the face of the waters.

19. And the waters prevailed to their fullest extent upon the earth: and all the high mountains were covered, which are beneath the whole heavens.

20. Fifteen mother-measure above them did the waters prevail: and the mountains were wholly covered.

21. Thus perished (disappeared) every corporeal form moving upon the earth, of birds and of quadruped, of terrestrial animality and of every creeping thing moving with reptilian motion upon the earth and all Adam (mankind).

22. Everything having an emanated essence of the breath of lives (spiritual comprehension), perished in the exterminating intumescence.

23. And everything (plastic, substantial nature) was effaced from the face of the Adamic element: from Adam (mankind) to the quadruped, from the reptilian kind to the fowl of the heavens: and they were effaced from the earth: and there remained only Noah (repose of elementary nature), and that which was with him in the Thebah (holy retreat).

24. And the waters prevailed upon the earth five tens and one hundred days (luminous periods, phenomenal manifestations).

CHAPTER VIII.

Accumulation.

1. And Ælohim remembered (the existence of) Noah and (that of) all terrestrial animality and (that of) every quadruped with him in the Thebah (place of refuge): and Ælohim caused a breath to pass over the earth, and the waters were checked.

2. And the springs of the deep (infinite source of potential existence) and the multiplying quaternion forces of the heavens were closed, and the falling of water (aqueous atmosphere) was exhausted from the heavens.

3. And the waters returned to their former state from off the earth by (the periodic movement of) flux and reflux: and the waters withdrew (shrank) at the end of five tens and one hundred days (luminous periods).

4. And the Thebah rested, in the seventh moon-renewal, on the seventeenth day (luminous period) of that moon-renewal, upon the heights of Ararat (first gleam of luminous effluence).

5. And the waters were agitated by (the periodic movement of) flux and reflux until the tenth moon-renewal: and in that tenth (month), on the first of the moon-renewal, the tops of the mountains (elementary firstlings, principles of nature's productions) became visible.

6. And it was at the end of four tens of days (the great quaternion), that Noah released the light of the Thebah, which he had made.

7. And he sent forth Ereb (western darkness) which

went to and fro (with periodic movement) until the drying up of the waters upon the earth.

8. And he sent forth Ionah (plastic force of nature, brooding dove) from him, to see if the waters were lightened from off the face of the Adamic element.

9. And Ionah found no place of rest to impart its generative force and it returned unto him into the Thebah, for the waters were still upon the face of the whole earth: and he put forth his hand (his power) and took it and brought it back unto him into the Thebah.

10. And he again waited a septenary of days (luminous periods) more, and again he sent forth Ionah from the Thebah.

11. And Ionah came back to him at the same time as Ereb (return of western darkness), and lo, an olive branch (a sublimation of igneous essence) was grasped in its mouth (its conceptive faculty): thus Noah knew that the waters were lightened upon the earth.

12. And he waited again a septenary of days (luminous periods) more, and he sent forth Ionah, and it (brooding dove, generative faculty) returned not again unto him.

13. And it was in the unity and six hundred cycles (of ontological mutation), in the very beginning, at the first of the moon-renewal, that the waters wasted away from upon the earth: and Noah elevated the shelter (vaulted superficies) of the Thebah and looked (considered) and behold they were wasted (the waters) away from upon the face of the Adamic element.

14. And in the second moon-renewal, in the seven and twentieth day of that moon-renewal the earth was dried.

15. And Ælohim spake unto Noah, saying,

16. Issue forth (produce thyself exteriorly) from the Thebah (sheltering place), thou and thine intellectual

COSMOGONY OF MOSES 337

companion (efficient volitive faculty), and thy sons (emanated productions) and the corporeal companions of thy sons (their physical faculties) with thee together.

17. All animal life that is with thee, of every corporeal form, of fowl and of quadruped and of every kind of reptile that creepeth upon the earth: let them produce (themselves exteriorly) with thee: and let them breed abundantly upon the earth and be fruitful and multiply upon the earth.

18. And Noah issued forth (was reproduced exteriorly) and his sons (emanated productions), and his intellectual companion (efficient volitive faculty) and his sons' companions (corporeal faculties) with him.

19. All terrestrial animality, all reptilian kind and every fowl: every thing creeping upon the earth after their kinds, issued forth (produced themselves exteriorly) from the Thebah.

20. And Noah raised up an altar (place of sacrifice) unto YAHWEH, and he took of every pure quadruped and of every pure fowl and raised a sublimation (caused an exhalation to rise) from the altar.

21. And YAHWEH breathed that fragrant breath of sweetness: and YAHWEH said within His heart, I will not again curse the Adamic element on account of Adam, because the heart of Adam (mankind) has conceived evil from his elementary impulses: I will not again smite all earth-born life (elementary existence) as I have done.

22. During all the days (luminous periods, phenomenal manifestations) of the earth, seed-time and harvest, cold and heat, summer and winter, and day and night shall not cease.

CHAPTER IX.

Restoration Consolidated.

1. And Ælohim blessed (the existence of) Noah and (that of) his sons (emanated productions), and He said unto them, Be fruitful and multiply and replenish the earth.

2. And the dazzling brightness of you and the awesome splendour of you shall be (impressed) upon all terrestrial animality and upon every bird of the heavens: upon all that receiveth original movement from the Adamic element, and upon every fish of the sea: into your hand (power) are they delivered.

3. Everything possessing in itself the principle of movement and of life, shall .be food for you: even as the green herb have I given unto you all.

4. But the corporeal form which has in its soul, its similitude (blood assimilation, homogeneity) you shall not feed upon.

5. For your homogeneity (likeness of your soul), will I require (avenge) it: from the hand of every living being will I require it, and from the hand of Adam (mankind) and from the hand of Aïsh (intellectual man) his brother, will I require this Adamic soul (similitude).

6. Whoso sheddeth the blood (homogeneous, corporeal likeness) of Adam (mankind), through Adam shall his own blood be shed: because in the universal shadow (image) of Ælohim made He (the selfsameness of) Adam.

7. And you, universal existence, be ye fruitful and multiply; bring forth abundantly upon the earth and spread yourselves thereon.

COSMOGONY OF MOSES

8. And Ælohim spake unto Noah and unto his sons (his emanations) with him, saying,

9. And I, behold I will establish (in substance) My Creative Energy in you and in your generation after you:

10. And in every soul of life that is with you, of fowl, of quadruped and of all terrestrial animality with you: of all beings issued from the Thebah, (including) all terrestrial animality.

11. And I will establish (in substance) My Creative Energy in you: so that every corporeal form shall not be cut off any more by the great intumescence (of the waters): and neither shall there be any more a flood to destroy the earth.

12. And Ælohim said, This is the symbolic sign of the Creative Force (law) which I appoint between Me and you, and every soul of life that is with you, for perpetual ages (immensity of time).

13. My bow, I have set in the nebulous expanse: and it shall be for a symbol of the Creative Force (law) between Me and the earth.

14. And it shall come to pass, when I bring a cloud over the earth, that the bow shall be seen in the nebulous expanse.

15. And I will remember this Creative Law which is between Me and you and every soul of life in every corporeal form: and the great intumescence (of the waters) shall no more destroy every corporeal form.

16. And the bow shall be in the nebulous expanse, and I will look upon it, to remember the Creative Law (established) for the immensity of time, between Ælohim and every soul of life in every corporeal form that is upon the earth.

17. And Ælohim said unto Noah, This is the symbol of the Creative Force (law) which I have established (in substance) between Me and every corporeal form that is upon the earth.

18. Now, the sons (emanations) of Noah (repose of nature) issuing from the Thebah (sacred enclosure) were Shem (that which is elevated and shining), Cham (that which is dark, curved and hot), and Japheth (that which is extended and wide): and Cham was the father of Chanahan (material reality, physical existence).

19. These three were the sons (emanated beings) of Noah and of these was the whole earth overspread (shared, divided).

20. And Noah released (gave liberty to) Aïsh (intellectual volitive principle) of the Adamic element: and thus he cultivated that which is lofty (spiritual heights).

21. And being steeped with the spirit of his production, he intoxicated his thought (attained ecstasy) and (in his exaltation) he revealed himself in the centre (most secret place) of his tabernacle.

22. And Cham the father of Chanahan (physical, material existence), discovered the mysterious secrets of his father and he divulged them to his two brothers exteriorly (materialized them).

23. And Shem and Japheth took the left garment and raised it behind them, and went backward, and covered the secret mysteries of their father: and their faces (were turned) backward, so that the secret mysteries of their father they did not see.

24. And Noah awaked from his spiritual ecstasy and he knew what his youngest son (the least of his productions) had done unto him.

25. And he said, Cursed be Chanahan (physical, material existence): a servant of servants shall he be unto his brethren.

26. And he said, Blessed be YAHWEH Ælohim of Shem: and Chanahan shall be servant unto them (his people).

COSMOGONY OF MOSES 341

27. Ælohim shall give extension unto Japheth and he shall dwell in the tabernacles of Shem (brilliant elevation) : and Chanahan (physical, material existence), shall be a servant unto them.

28. And Noah existed after the great intumescence (of the waters), three hundred and five tens of cycles (of ontological mutation).

29. And all the days (luminous periods, phenomenal manifestations) of Noah (repose of nature) were nine hundred and five tens of cycles (of ontological mutation) : and he passed away (returned to universal seity).

CHAPTER X.

Aggregative and Formative Energy.

1. Now these (are) the symbolic generations of the sons (emanated productions) of Noah (repose of nature): Shem, Cham and Japheth: and sons (emanated productions) were unto them after the great intumescence (of the waters).

2. And the sons (emanated productions) of Japheth (absolute extension) (were): Gomer (elementary cumulation, aggregative force), and Magog (elasticity), and Madai (infinite commensurability and sufficiency), and Javan (generative ductility), and Thubal (diffusibility), and Meshech (perceptibility), and Thirass (modality, faculty of appearing under determined form).

3. And the sons (emanated productions) of Gomer (elementary cumulation) (were): Ashechenaz (latent fire, caloric), and Riphath (rarity, centrifugal force), and Thogormah (density, universal corporization, centripetal force).

4. And the sons (emanated productions) of Javan (generative ductility) (were): Ælishah (diluting and moulding energy), and Tharshish (intense, sympathetic principle), of Chittim (Chuthites, Scythians, the rejected, the barbarous) and of Dodanim (Dardanians, the elect, the civilized).

5. By these (faculties, or powers of repulsion and attraction) were differentiated the centres of will (interests, opinions and ideas of peoples), of social organizations in their lands: every principle (acting) after its own tongue, toward tribes in general, in their social organizations.

6. And the sons (emanated productions) of Cham (dark, hot inclination) (were): Chush (igneous force, combustion), and Mitzeraim (subjugating, victorious, oppressing power), and Phout (suffocating, asphyxiating energy), and Chanahan (physical and material existence).

7. And the sons (emanated productions) of Chush (igneous force, combustion) (were): Seba (radical moisture, principle of all natural productions), and Hawilah (natural energy, travail), and Sabethah (determining movement, cause), and Rahamah (thunder), and Sabethecha (determined movement, effect): and the sons (emanated productions) of Rahamah (thunder) (were): Sheba (reintegration of principles, electric repulsion), and Dedan (electric affinity).

8. And Chush (igneous force) produced Nimrod (principle of disordered will, of rebellion, anarchy, despotism): he who strove to be the dominator of the earth.

9. He who was a lordly adversary (proud opposer), before the face of YAHWEH: wherefore it is said: Even as Nimrod (principle of anarchical volition), lordly adversary before the face of YAHWEH.

10. And such was the beginning of his kingdom, Babel (vanity), and Arech (softness, dissolution), and Achad (selfishness), and Chalneh (ambition, all engrossing desire), in the land of Shinar (civil revolution).

11. Out of this land issued Ashour (principle of enlightened government, and the order and happiness resulting from the observation of laws), and founded Nineveh (exterior growth, colonization, education of youth), and the interior institutions of the city, and Chalah (perfecting of laws, assemblage of wise men, senate).

12. And Ressen (legislative power, reins of the government), between Nineveh (exterior growth, colonization) and Chalah (interior action of deliberation, senate): a very powerful civil safeguard.

13. And Mitzeraim (subjugating, victorious, oppressing power) produced (the existence of) Loudim (physical pregnancies), and (that of) Whonamim (material heaviness), and (that of) Lehabim (inflamed exhalations) and (that of) Naphethuhim (hollowed caverns).

14. And (that of) Phatherusim (infinite fragments), and (that of) Chaseluthim (expiatory trials, forgiveness of sins) from which issued forth Phelishethim (rejected, infidels) and Chaphethorim (converted, faithful).

15. And Chanahan (physical, material existence) produced (the existence of) Tzidon (insidious adversary, ruse) his first-born, and (that of) Heth (moral weakness, debasement).

16. And (that of) the Jebusite (inward crushing), and (that of) the Æmorite (outward wringing), and (that of) the Girgashite (continuous gyratory movement).

17. And (that of) the Chivite (bestial life), and (that of) the Wharikite (brutish passions), and (that of) the Sinite (hateful, bloody passions).

18. And (that of) the Arwadite (plundering desire), and (that of) the Tzemarite (thirst for power), and (that of) the Hamathite (insatiable desire) : and afterward the tribes of the Chanahanites (physical existences) were scattered.

19. And such was the general extent of the Chanahanites (physical existences) through Tzidon (insidious adversary, ruse) : by dint of intestine convulsion (they came) unto consolidation, by intrigues, and tyranny, and unmercifulness and wars (they came) unto swallowing up (of riches).

20. These are the sons (emanated productions) of Cham (that which is dark, curved, hot) after their tribes, after their tongues, in their lands (and) in their universal organizations.

21. And unto Shem (brilliant elevation) were sons (emanated productions) : he was the father of all ultra-

terrestrial productions, (and) the elder brother of Japheth (absolute extension).

22. The sons of Shem (upright and bright) (were): Heilam (infinite duration, eternity), and Ashur (lawful power, harmony and the happiness which results), and Arpha-cheshad (restoring principle of providential nature), and Lud (intellectual generation), and Aram (universal elementization).

23. And the sons of Aram (were): Hutz (substantiation), and Chul (virtual travail), and Gether (abundant pressing), and Mash (harvest of spiritual fruits).

24. And Arpha-cheshad (restoring principle of providential nature) produced Shelah (efficacious, divine grace), and Shelah produced Heber (that which is ultra-terrestrial, beyond this world).

25. And unto Heber were two sons: the name of the first was Pheleg (separation, classification), for in his days was the earth divided (classified): and his brother's name was Yaktan (attenuation of evil).

26. And Yaktan produced (the existence of) Almodad (divine, probatory mensuration), and (that of) Shaleph (reflected light), and (that of) Hotzarmoth (division caused by death), and (that of) Yarah (radiant, fraternal manifestation, the moon).

27. And (the existence of) Hadoram (universal splendour), and (that of) Auzal (purified, divine fire), and (that of) Dikelah (sonorous lightness, ethereal rarifaction).

28. And (the existence of) Hobal (infinite orbicular diffusion), and (that of) Abimael (father of absolute fullness), and (that of) Sheba (reintegration of principles, restitution of repose, redemption).

29. And (the existence of) Aophir (fulfillment of elementary principle), and (that of) Hawilah (proved virtue), and (that of) Yobab (celestial jubilation): all

these were the sons (emanated productions) of Yaktan (attenuation of evil).

30. And such was the place of their restoring (reintegration), from the harvest of spiritual fruits, by dint of spiritual travail (meditation), to the height (generative principle) of the anteriority of time.

31. These are the sons (emanated productions) of Shem (sublime, exalted), after their tribes, after their tongues, in their lands, after their universal organizations.

32. These are the tribes of the sons (emanated productions) of Noah (repose of elementary existence) after their symbolic generations, in their constitutional organizations: and of these were the natural organizations (general and particular) divided in the earth after the great intumescence (of the waters).

THE END